W9-BUL-684

72000-1/2

STATE BUILDING IN REVOLUTIONARY UKRAINE

STEPHEN VELYCHENKO

STATE BUILDING IN REVOLUTIONARY UKRAINE

A Comparative Study of Governments and Bureaucrats, 1917–1922

UNIVERSITY OF TORONTO PRESS
Toronto Buffalo London

© University of Toronto Press Incorporated 2011
Toronto Buffalo London
www.utppublishing.com
Printed in Canada

ISBN 978-1-4426-4132-7

Printed on acid-free, 100% post-consumer recycled paper with vegetable-based inks.

Library and Archives Canada Cataloguing in Publication

Velychenko, Stephen
State building in revolutionary Ukraine: a comparative study of governments and bureaucrats, 1917–1922/Stephen Velychenko.

Includes bibliographical references and index.
ISBN 978-1-4426-4132-7

1. Ukraine – Politics and government – 1917–1945. 2. Public adminstration – Ukraine – History – 20th century. 3. Nation-building – Ukraine – History – 20th century 4. Comparative government. I. Title

DK508.832.V442011 320.9477'09041 C2010-907040-2

The research for this book was made possible by University of Toronto Humanities and Social Sciences Research Grants, by the Katedra Foundation, and the John Yaremko Teaching Fellowship.

This book has been published with the help of a grant from the Canadian Federation for the Humanities and Social Sciences, through the Aid to Scholarly Publications Programme, using funds provided by the Social Sciences and Humanities Research Council of Canada.

University of Toronto Press acknowledges the financial assistance to its publishing program of the Canada Council for the Arts and the Ontario Arts Council.

Canada Council for the Arts Conseil des Arts du Canada

ONTARIO ARTS COUNCIL
CONSEIL DES ARTS DE L'ONTARIO

University of Toronto Press acknowledges the financial support of the Government of Canada through the Canada Book Fund for its publishing activities.

To my parents and my children

Contents

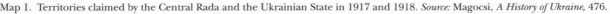

Map 1. Territories claimed by the Central Rada and the Ukrainian State in 1917 and 1918. *Source:* Magocsi, *A History of Ukraine,* 476.

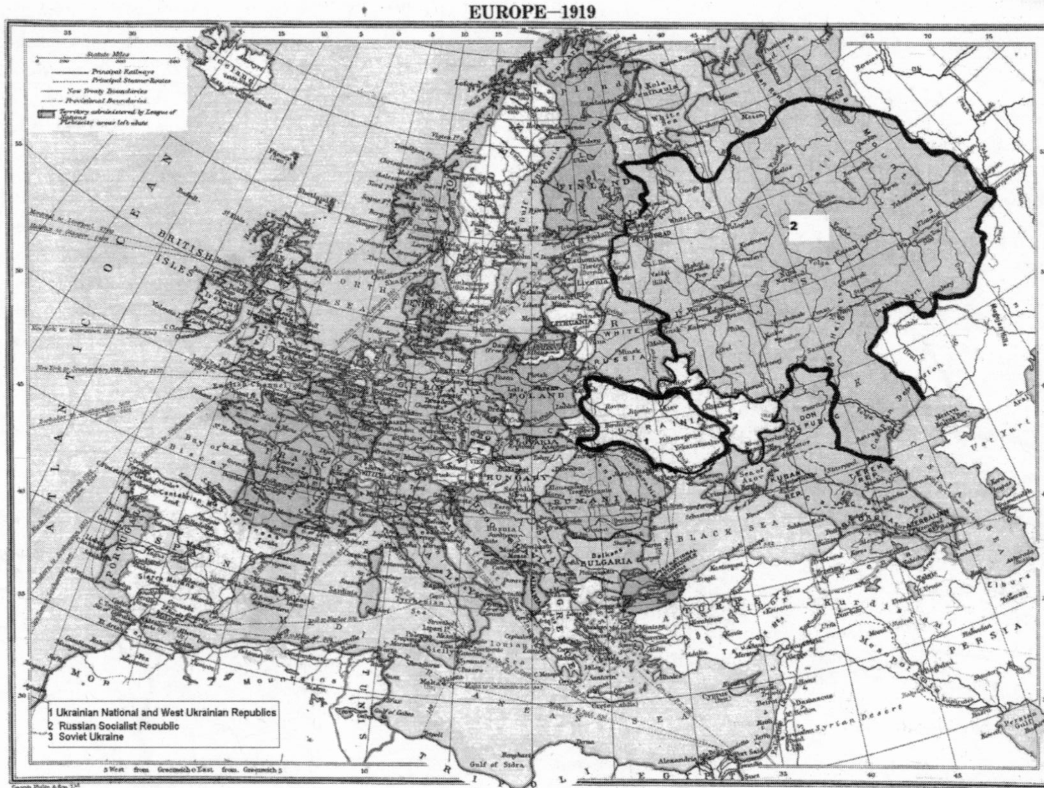

Map 2. Approximate territories controlled by the Ukrainian National and Russian Socialist Republics in January 1919. *Source:* http://commons.wikimedia.org/wiki/File:Europe_map_1919.jpg.

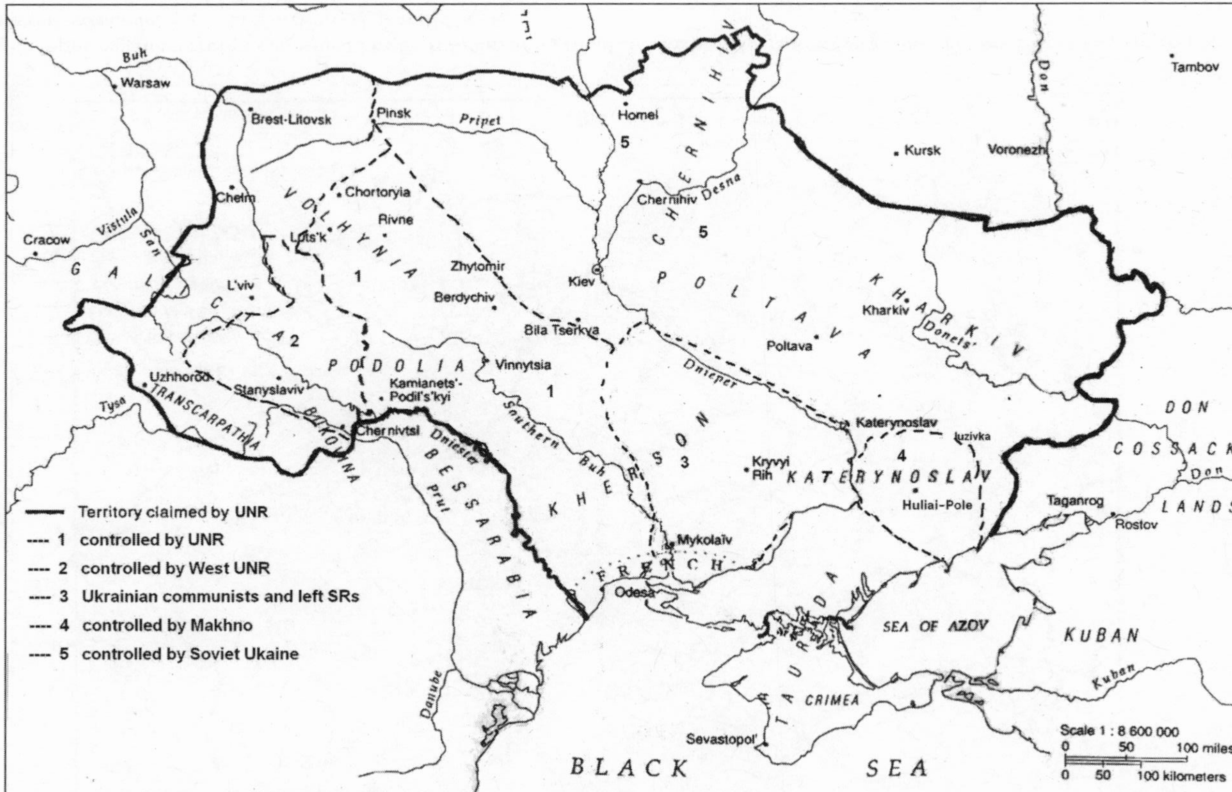

Map 3. Approximate territories controlled by governments and groups in March 1919. *Source:* Loza, *Ukraina, Istorychnyi Atlas*, 3, 5–7; Magocsi, *A History of Ukraine*, 496.

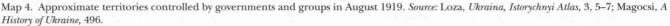

Map 4. Approximate territories controlled by governments and groups in August 1919. *Source:* Loza, *Ukraina, Istorychnyi Atlas*, 3, 5–7; Magocsi, *A History of Ukraine*, 496.

STATE BUILDING IN REVOLUTIONARY UKRAINE

Introduction

> In a modern state the actual ruler is necessarily and unavoidably the bureaucracy, since power is exercised neither through parliamentary speeches nor monarchial enunciations but through the routines of bureaucracy.
>
> Max Weber (1917)

During the four years following the October 1917 collapse of the Russian Provisional Government seven major groups and/or governments claimed political authority in some or all of the Ukrainian provinces of the former tsarist empire. These were the Whites; the Bolshevik Council of People's Commissars; the Ukrainian Central Rada (March 1917 to April 1918); the Ukrainian State (April to December 1918); the Directory (December 1918 to November 1919); the anarchists; and the Ukrainian Communists, former left-wing members (*Borotbists*) of the Ukrainian Party of Socialist Revolutionaries (UPSR) and the Ukrainian Social Democratic Labour Party (USDLP), who sought an independent communist Ukraine.[1] Between November 1917 and January 1920 some towns in formerly tsarist Ukraine changed hands as many as twenty times, and no one government controlled for longer than eight consecutive months any sizable core territory – that is, regions behind lines delineated by towns garrisoned by troops of a particular government (see Maps 1, 3, and 4).[2] In the eastern part of Habsburg Galicia Ukrainians established the Western Ukrainian National Republic (ZUNR), which lasted from November 1918 to July 1919. Later, Ukrainian national leaders would bemoan a dire shortage of Ukrainians able and willing to work as administrators as a major reason for Ukrainians' failure to attain independence in those years.

This book examines this claim and asks the following questions: Who were the administrators? What did they do? How did their nationality and interests affect their behaviour? How many stayed at their jobs despite the changing of governments? To better understand what happened, the book will compare not only the state-building efforts of rival sides in Ukraine but also state building in other countries at the time. It focuses on state-building projects, initiated and led by nationalist and/or socialist, educated elites, which were premeditated directed activities that involved making an administrative apparatus bigger, more complex, and more coordinated. These attempts to create or control government bureaucracies did not occur in isolation but within a larger context of state formation, that is, rival groups of educated minorities and their supporters, while engaged in state building, were fighting with each other for control over existing administrative organizations within specific territories. Ukrainian national state building began in June 1917 and ended in late 1921, when leaders failed at their last attempt to form a government and an army on Ukrainian territory. In December 1917 Russian Bolshevik armies invaded Ukrainian territory. Bolshevik state building and state formation that began that month in Ukraine ended successfully five years later, when the only powerful army and central bureaucracy left on formerly tsarist Ukrainian territory became formally subject to Kharkiv, the first capital of the Ukrainian Soviet Socialist Republic.

State building refers to a rational, formal, organizational 'top-down' activity often moulded by the pressures of war and diplomacy. From this perspective traditional politics based on kinship and clientism do not reinforce but obstruct or undermine government. Historians have shown, however, that central government leaders might also exploit or direct informal personal-patrimonial relations, 'old-boy networks,' in the interests of state building. Where central leaders were unable to control their formal subordinates, a group of associates at a local level who trusted each other and shared personnel, resources, and information among themselves on personal terms, outside the established legal-vertical ministerial hierarchies, not only could undermine and blunt central control over their territory but also could help establish that central authority. Bolshevik Revolutionary Military Committees (revkoms), responsible for organizing the seizure of power and/or administration at the local level in the wake of military occupation, for instance, were in practice neither hierarchic nor part of a hierarchy, rather, they were an informal association of acquaintances: 'personal network ties were used in such ways to facilitate the development of a capacity for territorial administration at a time when the state's formal administrative mechanisms were still not reliable beyond the central industrial region.' What ensured that such local people ultimately reinforced central authority were plenipotentiary agents sent by Moscow who, on the spot, using violence if necessary, made revkom personnel obey central orders.[3] Another approach to state building studies it as a 'bottom-up' phenomenon using ideas from Max Weber and, most recently, Michael Mann. This approach draws attention to the important role of self-discipline, what Weber called 'congregational discipline,' the self-discipline stemming from Protestantism. 'Congregational discipline' was enforced by the believers themselves, not an external authority and because it focused on morality and behaviour, not ritual, submitted Weber, it promoted order and trust.[4] Originally imposed in the eighteenth and nineteenth centuries by clerics at the parish level through the strict regulation of poor relief, religious education, sexuality and marriage, secular officials took on these tasks using secular institutions. Consequently, societies within which the individual behaviour of urban literate citizens was thereby 'disciplined' or 'internalized' via regulatory legislation could be governed less arbitrarily and with less direct violence than societies without such institutions. By drawing attention to political ethics and social structure in the creation of government power, historians explain why Britain and the Netherlands, the wealthiest, most orderly, and powerful European states, were neither centralized, nor absolutist, and had small as opposed to large bureaucracies.

State power cannot be understood only as elites using force or the threat of force via a bureaucracy to extract resources from a cowered populace. The power and authority of government also depends on socialization and voluntary cooperation for the public good in order to live in safety. Subalterns, informal organizations, ethics, and norms must interact for societies to establish working legitimate governments. In the face of violence and shortages, moreover, the self-discipline needed to organize at the local level is not repression but a means to freedom and constructive involvement. Organized interests and networks of associations facilitate cooperation and trust, and the closer they work with government bureaucracies, the more effective that government is.

This book uses the top-down approach and will study only one aspect of state building, namely, the forming and functioning of central government bureaucracy. It focuses on educated elites, describes what leaders thought about the government's administration, who worked in it, and what they did. It will attempt to identify administrators, their number, and where possible, their interests, job histories, and loyalties. Moreover, where possible, it attempts to determine the degree to which local officials could implement central policies and the impact of inertia, inefficiency, bad organization, wartime conditions, and staff shortages and overstaffing, as well as sabotage, on state building. The book focuses on central ministries within the borders of territories claimed by each of the various governments and their local agencies at the district (*povit,* Russ. *uezd*) and county *(volost)* levels. Attention here is given to local actors, interactions, and events outside the capital, rather than central elites, legislation, and proclamations. This is not a narrative political history of events, nor a study of the institutional legal aspects of state building, elected assemblies or ministers, civil servants, and party political appointees – who all came and left; city councils (*dumy*) are considered only in passing.[5]

The need to mobilize for war, provide minimal levels of subsistence for all, and then social services resulted in the expansion of government bureaucracy. As the number of functionaries increased, government became more effective from the point of view of central authorities, and more tangible from the point of view of the population. In response to this unprecedented growth of services and providers, the First World Congress of Administrative Studies was held in Brussels in 1910. Government jobs, in turn, provided desirable employment for the educated, particularly in countries with limited opportunities in the private sector. The politicization of national language and culture in the nineteenth century, furthermore, forced ruling elites in multinational states to consider not only the education of applicants, but also their declared nationality, and thus, not only whether applicants should be allowed into the bureaucracy, but also where in the empire they should work. National minority leaders were normally loyal and sought places for their nationals within government. Between 1916 and 1922, however, nationalists throughout the world attempted to create new states. Sixteen of these attempts succeeded – seventeen if we consider the Ukrainian Soviet Socialist Republic as a success.

Max Weber observed that no modern society can exist without bureaucrats and that only peasants do not need bureaucrats because they own their means of production. People seeking to escape from an existing bureaucracy have no alternative but to create one of their own. Implicit in Weber's reasoning is that bureaucrats are unmoved by political ideas like nationalism. Even in the case of revolution or enemy occupation they normally will continue to function as they did before because they are concerned primarily with their jobs, salaries, and pensions. An operative 'disinterested ideological factor,' Weber continued, involved civil servants' realization that they had to continue working to provide the necessities of life to the population – which included themselves. Bureaucracies continue to function regardless of who rules because a rationally ordered officialdom is of vital interest to all. Being indispensable, bureaucrats work for anyone who manages to gain control over them: 'Such an apparatus makes "revolution," in the sense of the forceful creation of new formations of authority, more and more impossible ... The place of "revolutions" under this process is taken by coup d'état.' Weber realized that bureaucrats had overthrown political leaders in the past, but he thought this improbable in modern societies.[6] After 1945 some academics questioned Weber's hypothesis in light of African and Asian decolonization and argued that during upheavals bureaucrats act as agents for party politics rather than as an institutional interest group.[7]

With the collapse of empires and the establishment of national states in their wake, by the turn of the millennium bureaucrats' loyalties and Weber's reflections about them no longer had the practical significance they once had. Nonetheless, the subject and the theory provide a useful perspective from which to examine a little-known aspect of the revolutions in early twentieth-century Europe. *State Building in Revolutionary Ukraine* is a study of the role of government bureaucrats in state building during the revolutionary years, seen in a comparative context and in light of archival sources. Ukrainian national, Bolshevik, and White state building in both eastern and western Ukraine (eastern Galicia) is compared with state building in Russia, Czechoslovakia, Ireland, and Poland. This book tries to determine the degree to which an alleged shortage of trained administrators holds up as a major reason for the failure of the Ukrainian national attempt at independence. The underlying theme is whether events in Ukraine support or refute Weber's hypothesis.

States have no life outside the people who incarnate them, and creating states means organizing people into an administrative bureaucracy that can provide services, impose a monopoly on violence, enforce justice, and collect taxes and military recruits in a given territory. In the case of the Union of Soviet Socialist Republics historians have studied how in Russia the Bolsheviks neutralized recalcitrant tsarist bureaucrats, staffed their new commissariats with persons prepared to follow their orders, and why former tsarist officials worked for them.[8] In Ukraine, unlike in Russia, the study of bureaucrats that was begun in the 1920s was not resumed after Stalin's death.[9] In the decades after the Second World War works from Ukraine dealing with 'the history of law and government' did not mention Lenin's dictum about using the services of tsarist specialists, or administrators' unions, or strikes. They described how local Bolsheviks followed Russia's lead, but not who worked for them. Studies on the soviets made little if any mention of their standing executive committees (*ispolkomy*, Ukr. *vykonkomy*) or salaried staffs.[10] Only after 1991 did historians begin examining the subject of bureaucrats and bureaucracy in Ukraine during the revolutionary years.[11]

The interests, behaviour, identity, and loyalties of the people who worked in the bureaucracies of the contending governments have not been studied in any detail by historians. The subject is mentioned often in Ukrainian national historiography, and here the judgment of participants remains influential, in particular that of Volodymyr Vynnychenko, who was in charge of the Central Rada's executive (the General Secretariat). Writing in 1919 Vynnychenko maintained that 'all the organs of state administration' had to be completely dismantled, all the personnel fired, and that everything then had to be rebuilt and staffed anew. At that time he claimed that the Rada did manage to 'Ukrainianize' the old government bureaucracy, but he later wrote that this bureaucracy had not been 'our state' because Ukrainians lacked the loyal trained personnel to staff it.[12] The latter opinion is similar to that of other educated observers at the time, for example, the Pole J. Hupka, who wrote: 'there are no state-building (*panstwotworczych*) materials in Ukraine.[13] Other participants who wrote histories of the revolutionary years shared Vynnychenko's views, and most historians today repeat the assessment that a key reason why Ukrainians failed to establish an independent national state was that there were too few educated, declared Ukrainians to organize and run a government bureaucracy.[14] During the last half of the twentieth century, some placed this opinion within a long-term structural interpretation. They imposed the characteristics of elite confrontations onto the mass of the population and the assumption that loyalties, language use, and identities are fixed and single rather than elective, variable, and multiple and that nation building must be a precondition of state building. Taking national consciousness to be very important, they have claimed that Ukrainians had too little of it. From this perspective state building failed because Ukrainians were underdeveloped, that is, in 1917 Ukrainian nation building was incomplete.[15] Dmytro Doroshenko, a minister in the Hetman government, held a different opinion. He argued that national governments lacked cadres not because there weren't any, but because the majority of political leaders were socialists with nationalist and anti-statist prejudices; thus, under the Central Rada and the Directory they failed to organize an effective bureaucracy because they hired as officials only socialist-inclined ethnic nationals motivated by cultural nationalism, while under the conservative Ukrainian State such people, as socialists and/or nationalists, refused to take government positions on principle.[16] Expressing a minority opinion, Nykyfor Hryhoriiv, minister of education under both the Rada and the Directory, explained that it was not a lack of educated Ukrainians or bureaucrats, but of political sophistication among educated Ukrainians who were officials that accounts for the failure of independence; with no political convictions and interested only in good pay and little work, they shifted their loyalty from government to government.[17] Although Hryhoriiv blamed career-minded opportunists for the failure of independence, Sergei Shtern, a moderate Russian member of the Odesa city council under the Central Rada, was of the opposite opinion; writing in 1922, Shtern thought that not only had Ukrainian separatism enjoyed success because it attracted opportunist Russians, but also because it gave jobs and status to thousands of 'semi-intellectuals.'[18] Osyp Nazaruk was a western Ukrainian who worked in a Directory ministry and observed its administrative shortcomings directly. In his opinion only a fool would attribute these shortcomings to an alleged unreadiness of the nation for statehood, for similar problems plagued revolutionary France as well as newly independent Poland and Bolshevik Russia; Ukraine's problem was not a shortage of educated men or administrative skill, but of competent political leaders. Oleksa Kobets would have agreed with Nazaruk: educated, and with pre-war experience as a clerk, he was unable to get a clerical job with the Rada in late 1917 because, as he later wrote, there were no vacancies.[19]

This book is based on memoir literature, the contemporary press, and the reports of government inspectors, local officials, and the secret police, as well as central ministerial and primarily, but not only, Kyiv and Podillia provincial records. Of all the governments examined it devotes the least space to the Whites because they could control only the eastern provinces for any length of time, and a full study of their rule would have to be based on those local archives. Particularly useful were the memoirs of Alexei Tatishchev, a native Russian who worked for both the Ukrainian State and the Directory, and the unpublished memoir of Dmytro Krainsky, inspector of prisons in Chernihiv province. Written in late 1918

Krainsky's memoir provides unique insight into work sites and events in a small town as observed by a middle-level professional Ukrainian-born government official.

A major problem with the remaining government sources is that ministerial personnel lists are fragmentary, incomplete, and scattered. Only the Bolsheviks were able to compile statistics relating to their first years of rule; there are very few comparable statistics from any Ukrainian national government.[20] As of 2009 ministerial records were still being made public, and naturally, many have been lost or destroyed. Moreover, not everyone in those uncertain times was prepared to have a written record kept of his or her past activities. At some time after 1927, for instance, someone removed from their archival folder eight pages with the names of Bolshevik sympathizers who had worked for the Rada in Kaniv district.[21] Soviet archival practice, meanwhile, kept personnel files (*lichnyi sostav*) separate from their respective ministerial and/or departmental files, and until 1991 access to them was restricted. They were filed in strict alphabetical order, thus including everyone from the caretaker to the commissar, and not catalogued; analysing these collections would be an immense undertaking, and it has not yet been done. Among records lost or destroyed during the revolutionary years important for the history of employees between 1914 and 1921 are the archives of most of Ukraine's central and local trade union organizations.[22]

There is the problem in contemporary reports of preconceptions and interests. The educated at the time, as officials of the new governments, thought that these governments should be bigger and more active and that their citizens should be more patriotic. They could be inclined to interpret the same behaviour that in peacetime they would have regarded as the tolerable administrative 'muddling along' characteristic of the tsarist system as indicative of breakdown, chaos, inefficiency, and disloyalty that was intolerable in wartime. In their regular reports officials on the spot did not normally list their shortcomings, while critical reports by centrally appointed inspectors were fragmentary because they only did random checks. In Bolshevik-controlled territories there was the additional problem of degrees of secrecy. Daily Communist Party intelligence reports from Katerynoslav province in June 1920, for example, note that better work and more officials familiar with Ukrainian conditions could create a 'strong revolutionary authority' in the province. A special secret report written a few days later for a select group of higher officials only, and based on reports from 226 of Katerynoslav's 278 counties between January and June 1919, was less optimistic: it characterized only three as firmly Bolshevik and 154 merely as 'peaceful'; six were said to be fully under partisan control and another sixty-four had significant partisan activity. Formally, local executive committees were functioning; upon closer examination, the report continued, it was clear that in fact better-off peasants ran the committees and carried out government policies in their interests: 'this crooked mirror does Soviet power more harm than good.' The secret police had begun to purge staff, but as of that summer this had not had any practical effect. A regular situation report from 20 March 1920 describes the administrative system in Kharkiv province as in place and functioning, although a secret report written three days later warns of serious hostility to food requisitions, notes prices rising by the hour on local markets, and categorizes local officials as mostly incompetent.[23] Faced with both sets of reports it is difficult to determine whether or not after six months of Bolshevik rule these provinces were under control or not. I was unable to find investigative-registration committees' (*anketno-slidchi komissii*) reports on officials compiled by the various governments during the revolution, which presumably contain the employment records of the officials they list. As a result, this book is based on only a random sample of central and local government personnel lists and cannot claim to be a definitive social history of Ukrainian bureaucrats between 1914 and 1921. Nonetheless, my review of previously unexamined information about administrations and administrators in a comparative context allows us to doubt some of the simplistic explanations of state building in revolutionary Ukraine and to determine if the reviewed cases confirm or deny Weber's hypothesis.

Given the importance of informal non-government networks in the Ukrainian national movement, in particular, its influential co-operatives, peasants' unions, and reading groups, once in power leaders obviously used those personal networks to implement their authority; however, the documents examined for this book revealed little of how such informal network ties intersected with formal impersonal lines of command. Although clientism regulated by leaders probably was a key feature of revolutionary politics, and perhaps made bureaucracies much less of a neutral civil service than before 1914, this book has little to say on the subject. If the fortunes of full-time rank-and-file bureaucrats were tied to those of politicians, it would follow that all leaders faced inherent administrative instability despite their best efforts to the contrary. Thus, the problem of relations at local levels between politically appointed central agents and ministerial chains of authority and procedure, which affect all governments, were probably compounded in Ukraine. Such practices by national leaders, for instance, could have easily alienated potential non-Ukrainian supporters. Practices inconsistent with declared principles would lead those who were indifferent or hostile to Ukrainian national aspirations to see the public sphere as something in which only those who national leaders considered to be 'Ukrainian' had a right to participate. Non-government hierarchic organizations like political parties were important during the revolutionary years – but their administrative activity is omitted from this book; also important, but omitted are the hundreds of unions that appeared, ranging from the powerful Peasants Union to the Thieves Union and the United Organization of Deserters. Each of these merits a separate monograph as do individual ministries.

No single government during the years examined here fully administered all of former tsarist Ukraine, or even all those parts that it controlled militarily. In particular, the urban-based government control of villages that was tenuous in 1917 had become very tenuous by 1919. Within weakly or completely uncontrolled regions distant from major cities were 'subaltern' counties that formed federations of walled villages and decided for themselves whether to recognize any outside government. Inhabitants carried on farming with their own militias and administrations built around kinship networks. If threatened, larger such entities could field as many as 30,000 men with artillery to repel outsiders and then return to their homes after the battle.[24] Such 'republics,' often along railway lines, used their strategic location to highjack trains – of all governments.[25] Perhaps the smallest was Kolosivka, north of Mykolaiv, with a population of twenty-five and a ruling council of eleven.[26] These 'subalterns' represent what today might be called 'mini state-building projects' at sub-national levels which central leaders at the time, and historians of successful state building subsequently, considered naive, misguided, or even malevolent. They all provide subjects for the bottom-up examinations of state building. However, this book will not study these projects or how local government councils (zemstvos) functioned in territories that were not formally controlled by a major claimant to central power.

This book omits Nestor Makhno's anarchist republic. For most of 1919 Makhno controlled a core territory in a 250 kilometre radius of Huliai-Pole. Lost between June and October to the Whites, this area included central Katerynoslav and northeastern Taurida provinces and almost three million people. Two years earlier anarchists happened to be the most numerous group in Huliai-Pole. By April 1917, primarily thanks to Makhno, they ran the local councils and soviets, which had been hastily formed throughout the Russian Empire by the Provisional Government and had overseen the redistribution of land. When Ukrainian and Russian Communist Party activists arrived they failed to turn the populace. In July and then again in September 1917 the local soviets explicitly condemned the Central Rada and the Provisional Government and declared it would obey neither.[27] Insofar as battles raged unceasingly, Makhno's army, via its Military Revolutionary Council, was the most important organization. During periods of calm Makhno never attempted to organize a standing civilian bureaucracy to back his authority: 'Free Russia does not need mail or telegraphs,' he purportedly told a delegation of postal and telegraph clerks who had come to see him after he had taken Katerynoslav. 'Our ancestors didn't write letters or send telegrams and were happier than we are. You are all free to go where you will.' In the towns that he took Makhno told the local populace that governing was not his affair and that 'if you need governing authorities (*vlast*), organize it yourselves.'[28] His associate 'Marusia' (Mariia Nikiforova) coined the phrase: 'unapologetic destruction of state institutions.'[29] The councils that ran Makhno's villages and regions, however, had 'civilian affairs committees' that apparently got things done. In theory these committees were supposed to be ad hoc bodies. According to published proceedings of the Army's Revolutionary Council, sanitary and army supply commissions seem to have functioned in the face of serious shortages of non-agricultural goods, but people ignored the orders of the local soviets. The Bolshevik commander in Ukraine, in a secret report dated May 1919, wrote that Makhno-controlled territory was superbly organized – noting schools, hospitals, and functioning arms factories in Huliai-Pole. A White prisoner who spent several months with Makhno remarked that he had a superb telephone system.[30] In the dozen-odd cities within Makhno's territory, except for Huliai-Pole, however, disorder and criminality appear to have been the rule. One of Makhno's leaders attributed this not to the practical results of anarchist theory but to conflicts between factional leaders and the remaining city authorities who could not agree on whether to organize urban administration on the basis of unions, soviets, syndicates, or the dumas. Nonetheless, a central social security department, of sorts, seems to have functioned in cities, using confiscated funds. 'Welfare' was distributed to thousands by a member of the Revolutionary Council, who judged claims on the spot, noted names from passports, and then instructed a 'treasurer' to give the person some money from a sack on the floor. An eyewitness noted that this department provided well for orphanages.[31]

Chapter 1 of this book surveys the place of government bureaucracy in society before the First World War. It discusses the norms, practices, shortcomings of, and complaints about the imperial tsarist administration and staff relationships to the national movement and questions of identity. A sizable group of literate Ukrainians worked as administrators, and Russian hostility to national demands must not be exaggerated. With the purpose of providing a better understanding of why leaders acted as they did during the revolutionary years, Chapter 2 summarizes the attitudes and policies of major thinkers and activists with regard to bureaucracy and bureaucrats. Subsequent chapters look at how each of Ukraine's governments attempted to create a bureaucracy, how they dealt with dilemmas of loyalty and competence, and how much continuity of personnel there was between them. Chapters 6 and 9 survey the interplay of identities, interests, principles, and loyalties between officials and rulers in four other new states that appeared at or about this time: Soviet Russia, Czechoslovakia, Ireland, and Poland. Although the book gives some attention to whether and how central policies were locally implemented, the main purpose here is to determine how officials came to be hired, who they were, how they worked, and what they actually did. The research suggests that no one government bureaucracy functioned exceptionally better than another. Within territories they controlled each ruling group or government managed to do some things sometimes, and the exceptional size and peculiarities of Bolshevik organization in Ukraine do not account for their ultimate victory there. The discussions of daily life and prices and wages in the appendixes give some idea of how on the local level people coped with life and interacted with government.[32] Throughout this book the focus is on the middle- and lower-level full-time administrative personnel, on the implementers and not the policy makers.

CHAPTER ONE

Ukrainians and Government Bureaucracy before 1917

At the beginning of the twentieth century Ukrainians were still often called 'Little Russians,' an eighteenth-century term for the inhabitants of Cossack Ukraine. Russian extremists advocated continued use of this term because in their view Ukrainians did not exist. Declared Ukrainians, however, considered the term anachronistic and demeaning and used it to refer to ethnic Ukrainians who did not consider themselves Ukrainian. Overwhelmingly rural and tending to Russify linguistically if they moved to cities, where strong anti-Ukrainian prejudices existed, Ukrainians at the time have often been described by historians as an 'incomplete' or 'underdeveloped' nation. When, however, available figures are examined, and considered in light of the bilingualism and multiple loyalties characteristic of all empires, Ukrainian society looks less incomplete, anti-Ukrainian prejudices seem to be less prominent, and national consciousness appears to be stronger than has been generally accepted. A comparison of 1897 census figures with figures from 1917, furthermore, indicates that the urban population grew significantly before the First World War; insofar as Ukrainian peasant in-migration 'ruralized' cities and, in particular, smaller towns the degree of cultural or political Russification and anti-Ukrainian sentiment should not be exaggerated.

Cities, Infrastructure, Language, and Bureaucracies

Tsarist Ukraine's population in 1917 was almost thirty million, of whom at least 5.7 million lived in 152 'towns.'[1] Twenty-two million declared Ukrainian as their first language. Ukrainian tended to be the spoken rural language of the illiterate and Russian the written urban language of the educated. Between 1861 and 1914 urban growth was phenomenal (see Table 1 in Appendix 1). The cities of Poltava and Vinnytsia, reflecting the Ukrainian and imperial average, tripled in size; Odesa quadrupled, and Sumy, Lutsk, and Kharkiv quintupled. The population of Kyiv increased seven-fold and that of Katerynoslav (today Dnipropetrovsk), ten-fold. Between 1897 and 1910, ten towns doubled in size and the population of Kyiv tripled. With over a million people, by 1917 Katerynoslav had become the third city, alongside Kyiv and Kherson, and the total urban population had doubled.[2] Although production fell the number of urban workers increased in the Ukrainian provinces by at least 100,000.[3] The typical capital of an imperial district (*povit*) had on average a population of at least 25,000 in 1914, with 2,300 buildings (20% of them brick), at least thirty-five inns, twelve churches, twelve schools, and at least one hospital and one pharmacy. Approximately half of the district capitals had a library and a printing shop, and almost all had night lighting. Five per cent had sewer systems, 20 per cent had piped water. However, no more than 3 per cent of the population could vote before 1917, and of that 3 per cent perhaps 2 per cent actually did vote in town council elections.[4]

Urban population figures published before the First World War must be considered to be minimal. Officially in 1897 west of the Urals there were 761 commercial-manufacturing centres with at least 2,000 inhabitants each, and these were listed as 'towns'; however, 227 of them had little or no trade or manufacturing, while 703 centres with trade and manufacturing and inhabited by more than 2,000 people each were officially listed as 'villages.' Accordingly, the Russian Empire west of the Urals actually had 1,237 towns in 1897.[5] In the Ukrainian provinces (excluding Taurida which included the Crimea), 111 commercial-manufacturing centres with at least 2,000 inhabitants each were officially considered 'towns.' But there were at least 700 settlements in Ukraine with more than 3,000 inhabitants each where as much as 50 per cent of the labour force worked in manufacturing, processing, or transport, and it was in such 'villages' that most peasant migrants sought their fortunes: places like Iuzivka and Kryvyi Rih, with factories and populations of over 10,000, were officially listed as 'villages.'[6] The 'village' of Huliai-Pole, which was within a two-hour ride of a train station, in 1914 had 16,000 inhabitants; it had three high schools, ten elementary schools, two churches and a synagogue, a library, a bank, a theatre, a printing press, fifty retail stores, a telegraph and post office, a doctor, a pharmacist, a lawyer, dozens of windmills, two steam mills, and two big agricultural machinery factories – which were converted to armaments works during the First World War.[7] The district of Uman in Kyiv province officially had sixty-one settlements listed as 'villages' and eight listed as 'towns,' which together accounted for 19 per cent of the district's population; in reality, one of these 'towns' had no trade or manufacturing and only 1,734 inhabitants, whereas four settlements with mills, schools, manufacturing, trade, a clinic or pharmacy, and at least 3,000 inhabitants each were called 'villages.' If we add to the number of urban dwellers these 14,628 people officially listed as 'rural,' the district's urban population would rise from 19 to 23 per cent – double that of 1897.[8] Similarly, recalculating the breakdowns for all of Ukraine suggests that its urban population was probably at least 25 per cent of the total population and that by 1917 more than the 2 per cent indicated in the 1897 census worked in the trade and manufacturing sectors; 41 per cent of the 'real' urban population lived in towns of at least 10,000 inhabitants and 18 per cent in centres of 100,000 or more. The two provinces with the most urban centres, each with a population of at least 5,000, were Katerynoslav and Kyiv (with 76 such centres), while Poltava and Chernihiv provinces had the fewest (with 35).[9] This breakdown cannot be compared to countries like Great Britain, France, or Germany, but it was comparable at the time to the situation in Canada, the United States, and smaller European countries.

Not all declared Russians were ethnic Russians. It is impossible to determine percentages for pre-revolutionary years, but in 1926 only half of those who declared Russian as their native language were ethnic Russians. We do know that in 1897, for example, 81 per cent of all first-generation urban dwellers were born in the same province as their city of residence and that 63 per cent of Kharkiv's population were born in a Ukrainian province – although only 25 per cent of that city's residents gave Ukrainian as their first language.[10] Accordingly, Ukrainians by 1920 were not a tiny but a sizable urban minority, averaging one-third of the official urban population, alongside Jews and declared Russians, who also averaged one-third. Although comprising less than 20 per cent of the population in the four Ukrainian cities with more than 100,000 inhabitants (Odesa, Kyiv, Kharkiv, and Katerynoslav), declared Ukrainians averaged almost 40 per cent in the remaining 148 towns – where culturally and/or linguistically based animosities were minimal.[11] The exclusion of de facto towns from the official category of 'town,' however, means that the proportion of Ukrainians in de facto towns was probably higher than indicated in the census.

Not only were there many more Ukrainian-speakers living in more towns than officially indicated, but also commercialization and industrialization began creating urban jobs at a faster rate in the 1890s than before. In the Ukrainian provinces this modernization did not leave out Ukrainians because most of it occurred either in places officially listed as 'villages' or in one of the 140 'towns' with 50,000 or fewer inhabitants. In both places Ukrainian-speakers were the majority, and they most likely constituted a higher proportion of those in trade and manufacturing than indicated in the census – 13 per cent and 30 per cent respectively. Except for Kharkiv province, where Ukrainians constituted 35 per cent of the total population, approximately 80 per cent of Ukraine's commercial and small manufacturing establishments, whose total number of employed individuals had doubled between 1885 and 1897, were outside provincial capitals. Only 43 per cent of Ukraine's factory jobs, meanwhile, were in the locations officially listed as 'towns,' and only Ukraine's four largest cities each had more than 5,000 factory workers living in them. The majority of factory jobs were in what were officially deemed 'villages,' where enterprises employed 5,000 or fewer people and where the population was Ukrainian-speaking. There is no record of which language was used in daily business outside the four big cities. Russian was likely used more in Kherson and Chernihiv provinces than elsewhere because there Russians dominated the commercial-manufacturing sector.[12] Sixty-four per cent of those in commerce were Jews; they were concentrated in the Pale, understood their customers' language, and usually could speak it.

As the census did not record national identity or bilingualism, the relationship between language use and loyalties must be inferred. Observed interaction between Ukrainian- and Russian-speakers and the grim squalor of bigger cities at the time adds credence to the populist-inspired conviction that capitalist modernization and urbanization were alien forces destroying 'traditional' society via 'Russification.' This view persists today although even at the time not everyone shared it. In the 1880s Vladimir Vernadskii observed that a Ukrainian version of Russian was emerging in cities, but he was also struck by the diffusion of Ukrainophile sympathies in central-eastern Ukrainian towns, where most people still spoke Ukrainian.[13] Mykola Porsh claimed in 1912 that Ukrainian towns were becoming 'Ukrainian' just as Bohemian towns had become 'Czech' and that landless Ukrainian rural migrants would swamp Russian immigrants. This was part of what historians now call the 'ruralization' of cities that was then occurring. Implicit in Porsh's argument was that since local Ukrainian merchants, markets, and labour were 'nationalizing' capitalism and leading Russian companies were beginning to advertise in Ukrainian, the government would inevitably have to administer in

Ukrainian.[14] These observations echoed those of the liberal Galician newspaper editor Konstanty Srokowski, who in 1907 explained that Poles had to accept that towns in eastern Galicia were becoming Ukrainian because of migration and that Ukrainian national leaders were their equals.

By 1914 the communications and transportation infrastructure allowed direct contact between major local administrative centres and St Petersburg. All provincial capitals were on the telephone line. The Ukrainian provinces had a total of 13,867 telephones, with Chernihiv province having the fewest (218) and Kyiv province the most (4,141), followed by Kherson province (2,878 – of which 2,236 were in Odesa). Twenty-four of the towns in the Kamianets-Podilskyi district were linked by telephone.[15] The ninety-nine district capitals and 1,811 county capitals were on the telegraph grid, and all of the provincial capitals were on a railway line. With approximately 9,000 kilometres of train track, Ukraine had less track per square kilometre than France or Germany but more than central Russia. Katerynoslav province (with 33 metres of train track per square kilometre) had the densest network, while Volyn (with only 12 metres) had the thinnest; Kyiv, Chernihiv, Kharkiv, Podillia, and Katerynoslav provinces averaged 20 metres or more track per square kilometre, while Kherson, Poltava, Taurida, and Volyn provinces averaged 17 metres or less. With roughly 5.5 million horses and mules in 1916, Ukraine had more horses and mules per capita (1:5) than any other European country. But with just under 17,400 telephones, Ukraine had 3 per cent of the number of telephones found in Germany. A contorted wartime railway system brought trains to the front, but returned few of them to their points of origin, which resulted in a glut of rolling stock west of the Dnipro. In 1914 the Ukrainian provinces had 132,041 freight wagons, 6,241 passenger wagons, and 4,983 locomotives. In terms of rolling stock per 100 kilometres of train track, Ukraine had more freight wagons and slightly fewer locomotives (with 27) than Russia (with 31). Twelve hundred of 4,000 locomotives and more than half to two-thirds of the 90,000 wagons in Ukraine were functional in 1920.[16]

During the revolutionary years the number of publications in Ukraine increased dramatically. In 1914 fifty-four Russian- and Ukrainian-language newspapers were published in twenty-eight towns; three years later 217 presses in forty-six towns published at least 346 titles. Ukrainian-language newspapers and journals jumped in number from seventeen in 1914 to 106 in 1917. In addition, in 1917 at least 751 Russian-language newspapers and journals appeared.[17] As far as can be determined, in 1914 approximately thirty-one (57%) of Ukraine's newspapers were published in its four largest cities (Kyiv, Kharkiv, Katerynoslav, and Odesa). In 1917 these cities published a minimum of 235 titles – 68 per cent of the total. Kyiv published the most titles both in 1914 (14, or 26%) and 1917 (126, or 36%). The number of provincial towns with at least one newspaper in 1917 was almost double the 1914 total. Of all the provinces, Poltava had the largest number (with 10) of district towns publishing one or more newspapers (see Tables 2 and 3). As of December 1917, however, neither the Central Rada government nor any Ukrainian group had a modern rotary press (which was able to print as many as 90,000 copies of a four-page newspaper in one hour). Because they had earlier models that printed only 1,000 to 1,200 pages per hour, Ukrainian national leaders reached far fewer readers than did Russian leaders who, in Russia as well as Ukraine, did have rotary presses. With the old-style press editors had to have copy ready by 8 p.m. to have newspapers out for sale by the next evening, as it took two machines sixteen hours to print 20,000 copies; with the new machines, copy in by 3 a.m. would be printed in as many copies or more and on the streets by morning.[18] By comparison, tsarist Poland published 330 newspapers and journals in 1914 (50 in Russian), of which 251 (80%) appeared in Warsaw; in 1919 approximately 1,000 titles appeared in independent Poland, of which roughly forty-five (5%) appeared in Warsaw.[19] Before 1919 local Bolshevik newspapers represented only a fraction of the total number of newspapers published in Ukraine.[20]

In absolute terms the tsarist bureaucracy appeared huge, and it was generally assumed that the Russian Empire had too many officials. Ministers knew that in proportion to the population the government's nine ministries actually had few employees (*sluzhashchie/sluzhbovtsi*, Ukr.), and none of them had permanent agencies at the lowest level (*volost*). Practical day-to-day authority extended normally only as far as district capitals. Below that after 1861 peasant judges, scribes (or secretaries or clerks), elders, and police deputies interacted increasingly with central officials but still administered themselves in a kind of indirect rule. The base of the tsarist bureaucratic pyramid was in the small provincial towns – it was here that the mass of officials interacted with the mass of the population and where, as a result of this interaction, people formed their understanding of what 'the state' and 'government' were and how to deal with them.

In 1900 the Ukrainian provinces averaged one official for every 1,668 persons. At the same time the per capita average was 1:555 in France,

Austria, and Germany; 1:1,063 in French Indo-China; and 1:1,903 in French Algeria.[21] Government staffing appears to have been weakest in the four left-bank provinces (1:1,885), dropping to 1:1,721 in the three right-bank provinces, and strongest in Kherson province (1:1,203). When private administrators, city dumas, and village council administrators are added to the government totals, Kherson province (with 1:298) remains the region with the most office workers, while the difference between the right-bank (with 1:404), which did not have zemstvos (provincial rural councils) until 1911, and left-bank provinces (with 1:414) decreases.

Provincial capitals could have thirty or more government clerks and/or secretaries in the governor's office. In 1914 each of the dozen-odd districts of every province averaged 1,000 officials (including judges, guards, and police). With between fifteen and twenty counties under their jurisdiction, each of which included thirty to forty villages, district officials rarely appeared in villages where the only full-time official was the council scribe or secretary (*pysar*) – who sometimes would have as many as five assistants.[22] Eleven of the fourteen secular officials in the chancery who actually made the decisions in the district capital were appointed and thus could be outsiders, including the police chief, military commander, bank manager, postmaster, chief of customs and excise taxes, high school principal, the school and tax inspectors, the town judge, the treasurer, and the attorney.[23]

Fourteen thousand government, zemstvo, city duma, and village council officials in the Russian Empire in 1897 gave their native language as Ukrainian. In the Ukrainian provinces, of the approximately 60,000 people who worked directly or indirectly as administrators, at least half were declared Ukrainian-speakers (see Table 4) and 38,000 were clerks in private companies. At least half of the other 21,000 or so individuals who worked in the central government, zemstvos, city dumas, and co-operatives were also Ukrainian-speakers – there are no published figures on language use for individual ministries, private firms, or co-ops. Again, there was a marked difference in staffing between Kherson in the south, the three right-bank provinces, and the five left-bank provinces. With 14 per cent of the region's population Kherson had 19 per cent of its government officials; with 41 per cent of the population right-bank Ukraine had approximately 41 per cent of the officials, and with 45 per cent of the population the five left-bank provinces had 40 per cent of the administrators. Whereas approximately half of left-bank government administrators declared Ukrainian as their native language, 41 per cent of right-bank officials did so. Attached to administrative institutions were 12,500 auxiliary personnel such as couriers, doormen, and security guards. Although officials were only a small percentage of the total workforce, in absolute terms there were almost as many administrators as there were metal and textile workers (59,000 each). Women comprised less than 1 per cent (at most 400) of those employed in administration, and at most 120 of these women were declared Ukrainian-speakers. No more than 250 Jews worked as clerks. Approximately 43,000 people operated the railway, telephone, and telegraph systems – with 64 per cent of the railway personnel and 29 per cent of the telephone and telegraph personnel declared Ukrainian-speakers (see Table 6).[24]

Of 2,500 lawyers in the Ukrainian provinces, 16 per cent were Ukrainian-speakers. This category, however, which includes 'private legal activity,' excludes thousands of non-licensed legal practitioners (*podpolnaia* or *nepatentovanna advokatura*), all of whom were at least semi-literate and passingly familiar with simple administrative and legal procedures. There are no data on this group – variously called *ablakaty, zhidomory, iazychniki, khodatai po delam,* or *khodatai po iz krestian* – which included not only Ukrainian-speaking Ukrainians, but also a disproportionately high percentage of educated Jews, whose petitions to enter the bar were no longer accepted after 1910 and who after 1912 were forbidden to become apprentice lawyers.[25]

With urban growth came urban problems. Together with the tendency of government to expand in both size and scope, these produced an unprecedented increase in the numbers of administrators in the decades before the First World War. In 1914 the number of central ministries increased to thirteen, and alongside them appeared four new central 'civil' organizations with branches and employees throughout the Russian Empire that became ministries in their own right during the war – the Military-Industrial Committee, the Army Supply Committee, the Union of Towns, and the Union of Zemstvos (the latter two together known as the *Zemgor*); 229,000 people worked for the latter two organizations by 1917 – with 63,000 in the Ukrainian provinces. Adding 109,000 Red Cross workers (38,000 in the Ukrainian provinces), the total would rise to 338,000. Seventy-six per cent of zemstvo staff in 1917 were peasants by origin, while 59 per cent had primary education or higher. Alongside these were 190,000 officials in the entire Russian Empire – almost twice the 1897 total.[26]

Thus, tsarist Ukraine in 1917 had more than 100,000 incumbents in state, civil, and private organizations, and at least 200,000 railway and communications personnel (see Table 6).[27] The city of Kyiv had approximately

26,000 administrative, legal, and police personnel – 15,000 more than there had been in the entire province in 1897. In addition, there were tens of thousands of civilian employees working for the army, enumerated as 'military personnel' in 1897 when they comprised approximately 2 to 4 per cent of that category. Between 1913 and 1917 the number of municipal employees in Kharkiv tripled, to almost 6,000, while the city's population had almost doubled, resulting in a small drop in the ratio of employees to population (1:119 in 1917 and 1:108 in 1913).[28]

Not all employment data are broken down by language use, but the proportion of Ukrainian-speaking Ukrainian officials probably increased during the war. This would have happened not only in the central government and municipalities, but also in the provincial zemstvos (which hired on average at least a hundred clerks and secretaries) and co-operatives (which increased in number from at least 7,100 in 1917 to at least 18,000 in 1919). By virtue of their semi-legal 'populist' aura co-ops attracted idealists and people who were unwilling to work in government offices.[29] Although only a small percentage of the total workforce, and including fewer individuals than the total employed in mining and heavy industry, the number of public and private sector administrators just before the Russian Revolution was about the same as the number of railway and food-processing workers (121,000 and 138,000 respectively). During the First World War yet more clerical jobs appeared as new institutions such as the county zemstvos appeared. Peasants' unions, soviets, and land and food supply committees all needed literate personnel. Inevitably, in 1917 administrators made up a sizable proportion of unionized public employees.[30] That summer the almost 400,000 public employees belonging to approximately 300 separate unions represented the third-largest group of organized workers in the Russian Empire, after textile and metal workers – also divided into approximately 300 unions.[31] In Ukraine by the following summer the almost 57,000-strong Public Employees Union was the third-largest group of unionized workers.[32]

The 1874 Conscription Law allowed exemptions for the skilled and educated as 'persons indispensable to the home front.' Among those who were drafted were between one-third and one-half of the land captains (*zemskie nachalniki*) and village elders (*starosty*) – important rural officials whose absence gave more tasks to those remaining in an already under-governed countryside.[33] Office employees, like almost anybody who could, tried to evade service by applying for deferment, exemption, and/or paying bribes.[34] Figures from Tambov province, which may be considered typical for non-industrial regions, reveal that many of the men there were successful in evading military service: between 1912 and 1916, while the total number of government and zemstvo employees increased by seventy-one (to 785), the number of administrators increased by almost twice that (by 137), from 564 to 701. We can only guess at how many incumbents still occupied the various auxiliary positions in 1917 since some positions were, and others were not, considered 'indispensable.' Wartime complaints suggest that many men moved to the 'indispensable' jobs: 'Throughout Kyiv province ... anyone who doesn't want to serve in the army serves on the railroad. On the railroads guards are freed [exempt] ... porters are freed ... guards for railway gardens ... gardeners, assistants, and others ... but mine's a good boy; he gave 100 roubles to the bosses and they put him [on the exemption] list and he didn't go.'[35] In 1916 as many as three million men had deferment status; four to five million more worked in supply transport and manufacturing. This meant that, overall, of every four men in the Russian Empire liable for military service, only one was in the army in 1917, and as many as one-third of those in uniform were not at the front. In the small northern Chernihiv province town of Zlynka, the budget shows a disproportionate increase in spending for administrators' salaries – which suggests that more people were in city hall than were perhaps necessary (see Table 7).[36]

The zemstvos and city unions exercised their draft-exemption powers liberally, and loyalist conservatives considered most of their employees to be draft dodgers or *zemgussars* (zemstvo hussars). Particularly galling to them was the massive draft evasion among the educated. Those not well disposed towards the regime made no secret of their intentions. Mykhailo Hrushevsky, who was to become head of the Central Rada, in 1916 recalled one man who knew him, who 'spoke with me ... at the moment when the possibility of mobilizing men over fifty was being discussed, about how he might get himself assigned as a clerk somewhere in the [general] staff or chancery.'[37]

The basic formal prerequisites for a clerkship were literacy in Russian and primary schooling. From 1831 anyone with primary schooling could join the understaffed bureaucracy, and as of 1871 all children could attend schools. In 1897 Russians and Jews as a group in the Ukrainian provinces had proportionately more literate individuals with higher education than did Ukrainians as a group. Of declared Ukrainians declared literate in Russian, 11 per cent lived in cities as did 54 per cent of literate Jews. Nonetheless, in the Ukrainian provinces, 60 per cent of all those who were literate in Russian and 25 per cent of the 916,141 urban literate gave Ukrainian as their native language; the respective figures for the Jews were 14 per cent and 29 per cent (see Table 8). A rare set of 1917 figures from Horodnia (pop. 3,892, in Chernihiv province) shows that 74 per cent of its declared Ukrainians were literate, as opposed to 80 per cent of the Jews and 84 per cent of the declared Russians (most of whom probably knew Ukrainian).[38] In absolute terms this amounted to at least two million literate Ukrainian-speakers between the ages of nine and sixty who could serve as a pool of candidates for desk jobs (see Table 8). This total would be higher if we add to it the unknown number of those people who knew Ukrainian but declared themselves Russian.

Schools legally had to teach in literary Russian but for Ukrainian-speaking peasants the language of instruction was not an insurmountable barrier to social mobility. Before the economic boom of the 1890s peasants as a rule took their children out of schools after only a few years, but not because they were Russian-language institutions. There was little practical need to learn more literary Russian in school than necessary to pass because everyone in any given vicinity knew vernacular Ukrainian. Since children understood little or nothing of Russian, teachers who knew Ukrainian used it surreptitiously before 1906 if they wanted the children to learn anything at all. When in1906 the government allowed teachers to use Ukrainian when necessary to explain lessons, many teachers took advantage of this loophole to teach as much in Ukrainian as was possible. In the years just before the First World War, the pages of the moderate Ukrainian-language daily newspaper *Rada* were filled with examples of teachers using and teaching Ukrainian; this would mean that in1917 there were many more literate bilingual Ukrainians able to work as bureaucrats than there had been in 1897.

Like their counterparts in most every non-industrialized country, Ukrainian peasants probably cared little about the language of instruction at school for as long as they saw little real need for learning. Parents were practical about schooling and did want some education and minimal literacy for their children; in the mid-nineteenth century, however, the only jobs readily available to graduates of village schools were not particularly desirable clerkships in local institutions. Peasants regarded the local clerks as leeches and drunks because they demanded bribes and, in keeping with custom, imbibed freely with each closed deal; furthermore, insofar as they were known to pass on information to the police, they were not trusted. Faced with a choice between respectability and the perks that relatives in office jobs would bring, most apparently chose the former. Formal instruction in village schools was essentially seen to be useless, even if free. Parents who set their sights higher, and could afford it, preferred to hire private tutors for their children.[39]

This attitude began to change after the 1861 emancipation when peasants found that they had less work to do on their farms, and in daily affairs written documentation began to displace the traditional verbal authority of the lord. No longer subject to forced labour, with plots of land that did not require more than 121 work-days annually, with increasing populations, and little or no local non-agricultural work available to them, the number of idle village youth increased with each decade.[40] One alternative open to such persons after 1861 was emigration. Within a generation, administrative reforms and the economic spurt of the 1890s brought more people into contact with more officials to do more things using written documents, and this opened up the prospect of private sector and higher-level government jobs for literate peasants. Primary school attendance, accordingly, more than doubled between 1890 and 1900.[41] Figures from Poltava, Kharkiv, and Chernihiv provinces reveal that in the 1890s the proportion of pupils who attended and then finished primary schools was the same there as in the rest of the empire – including the Russian provinces.[42] A Ukrainian Bolshevik writing in 1917 observed that ten years earlier life in villages had begun to improve markedly as brick houses with tin roofs began replacing thatched cottages. Anyone who could, rich or poor, wanted to give their children schooling and see them as clerks or professionals. The youth, in turn, outdid their parents' expectations 'and soon acquired all the mannerisms and traditions of the tsarist educated officialdom; awards, promotions, and privileges became their ideal.'[43] The more ambitious and able from among this generation got jobs as clerks in local small companies, larger estates, co-operatives, and town, city, and provincial government and zemstvo offices. Within the latter group, noted one observer, in the Ukrainian provinces for the first time since the abolition of the Cossack Hetmanate in the 1780s there were people who began to speak broken Russian instead of Ukrainian at work.[44] This shift underlay the above-mentioned pessimistic populist prognosis for the fate of the Ukrainian nation, but whether it reflected the dominant trend within the broader context that was cut short in 1914 remains an open question.

Some parents accepted that their children had to learn Russian to get a job. Others openly supported demands for Ukrainian-language schools, and in the decade before the First World War, the matter became a contested public issue. In February 1913 a Russian extremist newspaper in Volyn province published a letter signed by a peasant complaining about schoolteachers, employed by the local zemstvo, who spoke 'in the peasant manner' instead of in Russian. A Ukrainian activist went to the village, discovered that no such person lived there, that the people were satisfied with their school, and then published a letter to that effect signed by the villagers.[45] In April 1914, in an analogous situation, 1,727 peasants from villages in Katerynoslav province published a collective protest against their nominal Duma representative who had claimed in speeches in Galicia that there was no such thing as Ukrainian peasants in Russia: he was a liar, they wrote, and represented no one except the province's big landlords.[46]

The figures on language use by government employees in 1897 show that 52 per cent of Ukraine's administrative, legal, and police personnel were declared Russians or Germans; 40 per cent declared Ukrainian as their native language, and 5 per cent were Polish, of whom almost half were in the three right-bank provinces. Clearly, there was no systematic exclusion of Ukrainian-speakers from government service. Once hired, they faced no organizational limits to promotion, nor were their careers restricted to their territories of origin – as were those of native officials in Europe's overseas empires. Cultural identity was not a career impediment. More Ukrainians took government and non-government clerical jobs just before the revolution, but there does not seem to have been a sudden mass influx that would have made them conspicuous as a group among bureaucrats.[47] Consequently, there could not have been an internal backlash against Ukrainians in administrative positions that would have aroused a collective resentment based on national identity. Some Ukrainian bureaucrats undoubtedly suffered personal slight or insults from co-workers, whereas others might have been fired or imprisoned for nationalist activities, but there is no evidence to suggest that declared Ukrainians understood these to be measures directed against them as a group.

Despite Russian-language instruction in the schools there was a sizable group of declared Ukrainians who worked as government employees, some of whose careers can be traced through to 1922. In response to an advertisement for a clerical position, placed in *Rada* in 1912 by one of its Ukrainian directors, a railway company in the Kuban region received over thirty replies from village clerks and treasurers written in perfect literary Ukrainian. In 1910 Stepan Shevchenko, after graduating from the local school in Uman, went to work at the government's legal archive; he was active in the local national movement, subscribed to Ukrainian newspapers, and read to peasants in the reading club.[48] After graduating from Kyiv University in 1889, Apollin Marshynsky, who was born in a town in Kherson province, was unable to get a job in the Ukrainian provinces because he had been arrested for trying to smuggle Ukrainian-language literature from Austria; between 1891 and 1916 he had to work in the Baltic provinces and St Petersburg, and only in January 1917 did he obtain a position in a government finance office in Katerynoslav.[49] Roman Trofymenko worked his family's farm in Chernihiv province while attending the local primary school and then high school. Between 1900 and 1905 he held various clerical positions locally including that of village scribe and court clerk, and during the Russo-Japanese War he administered a hospital train. For the next seven years he studied law at Kyiv University and taught, and then with the outbreak of the First World War he joined the zemstvo and ran a food supply unit in Galicia, making 400 roubles a month.[50] In 1895 Makar Mokrytsky, aged nineteen, born in a village in Kyiv province and recently graduated from the secondary school in the town of Tarashcha, was hired as clerk in the provincial prosecutor's office. From 1900 he worked in the Zhytomir Provincial Court, and by 1914, when he was transferred to the civil administration of the newly annexed province of Galicia, he had won awards for diligence and was earning 130 roubles a month; in March 1917 Mokrytsky was the head secretary in the governor's chancery in Lviv. Before the war Denis Kirichok from Poltava province worked as a bank clerk and then for an insurance company, when he got a position as a military administrator; in 1917 he was an accountant with the General Ukrainian Military Committee. Kyryl Kuzmenko went to Kyiv, where, being illiterate, he worked in a factory for six years and during that time put himself through a local primary school, after which he was hired as a clerk with the police; in 1913 he went back to his native Bila Tserkva, worked as a clerk in the town's legal office, and from 1915 to 1917 he worked as a clerk for the Red Cross in Kyiv. A poor peasant from the small town of Malyn in Kyiv province, Vasyl Korenchuk finished primary school and six years of secondary school, and got a job as a telegraphist in his home town during the war.[51] Born in Dubno in 1898, Serhii Vishnevsky identified himself as a peasant in his 1920 job application form; he had only completed primary school, he stated, but knew Ukrainian, Russian, and Polish and before and during the war had worked as a clerk in a government office in his home town and had never belonged to any political party, while after 1917 he had worked in 'various cultural-educational institutions' as well as the local zemstvo. In Kyiv province Petro Kramar, aged eighteen, was hired as a clerical assistant in the local zemstvo in 1916, having finished his two-year village school.[52] These were presumably the kind of people who Pavlo Skoropadsky was referring to seven years later when he wrote: 'I know our class of lesser intelligentsia very well ... all lesser administrators, clerks, and telegraphists always spoke in Ukrainian, [and] received *Rada*.'[53] In short, Ukrainian-speakers had administrative jobs, and there do not appear to have been ethnic grounds for Ukrainians in bureaucracies to have developed a dissatisfaction predisposing them as a group to a Ukrainian national message.

Administrators as a Social Group

By the end of the nineteenth century the number of commoners in the imperial bureaucracy was rising while the number of nobles was falling. In the decades before 1905 those with completed secondary education, as a rule, were loathe to work directly for the government – which they despised for its failure to fully implement the Great Reforms. After 1905, in light of renewed liberalization, land shortages, and industrialization, a new apolitical generation were more inclined to work for the government – at least in the finance, justice, or agriculture ministries, which the educated considered more 'enlightened' than the Ministry of the Interior. Consequently, by 1914 the entire tsarist bureaucracy was socially democratized; not a caste apart from, but reflective of a new, more urban society. In 1913, 72 per cent of the empire's top 1,112 bureaucrats at central and provincial levels were noble-born, but only 54 per cent of these belonged to the old nobility. Only 32 per cent were landowners, and 65 per cent had no property at all; 84 per cent had finished university, and the majority depended on their wages for their livelihood – just like any other educated urban dweller.[54]

Life for a married lower-level official working on contract was hard. But it was less the pay difference than the marked distinction within the system between lower-level personnel without rank (*chin*) and higher personnel with rank that provided grounds for institutional group dissatisfaction among the thousands who found themselves in the former group. These were people like Iakiv Stepanchenko,who village-born and self-educated, in the ten years before the First World War worked on contract in various district offices in Kyiv province, or Ivan Troshchynsky, aged forty-eight and also self-educated, who worked on contract as a county clerk for twenty-five years until January 1917, when he got a job with the Kyiv district zemstvo. A Kyiv-born Russian who was fluent in Ukrainian and had finished secondary school, Iakov Sviridov was no better off – working on contract in provincial government offices from 1902 through to 1914.[55]

Invaluable insight into bureaucrats' working conditions is provided by *Sputnik chinovnika,* a small professional journal that was published in Kyiv between 1911 and 1914 by Aleksander Miretsky. While working as a clerk in Kyiv's provincial Finance Office he decided to publish his journal using some of his own money. When his superiors offered him the choice of either shutting down his publication or being fired, he chose the latter option. Self-educated and not affiliated with any political party, Miretsky sympathized with the left-leaning Constitutional Democrats (Kadets). He circulated his journal in Mogilev and Perm provinces and in the Ukrainian provinces of Volyn, Katerynoslav, and Kharkiv. He also sent 200 free copies to the Third Duma. Born in Kyiv province near the town of Skvyra, where he finished primary school, Miretsky possibly was an ethnic Ukrainian, but he was not involved in the national movement. His close associate was an assimilated Jew, Artem Moiseevich Liubovich, residing in Bratslav, where he worked in the telegraph office. Miretsky included many articles favourably contrasting the working conditions of French, British, and German civil servants with those of their tsarist counterparts. Through his publication he urged public employees to form professional clubs and credit and self-help associations to alleviate their plight. Despite fear and indifference by 1909 Miretsky had managed to mobilize 300 of Kyiv's approximately 10,000 bureaucrats into the Russian Empire's first organization of administrators – the Kyivan Chinovnik Club. Four year later he claimed that by 1913 almost every provincial capital had such an organization and announced his intention to call an all-Russian congress of government administrators.[56] Repeatedly fined and imprisoned for his investigative exposure of working conditions, Miretsky and his journal provided educated readers with a picture of their co-workers that was totally at odds with the received image of tsarist officials as mindless, inhuman martinets. In May 1914 in St Petersburg he organized the first ever public lecture on the plight of lower-level government officials where the audience learned that this group had little in common with their superiors (*vlast*) and shared common interests with moderate liberals (*obshchestvo*).[57] In response to Miretsky's exposés in 1912 the governor general of Kyiv specifically forbade bureaucrats from meeting with reporters and reporters from entering government offices. In December 1913 Miretsky's journal was shut down, its archives seized by the secret police, and as a result, Miretsky moved his operations to the capital (see Chapter 6).[58] Miretsky's efforts bore fruit in the Fourth

Duma, where delegates organized a special commission on employees' grievances and passed a resolution advocating more pay, pensions, and better hiring and working conditions, which, however, was not enacted because of the war.

Sputnik chinovnika informed the public that government officials were paid according to rates compiled before 1900. It demonstrated statistically that whereas single men might be able to survive on a wage that averaged between 10 and 30 roubles a month, married men could not. In Kyiv province, it revealed, postal and telegraph apprentices, who were forced to live in their offices, were made to work for months for nothing at all while learning their jobs.[59] The journal claimed there were clerks who worked eight-hour days, had regular holidays, little to do, and paid little attention to their clients, but as often as not, these were the pampered favourites of some office potentate. Postal and telegraph clerks and civilian police administrators, by contrast, worked seven days a week, ten to twelve hours a day and with added hours for night-duty – which could amount to as much as a hundred hours of work per week. They had to work overtime without pay, and although in theory they had three days' holiday annually, they were obliged even then to work if necessary.[60] Village clerks (*pysari*) were similarly burdened. An exposé from Lodz province showed that in return for a salary of 15 roubles a month the average clerk had to deal with 25,000 incoming and 30,000 outgoing documents a year and maintain 229 books and ledgers. With five or six days off annually, the normal work-day was ten hours long – three hours on holidays and Sundays. Sometimes the clerk had assistants, who got 10 roubles a month for their efforts.[61] Working conditions were unpleasant, not only because offices were normally cold, damp, dirty, and small, but because the internal atmosphere was stifling. Employees hated each other and were petty and spiteful. Losing themselves in their tiny worlds of boring routine, the journal's contributors informed readers, they ultimately lost their sense of humanity and ability to interact normally. Where individuals managed to rise above their circumstances and informally organize friendly gatherings outside the office, their superiors eventually instructed them either to desist as their meetings were illegal, or to formally register with the police and get a charter – which involved long arduous procedures that few wanted to undertake.[62]

Particularly informative are *Sputnik's* revelations about the breakdown of entrance and promotion procedures in the pre-war bureaucracy. By 1900 official rank no longer guaranteed a full-time well-paid position with a pension, and few individuals could afford either the time or the money necessary to take the examination for rank. As a result, there were thousands of petty clerks and secretaries who worked for low wages, sometimes on contract, with no prospects for normal promotion or a pension – regardless of their education. Interested in saving money, senior bureaucrats would often fire such persons after they had worked a number of years and then hire new people at the starting rate rather than giving the older ones a pay increase. In the State Bank the recommendation of a well-positioned person could replace the higher educational requirement for applicants. As a result in 1911, of 117 heads of departments, fifty-nine had no higher education whatsoever, while twenty-two had degrees unrelated to banking; of those remaining, few had formal qualifications in accounting or commerce.[63] In general, entrance and promotion depended on bribes and/or protection, and those without either could find themselves in the position of an anonymous writer who, in a heart-breaking letter, told *Sputnik* readers that at age fifty-six, after thirty years of service, and still single, he was without prospects or a pension.[64] The fate of bureaucrats without ready cash, patrons, or rank depended exclusively on the office secretary, as the senior official formally in charge rarely if ever actually entered his offices or interacted with his employees. The head of the Warsaw Treasury Office, for instance, went into his offices no more than five times during the entire fifteen years of his tenure. The future of local senior bureaucrats suffered whenever newly appointed senior officials arrived: they would bring in their favourites, who were either relatives or clients, and these would then be the first in line for pay raises and promotion.[65] In 1912 *Sputnik chinovnika* made public information about the buying and selling of rank within the system. The long exposé concluded that nothing could be done about the problem legally, because the law as written punished plaintiffs. Inspections and complaints by those who lost out in the trading merely resulted in a quiet removal of the guilty and their later reinstatement somewhere else.[66]

Sputnik was critical of attempts by extreme right-wing politicians, via their supporters in the higher bureaucracy, to intimidate lower-level officials to support their aims. The editors regretted that some people gave in to such pressure and said that this had to stop as a man's conscience belonged only to him. A caption beneath a cartoon of a lower-level bureaucrat replying to a superior who asked him if he was a nationalist reads: 'It's all the same to me, your excellency. [If you like] I could be a Decembrist.' The editors bemoaned such occurrences and asked how bureaucrats had ever allowed themselves to fall to such depths. It was submitted that officials should concern themselves exclusively with their jobs and their professional interests.[67] *Sputnik chinovnika* never ran articles related to Ukrainian issues per se but throughout 1912 and 1913 it did run Ukrainian-language advertisements for *Rada*.

Besides publishing numerous anonymous letters describing the internal mechanisms of the tsarist administrative system, in 1912 *Sputnik* released the results of a poll it had organized inquiring about readers' demands and conditions of work. Government clerks, it emerged, wanted the right to organize unions and a say in the running and staffing of their offices. They wanted assemblies of peers to deal with issues related to disagreements and dismissals, courses to improve their qualifications, compulsory confirmation of all qualifications, a five- or six-hour work-day, realistic pay rates related to costs, overtime pay, holiday bonuses, higher pensions, fewer pay differentials, no arbitrary dismissals without cause, day care, medical care, and the right to holidays.[68]

Alongside the dissatisfactions of those who were employed must be added the frustrations of those unable to get jobs. Every year hundreds of letters of application flowed in to gubernatorial and general-gubernatorial offices. Letters from Kyiv province between 1910 and 1914 show applicants who had finished at least a village school, many who knew office procedures and could type, and some, like Kuzma Derkach, who were already working as secretaries or assistants in small towns or villages and wanted to move to the capital. Many pleaded hardship and, for them, the application fee of 1 rouble 50 kopeks represented a significant sum. Pavlo Nekrashchuk, aged nineteen, sent no fewer than four letters between March and October one year in which he explained that his father, who had worked for the Excise Office in his village, had died and that he, his mother, and four siblings had nothing to live on. While Nekrashchuk may have wondered why he was constantly rejected, Oleksandr Rokytiansky, aged twenty-seven, who had been unable to complete secondary school in Kharkiv province because of poverty, was perhaps hoping against hope when he sent in his application: 'Everywhere I have turned to ask for a job they told me I needed contacts (*protektsiia*). I don't have any.' Applications continued through 1917 and then declined sharply after that August. The last recorded application to the governor's office, by one A. Godovamok, a clerk in the town of Balyn since 1907, is dated 9 December, and his rejection was mailed out 9 January 1918.[69] In their letters applicants not only included qualifications and sponsors' names, if they had any, but also references to hardship and fear of dying of hunger and cold unless they were hired. Normally one-page long, some included heart-rending details about experienced misery and how their authors proposed to pay the application fee which they could not afford for four double-sided single-spaced folio pages. In July 1911 'the son of Major Aleksandr Panchenko,' who had to drop out of school to take care of his mother when his father died, wrote that he was willing to take a job without pay if none with pay were available because he wished to serve 'with honour.' Feodosii Hlushko from Lubny in Poltava, educated and qualified, was much perturbed by the refusal of the police to explain why his applications for promotion to Kyiv were rejected. The reasons were mundane; in response to his letter, the governor general ordered an inquiry and learned that the man was forty-five years old and that there were no openings.[70]

Identities

Where loyalties were multiple and concentric, rather than exclusive, patron-client networks easily crossed national lines. The empire was still a place where local people who would not condemn a local official for using his position to favour his kin would roundly condemn an official brought in from outside if he favoured his. In other words, any assessment of the influence that administrators had on local events in non-Russian areas must consider that the relationship between language use, identity, and political loyalty was still mediated by kinship and clientism. There was no necessary direct relationship between the language used in public and national affiliation. Long-time residents could switch languages, and change was not necessarily tantamount to repudiation of heritage or the destruction of the soul. The words of an anonymous Slovak peasant replying to a Czechoslovak government enumerator's question about nationality in 1919 sum up the situation: 'I did not ask which language you speak but whether you are Hungarian or Slovak,' said the official. 'If the bread is buttered on the Hungarian side I am Magyar, if it is buttered on the Czech side, I am Slovak.'[71] In Chernihiv province in late 1917, reported an eyewitness, 'Ukrainians particularly feared the Bolsheviks who dealt with them with exceptional ferocity.' National activists in response 'changed their faith' or, in today's terms, changed their identities. Women previously active in Ukrainian social and cultural work suddenly began saying publically: 'What kind of Ukrainian am I? My father was born in Petrograd and my mother in Voronezh. I was only born here.' A Ukrainian former minister and historian put it this way: 'today's "Russian" or "Little Russian" could tomorrow become nationally conscious and "Ukrainian." Conversely, today's nationalist Ukrainian upon becoming a Bolshevik looked at "Ukrainian nationalism" as a reactionary phenomenon hostile to the interests of the "working mass" and took up arms against the Ukrainian movement.'[72] Russian children, finally, insofar as they were exposed to Ukrainian, could easily learn Ukrainian if they wanted to. Alexei Tatishchev was a boy when his father became the governor of Poltava province, and during his three years there Alexei learned to understand Ukrainian, as his mother had relatives living in the nearby town of Myrhorod; after 1905 he worked in the Settlement Bureau of the Land Ministry, where he perfected his Ukrainian as most of the people he dealt with were Ukrainians.[73]

In the nineteenth century literate non-Russians acculturated to imperial Russian ways were usually bilingual, and use of a native language did not imply that a person was nationally conscious or that the person's primary loyalty was to that language group. For the literate and illiterate alike, imperial and regional identities could coexist for as long as ministers believed that the unity of the state should depend on loyalty to the tsar and not on uniformity of language and culture. Regional and/or national backgrounds provided a basis for 'dual loyalty,' and Russians who lived in non-Russian areas, or non-Russians who used literary Russian, did not necessarily consider themselves to be Russians or devoid of a regional loyalty to which they might tie their professional activity. Region and social status were at least as important as language in determining political attitudes, and perceived differences of themselves were not a basis for conflict.

The relationship between cultural and political loyalties was not fixed. Someone opposed to Ukrainian political separatism was not necessarily opposed to Ukrainian cultural demands or territorial autonomy. Katalina Sobieska, Dmytro Pikhno, and Aleksandr Savenko were notorious for routinely denouncing national activists to the secret police. Baltic Germans like the Gesses, settled for generations in the Kyiv region, were unambiguously loyal to St Petersburg. But foreigners and locals in non-Russian regions, who identified with a political-legal historical entity such as the Cossack Hetmanate and did not think cultural and linguistic distinctions were politically significant, could have advocated or supported two kinds of regionalism even if they did not support Ukrainian cultural demands. Proposals by powerful 'Little Russian' nobles in the mid-nineteenth century for railroads in their provinces are an example of regionalism based on geographical and economic considerations, for instance. Count Vasyl Kapnist, a Duma delegate from Poltava province and descendant of a famous Cossack family, provides an example of traditionalist regionalism. In a 1914 speech protesting the prohibition of public celebration of the centenary of Taras Shevchenko's birth, Kapnist distinguished between the dangerous political separatism of the 'so-called Ukrainian movement' and the 'natural affinity of every Little Russian to his native country,' which if repressed would constitute an insult to his patriotism.[74] Oleksandr Afanasiev-Chuzbinsky, who argued that modernization would succeed only if the central government utilized local traditions and knowledge, advocated both kinds of pre-national regional interests. The German landowner in Volyn province, Baron Shteingel, was active in the national movement and later joined the Central Rada, even though he never learned the Ukrainian language. Russians in Ukraine like princes Kurakin, Rumiantsev, and Repnin represented regional concerns and placed estate above state interests. Prince Dolgorukov, a Chernihiv gentry marshal in the 1890s, participated in the national movement, and his successor A. Mukhanov supported it in the First Duma.[75] Russians like Tikhon Rudnev, head of the Poltava Appeals Court, sought out and worked with Ukrainian intellectuals to stamp out speculation. In New Russia (Taurida province) Mikhail Vorontsov was the first to propose building railway lines in his jurisdiction to facilitate industrial development – rather than grain export – and he later financed an unsuccessful project to build such a line. In Kharkov province Governor Obolenskii, who had no compunctions about ordering brutal floggings for rebellious peasants, chastised the local zemstvo for not providing adequate services for the taxes that it collected.[76]

Some changed with the times. The writer Borys Antonenko-Davydovych related how his Russified ethnic-Polish high school principal and teacher in eastern Ukraine, by the end of 1917, had changed from a Russian-speaking monarchist who had warned his students about the dangerous consequences of Ukrainian sympathies into a Ukrainian-speaking supporter of the Central Rada who wondered why there was no statue to Hetman Mazepa in Kyiv.[77] An examination of 170 personnel forms completed by Kyiv district zemstvo staff in October 1918, which asked applicants about place of birth, native language, language competence, and language use at home, reveals that of forty-six Russians only thirteen could not speak or write in Ukrainian – although they all could presumably read it since they did fill out the form. These thirteen were either Kyiv-born or immigrants, like self-taught Olga Bugachova, who was nineteen years old when she arrived in Kyiv in 1905. All the other Russians, like the eight Poles who filled out the forms, were born in small

Ukrainian towns and could read, write, and speak Ukrainian. Among them were sixteen-year-old Tetiana Gorbanova from Bohuslav, who after finishing Kyiv's girls' high school and conservatory in 1916 was hired by the district zemstvo as a typist, where a year later she was joined by Vira Vintskovska from Volyn province, who besides Ukrainian, knew Polish and French. Some Russians filled out their forms in Ukrainian.[78]

In short, dynastic-imperial, community-regional, and familial-national loyalties crisscrossed and interrelationships between territorial, cultural, professional, and group identities and loyalties often depended on circumstances. Language use and/or identity did not always define political attitudes and/or loyalty, and to assume that people opposed or supported Ukrainian-related issues exclusively on the basis of language-use statistics is tenuous. Accordingly, the loyalties of educated declared Ukrainian and Russian activists in Ukraine should not be read into the loyalties of the population at large. Declared Russians, moreover, did not create a territorial 'creole nationalism' to distinguish them both from the native population and the imperial metropole, which would have made them similar to third- or fourth-generation Spaniards in Latin America or Anglo-Scots-Irish in North America. Most identified with the empire, and some with 'Little Russian' in a regional sense. Analogously, not all government employees in Ukraine necessarily shared the Russian extreme right's hostility to Ukrainian national issues. Behaviour depended on local circumstances, personal attitudes, and the affiliations of superiors and patrons.

Obviously there were notorious individuals for whom identity was simply irrelevant and whose opportunism and ambition overrode all concern for any greater social good. Yet, there were also bureaucrats who were not indifferent to their society's welfare. The structural weaknesses of the tsarist administration, despite the improving communications system, in turn, allowed such people the possibility of softening and/or frustrating formal authority. Covert evasion, false reporting, collusion, and bribery mediated relations between subjects and officials and superiors and subordinates. Although hardly conducive to public morality or civic culture, such practices tempered central authority, and those concerned thought they were better off because of them. In 1911, for example, three bureaucrats from near Bratslav were tried and punished for ignoring the existence of a village school run by a Polish Catholic priest who since 1907 had been teaching Polish and catechism to approximately fifty children. The school was discovered one day by the provincial superior who noticed it when he happened to be visiting. Although the bureaucrats pleaded ignorance, it appears that they actually did know about the school and the priest but had simply ignored them.[79]

The bureaucracy did not meet the exacting standards of reformist Petersburg ministers. Authority remained personal and arbitrary, rather than procedural and impersonal, and particularly at the rural level, decisions often were left unimplemented because bureaucrats preferred the safety of inactivity to the risk of initiative. But the system muddled along well enough to bring in taxes and conscripts and few considered the dysfunctions intolerable. Accordingly, government institutions in the Ukrainian provinces cannot be regarded as agencies of relentless Russian nationalization – particularly at the lower levels, where most clerks invariably were local-born. Confrontations between specific elites, or between declared Ukrainian and extremist Russian activists, must not be read into the political behaviour of the majority, who were sooner motivated by circumstances and interests than by ideology or convictions. Administrative offices can arguably be treated as 'sites of contact' where people worked out their own understanding of what 'government' was and what it meant to be 'Ukrainian' or 'Russian' or 'Little Russian.' This, in turn, did not necessarily correspond to what nationalists or imperial loyalists thought 'Ukrainians' or 'Russians' or 'Little Russians' should be.

On the one hand, local Ukrainian-born rural officials who read *Rada* could have impeded the dissemination of Ukrainian-language publications and education. Before the First World War almost every government office in the Ukrainian provinces had to subscribe to the Russian extremist newspaper *Kievlianin,* for example, which regularly contained articles accusing the Ukrainian movement of treason. After reading such diatribes some local officials were unable to understand why the central government tolerated national activists and saw no reason why they could not do something about such people on their own initiative. Thus, contrary to the desires of their more moderate superiors in Kyiv and St Petersburg, village policemen and postmasters would arbitrarily confiscate any published Ukrainian-language material that they found.[80]

On the other hand, some individuals surreptitiously manipulated the system in 'Ukrainian interests' as defined by activists at the time. Government administrators could influence local affairs in general, and Ukrainian cultural issues in particular, because in practice it was often up to them how they implemented or delayed implementing rules and policies. The scope of their influence was related to considerations of space, technology, and organization which ensured that tsarist central rule did not always mean central control. Regularity in policy was impeded also by the vacillation of ministers and general governors in Kyiv and St Petersburg who, in cultural-linguistic matters, wavered between repression and tolerance. Moreover, regardless of what the ministers decided, the inertia, feuding patronage systems, nepotism, corruption, clientism, and overlapping jurisdictions that plagued the tsarist administration gave scope to locals to act as harshly or as leniently as they thought they should. Regions were subject to arbitrary intervention but little administrative due process, which meant that local elites and full-time bureaucrats had more influence on local affairs than the law or their formal status allowed. Particularly influential were provincial permanent secretaries and office heads who worked for indolent, incompetent, or indifferent political appointees or elected heads.

Recently examined police files reveal that between 1900 and 1908 hundreds of civil officials either actively sympathized with, eagerly took bribes from, or had close relations in one or another revolutionary group. Such work is yet to be done for Ukraine, but in 1910 extremist Russian bureaucrats in the right-bank Ukrainian provinces expressed concern to the Kyivan governor general about the shortage of native Russians in the local administration. They pointed out that local Poles and Ukrainians working in government offices could not be expected to implement policies made 'in the spirit of the Russian national idea,' since they were little influenced by Russia's 'national state ideals.'[81] The complaint of one Leonid Karchevsky to the Kyivan governor general in 1911 confirms that by 1900 nationality was playing a role in office politics. Karchevsky claimed that while serving as a police officer in Perm province he had been unjustly framed and then fired thanks to the machinations of an anti-Russian Polish colleague with 'radical left inclinations.' Having returned to what presumably was his home province of Podillia, he related in his letter that he had been unable to get a local job because he had no 'protection' and his former chief, who was the patron of his old Polish nemesis, gave him bad references – despite an acquittal for his alleged misdeeds in Perm. Karchevsky went on to write that in Podillia local Poles had formed cabals within offices and via their family ties did what they could to exclude 'outsiders.' It was consequently very hard for a 'native Russian man' to get an office job, and he begged the governor general to see to the situation and intervene on his behalf.[82]

Memoir literature suggests that there were slowly increasing numbers of men before the war who, before they took their jobs, already considered themselves Ukrainian. On the local level in the 1870s, for example, Illia

Hladky, a clerk in the Nizhyn province Excise Office and an activist in the Ukrainian movement, used his office to influence the local student and populist movements. In the 1860s Fedir Rashevsky, head of the Chernihiv province Excise Office, gave positions to activists in fifteen local districts; while performing their professional duties they promulgated the use of Ukrainian books and language among the peasants. Working in the provincial administration in the 1870s, Ivan Rashevsky got permission for Ukrainian concerts and intervened on behalf of anyone who fell foul of the authorities. A statistician in Chernihiv and later Poltava, as a zemstvo employee A. Rusov disseminated illegal Ukrainian-language material; his sister's comments about him could well apply to Ukrainian-speaking government bureaucrats as well, who 'opposed the administration on the basis of its own laws.' A member of the first Ukrainian political party, the Revolutionary Ukrainian Party (RUP, established in 1900), K. Kokhlych, worked in Kyiv's Post Office where after it had been screened by censors he slipped illegal publications into mail for activists. From the 1890s the informal and semi-legal All-Ukraine Non-Party Organization traced openings in the administration in order to place activists. Police reports reveal that this network was strong enough to be able to forewarn its members of all raids – men from this organization later formed the Ukrainian Democratic Workers party (UDWP). In Kyiv Ivan Rudchenko, a colleague of Mykhailo Drahomanov and the brother of a leading writer (Panas Myrny), worked in the governor general's office in the 1880s; rumour had it that through his friendship with the powerful chancery secretary, M. Merkulov, Rudchenko influenced the governor general to enact pro-peasant policies in right-bank Ukraine. In the 1890s an activist with the name N. Molchanovsky met A. Ignatiev when he was the governor general of Siberia. When Ignatiev was appointed governor general of the Southwestern Region in 1894, he took Molchanovsky with him to Kyiv and placed him in charge of the chancery; in office until 1905, Molchanovsky did what he could to support Ukrainian cultural interests.[83] Noteworthy is the behaviour of Pavel Beliakov, father-in-law of Lenin's polemical rival Lev Iurkevych. In charge of conscription in Nizhyn district Beliakov survived thanks to the bribes he took from Jews to keep their sons out of the army. They particularly honoured and respected Beliakov because after taking their money he always kept his side of the bargain. To show their appreciation the local Jewish band conscientiously played at his house on all holidays because they wanted to – not because they had to.[84]

National activists exploited friendships and/or Masonic ties with officials at all levels. After 1910, when peasant reading clubs (*prosvity*) were formally dissolved, they continued to operate throughout Katerynoslav province thanks to the efforts of Octobrist historian Dmytro Iavornytsky, a close personal friend of the provincial gentry marshal and governor – both of whom were Russians. That same year Dmytro Doroshenko, a future Ukrainian foreign minister, was denied permission to head the reading clubs in the city of Katerynoslav by Governor Shidlovskii because he was 'undesireable' (*neblagonadezhnyi*). Shidlovskii, however, was fond of the ladies. Caught by a husband one evening, he made his escape through a window and was seen running down the street half-naked. Doroshenko, taking advantage of the governor's dismissal, arranged through friends to have the head of the provincial chancery mislay the disgraced governor's file on himself. His grandfather, meanwhile, obtained a certificate of reliability from the home town police constable, who was a friend of the family, and then got Governor Maklakov, another family friend, to vouch for his grandson. A new governor confirmed Doroshenko's appointment.[85] Naturally, not everyone was as well connected. Although no one seemed to mind what Stepan Shevchenko was doing in Uman province, three months after he was hired by a Kyivan government office in May 1903, Symon Petliura was dismissed for the same reason Doroshenko had been.[86]

Panas Myrny, the first writer to develop the character of the Ukrainian petty official in Ukrainian literature, worked as a clerk and he provides an example of an honest declared-Ukrainian official. While drawing due attention to the scoundrels, in his stories Myrny also demonstrated that some officials were basically good men destroyed by circumstances. Personally, Myrny became depressed and sad whenever he reflected on the drudgery of his job. Yet, he was a loyal and efficient provincial bureaucrat under the tsarist and Soviet governments who seems to have balanced political loyalty, national affiliation, bilingualism, and professional interests. After 1917 he seems to have worked through all the regimes that occupied his province during the revolutionary years. Analogously, Mykola Tairov, who in 1910 finished his law studies and then worked at the Kyiv District Court, seemed to be an honest man. He explained in his April 1918 application letter to the Central Rada that he had left his job when he realized that what mattered for advancement was not knowledge or work but the favour of a superior and protection 'which was against my conscience.'[87]

Few 'Little Russians' or declared Ukrainians who were employed in government offices left accounts of their experiences and milieu that would allow insight into how bureaucrats navigated between political loyalty, professional grievances, and national affiliation in their native provinces. What does seem certain is that no tsarist bureaucrat was assassinated in the Ukrainian provinces because of his nationality. Nor does it appear that declared Ukrainians or 'Little Russians' before 1917 decided not to work for the government because they feared that would make them targets for assassins.

The nationalist idea that faithful service to the tsar and 'Rossiia' was incompatible with concern for the native group and its territory took root late in Ukraine. Up to the twentieth century national leaders (sometimes called Ukrainophiles), notwithstanding Shevchenko, were moderates who considered government work a legitimate activity, and they did not consider those who worked within a government, which they did not consider 'foreign,' to be national apostates or renegades. The Austrian consul in Kyiv, a Czech, observed in 1893 that national activists strove to occupy any government positions that they could. While remaining true to their ideals they behaved correctly at work: 'I personally know many bureaucrats and teachers whose professional behaviour is impeccable, yet who, in private express views about the government that can hardly be considered favourable.'[88]

Lines between Russians, 'Little Russians,' and Ukrainian national activists began to harden at the beginning of the twentieth century. The RUP claimed in its manifesto that only Russians and 'Russified renegades' staffed government offices in Ukraine. Twelve years later, a public protest, signed among others by Hrushevsky, condemned a Duma delegate named Skoropadsky for claiming that he represented Ukrainians/Little Russians. He, like all 'conscious turncoats' from among the intellectuals and 'the dark masses,' could not voice the views or wishes of Ukrainian intellectuals and declared Ukrainians.[89] In a letter to a Russian newspaper, an anonymous group in 1914 threatened with imminent horrific punishment the 'many scoundrels' who, out of selfish personal interests, had forsaken 'Mother Ukraine,' 'held on to Muscovite pockets,' 'fawned before torturers,' and enjoyed ruling while 'standing on foreign shoulders.'[90] Between 1905 and 1910 revolutionary terrorist groups killed at least 17,000 people throughout the Russian Empire. Approximately 6,000 of these were civilian government officials of whom an unknown number were middle- and lower-level bureaucrats. Ukrainians were among the assassins both within all-Russian and Ukrainian parties or groups, but whether any of them killed their victims because they represented a 'foreign' authority is not known.[91]

Under a common veneer of Russian-language use and indifference, if not hostility towards public expressions of Ukrainian national identity, bureaucrats' behaviour varied from province to province. In 1905 zemstvo, duma, postal and telegraph, and private sector employees formed unions, but only one instance is known, in Poltava province, of government clerks taking such an initiative.[92] In Podillia province, where Little Russians were a majority in many offices, the atmosphere was not 'official petersburgian,' but specifically local. Declared Ukrainian students promulgated their ideas among Russian-speaking Little Russian acquaintances who worked as clerks, for instance, by organizing parties where they explained to them that everything they had heard about 'Ukrainians' was wrong. Declared Ukrainians who worked as clerks were openly active members of legally permitted national organizations and subscribers to Ukrainian-language publications. Some were prepared to suffer imprisonment or dismissal for their beliefs. Others were not. In one case, an active member of the local reading club quickly ran to its office on the morning after he had heard that its other members had been arrested and erased his name from all records. Other employees kept a poker in all fires, and their braver colleagues fully sympathized: advising them to participate in national activities and read the literature, without actually becoming members or taking out subscriptions.[93] An account from Chernihiv province suggests that the gap between national activists and a-national clerks could be wide. The author here saw his colleagues as overwhelmingly 'men of the twentieth' – a phrase used in tsarist times to refer to bureaucrats who sprang to life only on the twentieth of each month because that was payday. These were people of limited abilities and horizons who could be properly described only by a Gogol, he continued: 'Many of them were primordial (*stykhiini*) Ukrainians unconscious even of their Ukrainianism; they could not even speak Russian correctly, and they probably heard real Russian very rarely. There were among them some nationally conscious Ukrainians of the "educational" sort [interested exclusively in cultural activities] ... but this entire milieu was so singular and foreign to me that I could not bear it very long and [within a year] I resigned.'[94]

Cities, Identities, and Attitudes

Some insight into the sympathies of government administrators might be inferred from statistics on the occupations of political party members and government policy on party membership. Between 1905 and 1917 approximately 250,000 people, 1 per cent of tsarist Ukraine's population, belonged to political parties.[95] Incomplete data at the imperial level from 1906–07 show that fewer than 5 per cent of the members of the Russian Social Democratic Workers' Party (RSDWP) and the Russian Party of Socialist Revolutionaries (PSR) were bureaucrats.[96] No more than 10 per cent of the Kadets (Constitutional Democratic Party) and Octobrists were bureaucrats – but whereas few if any in the Ukrainian provinces belonged to the former, many belonged to the latter parties.[97] There are no occupational data for the rank-and-file members of extreme right-wing parties other than the tiny *Russkoe Sobranie,* where on average 30 to 40 per cent of the members were bureaucrats.

After 1906 only the Octobrists and extreme-right parties were legal. That September Prime Minister Stolypin specified that government administrators could not join any political organization advocating revolution or 'struggle against the government (*borbe s pravitelstvom*).'[98] Extreme-right party leaders did not think this injunction applied to them, and they even sent Stolypin a telegram praising his initiative. The police considered extreme-right parties exempt from this restriction and reportedly gave speeches to bureaucrats urging them to join, while sympathetic senior officials tacitly supported extreme right-wing groups without formally joining.[99] Unsympathetic senior bureaucrats, however, did consider them involved in the 'struggle against the government' and steered employees away from them and towards the Octobrists, at least until 1911. In the years before the First World War the fortunes and numbers of the extreme right declined as the indulgent attitude of the powerful towards them dissipated. Ministers now began to receive complaints from extreme-right leaders asking them to rescind Stolypin's injunction because local bureaucrats were using it to prevent government employees from joining their parties. Such complaints increased after 1915 but, by then, the right was no longer a major political force, and most of its powerful sympathizers and supporters had joined the Kadet-led Progressive Bloc, formed that summer.[100] By November 1917 all extreme-right parties had been dissolved.

In the Ukrainian provinces extreme-right party membership dropped from almost 250,000 in 1906, when it was strongest in Volyn province, to no more than 9,000 by 1916 – with the largest group of 1,000 in Kharkiv province.[101] Local leaders, who wanted a regional congress that year, did not know which governor would allow it.[102] In light of the above, apparently by the time that war broke out, rank-and-file bureaucrats avoided direct political activity according to the letter of Stolypin's injunction. Articles in *Sputnik chinovnika* suggest that most of those administrators who were active before the war inclined towards the Kadets or Octobrists rather than towards the extreme right.

Besides political parties, the educated and politically active were also attracted to freemasonry. With perhaps 400 members throughout the Russian Empire in 1914, Freemasons provided a conspiratorial milieu of important persons that was open to all except monarchists, Bolsheviks, and anarchists.[103] Few in numbers, Masons were influential by virtue of their status. They influenced events by persuading important non-members to see things their way and by placing their own into positions of power when possible. Leading Russian Liberals and Ukrainian national activists were Masons and, up to October 1917 when they divided over the issue of separatism, they agreed with each other as Masons on non-Russian national rights and territorial autonomy. This agreement found political expression before the war in jobs and protection for national activists or sympathizers both in and outside government. In early July 1917 this agreement played its role in leading the Provisional Government under Aleksander Kerensky, a Mason, to recognize in principle the political and administrative authority of the Central Rada under Hrushevsky, also a Mason. Because France and French Masons supported this recognition, Russian leaders had to take Ukrainian autonomy seriously.[104]

Insofar as most bureaucrats lived in towns, it must be added that not all Russian-speaking urban dwellers were uniformly hostile to or intolerant of Ukrainian issues. Russian and/or Russian-speaking urban leaders, for their part, moved from supporting cultural demands before the war to by late 1917 supporting Ukrainian territorial autonomy. Almost no one yet advocated political separatism. *Rada,* in its 1913 annual survey of national issues, reported that in terms of resolutions supporting or rejecting national cultural-linguistic demands, provincial zemstvos were the most hostile. In Poltava province the zemstvo had refused to publish anything at all in Ukrainian that year. District zemstvos and city dumas, for their part, were exceptionally sympathetic and consistently voted funds for national projects.[105] The July – August local duma election returns confirmed this trend and its extension to the issue of Ukrainian political autonomy.[106] After weeks of massive pro-Rada demonstrations in Kyiv and the Provisional Government's recognition of the Central Rada, the local regional branches of all but two all-Russian political parties accepted the legitimacy of the Rada and its demand for autonomy. Instead of opposing the Rada, they began seeking places in it and supporting imperial decentralization.[107] The two major groups opposed to autonomy and decentralization got the least votes that summer: the Bolsheviks, who averaged approximately 10 per cent of Ukraine's urban vote, and the extreme-right candidates, who garnered no more than 3 per cent.[108] In short, election returns suggest that by 1917 the climate of urban opinion was more sympathetic towards Ukrainian national issues than had been the case before 1914.

Incomplete returns that summer from major towns show Jewish parties, together with the Ukrainian political parties, which they supported, averaged 25 per cent of the vote – and often approached 50 per cent in towns with 50,000 or fewer inhabitants. Kadets in Kyiv province voted at their party meeting to support the Rada and Ukrainian autonomy as defined in the 'Instruction' of August 1917 (see Chapter 3).[109] Together with the local pro-Rada PSR, Kadets held approximately 50 per cent of the vote in Kyiv province. In August 1917 the Ukrainian branch of the PSR opposed the restricted autonomy of the 'Instruction' and voted against its right-dominated parent party in Petrograd on the issue.[110] The PSR dominated the soviets throughout 1917 – even in Kharkiv and Katerynoslav provinces. In Kyiv, where less than half the population voted, Ukrainian parties averaged 25 per cent of the vote, which was almost the same as the combined total of the Bolshevik (left wing of the RSDWP) and extreme-right parties (see Table 9). However, Ukrainians had the support of local pro-Rada, pro-autonomy Kadets, the PSR, and the Menshevik (right wing of the RSDWP), Polish, and Jewish parties, which together probably accounted for the other 50 per cent of the votes.[111] In the smaller towns the situation was radically different, and no analogous generalizations can be made because few of the major central political parties ran candidates there. Reports from Central Rada organizers from almost every town emphasize that alongside considerable indifference on the part of voters, candidates normally ran in blocs determined by their personal interests or as independents, and not on party slates for specific programs. The Russian and Ukrainian Socialist Revolutionaries, Social Democrats, local soviets, and Kadets appeared most often in local town lists, but by no means in all of them. Government and zemstvo employees frequently formed their own electoral group. Seven towns in Volyn province had a total of seventy-eight groups running for seats, for example, and of those, the Kadets, Socialist Revolutionaries, and Jewish Social Democrats (the Bund) had a total of six. For this reason, it is impossible on the basis of the municipal election returns to infer non-Ukrainian attitudes towards Ukrainian national issues in small towns.[112]

In the Russian Constituent Assembly elections in November 1917, when all men over the age of the age of twenty-one were eligible to vote, in the Ukrainian territories the share of the vote given to Ukrainian and Jewish political parties together had doubled to average nearly 50 per cent, and it was probably higher in the smaller towns. Support for the PSR had dwindled, but when grouped together with Ukrainian and Jewish parties, put roughly two-thirds of the urban vote behind the Central Rada and autonomy. Kadets got 15 per cent. The extreme right averaged no more than 3 per cent, and the Bolsheviks roughly 20 per cent of the votes.[113] In Kyiv the extreme right and Bolshevik vote (18%), increased to 38 per cent, while the federalist-autonomist pro-Ukrainian share dropped from 64 per cent to 44 per cent. The Kadets, with 10 per cent, could decisively influence outcomes.[114] The Mensheviks won few votes in either the summer or November 1917 elections but were influential in unions; they opposed separatism, yet, until January 1919, they backed Ukrainian independence as a lesser evil than Bolshevism.[115]

CHAPTER TWO

Bureaucracy, Law, and Political Parties in Ukrainian Thought

At the beginning of the twentieth century Ukrainians with practical administrative experience subscribed to a variety of prevailing ideas about administration and bureaucracy, ranging from traditional or classical theories advocating hierarchy and centralized control to radical theories calling for local self-government or no government at all. To better understand how men who found themselves claiming power after 1917 reacted to and tried to deal with the government bureaucracies that they inherited this chapter reviews those theories and ideas.

In the eighteenth century cameralism taught that officials had to rationally use central state power to actively provide for the well-being of citizens, promote economic development, and in general, to organize society. These principles heavily influenced tsarist administrative practice, and among its leading advocates were 'Little Russians' like Semen Desnytsky, Oleksander Bezborodko, Vasyl Kochubei, and Dmytro Troshchynsky.[1] Throughout the nineteenth century central and municipal governments grew in size and scope as they either organized new services or took over family-related activities. Between 1890 and 1914 thinkers like Sidney Webb and Adolph Wagner advocated and justified such interventions in the cameralist tradition. Europe's foremost Social Democrat Karl Kautsky initially considered administrators, or what we now call civil servants, a threat, but later, like Weber, saw them to be a necessary group requiring control. Kautsky argued, contrary to Marx, that socialists could not destroy government bureaucracies given the complexities of modern society. In *Die soziale Revolution* (1902) and *Die neue Zeit* (no. 46, 1912), Kautsky explained that bureaucracies could only be taken over and then placed under parliamentary dominance. Socialists should not strive to abolish the bureaucracy, whose importance and size would not diminish after they took power, but to open entry into it for all. The demands of the First World War reinforced centralist-interventionist practices within all belligerent states. Even in Britain the scope and scale of government activity increased stupendously: in 1914, for instance, the Contracts Department in the United Kingdom had twenty clerks; renamed the Ministry of Munitions in 1915, by 1917 it had 65,000 employees in charge of over three million workers.[2]

The Anti-statist Background

Radical educated declared Ukrainians in the national movement saw government from a romantic-populist perspective that was critical, if not hostile, to the cameralist type of interventionist state. They would have applauded Benjamin Tucker, Jan Machajski, and Lenin, who opposed what before 1914 they called bureaucratic 'state socialism.' The writer Taras Shevchenko played an important role in spreading this understanding of government among the population: 'Scribes (*pysari*) and scribblers rule,' he proclaimed in 1860. In another poem written two weeks later he asked why scribblers and tsars were necessary: '*Oi liude, liude neboraky / Na-shcho zdalys vam tsari? / Na-shcho zdalys vam psari?*' Because in his early poetry images of a suffering nation included references to an oppressive state whose personnel included obsequious Russified renegades, Shevchenko also might be considered to have reintroduced into modern Ukrainian thought the idea that Russian/Muscovite rule was foreign rule.[3] Mykola Hohol's (Nikolai Gogol) characterization of officials in his *Dead Souls* was also influential: 'I know them all,' said Sobakevich to Chichikov. 'They are all crooks ... There is one decent person, the Procurator, but quite frankly, he too is a swine.' Panteleimon Kulish, annoyed by the censors' refusal to approve for publication his historical novel *Chorna Rada*, and disillusioned by the lack of reform in general after the death of Nicholas I, concluded in 1857 that politics was pointless and that only writers involved in the apolitical creation of literature could lift Little Russia/Ukraine from decline. Kulish in principle distinguished between a state that was 'good' because its ruler was moral and a state that was 'bad' because its ruler was immoral.[4] His implicit identification of the state as it existed with evil, and his claim that writers would do best to avoid it and devote their energies instead to the search for the 'national soul,' alongside the ideas of Shevchenko and Gogol, formed and reflected a powerful anti-statist current in Ukrainian thought. Ivan Nechui-Levytsky considered service in the tsarist government to be a form of treason: 'And when they [tsarist officials] choose one of our Ukrainians for a higher administrative position, then it is one whose scrupulousness, obsequiousness, policing, and Russificatory zeal outdoes that of even the most committed Katkovite [follower of Russian conservative Slavophile Mikhail Katkov]. So eager is he to make a career that his brow sweats at the thought of it ... These fellow-countrymen are even worse than the foreign Russifiers [who come here from] Russia and other Slavic countries.'[5]

Although Ukrainian nationalists by the end of the nineteenth century began to regard tsarist domination as 'foreign rule,' treason and betrayal remained but marginal themes in Ukrainian literature and letters. The literati did not attempt to formulate, and then enforce by moral censure, a 'code of national behaviour' for Ukrainians, as did their Polish counterparts. Furthermore, there is no evidence of public debate around 1900 between those who advocated participation in the tsarist government as a means of promoting the national interest and those opposed to such participation on any grounds.

Nineteenth-century historians who wrote that in Kyivan Rus', eastern Galicia, and Cossack Ukraine the native population had survived well enough without states in the past, added legitimacy to this anti-statist attitude. Initially formulated by Mykola Ivanyshiv (Ivanishev), Ivan Kamanin, and Volodymyr Antonovych in their work on peasant, burger, and noble self-government, this idea became a key element in the grand narrative of national history elaborated by Mykhailo Hrushevsky, who was the leader of the Central Rada (see Chapter 3). According to this interpretation of the past, a peasant/noble communal-civic order had always coexisted and functioned alongside each successive 'foreign' government that had ruled Ukrainian territory. This 'civil society' in the past had not threatened its foreign rulers and had enabled Ukrainians to survive even though they had not been politically independent. The subtext to this interpretation was that analogous behaviour would enable Ukrainians to survive as loyal subjects in the present under Russian and Austrian rule. Within this scenario communities revolted only when officials infringed upon what the locals considered to be their legitimate prerogatives.

Inasmuch as nineteenth-century national activists reflected politically on state power as it existed, most understood it as domination built on force and not as the exercise of authority via the rule of law. Centrally appointed bureaucrats figured as instruments of domination rather than as agents of benevolence. From this participatory ethnic-communitarian perspective an ideal 'popular government,' once established, would reflect the power of the nation. Such a popular government would be one and indivisible like the nation, democratic by definition, and would not legally define relationships between people with different functions – a view that echoed Rousseau. Because all citizens were bound together by indissoluble ties of nationhood, which represented the ultimate fount of all authority, imposing legally based distinctions would only sow distrust among the people. Since administration in this envisaged democratic order would not be repressive because administering would be the task of the citizens and their representatives, society would not need a hierarchic organization of full-time professionals set apart from the citizenry to ensure that legislative proposals became reality. This Slavophile-socialist variant of romantic nationalism that defined the national movement, in addition, accentuated the political division between the non-national state and the nation, with a class division that included only peasants into 'the nation' – not the 'exploiting' upper and middle classes. This current in nationalist thought also had roots in the anarcho-syndicalist opinions of socialists like Proudhon, who pointed to the Paris Commune, labour parties, unions, and co-operatives as proof that spontaneous, popular, de-centralized self-administration worked in practice:

> To be GOVERNED [sic] is to be watched, inspected, spied upon, directed, law-driven, numbered, regulated, enrolled, indoctrinated, preached at, controlled, checked, estimated, valued, censured, commanded, by creatures who have neither the right nor the wisdom nor the virtue to do so. To be GOVERNED [sic] is to be ... counted, taxed, stamped, measured, numbered, assessed, licensed, authorized ... forbidden, corrected, punished ... It is, under pressure of public utility, and in the name of the general interest, to be placed under contribution, drilled, fleeced, exploited, monopolized, extorted from, squeezed, hoaxed, robbed; then at the slightest resistance, the first word of complaint to be repressed, fined, vilified, harassed ... outraged, dishonoured. That is government; that is its justice; that is its morality.[6]

Mykhailo Drahomanov regarded the state as a necessary evil whose scope had to be as limited as possible. In 1878 he wrote that western Europeans had 'outgrown' the state and were now aspiring to other forms of organization. He advocated decentralized leaderless communal self-government on the grounds that people were striving towards better, more just forms of organization without directors, nobles, or centralized states. As in the cossack *Zaporozhian Sich,* in the future, officials elected by society and subject to instant recall would administer services in an order without hierarchic form: 'no boss, no lord no state (*beznachalna, bezpanska, bezderzhavna*).' In the interim, Ukrainian socialists should attempt to create a non-hierarchic, non-government system of social services based on civilian associations parallel to the state bureaucracy. In keeping with his federalism and distrust of centralized bureaucracy Drahomanov explicitly rejected the notion that Ukrainians should attempt to unite their provinces into a single administrative unit within Russia, as Hungarians recently had within the Austrian Empire, with the aim of future separation.[7] Serhii Podolynsky, an associate of Drahomanov, disseminated a simplified overview of this national-populist view of society and government in his Ukrainian-language pamphlet: *The Steam Engine* (*Parovaia mashyna,* 1875). Read by activists and disseminated among peasants, it tells the story of a peasant who dreams about waking up in the future. He learns that previously bureaucrats, judges, and lawyers had all been in the pay of Jews and landowners who conspired together to exploit the peasants and to jail them for demanding justice. After the peasants realized that they could order their lives without lords, Jews, or bureaucrats, like the Cossacks of old, they took up arms, and once the soldiers sent to suppress them had defected to their side, they took power and established their ideal order. Enemies who surrendered were forgiven and freed. 'We found only landowners, Jews, and bureaucrats insufferable, because they are the source of all evil.' Those who were not killed were given one week to leave 'Ukraine,' so not one of them would remain. For another week, the dream continued, trains left every hour for Germany filled with 'landlords and Jews.' Revolutions in Russia and Germany ensured that Ukraine would not fear invasion. Thereafter, the people decided that the best way to run their lives would be to elect officials from among their own 'to see to minor occasional daily affairs' and to decide on major issues by calling general meetings of all inhabitants.[8] Ivan Franko in his critiques of the 'state socialism' envisaged by German Social Democrats equated administration (*pravlinnia*) with oppression and claimed that a true socialist order would have no government bureaucracy. Society would be based on self-administration by directly elected local councils. There would be no bureaucracy because every citizen would be an unpaid bureaucrat – an idea adopted by the Ukrainian Socialist Revoutionaries in 1918.[9]

Ukrainian SRs published pamphlets in 1917 that spread among the population a critique of tsarist officialdom together with descriptions of a democratic order with elected bureaucrats.[10] Ukrainian Social Democrat leader and spokesman Mykhailo Tkachenko similarly envisaged annual elections of all bureaucrats in a national republic, and these bureaucrats would be subject not only to the voters but also to elected judges. He specified that even standing executive committees could not include appointed officials but should have their officials elected as well. This was in keeping with his party's 1905 program, which envisaged citizens personally taking officials to court if they thought their rights had been violated, but not with its 1916 program, which foresaw the election of higher officials only, and referred only to officials being subject to the law – not to the possibility of making personal suits against them.[11]

Some of Drahomanov's followers did not go on to join or form moderate political parties, nor did they all share his condemnation of violence. V. Debohorii-Mokriievych and V. Kovalik formed conspiratorial terrorist groups whose members and followers became anarchists. In the decade before the First World War groups like 'The Leaderless' (*Bezhnacheltsy*) and the Union of Poor Farmers (*Soiuz bidnykh khliboroiv*) in central and southern Ukraine disseminated not only the writings of anarchists Mikhail Bakunin and Petr Kropotkin but also of Apollon Karelin. Before he returned from France to Russia in 1917, Russian left-wing SRs and the South Russian Group of Anarchists-Syndicalists smuggled in Karelin's writings through Odesa and circulated them in southern Ukraine. He was widely read at the time and influenced Volin, Nestor Makhno's ideological mentor. For Karelin state and society were incompatible, like wolves and lambs: 'The state is a group of criminals at work.'[12]

Makhno, leader of the Ukrainian anarchists, was himself of the opinion that the state and capitalism could not exist without each other and that it was simply impossible for a state to be socialist. In his brand of anarchism no party members were to be admitted into elected councils, and unions were to administer whatever had to be administered. Organizations formed to carry out specific tasks were to do only that task and were not to be allowed to contact or interact with other such organizations. Under no circumstances were such organizations to regulate society.[13] Decrees during the revolutionary years refer to executive organs that carry out co-ordinated administrative functions on a wide scale, but that are not supposed to have power *(vlast)*. Under the authority of soviets/councils, these 'advisory-executive organs' were described as free 'organizations without power (*volni bezvlastni organizatsii*).' The stated underlying assumptions were that the people would spontaneously organize themselves in this manner and that freely undertaken personal initiatives to that end would be forthcoming.[14]

Radicals could also consult the writings of their Russian colleagues for extended explanations of how people could manage their lives without hierarchically organized full-time professionals performing specialized tasks. Russian and Ukrainian socialists, including Podolynsky and Drahomanov, had initially cooperated with each other. They eventually split because of differences over nationality and the peasant commune, not over the role of government. Thus, Russian populists, and later the Russian Socialist Revolutionaries, which attracted Ukrainian-born activists and sympathizers, disseminated ideas about political organization in the Ukrainian provinces that were not much different from those of Ukrainian populists or, for that matter, from those of the anarchists. The man most responsible for the SR credo was Petr Lavrov, founder of Russian populism, whose widely circulated journal *Vpered* influenced thought and debate until the 1900s. In 1876 Lavrov devoted an entire issue of his journal to a closely typed 200-page treatise on the role of the state in future society. Here he explained in detail that after the revolution there would be no such thing as a group of bureaucrats. Everything would be done voluntarily, and work norms agreed upon by all would include a given number of hours for each individual to do office work. No one would have any authority for any longer than needed to fulfil a particular task and that authority would not apply to anything beyond the immediate task. Subordinates could leave at any time but, until they did, they had to unconditionally obey their superiors.[15] A characterization of eighteenth-century French radicals seems applicable to those activists raised on a diet of Shevchenko, Podolynsky, Karelin, and Lavrov: 'They rather give the impression that they believed that merely posting the latest laws on a convenient tree would automatically lead to these being implemented and obeyed.'[16]

In the decades before the First World War people had more frequent interaction with government officials than did their grandparents, including peasants in villages where the scribe, clerk, or secretary was a very important person. The scribe's influence was also crucial in local courts, where increasingly decisions depended not only on vodka and bribes but also on how the scribe had phrased the pertinent documents. Those who otherwise might have cursed the clerk's misdemeanours, meanwhile, would do nothing to him if their families had to get along with each other as neighbours.[17] When after 1917 post-tsarist governments could not continue the pre-revolutionary policy of subordinating village secretaries to county councils, peasants nevertheless effectively retained control over their secretaries in the traditional manner, via their village councils.[18] Thus, secretaries and treasurers, in practice, remained as local rather than central officials.

Whatever its attitudes to bureaucracy, by 1905 the peasantry definitely had been influenced by the idea that the cure for its ills was elections. Peasant delegates to the 1907 Duma wanted to try 'all torturers and bureaucrats from the lowest to the highest' and in their place directly elect all bureaucrats 'from the lowest to the highest.'[19] Popular opinion on the subject was also expressed in countless letters to newspapers in 1917. According to Hnat Zhurybida, for example, the country needed a 'national administration (*uprava*)' elected on the basis of universal suffrage to run its affairs. No one should listen to government commissars because no one elected them.[20] The Socialist Revolutionaries called for all administrative officials to be elected and subject to immediate recall as well as private prosecution in cases of malfeasance. These officials, meanwhile, would presumably be those responsible for running the water, electricity, education, and housing services that the SR wanted placed under duma and zemstvo control.[21] Those leaders who realized that controlling a state meant having an appointed, hierarchic, central organization with a division of labour working according to impersonal rules, able to impose authority and implement decisions among an entire population, and not only party supporters, were few in 1917 and they faced no easy task. They lived in a society where peasants saw no need to subordinate their village councils to county councils and where urban populations also still thought of politics in terms of traditional patronage/client networks. Party political leaders within such an environment who restricted themselves to modern party building based on impersonal ties, interests, and class risked alienating peasants if they tried to subordinate traditional communal to *new* county officials. Circumstances arguably forced them, in turn, to devote more energy to building rival new patronage/client networks than the modern impersonal political organizations based on interests that they knew existed in western Europe. What Ukrainian leaders and intellectuals did share with their counterparts in Europe, however, was ignorance of the link between the expansion of the government activities that they called for and the numerical increase of bureaucrats.

The Ukrainian Communist Party (UKP), formed in January 1920 by the left wings of the Ukrainian Socialist Revolutionaries (*Borotbists*) and the Ukrainian Social Democrats, was the only Ukrainian political party during the revolutionary years to include explicit anti-statist ideas in its program. The UKP sought an independent Ukraine with its own independent Communist party, and its program reflected the radical national anti-statist traditions. The UKP borrowed heavily also from the March 1919 Russian Communist Party Congress resolutions and Nikolai Bukharin and Evgenii Preobrazhenskii's *ABC of Communism,* published that summer – both influenced by Lavrov's ideas. In the envisaged Communist order, officials would not be elected as much as compulsorily assigned administrative jobs on a rotational basis. The book did not mention who would do the assigning. While initially the candidate pool was to include only soviet members, Communist leaders envisaged expanding it to eventually include all citizens, and turning the 'state apparatus' into an 'apparatus of workers.' Officials were to be subject to immediate recall, not law.[22]

Moderate Opinions

Under the influence of classical liberal theories about government as a 'night watchman' controlled by the rule of law and public debate, Drahomanov in 1884 modified his earlier ideas on bureaucracy. In his project for a Russian constitution – a copy of which Prime Minister Serge Witte allegedly kept in his drawer – Drahomanov did not actually discuss relationships between standing committees staffed by full-timers and elected part-time deliberative bodies. But he did isolate three cardinal principles related to government and bureaucracy that were ignored by his later anarcho-communist followers. First, divisions of function between elected and appointed officials had to be worked out between all concerned and clearly specified. Implicit here is the understanding that administrative appointments should not be subject to political parties and that local bodies would both appoint and train some full-time staff. Second, all administrators had to be subordinate not only to voters but to the courts. Third, although all citizens could be administrators, they had to be literate and educated beyond their particular trade or profession.[23] This project reveals that despite his communalist-egalitarianism Drahomanov did not see good government as 'no government,' but as something whose powers were limited by courts, elected representatives, and the division of responsibilities between trained executive, legal, and administrative officials. Bureaucracy was a useful tool, not a dangerous institution. Like aristocratic British and radical American critics at the time, Drahomanov was suspicious of full-time unelected merit-based bureaucrats and preferred a rotation or 'spoils system' wherein bureaucrats, as agents of political parties rather than governments, would change after each election. This kind of system allowed elected leaders to appoint people who they trusted to serve them. It would keep central power weak by ensuring that officials in office would be more interested in cultivating post-government employment for themselves than in trying to protect their government jobs and increasing their prerogatives. It guaranteed the balance of power at the cost of administrative continuity and efficiency. Ironically, however, from the 1880s to 1914, in response to critics in their countries who condemned the rotation system as corrupt and inefficient, both American and British governments steadily increased the percentages of their administrators hired by merit and competitive examination, and decreased those appointed according to elections and political party affiliation.

Drahomanov's account of the United States and Switzerland as idealized countries, where representative assemblies fulfilled executive and administrative functions through elected bureaucrats, influenced moderate pre-revolutionary activists. In 1905 they republished his *Shvaitsarska respublika* (1899). In their pamphlets and programs that year, like their mentor, they pointed to Switzerland and America as political models, but in general, administrative matters received little mention. Those who do mention government services clearly show that they thought their future ideal state should have many more functions and duties than the tsarist state had. They wanted bureaucracies to be subject to locally elected assemblies, rather than to a federal or imperial centre, bureaucrats to be made subject to the law and liable for prosecution by any citizen, and all elected officials as well as bureaucrats to be local people. While the more radical among them also mention the election of officials, this demand was not characteristic of the moderates. Under the existing system, their readers were told, each official was a tsar unto himself and interested only in bribes and spying.[24]

Drahomanov's ideas are also found in the writings of Ukrainian liberals Bohdan Kistiakovsky and Maksym Kovalevsky. The stillborn Ukrainian Federal Democratic Party (UFDP), which included Kistiakovsky among its founders, differed from the socialists inasmuch as the UFDP specified that administrative courts, not citizens, should charge and prosecute officials.[25] The centrist Ukrainian Party of Socialist Federalists (UPSF) and the Ukrainian Democratic Agrarian Party (UDAP, formed in 1917) did not directly deal with bureaucracy or administration in their programs. They only implied that positions would be appointive and subject to the courts.[26]

National leaders in Habsburg-ruled western Ukraine agreed with their moderate eastern co-nationals that the bureaucracy had to be subject to the law, and unelected.[27] The major Ukrainian political party in that region, the National Democrats (UNDP), explicitly demanded a national bureaucracy to administer a separate province named Eastern Galicia. In the interim, the party wanted as many Ukrainians in the local bureaucracy as warranted by their share of the population in the Austro-Hungarian Empire. In the years before the First World War the UNDP regarded the local Polish-dominated bureaucracy in Galicia as even more arbitrary, unaccountable, corrupt, and omnipotent than the central bureaucracy. They argued that since Ukrainians had attained parliamentary representation and the bureaucracy could not be changed, it was now time to influence the mechanisms of policy implementation such as they were, as without such influence, laws could never be implemented. Pointing to the impact of Czechs and Poles in the bureaucracy, the UNDP argued that it was wrong to ignore the importance of bureaucracy. Education in the native language, accordingly, should be valued as a means of educating patriotic administrators.[28]

National leaders, as will be shown, realized that they had to deal with the relationship between ministerial bureaucracies and federalism, but in their first talks with the Provisional Government in April 1917 they made no mention of subordinating ministerial offices in Ukraine to the regional Ukrainian Assembly in Kyiv that they demanded.[29] They referred only to persons familiar with the country staffing central offices in Ukraine and to Ukrainian being recognized as an official language. This arguably stemmed from tactical considerations – a desire to keep Ukraine's Russian-speakers behind the Rada. But the idea was 'in the air.' Max Weber that same spring had observed that creating autonomy in the tsarist empire would require replacing Russian officials with elected Ukrainian civil servants, and not establishing a parallel territorial ministerial structure.[30] In the May and June 1917 issues of the German newspaper *Frankfurter Zeitung* Weber explained that the actual ruler of the modern state was the bureaucracy and that it was 'a horrendous error of the literati' to think that a large organization like a state could be governed without a core of full-time salaried career bureaucrats to execute the decisive everyday routines. Explicitly referring to Drahomanov, Weber wrote that unpaid party appointees and elected respectable citizens still had a role in medium-sized cities alongside bureaucrats, but as such people were doing less and less work, this kind of amateur administration was doomed. Only private bureaucracies and central parliaments could check the power that fell to government bureaucracy by virtue of its functions and knowledge. Weber did not think a 'hierarchic organization of elected officials' was even possible. They existed in the United States but were 'greatly inferior as an instrument of precision compared with ... appointed officials': 'It is in general not possible to attain a high level of technical administrative efficiency with an elected staff of officials.'[31] Thus, moderate socialist leaders during the first weeks of the revolution, who imagined Ukraine as part of a decentralized multinational democratic liberal Russian state with full-time centrally appointed bureaucrats within a single centralized ministerial system, were thinking along the same lines as Weber. The differences lay in emphasis. National leaders allotted bureaucrats narrower spheres of jurisdiction and greater powers to various civic and elected organizations.

Mykhailo Hrushevsky in his constitutional writings stressed the role of elected representative bodies. Like the socialists, he seemed to believe that these public agencies would at some point become coterminous with the state. As president of the Central Rada, in a series of pamphlets published in 1917, he expressed the same disdain of 'traitors' as did Shevchenko and Nechui-Levytsky, and he condemned an entire generation of 'demoralized' Ukrainians who, by the nineteenth century, from greed and fear, had developed the conviction that the purpose of life was defined by service to the tsar. Yet, he also cautioned Ukrainians that their populist anti-statist attitude towards organized government, much influenced by radical Russian ideas that identified the state exclusively with destructive bureaucratism and imperialism, was both erroneous and dangerous. Echoing Drahomanov, Hrushevsky in March 1917 called for the creation of a hierarchic network of non-government national-civil organizations throughout Ukraine with broad areas of competence, and parallel to these, a hierarchy of non-Ukrainian organizations. He did not specify how this chain of committees related to the established government bureaucracy. But, in an important departure from Drahomanov, presumably resulting from the pressure of events, a few months later Hrushevsky did specify that true autonomy required Ukraine to have its own ministerial administration parallel to that of the Russian central government. This would have given it a status within a decentralized federal Russia similar to that of Hungary in the Dual Monarchy – although he nowhere explicitly made such a comparison.[32]

Hrushevsky did not elaborate upon what he thought the relationship between public, elected- deliberative, and standing appointed executive bodies, the bureaucracy, was supposed to be within the envisaged autonomous Ukraine. In the Third Universal of November 1917 he specified that the locally elected bodies would be formally under the jurisdiction of the Rada's General Secretariat (the Ministry of Internal Affairs), but he nowhere explained how elected officials were to prevent appointed officials from taking over their authority. The gist of his writings suggests that, in the liberal tradition, he hoped that the legislative, executive, and representative branches of government would balance each other. In a phrase reminiscent of Lenin's utopian belief expressed in his *State and Revolution* about everybody who was literate working part-time as bureaucrats so no one could become a bureaucrat, Hrushevsky referred to a society where 'the state was socialized and society statified.' This cryptic formulation echoed pre-war populist ideals, but it also reflected a pre-war liberal-technocratic understanding of 'organic' or 'cultural' work and a wartime experience that seemed to confirm that bureaucracy was both necessary and desirable, as long as it facilitated rather than hindered civil and public organizations involved in administration.

The army's usurpation of the civilian administration as of 1914 severely hampered the tsarist government's ability to manage the war effort. Liberals filled the administrative vacuum with a host of voluntary public organizations co-ordinated by the Union of Zemstvos and the Union of Towns (together, *Zemgor*). Supported by the tsar and the ministers of war and land use to the tune of more than 500 million roubles, which was fifty times more than the unions had received from voluntary donations, these auxiliary, nominally non-government organizations dealt with welfare, production, and procurement, but they did so not very much more honestly or efficiently than did government agencies. Organizationally, the significance of the Zemgor administrative structure was that, despite being paid by the government, its thousands of employees were independent of it because they were hired through the Socialist Revolutionary, Kadet, and left Octobrist parties that controlled it. Kadet leaders already in 1915 were beginning to see the Zemgor bureaucracies as the basis of a future republican government.[33] Two years later, when the tsar fell, the Provisional Government formalized the existing interaction between government and nominally non-government organizations and declared its intention to ultimately transform the entire Zemgor structure into a government agency.

The theoretical implication of this activity was important as it convinced leaders that they were creating a new kind of government: 'a free civic organization' that would mediate in the general interest rather than repress in the name of a particular interest.[34] Perhaps this is what Hrushevsky had in mind when he described the new democratic Ukraine as a place with public organizations, an elected local bureaucracy similar to America's and England's, working alongside a professional salaried bureaucracy. Balanced by this division of power and subject to law, the bureaucracy would not dominate the other two bodies by virtue of its function. Thus, as the main author of Ukraine's 1917 Constitution, Hrushevsky ensured that it contained a provision in Article 26 subordinating full-time bureaucrats to the law. On this issue Ukrainian political leaders demonstrated more sophistication than Lenin in power, who, although a lawyer by training, thought that one government bureaucracy was best controlled by another government bureaucracy rather than by laws or private corporate bureaucracies – which in any case would not exist under socialism. In his criticism of socialists in 1917 Weber predicted that such a situation would make the population 'as powerless as the fellahs of ancient Egypt.' The 'shell of bondage' would be reinforced by fettering every individual to his job and occupation.[35]

The man in charge of the General Secretariat under the Central Rada, Volodymyr Vynnychenko, before the revolution wrote nothing on state and bureaucracy. As a member of the Social Democrats' central committee, living in exile in western Europe between 1907 and 1914, Vynnychenko was likely influenced by Karl Kautsky. The 1905 USDP party program assumed that bureaucracy would continue to exist and demanded that bureaucrats be legally accountable not only to the courts but also directly to individual citizens. Vynnychenko later condemned the Rada's failure to dismantle the existing bureaucracy, as advocated by Marx, and as he thought the Bolsheviks had done.[36] Writing in 1919 in exile, just after his conversion to communism, Vynnychenko was actually criticizing his own policies enacted two years earlier as party leader and head of the General Secretariat. Those policies, in turn, as expressed in the Rada's and the Secretariat's declarations, which Vynnychenko either authored or co-authored, reflected Drahomanov's and Hrushevsky's ideas – not the ideas of Shevchenko, Gogol, or Franko. Lenin, of course, within days of taking power dropped the extreme anti-bureaucratism he had espoused in *State and Revolution,* but there was to be no legal-parliamentary control of the bureaucracy in his regime of the sort that Ukrainian leaders, including Vynnychenko, had planned in theirs. By deciding to use existing bureaucrats, Lenin effectively ended up following Kautsky, just as Vynnychenko had done, although Vynnychenko did not admit this in his book – written while he was enamoured of Bela Kun's Communist Hungary.

One of Vynnychenko's conservative postwar critics, therefore, is unfair in condemning Vynnychenko's actions in 1917 on the basis of what he wrote in 1919. Vynnychenko's views on government when he was in exile were not the views he held when he was in power:

> And when according to the head of the Ukrainian government Vynnychenko all administrators, liberal or reactionary ... were 'the worst and most pernicious people' towards whom he 'immediately felt revulsion and disgust,' then how could people [like him and his socialist associates] be expected to regard the government bureaucracy in Ukraine ...? Obviously they thought that they could eventually throw out the old administrative apparatus to the last clerk ... and place their hopes on 'the people,' saying 'the nation gives and creates everything. Intellectual forces will appear. Our Russified intellectuals will join us. We will ... put them to work.'[37]

After two years of upheaval and party splits between their left and right wings, Ukrainian leaders changed their ideas about administration. Left-wing SDs and SRs, as noted above, adopted the pre-revolutionary anti-statist approach towards bureaucracy. Centrists and moderates decided to curb zemstvo and urban autonomy and tried to centralize. Thus, the Ukrainian right SDs reaffirmed at their January 1919 conference that Ukraine was still not yet ready for socialist revolution and that the country's proletariat had to participate in national state building via 'bourgeois democratic' government and its centralized professional bureaucracy.[38]

Government Size and Party Politics

Before 1917 national leaders represented a dominant minority in an empire. They were concerned primarily with cultural issues and devoted little thought to problems of practical politics such as bureaucracy. Even among those who had given some thought to bureaucracy, and accepted that it should exist, not many had reflected in much detail on how the duties and services that they wanted government to provide were to relate to its size and how it should be controlled. Here, after 1917, national leaders acted by trial and error. As it turned out, their ad hoc solutions resembled those of other governments.

Three weeks before taking power, Lenin explicitly stated in *Can the Bolsheviks Retain State Power?* that he would make the government administrative apparatus as big and all-encompassing as possible. No Ukrainian leader is known to have made a similar pronouncement but the policies of Ukrainian leaders set them in this same direction. Most activists and leaders were leftists, and as demonstrated in the RUP's program, they sought improved standards of justice and social well-being for the population. Like socialists and liberals elsewhere they wanted the government to take on those obligations – which meant that the 'good government' that they wanted to create for an autonomous Ukraine would have been bigger in size (per capita) and scope than the tsarist or Habsburg governments. The programs of the four largest political parties that were to play key roles in the years 1917 to 1921, namely, the Social Democrats, the Socialist Revolutionaries, the National Democrats, and the Socialist Federalists, all included demands for the provision of welfare, minimum wages, factory inspections, and universal free education – which needed people in offices to plan, implement, fund, and supervise the implementation of these demands. The SFs called for 'socialization' of the means of production in order to overcome Ukraine's legacy of economic colonialism. The SRs specified that they stood for 'nationalization,' state monopolies, and supervision. In both cases, their governments would inevitably be bigger than the tsarist government.[39]

This trend reflected the times, and if Ukrainians had been able to successfully defend their borders, it is unlikely that their state would have been much different from those of their neighbours. Before the First World War Ukraine's future leaders, like most educated Europeans, believed that societies ruled by skilled managers and/or technocrats were preferable to societies dominated by wealthy owners of private factories and land. This predisposition was reflected in and disseminated by the incredible popularity of Edward Bellamy's *Looking Backward* (1887), a novel that depicted how a future state had emerged peacefully from an old order and was run as if it were one big national co-operative, where the only thing government officials administered was the economy. Between its appearance and 1917 the book was published in 1,250,000 copies in English alone. It had ten German printings, four Polish printings, and eight abridged Russian printings, with a combined run of over 50,000 non-English copies. Among its reviewers was a future Ukrainian minister, Mykhailo Tuhan-Baranovsky, who in 1906 confirmed the profound impression that Bellamy's ideas were making among Ukrainian intellectuals and workers alike.[40]

Faced with the demands of war, like all belligerent governments, the Central Rada began building this previously imagined huge interventionist bureaucracy during its last weeks in power – but its place in the envisaged constitutional order was unclear. Topped by a Main Economic Council, this monolith was supposed to control prices, transportation, hours of electricity use, and food production, as well as prevent people from speaking on the telephone for longer than fifteen minutes at a time.[41] In January 1919 the Directory developed a plan for a system of public surveillance and concentration camps. Political Information Bureaus attached to the Ministry of Internal Affairs and the army sought detailed information about everything, much like the surveillance organizations of other powers at the time. Agents reported not only about political parties, popular sympathies, and morale, but about what co-ops were doing, prices, and the conditions of kindergartens. Those who finished the course at the Directory's intelligence school had no illusions about their tasks. They were told that if they refused to work where they were sent they would be arrested and shot as deserters.[42] In October 1919 the Directory introduced forced labour on railways – like the Bolsheviks had done – and during its successful 1920 summer offensive the Directory decided to require everyone in its territory to register with the government on penalty of fine or imprisonment.[43]

All of this resembled the cameralism practised by their 'Little Russian' tsarist precursors and the interventionism of the Provisional Government, more than it did the non-interventionist principles of pre-war socialist populism. Hrushevsky and Vynnychenko attempted to resolve the tension between Ukraine's populist-federalist intellectual traditions and the practical demands of politics in a time of crisis. As an emigre, Hrushevsky inclined to the cameralist side. In keeping with the practice of his last days in power he called for a 'dictatorship of the working people in the form of a soviet socialist republic.'[44] His fellow right-wing SRs seemed to be oblivious to the problem. Retaining, on the one hand, their anarcho-syndicalist federal vision of a decentralized participatory democratic Ukraine, they also stressed that their new state would use more force than the old one that it would replace: 'This will really be a dictatorship,' wrote a former minister, Mykola Shapoval, in 1920. 'The socialist state will be a real state, that is, a forced union with a developed technical apparatus of force.'[45] The western Ukrainian government was moving along parallel lines, although its ultimate size would probably have been smaller inasmuch as it recognized private ownership.

Conservative critics of the SR- and SD-dominated eastern Ukrainian government observed another characteristic of their leaders that was not elaborated in print but gives an insight into their understanding of politics and administration. Conservatives thought that because tsarist Ukrainian political parties had emerged so recently, they were not political parties in the western European sense of the term but, rather, conspiratorial clubs. Easterners, unlike westerners, who had been activists before the First World War regarded government positions as sinecures, that is, as rewards for years of service to the Ukrainian cause.[46] Related to this was the Directory's tendency to hire only SR and SD party members as administrators, and for SR and SD party leaders serving as government leaders in 1919 to disperse huge amounts of government money to their own parties, but not to others.[47] When to cope with a numbing workload western Ukrainians sought to hire according to ability from a huge pool of willing candidates, rather than according to political affiliation, eastern Ukrainian leaders became displeased. 'Lazy slaves without education' wanted to, but could not administer, complained critics, yet in all offices these 'eternal students, chauffeurs and accountants,' who knew only how to 'take car rides to lunch,' lorded it over university-educated western Ukrainians.[48] It is unclear whether such practices characterized appointments to higher-level positions only or to middle- and lower-level positions as well. Either case would point to the lingering influence of the traditional idea of politics as personal, and that as leaders of governments eastern Ukrainians still thought of politics in terms of personal coteries. What mattered was not hierarchy and rules, but to whom one owed loyalty and friendship. This ideological/traditional preference to use informal personal networks rather than impersonal organized officials would have been reinforced by the success national activists had with co-operatives and self-help groups.

This personal-traditional conception of politics identified by western Ukrainians had similarities to the early American and British spoils system of bureaucracy favoured by Hrushevsky and Drahomanov, and not unknown in Bolshevik practice during the revolutionary years.[49] But to anyone raised in the professionalized Austrian administrative system, these populist and 'spoils system' ideas of administration were tantamount to chaos.

CHAPTER THREE

The Central Rada, March 1917 to April 1918

After the abdication of the tsar in March 1917 Ukrainian leaders in Kyiv created the Central Rada and that November proclaimed the Ukrainian National Republic (UNR). The Rada, composed of socialists, claimed authority over the Ukrainian provinces of the Russian Empire – including the Crimea (see Map 1). From the summer of 1917 the Rada was one of six organizations nominally responsible for administering the empire alongside commissars appointed by the Provisional Government, the central government ministries, the army general staff, the newly elected city dumas, and provincial rural government councils (zemstvos), which the Provisional Government had begun to extend to the *volost* (county) level as its local agencies. Although national leaders realized the importance of government bureaucracy, for political reasons they delayed creating one and then, for ideological reasons, delayed centralizing it until after they declared independence. Under the Central Rada Ukraine arguably had too many rather than too few bureaus and bureaucrats and, in practice, who obeyed whom depended on circumstances.

Functioning, Order, and Disorder

In theory the zemstvos were subordinate to Petrograd-appointed Interior Ministry commissars, and the intention was that at some point they were to take over all provincial administration; nevertheless, the zemstvos were not formally incorporated into the administrative bureaucracy. Furthermore, local ministerial personnel were supposed to be subordinate to the commissars, but because other ministries regarded zemstvo personnel as only Interior Ministry officials they kept their own personnel separate from the commissars. Army officers could override any civilian official at any time. In addition to these centrally linked organizations and the Rada and the dumas there were a maze of councils and committees affiliated to one or another of at least nine civilian central hierarchies some of which were, and some of which were not, part of imperial organizations (all-Russian). Imperial structures included soviets, co-operatives, trade unions, some political parties, and the Russian Peasants Union (*soiuz*). The Central Rada, various national-minority organizations, reading clubs, the Ukrainian Peasants Union (*Spilka*), and Ukrainian political parties limited their activity to the Ukrainian provinces.[1] Throughout 1917 the number of sub-imperial entities increased as Ukrainian and non-Ukrainian organizations formed either Ukrainian territorial sub-units within imperial structures or organizationally independent national institutions. All local organizations were usually represented in a local Committee of Public Organizations.

Every group that could do so sent its activists throughout the country, and many published pamphlets and articles explaining in detail how people were to organize themselves and carry on under enemy occupation.[2] Not everyone understood what was what. In mid-June 1917, for instance, a provincial district Rada representative urgently requested Kyiv to send an agitator/instructor because peasants were confused by the myriad of councils and committees that had appeared and had no idea whom to turn to for what. One eyewitness reported that by the end of 1917 there were so many instructions and explanations from so many authorities that even lawyers could not understand them and that the result was chaos. In the avalanche of messages items obviously got lost. Among the thousands of complaint letters sent by ordinary people to the Central Rada, one from a soldier who had travelled through Podillia province that autumn noted that county and district committees did not transmit village resolutions up or government instructions down.[3]

This plethora of officials and new offices in 1917 inevitably contributed to weakening vertical authority. Officials could not always implement the decisions of their superiors: they got contradictory instructions, or they got no decisions at all to implement, or they spent more time feuding than working. The roots of this administrative collapse had little to do with the Ukrainian movement or the Central Rada. They go back to 1914, when the army placed hundreds of miles of territory behind the front under military command – which included the provinces west of the Dnipro. Within this territory any officer, at any level, at any time could command civilian officials, or dismiss them, without having to account to any minister. Within a year ministers were using words like 'chaos,' 'anarchy,' and 'madhouse' to describe the administration. The situation was worsened by the ministerial leapfrog that characterized the last years of the tsarist regime – between 1915 and 1917 the head of the Interior Ministry, for example, went through six incumbents. As each official had coteries of clients and favourites, he brought with him new assistants, who in turn hired new directors, who in turn brought in their subordinates. The changes wrought havoc with routines as people either moved after they had learned their jobs or did not even stay long enough to learn them. Due procedure disintegrated. Not knowing whom to turn to lower officials stopped referring to immediate superiors or local associates and instead sent telegrams directly to Kyiv about the various problems that they faced which they inevitably labelled as serious. In response the Rada Secretariat sent commands to the immediate superior commissar concerned to 'do something.'[4]

Failures in implementation cannot be isolated from the broader social context born of political uncertainty and a general quest for democracy. By the end of 1917 officials either feared or already experienced disturbances in the accepted patterns of security, tenure, pay, assignments, and promotions. The situation was characterized by rapid promotions, a breakdown of the division between the personal and the professional due to increased interference in hiring and functioning by party and family interests, intensified clique animosities, and slowed down office work, as aggrieved individuals complained to office committees which, in turn, called meetings to resolve issues. Finally, problems can be traced to bad organization rather than no organization. On 4 January 1918, for example, the day the Bolsheviks formally declared war on the Central Rada, its new war minister declared demobilization; because officers duly implemented the command the resulting organizational chaos helped the Bolsheviks take over most of the country with only minimal resistance from newly formed units who lacked a central command.[5] Related to this were overlapping authorities that seriously impeded troop deployment, as pointed out by the Koziatyn military commissar in his urgent complaint to the general secretary of the army in January 1918: staff headquarters was far away (in Bila Tserkva); the army commander gave orders contradicting it; Kyiv issued different orders; while he, others, and civilian commissars interfered with military commissars. There were no commanders at vital communications nodes that could give commands related to a general strategic plan.[6] That February, to give another example, the Central Rada declared something that might be best termed 'partial' martial law and gave a chief commissar attached to the general staff full civilian authority, which included the right to appoint and dismiss officials. Provincial and district military commandants, meanwhile, were to be appointed by the War Ministry. However, the authority of these commandants was conditional, and they could command civilian authorities only in times of emergency. They otherwise were envisaged as functioning alongside, not above, their civilian counterparts, except in military matters – but the decree did not specify what constituted 'military' as opposed to 'civilian' matters in time of war. In the event of conflicts, both sides were to refer to the relevant civilian ministries. The desire to balance democratic accountability with central control by limiting the authority of the commandants was perhaps commendable but, administratively, it made conflicts and deadlock inevitable.[7]

The Provisional Government formed new agencies, but then for as long as two months did not give them rules delineating procedures, functions, and tasks. Rationing was declared in April, but not until June did orders come to organize a survey of supplies, stocks, and needs. The establishment of a separate Ministry of Food Supply resulted in duplication and overlap of functions with the Ministry of Agriculture, while the establishment of Land Committees alongside Food Committees further muddied lines of authority and tasks. The decision to delegate a group of people to control grain prices was not matched by establishing a parallel group to control the distribution and prices of manufactured commodities. Since local committees ultimately could only rely on persuasion, peasants quickly learned that they were unlikely to face sanctions if they did not carry out instructions they disliked – which discredited government authority in general.[8]

When the tsar abdicated Dmytro Krainsky, inspector of prisons in Chernihiv province, observed that 'the people became primitive (*prostoi narod dikoval*)' primarily because of the impact of thousands of mutinous and deserting troops which poured into local towns by the trainload as they made their way home. Political positions became mere titles as authority devolved to committees, and the rule of thumb was that whoever had the lower social status was right: 'Every group of individuals related to each other in some way, whether socially or officially, formed committees that controlled all within their respective spheres.' Centrally appointed commissars at all levels served simply as intermediaries between these groups and Petrograd: 'In these conditions, naturally, every group, every organization, left the sphere of general government administration, and represented an individual entity subject only to itself, and it had power (*sila*) if it could win the support of other groups.' When the municipal elections ended, the still mostly non-Bolshevik soviets became the de facto local executive authorities and, implicitly, according to Krainsky, if bureaucrats in provincial towns agreed to obey anyone it was these soviets, who did attempt to keep services and administration functioning. He himself related that he still took orders from Petrograd that summer. This disinclination to obey authority existed in tandem with 'administrative democratization,' that is, the subordination of office heads to committees of clerks, which in Krainsky's view, undermined efficiency.[9]

In response to the prevailing situation, by 1917 village councils were beginning to run their own affairs and, with the abolition of the police, the village scribe or secretary, usually loyal to the council, became particularly influential. Which officials were obeyed, and whether villages obeyed any officials at all, depended on the local government council. An eyewitness that spring noted that village clerks in Radomysl district in Kyiv province were all hostile to the Central Rada.[10] In towns official relations between centrally appointed commissars and the elected duma, which ran the municipal bureaucracy, depended on the personal relationships between the men involved. As one peasant conference delegate quipped, everyone was now a tsar and all were equal.[11] How long a given group dominated a local council depended on the influence of its activists and on how many local people were willing to devote more than a few hours a week to their group. All, in turn, thought it their right to give instructions to the bureaucrats. Apparently provincial gubernatorial staff decided when they would work for their commissars, but they could just as well take orders, initially from their local executive committees of representatives of social groups and/or soviets. All ministries were supposed to provide personnel for the local Committee of Public Organizations. While soldiers had to swear allegiance to the Provisional Government, officials were expected to take their loyalty oath only after the Constituent Assembly had gathered.

In Russia by November 1917 most of the thousands of committees that had formed during the previous eight months had either disappeared or been subordinated, at least in theory, to a larger centrally controlled union and/or party organization that had full-time staff.[12] The issue has not been studied in Ukraine but by the end of 1917 most of its rural councils, and possibly many other organizations, were probably dominated by Ukrainian Socialist Revolutionaries whose members made up most of the Rada's travelling agitators and who usually dominated local Land Committees, village councils, newly formed counties, local governing councils (zemstvos), and Peasants Union councils. Since they were the majority in the Central Rada, how did the SRs cope with this organizational issue?

National leaders were thinking about government bureaucracy already during the first days of the Rada and in their brief to the Provisional Government that April they specifically referred to the possibility of establishing a 'Regional Commissariat' for their provinces and a 'Ukrainian ministry' as part of the Provisional Government.[13] Yet, they did not attempt to subordinate local offices of central ministries and organizations to themselves. Until the autumn of 1917 most regarded the Central Rada as a 'public organization,' and even afterwards the Provisional Government regarded it as a government agency staffed by its nominees. Senior Socialist Federalist Party leaders in St Petersburg, accordingly, decided that coalition building with non-Russian political parties would give the Rada a legitimacy that it lacked and instructed its president, Hrushevsky, and his SR associates in Kyiv to form coalitions with non-Russian parties rather than trying to take over the administration.[14] The Rada thus put itself forward as representing only Ukrainians in Ukraine, and in the First Universal of June 1917 it made no explicit demands for territorial administration. With respect to government bureaucracy, the First Universal only stated that local populations could elect new administrations where incumbents were hostile to 'Ukrainian interests.' In March 1918 Hrushevsky observed that the imperial bureaucracy would continue to treat Ukraine as a 'colony' regardless of who ruled, and in mid-June he wrote that during the first months of its existence the Central Rada could not count on either 'the entire Ukrainian administrative machine' or that 'passive civilian mass whose behaviour is determined by the government's position and will.'[15] In practice, Hrushevsky accepted the situation in the name of political expediency.

Refusal to take resolute administrative initiatives stemmed not only from tactical reasons. Political rivalry played a role. As the biggest Ukrainian political party, the Socialist Revolutionaries had the most sympathizers and activists at the local level. SRs could dominate provincial administrative organs and ignore political parties and central ministries in Kyiv whenever they chose to do so.[16] In many villages through the summer of 1917 the Ukrainian SRs and their *Spilka* also managed to co-opt or defeat the Russian SRs and their peasants' unions. While the Ukrainian SRs sat on the Central Rada, they often opposed the Rada's policies because they were enacted by its rivals the Ukrainian Social Democrats and the Socialist Federalists, who dominated the Rada and its Secretariat, but had minimal if any influence in local districts and villages.[17] The SDs and SFs were numerically small. They focused their activities in Kyiv on winning the support of non-Ukrainian moderates, and they would control any central administrative organs. But they lost the organizational initiative in the rest of Ukraine to the SRs, for whom political freedom was pointless without land reform.[18] Bureaucrats in this situation could choose to implement whatever they wanted to, or in the face of conflicting instructions, do nothing at all.

The Central Rada's first practical administrative measure, in April 1917, was to dispatch into the country hundreds of volunteer travelling agitators ('instructors') to form a countrywide hierarchy of elected pro-Rada committees. There are no studies of the impact of these agitators, but in some areas they seem to have had success. In the wake of the municipal elections, for instance, they managed to forward reports of local results from the entire country to the Rada's Organizational Bureau, which as noted in Chapter 1, were sometimes very detailed. Their reports on village attitudes show that at least some were competent and able. Programs were less crucial in determining village loyalties, they suggest, than who arrived first and their personal speaking and organizational abilities. Reports frequently mention how after hours of stubborn argument a persistent Rada activist could swing meetings from hostility or suspicion expressed in Russian, to support expressed in Ukrainian.[19] One young student in a group of travelling instructors related how at their first meeting he spoke in Russian. After asking the assembled crowd whether he should continue '*po rusku*' or in 'Ukrainian' – a word few peasants yet applied to themselves – as he expected, they replied, 'po Rusku.' Learning their lesson, in the next villages the Ukrainians would ask if they should speak 'in the landlord's language (*po pansku*)' or 'in our language (*po nashomu*)' – the crowd replied 'po nashomu' and meetings went on in Ukrainian.[20]

Evaluations of these Rada activists vary. A supporter of independence who worked in a zemstvo was critical of the 'Ukrainian populist intelligentsia' among whom political illiteracy, lack of education, and administrative incompetence existed alongside 'the energy and temperament of chauvinists.'[21] A Ukrainian Bolshevik was impressed and dismayed at how the SRs had established themselves throughout the country via their peasants' unions. Working in villages presumably loyal to the Central Rada, he explained in December 1917 that they were dominated by the local educated, who after the fall of the tsar were joined by local bureaucrats: 'In strictly national terms, the Ukrainian poor and Ukrainian proletarians cannot muster the intellectual (*intellihentnykh syl*) or the organizational talent to counter the [combined] pressure of the recently red-painted bureaucracy and ... the rural educated. The Ukrainian Republic's entire state apparatus, in this situation, will fall into the hands of the slightly renewed and slightly improved old class.'[22]

The vertical civil organizational tie between the capital and the provinces that these Rada activists established could apparently implement some of the instructions issued by the General Secretariat in a working relationship with society that was governmental in practice if not in law. The Secretariat ran a Refugee Department through an already existing volunteer organization of Galician Ukrainian refugees, for example.[23] The Postal and Telegraph Workers Union, under Andrii Makarenko (who did not actually sit in the Rada), supported the Central Rada, and through it 'rail commissars' simply bypassed the regular personnel and until November 1917 made trains throughout Ukraine run on schedule.[24]

On 15 June, five days after proclaiming the First Universal, the Rada's ten-member standing committee (*Komitet*) decided to create a General Secretariat to serve as an executive. Five days later the leaders of all Ukraine's moderate Russian political parties, after informal talks with national leaders, agreed to de facto recognize the Central Rada and its Secretariat as a territorial and not merely a Ukrainian national organization. There is no record of these talks but possibly the Ukrainians agreed not to claim legal-administrative authority in the interests of de facto co-operation with the local Russian elites.[25] Thus, when Hrushevsky announced to the Rada the formation of the Secretariat on 23 June, members reacted with surprise and caution. An SD representative, perhaps making public a condition reached at the earlier talks with the Russians, stated that his party would support the creation of the Secretariat only if it was not described as an 'administrative' organ. The SRs agreed, saying the wording was tactically necessary. Accordingly, the 'Declaration' of 26 June (9 July) announcing the creation of the General Secretariat referred to it as the highest executive and legal organ of the Ukrainian nation whose immediate task was to 'organize and educate the masses.' This work was classified as 'moral' rather than 'public-judicial' in nature and was supposed to be done through provincial, district, county, and city executive committees that were eventually supposed to be subordinated to the Central Rada and to become the basis for Ukraine's future new decentralized territorial autonomy. Significantly, these committees were not local agencies of central ministries, and they were only nominally under the Ministry of Internal Affairs. The 'Declaration' included no central ministerial agencies within its envisaged immediate tasks, nor did it mention administrative separatism but carefully noted that only in the future did the Secretariat hope that local agencies of central ministries would assist it in forming a new regional administrative order.[26]

Hrushevsky's position on what to do with the existing administrative bureaucracy is unclear. However he did, apologetically, explain that Vynnychenko, the man in charge of the General Secretariat, had no desire to present the Secretariat as a threat to the regional bureaucracy. He explained that Ukrainian leaders had neither the will nor the ability to suddenly take over the imperial bureaucracy – which would have made them seem responsible for the collapsing public order. He doubted, in particular, whether the Central Rada could have exercised any authority over demobilized soldiers, among whom there were many non-Ukrainians. To illustrate the Secretariat's helplessness Hrushevsky notes that it could not even procure more space and typewriters for its officials in the building where the Secretariat convened.[27]

Nevertheless, on 3 (16) July, the Provisional Government did recognize the Secretariat in principle as the regional administrative authority, and within three days Vynnychenko requested permission to sequester men drafted into the army to staff the bureaucracy that the Rada now needed. Neither Petrograd's statement of intent, nor Vynnychenko's later letter, specified how this 'temporary executive apparatus' related to central ministries or which provinces were included into 'Ukraine.'[28] Only on 16 (29) July did the Secretariat explicitly claim twelve ministries for Kyiv, and full territorial administrative authority within all Ukrainian provinces including the Crimea, in its Statute of the Higher Administration of Ukraine – which also specified that laws would come in to effect in Ukraine the day that they were published in Ukrainian.[29] Petrograd rejected the Statute and on 4 (17) August issued instead a Temporary Instruction. This document restricted Kyiv's administrative authority to internal affairs, finance, agriculture, education, labour, and trade in only five provinces – excluding among others the Crimea. The Secretariat protested but accepted. In lieu of a precise delineation of functions, and despite Article 9 of the Instruction which allowed central ministers to ignore the Secretariat, it requested the Provisional Government to explicitly instruct ministry officials in the five designated provinces to obey Kyiv and accept correspondence in the Ukrainian language. Among the last laws passed by the Provisional Government was one requiring all ministries subject to Kyiv to use Ukrainian in dealing with citizens and in internal correspondence related to local affairs.[30] Local officials, meanwhile, did not know what to do. The Bohodukhiiv district commissar reported to his provincial superior that the Central Rada's instructors had arrived and that they were organizing a 'Free Cossack' militia in his territory with men from another province. He characterized their attempts to get the local teacher to teach in Ukrainian as 'nationalist propaganda' that could add to the existing disorder 'conflicts of a national nature.' He asked what he should do, but there is no record of an answer.[31]

As of September 1917 government provincial newspapers in Ukraine, the *Gubernskiia vedomosti* and *Vestnik* of the commissars, began to appear in both Russian and Ukrainian. *Kyivski huberniialni visty* appeared above the Russian version of the title. On 13 September *Vestnik Volynskago gubernskago kommisara* introduced its Ukrainian-language section with a note saying that three-quarters of its readers did not understand Russian. In their September issues all these newspapers printed a notification from the General Secretariat declaring that as of 4 August the Rada was the highest administrative authority in Ukraine. No such notification appeared in the official *Vestnik Vremennago Pravitelstva,* which that month, instead, notified readers about the formation of two committees within the Interior Ministry to study nationalities and provincial reform.

Local Masons, Kadets, right-wing Mensheviks, and Russian Socialist Revolutionaries, who dominated the municipal dumas, resigned themselves to Ukrainian territorial autonomy from early June 1917 and worked with the Central Rada. This meant that municipal bureaucrats were subject to Kyiv. In Kharkiv during the summer of 1917 the Russian or Russian-speaking citizenry, officers, and officials, as much concerned about their jobs as about public order, were also prepared to recognize the Rada insofar as it could meet these desires. The Rada's officer in command of the city accepted their loyalty and left them at their jobs.[32] Indicative of the broader trend in towns was the Berdychiv duma: elected in July, at their first sitting on 2 September its fifty-seven Jewish, thirteen Russian, and eight Ukrainians recognized the Central Rada. Municipal officials, in practice, worked for the Rada.[33] At the end of July the five provincial commissars appointed by the Provisional Government were Ukrainians – of whom three were Masons – declared themselves and by extension their staffs subject to Kyiv.[34] By publishing statistics showing that Ukrainians were the overwhelming majority of the province's inhabitants, Katerynoslav's major Russian daily *Narodnaia zhizn* (on 8 October) signalled that the local Russian elite considered themselves to now be under Kyiv's rather than Petrograd's administrative jurisdiction. Fifteen days later Katerynoslav's duma voted in favour of inclusion into Ukraine.

Finally, Hrushevsky wrote that the Secretariat informally attempted to expand its area of competence beyond its legal limits on both the central and local levels by relying on Ukrainian staff, who sometimes were able to bring their particular offices under Kyivan authority.[35] In a memorandum of 13 (26) October the General Secretariat noted that government commissars, zemstvos, dumas, and co-operatives, who between them provided goods and services, and 'some government agencies' who had recognized its territorial administrative authority, did not understand why they were still getting instructions from Petrograd.[36]

By late 1917, therefore, despite central ministerial orders, legal limbo, administrative disruption, and some sabotage, there were officials who were obeying Kyiv's Central Rada, and horizontal ties between organizations on Ukrainian territory were beginning to replace the old imperial vertical ties. A zemstvo-sponsored survey of language use by local rural officials in Kyiv province, undertaken that autumn, suggested that approximately half of them used Ukrainian. Nevertheless, in Kyiv that same autumn an educated veteran with pre-war experience as a clerk was unable to get a clerical job with the Rada, as everywhere he went officials told him day after day that there were no vacancies. Watching them at their desks, he observed how laboriously they used Russian-Ukrainian dictionaries to write their documents in Ukrainian.[37] An administration independent of Petrograd was beginning to function. The Russian Senate never ratified the Temporary Instruction. Central ministries continued to deal directly with officials in the Ukrainian provinces, told their agents specifically to ignore Kyiv, and presumably, paid them as well.[38] The Rada got only 300 000 of the the 2,300,000 roubles it requested to fund its needs and 144 staff.[39]

From September 1917 Ukrainian leaders could begin legally subordinating government officials in five provinces to themselves, and localities were recognizing the Central Rada. But as yet little is known about what happened outside the three big cities. The records of central ministries in Kyiv province under the Provisional Government, for instance, have been lost; not all urban administrations have been studied, and there is as yet no synthesis generalizing about the achievements of those that have been studied.[40] On the one hand, it seems that throughout the former empire ministerial personnel by late 1917 were not attempting to exercise any authority beyond district capitals. An eyewitness in Katerynoslav confirms Krainsky's claim that already that summer Petrograd was ignoring provincial capitals, which in turn ignored their respective districts and villages, which in turn lived according to their own rules and regulations.[41] Lower agencies themselves decided whether to comply with instructions, and whether officials obeyed Kyiv or Petrograd when instructions conflicted was often up to them. There were lots of authorities, but little authority. Politicians formed committees, held meetings, and chaired meetings, reported Krainsky, but other than knowing that these organizations were linked to the Rada, no one knew why they existed.[42]

On the other hand, an increase in bureaucrats and organizations, paralleled by a decline in the amount of work, was balanced by an evident faster turnover of what was done – which indicates that things were being done. Before the revolution, as noted in Chapter 1, a provincial office averaged 2,000 incoming and 2,500 outgoing items a month. This apparently continued until the tsar's abdication in March 1917, as suggested by the figures from the Kyiv provincial governor's office. Averaging 2,000 incoming and 1,000 outgoing items for the first two months of that year, the total number of incoming items fell from 1,480 in March to 892 in August, while the number of outgoing items, which had fallen to 399 in March, rose to 907 by August. Other government wheels also kept turning throughout 1917 – as in the Kharkiv Provincial Customs Office, where citizens despite events duly submitted their requests to buy, sell, and trade products containing alcohol.[43] The postal service worked. Letters took between five and seven days to arrive in Kyiv from Podillia, Kharkiv, and Katerynoslav in 1917. In early 1918 a letter from the small town of Okhtyrka in Kharkiv province took two weeks to get to Kyiv. Interestingly, correspondence mailed from towns in Kyiv province to the capital before or during the Bolshevik invasion of 1917–18 began arriving after they left, in April 1918. A letter sent from Vladimir, Russia, on 16 January arrived in Kyiv on 9 March.[44] Although there was a tannery in Chyhyryn, to take another example, that regularly shipped its production to Moscow, the local population of Chyhyryn could not obtain any leather goods. Responding to protests, in October the town council decided to expropriate the tannery. The factory then complained to the district commissar who discovered that it was owned by a Moscow-based company and had no authority to sell locally. He then telegraphed the owners requesting permission to sell locally, and in the interim, ordered the factory to sell whatever surplus it had in stock.[45] Officials of the old Office of Royal Domains (*Udelnyi okrug*) remained at their jobs and quietly kept the thousands of acres of land and millions of roubles under their control out of Ukrainian hands – and then out of Bolshevik hands.[46] The Kadet *Volnosti* in the winter of 1917 described the Rada, alongside the anti-Bolshevik Southeastern League of Cossack Armies under General Kaledin in southern Russia, as one of 'two state organizations with the actual power to realize general tasks of state.'[47] Requests from the Secretariat sent to all provinces in early December 1917, asking for detailed descriptions of local administration, began returning four months later, and those from Kyiv province reveal that there were central institutions in the major towns and at least one co-op or *Spilka* organization in every village.[48]

Despite its differences with Petrograd over territory, language, and jurisdictions, the Central Rada did not contest the need to continue the war, supply the army and cities, delay land reform until the Constituent Assembly convened, or presumably, any other non-national issue. Accordingly, what remained of the local agencies of central ministries in Ukraine tried to carry out the same policies in 1917 as in 1916, regardless of who their formal superior was. Officials hostile to the Rada and local representative organs controlled by opponents did sabotage or ignore educational, cultural, and language directives before and after August 1917. In Lypovets in Kyiv province non-Ukrainian postal and telegraph staff refused to accept Ukrainian money into 1918, and not all of them attended the Ukrainian studies courses they were supposed to attend.[49] But, since tax collection had collapsed, the only other major non-culturally related government task that affected the entire population directly was the collection and distribution of foodstuffs through the zemstvo (renamed *narodni upravy* [people's adminstrations] in July) and the Food Supply and Agriculture ministries. On these policies the Rada had no differences with Petrograd. If these organizations worked badly, as noted, it was not the Rada's fault. The General Secretariat's decree of 23 July 1917 threatening anyone caught hoarding grain with confiscation was not at odds with Provisional Government policy.[50] Troops began to be used to collect grain in Ukraine from August 1917. Against the backdrop of general decline we know that central food supply officials did their utmost to make local zemtsvos comply with the unpopular supply measures involving state monopolies, fixed prices, and requisitions, and we know that results varied. The Russian minister of supply concluded after an inspection trip in September 1917 that in Kyiv, Poltava, and Katerynoslav provinces food supply personnel were working 'magnificently.' The Podillia commissioner reported the same for his province. Between November 1917 and its demise in April 1918 the Central Rada continued policies enacted originally by the Provisional Government to supply the Ukrainian army, and presumably, the same people that had to carried out these policies before November had to carry them out afterwards.[51]

Staffing

Government bureaucrats like everyone else in the Russian Empire had their professional grievances, and by the end of 1917 in a random sampling of newspapers at least two dozen of their unions and professional organizations can be found. Already by 1916 lower-level bureaucrats were demoralized because huge price increases had left them in penury and malnourished. Secret police reports characterized them as profoundly hostile to the government and a ready audience for revolutionaries.[52] Local newspapers mention pay, an eight-hour work-day, and Sundays and holidays off as their major demands. It is likely that urban administrators in Ukraine, like their Russian counterparts, wanted, in addition, the right to form unions, elect their own superiors, and to have a say in running their offices and in hiring and firing.[53] Underneath the uniforms and impressive long titles, wrote their Petrograd union leaders in July 1917, 'the most refined oppression has remained together with a long list of savage vestiges and pay rates lower than in any [private sector office]. Additionally, nowhere have so many old regime leftovers remained as in the labyrinth of departments and quiet directors' offices, where, hiding under the sobriquet "republican," are the old wolves of reaction ready to throttle all who are striving for real freedom and to impede the spontaneity of the masses by deflecting their efforts from the straight and narrow into narrow tangled paths.'[54]

Annoyed and fed up, many men had quit during the war for jobs in the zemstvos, where 'people were treated like human beings' even if they did not have rank. Some towns, as a result, already short of bureaucrats because of the draft, allegedly had no administrators even before the tsar had abdicated.[55] Those that remained formed office committees which even in the central provincial commissars' offices decided when and what orders they would implement. How many bureaucrats remained in place at local levels is unknown. An invaluable survey of peasants' attitudes, done in the summer of 1917 by the Kyiv Zemstvo, suggests that there was considerable turnover of officials in that province. This survey of 887 respondents in twelve districts shows that 506 reported some change of personnel and that 658 reported that those officials were changed either at the request of government commissars or local peasants' committees.

It also revealed that 356 of the respondents wanted Ukrainian to be the language of administration.[56]

Isolated extant statistics suggest that despite some staff losses the phenomenal increase in the number of administrative personnel that began before the First World War, and then seen in wartime organizations, too, continued through 1918 at least. The number of staff in Kyiv Province's Tax Collection Office (*Kievska kazenna palata*) increased from 802 in 1916 to 1,599 by September 1918, and of these the greatest increase was among the common clerks, typists, and copyists whose number had risen from eighty to 224.[57] Although the counties lost their land captains and elders, in addition to their ministerial officials and duma or zemstvo staff geographical units above that level also had a soviet, at least one trade union, a co-op, a reading club, political party organizations, a Rada committee, and a peasants' union cell – each of which needed someone to do the administrative and organizational work. Not all who were unemployed registered, and as of March 1918 Ukraine had only forty-two unemployment offices of which only fifteen were able to submit data before the Rada fell. What that information for this limited sample shows is that more clerks were employed than were other social groups. In Mykolaiv 50 per cent of the 6,994 registered unemployed between January and March 1918 were soldiers, 60 per cent of the men were single, and 82 per cent were non-union – which meant that they collected no benefits. Whereas between 40 and 60 per cent of all Ukraine's registered unemployed were skilled and unskilled workers, only between 11 and 15 per cent were clerks – who apparently found jobs more easily than did others.[58]

In the towns, in theory, bureaucrats worked for SR- and Menshevik-controlled councils. In practice, as suggested by the situation in Chernihiv, their committees ran their offices. There, employees' committees during the course of 1917 had subordinated their department heads to themselves, and by that December employees' committees were responsible for almost every facet of office work from hiring and firing to finance. In small offices with few staff, collective decision making had become customary by the end of 1917. Krainsky does not mention what, if any, political affiliations clerks had. For him, their activity amounted to Bolshevism, and because of it, he wrote, Bolshevism effectively existed in Chernihiv before the Bolsheviks.[59] Krainsky implies that whereas higher provincial officials had almost all been replaced by 1918, lower- and middle-level officials remained in place – an observation confirmed by the provincial unemployment statistics cited above. We don't know which political parties controlled appointments to which administrative positions and the intensity and frequency of horizontal ties between administrators and party activists.

Little is known about the village secretaries, who besides fulfilling an important function before the revolution were agents of Russification, because to demonstrate their superiority, they spoke a Ukrainian version of Russian that native Russians could not understand. Although the secret police viewed village secretaries as potential organizers of resistance, in 1917 there is a reference to most of the secretaries in Radomysl district in Kyiv province being opponents of the Rada. How representative this was is unknown. In one of the hundreds of accounts of village meetings printed in Ukrainian newspapers in the summer of 1917, one reporter mentioned the opinions of a village secretary in Katerynoslav province: 'Much respected,' he gave a speech at a meeting of two villages attended by an estimated 6,000 people. In response to a Russian Bolshevik, he argued, in Russian, that the people should support federalism and Ukrainian autonomy.[60] The author of a critical article written that same year, meanwhile, repeats the arguments of the pre-revolutionary reform movement that called for the professionalization of the village secretary function, that is, changing the position from a poorly paid elected one to a centrally appointed well-paid one, and open only to those with professional qualifications. He claimed that secretaries used their literacy and knowledge to exploit their fellows. Working ten- to twelve-hour days for 10 to 20 roubles a month, they understandably demanded bribes. As slaves of the old regime, the author continued, these secretaries treated their fellow citizens despotically because that is how their superiors treated them, and they would disappear only when the old regime disappeared. Until then they and their old practices would remain. Receiving an order to submit within three days a full account of all planting, harvesting, costs, and profits for the year 1917–18, for example, the secretary would produce a report in three hours and then submit it knowing he would still be judged for submitting the report – not for its contents. The only solution was to change the *pysari* into bureaucrats. He concluded that since changes of such magnitude could not be done overnight, and all secretaries could not be summarily fired, the best way to begin would be for zemstvos to establish improvement courses for them.[61]

Former tsarist officials, as mentioned in Chapter 1, worked for the Central Rada. A peasant in Valky district in Kharkiv province, Mytrofan Kotliar began working as a secretary for the local council in 1915, stayed on under the Rada, and then kept working for the Ukrainian State.

Remaining in western Ukriane, Makar Mokrytsky was employed by the Rada's Military Secretariat and worked as an assistant to one of its district commissars. In March 1918 he addressed a letter in Ukrainian to the Rada's Ministry of Internal Affairs requesting a transfer so that he could 'work for the benefit of my native Ukraine.' That April he became head of the Personnel Office in that ministry's General Affairs Department earning 600 karbovantsi a month. With twenty-five years' experience Apollin Marshynsky moved to Kyiv in November 1917 to head the Rada's Tax Department; for a short time in January 1918 he was moved to the Ministry of Justice, but by April he had returned to his previous post. When his Zemgor section was dissolved in September 1917 Roman Trofymenko, aged thirty-six, moved to Kyiv and that November applied for a job to the Rada. On 1 December he was appointed head of the chancery at the Third Department of the Ministry of Food Supply at a salary of 600 karbovantsi a month, and still attending university classes, he requested leave the following January to sit his exams. Having transferred in November 1917 to the administrative-political section of the Rada's Ministry of Internal Affairs where, as a secretary, he earned 300 roubles a month, in April 1918 Denis Kirichok was promoted and put in charge of the section's secretariat and his salary was doubled. In 1917 Vasyl Korenchuk was hired as a telegraphist in Kyiv. Of the thirty-seven members of the Kyiv provincial commissar's office in March 1918, eleven had worked there since April 1917.[62] Of the 163 men who worked as tax inspectors in Kyiv province in the autumn of 1918, all but fifteen had been at the same job before the Rada was formed.[63] Among the tsarist clerks in Kyiv province who continued on under the Rada were Vasyl Klokosos, Oleksander Kuzminsky, Fedir Borodenko, Zotyk Korotiuk, and Andrii Rozhko. However, Kyryl Kuzmenko, who was working as a clerk for the Red Cross that year in Kyiv, did not work for the Rada. When he applied and admitted that he did not know Ukrainian he was rejected. Arguing that as a citizen he had his rights, he was apparently thrown out of the office, and in January 1918 he got a job as a mailman.[64]

The 1918 Treaty of Brest-Litovsk made the former civilian employees of the military redundant. With demobilization newspapers began posting advertisements informing previously drafted bureaucrats who were still on government payrolls that if they reported to their original places of work by April they would get their jobs back. Unemployment registers at the time included no former government bureaucrats but saw a sharp increase in the number of former private sector bureaucrats – either returned veterans or administrators of private estate not rehired by local Land Committees.[65] The Rada's General Secretariat, with seven employees in March 1917, had thirty-one by 31 August, sixty-five in December, and ninety by February 1918 – including six chauffeurs, one doorman, and a mechanic. Dementii Lytvyn, from a small town in Tarashcha district, complained in a letter sent to the Kyivan provincial commissar in January 1918 that he had been unable to get a job since October 1917 even though there were offices where one person held two or three jobs simultaneously.[66] Letters requesting employment sent that spring to the Rada normally focused on qualifications. A typical applicant was Katerynoslav-born Ukrainian-speaking Vasyl Vasylenko. A seminary graduate, he had finished teachers' college, knew how to type, and had worked in the local zemstvo. Some claimed hardship, and of these, two stand out. Feodosi Pasko, the former president of the Ukrainian students' club at the Kyivan Theological Seminary wrote that he would starve if he didn't get a job. In another letter, a refugee western Ukrainian priest in the village of Okhtyrka, with a family of eight, stated that he too feared starvation, if he did not get work.[67]

How many tsarist bureaucrats were still at their desks by the spring of 1918 is unknown. There are no known statistics on how many people were involved in administration, nor information on how they were appointed, or the role of such key figures as permanent secretaries (*tovarysh ministra*). On the one hand, central newspapers do not mention any shortage of ministerial staff, and archival records include hundreds of applications at all levels. Apparently there were so many applications that the Ministry of Internal Affairs announced it would no longer accept them. By April 1918 Ukraine's War Ministry alone allegedly had almost 15,000 personnel.[68]

Ukrainian leaders do not appear to have hired women and Jews en masse to their incipient central administrative structures. The Central Rada, like the Provisional Government, declared women and Jews to be equal citizens and eligible for government jobs. However, the Rada's published personnel lists contain almost no Jewish names and few women's names.[69] Educated secular Jews represented a particularly valuable potential source of bureaucrats. From no more than twenty (0.5%) Jewish urban administrators, legal personnel, and police in all of Kyiv province in 1897, the number of Jews in the same category in September 1917 in the city of Kyiv alone had ballooned to almost 2,600 (10%). Jews also comprised as much as one-third of the Southwestern Front Zemgor staff – who presumably remained at their posts through 1917.[70]

Few Jews figure in central organs. One, Cherkasy-born Solomon Abramovych Zalkind, a graduate of Kyiv and Moscow universities, became a sub-section head in the Ministry of Food Supply in April 1918.[71] The situation was apparently different in provincial administrations. Kyivan-born Haia Liebishevna-Freilikh, a university student, worked in the Kamianets city hall statistics office from 1917.[72] In Lypovets district in Kyiv province Isaak Sokoletsky was secretary to the local commissar from April through December 1917. His brother was the assistant secretary, and a Jewish girl worked as a clerk. Fired in December, together with his brother, without pay by a new commissar, he complained to the governor, and the ensuing correspondence provides insight into local government offices. In his complaint Sokoletsky stated that the new commissar had 'always been hostile towards other [non-Ukrainian] nationalities,' that he had referred to his office as being 'full of yids,' and that he had given his own brother and another relative jobs in his office as soon as he had been appointed. Sokoletsky wrote that he was hard-working, honest, respected by all, and that he was fired because he had complained to the commissar about the hostility towards him of the new appointees. His dismissal was illegal and intolerable in light of the Rada's Third Universal, he wrote. In his rebuttal, sent 13 January, but received only one month later, the new commissar stated that Sokoletsky was sloppy and derelict in his duties, that he himself had nothing against Jews, because the Jewish girl was still employed, and that his own brother and relative were the only persons immediately available to put affairs into order. Sokoletsky, one week later in a reply, dismissed everything that the commissar wrote as a lie. There is no further record of what happened other than a note dated 16 April from the governor firing the commissar – with no reason given. His relative, Ivan Romanivsky, the former assistant secretary, was appointed in his place. In his March 1918 application letter for work in the Kyivan commissar's provincial office, Mefodii Kucherenko, from Cherkasy, mentions that 'all the institutions' in his town were filled with Jews.[73] In right-bank Ukraine, however, no officials had any illusions about the importance of Jews to the functioning of their government. Accounts from the district of Letychiv in Podillia from January 1918 show that Jewish merchants and artists provided stationery, printed copies of the Universal, as well as Ukrainian flags and signs, and portraits of Shevchenko.[74]

Co-op officials, who either belonged to or sympathized with the Ukrainian Socialist Revolutionaries, were a particularly important non-government institutional group that functioned throughout the revolutionary years and provided services. At their first congress in March 1917 eighteen of the empire's forty-six co-op unions formed a separate Ukrainian organization with its own central standing executive committee (*Kooptsentr*). Six months later, at a second congress, twelve more co-op unions joined this national organization. *Kooptsentr* envisaged its local branches as the local agencies of government and in its circulars did not even refer to non-elected government officials. Both the Provisional Government and the Central Rada encouraged and supported co-ops to take active roles in regional administration. Co-ops not only provided jobs for the educated but co-op leaders, frequently SR activists, were ministers, assistant ministers, and permanent secretaries. By 1919 co-ops had actually turned into de facto ministries of education, economics, and trade with full-time personnel in centralized hierarchic organizations that were also well integrated horizontally with the organizations they had to work with. From an estimated total of 8,100 in 1914, the total number of credit, consumer, and agricultural co-ops in Ukraine had increased to approximately 22,000 by 1919. Total membership figures are unknown, but consumer co-ops alone in 1919 had four million members. If we count each member as the head of a family averaging four persons, then at least sixteen million people, roughly 60 per cent of tsarist Ukraine's population, might have been part of the co-op system. Co-ops were divided between national and imperial (all-Russian) unions, and although there was overlap, an estimated one-third to one-half of co-ops belonged to the former.[75] National co-ops in pre-war tsarist Ukraine, accordingly, not only included at least as many people as did eastern Galicia's Ukrainian co-ops, but unlike their Galician counterparts, they were bigger, wealthier, and expanded and flourished during the war.[76] While *Kooptsentr* offices probably controlled nothing, the central organizations of credit, consumer, and agricultural societies did function as institutional networks on a regional if not national level without a break from 1917 through to 1921, when the Bolsheviks abolished them. Co-ops were perhaps the only horizontally integrated central administrative networks that functioned continuously through those years under all governments.

Ukraine under the Rada clearly had bureaucracies and bureaucrats. As of September 1917 its General Secretariat had some authority over part of the old imperial bureaucracy which was formally subject to it. As of November it ran what remained of the entire tsarist system and was planning its own state structure. While some government officials left their jobs for more pay elsewhere before March 1918, afterwards there appears to have been an influx into these positions. On the Ukrainian side, local papers began running numerous advertisements that summer for bureaucrats and announcements about pay raises. Some counties offered new salaries for village scribes ranging from 600 to 1,800 roubles a month. Policemen, we read, had to be 'politically conscious Ukrainians.' Reports from the provinces complain about local 'Little Russians' who suddenly became exceptionally public in their manifestations of national loyalty – only because they wanted government jobs – and then, behind their desks, used Russian because they did not know Ukrainian. In an attempt to coordinate this activity, the Rada established a Labour Office exclusively for officials and clerks which advertised in local newspapers.[77] A hostile Russian eyewitness noted that government offices were full – occupied by incompetent youth who had forsaken their studies and had nothing to commend them except their nationalism. Government offices, he complained, closed their doors to masses of Russian officers seeking work because they only spoke Russian. He also observed that because of the language regulations, many got work as translators.[78] In Chernihiv Krainsky reported that 'people with socialist sympathies' in social and political institutions quickly Ukrainianized social and political life. The best way to a job and promotion was to profess a knowledge of Ukrainian. These people, he continued, were primarily rural teachers and secretaries, clerks, office workers, scribes, and seminarians 'who considered themselves specialists in Ukrainian.' These 'half-educated (*polintelligentsia*)' people had little to recommend them, he wrote. They were democratically inclined, with little or no education, 'ignorant of affairs and totally unprepared for serious work' but they moved up fast and by the end of the year were in charge of affairs and dominated government administration. Office attire, he complained, was no longer formal but casual, the accepted clothing being uniforms without insignia.[79] At the end of December 1917 the Central Rada's Labour Office announced that there were lots of men literate in Ukrainian looking for office positions.[80] The role of the Ukrainian Union of Clerks in Government, Private, and Civil Organizations, in channeling Ukrainian administrators has yet to be examined. Formed by Ukrainian activists in Petrograd in June 1917, its objective was to facilitate the return of Ukrainian bureaucrats scattered throughout the imperial bureaucracy to Kyiv. Members came to Kyiv that December and established a branch there on 1 March 1918. A subsequent call for a general meeting was later reissued because so few people showed up and thereafter newspapers stopped mentioning it.[81]

In addition, despite internal opposition, the Rada began hiring fugitive officials from Russia. Vynnychenko later called these people 'garbage' but also admitted that they wanted jobs with the Rada.[82]

As of September 1917 leaders might not have had a national government functioning in Ukrainian, but in addition to civilian organizations working for it at all levels, they had lots of government bureaucrats some of whom were doing what they could in conditions of war. On 1 (14) September *Narodnia volia* reported that while there was no order in Poltava province, administrative posts were a big pork barrel (*koryto*) for the literate. From this perspective, it was the wartime proliferation of offices and officials that represented a serious impediment to Ukrainian state building. If things did not get done it was not because of a lack of administrators. The war and later democratization not only had left bureaucrats in place, but produced more of them, both government and non-government, together with heads and directors often more interested in politics than administration. With each passing month people who may or may not have had relevant experience came to and left offices. They would then get in each other's way because their organizations had ill-defined functions, because of rivalries, or simply because they did not know each other. And by the time they re-established routines they were shifted again. Commissars were at odds with zemstvo and duma officials, and all three could find themselves at odds with local military commanders, radical county Land Committees who would be at odds with the more moderate provincial Land Committees, and radical SR officials in the Ministry of Agriculture who would be at odds with moderate Kadet commissars. Officials forming a new militia to replace the standing army would find themselves at odds with others carrying out orders to demobilize and with individuals raising volunteer units. All of this contributed to administrative breakdown. In light of the glut of pre-war educated applicants for government positions, the qualifications listed by applicants in 1917–18, and the presumably very high number of educated tsarist bureaucrats who remained at their desks, Krainsky's caustic dismissal of the abilities of entrants was perhaps an exaggeration.

Nationality, Legitimacy, and Loyalty

In light of the above it would seem that in 1917 the radical pre-war anti-bureaucracy trend in political thought had little impact on the behaviour of central government leaders towards administrative issues. The moderate trend dominated, reinforced by the general impression of the educated that the wartime public organizations were working. In the spring of 1917 the Rada's decision not to try and subordinate the existing administrative system to itself was not ideologically but politically motivated and was reinforced by the belief that public calls for independence would be disastrous: 'the Russians and our Russified citizens will obliterate us because the struggle against them is harder than the one against the tsarist administration.'[83] That June the Provisional Government secretly dispatched a military intelligence team to Kyiv with instructions to gather evidence of Ukrainian pro-German sympathies – and those men eventually began working with local Russian extremists against the Rada.[84] The knowledge that they were under surveillance by military counter-intelligence as possible 'German collaborators' reinforced their conviction to avoid any actions that Russians and Russian-speakers might use to justify armed repression against them – which included attempts to take over or create a government administration.

Ukrainian leaders, as moderate socialists, were aware of the importance of bureaucracy, and they rejected anything that smacked of Jacobite conspiracy, elitism, compulsion, and radicalism. 'The nation' was something that the educated had to lead to a suitable level of self-awareness, and therefore independence would be just only if it were the product of a spontaneous, representative, popular mass movement. Additionally, they thought it best not to advocate separatism for tactical reasons so as not to alienate Russian-speakers sympathetic to Ukrainian cultural demands and a federal restructuring of the empire. Since they had ruled out political separatism, the only way that they could legally subordinate municipal bureaucracies and local branches of ministries to themselves was to be recognized as a federal administrative unit by Petrograd. Apparent administrative inactivity, therefore, was actually political strategy. Even so, during that time the Central Rada did begin creating a hierarchy of civil organizations parallel to the Russian central government administration. This suited the intellectual heirs of Drahomanov, who envisaged their future political independence as one built on elected majorities in administrative organs and public organizations – 'civil society.' Like their mentor, Central Rada officials presumably imagined that these elected local organs of self-government could simultaneously serve as executive and administrative organs. Accordingly, through most of 1917 they attempted to build an autonomous administrative order around city dumas, zemstvos, and land committees rather than central ministries. Their socialist and democratic convictions might also explain why national leaders restricted the authority of the military commandants who they hoped would establish order and control at local levels.

The Temporary Instruction allowed the Central Rada to legally deal with bureaucrats, and as of autumn 1917 there do not seem to have been outstanding differences between it and bureaucratic officials. That September the Rada declared that government office hours would remain unchanged. What effect this had on bureaucrats who still worked ten to twelve hours a day, six and even seven days a week is unknown, but that same month administrator's unions in the town of Kupianka passed a resolution requesting Sundays and holidays off.[85] Pay doubled in August 1917. In April 1918 the government increased monthly wages again: 250 karbovantsi for the lowest-level clerks (8 karbovantsi a day), 400 to 600 for middle-level officials, and 1,000 to 1,200 (33–40 a day) for directors and permanent secretaries.[86] Those who did get paid would not have been displeased.

How did bureaucrats react to the Cantral Rada? In its first month of existence the Rada had apparently wanted Ukrainian bureaucrats to sign a Ukrainian-language version of the new oath, and it was much perturbed when it learned that certain Ukrainian Kyiv province officials had refused to do so.[87] But there is no record of resignations or protests among government administrators in response to this or to the Statute or the Temporary Instruction. Krainsky, who opposed independence, but was prepared to accept autonomy, stayed on at his job. Occasional published lists of resignations that sometimes included reasons, mention only 'health.' Many also resigned because of bad pay and poor working conditions. In general, given the begrudging recognition of the Central Rada by the major local non-Ukrainian political parties, at most there would have been isolated incidents of sabotage within the local bureaucracy because, in theoretically autonomous Ukraine, Petrograd was still the capital and had to be obeyed.

Published accounts give no indication that in 1917 a 'territorial bureaucratic nationalism' might have prompted old regime officials to work for the Ukrainian cause. In addition, cited examples of 'anti-Ukrainian prejudice' among rank-and-file administrative functionaries relate to linguistic, cultural, educational, and legal issues, rather than to social-political-economic matters. There is evidence of monarchist-loyalist hostility to the Provisional Government among local officials during the first weeks of March 1917, which implies hostility to the Rada as well. In Nemyriv, where Russian extremists had a strong cell from before 1914, they managed to get control of the county executive committee and in

July 1917 sent a message to Kyiv saying that the committee would not recognize the Rada because it 'did not reflect the attitudes of Ukraine's native Little Russians.' There are references to refusals by rank-and-file bureaucrats to counter 'anti-Ukrainian' activities, and in Podillia province town Committees to Save the Revolution, formed that summer, subordinated municipal bureaucracies to themselves and ignored the local Rada commissars.[88] Regardless of such incidents from that summer there was a distinct trend among the newly formed administrators' unions to recognize the Central Rada as the highest administrative authority in Ukraine and the need, at least in principle, to function in Ukrainian. Significant as well was that local agencies of central Petrograd ministries, for example, the Central Sugar Agency (*TsentroSakhar*) in the Ministry of Agriculture, were restructured to give the deciding voice in their operations to representatives from all local organizations and committees relevant to its operations.[89] Two initiatives stand out in particular. The first, in Kyiv in April 1917, was an attempt to form Ukrainian branches of the All-Russian Union of Unions. The second, presumably a renewed effort eight months later by G. Arkhangelskii and A. Stepanov-Melnikov, was to centralize all Ukraine's administrators' unions into one organization. After a first meeting that included representatives from thirty unions, this new group demonstrated its position during pay negotiations between the Central Rada and its Ministry of Education employees, when it convinced the latter not to go on strike in face of the impending Bolshevik threat.[90] In July the Poltava provincial zemstvo adopted Ukrainian as its official language, and the local Treasury Officials Union agreed to donate 0.5 per cent of each official's pay to the Rada.[91]

The case of Russian-born Ivan Illin, who applied for a job in the Ministry of Finance, is likely illustrative of a broader trend. After finishing the Artillery School in St Petersburg in 1911, Illin moved to Kyiv, where from 1914 to 1917 he worked as a clerk in the city's Artillery Park. On 12 March 1918, 'being in very difficult material straits' he mailed his application letter, in Ukrainian, asking for a job. The letter was forwarded to a departmental employees' committee which noted that he should not be hired because he was not a citizen, and as a native Russian he could not be loyal. The department head decided to hire Illin, however, noting that he had applied for citizenship and had family ties in Ukraine. Hired on 2 April, Illin worked until July 1918 when he resigned saying that he had to care for his injured wife.[92]

Anti-Rada officials could and did subvert or ignore Kyiv's instructions and, after July 1917, could question the Rada's legal authority until the Russian State Council actually ratified the Temporary Instruction. Nonetheless, the apparent limitation of most bureaucratic opposition to linguistic Ukrainianization only from the summer cannot be construed as mass opposition to ministerial decentralization or to the Rada as such. Hrushevsky himself, who knew that Jewish clerks not only refused to learn Ukrainian but agitated against doing so, waxed philosophical about them in February 1918. He admitted that it was not easy to rise above imperial russocentric prejudices and that in the short term learning a language could be a nuisance. Yet, he warned that those who practised such short-sighted self-interest placed themselves among the ranks of Ukraine's enemies and risked provoking a backlash.[93] The daughter of the Rada's governor in Poltava province in the autumn of 1917, who related that the province's entire staff were former tsarist officials who did not know Ukrainian, made no mention of any antipathy or hostility on their part towards the Rada.[94] Krainsky wrote that although everyone in his office was local Ukrainian-born, none could either read or write Ukrainian as government ministries demanded. He personally considered Ukrainian a 'Galician peasant dialect.' But he did not protest nor record any complaint and regarded the Rada as a central authority representing an alternative to the disorder represented by the Bolsheviks.[95] A June 1917 report from Kaniv district notes that the local authorities had organized Ukrainian language courses for administrators and it makes no mention of resistance.[96] As the Rada's policies usually matched Petrograd's it is likely that administrators probably tried to implement more than they rejected.[97] Intergovernmental correspondence written in Russian did not mean that the officials who wrote that correspondence were not performing their duties.[98]

The Kyivan Jewish lawyer Aleksander Goldenveizer observed that officials, 'as one might expect, were not particularly opposed to Ukrainian power.' While all lawyers opposed linguistic Ukrainianization, he added, not all refused to recognize the Rada.[99] An article in the semi-official Ukrainian newspaper *Narodnaia volia* urged readers to dispense with their pre-war anti-bureaucrat prejudices. To categorize bureaucrats by their European-style suits, collars, and ties as 'exploiters' or 'bourgeoisie,' it wrote, would be as unjust as the pre-revolutionary practice of summarily firing any newly hired clerk who came to work wearing peasant-style shirts and trousers. Bureaucrats, the article noted, had to be judged not on the basis of how they looked or what they wore, but on their miserable salaries which made them the natural allies of the working population.[100]

Rather than sabotage, difficult to trace and prove, more important reasons for Ukraine's administrative problems in 1917, as noted, were three years of ministerial leapfrogging and military mismanagement compounded by bad bureaucratic planning, organizational inefficiencies, and too many rather than too few officials and organizations. Some might add employee committees/unions to this list. Districts and villages, consequently, ran themselves according to their own rules, or decided for themselves which central instructions to accept, sabotage, or ignore, and interacted with each other directly rather than through vertical intermediaries. All these factors were more detrimental to Ukrainian state building before November 1918 than opposition to Rada policies that they disliked by anti-Rada tsarist officials who were formally subject to the Secretariat.

In general, as far as is known, in response to Bolshevik seizures of power, office staff usually decided to ignore them and either go on strike or keep working for the public good. In the latter case, as happened in Lutsk and Kharkiv, and the Kyiv food supply and postal and telegraph workers, many did go on strike if the Bolsheviks tried to interfere with the work or take over their offices. Which tactic dominated in Ukraine remains unknown. Significantly, anyone interested in the bureaucrats' strikes against the Bolsheviks in Petrograd and Moscow could read about them and their appeal for an empire-wide strike. At least seven of Ukraine's major urban newspapers (in Kyiv, Katerynoslav, Kharkiv, and Chernihiv) carried detailed accounts about them. In the first weeks of December 1917 even the Odesa and Kherson provincial unions joined those that had recognized the Rada, as did the Kyiv Union of Municipal Officials. The Chernihiv Union of Municipal Officials voted to strike in support of the Rada should the Bolsheviks attempt to seize power.[101] Kyiv's city soviet clerks resigned in protest when the Bolsheviks made their first attempt to seize power there in November 1917.[102]

Despite opposition in places, in the few reported published proceedings of employees' meetings in a country where pay could be months in arrears, principles or loyalties figured rarely. At the January 1918 organizational meeting of the Kharkiv-based Officials of the Southern Land, one speaker is on record saying: 'We don't care whether Lenin, or Petliura, or Trotsky, or Vynnychenko is in power ... this doesn't concern us. We will follow whoever suits us best because we must eat.' Supposedly few at the meeting supported him, but similar attitudes were voiced elsewhere. The previous November in Kherson, where Russian Socialist Revolutionaries dominated administrators' organizations, spokesmen told Ukrainian representatives that they would work for the Rada and learn Ukrainian if they were guaranteed 300 roubles a month.[103] In Chernihiv, on the eve of the Bolshevik invasion in December 1917, prices suddenly tripled and the worst hit were government clerks, who began to starve. When the Bolsheviks arrived the various office committees promptly recognized them, submitted requests for pay raises – and got them. When the Rada returned in March 1918 it promptly declared an across-the-board bonus equal to forty-seven days' pay for all employees.[104]

Ukraine's Bolsheviks encouraged sympathizer minorities within established unions to form splinter groups within their organizations that would then claim to represent the entire group; where this happened, as with the Kharkiv Postal and Telegraph Workers Union, the majority would then declare that it was no longer responsible for services, as strikebreakers were taking them over.[105] Newspaper reports during the pro-Bolshevik strikes in Kyiv that winter do not mention administrators as participants – one specified that all ministry employees were at work.[106] On 5 (18) January 1918 the Rada paid ministerial officials, and at 2 p.m. on 16 (29) January, when the shooting began, government offices closed. Clerks who remained in office buildings for the next three or four days did so because they could not get home. Finance Ministry workers agreed to return to work on 25 January – two days after the Bolsheviks had accepted all their terms.[107] The bulk of Kyiv's office workers went back to work on 29 January, however, despite earlier calls for strikes against the Bolsheviks. Their decisions should be seen in light of the collapse of the central strike in Petrograd on 12 January, the dissolution of the Constituent Assembly, and the position of their city duma.[108] Bolshevik manifestos included 'officials' among 'those defending the all-Russian bourgeoisie and bureaucracy who sit in the Central Rada.' These manifestos contain no hint of support for Russians as a nationality.[109]

Although most bureaucrats were Russian-speakers, this group was not necessarily uniformly hostile to the Rada or to Ukrainian autonomy, and the influence of umbrella organizations like the Russian National Union in Kyiv or other extremist groups created in November 1917 in Odesa to work for imperial unity should not be exaggerated.[110] Discussion about why declared Russians and/or Russian-speakers did or did not support the Rada became intense during and after the first Bolshevik occupation. Pro-Rada Ukrainians later claimed that Russians supported the attempted coup in Kyiv on 5 (18) January 1918 and, implicitly, in other cities as well, for imperialist reasons.[111] Perhaps the first printed article implicitly accusing 'Russians' in general of disloyalty was written by Vynnychenko that

January for the Ukrainian SD newspaper *Robitnycha hazeta.* He claimed that because the Kadets knew they could not destroy the Central Rada they supported the Bolsheviks, who could, and that anticipating that the ensuing anarchy would then sweep away the Bolsheviks, the Kadets planned to put the extremist Black Hundreds into power to restore the Russian Empire.[112]

Although compelling, there is little evidence supporting this observation or indicating that bureaucrats were involved. The attitudes of dumas, which had just recognized the Rada weeks earlier, towards newly arrived Bolsheviks in their towns ranged from non-recognition and subsequent dissolution, as in Kharkiv, to submission in response to threats of violence, as in Proskuriv. In Kyiv the situation remains unclear. Apparently local Bolsheviks exploited Russian soldiers' dislike of the 'Ukrainianization' of army detachments that had been occurring throughout 1917. City officials, most probably, like in Zhytomir, decided to keep working in the interests of order rather than because of feelings of national affinity with the Bolsheviks. National leaders accused city officials of making anti-Rada speeches, not pleading for amnesty from the Bolsheviks for arrested Ukrainians, and greeting the Bolsheviks much the same as they later greeted the returning Rada, as liberators. Apparently the mayor, K. Riabtsov, a Russian right-wing SR, sent a letter to the commander of the Bolshevik forces on 26 January referring to his victory as 'the re-establishment of the tight union of the all-Russian proletariat,' and that same day the Russian left-wing SR Frumin made a speech saying that the Duma had always been loyal towards the Soviets. When a Ukrainian SR deputy resigned in protest at Riabtsov's letter, his gesture was dismissed as meaningless by the Duma's speaker, who confirmed the notion of a 'tight union' and got an ovation for it from the members.[113] Riabtsov was sacked together with the entire Kyivan organization by his party for supporting the Whites in 1919 but, when the Rada returned to Kyiv in March 1918, he claimed that the Duma had done what it could with the help of 'civilized Bolsheviks' to save arrested Ukrainian and Russian officers, just as under the Rada it was making similar initiatives for those arrested by the Rada with the assistance of 'civilized Ukrainians.' In an earlier note he had pleaded with the returned Rada to halt arbitrary arrests and shootings of suspected Bolshevik sympathizers because such activity would compromise the 'young Ukrainian Republic' and make it seem no different from the Bolsheviks.[114]

As mentioned previously, there was no direct relationship between language-use, attitudes, or loyalties. Left and right factions of the

Russian SRs each had a Ukrainian party organization and neither formally recognized Ukrainian independence. But the right was prepared to support it as a lesser evil to the Whites and because they approved of the Ukrainian government's commitment to seek confirmation of independence from a National Constituent Assembly. The Jewish Bund was divided over support for autonomy as well as independence. Ukraine's Kadets and right-wing Mensheviks did recognize independence, as did Ukraine's key social groups. The statements of the Union of Towns and spokesmen for administrators have been noted. In Kyiv an important Jewish credit association did not send its incorporation charter for ratification to Petrograd but to the Rada.[115] The All-Russia Professional Union of Administrators in all Branches of Agriculture did not recognize the Central Rada, not because of the national issue but because it opposed the Rada's land policies which had made tens of thousands of its members unemployed. Even so, the organization's local branch addressed its requests and demands to Kyiv and not to Petrograd. Officials of the Food Supply Committee of Kharkiv province, who formally did recognize the Rada, meanwhile refused to obey its directives not to ship food to Russia.[116] Sergii Shtern, a Kadet member of the Odesa city duma, was opposed to separatism and critical of attempts to linguistically de-Russify government administration; nonetheless, Shtern believed that pragmatic Russians had to come to terms with the Ukrainians. Because most of them were more anti-Bolshevik than anti-Ukrainian, and as such, preferred federalist-autonomy to separatism, Russians had to accept that the empire had to be decentralized and that compromise was necessary if they wished to save anything at all of the Russian state.[117] Shtern's opinions echoed those of Ukraine's representative in the Provisional Government, Petro Stebnytsky, who in October 1917 warned Petrograd against restricting Ukrainian autonomy. The Rada and the Secretariat, he explained, were moderate forces for order and by virtue of their authority promoted legality and restrained anarchy.[118] An anti-Rada Russian eyewitness claimed that the Russians hated the Rada for its 'chauvinist' nationalism and social radicalism and were attracted by Bolshevik slogans, but he himself revealed no nationally motivated sympathy for them. Cryptically noting that Russians who were willing to work for the Rada because it was anti-Bolshevik were repelled by its 'chauvinism,' he went on to specify that educated people passively accepted 'the Ukrainian yoke,' while workers, the general population (*gorodskie meshchane*), and small traders, openly organized against it. Stebnytsky called the pro-Bolshevik soldiers and students behind the uprising 'scum.'[119] A pro-Russian 'Little Russian' landowner in southern Ukraine complained that the Provisional Government had not placed Kherson province under the Rada and thus forced him to deal with far-away Petrograd instead of nearby Kyiv. When the Provisional Government collapsed, he supported Ukrainian independence because it represented a uniting with Europe: 'otherwise we will die at the hands of the asiatic muscovite Bolsheviks.'[120] There is every reason to think that had it existed longer, Ukraine's non-Ukrainians would have made their peace with the Rada.

The pressure of events presumably increased the number of Russians who began to imagine Russia as a national-territorial unit distinct from, and not coterminous with, the empire, and thus, see Ukraine as a national-territorial unit in its own right. While individuals through the nineteenth century had reflected upon where exactly 'central' or 'great' Russia was, in the summer of 1917 members of the centre-left Russian Radical Democratic Party (RRDP) began to see it as a political-administrative unit. Maksym Slavinsky, one of its founders and a Ukrainian national-activist and left-wing Kadet, was in charge of a special commission on territorial reform attached to the Provisional Government. In his draft project Slavinsky proposed that Russia have separate representation on the commission from other regions of the empire. Nothing practical emerged from this project, and the RRDP collapsed by the end of the year. Nonetheless, those discussing federalism, autonomy, and national issues inevitably had to consider whether 'Russia' was to be centralized or decentralized.[121] That autumn the leaders of the zemstvo in Kaluga province formed a 'Great Russian Union' that took Slavinsky's idea a step further: it sought to establish a separate Russian territorial-administrative unit. This idea of creating a Russian national state was never realized, but it showed that Russian liberals were beginning to think of a separate Russian republic in a confederated arrangement with Ukraine. The Bolshevik invasion, finally, prompted the Kadets to recognize Ukrainian independence in January 1918 – which they saw as a first step to the formation of a federal confederation on the territory of the old empire. Clearly, some Russian liberals at last realized that restoration was not an option and were trying to come to terms with the new administrative reality.[122]

Even the Ukrainophobe Vasilii Shulgin realized restoration was no longer an option, and it seems doubtful that his sympathizers in the Russian National Union helped the Bolsheviks that winter out of national feeling and the hope that they would restore 'Russian unity.' Russian extremists, it must be remembered, considered Bolsheviks to be sooner Jews than Russians. In 1918 Shulgin was rumoured to have met the Bolshevik commander and told him that his 'all-Russian party bloc' was doing with its pens what his troops were doing with their swords. Shulgin himself denied this. In a long front-page editorial in his newspaper *Kievlianin,* Shulgin explained that the Bolsheviks had imprisoned him during their occupation, and he denied complicity with them. In a speech in the Kyiv duma Savenko, one of Shulgin's anti-Ukrainian associates, said that the Bolsheviks had destroyed his party's offices and seized all its documents and property.[123] Shulgin, as a right-wing Kadet, did oppose uniting the Ukrainian-speaking provinces into one unit of a federal Russia administered from Kyiv. He instead wanted to divide the region into two or three autonomous provinces each with its own administrative capital. This coincided with how the Bolsheviks had divided the Ukrainian provinces that winter, and a similar project was later adopted by General Denikin.[124] It may be that Shulgin discussed collaboration with the Bolsheviks on the basis of this common interest while in prison – but there is no record of this. This possibility, additionally, has to be weighed against the circumstance that, faced with the Bolshevik advance during the Rada's last days in Kyiv, Shulgin secretly came to a tentative agreement with Petliura, then a Rada minister who was planning a coup against Hrushevsky, to recognize Ukrainian independence on condition that it officially be a bilingual-bicultural country.[125]

The left wing of the Russian Socialist Revolutionaries would have helped the Bolsheviks between November 1917 and March 1918 for doctrinal not national reasons, but Ukrainian government newspapers identified only monarchists and the extremist Black Hundreds as Bolshevik supporters. One referred to events that January in Kyiv as a 'Bolshevik – Black Hundreds' uprising. Reporting on events at the city's electricity-generating station the paper identified the leader of the pro-Bolshevik strike there as Globa-Mikhailenko, a known member of the Black Hundreds who had convinced his fellows to pass a resolution specifying that they opposed not 'the bourgeois Rada' but 'Ukrainian government.' The same man, an accountant at the power station, was also identified in the Duma and the Russian liberal press as a leader of the Bolsheviks' failed November coup in Kyiv.[126] But Ukrainian newspapers also reported that there was nothing in the Russian press about Russians as a group in Ukraine supporting the Bolsheviks. In light of this, the dissolution of Black Hundred parties as organizations by November 1917, the appearance of a 'Russian Republic option,' and Shulgin's position, it seems unlikely that educated Russian-speakers as a group in Ukraine would have supported the Bolsheviks that winter for purely national reasons. What does appear likely is that there were individual Russian or Russian-speaking former members of the Black Hundreds who supported the Bolsheviks for national reasons. But it is impossible to determine how many there were, who among them were bureaucrats, and to what degree they contributed to the collapse of the Rada. Vynnychenko's claim about Russian liberals restoring the empire with the help of Bolsheviks and right-wing extremists seems therefore dubious.

The Attempt to Centralize

As part of the Provisional Government the Central Rada could not demand that bureaucrats, in legal limbo until the Constituent Assembly met, swear an oath of loyalty to Ukraine and threaten them with dismissal if they did not so swear. The Rada did not even call its Secretariats 'ministries' until it declared independence in 1918. But neither could officials go on strike against the Rada simply because it was Ukrainian. Given its legal status from July 1917 this would have been tantamount to a strike against the Provisional Government – which no bureaucrats undertook, even in Russia. There is no research on the subject, but after the fall of the tsar probably all administrators' unions were dominated by the Mensheviks, who supported Ukrainian autonomy. As noted, on local levels, individual offices and groups did begin to recognize Kyiv as their superior instance. This should be considered when judging evidence of bureaucrats' hostility towards Rada instructions and animosities between it and rank-and-file bureaucrats. Despite individual opposition to the Rada government bureaucrats as a group apparently never went on strike against it.

The legal-administrative situation changed dramatically after the Bolsheviks took power and the General Secretariat decided on 1 (14) November 1917 to take over those ministries that it had been denied earlier as a 'temporary measure' – presumably meaning that any final division of administrative authority would be done after the Constituent Assembly met. Two days' later the Rada claimed authority over the four provinces (including the Crimea) that the Provisional Government had denied it.[127] That same day the commander of the Southwestern Front and the Kyiv duma recognized the Rada as the only remaining legal local representative of the Provisional Government.[128] After it declared autonomy on 7 (20) November, the Rada announced its desire for relations not only with the Bolsheviks, but with the Southeastern League.[129]

Russian Masons, in keeping with their October decision, did not recognize Ukrainian autonomy nor did local Kadets on 11 (24) November.[130] Nevertheless, on 24 November (10 December), two days after the Senate in Petrograd at its last meeting declared the Bolshevik government illegal, ten leading ministerial officials in the Ukrainian provinces claimed by the Rada formally recognized the Rada as the highest local administrative authority. They stated in a declaration to the Secretariat that since the Provisional Government was no longer functioning normally, they, as 'official representatives of institutions residing in Kyiv,' had unanimously decided for the sake of public order to recognize the 'General Secretariat of Ukraine as the country's highest administrative organ.' The next day the Rada explicitly instructed all bureaucrats to remain at their jobs.[131] Within the week Kyivan Kadets reversed themselves and decided to accept Ukrainian autonomy on condition that it be accepted by the All-Russian Constituent Assembly and that Ukraine's borders be ratified by the Ukrainian Constituent Assembly. In Chernihiv province local Kadets not only declared themselves to be behind Ukrainian territorial autonomy but formed a Ukrainian Association for the Defence of Statehood and the Economy.[132] *Kyivski hubernialni visti* continued to print Provisional Government decrees and notifications through December 1917. Throughout the autumn, the number of town dumas, which included their administrations, formally recognizing the Rada increased and by December included Kharkiv and Katerynoslav. That month Ukraine's duma representatives voted to replace their regional branch of the All-Russian Union of Cities with a national organization, the Union of Cities of Northern Ukraine, and to recognize the Central Rada as the highest local administrative authority.[133] In November the Rada created a special department within its Ministry of Finance under Marshynsky whom it charged with the task of literally creating a national central and local governmental administration. The *Komissia po rozhliadu i ukhvaliuvanniu shtatov uriadovstsiv ministerstv* included representatives from government employees' unions, and its work was completed under the Hetman. On 22 January 1918 newspapers published a Ministry of Internal Affairs circular instructing officials to follow channels and due procedure.[134]

The organizational significance of these events was profound. On the ruins of the old vertical imperial bureaucracy partially destroyed already by 1917, elements of a new national bureaucracy were appearing. As of November the Central Rada had what was left of the local tsarist administrative system at its disposal, and the bureaucrats who ran it recognized the Rada. Even Krainsky admitted that the Ukrainianization of the army and public life saved Ukraine from the Bolsheviks temporarily and restrained the 'animal instincts of the masses' at least until January 1918. He got his first Ukrainian-language official letter on 4 November. Only in January did he observe that although institutions existed they had no authority, functioned by inertia, and did almost nothing. The one activity that did not cease was departmental correspondence, and the only authority that the urban masses recognized by then in Chernihiv was the local soviet.[135]

When the Rada declared independence on 9 (22) January 1918, its formal control was limited to right-bank Ukraine, and within the week it would lose southern Ukraine to the Bolsheviks. That same day General Denikin, in Novocherkassk, announced the creation of the anti-German Volunteer Army and the Don Government. Since this organization included a council of Kadet ministers it could claim continuity with the Provisional Government and serve as a legal focus of loyalty. On 12 (25) January bureaucrats in Petrograd declared their strike formally ended. By the end of that month the Bolsheviks had occupied Kyiv.

When the Rada returned to Kyiv in March 1918, under German protection, offices were functioning within four days and it began a review of personnel.[136] Having just enacted a law that granted citizenship to those who were born in or long resident in Ukraine, the Rada could begin legally dismissing bureaucrats as 'foreigners' (it also provided them with a ticket to the Russian border and a certificate specifying how long they had worked). Ukrainian citizens dismissed for working for the Bolsheviks could be rehired after investigation.[137] The Land Ministry began dismissing anyone hired by the Provisional Government as 'representatives of a foreign government.' In Volyn the entire provincial administration except for nineteen persons was dismissed, and there were too few local commissars. While some condemned 'opportunists' seeking government jobs, it must also be noted that the Ukrainian Socialist Revolutionaries opposed such condemnations as destructive of Ukraine's 'young state-building' efforts.[138] Thirteen bureaucrats were dismissed from the Kyiv provincial commissar's office in March 1918, but these were all soldiers who had not returned from the army.[139] These dismissals coincided with ministry building. The Rada, like the Bolsheviks, had thousands to choose from. By April 1918 the Rada had established terms of employment for its employees that incorporated their pre-war grievances. Employees had to belong to unions; unions had a say in hiring, promotion, and firing; and all dismissals were to be judged by an administrative court. Money for pay began arriving in Kyiv province's towns in mid-May.

Application letters suggest that most applicants were educated and had previous clerical experience. Krainsky complained that the newcomers were mostly incompetent and that office committees only created chaos in ministries. Unqualified and unwilling to work, voting to cut hours, and leaving work by two in the afternoon, these people destroyed professional standards, he continued. Those who protested they condemned as extremist Black Hundred reactionaries and subjected to office sniping and intrigues, and firing someone was impossible: 'in the provinces all those undeserving of work, all the losers and uneducated, occupied well-paid jobs.' However, although Krainsky complained that lower-level incompetent clerks were paid more than higher-level competent officials, he also complained that no one in Chernihiv had been paid at all for two months in 1918. Thus, he never specified whether people were unwilling to work because they did not want to work or because they were not getting paid.[140]

In cities under German control a sense of government returned, showing that work could be done where there was political will. Within days of arriving in Kyiv the Germans hired women to scrub down the main station for the first time in living memory and repaired dilapidated rolling stock untouched since 1914 – which included new windows and clean white sheets for first-class compartments. In Katerynoslav they supervised the cleaning of the governor's office and the post office. In provincial towns teams compiled lists of population and material damage, which were later forwarded to Ukrainian officials, and cleared pigs from the streets.[141] Residents of Kharkiv were astounded how, within hours of taking the city, the Germans began to re-establish administration and communications and got all public spaces swept. By next day all could safely sleep again at night and walk the streets in daytime. Already that January the records of the Iarmolynsk county office in Podillia province show that commands, detailed instructions, and central publications were arriving.[142]

Outside the major towns, in the wake of the Bolshevik occupation and change in government, the establishment of central communications and administration in the spring of 1918 took longer. Correspondents reported that mail was not getting through and that to find out what happened villages had to send delegations to Kyiv. The commissar in Balta district did not know that the Rada had returned to Kyiv until one month after the event.[143] Nor was the German commander impressed, as he apparently thought the entire country could be as easily stabilized as the major cities had been: 'The people who are unsuccessfully attempting to rule Ukraine are like children. They believe they will be able to exercise power without a professional bureaucracy.'[144] Rural resistance to the returned Rada stemmed as much from matters of land and forest use as from refusal to surrender arms and stills – although people normally complied when they knew officials could use German and Ukrainian troops to enforce their authority.[145] Reports from some provinces that spring claimed that Bolsheviks and Black Hundred sympathizers in the wake of the German advance exploited the collapse of vertical control to do as they willed. Others complained about arbitrariness by tsarist personnel returned to office in the wake of the returning Rada and brutal requisitioning by its own troops. Self-appointed 'commanders' allied with local landlords to take revenge on rebellious peasants. In April 1918 the Food Supply Committee in the town of Fastiv complained to their Kyiv superiors about the odd behaviour of a recently arrived plenipotentiary who regarded all the peasants as 'bourgeoisie.' As such, they had to eat little and to give foodstuffs only to him, because he represented authority and had 580 machine-guns and two German divisions behind him. Anyone who sold goods privately was a traitor.[146] In Volyn province 'Ukrainian' policemen no longer took bribes and then left people alone as they did when they were tsarist policemen but kept pestering even after they were paid. In Poltava province 'the serving intellectuals don't do anything, are not interested in anything, have a Ukrainian government yet sabotage its policies (*maie ukrainsku vladu i ... sabotuie polityku Pravytelstva*).'[147] In Berdychiv the local commissar reported that the Bolsheviks had not totally disbanded the administration, it had functioned under their rule, and was able to function after they had left. However, confusion was perpetuated by the liberating commander, who first established military rule and then left in place after his departure his appointed officers with no instructions – and no money.[148] In some rural districts locals refused to take government positions for fear of reprisals from the more radically inclined.[149] More villages and counties fell under the control of local strongmen or political party organizations, of which the strongest were still the Ukrainian Socialist Revolutionaries. 'Ukrainian organizations' in the countryside, dominated by the SRs or their sympathizers, were disparate, and not necessarily pro-Rada. In response to the disorder people began digging trenches around their villages, arming themselves with whatever weapons they could find, and refusing admittance to outsiders.[150]

Reports of misrule from the provinces that spring confirmed what national leaders had already concluded: that their civil, decentralized, administrative model did not work in conditions of war and shortages and had to be changed. Ukrainian organizations based on personal networks, like the co-ops, Rada committees, and various elected councils may have worked at local levels, but they had not evolved into the vertical and parallel system of civilian administrative associations that Drahomanov and Hrushevsky had envisaged and, without police and troops to enforce order, violence plagued daily life. In response the Rada attempted to displace these various organizations with a single centrally controlled vertical bureaucracy. Leaders began enacting policies that would have created as vast a bureaucracy as that of any other belligerent state. To this end during the last month of its existence the Central Rada established an investigative commission (*anketno-slidcha komisiia*) with extensive powers to observe and interrogate all government employees, and if necessary, forward cases for prosecution.[151] It gave its commissar to Odesa in March 1918, for example, full authority to do as he saw fit, including the power to fine and arrest. Other initiatives, however, obfuscated lines of authority and produced confusion. A February decree that gave military commandants full authority in emergencies did not define 'emergencies' and left local police forces under duma authority. By the spring commandants were giving orders to civilian commissars and local dumas that the latter then ignored because they considered them unwarranted and illegal.[152] The presence of German troops was a mixed blessing. The German military administration did enforce order but it functioned in parallel with the civilian administration at all levels. German officers imposed military law on civilians and requisitioned at will, ignoring civilian officials.

City duma and zemstvo leaders protested as they had become accustomed to independence from central control, and this is often interpreted in national terms. Ukrainians in city dumas and zemstvos at the time, however, also saw this attempted curtailment of their administrative authority as an attack on federalism and democratic rights – that is, as a sociopolitical not a national issue.[153] Vladimir Vernadskii, a Ukrainian Kadet leader sympathetic to self-determination, thought that national leaders had brought misfortune upon the country because of their ineptitude and ignorance. While surrounding themselves with a mass of well-paid bureaucrats whose only merit was their knowledge of Ukrainian, these same leaders sabotaged loyal Russian-speaking officials. No less alarming, he claimed, were the Central Rada's attempts to replace local self-government with centrally appointed bureaucrats. Regardless of how corrupt and venal local officials were, the central appointees were no better and usually were worse, he claimed.[154] True or not, the key issue here is the national leaders' abandonment of their earlier Drahomanov model of bureaucracy and their attempt to establish strong central control. Against this background it is possible to seriously doubt the wisdom of the German decision in early March 1918 to intervene directly and take over a considerable portion of internal administration on the grounds that the Rada was woefully inept. How administratively efficient could any government be within one month of being re-established?

When national leaders in November 1917 got control over the entire tsarist administrative system in Ukraine there was no shortage of personnel, and nationality was not the sole determinant of loyalty. The Central Rada collapsed in face of the Bolshevik invasion that December, but when it returned to power in early 1918 its leaders realized that the administrative system had to be centralized. The major administrative problem was to subordinate elected organizations and their full-time staff to the government bureaucracy, not to replace Russians with Ukrainians. Ukrainians and Russians in elected institutions, meanwhile, condemned the Rada's centralization policies as anti-democratic and dictatorial. National political parties in 1917 may have lacked activists but Ukraine's institutions did not lack literate apolitical persons able to work as administrators who, given their tsarist-era behaviour and attitudes, worked as well as might have been expected in those circumstances.

CHAPTER FOUR

The Ukrainian State, April to December 1918

With the backing of German generals and Ukraine's financiers, industrialists, and landowners, on 29 April 1918 the Ukrainian-born former tsarist general Pavlo Skoropadsky overthrew the Central Rada. He established a neo-monarchist regime called the Ukrainian State (*Ukrainska Derzhava*) with himself, as Hetman, at its head. A major issue of contention surrounding the Ukrainian State from the point of view of administration was the national composition and loyalty of its bureaucrats. The Hetman's opponents refused to recognize his government as a national state and rejected the idea of an officially Russian-Ukrainian bilingual country. They condemned the many Russians and Russian-speakers in Skoropadsky's administration, the dismissals of Ukrainian personnel, which the critics claimed were made according to ethnic criteria, and the importation by the trainload of 'Russian monarchists' – a practice that they claimed the Bolsheviks, in turn, supported to destabilize the country. Skoropadsky and his defenders retorted that because national leaders had refused to join his government, and many of them were administratively incompetent, Russians and Russian-speakers represented the only source for higher administrative personnel and that they had created as efficient a government as was possible. This chapter notes that the relationships between loyalty identities and competence were not as simple as suggested in the historical polemics. Most middle- and lower-level government personnel probably remained at their jobs after April 1918. By late summer the worst anti-Ukrainian provincial and district (*povit*) heads (*starosty*) had been replaced, and well-paid, higher government officials had strong material incentives to be loyal to the Ukrainian State.[1] Not all Russian officials were necessarily disloyal or engaged in sabotage.

Functioning and Staffing

Skoropadsky's newly appointed minister of the interior told him shortly after he took power that he had no ministry because all of its former employees had fled and that, except for Finance, all ministries had to be built from nothing. Skoropadsky himself in the final version of his memoirs changed his description of the situation in the Rada's central ministries during its last days from 'absolute chaos' to 'indescribable.'[2] German bureaucrats were disillusioned with the inefficiency that they saw during the first weeks of the Hetman's rule and attributed it partly to staffing: 'The ministries work slowly, if at all. This stems from a lack of middle- and higher-level personnel ... Yet, these gentlemen do not want Muscovite or Petersburg personnel for officials, fearing that they would be too [Russian] nationalist or Bolshevik. A second problem is that ministers in central offices are totally inexperienced and despite good intentions cannot identify what is urgent and requires haste nor expeditiously conclude specific matters.'[3]

The Hetman's socialist opponents had their supporters in government sabotage the policies that they disliked and, both at the time and subsequently, they publicized every instance of corruption and breakdown that they could to discredit the regime. In the winter of 1919, after Skoropadsky's fall, newspapers reported that under the Hetman criminal gangs with the collusion of the local police had established their own 'republic' centred on the village of Sokul. The local populace, as a result, blamed the disorder on the Ukrainian State and wanted the tsar back.[4] In Katerynoslav a local nationalist activist and head of the Rada committee claimed that 'reactionary Russian elements' dominated the provincial administration under the Hetman.[5] The Ukrainian mayor of Volodymyr-Volynskyi stated that although there were Ukrainians that he could have employed as bureaucrats, officials during the last weeks of the regime gave the jobs to Russians and Poles.[6] A non-government refugee organization, for instance, collapsed because it got almost no money from the government. Its leaders finally turned over what was left of their organization to another group and resigned. Because only at that point did the government Refugee Department finally intervene, take over what was left of the old organization, and begin financing it, critics used the affair as an example of 'anti-Ukrainianism.'[7]

Secret police reports contain accounts of misrule and corruption. In Volyn province they identified Rada sympathizers in administrative positions sabotaging policies. In Zhytomir eight Jews, some of them in city hall, reportedly were involved in shady dealings but at large because the local police chief was corrupt; he, in turn, had been appointed by the governor on the recommendation of another rich local Jew who split bribes with him and reserved the right to intervene in any decisions that interested him.[8] Any discussion of Ukraine's bureaucracy in 1918, however, must consider its shortcomings and inefficiency not only in light of structure and personnel, but of German interference: the arbitrary intervention at all levels by German military commanders who imposed martial law and requisitioned at will undermined Ukrainian civilian ministries. The government, for instance, could not export the amount of foodstuffs stipulated in the Brest-Litovsk Treaty. Yet, if incomplete figures on illegal exports done by the German Army are included in total export figures, they would show that Ukraine provided Germany with much more than it was obliged to. The Ministry of Trade functioned well enough to provide weekly reports on all foreign trade, and in these reports we see German violations and that German officers totally ignored the Hetman's officials. Although the ministry could do nothing, the Germans, nonetheless, complained about it and demanded that the Hetman abolish it because it was 'interfering' with trade.[9]

Nonetheless, by autumn 1918 German reports, which were later confirmed by historians, noted that a bureaucracy had been established and was functioning tolerably well. In Podillia province eighty-eight regional tax collectors, who were paid 375 karbovantsi a month, were managing to collect some taxes. A 22 May request from Kyiv for Rzhyshchiv county to compile a personnel list of its fourteen village councils was completed and delivered on 10 June, while long lists of local council electors compiled by bureaucrats during the summer undoubtedly later helped the Bolsheviks identify opponents when they took power. Not the least of the Hetman's accomplishments was the creation of Ukraine's first Department of Public Health, which managed to repair the wartime destruction of the medical system and restore some basic free services and the massive stores of arms, clothing, medicine, and munitions that officials assembled in Kyiv's depots by November 1918.[10] With the help of the German Army, the Hetman government that summer disbanded the railway commissars and ran trains on time. By September railway traffic had to be cut by more than half not because of inefficiency or staff shortages, but because of a shortage of grease. Material shortages rather than administrative disorder also account for other problems. In a village near Kherson in August 1918 it was impossible to obtain items like boards, nails, tiles, or whitewash, all of which were readily available before the First World War. Land reform could not be implemented because the ministry in Kyiv had no statistics, while in all Ukraine there were only 1,000 sets of surveying instruments.[11]

Nationality aside, senior government officials were quick to take their subordinates in hand strictly and instructed them to work properly or face the consequences. The Proskuriv district head told his staff to stop carrying out orders as if they were 'waiting for something to happen.' The 'strong authority' we have wanted is now here, he continued, and anyone who doubted that should resign. He added that five people had recently been arrested for five days because they had failed to appear for a regularly scheduled meeting. Similar imposition of discipline that summer occurred in Kherson province.[12] In July in Kyiv province Vasyl Steblovsky, who had fifteen years' experience as a county secretary and had been unemployed for the previous year, pointed out in his application letter that he had to be hired because 'today's secretaries do not meet the requirements of their job,' and continued, 'the young Ukrainian state cannot allow this.'[13]

In light of such accomplishments Skoropadsky's supporters have a strong case. They claimed that they had sought to attract professionally competent individuals who were tied in some manner to Ukraine and that they had given the benefit of doubt to Ukrainian-born conservatives like Bohdan Kistiakovsky and Fedir Lyzohub. They admitted that some appointments were wrong, but that these represented mistakes inevitable under the circumstances. All but one of the government's twenty-nine permanent secretaries (*tovaryshi ministra*) were Ukrainian-born, they noted.[14] Skoropadsky later maintained that there were too few educated Ukrainians and that it had been impossible to create 'anything serious' using only Ukrainians: 'But there are many who deeply love Ukraine and desire her to be culturally developed who identify with Russian culture, which will care for Ukrainian culture without in any way betraying Russian [culture].'[15] According to Alexei Tatishchev senior Ukrainian-born bureaucrats were culturally Russian, but when they became ministers 'they tried to behave as they thought a Ukrainian nationalist should and, while slowly building the new "state" their new offices penetrated their psychologies, and they forgot, or tried to forget the habits and traditions of their former life and activities.'[16] Russians and Russian-speakers began seeing to their own interests only on the eve of the Hetman's fall. Accusations concerning the dismissal of Ukrainians and the influx of Russians, according to defenders, were either inaccurate or exaggerated, as most all of those who had worked for the Rada remained at their posts. Russian Kadet complaints about the Hetman add credence to his defenders. While initially urging their 'Little Russian' compatriots to join the Hetman's government, within a few months they began complaining about them. Skoropadsky had let power go to his head, they wrote. His 'careerist' ministers were taking linguistic Ukrainianization too far, and both were making totally unnecessary speeches about Ukrainian independence and Russian oppression![17] Noteworthy also are the complaints in Russian newspapers made by former tsarist officials about unqualified personnel taking 'their' jobs. Russians were being fired just because they were Russian. From their point of view, there were too many Ukrainian nationalists and Bolsheviks in lower-level positions.[18]

The minister of labour, a Russified German who in the spring of 1917 had signed a protest against the national movement, within a few months of taking office was circulating memos to his staff instructing them not to joke about Ukrainian or Ukrainians. He later signed a circular on the compulsory use of Ukrainian in the ministry.[19] A Colonel Pasyk at the Congress of Agriculturalists in November 1918 got a standing ovation when he said that although clerks could start using Ukrainian because they could keep a dictionary on their desks, the language should not be forced on the general staff for whom time was at a premium. Eventually, he concluded, 'we will all learn Ukrainian.' Konstantin Glukhovskii, who had finished St Petersburg University and then worked in the imperial Finance Ministry between 1913 and 1917, decided to go to Ukraine after the Bolshevik takeover. He seems to have regarded using Ukrainian as simply another job requirement. He explained in his letter of 4 June 1918 that he could read Ukrainian and that with some on-the-job practice he would quickly learn how to write Ukrainian. On 1 July Glukhovskii copied out and signed his oath in Ukrainian.[20] Russians Ivan Nikishin, Viktor Maliavkin, Fedor Mitenskii, and Iary Malygin also took learning Ukrainian in stride.[21] Hired under the Rada, they all worked for the Ukrainian State and then for the Directory. A June 1918 letter from the clerks' union in Vinnytsia complained that its members had not the time, money, books, or teachers to learn literary Ukrainian, which they said was vastly different from the vernacular. Although not opposed to learning Ukrainian, they wanted the legislation delayed a year and then implemented slowly. October data from Kyiv district show that of 170 zemstvo staff who filled out personnel forms, only thirteen could not speak or write in Ukrainian; meanwhile, district-level official correspondence was just as often in Ukrainian as in Russian.[22]

A declared-Russian officer with a Ukrainian name claimed that pre-war local-born bureaucrats predominated in offices. Before the war many had sympathized with Ukrainian cultural nationalism, he continued, and although they sweated and swore as they tried to write in Ukrainian under the Hetman, they did write in Ukrainian. He also adapted in his own way, he said. Because he himself had finished high school in Lomza he knew Polish and used it to make practical adaptations during a stint of office work. To write up documents he would take Polish words, attach Ukrainian prefixes or suffixes, and then string them together using Russian bureaucratic expressions. His fellow workers soon began turning to him as their 'Ukrainian specialist.' His superior confidently signed all his documents convinced that since he could not understand them they had to be in Ukrainian.[23]

Application letters for middle- and lower-level positions began arriving in offices within days after the takeover of power. Many were in Ukrainian, and like some of those in Russian, contained expressions of Ukrainian patriotism. In September 1918 districts in Kyiv province were still getting so many qualified applicants, some of whom were willing to work for nothing, that the secretary requested ministerial permission to take them on.[24] In his letter Mykhailo Novikov, who had refused to work for the Bolsheviks in Russia, pointed out that he was Kyiv-born and a 'native Little Russian.' Nikolai Glavatsky, a guards' officer and Kharkiv province nobleman, emphasized that he was a native of Ukraine and that he wanted to use his talents 'for my country's benefit.' Vladimir Krotkovsky, who had twenty-five years' experience working in various positions in the pre-war Polish provinces, wrote his letter of application in Ukrainian and stressed that he was Ukrainian-born from Podillia. Ivan Strizhev was a Russian official who had worked in Astrakhan and was living in Odesa that summer; he let it be known that he had taken Ukrainian citizenship and wanted to 'truly and faithfully' help build Ukraine.[25]

On lower levels there is little evidence of a massive Russian presence in government offices. When Skoropadsky took power he announced that all officials were to remain at their posts. Some accounts claim that most did, while others note that many left-wing Ukrainian bureaucrats resigned in protest at his coup. Recent work suggests that most of those who left did so because of low pay, age, or incompetence. 'Little Russian' permanent secretaries observed that the number of Ukrainian-speaking Ukrainians increased the lower down the hierarchy one looked. The staff of the Ministry of Education remained at their jobs. During the last months of the Hetman's rule the number of pre-1917 employees still working in the Poltava, Chernihiv, and Katerynoslav offices of the Customs and Excise Department were respectively 191 of 193, 167 of 171, and 114 of 116. In Katerynoslav and Chernihiv ninety staff members had completed or at least attended universities or technical colleges, and only twenty-three declared that they had been 'educated at home.'[26] The staff of the Land Ministry were almost all Ukrainian Socialist Revolutionaries or sympathizers. Opposed to the regime's land policies and their minister's refusal to communicate in Ukrainian, they refused to obey his instructions. In response the minister unilaterally dismissed all of them – later rehiring only secretaries and typists after the Hetman had intervened. A Socialist Revolutionary headed the General Affairs Department of the Ministry of Internal Affairs. Not only did he place fellow party members into the ministry, but also he managed to channel all correspondence directed to the minister and the Council of Ministers through himself – this included all intelligence about immigrants and fugitives from Russia.[27] One contemporary wrote that except for the ministers themselves and their personal secretaries, and the Agricultural Ministry staff, the bulk of the Rada's central ministerial officials remained at their jobs.[28] Among them was Apollin Marshynsky in the Tax Department, and in July 1918 Makar Mokrytsky was still in the General Affairs Department of the Ministry of Internal Affairs – but as a senior secretary, not head of Personnel. Roman Trofymenko appears in documents that March as one of the members of his ministry's rehiring committee and then again in May as the head of the Food Supply Ministry's Personnel Department, with a salary of 700 karbovantsi a month. After coming back from holiday in August Trofymenko requested a raise according to a new pay scale, but was dismissed as part of a general reduction of staff made at the time. Denis Kirichok was transferred to the Insurance Department of the Ministry of Internal Affairs in September, where he seems to have been demoted to assistant clerk. Serhii Vyshnivsky remained at his desk in Dubno, while the four clerks in the Iarmolyntsi county office in Podillia, who had been there since before 1914, were still there as of June 1918. Kyryl Kuzmenko moved to Kaniv where he worked in the Post Office, while Vasyl Korenchuk, hearing that his three brothers had been arrested on charges of Bolshevism, decided that the Hetman's regime was not to his liking and applied for a transfer to Podillia, where he believed he would be safer.[29]

Staff changes in the Refugee Department of the Ministry of Internal Affairs support the claim that natural attrition, promotions, and resignations rather than dismissals underlay the fast staff turnover. In April 1918 staff numbered fourteen men and nine women. By June that number had expanded to thirty-eight, of whom seventeen had been there since March, and by August the department had forty-one people employees, only ten of whom had been there four months earlier. By November the staff numbered forty-six, of whom only eight were 'old-timers.'[30] The Ordinary Tax Department of the Ministry of Finance had forty-eight employees under the Central Rada in April 1918; thirty-nine of them were still there three months later when the department had expanded to ninety-five, and twenty-six were still there in September out of the new total of 144. Personnel lists show that six of the original forty-eight staffers had quit or been dismissed because they had stopped coming to work. In November 1918 of the 275 personnel of the Kyiv district council, 126 had worked for the Central Rada.[31] In the fourteen counties of Rzhyshchiv district in Kyiv province, all of the officials appointed under the Rada were still in office in June 1918. Fourteen of the staff of twenty-eight that the Kyiv governor's office had in August 1918 had been there since April, and of those, five had been there since June 1917 or earlier; the same fourteen were still there in September – although by then, the total number of employees in the governor's office had risen to forty. Turnover was high. Where letters of resignation included a reason for resigning, these reasons were mundane rather than political – health, age, wages, and different jobs. As far as can be established all forty-three of the Podillia provincial governor's office staff employed in September 1918 were hired only that summer; since most application letters came from the city, the chosen were hired within weeks if not days.[32] Of the forty-one administrative personnel in the Kyiv province Peasants Affairs Office in July 1916, thirty-two were still there in July 1918.[33] Incomplete lists compiled that October show that all but three of Kyiv province's Draft Board's seventy-five officials had been hired before 1918, with twenty hired in 1917 or 1918; all seventy-nine staffers of the provincial governor's office were there before the Hetman took power, and nineteen of the twenty-six members of the province's Prisons Inspectorate had been employed there since before 1917.[34]

One example of firing for political reasons is recorded from Lypovets district, fifty kilometres east of Vinnytsia: in 1904 Foma Dzuibenko was appointed assistant secretary in a county office, where he worked until he was drafted in 1915. Demobilized in March 1918 he returned to his old post. When he appeared to swear loyalty to the Hetman in July he was fired. The next day Dzuibenko protested his dismissal, and the police investigation later explained that he had been fired because he had been rehired under the Rada which the police termed a time of 'liberty and anarchy.' After the Directory took power in December 1918 and recalled all old Rada officials to their positions, Dziubenko's name does not reappear. Aleksander Okunov, however, the county secretary since 1911, did continue in his position under the Directory. Petro Iamkovy and Mykhailo Zhurba, who since 1914 had been working as clerks in the Kyiv governor's office, were still there in September 1918.[35]

The Citizenship Law of July 1918 declared that all former tsarist subjects living in Ukraine on the date of issue were citizens and thus eligible to hold government jobs. Although the Hetman rehired pre-revolutionary lawyers for the Ministry of Justice, he did retain Ukrainian-speaking lawyers that had been hired by the Central Rada.[36] He also hired refugees from Russia, where consuls had instructions to provide passports without scrutinizing too closely whether applicants in fact had been born in Ukraine. For a few weeks, until they realized that too many were fleeing with their assets and introduced restrictions, the Bolsheviks permitted anyone who wished to do so to leave. Not all of these people were Russians. Petro Kornienko had worked for fifteen years as a district secretary in Russia, and he explained in his May 1918 letter of application that he had been fired by the Bolsheviks because he was Ukrainian and that he now again wanted work as a local secretary in Kyiv province.[37]

Ukraine apparently had a considerable number of educated unemployed people, and ministerial records reveal applicants pleading destitution as a motivation for applying for jobs, while incumbents were quitting for higher-paying positions elsewhere. Eighty per cent of the 6,000 members of the Union of Government Administrators were unemployed. In November 1918, of an estimated 40,000 to 50,000 registered unemployed workers in Kyiv, only 1,162 got benefits of 14 roubles a day, and this implies that there were lots of frustrated educated people in the capital. Local provincial office records show no shortage of application letters for government jobs – which began arriving within days of the Hetman's seizure of power. These applicants included qualified Ukrainians like Mykhailo Hrebeniuk, who had been working in government offices in Ukrainian provinces since 1912 and, just before the position was abolished in May 1918, had been secretary to a district commissar in western Ukraine.[38] The government hired women typists, but there is no record of its organizing schools to train administrators. Central officials issued secret instructions not to hire Jews as bureaucrats and to release those that had been hired by the Rada. A report from Rivne in Volyn province, however, claims that the city's police chief, a Russian officer hired under the Hetman who remained at his job under the Directory, hired Jews as policemen supposedly because no one else would work for such miserable wages. Secret police reports on corruption and embezzlement in the Ministry of Food Supply also mention Jewish employees. Solomon Zalkind, a section head hired under the Rada, remained at his post in the ministry.[39]

The probability that nationality figured little in appointments to middle- and lower-level positions is supported by evidence from audits of local elected bodies. New research suggests that dismissals there were not made for national reasons and that they have to be understood as a renewed attempt at administrative centralization that was begun by the Central Rada. Faced with paralysis of services and resistance to centralization, the Hetman shortly after taking power sought to replace incompetents and political opponents. Ukrainians and non-Ukrainians, who united in this matter, condemned the move as an attack on democratic rights and local autonomy. The audits reveal widespread absenteeism, incompetence, corruption, illegal commerce, cronyism, and criminality among elected and appointed governors (*starosty*) and city duma and zemstvo personnel. Regardless of claims to the contrary by the Hetman's opponents, what these audits show is that only those who broke a law, regardless of their nationality or position on independence, were subsequently charged and dismissed – although entire executive committees were sacked too. In twenty districts of Kyiv province only two zemstvo were actually dissolved, while two dumas saw no arrests or dismissals whatsoever. The Kamianets-Podilskyi duma seems to have avoided the Hetman's purges, yet its behaviour apparently remained unchanged after his demise, as the Directory newspaper criticized its inactivity. In three consecutive daily six-hour sessions instead of enacting legislation and giving instructions to its officials for implementation, this duma debated political matters – despite the fact that 80 per cent of the population was apolitical and did not understand the difference between Socialist Revolutionaries and Social Democrats, but did realize that they were getting no services for their taxes and therefore had stopped paying them.[40]

These audits substantiated newspaper reports that complained about local services functioning badly or not at all primarily because of politicized executive and representative bodies. When local commissars or military commanders tried to establish services, personnel and activists would condemn their initiatives as dictatorial and counter-revolutionary.[41] Most members, both non-Ukrainian and Ukrainian, it transpired, were usually absent from most sessions, while those that did attend spent more time debating political issues and pay raises for themselves than supervising their subordinates or assigning them tasks. On average no more that 30 to 40 per cent of members were present in the country's dumas and zemstvos when they were supposed to be. Inspectors' reports condemned the work of the Zvenyhorod town council, elected in August 1917, and noted that its office work had deteriorated 'to the extreme,' yet nobody was fired. Of the council's thirty-nine members, eighteen were 'from Ukrainian organizations' and fifteen were from one of the town's six Jewish organizations. The report characterized the council as apolitical because it appointed a Bolshevik as a commissar before the Bolsheviks took the city and then declared its loyalty to the Hetman as soon as he had taken power. The work of the district zemstvo, on the other hand, was characterized as nationalist and pro-Rada, because it was dominated by the Ukrainian SRs, judged to be acceptable, and none of its members were dismissed.[42] Only in May 1918, which was almost one year after it had been elected, did Kyiv's duma finally agree on the composition of its standing executive committee. With no instructions from their superiors officials presumably limited themselves to routine functions. Local inhabitants, meanwhile, in receipt of minimal if any services, stopped paying their taxes. Administrative problems here had little to do with bureaucrats or nationality.

In their complaints and protestations Ukrainians and non-Ukrainians alike ignored the relationship between their opposition and administrative-organizational problems, and both condemned the Hetman's centralization initiative, as they had the Rada's. National leaders added the charge that they were being victimized by an anti-Ukrainian regime and that the country did not have enough loyal bureaucrats. Nonetheless, a strong case can be made for the Hetman's dismissals policy at the higher and middle levels as a consequence of state building, that is, rationalization and centralization, not as a manifestation of anti-Ukrainian politics. It is unlikely that government appointments were much different. At the county level centrally appointed heads (*starosty*) were to ensure only that no clerks were hired either with Bolshevik loyalties, which was specific, or with unspecified 'dubious loyalties.' The latter term was obviously open to interpretation, but there do not appear to have been mass dismissals of Rada-appointed Ukrainian officials at lower levels. In a list compiled in August 1918 of the clerks in eleven villages in the Vinnytsia district, only three had apparently held these posts before Skoropadsky came to power, and there is no evidence that any of the three secretaries of the Kalynivka county council had worked for the Central Rada. But rather than speculating on the dismissal of the others in those places, it would be wiser to try to discover reasons for their leaving in the evidence that does remain.[43]

Loyal Russians?

Opponents accused Skoropadsky's senior- and middle-level bureaucrats of being sympathetic to the Whites and of sabotaging policies; however, the behaviour of these men must be judged in light of three considerations. First, powerful Russian-dominated groups had agreed not to sponsor or organize anti-Hetman activity. Second, declared Russians were divided over supporting the Hetman. Skoropadsky for his part, being mindful of the future, White connections to the Entente, and their potential as an anti-Bolshevik ally, financed White paramilitary formations in Ukraine indirectly as well as secretly. Most of the members of the Hetman's 60,000-strong police force were former tsarist personnel who worked for pay; nevertheless, their standing orders identified anarchists and monarchists alongside nationalists and Bolsheviks as the enemy, and if monarchists and Russian extremists actively involved themselves in explicitly anti-government plots, they were arrested. In one curious letter, the Lypovets district official in August asks the governor what he should do about a strange officer who had arrived in town and recruited a few hundred 'criminal and disreputable' men as volunteers. Three months later the governor replied, telling him to ask the officer for identification. Presumably, if there were plots, lower-level officials were either excluded – or like this fellow, they were too dim-witted to know about them.[44] Excesses against peasants, committed by German or Ukrainian troops paid by returned landowners (some of whom held district or provincial posts), cannot be automatically categorized as 'anti-Ukrainian' and blamed on the central government – except insofar as it failed to prevent them.[45] In addition, historians must not overlook the issue of self-interest. Secret police investigations from the Hlukhiv region, for instance, explain that the violence and discontent reported by its zemstvo head were unfounded, as they were unsubstantiated by the local governor.[46] Whatever the case may have been, violent rural opposition was subsiding by autumn 1918, and the then new prime minister Kistiakovsky began dismissing the officials responsible. Skoropadsky's claim to this effect is supported by Russian Bolshevik leaders. While planning their invasion in early November 1917 Aleksandr Iakovlev stressed to all present that although the Bolsheviks had the support of workers and peasants in Chernihiv province, they should have no illusions: without the presence of a powerful Red Army there would be no revolution in Ukraine.[47]

Third, Germany influenced the composition of the Hetman's higher administration. Ukraine's moderate Russians and Russophiles regarded the Hetman as a lesser evil to Lenin or Ukrainian socialists, and by working in Skoropadsky's government, they reasoned, they were preserving 'a part of Russia,' its breadbasket, from catastrophe. When the Hetman took power Russian Masons in Ukraine reversed their earlier position and supported independence as a lesser evil to Bolshevism.[48] While the Mensheviks refused to recognize the Ukrainian State, most Kadets in Ukraine did recognize it, and they were supported by the German Foreign Office, which in face of serious peasant revolts protesting requisitioning encouraged the Hetman to hire Ukrainians as administrators. At their party conference Ukraine's Kadets agreed to work with the Hetman, and they separated from their anti-Ukrainian pro-Entente parent organization – which was backed by the pro-Russian-monarchist German General Staff. Pavel Miliukov, involved in secret talks that summer on the possibility of a German-supported Russian constitutional monarchy, was also prepared to accept limited autonomy for Ukraine more or less according to the Provisional Government's Temporary Instruction of the previous August.[49] By October, faced with defeat and recognizing the strength of the Hetman's socialist opponents, the German generals shifted from their earlier position and also began encouraging the Hetman to hire more Ukrainians.[50]

The coalition of Ukraine's financiers, industrialists, and landowners (PROTOFIS), who found themselves having to depend for law and order on a Ukrainian government, published a statement in February 1918 declaring that they would support independence if the Central Rada reversed its socialist policies. It supported the Hetman thereafter and that September, facing the possibility of German defeat, the PROTOFIS declared that it supported an officially bilingual Ukrainian state and that it would repay Ukraine's portion of the tsarist debt.[51] The chair of the coalition, Aleksandr Golitsyn, was also head of Kharkiv province's Assembly of Gentry. Opposed to independence Golitsyn later wrote that he had recognized that the country was different from Russia. He accepted the official status of Ukrainian and thought that the country had to have autonomy under Russian rule, like Finland.[52] Although condemned by national leaders who wanted independence, it must be stressed that the men who in 1918 were prepared to finance the debt of a bilingual Ukraine federated with Russia along the lines of the Third Universal had evolved significantly. Two years earlier they were willing to support little more than cultural autonomy for 'Little Russians.'

Pro-Skoropadsky Russian-speaking Ukrainians were divided. Some regarded the Ukrainian State as a temporary necessity that should be dissolved once the Bolsheviks were overthrown in Russia, and others, who accepted it in principle, claimed that post-Bolshevik Russia would enjoy stability only if it accepted Ukrainian political autonomy. Such men, like Vladimir Vernadskii, saw themselves much as did the Anglo-Irish in Ireland – a group with two compatible loyalties.[53] Non-Ukrainian supporters like Shtern elaborated upon the pragmatic political rationale for backing independence that influenced men like Golitsyn. Since Skoropadsky had established order in the region, it was in Russian interests to support him because a strong independent Ukraine could serve as a stepping stone to overthrow the Bolsheviks in Russia. Given the distance to Petrograd, Shtern continued, it was desirable, reasonable, and practical for cities like Odesa and Kharkiv to look instead to Kyiv as their administrative centre. Russians mindful of these considerations, he added, had willingly learned and begun using Ukrainian.[54] Alexei Tatishchev was in Ukraine when the Germans arrived, and one of Skoropadsky's ministers invited him to be a ministerial secretary. Reflecting on Ukraine's statehood he concluded that it had a rationale and that independence was an understandable reaction to tsarist policies. As he knew Ukrainian, and was aware that it was very different from Russian, he was not troubled as much by Ukrainianization as by the refusal to give Russian status as the second language. Chancery Ukrainian may not have been fully understandable to Ukrainian peasants, he continued, but then Russian peasants did not fully understand chancery Russian either.[55]

On the one hand, there were people like the permanent secretary to the minister of the interior, who chastised Russians for refusing to work as bureaucrats and thus ensuring Ukraine would have a 'Russian physiognomy.' In his opinion, Russians had to take jobs to keep out incompetent Ukrainians whose only qualifications were their knowledge of Ukrainian.[56] Having to use 'Mr Hrushevsky's Ukrainian language' was annoying and necessary, but probably temporary.[57] On the other hand, the editor of *Russkii golos* observed, on 14 November 1918, that 'we liberals must support the Ukrainian national idea.' A Katerynoslav newspaper noted that since no Ukrainian political leaders were skilled administrators, Russians had to be in the government which, therefore, had to be bilingual.[58] While some rationalized their position in anti-Bolshevik terms, a provincial journalist from the town of Kupchynsk in eastern Kharkiv province expressed his territorial patriotism as follows in October 1918: 'Russian Ukrainians, or more precisely, Little Russians proud of Kyiv as the source of all-Russian culture and statehood, will never regard themselves as "Muscovites" or "Zaporozhians" or "Galician-Ruthenians" but as Russians (*russkimi*), regardless of what political forms the various parts of Rus adopt ... The best guarantee of this brotherhood would be the adoption of the Russian and Little Russian languages as official languages, because these are the languages of the majority.'[59] Although some government employees in the eastern provinces did quit in protest over having to learn a language that they said no one ever used to address them, secret police files reveal that lower-level bureaucrats who complained about what they thought was too little time to learn Ukrainian were nonetheless loyal.[60] Anyone entering the city of Poltava in June 1918 would have found all of its signs painted over white, not because their owners opposed Ukrainianization, but because financially pressed city officials had decided to tax the words on signs.[61]

Although there were few declared Ukrainian high officials, many Ukrainian government employees at lower levels evidently remained in their positions after the Central Rada fell. Moreover, a significant number of declared Russians and Russian-speakers had territorial patriotism, worked for the Ukrainian State, and were willing to learn and to use Ukrainian. Complaints about this group by the Whites indirectly confirm the applicability of Weber's hypothesis about interests trumping principles. They condemned pro-Hetman Russians and 'Little Russians' as 'degenerates' concerned about their wealth whose fear of Bolshevism was stronger than their Russian patriotism. By this logic it was not Ukrainians who created Ukraine, but these 'degenerate' Russians – whose faith in Germany was merely a grasping at straws.[62]

CHAPTER FIVE

The Directory, December 1918 to November 1919

Pavlo Skoropadsky abdicated one month after Germany's surrender in November 1918. In his place Volodymyr Vynnychenko and Symon Petliura re-established the Ukrainian National Republic and declared themselves as heads of its temporary government – called the Directory. Whereas the Ukrainian State and the Central Rada had controlled a core territory of five tsarist provinces for at least six months each, the borders of the Directory-ruled UNR fluctuated with the fortunes of war. The new republic fought against the Bolsheviks, the Whites, and the anarchist Nestor Makhno (see Chapter 7). The Directory's core territory was limited to an area of land measuring roughly 200 square kilometres, including most of Podillia province and parts of Volyn and Kyiv provinces which it controlled for two periods of no longer than five months each – between December 1918 and April 1919 and then from August to November 1919. The total population in this area varied between three and ten million. The only territory the Directory controlled with but a few weeks' interruption was the area around the city of Kamianets when it was the capital, consisting of no more than 100 square kilometres (see Maps 3 and 4). During 1919 the extent of Bolshevik- and Directory-controlled regions fluctuated, and both were about equal in size and population. That December the Directory allowed Polish troops to occupy territory as far east as the Zbruch River. Contrary to their agreement Poles summarily confiscated and shipped to Poland office materials and dismissed all Ukrainian officials within the region and replaced them with their own civilian administration.[1] The issues concerning the UNR and its bureaucrats involve not only loyalty but whether the Directory could do anything at all, how it compared with its Bolshevik rival, and the degree to which bureaucratic incompetence might account for its demise.

The Directory never clearly demarcated civilian and military spheres of competence in the republic. A 24 November 1918 army decree reinstituted the situation of 'dual power' that had existed under the Central Rada earlier that year. Petliura, without the agreement of the other members of the Directory, declared a 'partial' martial law that allowed local commanders – otamans, a term that referred to a military rank as well as to any commander, self-appointed or otherwise – temporary administrative and judicial authority. This included the right to try 'treason' and plundering by martial law and to execute by firing squad. Otamans were allowed to decide among themselves on the territorial limits of their authority, and during military operations military commanders had total authority in their areas of operation.[2] Indicative of the vague lines of authority that plagued the Directory is that by the autumn of 1919 Petliura had arrested over a dozen of his major otamans. That November, on the eve of the UNR's collapse, his Interior Minister Isaak Mazepa ordered them all released.[3] Military commanders and/or otamans acted as or gave orders to civilian administrators. Colonel Bolbochan in eastern Ukraine instructed Hetman officials to remain. He ended a Bolshevik-organized municipal workers' strike in Kharkiv against the Directory by threatening strikers with court martial, and the administration functioned normally thereafter until the Bolsheviks retook the city.[4] In right-bank territories, in the first weeks after the Bolsheviks were evicted from a region, soldiers were the Directory's only representatives on the spot. Partisan commanders would even declare themselves dictators of entire provinces. But, simultaneously, officers themselves complained about being forced to administer. Despite the martial law decree civilian commissars, for their part, complained that military officers interfered with their authority, and it seems that in some places civilian officials actually did take over. Already on 30 December 1918 the chief of the General Staff issued a clarification to the original decree stipulating that commanders securing rear areas were to exercise their authority only temporarily and were not allowed to exceed their authority nor override civilian officials.[5] Otamans were strongest not in Directory territories in 1919 but in Soviet Ukraine through to 1922 where they led the armed opposition. Outside the major cities people as a rule supported them and at least half claimed they were fighting for what by then was a government-in-exile. By 1921 there were fifty-eight otamans, but the details of civil authority in their regions are unknown.[6]

Staffing

When they were in opposition the future leaders of the Directory alleged that ministers intentionally dismissed Ukrainians. They also called for bureaucrats who had broken the law to be brought to trial – which implied that they did not distinguish between them solely on national grounds.[7] On 2 December, the day after taking power, the Directory allowed its ministers to dismiss at will any officials, yet Land Minister Mykola Shapoval declared that he would discriminate. At his first meeting Shapoval was asked if he would stop importing trainloads of bureaucrats from Moscow and reinstate Ukrainians fired under the Hetman and allow them to re-establish their professional committees. He replied that all Ukraine's nationalities could take part in building its state and invited all except those who felt they could not accept the new government to remain at their jobs. Having defeated the enemy, 'Ukrainian revolutionary democracy' sought to create, not to destroy or seek revenge. Shapoval recognized that it had been difficult for some to work under the Hetman, although he did not call them Russian-speakers, and he assured his audience that he would listen to all languages and could be approached in any language: 'At work I recognize one language – honest work for the great national cause.'[8]

A 14 January 1919 decree summarily dismissed all officials hired under the Hetman, and in February all those who had remained in recently Bolshevik-occupied territory were also dismissed. Presumably because of complaints from local officials about disruptions caused by arbitrary dismissals and appointments by commissars, rehiring was made subject to consultation with, as well as review by, a superior, and the recommendation of a pro-national civil organization.[9] Unlike the Bolsheviks, Directory officials did not direct applicants through a labour exchange, but told them to apply directly to their ministry. Supporting statements from civil organizations or leading citizens were acceptable in lieu of missing documents. A government newspaper argued that since non-Ukrainians in responsible positions had demonstrated disloyalty, even after formal declarations of loyalty they could only be allowed into lower-level positions. Newspapers refer to the Ministry of Roads releasing only higher officials, to the formation in all offices of councils of trusted superiors to decide on staffing, and that despite vetting the same people that had held jobs previously remained at their posts.[10] In similar fashion when the Directory reoccupied Kyiv in May 1920 it dismissed all bureaucrats hired by the Bolsheviks and required all those who wanted to work to reapply to local vetting committees and to explain why they were important to the government. In exile in October 1920 the Directory again summarily dismissed bureaucrats that had remained in Bolshevik-controlled territory; upon its return the Directory had intended to allow ministers to rehire at their discretion.[11]

Historians have claimed that the Directory's measures applied primarily to ministers and higher officials.[12] Others have said that staffing decrees had little impact. Vynnychenko claimed that adventurers, Russifiers, and right-wingers kept their jobs in Directory territory: 'the worst elements of the national petite bourgeoisie.'[13] Isaak Mazepa stated that it was impossible to staff the bureaucracy with loyal Ukrainians and that non-Ukrainians used their positions to sabotage the government: 'Almost every government institution was overflowing ... with Russians, Poles and "Russified Little Russians" that cared little for Ukrainian interests.' A Russian in Katerynoslav noted that the Directory's local representatives issued orders that were never implemented but that they did dismiss all non-Ukrainian-speaking bureaucrats.[14]

What actually happened remains unclear. Although some have noted that higher Russian/'Little Russian' bureaucrats throughout Ukraine usually fled oncoming Directory troops,[15] remaining central ministry records give little detail about who was fired at local levels and why. They do not give totals and percentages but do reveal that employees suspected of sedition were not shot – a common fate in Bolshevik territories: 'We are not Bolsheviks and have no reason to resort to unlimited terror' on pro-Russian bureaucrats, whose presence became more threatening once the Directory faced not only the Bolsheviks but Denikin, wrote a critic in the autumn of 1919. He wanted all politically loyal Ukrainians in government offices to organize themselves to work together with the recently created government inspectorate and watch Russian and former tsarist employees. If this were not done, he claimed, soldiers would purge on their own initiative. Although security officials arbitrarily may have shot individual officials for disloyalty, the Directory never threatened any of its officials with the death penalty.[16]

What probably happened was that despite official decrees institutions contained a mix of bureaucrats left over from each preceding government. Of twenty-nine permanent secretaries in the Hetman's central ministries, eight continued working for the Directory.[17] Pro-German

Masons who had worked for the Hetman and were unable to come to an agreement with Petliura were dismissed.[18] On the lower levels of some central ministries most employees were quickly rehired. Tatishchev had initially been prepared to remain but was dismissed by Vynnychenko. Realizing that the Directory would fall to the Bolsheviks, he decided to remain in Kyiv until then so he could later travel to Kharkiv to his family. In the meantime Tatishchev was hired as a librarian by his old Ukrainian friends in the ministry. In the Refugee Department of the Ministry of Internal Affairs under the Hetman, three employees were fired with no reason given while others who left quit at their own request, and by January 1919 only five were left of the department's original twenty-three members. Twenty-three hired under the Hetman had to reapply that month and be vetted by a local committee of the Employees Trade Union (*Spilka spivrobitnykiv MVS*); of those, four did not reapply, and of the remainder, only three were not rehired.[19] Those who stayed included the head Iury Starytsky, his chief secretary, and the faithful office secretary, a twenty-year-old Polish girl Wanda Slabowska. Beginning as a typist making 250 karbovantsi a month in March 1918, fired during the summer just after returning from a paid holiday, she was rehired three months later and that December was working as a clerk 2nd class, with a salary of 300 a month.[20] During the tense days between 21 December and 6 January a considerable number of the Ordinary Tax Department's staff of 137 applied for temporary leave. After vetting (18–26 January) the majority (83) of those hired under the Hetman were rehired; thirty-four of these were 'old-timers' from March 1918. Of sixty-one people in three central Finance Ministry departments in 1919, only six had worked for either the Central Rada or the Hetman;[21] of the fifty-five in the ministry's Credit Office that January, only six had been there in 1918, and by the next June that number had shrunk to twelve, of whom only six had been there since 1918. Those rehired included Poles and Russians. In Radyvil station in Volyn, out of a staff of sixty, only nineteen reapplied and they were all rehired.[22] In three local branches of the Excise Department only one of almost 200 employees who had to reapply was not rehired, while in the central office forty of the total of sixty were rehired. The Land Ministry in 1919 had eighty-one central officials; of these, nineteen had been with it since the Rada. Ten of those had quit when the Hetman took power and then returned to their jobs after his fall; the remainder were all Directory appointees. Two of the four officials employed in the Kamianets Market Gardening Subsection of the Land Ministry in late 1919 had worked there since 1917.[23]

Apparently almost all the personnel and material of the medical services of the River Transportation Department of the Ministry of Roads and the Kyivan section of that ministry managed to survive and function from 1917 through to May 1920. Of the thirty-one in the Podillia governor's office in July 1919, twenty had worked for the Hetman and among them was sixty-three-year old Trentyi Smetana.[24]

Staff turnover in central offices, as suggested by the above figures, was fast. In April 1919, after it had fled from Kyiv, the General Affairs Department of the Ministry of the Interior, where Mokrytsky worked, had a staff of eight; that September this number had grown to fifty-two, and then to sixty-three by November. During the 1920 summer campaign Mokrytsky drew up a plan to expand the central staff of the ministry by ninety-six people to 207.[25] The Department of Political Information was to expand to at least 4,000 officials.[26] In June 1920 a staff of 232 still managed to keep six trains running in Directory territory; this was only 52 per cent of the 1914 staff but, according to the chief engineer, they sufficed. The number of telegraph and medical personnel in 1920 was almost the same as it had been in 1914; of the 220 in the Maintenance Department, sixty-eight were women.[27]

Officials were sometimes surprised by what they found in their offices. In February 1919 the Podillia provincial commissar discovered that the old tsarist provincial chancery still existed even though it no longer did anything; of its 1917 staff complement of 102, forty were still coming to work and getting paid according to 1917 pay rates. Alongside them another sixteen of the Agricultural Office staff were also still working for 1917 salaries – although they administered aid programs to soldiers' families. The lowest-ranking clerk, Lukasz Jaworski, who had begun working there in 1903 and had seven children, was making the same 130 karbovantsi a month in 1919 as he had been making in 1917. That year one egg in Kyiv cost one kopek; in 1919 in Kamianets it cost one karbovanets.[28]

Perhaps the only generalization that the examined data allow is that turnover seems to have been less on lower levels. An otherwise detailed account of the district of Vinnytsia's five-month experience of Bolshevik rule in 1919, made by the city's mayor, does not mention what the clerical staff there did. Reports from some of the districts retaken from the Bolsheviks in August 1919, meanwhile, imply that all of their employees had worked through the occupation and then continued working for the Directory. The Directory's commissar in Volyn declared in his newly retaken province that all Bolsheviks previously employed by the UNR who were competent and loyal could continue working.[29] In Bratslav a list of the fourteen members of the board of the local Professional Clerks Union shows that nine were communists, of whom seven fled with the Bolsheviks. Besides the two communists among the five who remained were two Russian SRs and one Ukrainian SR.[30] Most personnel in Kyiv and Zhytomir also appear to have remained at their desks when the Directory arrived – and when it departed.[31] In the Podillia provincial governor's office in March 1919 the staff had dropped from its total of forty-three under the Hetman to twenty-eight, and of those, twenty-five had worked for the Hetman. In the Vinnytsia district council as of February 1919 twenty-four of the 113 staff members had been at their jobs since before 1914.[32]

Random lists of bureaucrats in Podillia province compiled in July 1919 indicate that of ninety-three, fifty-one (79%) had been clerks on or before 1917. Ivan Romanivsky, an assistant secretary in a commissar's office in a district in Kyiv province, provides an example of continuity. Beginning work in his district Tax Office in 1908 Romanivsky was drafted in 1912 and served as a regimental clerk. In December 1917 he returned home and, aged twenty-seven, was still at his desk in April 1919 earning 275 karbovantsi a month.[33] Oleksandra Vinober joined the Podillia provincial zemstvo as a clerk in 1913, applied to work in the Hetman's Ministry of Internal Affairs in July 1918, and was still working when the Ukrainian State collapsed that December. Fired because she had worked for the Hetman, she wrote a letter on 20 January 1919 requesting that she be rehired, with an attached reference noting she had been active in Ukrainian civic organizations. Serhii Vyshnivsky was now working for the Directory in Dubno, while Makar Mokrytsky appears in government records again in February 1919 as the head of his department – with permission to carry a revolver. Not everyone could cope with the difficult conditions of the time. In early December 1919 Mykola Havryliv, the permanent secretary of the Food Supply Ministry, submittted his resignation. Working since 1914 he had lived through thirteen ministries and complained that his health and nerves were ruined; however, if asked he was prepared to work part-time without pay.[34] Apollin Marshynsky remained head of the Tax Department. Kyryl Kuzmenko shifted from town to town in 1919 following the Directory's retreat, and in Proskuriv that spring remarked that there were so many clerks in the Post and Telegraph Office that they had nothing to do. Roman Trofymenko appears in documents for the last time in January 1919; just hired, he was appointed the Directory's head of food supply in the ZUNR with a monthly wage of

1,500 karbovantsi. Vasyl Korenchuk supported the Directory insofar as it overthrew the Hetman. With the evacuation from Kyiv that January he was put in charge of the government's telegraph machines, and for the next nine months he travelled with the Directory taking care of them. As he explained to the Bolshevik secret police (Cheka) in a later interrogation, although he was apolitical and uninvolved, he was interested in events and followed them closely. Korenchuk explained that he decided to travel for the Directory to see the country and to learn and understand what was happening. During the conflict between Petliura and his left-wing rivals that autumn, Korenchuk sympathized with the latter. He used his access to official communications to supply them with information and finally fled to Bolshevik-controlled territory and returned home.

In some counties and villages in Podillia province, curiously, there seem to have been no holdovers. A comparison of two lists of village heads and assistants and/or secretaries in Kalynivka district from June 1918 and September 1919 reveals only two names on both lists. During that time the two clerks in the Kalynivka county office had become assistant heads, while three new people had taken up the duties of secretary.[35]

Letters of application letters for Directory administrative positions began arriving shortly after it took power and continued to arrive until it fell. They were written in Ukrainian and tended to be matter of fact, focusing on qualifications and career history.[36] Some do mention material hardship and/or patriotism as reasons for reapplication. Nineteen-year-old Francine Karvovska in Mohyliv-Podilskyi, hired in August 1919, emphasized in her letter that she was 'a real Ukrainian not mixed up in any politics.' Her co-worker Afanasia Kadai-Atamasov, who had worked in the local government office since 1904, noted in her letter of application that besides Russian and Ukrainian she knew eight other languages.[37] A complaint about opportunists quotes the following sentence, which the author claimed could be heard often in different variants in many offices: 'Dear sir, Could you not tell me who to see [about a job]. I worked for the Rada, and for the Hetman my work was also for the good of Ukraine.'[38] The impact of the presence of hundreds of fugitive western Ukrainian bureaucrats after July 1919 has yet to be studied. On the one hand, anonymous letters asked why they were not being hired. On the other, later, in emigration, one such official claimed that they had been sent to rural regions because the hundreds of eastern Ukrainians who populated city offices had refused to go.[39] With the assistance of western Ukrainians the Directory opened a school for bureaucrats in August 1919 that is on record as graduating forty students.[40]

Reasons for dismissal appear infrequently in the examined documents. Politics or nationality are rarely given as the cause for being let go. In her application letter Ielysaveta Nesterenko, a Kyiv University student, wrote that she had worked the two previous years in Kyiv as a copyist/typist. Yet, she was fired after a three-day period of probation because her typing was said to be unsatisfactory. Vira Melnyk, hired on 29 September1919, reported sick the following week; after a co-worker sent to confirm her illness reported that she was not at home, she was fired on 16 October.[41] In response to complaints about them in Podillia province the government replaced former Hetman bureaucrats that it had earlier retained and reappointed.[42] Denis Kirichok, who had been away on leave during the autumn of 1918 returned to Kyiv in December; he appears on Directory lists as the head of the general section of the Political Administrative Department of the Ministry of Internal Affairs. On 26 January 1919 he seems to have decided that the Directory's days were numbered and confided to the department's assistant head that he should 'not be naive' and use his authority to channel government money into both their pockets. It was Kirichok's misfortune that his superior complained to the minister the next day, and he was fired on 5 February.[43]

Since allegations of sabotage are difficult to trace historians will probably never know the degree to which hostile intent, general collapse, mundane bureaucratic inefficiency, or even people using regime change to settle personal scores best explain administrative breakdown and staffing. The evidence that does exist about disloyal non-Ukrainian employees does not permit generalizations about their impact. Rare proof of planned bureaucratic disruption is provided by Colonel Makogon, who sat on the Directory's general staff for most of 1919. In a report written shortly after he had fled Ukraine for Warsaw, he related that his organization had effectively prevented tens of thousands of recruits from reaching the army and ensured that the army received no supplies, that its innocent quartermaster general was tried and dismissed, and that few supplies had reached the cities – thus provoking anti-Ukrainian attitudes among the populace.[44] In another instance of sabotage the local populace complained about one Karbovsky, head of the Investigative Committee of the Ministry of Internal Affairs in Vinnytsia in 1919. The Jewish Socialists he hounded claimed that he was a vicious anti-Semite who had been active in the prosecution of the notorious Beilis case.[45] Similar accounts about suspicious holdovers appeared in press articles at the time, together with complaints about ignored dismissal decrees and 'opportunists' who made false overtures of loyalty and then hired Ukrainophobes. District commissars who complained about, or arrested, hostile Hetman officials, claimed that they were either left in place or released by higher-ups – in one case by the provincial commissar and the minister of justice.[46]

In western regions near the newly formed Polish state, local Polish employees of the Directory actively sabotaged its policies. One Polish report dwells on the mutual butchery that broke out in late 1918 during which Ukrainian peasants targeted Polish bureaucrats.[47] Ministers, meanwhile, clashed over whether to fire all Poles or only those actually caught in wrongdoing – which implies that some were loyal.[48] That August the Directory's provincial commissar reported dismissing four pro-Russian officials. One, the head of the Customs Office, preferred teaching to administering and in his absence 'the huge staff' did nothing; a Kadet, he was not openly anti-Ukrainian but appointed such people to other positions.[49] In Mohyliv, by contrast, an anonymous letter protested that although thousands of officials hired by the Rada in March 1918 had all described themselves as 'Ukrainian' in their files, two years later, despite having promised to learn Ukrainian they had not done so.[50] When the Bolsheviks left Boryspil, near Kyiv, in August 1919 to the Whites, all their soviet executive committee personnel remained and renamed themselves the Committee for Social Safety.[51] The Directory replaced Russians with Poles and Ukrainians who had previously staffed Bolshevik executive committees, yet a Bolshevik agent reported that 'Black Hundredists and Denikinites control all the apparatus.' An undated inspector's report from Podillia province identified the elected officials, but not their full-time staffs, as loyal.[52]

Distinctions between extremist Russian political activists and apolitical Russian-speakers existed and were important but not easy to make and not everyone tried to make such distinctions. The official newspaper *Trybuna,* on 4 January 1919, for example, reprinted some discovered protocols of Russian party meetings. Although the document stipulated that all political parties 'except' the extreme right had attended, the accompanying editorial, in its attempt to cast aspersions on the loyalty of all Russians, claimed that the meeting 'included' the extreme right. Some used political rationales to settle personal scores. In Podillia province local activists had a police chief removed on the grounds that he had abused his authority under the Hetman. The man in question, in response to his accusers, informed the public that he had launched a libel suit against them. He claimed that he was a patriot originally appointed under the Rada by respected local national activists, had remained in office under the Hetman because he had chosen to do so, and had done nothing during those months to be ashamed of.[53] Georgii Korchagin, born in Poltava province, was an officer cadet in Petrograd when the Bolsheviks took power. He applied, in Russian, for a position noting clerical experience with the Orel province zemstvo; in March 1919 in a letter to his superior written in Ukrainian, Korchagin also used the Ukrainian form of his first name – Iurko.[54]

In Iampil district near the town of Mohyliv-Podilskyi one report explains that the commissar, a declared Ukrainian, was an incompetent and arrogant bureaucrat who used the considerable funds he obtained from unknown sources to buy expensive clothes and parade around town with an entourage of horses and escorts. Local elected officials, and three-quarters of the administrators, were pre-1917 personnel sympathetic to the Whites or Bolsheviks, who all functioned in Russian, while the Polish mayor was politically pro-Polish. Local bureaucrats destroyed or hid instructions arriving from the Directory and decided everything among themselves informally, over vodka. They told the populace that conscripts would not be punished if they did not arrive when called and that they did not have to pay taxes or deliver or sell their obligatory quotas to the state. There were too few local personnel and police loyal to the Directory to do anything to change the situation. In January 1919 the Katerynoslav state zemstvo bank had over 300 employees, most of whom had arrived from Russia under the Hetman, who were getting paid but did nothing. One Orkhovsky, a district police chief in Kamianets-Podilskyi from the summer of 1919, according to the complaints from his subordinates, was a Bolshevik military officer who sold jobs in the police, extorted money and food from his staff, and rehired Bolsheviks dismissed by the Directory when it retook the city in June. Also missing from his precinct were millions of karbovantsi worth of civilian and military supplies. The files from the case have been lost, but it appears that despite the complaints and an investigation begun that autumn, Orkhovsky was still on the job in March 1920 – having been appointed temporary provincial police inspector by the governor.[55]

Despite such incidents, in an exchange between the ministers of labour (Bezpalko) and land (Kovalevsky) in June 1919, the former informed the latter that officials were not be dismissed solely on the basis of hearsay but had to be accused of specific crimes and tried. Kovalevsky replied that he could not keep people who were sabotaging land reform, and he issued a secret circular to dismiss all Poles and Bolsheviks. He claimed that he knew what had to be done 'in the social interests of the state' and would not be instructed by another minister to whom he was not subject.

In reply Bezpalko wrote that he had to defend the rights of all officials and that he would submit the issue for resolution to a cabinet meeting.[56] That September Bezpalko referred another case to Kovalevsky, asking what to do about a complaint to him from the Bratslav employees' union about an illegal dismissal that was accompanied by a request from the local criminal investigator for files on all of the union committee members. Although the minister himself thought the official was unjustly dismissed, the local district commissar who fired him, he continued, considered all non-Ukrainians to be traitors and acted accordingly.[57]

Generalizations about identity and loyalty must consider the reality of shifting political alignments among bureaucrats. In Zhytomir non-Ukrainian 'revolutionary democrats' apparently supported the Directory.[58] P. Vyrzhykovsky in Kamianets-Podilskyi explained that the loyalties of his Russian newspaper should not be judged by its language. He had no subsidies, no one on the staff who knew Ukrainian, and he did not represent any political party. His paper was for 'pragmatic democrats.'[59] In Kyiv itself in December, after the Directory issued its decree regarding the language on signs, the Russian-language daily *Posledniia novosti* published Russian-Ukrainian word lists for its readers. Moderate Russians that spring, in the wake of an informal agreement with the Socialist Federalists, published a series of articles that urged the Directory not to discriminate on the basis of nationality or religion. This, claimed the moderate Russians, would allow all residents of Ukraine to work for the good of their country. Developing their earlier idea about the national states that emerged from the tsarist empire as transitional entities in a political process that would see the formation of a confederation, they now rejected 'Bolshevik imperialism' and 'Denikin's Little-Russianism' and urged all Russian democrats 'to help build democratic statehood in Ukraine.' Ukrainian democrats, for their part, had to understand that for the moment they simply did not have enough competent people 'to create new forms of statehood,' wrote journalists. This meant that hiring only nationals would be folly. Ukraine, as all governments, should hire those of its loyal minorities who recognized its independence.[60] Rather belatedly, in September 1920, the Russian Socialist Revolutionaries recognized Ukrainian independence.[61]

Two valuable comments by outsiders provide a glimpse into the attitudes of educated Ukrainians who worked for the Directory in 1919. One, by I. Popov from Moscow, who travelled in Directory-controlled Ukraine that autumn and spoke with Ukrainian SRs, related that after the Whites took Kyiv from the Bolsheviks that September many Ukrainian bureaucrats had fled with Directory troops. Most had worked in Soviet offices and then taken jobs with the Directory. But 'suffocating from its deathly atmosphere (*zadykhaiutsia v tsariashchii tam mertvenyne*)' they had begun to wonder whether it made more sense to work for the Soviets: 'We can confidently assert that in connection with recent events, we can see an important shift in the mentality of educated Ukrainians in favour of Soviet power,' Popov concluded. A second observation, made by a Jewish teacher in an affidavit about a pogrom in his native town of Slovechna in Volyn province – untouched by violence until July 1919 – described the local educated Ukrainians as pro-Petliura and accustomed to work on their own without direction from above. Only when under the Bolsheviks they began getting orders that they did not like, and from officials who were Jews to boot, did they became hostile towards Jews.[62]

Besides new applicants and experienced clerks, another important source of bureaucrats were co-operatives and civic organizations. Thus, the interior minister turned to the main Ukrainian co-op organization in Kyiv shortly after coming to power on 11 January 1919 with a request for instructors/agitators. Its committee replied that a considerable number of it members had already taken jobs in government and other civic organizations: 'If more people leave the committee the existence of the centre of the Ukrainian co-op movement, upon which the government has placed many obligations, will be threatened.' There is no record of a reply from the Ukrainian organization *Pratsia*, which the minister hoped would serve as a source of qualified staff for all levels of government.[63]

Educated young Jews, who desperately needed employment to survive, were another potential source of candidates for government office jobs, and here, again, it is difficult to generalize in light of limited evidence. Some, like Russians and Poles, worked for the Directory after March 1919 in Podillia province in central and local offices. Alongside Solomon Zalkind, who was still in the Ministry of Food Supply, and Haia Freilikh, who that year was in the Ministry of Labour and was to continue working until July 1920, was Eva Abramovna Kogan-Marianovska. Finishing secondary school in her home town of Vinnytsia, she went on to Odesa University and from 1917 to 1919, when she also got a position in the Directory's Ministry of Labour, she worked in Vinnytsia province's Food Supply Office. Khaim-Hersh Shvarts was hired as an assistant to the Berdychiv town commissar – and had no less than seven local dignitaries witness that he had neither belonged to the Bolshevik party nor worked for its government.[64] Understandably, little Jewish sympathy towards the Directory survived as news spread of the unprecedented pogroms that occurred in its territories. So many Jews subsequently flocked into Soviet offices in the spring of 1919 that Bolsheviks feared that they would compromise the 'proletarian' nature of their regime. In territories that they recaptured the following spring arriving Ukrainian officials, for their part, fired and/or tried Jews who had worked for the Bolsheviks. However, in the wake of Ukrainian efforts to compensate victims of pogroms and prevent new outbreaks of them, which began in June 1919, pro-Directory Jewish political parties, the leftist Zionists and rightist Bundists, backed the Directory's July calls for Jews to enter government service.[65] After the May 1920 Polish-Ukrainian offensive drove the Bolsheviks out of Kyiv, however, the city's Jews refused to work for the Directory. Soviet employees who had not fled boycotted the Directory, while Ukrainian-speaking Ukrainians in the capital formed a citizens' committee to administer Kyiv – rather than doing it through city hall. When the Bolsheviks returned, many Ukrainians decided to flee. Many of those who did not flee were later shot.[66]

Functioning and Competence

What could the Directory do in the core territory that it controlled between December 1918 and November 1919? Accounts vary. The Hetman claimed that during the three weeks that the Directory held Kiev, in early 1919, 'all semblance of Ukrainian statehood disappeared.'[67] Similarly, eyewitnesses a year later said that everything in the capital had broken down during those weeks. Bolshevik reports noted that ten days after their arrival services were still not functioning. Directory inspectors' reports from October 1919 indicate that two months after the Bolsheviks had been pushed back to the Dnipro, officials had not re-established its authority in its reclaimed easternmost territories. A trade union official claimed that in August 1919, when its army was approaching Kyiv, the Directory could control only a 15-kilometre radius of territory around its capital, Kamianets-Podilskyi. In Podillia province towns were filled with young draft dodgers, few educated declared Ukrainians were willing to work for the government, and since professionals did not get paid, they preferred to do manual work for peasants who at least fed them. In some provinces peasants would wander from district to district desperately looking for a civilian official. Complaining to inspectors, they explained that whereas district heads under the Hetman and Bolsheviks would inevitably appear within days of taking the local towns, they only heard about the existence of Directory commissars – but never saw them. In his defence the Kamianets district commissar in the summer of 1919 said that he had no car or horse and that his annual travel allowance was enough for one-way trips only.[68]

Fugitive government commissars in the spring of 1919 reported that the Directory had been unable to control what, by then, were the territories lost that January and February. Former Hetman ministerial bureaucrats still in office ignored Directory commissars, who argued that all government offices had to be summarily purged of all former tsarist officials – which suggests that the measures decreed four months earlier had not been very successful.[69] Audits repeatedly mention low pay as a reason that local educated Ukrainians preferred work as hired farm hands to taking government jobs. By 1919, in addition, many of the literate and educated people in small towns and villages had either fled or been shot. A military commander reported than in territories that he had recently freed from the Bolsheviks, educated Ukrainians were in a 'state of shock (*ne zdibni zrazu opamiatatys*).'[70] Audits identified absenteeism, idleness, complete disorder, bad organization, massive overstaffing, colleagues smoking and chatting in offices, and forms filled out incorrectly and ungrammatically. Dismissed officials, apparently, kept their identity papers in order to hold on to their quarters, because personnel lists were not regularly updated or checked.[71] In some offices, nonetheless, the total number of employees seems to have risen. Thus, in the Letychiv district office the total number of staff increased from three to eleven between February 1918 and the beginning of 1919.[72] In villages isolated from local capitals in July 1919, weeks after the front had moved east, Bolshevik commissars and Committees of Poor Peasants still existed, and the local heads and secretaries made no effort at all to either mobilize recruits or catch deserters.[73]

Where commissars with funds did arrive in the wake of the army, they were inevitably short and had to request credits. Told to follow due procedure in making such requests, some did little, and in the meanwhile, poverty-stricken staff left their jobs. Commissars who requested permission to use force against civilians were refused and told instead to hold meetings and convince locals to pay their taxes in order to pay wages, or to surrender deserters – despite the martial law declaration. When in August 1919 the Podillia provincial council informed the government that they needed troops to collect taxes, the minister of finance instructed them the next month that they could use the police if problems arose, but only as persons 'who represent the local authority.' They were not to be used 'as an armed force.' Yet, ironically, local officials informed their superiors that when they did use force to round up draft dodgers or deserters, people responded favourably because this demonstrated to them that laws were being enforced: '[This] influences the peasants much and leads them to reflect upon the fact that there is an authority able to punish to the full extent of the law.'[74] County heads from the Kamianets-Podilskyi district in June 1919 voiced similar opinions. The peasants, they reported, were tired of war and politics and only wanted order so that they could harvest their crops. They wanted a firm and just, but not harsh government 'that would use force when necessary and not appeal to human conscience as the Ukrainian authorities have been doing up to now.'[75]

In Mohyliv-Podilskyi district in July 1919, just after the Bolshevik occupation, five counties mentioned the condition of their administrations in reports, and of these, four had only one or two staff members, if any, and no office supplies.[76] In the summer of 1919, after the Bolsheviks had left them, the districts of Kamianets, Letychiv, and Nova Ushytsia were apparently ungovernable. Not the least of the latter's problems was that Ukrainian troops had evicted the region's civilian bureaucrats from their offices. Reports on these areas refer to few, badly paid and badly armed police, and the indifference of pro-Bolshevik officials still on local boards as reasons for disorder. A perceptive analysis of Kamianets district, made by its commissar after one month of Directory rule, cited as the main causes of disorder the refusal of local military officers (who literally robbed the population and treated the region like an occupied territory) to recognize civilian officials and a totally ineffective police force that showed people that laws could not be enforced. A government that appealed to hearts with slogans, instead of issuing concrete rules and commands, and in which ministers decided whether or not to send a cavalry unit to enforce mobilization in some isolated village, only undermined its authority and hardly helped the situation, added the commissar. Bureaucrats worked unsatisfactorily, he continued, not because they were incompetent, but because they were not paid, and they were not paid because no taxes were being collected.[77] In Proskuriv county councils began being formed in early January 1919 and were in place by mid-March, but whether and when they were able to function depended on when they got cash from the central government. In Bratslav district only one month after evicting the Bolsheviks the county but not the district council had been re-established – presumably because the town of Bratslav itself by September 1919, after four destructive occupations, 'resembled a graveyard,' in which all the educated were pro-White.[78]

Centrally appointed commissars and/or governors with local bureaucrats but no military detachments had to deal with towns or villages that had their own militia. They faced people like Foma Mykoliuk, Vasyl Chumak, and Makar Monastyrsky. When ordered by their village head in February 1919 to deliver wagons and wood to a nearby hospital, they simply refused. As noted in the head's report to the county commissar, they told him: 'I did not make you head and [therefore] I am not subject to you.'[79] In villages 16 kilograms of grain could be sold to the government as grain for 40 or 50 karbovantsi; but since the same amount sold as liquor could fetch 200 karbovantsi peasants avoided meeting government delivery quotas.[80] To make farmers deliver quotas or sell their surplus at the fixed government price, or to arrest them and confiscate the surplus if they did not, the official had to rely on persuasion and patriotism. Although local officials were prepared to use force and even the threat of execution to collect recruits and deserters, Directory ministers explicitly instructed them not to use force to collect taxes except as a last resort – even in October 1919 when the Directory was on the verge of collapse. Provincial commissars were not to overstep their authority unless it was absolutely necessary to do so, while all lower-level commissars were told not to overstep their authority under any conditions whatsoever. Despite having decreed martial law seven months earlier, Petliura on 31 August 1919 ordered officers not to interfere in civilian administration without cause.[81] One key reason why the army lacked food was that the government simply could not pay workers to produce it. In Proskuriv district during the autumn of 1919, for instance, grain collected for the government from forty of the area's 165 estates could not be ground because the local officials were bankrupt.[82]

In September 1919 reports from Tymanivka county attribute bureaucratic chaos to the refusal of both elected and appointed officials to carry out instructions. After seeing governments shift so often, they simply refused to do anything and waited. Another problem was the rivalry between local officials which reinforced among the populace the idea that the strong authority that they wanted was lacking. District commissars, as one peasant wrote in a letter to a newspaper, would issue an order. Rather than comply with it, some people would complain to the local military commander, who then would countermand the original order and issue another one. Analogously, village and county commissars would issue contradictory commands. Such behaviour undermined authority in general, the peasant continued, because instead of obeying whom they were supposed to by law, it led people to debate who was stronger and then to obey them.[83] From the other perspective, clerks were too few, overworked, and underpaid. In November 1919 in Kamianets-Podilskyi itself the staff of the Press and Information Ministry's Accounts Office worked in a building with no heat and no electricity; they spent most of their time compiling pay lists, because they daily had to add or remove the dozen or so names they received of people hired or fired. With half his staff absent, the man in charge, Vasyl Lytvyn, complained that he ended up working seven days a week from 9 to 9, and he told the minister not to be surprised if pay was not forthcoming even if the payroll did arrive from the bank – which sometimes it did not.[84] Nonetheless, job application letters continued to arrive, and ministers were still hiring new people and ordering documents printed even while Bolshevik troops were gathering on the outskirts of their capital.[85]

The Directory provided paper and millions in funding for publications, and 2,000 people staffed its Information Bureau. Sometimes the central office worked 24 hours a day. But apparently few of the hundreds of thousands of copies of its publications got to readers. This was because local pro-Russian bureaucrats still at their jobs sabotaged local agents, calling them 'Bolsheviks' because they exposed their pasts; the post office and railway worked only sometimes and could not always transport literature; or train commandants would often refuse to carry what they thought was the literature of political parties other than theirs. Not the least of the Information Bureau's problems was that, except for Vynnychenko, no other Ukrainian minister saw any need to give interviews, and thus, its agents had to get what information they could about what was happening second-hand and late. That meant that often they had no answers to people's questions on the spot.[86] Kamianets-Podilskyi, the temporary capital, where eighty to a hundred barrels of waste had to be removed daily, only had enough wagons and horses to remove no more than eight to ten barrels – with the results clearly visible on the streets.[87] To clean the railway station, the police mustered a hundred people each morning with the threat of three months' arrest if they refused.[88]

The national government bureaucracy shared with its Bolshevik rival, as will be shown, rife corruption, graft, nepotism, sloth, incompetence, and overstaffing. Newspapers pointed to city streets filled with beggars and orphans, stores filled with expensive delicacies, and asked why this was so and what had happened to six million kilograms of recently arrived foodstuffs from western Ukraine? In Germany during the First World War reporters had noted that the ration system provided rich and poor alike with the same amount of black bread.[89] An anonymous whistleblower, who called himself Okhrym Perchytsia, provided insight into bureaucratic realities under the Directory in a letter published by a newspaper. This 'average man' of socialist-republican convictions working in an 'average office' described how his bosses hired dozens of totally unnecessary friends and 'nice ladies' who showed up only on payday to collect 600 karbovantsi. When told after complaining to mind his own business, because it was not his money, he responded to his superiors that because wages were paid from the 237 karbovantsi that he paid in taxes last year it was his business. He added that while his superiors made three times what he did, they neither paid taxes nor filled out declarations. His boss finally called him in one day and said that if he did not stop complaining he would label him a Bolshevik and have a friend who was an otaman shoot him. 'Now I shut-up,' Perchytsia wrote, 'I see nothing and hear nothing.'[90] Under the Directory money for military supplies was not given to the army, but to the co-operatives. An inspector reported that Kamianets district officials, at the Directory's end, sat in cold dilapidated offices without ink, pens, or glue, and explained that they did nothing because they had not been paid for a year. Some investigation on his part, however, revealed that the heads and secretaries in question had fiddled the books and pocketed the funds that had arrived.[91] In August 1919 a long-serving legal investigator Dmytro Vodopianov applied for a passport in order to go to Western Europe for a year. He explained that he wanted to study governments there with the purpose of using the knowledge thus obtained to improve the Directory's state-building efforts; unfortunately, there is no further reference to this pioneer in the archives.[92]

Offices were filled with educated men avoiding military service. During the Directory's last days in Kamianets-Podilskyi, in the last three districts of Podillia province still under its control, critics said it had enough bureaucrats for all Ukraine – the landlocked regime even had a fully staffed Naval Department. The Ministry of Internal Affairs allegedly had 950 employees. Throngs of inactive incompetent paid 'officials' in 1920 were ready to take ministerial positions, but not local appointments, and they did little except shuffle papers and plot and arrest each other in their overcrowded offices. This is corroborated by a plea from the Kamianets district Land Committee in August 1919 begging for more office space, because in order to deal with the harvest, it had to double its staff to sixty and that as a result they were sitting three to a desk. That spring saw a huge influx of men seeking office jobs to avoid military service.[93] But not all ministries were necessarily busy. The Ministry of Labour averaged four to five incoming and two to three outgoing items of correspondence daily through 1919.[94] While the Directory's 40,000-strong army's Quartermaster Corps had 1,800 officers, the 85,000-strong Ukrainian Galician Army managed with only forty-five. Why, critics asked, could Denikin form a fighting unit out of 11,000 officers, but not the Directory, which had the same number walking around Kamianets or Vinnytsia, getting paid and doing nothing while the front was collapsing? What effect a quartermaster-general's office circular had that warned any of its personnel caught wandering around city streets during working hours would be transferred to a front-line detachment is unknown.[95] In Kyiv in January 1918, while the Bolshevik army was approaching and its agitators in the city were at work demoralizing troops and workers, Ukrainian party activists were enjoying themselves in the bars and restaurants. Similarly in the spring of 1919 Petliura's head of counter-intelligence observed that while Bolshevik armies were beating the hard-pressed army and closing on Vinnytsia and Kamianets, those towns' streets, bars, and restaurants were overflowing with soldiers.[96]

Although the government had difficulty in organizing supplies for the army and resorted to calling for voluntary donations, sober critics realized that wartime conditions only partly explained the condition of the army. The appalling conditions in military hospitals, for instance, can be attributed to functional overlapping that produced bureaucratic infighting. Thus, besides the Ministry of Health, the army and the Ministry of Roads were also responsible for health, hospitals, and sanitation. But all three structures were independent of each other and fought over resources. So intense was their rivalry that between June and August 1919 they were able to bury a government plan to unify them. The situation was made worse by civilian resistance to generals' attempts to militarize the entire health system in order to deal with the disastrous situation in the army. Thanks to this organizationally based rivalry and chaos, medical services were decentralized, underfunded, and uncoordinated, and thousands of troops and civilians died unnecessarily in Directory territory.[97]

While serving the tsar Ukrainian soldiers, for their part, had learned the common Russian practice of selling all their clothes and weapons for ration cards and vodka – a habit they did not lose when they were in the Ukrainian army.[98] As a result, town bazaars were well stocked with arms, ammunition, and uniforms at high prices, while soldiers made do without. In October 1919, when the Ukrainian army had practically collapsed and was in dire need of everything, the General Staff decided to obtain supplies from contractors directly. The government duly sent the army the money, but before the money got to the army, it somehow found its way to the co-ops as payment for a massive order of jams and marmalades.[99]

Western Ukrainians working for the Directory placed its failings at the feet of its leaders, whom they condemned as incompetents:

> What kind of internal politics could the eastern Ukrainian government follow when its ministers of internal affairs did not know the difference between an administrative rule and a law ... How can one speak about consistent internal policy in such conditions? About administration? First one must know what administration is. But neither Petliura, the geology professor Shvets, the rail administrator Makarenko, nor Mazepa, the minister of internal affairs, did, just as Petliura knew nothing about military matters, like the minister of external affairs did not even know one foreign language, let alone anything about foreign affairs, and the minister of labour, Bezpalko, had no idea what a Ministry of Labour should be.[100]

Western Ukrainians also found eastern Ukrainians' attitudes and work habits annoying. In eastern Ukraine during the revolutionary years everyone thought themselves able to occupy any position, often held two or three, took the pay, and did nothing in any of them. Offices were filled with people with lackadaisical work habits and no sense of professional duty. In the midst of war and revolution the work-day of government offices formally ran from 11 a.m. to 3 p.m. and was punctuated with lots of tea drinking – while people outside waited. All offices were closed on Sundays and holidays. Nazaruk was able to get his clerks in when they were supposed to, at 10, only by threatening to shoot latecomers – and this worked only because everyone knew that as a military officer he had the connections to be able do it.[101] 'Ukraine should be ashamed of its government,' observed one critic. Another remarked that the only Directory personnel who worked tirelessly and effectively were the agents of the Supreme Investigative Commission (the secret police).[102]

Against these gloomy accounts there are other reports that tell us that although central ministries might not have worked very well everywhere, they did some things in some places and worked better where they functioned longer. For instance, where Information Bureau agents arrived immediately behind the army with ample amounts of literature and good answers, the local populace normally acquiesced to reasonable government demands for food, taxes, and recruits.[103] I found only one report, from the town of Lypovets, in which the commissar complained that he had to hire semi-literates as administrators because of the absence of educated people. Nonetheless, he continued, he managed to establish the district administration in a week.[104] Like other local city, district, and county bureaucracies, with as many as 1,000 officials in a given province, this commissar evidently managed to get some things done. By the end of its last four-week period of rule in Kyiv, in January 1919, the Directory had managed to organize a police force and begun to restore public services. Since some Bolshevik reports state that services were functional within three days of their arrival, presumably they had already existed and some staff remained after the Directory left.[105] A Bolshevik military inspector's description of some of the departments of the Directory's War Ministry in Kyiv in February 1919, written just after taking the city, suggests that its officials were organized and able. Approximately 1,000 administrative staff had either failed to leave or had been ordered to remain, and the inspector described their abilities as ranging from competent to very well qualified. Their various departments were well organized and implementing detailed plans when they had to retreat. Only time had prevented the fleeing Directory to take more of the Hetman's carefully collected supplies than it did.[106]

On 23 December 1918 the army's quartermaster-general complained to the Ministry of Food Supply that his horses had no fodder. On 11 January he wrote they were dying because of corruption and treason. He called the held-over staff 'thieves and loafers' and arrested those in Bila Tserksva, where he happened to be, for 'shady dealings,' claiming that they were selling state property to local landowners. He also claimed that the Food Supply Ministry was riddled with 'people hostile towards the UNR.' Two days later he wrote that his stores were empty because he got nothing from the ministry. These accusations would suggest the ministry was not doing its job. However, the Food Supply Ministry records for December and January have survived. They indicate that it is possible to give the benefit of the doubt to the ministry and that it was more circumstances than sabotage or inefficiency that underlay the shortages. On 16 January the food supply minister replied, asking for names, and he requested the general not to arrest civilians outside his jurisdiction. The next day, in a detailed letter to the war minister, he explained that 329 wagonloads of foodstuffs had been delivered to army stores in nine provinces that month and that his people had received no requests for fodder until 13 January – when they promptly began meeting them. He added that fodder had been sent to the army the preceding month and that shortages were the result of circumstances. Under the Hetman, that autumn, responsibility for the provision of fodder had been given to the army, and fodder had been sent to ports for shipment by boat. But because the army had failed to arrange shipping, the fodder was left standing in storage some distance from railway stations. Related correspondence, beginning 2 January, shows that central officials were sending commands to local officials to ensure the collection and distribution of foodstuffs. Among these were instructions to find and arrange river transportation, giving priority to shipments to Kyiv, and sending plenipotentiaries.[107] This correspondence suggests that bureaucrats were collecting, tracing, identifying, storing, shipping, and receiving foodstuffs and that problems were technical. A note from Chernihiv stated that grain could not be shipped because there was not enough rolling stock. Not only were officers requisitioning stores on their own for their men, but troops were seizing trains and then selling their cargoes. In Kyiv so many trains had arrived that they could not be unloaded, and not the least of the problems was that the loading vehicles had no gasoline because the army had requisitioned it. The Ministry of Food Supply itself had moved from its old premises and had no telephone. It had to send a request to the Post and Telegraph Ministry not only to move the apparatus but to find the necessary cables and wiring. By 16 January the food supply minister called the situation in the Kyiv yards 'catastrophic.' He realized that the army needed the gas and explained that the loaders could run on naphtha – if it was diluted with pure alcohol. However, alcohol could not be obtained without permission from the Ministry of Finance.

Outright theft was also an issue. Besides small-scale theft en route, which meant that railway stations had to order scales to check shipments, which delayed expedition, bands of 300 or 400 men would unload entire trains, and the local police could do nothing. Rivalry between local food supply and road ministerial plenipotentiaries also slowed down collection and transport, as both made requisitions that the other considered to be illegal.[108]

The correspondence registry of the Labour Ministry's General Affairs Department indicates that there were 1,228 items of incoming correspondence and 933 outgoing items for a nine-month period in 1919. This averages 123 incoming and ninety-three outgoing items a month – which was less than the average flows in tsarist offices, but comparable to that in Bolshevik offices. The postal system was slow but it worked until the autumn, when local authorities stopped paying carriers. A letter took five days to travel the short distance between Vinnytsia and Kainivka in December 1918. Mail delivery in 1919 averaged two to five days between

Kamianets and Proskuriv, and three to six days between Kamianets and towns further away such as Berdychiv, Mohyliv, and Vinnytsia.[109] In September 1919 the railway system suffered from staff shortages, no coal, almost no grease, and no big repair workshops. The army de facto controlled traffic and had commandeered 2,032 of the available 4,976 freight wagons for itself. Nonetheless, with 3,176 functional wagons and 536 locomotives, the government was able to run sixty-nine trains daily within its territory.[110]

Official publications were few and arrived irregularly in some places, yet hundreds of titles in thousands of copies did get printed and were delivered to other places thanks to heroic couriers who managed to drag their huge loads on and off overloaded trains.[111] Between January and May 1919 the Ministry of Food Supply could transport goods between the territory it controlled and western Ukraine. This included the transfer of huge stockpiles of sugar used to back the currency and 1,168 wagonloads of grains shipped between January and April. In July the government could provide all its bureaucrats with their flour ration.[112] In Letychiv, where 30 per cent of the criminal cases were solved, an inspector reported that the government should be pleased. A September report made by a Ukrainian left SR agent (*Borotbist*) claimed that recruit turnout had been good, the army was training near Kamianets, had high morale, and was well armed and provisioned thanks to supplies from Romania, Poland, and Germany (by air). He claimed that it was approximately 20,000 to 30,000 strong and would be used once the Bolsheviks, the partisans, and the Whites had worn themselves out fighting each other. He stated that the small territory that the Directory did control was well run because it made good use of the educated and that a successful purging of all potentially disloyal incumbents from offices was going on. Fighting under the slogans of all power to the soviets in an independent Ukraine, the mass of the population in Denikin-controlled territory would support the UNR because they were decidedly anti- Bolshevik – unless Moscow changed its policies regarding Ukraine.[113]

Individual beliefs, personality, and behaviour were often decisive in getting things done. In Podillia and Volyn provinces the Directory governors condemned pogroms. In Proskuriv the subordinate commissioner was able to stop the massacres – started by the local military commander. The Zhytomir district commissar could not stop them. In Khmilnyk, a town of 25,000 Jews living in destitution after Bolshevik pogroms, the Directory commander, a western Ukrainian who had earlier won their gratitude by preventing a pogrom, threatened the local rich Jews with arrest for treason unless they collected one million hryvnia to help their poor co-religionists. They delivered and he duly allocated the funds for services and relief work. In Ovruch the commissioner ignored his superiors and took part in pogroms.[114] Much also depended, as in Uman, on the commitment of the local educated. One inspector observed that while elected representatives did nothing but debate their own pay, their hired bureaucrats did work. He complained, however, that often the latter worked not as agents of the local council but of the central government, inasmuch as the theoretically elected local council head was often, in practice, the government commissar and thus was more concerned with central demands than with local needs. In a letter to his superiors in the Land Ministry in September 1919 a local sub-section head explained that he had had no funding for two years, but that during the previous year he had borrowed from what funds remained in his budget and allotted them to his subordinates so that they could stay on the job and provide their local populations with some semblance of a working administration.[115]

In some places Bolshevik and White agents were eventually discovered without resorting to terror, and rural commissars in Kamianets district apparently could collect money for the army and provide grants and subsidies and pay to local bodies. Some corrupt and/or disloyal officials were fired. Submitted reports were read, considered, and then instructions with suggestions and orders were returned a few weeks later – by courier or telegram. In January 1919 the Haisyn district commissar requested survey lists of estates from all his counties, including details of administrative staff. They duly arrived that March.[116] That same month the Novhorod-Volynskyi county council submitted a 1,152-page budget in its request for funding from Kamianets. One month later the request was approved, but apparently no money was sent, as that October the council sent a renewed request in a short letter that arrived in Kamianets four days later – explaining that since Bolsheviks had just taken the local capital, it could not provide the necessary paperwork.[117] The work of the Vinnytsia district executive council under its energetic head Iosyf Lozynsky shows that some officials took their jobs seriously and thought the government would survive and be able to implement projects. Plans for 1919 included increased support for orphans, a detailed listing of rules and procedures, detailed plans for repairs to the regional roads and communications systems, and provision for a small workshop to produce concrete crankshafts for village wells.[118]

Ivan Kryvorot arrived as district commissar in Letychiv on 7 August 1919, just after the territory had been retaken from the Bolsheviks, and he found one secretary and an assistant ready to re-establish the administration. Unable to ask them to work more than the six hours daily stipulated by law, he found that he could not cope with the workload. When he asked people to work, they asked how much they would be paid, to which he replied that Ukrainians should help their government as much as they could to free the country from Bolshevik terror and rebuild the administration. A week later he still had only two clerks in his office. He then turned to friends in companies and non-government agencies, and by 23 August he had put affairs into order and was able to claim that he had re-established a tolerably functioning administration throughout his district thanks to nine volunteers – despite lack of space, supplies, broken down communications, and no transportation. Like almost all reports at the time Kryvorot's ended with a request for funds. He found his two newly hired lower-level clerks inexperienced, while his experienced senior people were soon requesting permission to resign because of their miserable salaries. Not the least of the government's problems was office supplies. County offices, in the wake of the Bolshevik occupation, unlike under the Hetman, no longer had typewriters, which remained only in some district offices.[119] The Letychiv district commissar, meanwhile, explained to the provincial governor in late September that not only had all his county offices literally run out of paper, but that there was none anywhere to be bought.[120] During the summer of 1919 telegraph lines were overloaded, and the army ordered its units to cut usage and content or face fines, while the Ministry of Economics ordered all government departments to 'reuse and recycle' paper.[121]

In Uman district in July 1919 we find a different history. After evicting the Bolsheviks, local leaders established an executive committee and the Committee to Defend Public Order under the protection of the partisans that had freed the region, and within five days, they had re-established the pre-existing administrative system. This was possible because, during the five months of Bolshevik rule, the incumbent UNR activists and officials had remained at their jobs. They kept services running under, got funding, and then prevented the Bolsheviks from taking public assets with them when they retreated. The peasants, moreover, had apparently continued to pay their taxes – which these bureaucrats hid and then forwarded to the provincial treasury after the arrival of UNR troops.[122]

Commissars' reports from the districts of Letychiv, Lityn, Ushytsia, and Proskuriv reveal administrations organized, at work, and meeting recruiting and requisitioning demands. The district commissar stated on 13 September that in the town of Lypovets, just after it was freed from the Bolsheviks, there were no educated people left; this implies that most of the bureaucrats were only semi-literate, and that although people supported the Directory, they were hostile towards its officials. To add to the confusion there were no instructions about which pre-revolutionary regulations were in force and which were not. Yet, a week later, the same man claimed that the town administration was functioning. January and February 1919 reports from Ushytsia district were positive. Just before the Bolshevik takeover in April they noted breakdown and rising criminality. In July and August, after the Bolsheviks had left, an eyewitness report stated that the area had no authority whatsoever and that the consequences were catastrophic. Yet, a month later, another report claimed that order had been re-established. In September the provincial commissar went there in person, and on 22 October he noted that the Ushytsia district administration was functioning as best as could have been expected. Within weeks of taking back Kalynivka county, just north of Vinnytsia, officials there could respond to orders from the capital about identifying village appointments and duly return lists with names. The same village officials were also able to compile lists of their conscripts, and the Kalynivka county office could produce a handwritten list of the 373 individuals who appeared in town when they were supposed to muster – alongside eighty-four draft dodgers. Oddly, none of these lists were in alphabetical order.[123] Apparently the Directory was able to collect approximately 30 per cent of its planned grain quota, more than twice as much as the Bolsheviks were able to collect that year in the part of Ukraine that they controlled.[124]

People clearly regarded the Directory as their government, sent complaints and requests to it, and their letters duly circulated between offices. There is evidence that workers turned to the Ministry of Health with grievances and that local officials requested and got funds from the centre which they then used to carry out projects.[125] As one inspector observed in the summer of 1919, people preferred the Directory to the Bolsheviks, but feared that it was unstable, and they were reluctant to show more than passive compliance so that if it collapsed the Bolsheviks would not murder them when they arrived.[126] A Ukrainian citizen residing in Tbilisi, Georgia, sent a letter to the Directory with a request to change his surname from Levenshtein to Sulyma-Sulikovsky. In July 1919 Victor Pote, a Frenchman residing in Kamianets-Podilskyi, wrote directly to Petliura asking for 20,000 karbovantsi as compensation for dispossession and robbery by Ukrainian troops. After teaching French for twenty years he had retired and ever since had been living on his monthly pension

— Папаша, вы либералъ или консерваторъ?
— Это что за дичь? Развѣ ты не знаешь, что я дѣй-
стви-тель-ный статскій совѣтникъ.

1 Pre-1917 caricature of bureaucrats' indifference to politics. [Translation:] 'Dad. Are you a liberal or conservative?' 'What nonsense is this? Don't you know I am a state councillor.' *Source: Otechestvennye zapiski*, no. 2 (2004).

2 Ukrainian depiction of national statehood with Russian eagle hovering ominously in the north (1917). [Translation:] 'Our warriors die like dew in the sun. We brothers in our turn will rule.' *Source:* http://www.geocities.com/ua_ukraine/ukrayinarus090.html.

3 Cartoon of Hetman government importing officials from Russia. [Translation:] 'The Mobilized. From Muscovy to Ukraine "for feeding."' *Source: Gedz,* Kyiv, July 1918.

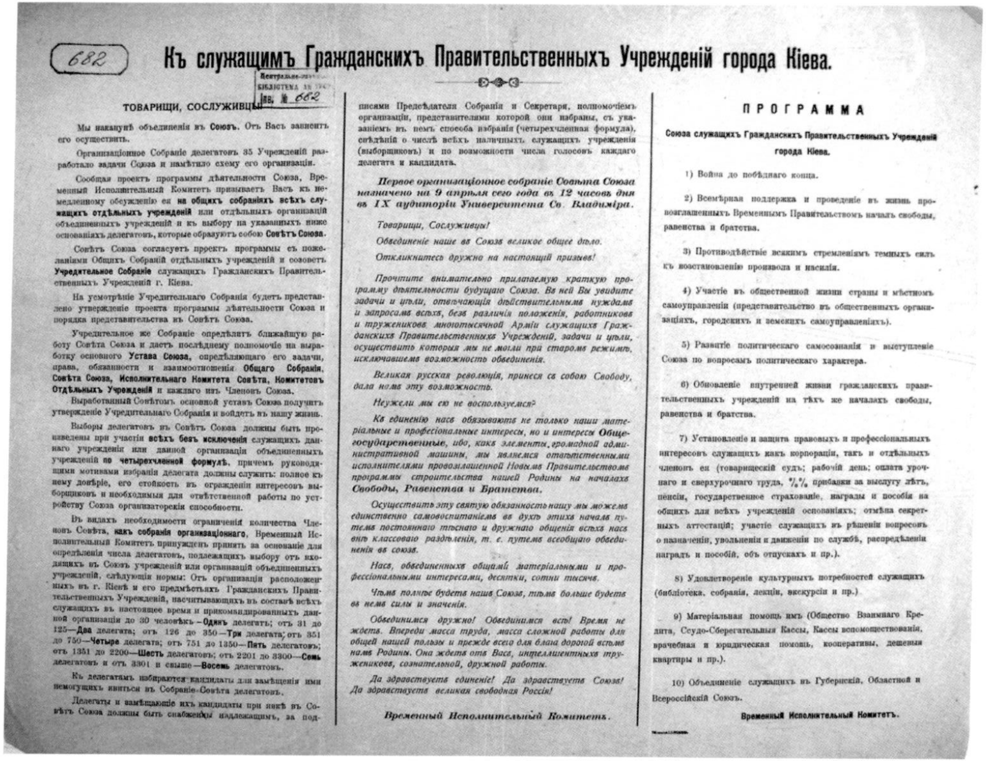

682

Къ служащимъ Гражданскихъ Правительственныхъ Учрежденій города Кіева.

ТОВАРИЩИ, СОСЛУЖИВЦЫ!

Мы наканунѣ объединенія въ **Союзъ**. Отъ Васъ зависитъ его осуществить.

Организаціонное Собраніе делегатовъ 35 Учрежденій разработало задачи Союза и намѣтило схему его организаціи.

Сообщая проектъ программы дѣятельности Союза, Временный Исполнительный Комитетъ призываетъ Васъ къ немедленному обсужденію ея **на общихъ собраніяхъ всѣхъ служащихъ отдѣльныхъ учрежденій** или отдѣльныхъ организацій объединенныхъ учрежденій и къ выбору на указанныхъ ниже основаніяхъ делегатовъ, которые образуютъ собою **Совѣтъ Союза**.

Совѣтъ Союза согласуетъ проектъ программы съ пожеланіями Общихъ Собраній отдѣльныхъ учрежденій и созоветъ **Учредительное Собраніе** служащихъ Гражданскихъ Правительственныхъ Учрежденій г. Кіева.

На усмотрѣніе Учредительнаго Собранія будетъ представлено утвержденіе проекта программы дѣятельности Союза и порядка представительства въ Совѣтъ Союза.

Учредительное же Собраніе опредѣлитъ ближайшую работу Совѣта Союза и дастъ послѣднему полномочіе на выработку основного **Устава Союза**, опредѣляющаго его задачи, права, обязанности и взаимоотношенія **Общаго Собранія, Совѣта Союза, Исполнительнаго Комитета Совѣта, Комитетовъ Отдѣльныхъ Учрежденій** и каждаго изъ Членовъ Союза.

Выработанный Совѣтомъ основной уставъ Союза получитъ утвержденіе Учредительнаго Собранія и войдетъ въ нашу жизнь.

Выборы делегатовъ въ Совѣтъ Союза должны быть произведены при участіи **всѣхъ безъ исключенія** служащихъ даннаго учрежденія или данной организаціи объединенныхъ учрежденій **по четырехчленной формулѣ**, причемъ руководящими мотивами избранія делегата должны служить: полное къ нему довѣріе, его стойкость въ огражденіи интересовъ выборщиковъ и необходимыя для отвѣтственной работы по устройству Союза организаторскія способности.

Въ видахъ необходимости ограниченія количества Членовъ Совѣта, **какъ собранія организаціоннаго**, Временный Исполнительный Комитетъ принужденъ принять за основаніе для опредѣленія числа делегатовъ, подлежащихъ выбору отъ входящихъ въ Союзъ учрежденій или организацій объединенныхъ учрежденій, слѣдующія нормы: Отъ организаціи расположенныхъ въ г. Кіевѣ и его предмѣстьяхъ Гражданскихъ Правительственныхъ Учрежденій, насчитывающихъ въ составѣ всѣхъ служащихъ въ настоящее время и прикомандированныхъ данной организаціи до 30 человѣкъ — **Одинъ** делегатъ; отъ 31 до 125 — **Два** делегата; отъ 126 до 350 — **Три** делегата; отъ 351 до 750 — **Четыре** делегата; отъ 751 до 1350 — **Пять** делегатовъ; отъ 1351 до 2200 — **Шесть** делегатовъ; отъ 2201 до 3300 — **Семь** делегатовъ и отъ 3301 и свыше — **Восемь** делегатовъ.

Къ делегатамъ избираются кандидаты для замѣщенія ими немогущихъ явиться въ Собраніе-Совѣта делегатовъ.

Делегаты и замѣщающіе ихъ кандидаты при явкѣ въ Совѣтъ Союза должны быть снабжены надлежащимъ, за подписями Предсѣдателя Собранія и Секретаря, полномочіемъ организаціи, представителями которой они избраны, съ указаніемъ въ немъ способа избранія (четырехчленная формула), свѣдѣній о числѣ всѣхъ наличныхъ служащихъ учрежденія (выборщиковъ) и по возможности числа голосовъ каждаго делегата и кандидата.

Первое организаціонное собраніе Совѣта Союза назначено на 9 апрѣля сего года въ 12 часовъ дня въ IX аудиторіи Университета Св. Владиміра.

Товарищи, Сослуживцы!

Объединеніе наше въ Союзъ великое общее дѣло.

Откликнитесь дружно на настоящій призывъ!

Прочтите внимательно прилагаемую краткую программу дѣятельности будущаго Союза. Въ ней Вы увидите задачи и цѣли, отвѣчающія дѣйствительнымъ нуждамъ и запросамъ всѣхъ, безъ различія положенія, работниковъ и тружениковъ многотысячной Арміи служащихъ Гражданскихъ Правительственныхъ Учрежденій, задачи и цѣли, осуществить которыя мы не могли при старомъ режимѣ, исключавшемъ возможность объединенія.

Великая русская революція, принеся съ собою Свободу, дала намъ эту возможность.

Неужели мы ею не воспользуемся?

Къ единенію насъ обязываютъ не только наши матеріальные и професіональные интересы, но и интересы ***Общегосударственные****, ибо, какъ элементы громадной административной машины, мы являемся отвѣтственными исполнителями провозглашенной Новымъ Правительствомъ программы строительства нашей Родины на началахъ* ***Свободы, Равенства и Братства.***

Осуществить эту святую обязанность нашу мы можемъ единственно самовоспитаніемъ въ духѣ этихъ началъ путемъ постояннаго тѣснаго и дружнаго общенія всѣхъ насъ внѣ классоваго раздѣленія, т. е. путемъ всеобщаго объединенія въ союзъ.

Насъ, объединенныхъ общими матеріальными и профессіональными интересами, десятки, сотни тысячъ.

Чѣмъ полнѣе будетъ нашъ Союзъ, тѣмъ больше будетъ въ немъ силы и значенія.

Объединимся дружно! Объединимся всѣ! Время не ждетъ. Впереди масса труда, масса сложной работы для общей нашей пользы и прежде всего для блага дорогой всѣмъ намъ Родины. Она ждетъ отъ Васъ, интеллигентныхъ тружениковъ, сознательной, дружной работы.

Да здравствуетъ единеніе! Да здравствуетъ Союзъ! Да здравствуетъ великая свободная Россія!

Временный Исполнительный Комитетъ.

ПРОГРАММА

Союза служащихъ Гражданскихъ Правительственныхъ Учрежденій города Кіева.

1) Война до побѣднаго конца.

2) Всемѣрная поддержка и проведеніе въ жизнь провозглашенныхъ Временнымъ Правительствомъ началъ свободы, равенства и братства.

3) Противодѣйствіе всякимъ стремленіямъ темныхъ силъ къ возстановленію произвола и насилія.

4) Участіе въ общественной жизни страны и мѣстномъ самоуправленіи (представительство въ общественныхъ организаціяхъ, городскихъ и земскихъ самоуправленіяхъ).

5) Развитіе политическаго самосознанія и выступленіе Союза по вопросамъ политическаго характера.

6) Обновленіе внутренней жизни гражданскихъ правительственныхъ учрежденій на тѣхъ же началахъ свободы, равенства и братства.

7) Установленіе и защита правовыхъ и профессіональныхъ интересовъ служащихъ какъ корпораціи, такъ и отдѣльныхъ членовъ ея (товарищескій судъ; рабочій день; оплата урочнаго и сверхурочнаго труда, %% прибавки за выслугу лѣтъ, пенсіи, государственное страхованіе, награды и пособія на общихъ для всѣхъ учрежденій основаніяхъ; отмѣна секретныхъ аттестацій; участіе служащихъ въ рѣшеніи вопросовъ о назначеніи, увольненіи и движеніи по службѣ, распредѣленіи наградъ и пособій, объ отпускахъ и пр.).

8) Удовлетвореніе культурныхъ потребностей служащихъ (библіотека, собранія, лекціи, экскурсіи и пр.)

9) Матеріальная помощь имъ (Общество Взаимнаго Кредита, Ссудо-Сберегательныя Кассы, Кассы вспомоществованія, врачебная и юридическая помощь, кооперативы, дешевыя квартиры и пр.).

10) Объединеніе служащихъ въ Губернскій, Областной и Всероссійскій Союзъ.

Временный Исполнительный Комитетъ.

4 Leaflet (summer 1917) announcing formation of an organizing committee of a Union of Kyiv's government officials and its program. *Source:* Tsentralna Naukova Biblioteka im. Vernadskoho, viddil starodrukiv, no. KL 682.

5 Monarchist caricature of stereotypical Ukrainian teaching officials Ukrainian. [Translation:] 'Studious youth. Ukrainian lessons in the ministries.' *Source: Urod*, Kyiv, 1918.

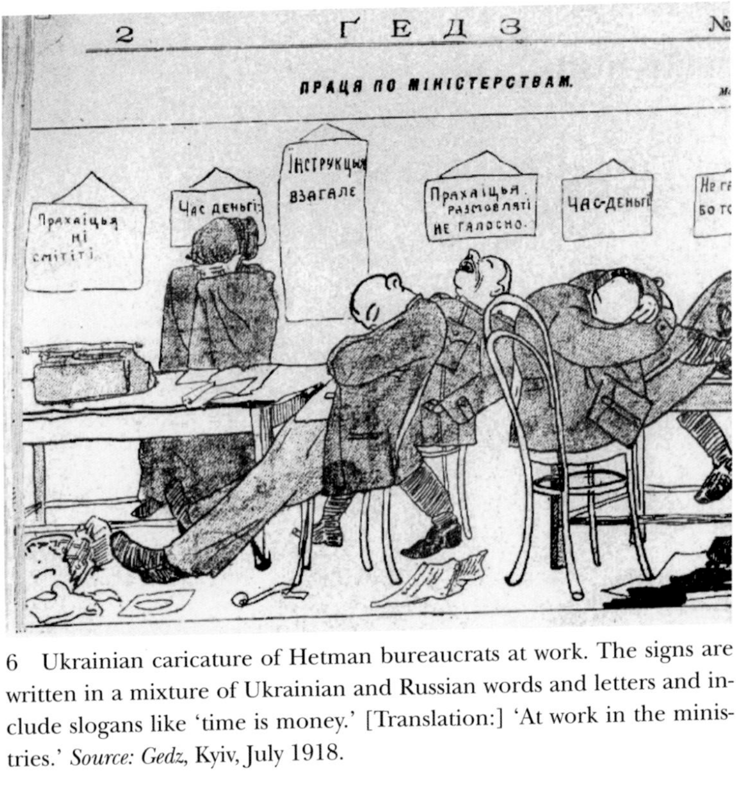

6 Ukrainian caricature of Hetman bureaucrats at work. The signs are written in a mixture of Ukrainian and Russian words and letters and include slogans like 'time is money.' [Translation:] 'At work in the ministries.' *Source: Gedz*, Kyiv, July 1918.

7 Ukrainian depiction of Russian invaders in 1917. *Source: Gedz*, Kyiv, Dec. 1917.

8 Ukrainian Directory depiction of Russian-Ukrainian brotherhood. [Translation:] 'Fraternal relations between Russkies and Ukrainians.' *Source:* Tsentralna Naukova Biblioteka im. Vernadskoho, viddil plakat no. 2755.

9 Bolshevik administrative reform. Inscriptions are in Russian. Reproduced in *Ukrainske mystetstvoznavsto* 1 (1967) 81. [Translation:] 'Cleaning out Soviet offices.' *Source: Bolshevik* [Kyiv], June, 1919.

10 Bolshevik depiction of Soviet statehood (1921). [Translation from Russian:] 'Look. The wealth of the Soviet Republics awaits exploitation. Comrades. Fight the devastation. With a powerful effort we will attain a prosperous and plentiful life.' *Source:* Tsentralna Naukova Biblioteka im. Vernadskoho, viddil plakat.

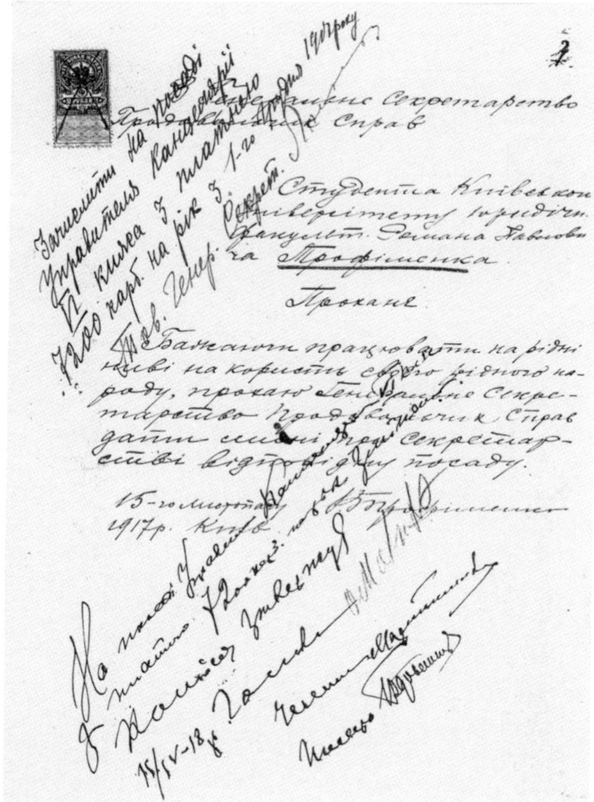

До Генерального Секретарства Продовольчих Справ

Студента Київського Університету Юридичн. Факультет. Романа Павловича Трофименка

Прохання

Бажаючи працювати на рідній ниві на користь свого рідного народу, прохаю Генеральне Секретарство Продовольчих Справ дати мені при Секретарстві відповідну посаду.

15-го лютого 1917р. Київ

Р. Трофименко

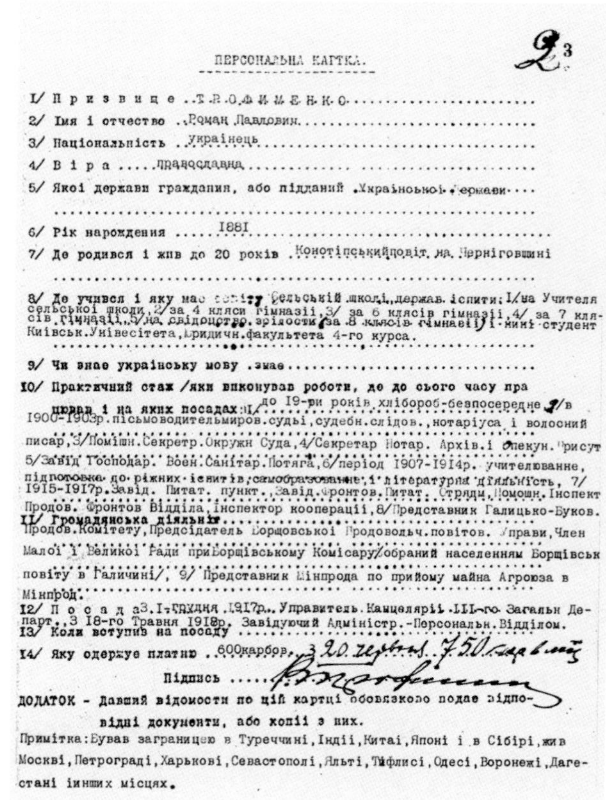

ПЕРСОНАЛЬНА КАРТКА.

1/ П р и з в и щ е . Т Р О Ф И М Е Н К О ....

2/ Імя і отчество . Роман Павлович ....

3/ Національність . Українець ....

4/ В і р а ..... православна ....

5/ Якої держави громадянин, або підданий . Української держави ...

6/ Рік народження ..... 1881 ....

7/ Де родився і жив до 20 років . Конотіпський повіт, на Чернігівщині

8/ Де учився і яку має освіту . Сельській школі, держав. іспити: 1/ на Учителя сельської школи, 2/ за 4 кляси гімназії, 3/ за 6 клясів гімназії, 4/ за 7 клясів гімназії, 5/ на свідоцтво зрілости /за 8 клясів гімназії/ і нині студент Київськ. Унівесітета, Юридичн. факультета 4-го курса.

9/ Чи знає українську мову . знає ....

10/ Практичний стаж /яки виконував роботи, де до сього часу працював і на яких посадах: 1/ до 19-ти років хлібороб-безпосередне 2/ в 1900-1903р. пісьмоводитель миров. судьі, судебн. слідов., нотаріуса і волосний писар, 3/ Помішн. Секретр. Окружн Суда, 4/ Секретар Нотар. Архів. і Опекун. Присут 5/ Завід Господар. Воен. Санітар. Потяга, 6/ період 1907-1914р. учителюванне, підготовка до ріжних іспитів, самобразованне і літературна діяльність, 7/ 1915-1917р. Завід. Питат. пункт., Завід. Фронтов. Питат. Стряды, Помошн. Інспект Продов. Фронтов Відділа, Інспектор кооперації, 8/ Представник Галицько-Буков.

11/ Громадянська діяльність Продов. Комітету, Предсідатель Борщовської Продовольч. повітов. Управи, Член Малої і Великої Ради при Борщівському Комісару/обраний населенням Борщівськ повіту в Галичині/, 9/ Представник Мінпрода по прийому майна Агроюза в Мінпрод.

12/ П о с а д а з 3.1. грудня 1917р. Управитель Канцелярії III-го Загальн Департ., з 18-го Травня 1918р. Завідуючий Адміністр.-Персональн. Відділом.

13/ Коли вступив на посаду ...

14/ Яку одержує платню . 600 карбов. з 20 червня 750 карбов.

Підпись ..... Р. Трофименко

ДОДАТОК - Давшій відомости по цій картці обовязково подає відповідні документи, або копії з них.

Примітка: Бував заграницею в Туреччині, Індії, Китаї, Японі і в Сібірі, жив Москві, Петрограді, Харькові, Севастополі, Яльті, Тифлисі, Одесі, Воронежі, Дагестані і инших місцях.

11 Typical application letter and personnel form of Roman Trofymenko, who worked in the Food Supply Ministry. The first line of the letter reads: [Translation:] 'Wishing to work in my native land for my nation ...' *Source:* TsDAVO, f. 2198 op. 2 sprava 131.

26

КОРОТЕНЬКА ЗАПИСКА
по службовому і громадському стажу
Евгена Івановича С І Р И К О В А.

Родився на Украіні в м. Харьківі. Мае 35 років. Женат.

По скінченні середнего комерціяльного училища поступив в Висщу Школу Мистецтв, але ж вийшов зі 2-го курса по семейним обставинам, після чого занявся службою, що вимогалось в тоі час скрутним матеріяльним становищем.

працював в ріжних відділах на посаді діловода по Мійскому Самоврядуванню біля 4 років.

Потім був запрохан в Губерніяльне Земство, де заняв посаду Керуючого Канцеляріею і бухгальтеріею Агрономічеського відділу, після чого в час війни був переведен на посади помішника завідуючого по заготовкам скоту, свиней, сала и др. в Харьківськоі губ. Потім після виходу в відставку завідуючого заготовками скоту і вибрання його Головою Харьківськоі Губерн. Земськоі Скарбниці дрібного кредиту, був призначен завідуючим відділа по заготовкам скота в Харьківськоі губерн. Після революціі, згідно роспорядження бувшого Міністра Російского Тимчасового Уряду Шангарьова був переведен зі всім відділом в улаштований в тоі час Губерніяльний продовольчий Комітет, де після переформування Комітету,

одержав призначення на посаду керуючого ліквідаційно-ревізійним окремим відділом, котрий і організував при допомоги бувшого въ той час Головного Інспектора В.К. Заіковського. Сей відділ мав компетенцію по обревізуванню діл всіх уповноважених і Земств по заготовкам всього військового часу. Зазначену посаду займав до останнього часу, коли був запрохан до Міністерства Продовольчих Справ, поперва на посаду урядовця особл. доручень V кляссу, з призначенням потім и на посаду керуючого адміністративною частиною Міністерства.

По громадському стажу працював не довгий час.

1/ Состою Членім " Просвіти" населення " Южний", від якоі виставлявся кандідатім по виборам в Волостне Земство.

2/ в час большевизма з'організував в м. Харькові по власній ініціативі Українську Раду співробітників державних і громадських інституцій, де стояв головою до призначення по Міністерству Продовольчих Справ.

20/XII [signature]

12 Work history of Evhen Sirokov, who was employed in the Ukrainian National Republic's Food Supply Ministry. He notes in the last sentence that under the Bolsheviks in Kharkiv he organized and headed a Ukrainian council of state and private office employees. *Source:* TsDAVO, f. 2198 op. 2 sprava 114 no. 26.

of 67 roubles. Fifty-nine-years old, crippled, ill, without family, and living with his common law wife on the verge of starvation, he begged for assistance on humanitarian grounds. Four months and one investigation later, he got a letter saying that his case was being examined – at which point the paper trail ends. In June 1920 a Ukrainian living in Warsaw, who had worked as a policeman in Moscow before the war, sent a letter via the embassy to the Directory asking for a job.[127] During the winter of 1919 in Kamianets, townspeople creatively complied with the Directory's decree ordering the Ukrainianization of street signs. Some painted over their signs and replaced lettering with pictures. Others pasted over their permanent Russian-language metal signs with Ukrainian-language paper signs, while others painted out only individual Russian letters. One reporter observed in the summer of 1920 that the only group in the city that consistently advertised in Ukrainian were the Jews.[128]

The Central Council of Schools (*Rada Tovarystva Shkilnoi Osvity*), based in Kyiv, as much as the Ministry of Education, ran Ukrainian schools within and outside Directory territory. With co-op finance it supported institutions ranging from primary schools up to the Ukrainian Academy in Kyiv.[129] In the absence of central directives and finances, and short of technical personnel and equipment, the zemstvo in Podillia province tried to implement as best it could programs such as land division. Although the council needed at least two hundred surveyors, it had only fifty-six and fifty sets of instruments.[130]

Recruit turnout rates varied according to region and time. Some inspectors explained that although there was little enthusiasm for military service, turnout would improve after the harvest was in. Others noted that turnout was good where it was proceeded by a good propaganda campaign and that recruits were successfully processed where military detachments were present. Bolshevik intelligence reports in the autumn of 1919 also report the army in tolerable condition, though short of supplies, and an acceptable turnout of conscripts.[131] In Kyiv, Volyn, and Katerynoslav provinces the Directory got thousands of recruits to mobilization points between December 1918 and April 1919. The army could arm and clothe them, but was unable to feed them for more than a few days, or house them, with the result that men simply went home.[132] Although ministries could send papers and officials back and forth and to towns and villages, and some districts did send thousands of men into the army, most only provided a few dozen of the thousands of recruits on compiled draft lists. However, when weeks later a special commissar arrived with an armed detachment in villages and, after failed moral exhortation, threatened shirkers with death, men appeared.[133] Analysis of the failed July 1919 mobilization resulted in organizational changes. By that September a new official in charge of a new Mobilization Office had placed conscription under the exclusive control of the local commissar, who required that it be preceded by informational meetings, that provisions be in place for arrivals, and that people know about benefits for soldiers' families.[134] In September the Directory called for voluntary contributions of supplies for the army, but as people began bringing in items they discovered that there was no one to give them to. Some local draft boards had not been paid for two to four months, existed only on paper, and consequently, offices were empty and telegrams merely piled up on the unoccupied desks.[135] Not until October was the requisite organizational structure established at all levels, and then in another two weeks officials would have been able to receive and stockpile the goods. Clearly, things could be done. By November, however, not only had none of these supplies arrived at the front, but the front itself had collapsed. Supplies obtained via the co-operatives were stolen by them, while food that did get to army stores was pilfered, in turn, by the local civilian bureaucrats.[136] Mykola Chebotariv, the Directory's rear-echelon commander and in charge of military counter-intelligence, confirmed the prevalence of theft and added that party appointees in office either did not exercise their authority or spent their time in bars rather than at their desks. Without supervision, lower-level bureaucrats did as they willed.[137]

Besides doubts about the Directory's long-term survival, what also deterred peasants from appearing for mobilization was their apparent ignorance of laws passed that January providing benefits for crippled veterans, orphans, and widows. Local officials, meanwhile, apparently did not compile the lists of soldiers and families they were supposed to and did nothing to help soldiers' families. Nonetheless, in June the long-postponed law on pensions for veterans and war widows began its last trek through the bureaucracy. By September the request had gone to the Ministry of Finance for funding, and an order was sent for booklets to be published explaining the procedures and regulations surrounding the benefits; these apparently started to arrive to troops by the end of the month. In the interim, in August 1919 the Ministry of Internal Affairs had ordered villages to take over the responsibility of caring for veterans and soldiers' families – though how successful that initiative was is unknown.[138] Curiously, while in September 1919 the government managed to circulate in Podillia province 1,000 copies each of pamphlets about requisitioning horses and the obligatory selling of arms, it circulated only fifteen copies of the pamphlet describing benefits for soldiers' families to the civilian population. Nonetheless, in October the first payments were being made and the first complaints about delays began coming in.[139]

Were reports of government collapse exaggerated or did Directory bureaucrats create some order from chaos? Perhaps the only generalization that can be made from the scattered evidence is that some bureaucrats collected some recruits and grain, arrested some criminals, managed to send letters and instructions from town to town, and make some basic services work, some of the time, in parts of the Directory's core area. Inspectors' reports made after the Bolsheviks left were sombre yet noted that, as a rule, things got done where people had not sunken into apathetic cynical indifference and were willing to donate time and energy and suffer through pay arrears.[140] These accomplishments are noteworthy given that the formal work-day was only six hours long and the wider circumstances. First, the Directory's control over its territory was interrupted by war and enemy occupation, unlike central Bolshevik-controlled Russia, which meant that there was insufficient time to settle normal organizational problems of the sort the Ministry of Food Supply faced. On 3 February 1919 Bolshevik troops entered Kyiv. Second, besides the conflict between civilian and military authorities, and overlapping jurisdictions, the administration itself was not centralized. On the one hand, people organized soviets, which the Directory in principle recognized but in fact commissars often either repressed or ignored them, while on the other, it re-established zemstvos and dumas, which were often dominated by people opposed to Ukrainian independence. Accordingly, officials would get conflicting instructions or none at all, or face resistance insofar as they were perceived as illegitimate. Pogroms in Directory territory appear to have mostly been initiated by troops and individual commanders, rather than by civilian officials. Whether they occurred with the concurrence or despite the efforts of the UNR government, and were the result of control or breakdown, is unresolved.[141]

Presumably, had the Directory held on to power historians would have highlighted its achievements as 'reasons for victory,' and proof of talent and national commitment, rather than looking at its failures, listing them as 'reasons for defeat,' and indication of Ukrainian incompetence and lack of national consciousness. The better-run regions in western Podillia are probably what former ministers remember when they claimed that, thanks to institutions of civil administration formed under the initiative of the Socialist Federalist Minister of the Interior Prokopovych, and attached to the General Staff and front-line commissars, civilian life went on as best as could have been expected.[142]

Voluntary civic organizations, in particular co-operatives, provided goods and services on Ukrainian territory. These were particularly significant in 'nationalizing' people, as they could win support for the national government not by moral appeal based on cultural/linguistic matters, but in proportion to their success in distributing tangible aid, goods, and services. Uncommitted bilingual peasants or townsmen found it easier to speak Ukrainian and thus implicitly affiliate themselves with the national government if that gave them goods and services. It is unclear to what degree these organizations compensated for the failings of Directory ministries, however. The relationship between ministries and local co-ops was not ideal. The Directory contracted services with co-ops, for instance. The minister of the interior was also the head of the Peasants Union, and he thought that his civic organization should closely supervise his government ministry. In 1920 Ukrainian Bolshevik leader Dmytro Manuilsky referred to Ukraine's major central co-op organization Dniprosoiuz as 'a state within a state' in Directory territory.[143] A co-op spokesman explained in the autumn of 1919 that for the previous five years co-ops had been successfully providing food to the army, that they had expanded during the war, that they were trusted by the people, and that their staffs were loyal; nonetheless, he continued, they were unable to function properly in Directory territory because the Directory had not yet come to an organizational agreement with them on the issue of food supply – and that it should. A commissar's report that same month, meanwhile, noted that in Iampil district many Ukrainian organizations existed only on paper: the region had no more than five or six small reading clubs, and people had little interest in the local co-ops.[144]

Alongside co-ops there also existed political party organizations and the remains of the Peasants Unions which had played such a prominent role organizationally in 1917. But just what their condition was in 1919 is unknown. The most powerful party, the Socialist Revolutionaries, had become a collection of like-minded individuals with little organizational discipline, and it existed, at best, in only half of the Directory's district capitals.[145]

CHAPTER SIX

Bureaucrats and Bolsheviks in Russia

Historians of France, like those of Russia, have focused on political party organizations and militants in revolutionary government organization. Both have failed to illustrate how the success of the new government depended on a host of minor but full-time technical and administrative employees. These were the people who saw to it that services, of which the most important were those linked to the military, continued and they had their thousands of subordinates doing at least something of what they were supposed to be doing. Like many Jacobins in 1791 many Bolsheviks in 1917 imagined that their just social order would be decentralized and run by amateur administrators elected from among the working population. Like the pragmatic Jacobins Lenin overrode those opposed to bureaucracy in his party. He knew that he had to keep professional bureaucrats at their desks. After breaking their strike in January 1918 Lenin argued that professional administrators were necessary and acknowledged that administration required training, but he did retain his hatred of former bureaucrats and his conviction that force was needed to transform an inveterately hostile group into what Nikolai Bukharin had termed 'plain social workers.'

The demands of war forced all governments to increase the size and reach of their bureaucracies. Nevertheless, three weeks before taking power, in *Can the Bolsheviks Retain State Power?* Lenin explicitly stated that he sought to make the government bureaucracy as big and as all-encompassing as possible, 'with ten if not twenty million people.' One reason was he thought that socialism needed a huge 'state apparatus.' Within two years Lenin had created a bureaucracy of unprecedented size and scope. Although it does not appear to have been more efficient or effective than those of its rivals, by 1921 Lenin's bureaucracy did seem to include within it almost all of the urban educated – if only because there was little alternative to government employment. This, in turn, draws attention to a second reason Lenin advocated 'big government.' He realized that people could be better controlled if they were government employees, and dependent on the government for wages and rations, than if they were simply threatened with laws and execution: 'The guillotine *only* terrorized, only broke *active* resistance. *For us, this is not enough*' (original emphasis). This was the subtext to the slogan: 'He who does not work shall not eat.'[1]

The Administrators' Strike

By 1917 the middle level of the tsarist state bureaucracy had been socially transformed by an influx of commoners, professionals, and technicians produced by the industrialization of the 1890s. These were personnel from the lower-middle strata of the zemstvos, co-operatives, and peasants' unions. On the lowest levels of the government hierarchy an influx of former shop assistants, clerks, factory officials, co-op activists, and technicians had also created a new cadre of bureaucrats. The total number of public employees increased throughout the whole Russian Empire. After the tsar abdicated that March, the Provisional Government dismissed police chiefs, governors, and vice-governors and replaced the latter with 'commissars.' It left in place tsarist ranks, pay scales, and pensions, and middle- and lower-level personnel – people who continued working and began organizing anew around the old pre–First World War grievances.[2] The first government employees' union appeared in June in the Finance Ministry, but the Interior Ministry explicitly rejected postal and telegraph employees' demands for a say in running their offices.[3] In the summer of 1917 Miretsky (see Chapter 1), in Petrograd since 1914, began to publish a continuation of his pre-war journal *Sputnik chinovnika,* renamed *Tribuna gosudarstvennykh sluzhashchikh.* The first issue revealed that clerks were disillusioned by the lack of change within the bureaucracy and were at odds with the Provisional Government over pay and the continued enforcement of tsarist regulations and practices. Activists wanted to elect superiors, see reinstatements, and have a say in running offices and staffing. Articles and letters accused senior staff of sabotaging the new government and condemned the continued presence of secret police informers in offices. Administration was breaking down, they explained, because old department heads were refusing to change, and work did get done where heads had come to agreements with their staffs concerning office procedures and practices.[4] Initially organized into dozens of separate unions according to function and status, by the autumn activists had assembled all administrators' unions under a single umbrella organization (*Soiuz soiuzov sluzhashchikh gosudarstvennykh uchrezhdenii*).

After they took power on 25 October (7 November 1917 NS) in Petrograd Vladimir Lenin and the Bolsheviks formed the Council of People's Commissars (*Sovet Narodnykh Kommisarov,* SNK). It sent commissars to ministries who, in accord with Lenin's 'draft rules for office employees,' threatened staff with imprisonment and confiscation of their private property if they did not obey the new government.[5] Bureaucrats, who still considered themselves to be employees of the Provisional Government, ignored the orders and kept working as if nothing had happened. During the following week as the SNK tried to impose its authority government employees began going on strike, while higher officials and city dumas, supported by right-wing Socialist Revolutionaries, Mensheviks, and Kadets, coordinated this spontaneous opposition into an organized strike planned to last until the Constituent Assembly met. At least 44,000 bureaucrats in Petrograd including clerks in private companies eventually took part, and all services except electricity, water, finance, and those directly related to the war effort were affected.[6] Office shutdowns went as far as removing pens from desks. According to Korostovets, one of the organizers, the Bolsheviks feared the united power of the 'official intelligentsia' as the sole and most dangerous force organized against them.[7] One monarchist eyewitness noted in his diary that as of 7 (13) December all Bolshevik measures against the strike had been unsuccessful. Offices were still empty or were being slowly reoccupied by unqualified and semi-literate persons. Alexei Tatishchev noted that while formally a pro-Bolshevik committee was in charge of his bureau, in fact, it did nothing because the personnel had voted to strike and to maintain only a token skeleton staff in the office; however, a mass demonstration by bureaucrats in support of the Constituent Assembly called by their union passed without impact, he observed. A good half of the demonstrators were senior officials who were not much interested in the Constituent Assembly, and he did not think that their marching with red flags, shouting slogans, and singing 'The Marseillaise' seemed very convincing to anyone, including themselves. But in those times 'that is what one did.' On 29 December junior bureaucrats decided to end the strike, at which point Tatishchev stopped coming in to take his turn manning the desk and left the capital.[8] Newspaper reports referred to the Bolsheviks forming an Employee Mobilization Unit *(Otdel mobilizatsii sluzhashchikh)* which apparently had difficulty in finding strikebreakers during the first days of the strike.[9] In a dramatic show of support, of 250 serving bank clerks mobilized from the front by the Bolsheviks to replace strikers in Moscow 230 refused to go.[10]

Not all bureaucrats or their associated unions supported the strike, and a handful of pro-Bolshevik junior functionaries usually came to work. As observers of administrative practice for years, they were familiar enough with procedures to take over tasks alongside assigned Bolshevik party members. A fraction within the Petrograd branch of the Telegraph, Post, and Railway Workers Union, for instance, negotiated separately with the Bolsheviks and managed to take over the entire union by the end of February 1918, in a pattern repeated in other unions.[11] Bolsheviks also managed to hold a meeting of sympathetic junior clerks during the second week of December 1917 and form a Union of Junior Administrators *(Vserossiiskii soiuz mladshikh sluzhashchikh)* which then organized an anti-strike initiative.[12] The Bolsheviks won over private sector administrators' unions with promises that all administrators would be represented on workers' councils (*soviets*).[13]

Three days into the administrators' strike Lenin called on 'the population' to take over government and a Labour Commission, presumably the above-mentioned *Otdel,* began hiring new clerks for all of the old ministries.[14] When argument failed to turn the strikers, the Bolsheviks began to use force and cajolery. Between 12 (25) November and 12 (25) December 1918 all ministries formally announced to their employees, in the newspaper *Izvestiia,* that they would be fired without pay or benefits if they did not come to work or refused to obey the new government. Commissars with armed detachments began systematically going from office to office either threatening recalcitrant bureaucrats with arrest unless they swore loyalty or dismissal without pension and immediate conscription into the army. On 7 (20) December they required all bureaucrats to register with the government and carry their identification papers with them at all times – thus making bureaucrats the first group of people under Soviet rule to be placed under permanent control.[15] Fearing that the strike would spread throughout the whole country, Bolshevik leaders that same day decided to create a special commission to prevent this and named it the All-Russian Special Commission against Counter-revolution and Sabotage – the Cheka by its Russian acronym. With less than a hundred men, and limited as yet to the capital, within a week of its creation the Cheka began arresting the leaders of the Kadets and of the central strike committee.[16] By 24 December (6 January), when the Bolsheviks effectively declared city dumas and zemstvos illegal, their countermeasures finally seemed to be neutralizing the strike as central government offices remained open. The dissolution of the Constituent Assembly on 6 (19) January deprived the strike of a legal rationale. After shifting the capital to Moscow, in the face of protests from radical party members Bolshevik leaders prepared to retain all personnel until such time as they found reason to dismiss them, and they sought out and amicably tried to convince as a many non-Bolsheviks as possible that they could work for the new regime without fear. On 12 (25) January 1918 former senior and middle-level ministerial bureaucrats formally declared an end to their strike 'for the good of the country.' By March 1918, after the Germans had failed to take Petrograd, the last work stoppages in the capital had ceased.[17]

Strikers in Petrograd considered their initiative to be a moral example for other cities. On 8 (21) December 1917 they called for an empire-wide strike, and newspapers in the major cities outside the capital carried both news about it and the call for support. Outside the capital private and government bureaucrats went on strike in towns where local Bolsheviks took power before January 1918. No one has systematically studied them but administrators' strikes did occur in at least eight central Russian provincial capitals, one-third of the total. The strikes lasted no longer than a few weeks and were usually, but not always, stopped either by force or threat of force. Once news of a failed strike in a provincial capital reached smaller towns, local organizers usually gave up peacefully.[18] In Bezhetsk in Tver province public employees at the end of December 1917 refused to recognize the Bolsheviks. Within a week they had agreed to work on condition that the Bolsheviks not interfere in administrative affairs. If the Bolsheviks refused they were prepared to strike but only if they were guaranteed three months' pay. A situation of 'dual power' continued until 31 January, when the town duma, with only half of its members present, voted to recognize the Bolsheviks. The same bureaucrats all kept doing their old jobs – although not without many insults and much abuse from their new rulers during their first days at work.[19] In the town of Simbirsk well-organized clerks began a strike on 8 (21) January, with six months' advance pay. The next day the Bolsheviks fired them, four days later they arrested all the leaders, and on 15 January the strikers gave up. In Moscow bureaucrats called a strike on 15 (28) November with the financial support of local banks and businessmen. The strike committee forbade individual unions from negotiating separately and declared that it would identify all strikebreakers.

Reports from Petrograd said that the Constituent Assembly would put strikebreakers on trial.[20] Municipal workers, lower-level clerks, and some middle-level and higher bureaucrats decided to leave the strike on 1 (14) December. The Bolsheviks did not take measures against the strikers, and an estimated 20,000 officials remained on strike until the end of February 1918, when, almost out of money, they voted to stop striking.[21]

A special section of the Interior Ministry dispatched 'instructors' throughout the country during 1918 who by August brought local urban offices and officials in Bolshevik Russia under nominal central control. In June the Bolsheviks formally abolished zemstvos and city dumas and took over their assets and personnel. Urban resistance through 1918 was peaceful and spontaneous, with local Socialist Revolutionaries and Mensheviks unable to coordinate or organize it. A sample of 762 participants suggests that public employees as a group were the most active, but only thirteen of a recorded total of 344 incidents in 200 towns in fourteen central Russian provinces lasted longer than a week, and only thirty-five numbered more than 2,000 participants. Besides weak organization, another reason that resistance petered out within a few months was because unpaid employees were unwilling to ally with two other key groups – the merchants and traders, whom they disliked for what they regarded as profiteering, and local garrisons whom they linked to anarchy.[22] By the autumn of 1918 administrators had either reconciled themselves with their new master, fled, or been fired.

Some bureaucrats were pro-Bolshevik by conviction. Others worked for the new regime in the hope of making as much as they could in hard times. People like M. Petrov, who in Orenburg province remained a district head from 1917 through to 1920, simply changed titles with each regime change.[23] Still others continued at their desks because of a psychological need to work, and they were the most dedicated and efficient bureaucrats. Particularly committed were educated Jews happy to hold jobs for which they were qualified but had been denied by the tsarist regime.

The reasons why people who initially opposed the Bolsheviks changed their minds varied. Some thought it would do no harm to remain at their posts because Bolshevik politics were so suicidal and absurd that even if the Bolsheviks did remain in power eventually they would 'stop being communists,' and then life would return to normal. Inertia played its role. Once in a position people would conclude that their survival was linked to the survival of the regime that they worked for.[24] In Moscow some officials decided that in view of the terrible plight of the people, and because the main organizers of the strike (the Kadets) had averaged only one-third of the city vote for the upcoming Constituent Assembly, it was their moral obligation to work regardless of who held power.[25] Another former tsarist bureaucrat explained that intellectuals and socialists had a duty to work with the Bolsheviks regardless of how undesirable they were in order to save the revolution from the 'wretchedness that engulfed it.' In emigration another person noted that some people decided to work with the hope of undermining the new regime because they imagined that it would be easy to change policies while implementing them. Once in office, he lamented, most people ultimately chose to make rather than risk careers. The continuing terror, the merging in March 1919 of the Interior Ministry with the Cheka, under Feliks Dzerzhinskii as commissar of the interior, and a gnawing realization that the Bolsheviks would remain in power led the last diehards to accept that surreptitious individual sabotage of government policy was futile, and they stopped making such efforts. People who rationalized their service with the intention of neutralizing Bolshevism became its servants, while those who had joined to only survive followed their conscience, either doing nothing or working to rule, implementing as decently as possible decisions that they thought objectionable.[26] A White spy working in a Bolshevik office through 1918 confirms this assessment, noting that the key turning point in attitudes came that July: 'Once they got a job and "established themselves" the citizens quickly changed and began to worry that the situation not become worse in the event things changed ... The rationale was primitive: let what is remain or even that won't be.' This is confirmed by a diarist in Moscow, who noted in late September 1918 that people were saying that the Bolsheviks would save Russia. Who else, he bitterly asked, could have created what they did, from the secret police to the army? Hunger for the many and privileges for the few, he added, also played their role. An archivist in Petrograd wrote in the summer of 1919 that he hated the Bolsheviks to the depths of his soul, yet saw no alternative to them other than anarchy which he feared even more.[27] What is ironic about this shift in attitudes is that it occurred precisely when Bolshevik leaders themselves were so terrified of being ousted from power by massive peasant resistance and social collapse that they had secretly begun preparations to flee the country and organizing those chosen to remain into underground cells.[28]

Once individuals decided to acquiesce, getting hired was relatively easy – particularly outside major cities, where the new rulers were desperate for clerks and literate adults were few. During the early years of

Bolshevik rule, in addition, those who wanted postings also knew that there was little likelihood that anyone would check their particulars, so they obfuscated or lied on application forms. Anton Okninskii, a middle-level bureaucrat went on strike in 1917 and then returned to work in January. He decided to leave Petrograd in the autumn of 1918 to avoid problems with the Cheka and because his life savings had disappeared with the bank where they had been deposited. Hoping for a White victory he moved to Tambov province, where food was still affordable, got a job on a village executive committee and, apparently, won the affection of the locals as an honest clerk. Okninskii decided to emigrate when he concluded that the Whites had been defeated.[29]

For the average clerk a crucial factor in ending the strike was remuneration. As payday was the 20th, many got their month's wages, plus a two-month advance hurriedly arranged by the Provisional Government just before the Bolshevik coup. In early November the striking bureaucrats explained to the underground Provisional Government that they could remain on strike only if they were paid, as they had families to support. Most got their December wages and the State Bank did issue money to all except the SNK because 'it was not a legal person.'[30] On 9 (21) November the Bolsheviks expropriated the Moscow branch of the State Bank, and on 17 (30) November with the use of troops and support from sympathetic junior staff they began taking money from the Petrograd branch. Faced with a call for a general strike on 14 (27) December, the Bolsheviks seized all the banks in Petrograd that morning and that evening declared them all nationalized. Now, only those who worked for the new government would get paid, with lower-level officials getting more than they did previously and higher officials getting less. Seeing their offices filling up with new workers – the State Bank had hired 500 in one month – and faced with the prospect of penury and starvation, as Lenin had foreseen, striking administrators had strong material reasons that January to make their peace with the new rulers.[31] *Izvestiia* (on 28 December / 10 January) mocked the bureaucrats, noting that they struck only for as long they were paid and warned that those who feigned to work in Bolshevik offices only to get paid would be arrested for fraud. The newspaper claimed that 'the proletariat' was not averse to suffer shortages and hunger in the name of socialism.

By 1918 the simple prospect of a job was a strong inducement for those too weak or old for the army, former providers of services to the wealthy, and literate but destitute professionals to enter the quickly expanding commissariats in the capital. In the provinces penury and hunger drove bureaucrats and the literate sooner or later into the Bolshevik government in a standard scenario. Once Bolsheviks established their authority, they shut down private stores and enterprises in towns. State stores were usually empty, prices rose, and goods were available only on the black market. After a year of Bolshevik rule in Bezhets province, for instance, state stores were empty and cabbage, groats, peas, and soap had disappeared even from the local market – where prices had increased by anywhere from three (for meat) to 100 times (for tobacco).[32] In such conditions the literate but manually unskilled initially formed Manufacturing-Trading Co-operatives and did physical work, which the Bolsheviks tolerated for a time. Once these were banned the only alternative to black marketeering was to get a legal income, rations, and the opportunity to steal and collect bribes by working in one of the innumerable new government bureaus.[33] To induce the educated to work as bureaucrats, city authorities allowed them to purchase rationed food at fixed prices once. Within the bureaucracy, meanwhile, after they had successfully subordinated it, Bolshevik leaders sought whenever possible to meet the material needs of their new bureaucrats as best they could.[34]

Staffing and Functioning

In 1919 Lenin, like Maxim Gorky, identified secular Jews (who had flooded into cities during the war) as the group that had played the decisive role in keeping the bureaucracy functioning after he took power by 'sabotaging the saboteurs [striking bureaucrats].' In the words of Simon Dimanshtein, to whom he confided, Lenin 'stressed that we could take over the government apparatus ... only thanks to this reserve of literate and more or less sober and competent new functionaries.'[35] Lenin did not specify which cities or regions he had in mind, but presumably he was referring to the capital and Ukraine. In 1915 concessions and wartime deportations increased the number of Jews east of the front by at least 500,000. That year the government allowed approximately 150,000 Jews to settle in central Russia alongside the craftsmen, wealthy merchants, and academics there since the 1860s, and also raised Jewish entry quotas for state schools – thus ensuring that a substantial number of Jewish graduates would be looking for work during the first years of Bolshevik power. Although the total population of the two capitals dropped between 1917 and 1920, more Christians than Jews fled; thus, while in 1917 50,000 Jews averaged 1:50 of the population, 30,000 Jews represented approximately 1:24 by 1920.[36] In March 1917 the Provisional

Government repealed all anti-Jewish legislation and restrictions, and Jews became prime candidates for government jobs – although few seem to have been hired. In Petrograd on the morning of the 26 October, after hearing that the Bolsheviks had overthrown the Provisional Government, and just as, or even before they began advertising for administrators, hundreds of Jews began lining up in front of soviet and government offices hoping for jobs. In the 27 October edition of their newspaper the anti-Bolshevik Zionists expressed their disgust at the behaviour of their co-nationals 'racing' for places in the queues. Others were surprised that they 'showed no shame.' A Russian archivist in 1919 Petrograd observed: 'We are governed by Jews ... All the higher officials – Jews. All the lower ones – Russians. And they all steal.'[37]

Young women provided a vital source of clerks. 'Soviet ladies (*sovetskie baryshni,* or *sovbary*)' were barely literate and not particularly enthusiastic about their jobs. 'Yet, in essence the entire system of Soviet bureaucratism is built on these ladies: without them it is impossible either to write a document, send it, issue an order, or take out the garbage.'[38] 'Imagine a line of tables,' wrote another eyewitness, 'and behind each one a 15- to 17-year-old lady, inevitably with lipstick, a coiffure, and a stamp. It is a great good if that stamp quickly makes contact with your document, but if that lady, or more correctly "comrade," starts a conversation with another comrade, or lights a cigarette ... you're lost – you will wait endlessly. There are many such *sovbary* in all offices; one stamps, the other confirms or signs, and all this you must quietly bear.' Our Petrograd archivist remarked about 'these ladies in offices' that 'there is nothing more insufferable than these creatures. Arrogant, importunate, and unpleasant. And that is if you ever get to them. They often don't even talk to who comes to them.'[39]

In January 1918 Miretsky's *Tribuna* endorsed Bolshevik rule and condemned the strike as something organized by senior department heads. A lead editorial explained that as bureaucrats were now part of a workers' state they had to realize that wages, pensions, and hours were less important than the business of the new state.[40] But within a few months Miretsky became disillusioned and critical. For one thing there were the Bolsheviks' new rules of procedure *(Polozhenie o sluzhbe grazhdanskoi)* which were intended to replace tsarist office regulations. Miretsky dismissed these as a rewritten version of the tsarist regulations but worse because old senior tsarist staff would be implementing them despite the new regime. In particular he condemned the new rules for not mentioning unions and denying officials the right to strike. Second, in Moscow he observed that unions were all being phased out of government offices. He seems to have been particularly unnerved by seeing, at a Moscow train station that winter, the man who had arrested him in 1913, travelling as a Soviet official with the same kind of identification papers that he himself had.[41] Accordingly, alongside a steady stream of official notifications, issues of *Tribuna* began including articles and letters critical of the new bureaucracy, asking whether the reimposition of tsarist practices by individual ministers and department heads reflected inertia or official policy.[42] Although from the point of view of ministerial and department heads the new bureaucracy was not functioning because of 'anarchy,' *Tribuna* explained that the problem lay in centralization, the continued presence of unreformed tsarist officials in senior positions, and the massive apathy of the official administrators' union bureaucrats. In place of the *Polozhenie, Tribuna* argued, the new bureaucracy should adopt as the model for its regulations the 'collective agreement' worked out by the Union of Credit Institution Workers.[43] Opposition to the *Polozhenie* was apparently so massive that Bolshevik leaders had to quietly shelve it. However, *Tribuna* complained, directors continued to issue orders phrased to favour senior staff arbitrarily and without consultation.[44]

The last issue of *Tribuna* appeared in February 1919. It contained a speech by Zinoviev condemning the new bureaucracy and reflected Miretsky's cautious optimism that, perhaps, the new leaders would not allow old tsarist officials to make the soviet bureaucracy a copy of the tsarist one. Initially, some lower-level bureaucrats in provincial offices, ignorant of high politics, were pleased with the improvement in personal relations at work that they experienced after the Bolsheviks took over. Within months of the coup, however, other lower-level bureaucrats were complaining that the overwork, low pay, stupid rules, theft, bribery, and overbearing superiors of tsarist times had all reappeared.[45] The Bolsheviks, meanwhile, having broken the organized resistance of bureaucrats at their place of work and having successfully created dependent unions from pro-Bolshevik junior personnel in all the ministries, had begun amalgamating the new structures into a tame All-Russian Union of Officials whose leaders, unlike Miretsky, did not concern themselves with the demands of 1917. In September 1919 the Bolsheviks began registering former middle-level and higher state bureaucrats as 'former people' – those considered hostile to the Bolsheviks because of their pre-1917 wealth and status.

In 1918 the Bolsheviks represented but one of thirty-nine political organizations that were claiming territorial administrative authority within what had been the tsarist empire. By the end of that year they controlled the urban administration in a core area comprising thirty Russian provinces of the former empire with a population of approximately sixty-four million (see Map 2).[46] But although by 1919 they were able to fill urban offices with thousands of people, before 1922 these people did not constitute a fully functional central bureaucracy. Russia's new government had overlapping jurisdictions, was overstaffed in cities, understaffed in villages, corrupt, and frequently inept. Furthermore, overstaffing, centralization, and a bad division of functions produced inactivity and idleness among apathetic employees who came to work late and did little during their eight-hour day. Rules defined everything but to no avail, wrote a Petrograd archivist in 1919. 'Whoever must, can avoid everything.' Only those people suffered who had not lost their sense of disgust.[47] During his first days of employment in a village in Tambov province in early 1919, Okninskii expressed surprise that the entire staff appeared for work at 9 o'clock, when they were supposed to, but quickly discovered that this was because they made no distinction between their place of work and places of residence. Since their duties took only a few hours a day, personnel spent most of their time playing cards, smoking, and drinking in the three-room town hall.[48] The intensity of the populace's hate of rank-and-file soviet bureaucrats was matched by the hate of rank-and-file Bolsheviks for former tsarist bureaucrats – referred to as 'working cattle necessary for the dirty work.' The Cheka, on the one hand, issued special decrees forbidding the arbitrary dismissal of former tsarist officials from soviet agencies and, on the other, sometimes executed entire executive committees for malfeasance.[49]

As the Bolsheviks increased government functions so they increased the number of functionaries. Whereas in 1910 approximately 7 per cent of the working populations of Moscow and Petrograd were government employees, by 1920 that proportion had risen to 40 per cent. Of all the government employees in 1920, 53 per cent were party members, while workers made up 11 per cent.[50] In Voronezh province the total number of public employees almost doubled between 1917 and 1919 (from 1,336 to 2,653), while the number of government clerks increased from 1,000 to 1,051.[51] By the end of 1920 in all Bolshevik territories there were approximately 500,000 central and local government employees, of whom almost 38 per cent were women. Critics were as contemptuous of these people as were critics of the Ukrainian governments' bureaucrats, calling the government machine 'the domain of illiterate ladies and inexperienced youths.'[52] If in the towns, alongside secular Jews and women, pre-revolutionary junior and middle-level clerks benefited most from Bolshevik power in terms of promotion, in villages the key pro-Bolshevik groups were lower-level zemstvo personnel and young literate peasants returned from military service. With high expectations and able to do administrative tasks, the latter group enhanced their prestige as veterans by joining local Bolshevik organizations and then getting office positions.[53] 'Throughout the peasant world Communist regimes have been built on the fact that it is the ambition of every literate peasant son to become a clerk.'[54]

Appointed full-time clerical personnel were within the administrative sections (*otdely upravleniia*) of Soviet executive committee (*ispolkom*) departments and sections. Bolshevik Revolutionary Military Committees (revkoms), however, which began appearing in the summer of 1917, normally ran affairs. The revkoms were controlled by local party members and had the task of seizing power using local Bolshevized troops and unemployed workers organized into Red Guards. They then dominated local soviets until such time as they could impose a Bolshevik majority within them. Revkoms later had the task of imposing Bolshevik rule in front areas and, at all levels regions newly taken by the Red Army. Eventually, the local military commissar normally headed the revkom, which was directly subordinate only to the Revolutionary Military Committee in Petrograd, and while they existed, revkoms used ispolkom staff as they wished. Since the revkoms' arbitrary powers included expropriation and confiscation, they had funds to pay clerks during the crucial first weeks of Bolshevik rule in any particular territory. In theory, ispolkoms were freely elected by soviets; in practice, local commissars told the local soviets who to elect. Thereafter, executive committees reappointed themselves every three months, their formal length of tenure. As of 1920 ispolkoms, with between three and five sections or departments, depending on the size of the locality, averaged two or three members in villages, three to five members at the county level, twelve at the district level, and twenty-five at the provincial level.[55] At the provincial and district levels 80 per cent of government department heads were Bolshevik party members. Approximately 85 per cent of all local Bolshevik party members worked in ispolkoms. Former clerks who had worked in tsarist private and social organizations averaged 25 per cent of the personnel at the provincial and district levels, and of these, perhaps 10 per cent were former government bureaucrats.[56] Although almost no ispolkom departmental salaried staff were Bolsheviks, there are no statistical studies of this group. A shortage of personnel in small towns and villages led to priests doing the work. In many districts of Ekaterinburg province in 1919 priests remained after the Whites left and occupied many and sometimes all middle-level district positions, while some of them continued performing mass on Sundays.[57]

A survey of 25 per cent of the almost 25,000 central ministry functionaries in Bolshevik-controlled territory taken in August 1918 revealed that, except for the foreign and secret police ministries, and the highest positions, at least one-third of all central government personnel, as many as 90 per cent of railway and Finance Ministry staff, and 55 per cent of higher officials in central ministries had been in tsarist service. By social status over 50 per cent of these were bureaucrats, and 59 per cent of central ministry personnel in Moscow were former tsarist officials.[58] Two thousand surviving questionnaires from Moscow and Petrograd reveal that as many as 90 per cent of former tsarist officials living there in 1919, who were forty years of age or older, were working in Soviet ministries.[59] This 'reconciliation,' however, had been preceded by strikes, which suggests that Weber's hypothesis about bureaucrats being apolitical might not apply to Russia – even given the role of wages and destitution in explaining people's behaviour. In 1917 tsarist officials were politicized for and against the Bolsheviks. In Petrograd and Moscow in particular during the first two months of Bolshevik rule, striking office staff posed a serious threat to Lenin. This activism made revolutionary Russia different from revolutionary France where, despite leaders' fears and mistrust, old regime officials who worked for the new regime apparently did remain indifferent to politics. By 1793 pre-1789 personnel in France averaged 50 per cent of the staff in the Ministry of Finance and approximately 25 per cent of all government administrators; 75 per cent of all officials had been hired between 1789 and 1793, but this does not appear to have been the result of mass firings or resignations of old regime officials. In the Ministry of War, 60 per cent of the pre -1789 personnel left service by 1793 because of retirement or death, 20 per cent served through the revolution, and another 20 per cent were rehired soon after their dismissal. Those purged or dropped because of staff cuts after 1795 were not the pre-revolutionary cohort, but new people hired during the preceding three years.[60]

The Bolsheviks during the first year of their rule may have formally controlled their bureaucrats, but their bureaucracy does not appear to have controlled society below the district (*povit*) level. The first general conscription, announced in September 1918, provoked armed revolts and involved thousands of deaths. That summer on average no more than 40 per cent of conscripts appeared when called up. Grain deliveries, meanwhile, did not exceed 30 per cent of what had been expected. The next call-up that autumn coincided with severe hunger in Petrograd and Moscow which led to a suspension of the state grain monopoly, requisitions, and the abolition of the much hated Committees of Poor Peasants. Forced collectivization had not yet been proclaimed. Consequently, by the end of the year approximately 75 per cent of the conscripts did end up in the army – the wartime average. In 1919, however, turnout dropped drastically, again in response to requisitioning; the lowest turnout was in Tver province, where only 15 per cent of those called up appeared for mustering.[61] Had the Bolshevik regime collapsed in 1919 or 1920 historians might have pointed to the failings of its bureaucracy as a cause citing dire descriptions from the 1919 Communist Party Congress of duplication, parallel structures, overstaffing, inactivity, clientism, corruption, and red tape.[62]

In lieu of the bureaucracy the personal networks and contacts that local Communist Party members built around themselves were vital in effecting local implementation of policy. Through these contacts central leaders exercised some control over local agents. Horizontally linked individuals in the provinces, who were not always in contact with distant leaders and did not necessarily obey their nominal superiors, were eventually brought into line by plenipotentiaries dispatched from Moscow. Thereafter, through their control of jobs, services, and rewards local Bolshevik agents provided incentives for subordinates to comply. Much depended also on whether the local potentate, thanks to a patron's support in Moscow, was not only a party official but also in charge of a central agency or ministry. Thus, central leaders during the revolutionary years managed to implement some policies without a well-defined working vertical system of administration by offering locals central spoils. Central leaders created middle-level regional bureaus and then appointed local leaders to them. This involved one boss and his network displacing or absorbing another and that new network then would provide the social and/or friendship structure around which the regional political administration was built.[63]

In Nizhnii Novgorod province, which was about as far from Moscow as were Katerynoslav, Kharkiv, and Kamianets-Podilskyi provinces from Kyiv, it took the provincial Bolsheviks a year to take over the soviets to the county level. That control was extended to villages through 1919–20 with the help of armed squads, led by the Cheka, of 1,000 to 1,500 men systematically going to every settled point and installing loyalists. It was these squads and their readiness to shoot malefactors that brought the terror to all of the territories that the Bolsheviks claimed.[64]

Against this background by the end of 1919 the Bolsheviks could organize the production and distribution of munitions to the army. To some degree verification committees could ensure that conscripts got to the army. Finally, valuables confiscated from deserters' families were redistributed to some, if not all, families of serving soldiers – a policy that won grudging local support from those with serving relatives and stemmed the massive desertions that had weakened the Red Army through 1919.[65] No less important was the distribution of pensions and rations to army widows. But these latter policies were not always done by full-time government bureaucrats or the special commission set up to implement them. Just as often armed district anti-desertion patrols would assist the chosen by redistributing among them what they had just previously confiscated from their neighbours or their neighbouring village.[66] Turning a blind eye to gross official malfeasance, corruption, graft, and theft played a role in getting central commands implemented. Just about every reported instance of 'speculation' in 1918 and 1919, for instance, led directly to some government office. Senior Bolshevik leaders and Cheka commanders quickly realized that unless they focused their repressive activity exclusively on matters that were unequivocally treasonous, their entire system would break down. Officials simply could not survive unless they lied, cheated, and stole – and so they were allowed to do so.[67]

CHAPTER SEVEN

Bureaucrats, Bolsheviks, and Whites in Ukraine

Representing between ninety and ninety-five of Ukraine's 300 soviets Ukraine's Bolsheviks seized power in a coup d'état in Kharkiv on 12 (25) December 1917. They set up a government with the help of some 4,500 troops and Red Guards – of whom approximately 2,100 had arrived from Moscow the previous week. Of the twelve members of the newly formed People's Secretariat, four were Ukrainians and four were Ukrainian-born. Evgeniia Bosh, a Ukrainian-born German, was the de facto head of the Secretariat, but she was not publically proclaimed as such for fear that because she was a woman 'the masses would not understand.'[1] This People's Secretariat, with Kharkiv as its temporary capital, claimed to be the true government of the Ukrainian National Republic, that is, the five provinces that the Provisional Government had allotted to the Central Rada (see Chapter 3). Bolsheviks in the other provinces remained formally under the Petrograd SNK. The Kharkiv People's Secretariat arrived in Kyiv on 30 January (12 February) 1918, from where the Germans evicted them in March. With the signing of the Brest-Litovsk Treaty that month the Bolsheviks had to recognize all the provinces controlled by the Central Rada as an independent state. Moscow then placed all soviets in Ukraine under the authority of the Kharkiv Secretariat. The order amalgamating these soviets under Kharkiv explicitly avoided legitimating Ukraine's soviet republic in national terms and defined it as merely a 'soviet republic on Ukrainian territory' within which soviets in the previously excluded territories had to unite to better face the German threat.[2]

In January 1919 Ukraine's Bolsheviks proclaimed the Ukrainian Soviet Socialist Republic and created a Council of Peoples Commissars for it. Until August that year its core territory comprised a region of 300 square kilometres in northeastern Ukraine, centred on Chernihiv. In the west the border shifted back and forth following the war with the Directory (see Maps 3 and 4). In the southeast, between May and December, the border moved back and forth in the wake of war with the Whites and Makhno's anarchist army. By 1920 the Bolsheviks formally ruled all of what had been tsarist Ukraine. In fact, guerilla war led by Makhno and otamans raged through to 1922, and central control was tenuous despite the huge administrative apparatus that existed by then. All nationalities worked in the Bolshevik government but their bureaucracy, unlike that of the national governments, contained large numbers of Russians and Jews born outside Ukraine.

First Reactions to Bolshevik Rule

Like their Petrograd counterparts, despite internal dissension over the decision, the Kharkiv Bolsheviks accepted into government service all bureaucrats who stayed on. They made their first request for money from Petrograd on 14 (27) December 1917, and three days later got millions of roubles that had originally been intended for the Central Rada.[3] Ukraine's bureaucrats did not go on strike against the Central Rada, even after it declared Ukrainian independence on 9 (22) January 1918. Notwithstanding the efforts of Stepanov-Melanakov and Arkhangelskii in Kyiv, the call by the Petrograd Administrators Union for an empire-wide strike, and supporting declarations from some Ukrainian administrators' unions, it appears that few Kyiv public employees went on strike against the Bolsheviks – presumably following the lead of the city duma, whose majority of Russian Socialist Revolutionaries and Mensheviks announced that they would continue working for the public good. The city's food supply and postal and telegraph workers said that they would not oppose the Bolsheviks for the same reason.[4] City hall called for a return to work when the shooting stopped on 22 January (5 February) 1918, and within seven days all offices were open. That winter almost all Rada officials formally worked for the Bolsheviks. According to one account this was not by choice, as they had no idea that the Rada had left the city. Rumour had it that government employees had been paid in advance in gold and were instructed to stay. Apparently the majority of those Kyiv bureaucrats who did leave in face of the approaching Bolsheviks that January were younger staff. Older employees, western Ukrainians, and personnel in the Agriculture and Food Supply ministries stayed. The situation in small towns remains to be studied. However, despite the rumours to the contrary, documents indicate that before the Central Rada fled Kyiv it had not managed to pay its local officials for the month of January.[5] Whatever the case may have been, there was no central civilian Bolshevik government in Ukraine until after the Brest-Litovsk Treaty was signed in March: 'We called ourselves a government but regarded this as a bit of a joke. And, actually, what kind of a government were we without an army or even a territory because even the Kharkiv soviet had not recognized us. No administration ... the Secretariat was in our pocket.'[6] In reality the People's Secretariat could do little without the agreement of the commander of the Red Army Vladimir Antonov-Ovseenko and Sergo Ordhonikidze, the resident Russian plenipotentiary.[7]

Opposition occurred outside Kharkiv but it seems to have been sporadic. In Chernihiv all the employees' committees, apparently despite their earlier resolution to oppose, recognized the Bolsheviks and then immediately petitioned for, and were given, higher wages.[8] The rank and file of the Food Supply Committee in Katerynoslav belonged to the biggest single government employer in that province and apparently worked for all of Ukraine's governments. Together with the Food Supply Committee in Kharkiv province they did strike against the Bolsheviks – who broke the strike in January 1918.[9] Officials resisted in Lutsk, where later that year Directory clerks also struck against the Bolsheviks. The closest parallel in Ukraine to the Petrograd administrators' strike was in Kharkiv and Katerynoslav, where administrators refused to recognize the Bolsheviks for weeks after they had dissolved the city dumas. In Kharkiv the Post and Telegraph Workers Union persisted despite having been 'dissolved' by pro-Bolshevik splinter groups that then tried to run their offices; Bolsheviks used force to end strikes by other Kharkiv administrators after a few days.[10] In Poltava there appears to have been resistance because one month after the Bolsheviks took over the Post and Telegraph Workers Union issued a uniquely worded declaration pledging its support to 'the proletariat and poor peasants of our beloved Ukraine and fraternal Russia in the struggle against ancient oppressors.'[11] In Oleksandrivske (today Zaporizhzhia) postal and telegraph workers refused to recognize the Bolsheviks for five days until faced with armed troops and the threat of arrest they surrendered.[12]

More detail about reactions to the new rulers and their bureaucracy is available for the year 1919 when Ukraine's Bolshevik government had a more tangible existence. Among those who worked for it was Kyryl Kuzmenko, who decided that he disliked the Directory and in the spring of 1919 fled to his native Bila Tserkva, where under the Bolsheviks he worked as chief of police and then from January 1920 as a clerk in the provincial zemstvo office. A Russian born in Kharkiv with passive knowledge of Ukrainian, Nikolai Nikolaevsky had a law degree from the city's university; working in the provincial legal office from 1911 to 1917, he then joined the Union of Towns where he worked until 1919, when he became a secretary in the Soviet government's Justice Committee. Aged fifty-two, Nikolai Listov, also a Kharkiv-born Russian who knew Ukrainian, was a teacher before the First World War; between 1917 and 1921 he worked through all the political changes as an administrator in the city duma. Sofiia Polotska, aged twenty-seven and a stenographer, worked for a private company in Poltava through 1917; according to her employment application form from January 1918 through to 1921 she worked in the Finance Ministry offices in Kharkiv. However, since Kharkiv was under the Hetman until the end of 1918, unless she was in exile with the Bolshevik government, she must have been working for the national government before joining its rival – a possibility confirmed by the presence of a Soviet confirmation of loyalty in her dossier.[13] Records of 138 staffers of the Kyiv district zemstvo just after the Bolsheviks took over in March 1919 show that fifty-nine were women and sixty had been at their jobs since before March 1917. Among them were Petro Kramar, Tetiana Gorbunova, Vira Vintskovska, Ivan Troshchansky, Iakiv Stepanchenko, and Iakiv Sviridov. Vasyl Klokosos, Oleksandra Kuzminsky, Fedir Borodenko, Zotyk Korotiuk, and Andrii Rozhko also remained at their desks and worked for the Bolshevik government. A list of seven clerks from one county revkom in Chornobyl district in September 1920 shows that five of them had been had been there since before 1914.[14]

A statement by Vinnytsia district council administrators reflected another practice. On the eve of the Bolshevik takeover there, in March 1919, they pledged that they would work in Soviet institutions where they would defend and protect 'the institutions of self-rule' to the best of their abilities. Most were still there when the Directory returned four months later; what they actually did during the next Bolshevik occupation is not known.[15] In Zhytomir clerks kept working but did not recognize the Bolsheviks. In Cherkasy all twenty-two postal and telegraph workers were pro-Rada but continued working under the Bolsheviks in order to protect the equipment; with the approach of Ukrainian and German forces they all got their guns and helped chase away the Reds. Bureaucrats in Radomyshl stayed put when the Bolsheviks came, as did those in Bila Tserkva, who in addition, kept new Bolshevik appointees out.[16]

Of the 189 staff members in the Directory's Ministry of Justice, 159 remained and worked for the Bolsheviks when they took Kyiv in February 1919; of the Ordinary Tax Department's 137 employees, seventy-five remained in Kyiv, and of these twelve were original staffers from April 1918. Together with most of the employees of the Agriculture and Food Supply ministries, a total of 2,000 western Ukrainian administrators stayed behind.[17] Junior state chancery employees who stayed thought to secure their jobs under the Bolsheviks by forming the Union of Former State Chancery Employees and they elected Alexei Tatishchev, who just happened to be in the building at the time, head of its revkom. In the confusion of the first days of occupation Tatishchev was arrested, managed to escape, and then got himself a job in Kyiv city hall, via an old tsarist acquaintance, who was working there for the Bolsheviks; later he moved to Kharkiv, where he was employed as a clerk in a co-operative.[18]

The Bolsheviks arrived in Kyiv on 3 February 1919 and declared that all officials who did not report to work within ten days would be fired. On 12 February newspapers reported that while senior personnel had fled, taking all their typewriters with them, almost all of the staff in the Agriculture, Food Supply, Finance, Transportation and Roads, Railways, Education, and Land ministries remained, as did those of the Kyiv province zemstvo. In the Land Ministry, Ukrainian SR union leaders expelled all non-socialist employees. The 800 employees in the Ministry of Food Supply supposedly did nothing except take care of themselves, collect their pay, and steal from their warehouses.[19] Cheka reports confirm that the entire staffs of the Ministry of Internal Affairs and the Jewish Affairs Ministry continued to go to work, the employees in the Directory's Political Administrative Department of its Ministry of Internal Affairs were 'very eager to work,' and they added, except for some in the Land and Education ministries, these officials engaged in sabotage. Former Directory officials were also condemned for drinking and beating people up.[20] The Bolshevik Workers and Peasants Inspectorate with a staff of 150 in May 1920 grew to 324 in October 1921 and to 4,011 eight months later; of these 342 had worked for the tsarist government's Labour Inspectorate.[21] Detailed figures are also available on personnel from the central offices of the Directory's Ministry of Transportation and Roads: of a staff of 827, 489 (59%) remained in Kyiv in March 1919; pay lists, including 186 names, reveal that almost all were probably Ukrainians, and at least 32 per cent were women.[22] In their January 1919 report to Lenin Ukraine's Bolshevik leaders stated that an estimated 6,000 clerks had remained in Kyiv after the Directory had fled, and all of them would be incorporated into their administration. Despite the presence of all these people, however, the only institution that apparently functioned more or less as it was supposed to was the army.[23] A considerable number of Russian-speaking Soviet bureaucrats who had earlier manned the Hetman's desks seem to have changed sides willingly in December 1918, and they allegedly were the principal target of Soviet decrees that attempted to make the Bolshevik bureaucracy in Ukraine function in Ukrainian in 1919.[24] All of the republic's Telegraph Agency staff except for the director remained. The Bolsheviks put a Russian in charge, who then began replacing his Ukrainian subordinates with other Russians, who refused to either work in or learn Ukrainian and called Ukrainians 'chauvinists' for speaking Ukrainian; this, in turn, led Ukrainians to resign in disgust.[25]

Although holdovers seemed to dominate in all of the urban offices, the situation varied in small towns and villages. According to a December 1920 list of sixty revkom staff from Skvyra district in Kyiv province, none of the twenty village secretaries appear to have had their jobs before that June. Similarly, all of the seven clerks in the Kaharlyk county *vykonkom* (Ukr.; Russ. *ispolkom,* meaning executive committee) were apparently hired after 1920. In four of the counties for which there are records in Proskuriv district, the same men worked as clerks both before and after the Bolshevik occupation in May 1919.[26] A report in a Ukrainian Communist newspaper from Volyn province gives valuable insight into how the Bolsheviks established village administrations in 1919. First one or more outside agitators/instructors would arrive and recruit people to form a party cell whose members then formed the local revkom and appointed one of themselves as commissar. Informed of this meeting the people would then leave wondering what their elected soviet was supposed to do. Most often, according to the article, it was the local village secretary and two or three local clerks who ended up in the new government and, once in power, they would arrest the local Ukrainian teacher, restrict the activities of the local Ukrainian cultural group, and then begin requisitioning from everybody except themselves and their relatives.[27] In the spring of 1919 after Ukrainian left-wing SRs (*Borotbists*) allied with the Bolsheviks had taken the south-central Ukrainian provinces from the Directory, they apparently could find no administrative personnel in villages because these people had fled with the Directory. Forced to tolerate Bolshevik or Bolshevik-appointed bureaucrats, whose arbitrary brutality compromised their authority, these Ukrainian Communists were overthrown that summer, together with their Russian comrades, as the populace saw little if any difference between the two.[28]

Functioning

Reports from 1919 and 1920 indicate that in the territories they held Bolshevik administrative control during the first months of their rule was tenuous, much as was the Directory's control over its territory. Until such time as they could dominate the soviets what little authority the Bolsheviks could exercise had to be either through revkoms or Committees of Poor Peasants. In some areas there was no government at all for months after the Red Army left. As of early 1919 one editor observed that outside a 20 kilometre radius of Kyiv and more than 5 to 8 kilometres beyond railway tracks there was no government at all and that 75 per cent of Kyivan publications never got beyond the city's borders. A letter signed by Stalin, as well as the head of Ukraine's SNK Khristian Rakovsky and the head of its revkom Hryhorii Petrovsky circulated throughout Ukraine in March 1920 and revealed that overlapping authorities and rivalries were not limited to the UNR. These three leaders emphatically demanded that government, party, and military officials stop working at odds with each other and co-operate else they undermine Bolshevik rule.[29] The official Interior Ministry annual report, dated March 1921, stated that only in January 1921 could Ukraine's government finally claim that it controlled to the district level all Ukraine – then divided into twelve provinces, fifty-one districts, and 651 counties. Although cities had soviets they did not have a separate administration but were subordinated administratively to the provincial *vykonkom*. By the summer of 1919, nonetheless, the last of Ukraine's clerks were being incorporated into a new centralized union of public employees (*Vserossiiskii professionalni soiuz rabotnikov sovetskikh obshchestvennykh i torgovykh uchrezhdennii*), whose Ukrainian branch had called its first congress that May.

A rare glimpse of provincial staff and offices is provided by Fedir Kyrychuk, who wrote his memoirs in 1957. Graduating from Vinnytsia Teachers College in 1906, he was unable to finish Kyiv's Commerical Institute because of poverty. In 1913 he began work as a clerk in the Liatychiv district zemstvo in Podillia province, where he remained until 1919, by which time he was chief accountant. Unfortunately, Kyrychuk relates nothing about his activities during those years, but he must have worked for all the national governments. Although he never joined the Bolshevik party he was sympathetic to their cause, and with their arrival in his town in March 1919 he became the head of the local Land Office, head of the district's union of public employees, and in 1921 head of the local Workers and Peasants Inspectorate. Kyrychuk claimed that since he never got any instructions from his superiors he had to act exclusively on his own initiative. When the Liatychiv revkom office was destroyed and the town itself was retaken by the Directory, its staff of approximately 200 apparently left for the nearest neighbouring town, where they remained for the next six months until the Bolsheviks returned. Kyrychuk describes how he worked in offices so cold that ink froze and forms had to be written by pencil, and because pay was so low few of the clerks were willing to stay on the job. Having run out of paper by 1919, into the early 1920s staff used the blank side of documents from local archives – until they too were all used up.[30]

Vasyl Korenchuk explained to interrogators in the winter of 1920 that eight months earlier, after having returned home to Malyn, he had decided that the Bolsheviks best represented poor workers like himself, and so he became involved with his county's Committee of Poor Peasants, of which he became secretary. Not working during the short Polish occupation, he nonetheless helped local Communists hide and, when the Bolsheviks returned, took up his previous position. An extant collection of seventeen Kharkiv district executive committee members' dossiers from November 1920 shows that the only member who had clerical experience was its head of administration, who from 1914 had worked at a regimental hospital and then as a clerk for the Kharkiv soviet.[31] Clearly, there was staff carryover from national to Bolshevik regimes, but the scattered evidence gives no hint of its scale.

Although by the autumn of 1920 Kyiv provincial officials perhaps were doing what they were supposed to be doing, that summer Bolshevik leaders had no illusions about how questionable their control was in the other territories that they claimed, where not only provincial government officials but also those of the Workers and Peasants Inspectorate were apparently helpless. The former ignored the latter, complained the agents of the latter, who reported that investigative documents simply disappeared and that they 'sometimes got replies that are impermissible within the walls of Soviet offices.' Inspectors characterized the affairs of Kharkiv provincial offices as chaotic, and in their own offices in Kharkiv problems ranged from illegible writing in documents to no statistics in the reports submitted by the Food Supply Committee and no register of correspondence in the Legal Section.[32] In Kyiv city hall three months after the Bolsheviks took power offices had funds, were filled with personnel, and punishments included the death penalty, but no one really knew what anyone was doing, theft by heads was rampant, and millions were distributed on the basis of handwritten notes like 'Comrade Pavlov got an advance from Kanzi for. ... ' Confiscated items ranging from nails to tractors, taken from tens of thousands of acres of nationalized land, lay un-itemized in a city storage area, unused, and while arrangements were made to give them to collectives, the peasants from whom they were taken could not farm. In the villages of Poltava province during the summer of 1920 soviet or Poor Peasants Committee chairmen and vykonkom personnel retreated for safety to the woods at night taking their telephones with them so that they would have them in the morning. During the day they were careful to 'function so as not to suffer [reprisals] from either [their own local] soviet or bandits [i.e., anti-Bolshevik partisans].'[33]

Although in theory revkoms were supposed to immediately begin organizing administration, in practice, a shortage of personnel and/or funds meant that for weeks after the Red Army left a region local inhabitants were often free to administer themselves if they had the will to do so. During the summer of 1919 Communist Party reports list Kremenchuk, Poltava, and Huliai-Pole districts as ones without any Soviet administration. Another report that autumn claims that Bolshevik rear areas in most of eastern Ukraine actually were under Makhno's control. Tiraspol that summer had two revkoms that annulled each other's decrees.[34] In Trostianets district in Podillia province within a few weeks of the arrival of the Bolsheviks the revkom created chaos and pogroms. Two party instructors, who arrived in the wake of the army to organize the revkom and were unable to bring men with them, found no local party members: they ended up taking a local Pole, an emigre Jew just returned from America, one ex-convict, a Ukrainian Directory army officer, a drunk with no known political affiliations, and a man who happened to be in the room where the selecting was going on.[35] The Volyn provincial revkom reported in February 1920 that Red troops during the two to three weeks that they had been garrisoned in area towns had so pillaged, fouled, and damaged them so that not only could they not be occupied by troops following, but that local workers refused to enter the premises to clean or repair them except in return for astronomical wages. Local leaders begged that pillaging be declared tantamount to sabotage and counterrevolution and subject to the death penalty. In such conditions, understandably, administration was not possible. Not only was there almost no staff in June 1920, there were no wages or rations for the few employees that were there, nor paper, nor typewriters. Only in early August could office work begin.[36] In Novomoskovsk district in May 1919 peasants wandered for weeks from office to office looking for someone who could provide them with wood for rebuilding. Four months after the Red Army took Chornobyl an inspector reported that despite having lots of cash its local administration was in chaos. The secretary of Kremenchuk in November 1921 informed Kharkiv that eight months after the last hostile forces had been expelled from the area its administration existed only on paper and could do nothing. In right-bank territories during the autumn of 1921 county executive committee personnel changed weekly because no one wanted to take responsibility for implementing orders. As a result the Bolsheviks either gave the Cheka the task of administration or instituted the practice of 'decimation' (*desiatnyky*), whereby one man in ten was given responsibility for ensuring that recruits and supplies were delivered, and if he failed he was shot and his goods and property were confiscated. Locals who decided to take Soviet office jobs were despised by their neighbours, but they were not seen as perpetrators while they sat out of sight in offices. Ironically, insofar as they did not get paid and their rations were not delivered for months, sometimes those who initially weren't hostile became hostile to the government they worked for.[37] In the eastern Luhansk region after almost a year under Bolshevik rule a Communist Party report characterized local officials as either 'rotten intellectuals' or petty traders. Politically indifferent or anti-Bolshevik they were divided between supporters of the Whites, the Directory, and the Mensheviks, and worked from fear and want.

In the summer of 1919 village committees within a day's walk of Kyiv simply chased away Bolshevik officials using arms, if necessary, and then carried on as they had before. One such official relates that he managed to inspect his assigned area because he travelled alone, could speak Ukrainian, and told the peasants he was not a Communist. Nor did the prefix 'soviet' mean that councils were Bolshevik. Just after the Bolsheviks took most of Podillia province from the Directory in June 1919 inspectors complained that offices were filled with corrupt anti-Bolshevik bureaucrats sabotaging policies. While Communist department heads were hiring 'bourgeois girls,' the staff of the War Commissariat were all buying items from army quartermaster stores at officially fixed prices, while soldiers had to buy where they could at market prices. We are fortunate to have the reports of a Bolshevik plenipotentiary/inspector who travelled Chernihiv province just after it was taken by his army, and then again six months later, just before the Whites took it. In January 1919, he observed, none of the staff from the first Bolshevik administration in the province (from ten months earlier) was still there and that other than some little contact with the capital in Kharkiv the establishment of a bureaucracy was impeded by local agents of central Moscow ministries who were ignoring the officials placed by Kharkiv. To remedy the situation he ordered all local revkoms to ignore Moscow's ministries and arrest their agents. Six months later some district capitals were regularly reporting to the provincial capital, but overall administrative control from the provincial capital was weak and below the county level, almost non-existent. In Sosnytsia county both the Cheka and the local police officer had to be arrested for corruption and extortion, while the local Communist Party bureaucrats were inactive because they were always drunk. The inspector reported, on the one hand, that mobilization for the army that summer was successful but, on the other hand, that the provincial military committee in charge of it was not yet organized. This seeming contradiction is explained by his account of how mobilization was done. Apparently, initially as many as half of the recruits sent by train to their mobilization points deserted at the earliest opportunity, while recruits who did arrive there soon left thanks to the efforts of anti-Bolshevik agitators. Turnout improved once local officials began surrounding newly arrived draftees with armed troops, shooting agitators, and making local village officials responsible for any of their draftees who did not appear at the mobilization point.[38]

Conscription was declared in March 1919 but, where supplies did exist for arrivals, they were insufficient. The Red Army was no better supplied than its rivals and, like UNR soldiers Red soldiers sold their arms, rations, and uniforms. Turnout varied, as in the UNR; overall, perhaps between 30 and 50 per cent of those called up appeared. Supposedly in February and March the turnout was acceptable in the four eastern and southern Soviet-controlled provinces, yet in Zhytomir district, taken by the Bolsheviks in March 1919, no recruits at all appeared that July.[39] In Kyiv and Chernihiv provinces no more than 25 per cent of those drafted actually arrived at their units. Conscripts that summer refused to proceed to the Red Army in Chernihiv and Katerynoslav provinces because they got no uniforms, clothes, arms, or family assistance. The Chernihiv recruits said that they refused to fight until the Bolsheviks removed all the Jews, Lenin, and Trotsky from power. In Kharkiv that summer, of the 619 men on muster rolls 331 appeared, and only 190 were actually sent to the army. In Katerynoslav province during the first half of 1920 turnout averaged between 25 and 60 per cent.[40] Support for Red Army wives and widows was declared two weeks before the draft, but that May we find complaints from Katerynoslav province that soldiers' wives were not getting their allowances because local officials were spending the allotted money on administrative matters; by 1920 soldiers' families in Kyiv province, however, were getting at least some of their promised benefits.[41]

Ukraine's SNK does not appear to have been more effective in obtaining recruits and food through 1919 and 1920 than was the Directory. In 1919 seventy-one armed requisition squads, with a total of anywhere between 55,000 and 85,000 men, were supposed to seize 2,300 million kilograms of grain and direct 820 million kilograms of that to Russia. Forty-six of these squads sent all of their grain to Russia. Overall, they got no more than 14 per cent of their target of which no more than 49 million kilograms went to Russia. In June 1919 four army food supply detachments reported that they had spent two futile months trying to obtain grain from peasants who apparently refused both cash and manufactured goods. Another report describes the food shortage in towns as being so critical that one army commander in Lozova, near Poltava, in contradiction to Bolshevik policy issued a decree forbidding any restrictions whatsoever on prices or free trade.[42] Throughout 1918 Lenin instructed his subordinates to show no mercy to Russians who opposed requisitioning, but his instructions to his officials in Ukraine in July 1920 were unprecedented: in face of the truce with Poland, he ordered the armies of the Caucasian front to plan a march through Ukraine so that they would enter each of its 1,900 counties twice to requisition by force – and to return a third time to those counties that proved particularly 'stubborn.' While even in Russia proper the Bolsheviks used 40 per cent of their army against peasants in their rear, this order seems to have had no parallel in Russia and does suggest that Russian Bolsheviks considered Ukraine to be an occupied foreign territory subject to plunder by right of conquest.[43]

Minutes from Kyiv province local council meetings in the months following the Polish invasion of 1920 suggest that in conditions of shortages, which included everything from pay to clothes and ink, bureaucrats were, at best, sometimes doing some of things they should have been doing – much like their Directory counterparts. Inspectors' reports, to the contrary, charge that those same bureaucrats were doing very little, if anything. Interestingly, both reveal that as of 1921 there were still county-level offices without typewriters. In Zvenyhorod district in the beginning of that year the government could not supply local offices with ink, pencils, or paper – so local officials had to buy in local markets, although this was illegal.[44] In Malyn district the inspector bluntly wrote that nothing was being done and that offices were filled with incompetent people who had no idea of what they were supposed to do or how to do it. Inspectors' reports from Tarashcha district describe offices filled with people doing nothing and note that services and administration existed only on the papers that those bureaucrats sent to their superiors. Orders from the county capital for village activists to re-elect soviets and start carrying out orders, or face arrest, as revealed by another report that spring, were ignored. Analogously, in Hostomel county peasants were still ignoring the Bolsheviks in March 1920, two months after the Directory was evicted from there; only by the end of the year did the local administration in Hostomel appear to have been functioning.[45]

In accord with Lenin's dictum about control via employment, in Kyiv in 1919 the Bolsheviks 'truly built government bureaus without restraint.' Particularly numerous were 'educational sections' which the educated willingly entered after they had stopped trying to sabotage the new regime. Like statistics and welfare, educational units were considered 'neutral' and were part not only of the Ministry of Education, but of every other ministry, because they all had libraries or reading rooms, and printing, cinema, and 'enlightenment' sections. Although many such sections actually did nothing 'educational,' that was not the point.[46] Thousands of educated people coming daily into the rooms, sitting there, and registered for housing, rations, and pay may have been disgruntled, but they were passive and under control. A Kyivan Jewish student noted that the bureaucracy grew endlessly, with five clerks that year doing what one had done before the war, and 'unfortunately, the ranks of this bureaucracy are filled, primarily, by bourgeois youth, chiefly Jews.'[47]

The common route to a government job was through personal contacts. In Kyiv offices were filled with 'merchants and homeowners,' who had obtained clerical staff identification cards and, once hired, had then proceeded to hire as many of their friends and relatives as they could, as 'specialists.' Overstaffing was rife. Simple typists were recorded as 'specialists' and thus received more pay than the normal clerks. Few reported the irregularities, and even so it was apparently impossible to actually arrest anyone because those concerned inevitably had some commissar or party member ready to defend them. The entire staff of some vykonkoms, who were outsiders to the town where they worked, as in Vasylkiv, would be related to each other on a personal or family level, and thus people fired would be subsequently rehired by the same department. In January 1920 Kyiv's Communal Housing Department was ordered to purge itself of 'counter-revolutionaries.' In true dialectical fashion the department decided to declare all of its employees officially dismissed but still on the job (*zvilnenymy ale zalyshaiuchymsia* [*sic*]).[48] 'One of my wife's distant relatives ... sat through all the regimes in a "neutral" economics-related office,' wrote one observer. 'He is sitting there now – only its name has been slightly changed. He strongly urges me to join.' This writer's job involved setting ration norms, which as he and everyone else in his office knew, bore no relationship to reality because there was no food to be rationed. Approximately half of the twenty-five people under him were file clerks and typists who had nothing to do until the norms were actually tabulated. Sabotage, he continued, was very rare and did not even cross the minds of the young secretaries. Others considered it futile since 'in half a year' Denikin would be in Moscow, or so they believed. People worked carelessly without interest because everyone realized that their tasks were meaningless. In April 1920 nobody did any work at all in Izium county offices because there was no paper.[49] When the Bolsheviks were evacuating Kyiv in August 1919, however, the 'Soviet ladies' of the personnel department exhibited exceptional ardour when they worked through the night destroying personnel lists.[50] As in Russia, the Cheka in Ukraine considered former tsarist officials unreliable by virtue of their origins, created files on them, and kept them under surveillance.[51]

Graft, theft, corruption, and dysfunctioning were rampant. During the five-week Bolshevik occupation of Chernihiv in early 1918 local officials retained their office committees, and the idea of socialized offices with elected leaders, which took root initially under the Rada, 'entrenched itself deeper in employees' consciousness.' Although heads remained responsible for their offices, the employees' committees did the work, but according to Krainsky (the local prisons inspector), there was no longer any clear authority.[52] Official reports the following year refer to administrative chaos – 'a bacchanalia' within which petty affairs took days to settle. Antonov-Ovseenko wrote that in the summer of 1919 offices were full of staff doing nothing but moving paper around.[53] In Kyiv a sub-section of a central ministry sub-section was established in April 1919 with approximately 200 staff to register and distribute confiscated furniture to workers. After two months of work an inspector reported that little had been confiscated because the wealthy had managed to obtain exemption letters, while what was confiscated was not duly registered and ended up in the homes and offices of staff members, with the head of the department in which this particular office worked having the finest items of the lot. Bolshevik clerks in Vinnytsia fleeing Directory troops in August 1919 desperately carted away with them wagonloads of gramophones and recorded cylinders – ignoring trainloads of boots and other valuable supplies standing in the town's railway yard at the time.[54] An official report on the achievements of the Interior Ministry's Housing Department during its first five months of work has a list of some fifteen points, none of which mention the building or repairing of housing.[55] The commandant of the Kharkiv military district in July 1920 complained to central leaders that his engineering department could not obtain necessary stores despite a formal order issued over a year earlier to the departments concerned that military materiel was to have priority. Regardless of the order and protests the various departments persisted in dealing with military orders as they did with all others, in sequence, which led to nothing being issued, complaints, ready items being undelivered, and an endless circulation of papers that eventually ended up in their office of origin.[56]

Bolshevik leaders resorted to a number of measures to try and establish order. They hoped that local Communist Party members could keep offices working properly. As of April 1919 they decided that all offices were no longer only to have an employees' committee, but that all party members there had to form a collective and appoint a 'bureau' of three to six individuals that between bi-weekly meetings was to exercise daily control. One of these bureau members had to be on the non-party office committee, and he had the right of final decision on all matters decided by the committee. Besides controlling all hiring and firing the party collective reported weekly to the local soviet or revkom, promulgated Bolshevik propaganda, recruited new staff, supervised office discipline, and strictly controlled the non-party committee.[57] In June 1919 the party decided to reduce total office staff by 25 per cent. Bolshevik leaders also used the Cheka in offices – in marked difference to the national governments. On 20 August in Zvenyhorod district, three months after Polish forces had been repulsed and where counties still ignored orders, the local military commander decreed that all disobedience and negligence would be treated as sabotage.[58] The clerks' union condemned the 'exceptionally low productivity' of office staff in July 1919 and published a regulation detailing such disciplinary measures as sign-in attendance and firing for absenteeism. On 1 August, in face of the opposition of its Russian parent body, the Ukrainian branch of this union reintroduced the eight-hour day for office staff.[59] In Katerynoslav during the terror of 1920 an eyewitness wrote that offices were filled with hungry officials 'held in the iron pincers of Soviet discipline and under the clandestine observation of Cheka agents.'[60] In September 1920 the Chornobyl district commissar ordered that a Communist Party member be present in all county offices, with the authority to enforce 'merciless administrative repression' – which included publication in newspapers of incidents involving breaches of discipline.[61]

The party instituted daily reports in March 1920 but by that autumn leaders decided to impose a standard quantitative format because local officials were sending them reams of rubbish. By the end of the year all counties had to fill out detailed monthly forms on 'building the Soviet order.' These contained eighty-four categories for which numerical totals had to be shown and included items such as total hours spent on meetings, ratings of staff performance, and personnel totals. Local vykonkoms and revkoms, once established, compiled detailed monthly situation reports, using numbers on standardized forms to indicate frequency and efficiency. The subjects reported on included everything from partisan raids, police activity, and public health, to self-assessments and Poor Peasants Committees.[62] There was nothing comparable in the national governments, where office-level coercion practically did not exist, where new tasks were fewer, and where tasks were devolved to non-government organizations like co-operatives. Submitting false information subjected local officials to prosecution. In the wake of the failed 1920 Polish-Ukrainian offensive, orders were issued in Kyiv province requiring the registration of all residents, then all foreigners, then unions, then all co-ops, then all unemployed, then all employed, then all former nobles and tsarist officials, which meant that hundreds if not thousands of clerks were compiling, checking, classifying, copying, and cross-referencing endless lists of people. Control over the clerks, who used their public powers for their private purposes whenever possible, led to more detailed lists of rules and regulations and duties and more officials to draw up and enforce them. Rules included things like specifying that all offices had to have sign-in sheets, anyone more than ten minutes late for work was to be punished, all official trips had to be strictly controlled, all offices had to compile and submit weekly protocols, and local officials were responsible for repossessing stolen railway station clocks. These orders poured out of Bolshevik offices despite explicit instructions to use as little paper as possible. Extant records suggest that this massive wave of instructions, regulations, and decrees that poured into local offices from central organs within weeks of the re-establishment of Soviet control over a region, and then became a flood after a few months, was not equaled in any national government.

In a vicious circle more staff produced more paper, which in turn led to bureaucrats demanding more staff to deal with it. In July 1920 the staff of the Donets district Food Supply Committee, which increased in number from 212 to 332 that month, received one item of correspondence every five minutes of each working day and sent one item out every three minutes.[63] That year between September and November the number of cases coming into the administrative section of the Kyiv province revkom increased from 1,481 to 2,066. In 1921 the Volyn Provincial Court office processed an average of 1,300 letters in and out every month, fifty-two each working day; the volume at the Ministry of Education increased from 2,140 letters in the month of January to 4,540 a month by November.[64] Bolshevik rules of office procedure and control, including staff limits, were not matched by any national government – none of which had an equivalent to the Workers and Peasants Inspectorate, either. This huge Bolshevik bureaucracy with thousands of officials who were not necessarily obeyed by others, and who were not particularly efficient, was an organization that did at least leave a fairly detailed record of sloth that historians should not ignore when judging the achievements of the Directory.[65] In desperation local executive committee chairmen would issue decrees that included placing bureaucrats under martial law and threatening them with death if they did not work eight hours without breaks or as required.[66] Cheka reports on bureaucrats in Kharkiv suggest that even severe penalties did not appreciably change behaviour. In March 1921, in response to food shortages and delays in pay, lateness and inactivity in that city's offices had become a norm – an almost obligatory form of behaviour among staff. Most either did not come to work at all, or they would sign in and then leave after a few hours. The average rate of attendance at work was no more than 60 per cent. The entire staff of the Interior Ministry was categorized as apathetic and engaged in mass sabotage. The man in charge of the Telegraph Department was a monarchist, who apparently had been at his job since 1917; he staffed his office with his relatives who, like most everyone else, did not come to work either.[67]

Office behaviour in Bolshevik Ukraine during the revolutionary period can be judged in light of three conditions. First, in November and December 1919 in Kharkiv clerks and the educated in general were dying from starvation.[68] Because of food shortages in the summer of 1921 in Kharkiv, Donetsk, and Katerynoslav office workers were not getting rations for as much as two months running, and malnutrition resulted in less work being done. At the height of the shortage, just before the 1921 famine in southern Ukraine, there were no more reports of starvation, but besides grumbling and working to rule, hunger also drove clerks to leave their offices en masse to engage in street trading or to quit for jobs in what remained of the private sector. From May through to September that year government offices were frequently empty in these provinces. Although staff still feared arrest in Mykolaiv and Donetsk, Cheka reports list strong anti-Communist attitudes and sabotage among government administrators – with no reasons given. Second, while the Cheka apparently had enough informers to survey staff, it probably did not have enough agents to make mass arrests, because at the end of 1921 the organization was reduced in size from 34,000 to 18,000, including secret operatives. Third, as in Russia, staff soon realized that unless they got involved in outright treasonous activity, the local Cheka would most likely turn a blind eye to the dubious activities that people engaged in only to survive. Thus, in March 1922 in Zaporizhzhia province, Izrail Borisevich, who made no secret of his dislike of Communists, paid no attention to his workmates who whispered to him to watch his mouth: 'I spit on all of them,' he shouted back.[69]

Government inspectors were often as badly off and indifferent to their tasks as were all other employees. So staff, when they did come to work, spent most of their time using their positions to see to their own needs and only then to those of the citizens – and preferably of those who could pay bribes. One office in Kharkiv that reportedly did function more or less as it was supposed to was that of the Food Supply Committee. But it appears to have done so because 75 per cent of its employees were former private merchants and businessmen who, while themselves working for the government, had set up their wives in the city markets and thus could manage to survive and work without complaints. The situation in small towns was no different through 1921. In November of that year Huliai-Pole Cheka reports identify strong discontent among city clerks because their offices were unheated; however, they do not mention hunger, although peasants in the surrounding countryside were dying of starvation. Normally indifferent and apathetic, by 1921 bureaucrats expressed distinctly hostile attitudes towards the new regime whenever they discussed rations and pay. Nevertheless, 1921 secret police situation reports mention only one instance of clerks threatening to go so far as to strike because they had not received their rations.[70] Whether Ukraine's bureaucrats were better off than their Russian counterparts is unclear – and they do not seem to have published a Ukrainian variant of Petrograd's *Tribuna*.

Ukraine's Bolsheviks were divided over whether or not Ukraine should constitute a territory with a government clearly autonomous from Moscow.

In January 1918, for instance, Ukrainian Bolsheviks in the Kharkiv city soviet complained about Red Russian troops and issued a resolution stating that 'all troops who come to Ukraine from the north' had to be subject to Ukraine's People's Secretariat.[71] Moscow's Bolsheviks, for their part, considered 'Soviet Ukraine' to be merely part of the Russian Socialist Federal Soviet Republic and exploited Ukraine's formal status only to consolidate their rule over it. When this was no longer possible in April 1918 Stalin told the local Ukrainians: 'You have played enough at being a government and a republic, that's it, time to end the game.' The next spring the newly arrived Bolshevik government was dominated by Moscow appointees and the Ukrainian Bolshevik Dmytro Manuilsky frankly referred to the Ukrainians in it as mere decoration – like the natives that colonial powers invited to join local administration.[72] When stiff opposition finally convinced Russian leaders that they had to offer some autonomy to their Ukrainian republic in November 1919, the resulting agreement resembled the Temporary Instruction of August 1917. Alongside internal affairs, agriculture, justice, food supply, and education, the Ukrainian Soviet Socialist Republic formally got newly formed health and welfare departments. It included all Ukraine's provinces, instead of only five, and Ukrainian was to be the language of administration. However, unlike the Rada in 1917, Ukraine's SNK did not control finance, the economy, or labour, and the local Bolsheviks were part of a single centralized Communist Party based in a foreign country. A Russian Communist Party decision from January 1920 allowed its Ukrainian branch to appoint in reality only three commissars – justice, education, and agriculture.[73]

Ukraine's SNK had no control over its own finances or economy. Its Red Army throughout 1919 was primarily a partisan formation most of whose troops came from Russia and whose leaders were wary of recruiting Ukrainians in Ukraine. The few separate Ukrainian military formations that did exist got less pay than Russian formations in Russia, fewer provisions, and fewer arms from Moscow, while Russian formations sent from Russia were armed and provisioned.[74] The police in Ukraine was also Russified in 1919. Two ministers complained in a letter to Moscow that because the police were demoralized, were local, and could not deal with anti-Bolshevik threats, they had to be totally subordinated to Moscow. In an official Interior Ministry account of its history, compiled in March 1921, we read that because approximately 50 per cent of Ukraine's police force served under the tsar and General Denikin, 3,610 policemen were imported from Russia to reinforce it.[75] Throughout 1920, as in 1919, most of Ukraine was, in practice, still administered by revkoms directly from Moscow. In 1920, of all its provincial, district, and county executive committees, 10,310 (56 per cent) were revkoms subject only to Moscow (see Table 10, Appendix 1).[76] Lenin rejected complaints from Ukrainian Communists about the mass export of Russian party members to Ukraine as a breach of party discipline.[77]

The Ukrainian faction within the local Communist Party remained dissatisfied with Ukraine's subordination. The situation was described in their letter of resignation by the Ukrainian Communist minister of housing and his assistant in August 1920. Their ministry, like the rest, was simply a branch of the Russian Communist Party whose officials totally ignored them: 'The administrative division of Ukraine exists only for the eyes of the "citizen" idiot (*hlupaka*).' Formally established in December 1919, and thus existing for six months previous to their arrival in June 1920, their department, nonetheless, had no staff and no offices. The only way that they were able to get staff was via friends, who told them there were some western Ukrainians in Kharkiv – of whom eighteen were promptly hired. With no financing, and a cafeteria that provided only one lunch irregularly, the staff were undernourished and within a month began leaving in search of better jobs in a city where a loaf of bread cost a week's wages. They concluded that the only way to get their ministry functioning was to militarize it.[78]

Staffing

In general, between 1917 and 1925 an initial massive increase in the number of bureaucrats, as compared with tsarist times, was followed by a slow decline. Incomplete figures from four provinces in 1920 indicate that there were a total of 19,700 local officials (over double the 1897 total of 9,300 for the same provinces).[79] The staff of Ukraine's nineteen central ministries and central vykonkoms totalled 21,398 in May 1921. During the first half of that year the central staff of the Post and Telegraph and the Education ministries numbered 285. The staff of Ukraine's SNK numbered 4,540. The postal and telegraph office staff in the provinces of Chernihiv, Katerynoslav, Poltava, and Kharkiv numbered 150, 135, 148, and 230 respectively. The central staff of the Workers and Peasants Inspectorate, intended to supervise the bureaucracy, included 374 people. The Volyn Provincial Court offices included forty-seven people, of whom twelve were judges and attorneys.[80] All of these totals were subsequently reduced by a commission established in March 1921 to deal with inefficiency and overstaffing (*Kommissiia po uproshcheniiu sovetskogo apparata*) – whose own staff by that November was reduced to 165 from the 191 in July; this total included thirteen chauffeurs and four helpers, ten janitors, thirteen typists, seven telephone operators, and six section heads. The commission also had a barbershop, cobbler, and cafeteria. Its first step was to set up nine academics in two research teams to study the government bureaucracy, which, however, leaders decided to abolish four months later because they were displeased with the slow pace of research. Their final report identified incompetence, overstaffing, and a lack of systematization as major problems in the bureaucracy and included a description of its size and volumes of paperwork.[81] The commission pointed out that the increased scope of government activity in Europe had led to larger bureaucracies and that Europeans were coping with the same problems as the Bolsheviks.[82]

Although the Hetman's officials had all the office space they needed, observers noted that the Bolsheviks never did.[83] Like their rivals Bolshevik leaders had to cope with numerous educated men seeking government employment to avoid military service. Unlike the national governments the Bolsheviks were able to systematize and control their hiring. Within days of reoccupying Kyiv in 1919 Communist Party leaders first declared that enterprises and offices could hire only via government employment offices and then ordered members who worked as administrators to form party cells in their offices. In two weeks, at their first meeting, these activists complained that their offices were still hiring, although they were overfilled with officials left over from all previous governments who were quietly sabotaging the new government. The meeting resolved to begin questioning and registering all bureaucrats and firing 'hostile elements.'[84] Unlike their rivals the Bolsheviks engaged in mass campaigns of government hiring and firing. The statization of almost every activity and the use of government employment as a means of control massively increased the numbers of workers in innumerable offices who were to do endless new tasks that did not exist before 1914 – like a bureau to distribute railway tickets and another to plan the distribution of labour and tasks during voluntary Saturday work days (*subotniki*). The longer that Bolshevik rule lasted, the more duties did the endless demands for control create. Concern over sabotage, corruption, disloyalty, and an ideological commitment to 'abolish the state,' on the other hand, produced dismissals.

Investigative reporters in 1919 were already complaining about the size of the government. A 20 July item in the paper *Nachalo* that year observed that whereas before the war Petersburg had between 25,000 and 30,000 officials, Moscow now had 193,000. The writer cited no figures for Kyiv but, after giving some examples of his personal experiences in the city, concluded that 'bureaucrats remain bureaucrats under all regimes (*pri vsiakom rezhime*).' On the other hand, early 1919 figures from Poltava's Employment Office show that the largest group among the 2,107 registered unemployed were clerks (31%), followed closely by tailors (28%). By the end of 1921, just over a year after the Bolsheviks had conquered the UNR, at least on paper 929,000 employees (including staff in state-owned enterprises) worked for the government in Ukraine. By June 1922 as a result of dismissals and Lenin's New Economic Program (NEP) that number had decreased to 486,000 and included 12,846 central government ministry employees, reduced from 21,398 in July 1921.[85] The earliest census to include all of Ukraine's towns and data on social structure revealed an urban population of just over five million in 1923. Of the 197,712 urban bureaucrats (including clerks in economic enterprises) 20 per cent were female; among secretaries and typists females averaged 30 per cent, and women comprised 37 per cent of postal and telegraph workers.[86] Government bureaucrats comprised 3 per cent of Ukraine's urban population; 4 per cent if we include 37,377 officials in the state-run economy. This was double what it was in 1897, when all urban administrators comprised no more than 2 per cent of Ukraine's urban population, including those in private companies and city Dumas; government bureaucrats alone were 0.4 per cent of the urban population. More detailed 1925 figures on government employment indicate that 57,000 of 309,000 public employees in Ukraine were administrators.[87]

Despite the presence of former UNR employees in Kyiv when they returned in February 1919 the Bolsheviks immediately began creating more jobs, and there was no shortage of applicants for them.[88] I. Rappaport, a native Kyivan, observed that with the arrival of the Bolsheviks that month 'the entire city rushed into service.' He also observed that the extreme Russian right in the city preferred the Bolsheviks to the Whites and implied that those who worked saw their job as a way of surviving until the Bolsheviks collapsed. Being unemployed was not actually dangerous but did involve liability for work details and endless hassles like reporting daily to have a card stamped at an Employment Office. By writing 'I recognize Soviet power' on their application forms people got pay and rations – the 'armoured ration' system had not yet been established – kept their apartments, and were exempted from labour duties and requisitions.[89] People who preferred not to sit in an office were able to survive by trading and selling only for as long the free market existed and they had something to trade or sell, or until one of the decrees stipulating arrest for all members of a given group was issued targeted at their specific group.[90] A Russian who arrived from Moscow in the summer of 1919 noted that people in Kyiv had no sense of what Bolshevik power really meant or what was happening in Russia and regarded Bolsheviks as a group of bandits who had temporarily taken over the city. Although this was the second occupation, and people had experienced summary executions and requisitioning, they were still decently dressed and could shop in stocked private stores; while Muscovites had forgotten about baths and meat, Kyivans complained about sharing bathrooms and occasional meat shortages.[91]

In a letter to Stalin in February 1919 Ukrainian Communist Mykola Poloz drew attention to another problem. Unless local revkoms stopped dissolving non-Bolshevik soviets, imposing only Bolsheviks on them, and stopped persecuting pro-Soviet activists just because they were Ukrainian, he wrote, Ukrainians would see Russian rule as occupation by an armed foreign power. The prevalence of Jews in revkoms and vykonkoms, he continued, alienated the population, who grumbled: 'we expected the Bolsheviks but got instead some kind of Jewish communes.' A personal letter from the Ukrainian assistant to Ukraine's Bolshevik commissar for engineering, written that June, begged Rakovsky to replace Jews with Ukrainian and Russian officials to avoid bloodshed.[92] Two months earlier Grigorii Moroz, one of the twenty-one members of the central Cheka Collegium and himself a Jew, wrote to the Russian Communist Party's Central Committee after an inspection trip in Ukraine that he was shocked beyond description at how people identified Soviet power with Jews and hated Jews as a result. He recommended that Jews be removed from responsible positions and replaced by Russians from Russia. Russian party leader Lev Kamenev made a similar proposal to Lenin in August 1919.[93] Against this background the above-mentioned November Central Committee decision that sanctioned the delineation of Russian and Ukrainian ministries also specifically directed them to begin an energetic campaign to recruit a select group of activists for Ukraine and restrict their intake of secular Jews: 'Take Jews (to be properly referred to as: the Jewish petite bourgeoisie [added in marginal comments]) and urban dwellers in Ukraine firmly in hand,' it continued, 'transfer them [Jews] to the front and don't allow them into the organs of power – except in tiny percentages in exceptional circumstances and under strict class control.' This particular stipulation was substantially revised in the

Resolution on Soviet Power in Ukraine confirmed by the Eighth Russian Communist Party Congress ten days later. This published document did not mention Jews at all, and instead of almost totally excluding 'urban dwellers' (the phrase retained from the resolution as a euphemism for Jews) from the bureaucracy, only stipulated conditions intended to prevent this particular group from 'flooding' Soviet institutions. Continual control remained but competence and loyalty demonstrated primarily at the front became simply one condition of acceptance.[94]

Secular educated Jews represented a valuable source of personnel. Some, radicalized by their pre-war marginalization and persecution, joined the Bolsheviks out of belief. Others worked for them to survive. Although quotas (*evreiskii komplekt*) formally restricted Jews from entering secondary and higher schools before 1917, in practice the number actually enrolled exceeded the quota and, proportionately, of all the Russian Empire's nationalities Jews had the greatest number of literate and educated people. Before 1917 many had found employment in Jewish-owned stores and companies. Excluded from government employment until that year, after 1889 secular Jews had been excluded from the bar except by a special decision of the minister of justice, and after 1912 they had been excluded from becoming apprentice lawyers. Consequently, thousands of Jewish graduates either worked as clerks or notaries in private Jewish companies or as unlicensed legal practitioners (*podpolnaia advokatura*), where they could become familiar with basic office and legal procedures.[95] By 1918 at least 90,000 Jewish refugees had settled in Ukraine east of the Dnipro, and of these, at least 44,000 were non-Ukrainian. Between 1896 and 1923 the number of Jews had doubled in Artemivsk, Oleksandrivsk, Poltava, and Donetsk provinces. Their numbers increased from 32,000 to over 117,000 in Kyiv, from 1,505 to 5,106 in Luhansk, from 8,805 to 12,278 in Chernihiv, from 755 to 3,253 in Sumy, and from 11,013 to 55,474 in Kharkiv.[96] Thus, towns with few Jews before 1917 by 1919 when they fell to the Bolsheviks had large pools of prospective officials made up of people who not only might not have had favourable memories of their Ukrainian neighbours but also were totally foreign to Ukraine and often ignorant of its language.

Ukraine's Zionists were as appalled by secular Jewish job hunters as were their Russian counterparts. The unprincipled materialism of those motivated by their desperate need for wages in particular, they observed, lent invaluable support to the Bolshevik cause and turned indifferent Gentiles into anti-Semites. These 'helpless half-educated elements' in the struggle for survival were prepared to support anyone in power 'who would feed them and not beat them.'[97] In Uman, where Jews constituted almost half the entire population before the First World War, a Jewish eyewitness reported that 'a decided majority of the commissariats and other high offices was occupied by Jews. The Jewish element in considerable proportions was installed in all possible institutions and offices [during the first Bolshevik occupation] ... the preponderance of Jews struck one forcibly.' This not only shocked Gentiles, who before the First World War had never seen a Jew in a position of authority and had traded with the fathers of the new commissars, but confirmed the popular belief that communism was a 'Jewish plot' and provoked pogroms. Faced with hostility after the Bolshevik occupation of Oleksandrivske in early 1918 the city's Jewish Committee issued a statement explaining that the sins of individuals could not be blamed on groups: 'Allow us Jews to have our scoundrels and a nation that gave the world Moses, Christ, Marx, and Lasalle, to have its Trotskys and Zinovievs.'[98]

Secular literate Jews began flowing into Ukraine's Bolshevik administration again after mass pogroms erupted in Directory-controlled territory. Their main sponsor now became the Bund. Initially supporting the Directory alongside the left-leaning Zionists, by February 1919 a pro-Bolshevik minority under A. Kheifetz had swung the majority in the Bund to recognize Soviet rule and then convinced the Bolsheviks that they would not be able to man their administration unless they accepted 'experienced' Jewish workers into the bureaucracy en masse. Among these presumably were people like Hersh Kogan, aged twenty-seven in 1920, when he was commandeered into the Kharkiv-based Food Supply Ministry as an accountant. Having finished the local high school before the war he had first worked in a private store as a clerk and then from 1917 through to 1919 as a clerk in the local Food Supply Committee of all the governments that ruled Uman. Also in 1920 Elena Kompanets was assigned to the ministry as a statistician. Born in Warsaw, the daughter of a physician, her family later moved to Katerynoslav where her father taught at the university, while she herself went to university in Moscow during the war and in 1919 studied at Kharkiv's Commercial Institute.[99] A job did not guarantee survival. Since pay and rations were not always forthcoming, the difference between hunger and survival often depended on village relatives able to bring food to their relatives who worked in offices. Accordingly, urban Jewish officials who had no rural relatives able to bring them food, ironically, often suffered more than their Christian co-workers did.

By the end of 1919, faced with an anti-Jewish backlash among the lower levels of the state and party organizations, Bolshevik leaders, probably acting on secret directives based on the above-mentioned November 1919 decision that was excluded from the Resolution on Soviet Power in Ukraine, instructed local activists to limit the recruitment of Jewish officials. In response, the Ukrainian Bureau of the Jewish Section of the Russian Communist Party, which included Semen Dimanshtein and Moishe Rafes, protested. They pointed out in the middle of 1920 that Jews had been the Bolsheviks' main supporters in right-bank Ukraine because they constituted the overwhelming majority of the region's proletariat and dominated all 'Revolutionary organs' – not just Bolshevik ones. The pogroms of 1919 were not the result of anti-Semitism, they continued, as Ukrainian peasants had earlier readily followed Jewish Bolshevik leaders. They had erupted only after 'Soviet power presented itself to the peasants as communist [which people did not identify with 'Bolshevik'] and began forcing communes upon villages.' Analogously, they continued, in offices, the problem was not the presence of Jews per se as of too many 'demoralized petit bourgeois' specialists. Although these included some Jews, the real villains were educated petit bourgeois Ukrainians and Russians and their 'reactionary Ukrainian and Russian ideas.' Local offices did not have too many Jews, and Ukrainian anti-Semitism, they maintained, if an issue at all, was merely an ideological form of a deeper class reality. The problem was, first, a manifestly bad agricultural policy that alienated peasants and, second, the refusal to accept revolutionary Jews, among whom were locals who knew their regions, into the Bolshevik party – and thus into responsible local administrative positions. Dimanshtein and Rafes urged Lenin to hire more 'good' Jews and rid offices of 'bad' bourgeois Gentiles and Jews, who demoralized the government from within. Implicitly, in their reasoning, Ukrainian hostility towards Jews would then end.[100]

What impact the decision to restrict the hiring of Jews had is unclear. On the one hand, Bolshevik leaders continued to fear that the huge number of newly hired Jews staffing their offices would compromise their regime. Some allotted the majority of places in local executive committees to Ukrainian peasants and gave far fewer Jews responsible positions.[101] In Kalynivka village in Podillia province the Bolshevik commissar acceded to the refusal of local Ukrainians to have Jews on the revkom. Of the sixty-six members of the Kamianets district revkom in mid-1920, for example, only one had a possibly Jewish name.[102] On the other hand, reports throughout 1920 indicate that Jews were still being hired and complain that Ukrainians were anti-Bolshevik because of the continuing predominance of Jews in local positions of authority.[103]

An invaluable insight and analysis of secular Jews in local Bolshevik administration is provided by a Jewish doctor from Talne, near Uman, who in 1919 headed the town's Jewish Committee. Ukrainians' hatred of these people, who brought many of the Jewish ghetto's bad traits into offices, was unbounded, he wrote. People accustomed to look at Jews as pariahs were shocked to find them at all levels of the administration, including the hated secret police and food supply organs. Jewish youth, who had fled from villages to towns during the war and revolution, by 1919 were even more destitute than they had been before 1914, when unemployment had been disproportionately high among them. With few jobs in the local economy, an office position represented their only means of survival. Local educated Ukrainians, he explained, who were anti-Bolshevik, avoided working in Bolshevik institutions or had no need of state employment because they already worked in non-government institutions:

> Vulgar, uneducated, without vision, dazed, and embittered by their suffering in the pogroms they experienced in defenceless tiny provincial towns and villages, when in front of their own eyes their family and kin died horrible deaths, their homes were destroyed, and their accumulated wealth stolen; they entered Soviet service as morally crippled individuals intent on eating their fill and rewarding themselves for their losses ... [B]ut they brought with them an understandable feeling of hate and a burning desire for revenge as well as envy of co-religionists who had not suffered yet. And if in the army, thanks to Trotsky's energy, and vicious punishments for pillage and rape, it was possible to establish order and discipline, in the civilian administration, that had grown colossally ... no punishments, even shootings, could end the predation, bribery, and favouritism ... Lots of idle Jewish youth constantly hovered around the revkom [offices] ... drank free tea, flirted with the girl clerks, [and that's why] the revkom appeared like a Jewish institution. Even in the month before the [anti-Bolshevik] revolt when Christian commissars replaced the Jewish ones, these layabouts still hung out at the revkom.

This account is confirmed by a western Ukrainian officer who traversed right-bank Ukraine in April 1919, just after the Bolsheviks had fled. In Zhytomir and all of Volyn province, he wrote, administrative offices had been filled with nineteen- or twenty-year-old Jewish students, 'who by their inexplicable behaviour' provoked the violent hostility of Ukrainians and Poles to all the local Jews. The young educated atheistic

Jews fled with the army and left their religious elders and family members to face the wrath of local Christians, who refused to accept that the conservative 'older and wiser Jews' condemned and disagreed with their apostate deracinated radical youth.[104] Working religious Jews, whose livelihoods had been shattered by Bolshevik policies, had no love for their former co-religionists who sat in Soviet offices. When Directory forces reoccupied territory in 1920 religious Jews were not displeased, and there were instances of Ukrainian peasants and soldiers protecting captured former Jewish commissars and soviet office workers from the wrath of local religious Jewish militias.[105]

Besides former tsarist bureaucrats and secular Jews Russians from Russia took office jobs in Ukraine as local Bolsheviks repeatedly called for Russian staff. The demobilization after the Brest-Litovsk Treaty, meanwhile, had increased the pool of available prospective clerical and administrative employees with the unemployed clerical staff released from military offices. Soviet Ukraine's fictional independence posed no barrier for their employment. As of April 1918 Ukrainian unions were 'reunited' with their 'all-Russian' counterparts, and as of July that year Russian employees only needed the consent of their department head to move south. Thus, Ivan Kotov, a Russian Red Army veteran but demobilized and unemployed in Ukraine, first applied for Communist Party membership and three days later for a job as a clerk in Kharkiv.[106] As of March 1919, wrote a Red Army inspector, 'All Ukraine is inundated with "specialist" workers sent from Russia, frequently incompetent, as offices sending workers to Ukraine send their worst and keep the better ones.'[107] Ukrainians in Russia were also recruited. In December 1918 Lenin had refused an offer from Ukrainians in Samara province to fight with the Red Army in Ukraine on the grounds that there were so many Ukrainians fighting already that they could not all be armed. Three months later he claimed that the Soviet government in Ukraine lacked people in general and, specifically, personnel for requisitioning squads. In accordance with the November 1919 Central Committee resolution, Lenin that December ordered all available activists to Ukraine rather than elsewhere,[108] while the Russian Central Committee that same month ordered all of its provincial executive committees to dispatch at least ten people or more each to Ukraine. By June 1920 they had sent over 1,500 plus an unknown number of additional officials from various government commissariats.[109] Alongside unsubstantiated reports about Russian officials being obliged to attend compulsory Ukrainian language courses in Moscow there are also references to Ukrainians in

Russia either requesting or being sent to work in Ukraine. In early 1920 the Kharkiv government sought Ukrainian-speaking Communist Party members from Siberia.[110]

Between January 1919 and April 1920 Ukraine's Bolsheviks also brought in thousands of Russian Communist Party members and workers to man the food requisition organizations. Russians comprised the majority of these 'activists,' whose total number rose from approximately 3,000 in April 1919 to almost 40,000 by the end of 1920.[111] The personal qualities of these people varied. In 1919 the head of Ukraine's Cheka explained to Lenin that his organization was obliged to hire people rejected by the Russian Cheka.[112] Curiously, despite this influx of Russians, a March 1920 official Interior Ministry report claimed that because it was so short of staff during the first six months of its existence, when it in any case did nothing because it had no offices or equipment, it had to commandeer staff from the local concentration camp.[113]

A fourth source of bureaucrats were women, and the Bolsheviks hired more women than other governments in Ukraine during the revolutionary years. From no more than 1 per cent of all government employees in 1897 Ukraine, in 1920 women comprised approximately 26 per cent; of these, almost 50 per cent were clerks and lower-level staff, while 17 per cent held higher administrative positions. An inspector's report from the summer of 1919 complained that offices in Vasylkiv were filled with 'empty-headed girls.'[114]

A final source of personnel were the Committees of Poor Peasants (*kombidy/komnezamy*), established in 1919. Subordinated to local executive committees and given pay and rations by the Communist Party, their membership fluctuated between 500,000 and one million. These people served as a pool of administrative personnel. Outside Communist Party agitators sent by the higher territorial unit, and working to a timetable, arranged elections to these committees (which had arbitrary authority over the local landed peasants) from among the landless, marginal, immigrant-townsmen, craftsmen, the destitute, and sometimes, even from people without a hut in the village. This rural lumpenproletariat was ideal material for dictatorship: 'it was like a lump of clay or shit.'[115] In the summer of 1920 the relationship between this social group, plain bandits, and the committees was explained by the rear echelon commander of the Red Army's Southwest Front. He noted that 'the poor' preferred joining the committees to various bandit groups, where they existed, because as committee members what they stole via 'requisitioning' they could keep without fearing the punishment that they would face if as bandits they stole the same items.[116] Each committee had a minimum of three members, was subject to the higher territorial vykonkom, and acted as the local administration until pro-Bolshevik soviets and vykonkoms could be formed. In Pryluky, for instance, Communists had to form and reform the local revkom and vykonkom three times before their make-up suited them. For all the effort put into them, inspectors in southern Ukraine reported that one year after their establishment they had achieved little if anything administratively.[117] Until 1922, when all the Committees of Poor Peasants were purged, most of them were composed of marginals and undesirables. Yet, some were actually run by established villagers who managed to take them over despite the efforts of local Bolsheviks. As one inspector reported from Kharkiv province during the summer of 1919 the peasants did not seem to understand that they were supposed to elect the poor to the committees, as they did not understand how a landless peasant could farm better than an owner. Abolished in Russia after one year because of the hostility they provoked, in Ukraine the Bolsheviks retained the Committees of Poor Peasants for eleven years.[118]

Few young local-born declared Ukrainians appear to have taken government jobs during the revolutionary years. Some, like twenty-year-old Ivan Bahmut and twenty-two-year-old Ielysaveta Shkandel were high school students during the war and revolution, and they simply applied for employment to whichever government controlled the territory they lived in. Shkandel joined the Kharkiv city co-operative as a secretary when she graduated, and then in 1920–21 she worked as a secretary in the Izium district vykonkom.[119] Graduates of newly established administrative schools provided a future source of officials. Established in February 1919, by the end of 1920 they numbered twenty-five with approximately 3,500 students.[120] In dire cases leaders mobilized by decree. In the summer and autumn of 1921 in Poltava they ordered all those with accounting or legal experience to register with their local authorities within ten days for work in the provincial vykonkom, on pain of arrest.[121]

Like their opponents, local Bolsheviks were concerned about corruption, inefficiency, and large numbers of hostile and/or dubious sorts of people within their bureaucracy. Communist Party loyalists complained that Bolshevik power changed only the signs on the doors. Hiring 'bourgeois' financial specialists, one thought, had become 'fashionable' and was totally out of step with what he thought was happening in Russia. Military intelligence reported in February 1919 that all Soviet offices were filled with Ukrainian spies and sympathizers: 'Anyone who has been to one of our [Soviet] offices would have to be blind not to see it.'[122] In the capital Kharkiv, a May 1919 report describes the offices of the Economics Ministry (*UkrSovNarKhoz*) and the department in charge of eastern Ukrainian factories (*Prodonbass*) as filled by 'bourgeoisie' and former owners, who had never done any administrative work, and speculators and layabouts, who all gave their friends jobs and formed cliques. Additionally, the report identified provincial 'bourgeois' elements fleeing levies, flocking to the city, getting Soviet administrators' identification papers, and then abusing their positions to 'turn the workers against Soviet power.' That same summer the central offices of the nationalized sugar industry, another report states, were awash in an endless circulation of paper formalities. Staff did not know what they were supposed to be doing, permissions and credits for purchases took so long to issue that by the time they arrived the commodity was gone, and arbitrary, unregistered requisitions led to huge stores of goods piling up in warehouses rather than being sent to where they were needed.[123] The presence of dilettantes is confirmed by claims in the non-Bolshevik Ukrainian press condemning bureaucrats who had worked under all the national governments in Podillia province, then continuing on under the Bolsheviks when they arrived in the spring of 1919. A report on conditions in Katerynoslav province in the summer of 1920 noted that in the town of Berdiansk local Communists and anarchists had arranged to release each other when either of them came to power – but to shoot all outside Communists.[124] Secret police situation and inspector reports describe deliberate sabotage by staff through the 1920s. One inspector condemned the personnel on the Kharkiv – Oleksandrivsk – Melitopol railway line and recommended that they should all be deported to work on Siberian lines. He added that the situation in the local provincial offices that December (1920) was hopeless. The last thing any government bureaucrats thought about, including the local Cheka, whom he described as hopeless, were their duties. A provincial-level inspection of the Chuhuiiv district Workers and Peasants Inspectorate (Kharkiv province) from June 1920 reported that it had not done any inspections, had no competent staff, no contact with any government offices, no files, and not only ignored complaints but had not even registered them.[125]

Investigations into Directory-organized conspiracies aimed at overthrowing the Bolshevik regime that same year drew attention to sympathizers and activists 'in almost all government offices' who were supposed to serve as a skeleton administration for an expected imminent attempt to restore the Ukrainian National Republic. Of the almost

200 arrested conspirators, however, few actually worked as clerks.[126] Communist Party reports complain about 'saboteurs,' UNR and Makhno sympathizers, and extremist right-wing Russian anti-Kadet sympathizers in government offices. As explained by bureaucrats in Vinnytsia, a major cause of administrative disorder was the Bolsheviks' deliberate destruction of all existing institutions and relationships and their replacement by new structures. Accordingly, old rehired personnel were just as unfamiliar with the newly introduced procedures as were Bolshevik-hired novices – who in Vinnytsia turned out in droves as soon as government job advertisements were posted. Two hundred former Polish Legion soldiers managed to get office positions in Kyiv in 1919, using phony identification documents. In May 1919, three months after Bolsheviks had retaken Bila Tserkva, a Communist Party inspector reported that the city's offices were filled with former UNR personnel who had not been arrested by the local Cheka and who were simply a bunch of drunkards. We read about former deacons being vykonkom chairmen, police drunk on duty, and a former Black Hundreds activist serving as the deputy commander of the Odesa Military District. In the Poltava city administration, months after the town was retaken from national forces, Communist Party leaders reported that the portraits of Lenin and Trotsky remained torn down and that a commission established earlier to purge the bureaucracy had done nothing. Eleven months after the Bolsheviks took Katerynoslav the city prison still had no list of prisoners, and some prisoners had no files. Five months after Myrhorod was taken reports condemn its officials as corrupt drunkards.[127] Reports in the summer of 1919 from the small towns of Romny, Pereiaslav, Lubny, Pryluky, and Tarashcha complain about 'counter-revolutionary' or 'anti-Soviet' bureaucrats in some or all offices.[128] Although the Ukrainian press accused Ukraine's Russians of working for the Bolsheviks because they regarded that regime as Russian, I have not found any Bolshevik reports that made or praised this link.

In May 1919, in addition to political vetting, central leaders ordered an overall 25 per cent reduction of office staff in Kyiv, Kherson, and Chernihiv provinces. In June they ordered an overall reduction of 25 per cent of all bureaucrats and to that end a Revolutionary Tribunal with a Special Commission for the Cleaning (*vychyshchynnia*) of Soviet Institutions (*OsKomChyst*) was established to vet employees. It declared that all employees were duty-bound to report any suspicious activity or persons. This commission established sections of three to seven individuals in all government offices to carry out the work and published short articles specifying how the loyal servitor could 'objectively' identify anti-Soviet co-workers even without actual proof of any wrongdoing.[129] Heads who failed to provide lists of employees within sixty days were threatened with prosecution. This vetting and registering of employees was facilitated by the rationing system, which required confirmation of place of residence and employment for a card, as well as by the hiring system. That is, people could not merely register at an Employment Office and then show the associated document to the prospective employer. What had been the practice was that once people obtained their registration slip from the Employment Office, they then got themselves a job in an office either through bribery or contacts. To prevent this practice new rules specified that to be legal the entire hiring procedure had to be done via the office. People were to inform officials if they knew of hiring done in breach of this requirement.[130] The Party's Control Commission, in addition, urged all department heads to submit lists of employees that included dates of hiring, the names of sponsors, those fired, and the reasons they were fired.[131] A 30 July 1919 meeting of the commission in Kyiv reported that nothing much had changed in offices since it had been formed except that the number of bureaucrats had risen. Ukrainian Communists observed that staff could be purged ten times but that unless those at the top were replaced 'the Russian spirit' of Ukraine's new Bolshevik bureaucracy would remain untouched.[132]

By the end of 1919 each government office had to have a Communist Party collective comprised of party members and sympathizers. Their tasks, as noted, included supervising the rest of the staff, controlling their administrators committee, and deciding on all hiring and firing.[133] In the autumn of 1920 provincial labour committees ordered all office staff to report with their relevant documents and register by a certain day or face arrest.[134] In 1919, after the Bolsheviks retook Kyiv, they became less fastidious about procedure. On 5 February the city's *Kommunist* published a short notice from a Sub-section for the Registration of the Bourgeoisie located at no. 2 Musical Lane, Apt. 5, calling on Soviet office and party workers, in accordance with their duties, to report in writing any 'bourgeois and speculative elements' that they knew were 'hiding' in Soviet institutions. The notice ensured all readers that surnames would remain confidential. (Two years earlier, the Central Rada's Ministry of War had issued a public statement that it did not accept anonymous denunciations.[135]) By July 1919 newspapers were publishing lists of people who were fired alongside descriptions by activists appalled at how anyone facing censure or dismissal seemed always to have the necessary official papers.[136] In Poltava province in February 1920 the provincial newspaper ran a lead article condemning the presence of anti-Bolshevik 'bourgeoisie' in government offices as nothing better than prostitutes that had served all previous governments and should not be tolerated. On the back page of the same edition the local Attestation Commission printed the names of thirty officials on the provincial executive committee and invited anyone with any information about them to submit it – but not anonymously as such letters would not be accepted.[137]

One man, who presumably himself was a Kyivan bureaucrat, having read an article about staff cuts, wrote a letter to the government in April 1919 that gives us an insight into the people who worked for it. Kostiantyn Marchenko explained that honest men who did honest work, and who by a twist of fate and the need for survival had worked for non-Bolshevik governments, should not be dismissed. The criteria of selection should not be party membership, but competence and honesty. He wrote that there were many very competent men in the bureaucracy who were socialists but not members of the Communist Party and that not they but nationalists and monarchists and the incompetent should be dismissed. Three issues particularly irked Marchenko: First was low pay and corruption. The second was family-based cliques that controlled entire departmental subsections, and third was too many unqualified incompetents in offices.[138]

While Ukraine's Attestation Commission, with sections in all ministries, tried to reduce the bureaucracy again during 1920, department heads tried to keep as many of their employees as possible. From a sample of eighty-four Food Supply Ministry officials who were vetted that December, only sixteen were dismissed, eight without reason and the remainder because they had not been hired via the Employment Office. In a sample from January 1921 only one employee was dismissed of twenty because he was a 'counter-revolutionary.' Yet, simultaneously, between February and March 1920 the number of staff in the Organizational Section of the Food Supply Ministry in Kharkiv grew from thirty-three to sixty-two, while the number in its Economics Section grew from sixty-six in April to 102 that August. In November 1921 the head of the Workers and Peasants Inspectorate in Volyn province complained to Kharkiv that he needed more people and that the local Attestation Commission was acting beyond its competence when it attempted to fire three of his staff.[139] Provincial party officials, meanwhile, complained about shortages of skilled office personnel, noting that qualified people avoided such positions because of small rations and late or low pay.[140]

The proportion of Ukrainian-speakers employed in government offices was probably lower than it had been in the 1890s, and during the early

1920s they were restricted to lower-level administrative and technical positions. There were none among the twelve members of the Food Supply Committee in Olhopil district in 1921, for instance, of whom only two were local men. A random sample of sixty-nine applications to Ukraine's Central Executive Committee, which had a total staff of 430 – of which eighty were office personnel – included only twenty Ukrainian-speakers, and nineteen of the forty-nine declared Russians and Jews had a passive knowledge of Ukrainian.[141] A fugitive from right-bank Ukraine reported that the Bolsheviks refused to hire any local people at all for government jobs in the spring of 1920.[142]

In 1919 Bolshevik leaders formally ordered officials to either know or start learning Ukrainian and in September 1920 stipulated that all offices had to have people able to work in Ukrainian. In practice, Ukrainian language use in offices depended on who worked there. In 1919 a section head within the National Economic Council would refuse to accept correspondence written in Ukrainian. He would cross over the text and write: 'although we live in Ukraine the government here is Russian and that is why I can only accept correspondence written in Russian.' In Rivne in 1919 Land Ministry officials opposed using Russian and the commissar agreed to learn Ukrainian.[143] In the first Bolshevik government in Ukraine, 39 per cent of the Ministry of Labour staff were declared Ukrainians, who occupied only the lower positions; 21 per cent were Russians, and 34 per cent were Jews. The numbers of Ukrainians slowly decreased as left-wing Ukrainian SRs (*Borotbists*) and SDs quit their jobs when they saw that the Bolsheviks were not using Ukrainian for administration. A report from a Directory partisan detachment in Oleksandrivske district from September 1920 related that educated Ukrainians had taken office jobs the year previous, but that in the spring of 1920, in the wake of anti-Bolshevik uprisings, they were arrested en masse as counter-revolutionaries.[144] In Poltava province in the summer of 1920, on the other hand, Bolshevik leaders were worried about co-ops, which because of their higher salaries were attracting officials from lower-paid government jobs.[145] Lists of office staff at all levels in Kharkiv province in 1920 contain primarily Russian and Jewish surnames. Of the 220 members of Ukraine's Central Revkom in May 1920 sixty had Jewish surnames and thirty-four had Ukrainian surnames. Similarly, the surnames of ministerial, departmental, and section personnel in the Kharkiv central government in February 1921 were overwhelmingly Russian and Jewish. By 1922 the proportion of Ukrainians among the Central Executive Committee staff of 236 had risen from 15 per cent to 28 per cent, while the proportion of Jews had fallen from 27 per cent to 16 per cent.[146] Jewish names appear with particular frequency in the Workers and Peasants Inspectorate and in the Food Supply Ministry. In May 1920 sixty of the inspectorate's 150 central staff had Jewish surnames. A random review of eighty-six personnel forms from the central Food Supply Ministry, filled out in 1920, shows that fifty-one of the office staff were Jews, twenty-two were Russians (of whom eleven were from Russian provinces), and two were Ukrainians.[147]

In 1922 declared Ukrainians constituted 30 per cent of all officials in the Ukrainian Soviet Socialist Republic, with declared Russians and others (including Jews) 30 per cent each. When these figures are contrasted with 1920 figures on literacy (see Table 14 in Appendix 1) it would seem that many literate declared Ukrainians were apparently working for the government by 1922 and that if Russians and Jews were overrepresented it was because there were not enough Ukrainians to fill the vast new bureaucracy. How many of these Ukrainians were former tsarist bureaucrats is not known.[148] Although there were probably more ethnic Ukrainians in the early Soviet bureaucracy than there were ethnic Russians and Jews in the national governments, the latter two groups probably predominated only in big cities. There are no comparable figures on the nationality of the administrative staff in the various national governments. Statistics from central Ukraine in 1924 show that 62 per cent of all 'Soviet staff' (a category that probably included elected as well as full-time administrators) in the city of Kyiv were Jews or declared Russians (64% Russian-speakers), while 30 per cent were declared Ukrainians (of whom 23% were Ukrainian-speakers). In the small towns, Ukrainians probably predominated. In Uman province (then called *okrug*), declared Ukrainians made up 63 per cent of the total, of whom 63 per cent were also Ukrainian-speakers – although, as in Kyiv, the working language was Russian. Jews comprised 27 per cent of all 'Soviet workers' that year; 66 per cent of them declared Russian and 34 per cent Yiddish as their main language.[149] The 1923 urban census indicates 197,866 government bureaucrats, including approximately 40,000 clerks in state-owned industrial enterprises, which is approximately as many clerks as there were in private enterprises in 1897. Subtracting these would leave us with 157,866 urban government clerks in 1923. This was 50,000 more clerks than there were industrial urban proletariat that year, and over 140,000 clerks more than there were in 1897.[150]

Only in 1926 did Ukrainian-speaking officials in government offices approximate their 1897 share – 50 per cent. That year's census lists just over 126,000 administrators in central government and economic enterprise offices with functions comparable to pre-1917 categories (see Table 11). However, whereas in Ukraine before 1917 administrative positions were divided more or less equally between Ukrainian and Russian males, by 1926 declared Russian males, whose share of this group had dropped to no more than 17 per cent, had been replaced by women and Jews, who together constituted 40 per cent – while declared Ukrainian males made up 44 per cent.[151] On the local level 75 per cent of 11,300 vykonkom members were declared Ukrainians, 13 per cent were declared Russians, and 4 per cent were Jews.[152] How many of the 76,800 Ukrainian and Russian male administrators in 1926 had been tsarist bureaucrats is not known. After 1929 and an influx of 8,000 workers and peasants as new administrators, then a purge of some 40,000 'anti-Soviet elements' from the bureaucracy, the remaining pre-1917 personnel still at their jobs would have been but a tiny minority.

In conclusion it should be noted that these statistics possibly overstate the true number of Ukrainian employees. The head of the Poltava Zemstvo Museum, who stayed at his post throughout the revolutionary years, wrote that it was Bolshevik policy to appoint people with Ukrainian surnames to leading positions but without any sympathies whatsoever for, or even knowledge of, Ukrainian national or political interests. These were 'Little-Russian Muscophiles,' he continued, who spoke Ukrainian as if 'they had a mouthful of water or their tongue were swollen from bee-stings' and what came out was what Ukrainian peasant-soldiers spoke when they tried to speak Russian. Identities were now politicized. Russian-speakers, for instance, resented losing jobs because they did not know Ukrainian. In Poltava, he continued, almost all officials were either Russian or Jewish and that influenced decisions. The Jew in charge of the local Fuel Department, allegedly, supplied Jewish and then Russian schools, first, while Ukrainian schools got what was left over, or nothing at all. Analogously, the local Ukrainian commissar in charge of education and culture supported Ukrainian interests in schools and cultural institutions.[153]

Whites

The Whites in Ukraine did not represent a separatist territorial 'creole nationalism' but an imperial loyalist restorationist movement. They attracted those who were alienated by Bolshevik policies and included people who did not think that something called Ukraine existed as a distinct national economic unit separate from Russia. Under General Denikin between June 1919 and January 1920 the Whites created six administrative units in what had been southern Russia. In March 1920 this regime formally called itself the South Russian Government (*Iuzhnorusskoe pravitelstvo*). Whites under General Wrangel in August 1920 formed the Government of South Russia (*Pravitelstvo Iugo-Rossii*). Wrangel controlled the Crimea until November 1920 and recognized Ukrainian independence in theory – much to the consternation of other leaders. In areas held by the Whites the civilian authorities were subordinated to the military at all levels and in cases involving treason, aiding and abetting, or sabotage were subject to military law and summary execution. Borders fluctuated according to the fortunes of war, but three White provinces were in territory claimed by Ukrainian leaders: New Russia/Taurida (including the Crimea), Kherson, Kharkiv, and part of Kyiv provinces.

Like the Bolsheviks the Whites had to deal with officials who worked for earlier regimes and determine if they did so from conviction or necessity. Leaders did not welcome senior tsarist bureaucrats who for whatever reason had worked for the Reds, and during the first months of White rule local White commanders would arrest or execute any such people in territories they took over. Selection criteria were elaborated only at the end of July 1919 and initially did not specifically mention government officials. Besides Bolshevik political leaders, anyone guilty of consciously implementing Soviet policies in any way was declared subject to the death penalty. Anyone who had assisted and supported Soviet power was subject to a term of imprisonment depending on whether that activity was important or not. Only those people who could show investigative committees that they performed inconsequential duties because of need or circumstance were declared innocent of collaboration. At the end of November 1919 a new regulation specified that everyone who held and thereafter would hold government positions had to submit signed letters to their immediate superior detailing whether they had worked for the Bolsheviks, and if so, why and what they did. Investigative committees were to forward the names of suspicious individuals to the courts. General Denikin formally forbade any former Hetman officials from working in the provinces of Kyiv, Kharkiv, and New Russia.[154] When the Whites occupied Kyiv in August 1919 they seem to have followed procedure. They initially dismissed massive numbers of bureaucrats, and then in September 1919 their secret police directed employees' unions to compile lists of Communist Party officials. In a rare list of bureaucrats in the Leather

Department of the Military Requisitions Committee we see that twelve of its staff of sixteen, who had admitted to working for the Bolsheviks, were still working. In Mykolaiv, by contrast, the Whites unceremoniously shot all clerks who had worked in the soviets. [155]

The Whites did not hire Jews or non-government clerks and formally forbade members of political parties from holding government jobs. In practice, they ignored this latter stipulation in the case of the small Monarchist and Kadet parties, but applied it to the big Socialist Revolutionaries and Menshevik parties. As a result, they excluded the hundreds if not thousands of zemstvo, co-op, and private company officials from their government bureaucracy in White territories dominated by either Mensheviks or the SRs. Annulling Bolshevik nationalization, they emptied offices and left former occupants unemployed.[156] White leaders hired women applicants only reluctantly, although married men placed their often incompetent wives and daughters in offices whenever they could in order to augment the family income.[157] Conversely, many liberal-minded zemstvo and duma specialists refused to work for the Whites. Alexei Tatishchev remained in Kharkiv working for the co-op when the Whites arrived and refused to join the government bureaucracy out of principle. He disagreed with White policies towards non-Russians and senior bureaucrats' indulgence of the unnecessarily harsh behaviour of their subordinates towards the civilian population. He also disliked the leadership's intransigent attitude towards all those who had worked for the Bolsheviks – even if only to survive.[158]

Relative to prices bureaucrats were very badly paid and had to exploit their offices to cover living costs. The plight of clerks in Kyiv after two years of regime changes was described in a letter written by an A. Semenov in the wake of Denikin's capture of the city in August 1919: 'All of us officials in those few offices that functioned through "all possible authorities" and who were neither socialized nor nationalized nor communized ... have been reduced to a shadow of our former selves. We need help, we must be fed, clothed, and shod.' Continuing with a description of 'that nightmare time of revolution and the "socialist paradise" that followed,' Semenov pleaded for a month's pay advance to stave off further hunger.[159] Fates also hinged on personal factors, as suggested by the case of Mikhail Rzhevskii, who in September 1919 appealed the decision of the White Kharkiv zemstvo not to rehire him because he had previously worked for the Bolsheviks. As secretary of the provincial zemstvo, he explained, he had been ordered that January, along with the entire staff, to remain at his job if the government changed. Yet, although the entire staff had thus dutifully worked in the city vykonkom, and four of his colleagues had actually obtained higher, more important positions under the Bolsheviks than they had held previously, why, he asked, was he the only one who was refused reappointment when the Whites retook the city? Unfortunately, as the full text of his appeal is lost, we do not know the outcome of the case, who was refusing to rehire him, or just what exactly Rzhevskii allegedly did to interfere with the investigation of his case.[160]

The Whites controlled eastern Ukrainian regions for no longer than four months, and there is no study of how their administrative bureaucracy worked during that time. But their sorry administrative record in southern Russia and, later in Crimea, suggests that the presence of many experienced tsarist officials in their bureaucracy did not make their rule any more efficient or just than that of any of their rivals. Nor is it known if more tsarist bureaucrats worked for the Whites than for other regimes. Corruption, theft, and graft under the Whites reached limits unheard of before 1914 and grew with each new regulation and office introduced to try and curb it. The Whites' administration, additionally, was probably as big numerically as that of the Bolsheviks. As soon as the Whites occupied a region they began hiring as many bureaucrats as possible because they expected they would soon have to run the empire again. Local officials also sought to hire as many people as they could because then they could claim more funds from the central treasury.[161] In Ukraine they got some basic functions running in the territories that they controlled. In the summer and fall of 1919 mail took three days to travel the roughly 100 kilometers from Kharkiv to Okhtyrka. Conscription lists were published, individual draft notices were sent, and requests for exemptions were submitted, and decided on within two months. In Poltava district between August and October 1919 bureaucrats completed a survey of damage incurred as a result of the Bolshevik occupation. Overall, Tatishchev thought civilian affairs were badly run. In particular people hated requisitioning troops, who had to take what they needed directly because the White armies did not have a single proper quartermaster or paymaster corps. Regimental quartermaster units thus turned into huge business operations and commandeered trains and hundreds of railway wagons to transport their confiscated goods, which disrupted even further an already crippled transportation system.[162] Locomotives ran and burned coal rather than wood because the Whites controlled the Donbass mines. But tickets cost from 1,200 to 40,000 roubles and trains moved at about 7 mph. By that autumn, when White armies were in retreat, there was no guarantee that passengers would not be summarily thrown out to ride on the roofs in –15C temperatures by army commanders wanting to seat their families.[163] Nor could the Whites get significant numbers of Ukrainians into their armies. In territories claimed by Makhno the Whites could organize conscription only in the cities.[164] In White-held territories, accordingly, much as they did throughout the country, Ukrainian co-ops provided essential services. In Poltava those services included providing financing because as White 'rouble coupons' fell in value daily, co-op coupons took their place.[165] A shortage of paper, printing presses, and very bad communications meant that central orders either took a long time to arrive to Kyiv province, the westernmost White territory, or never arrived at all. Ministries had to use couriers and sent money via co-ops. An official in the Whites' Ministry of Propaganda wrote: 'Was there any administration at all? Of course not. There was a convulsive uncoordinated movement of a huge unorganized mass of more or less impoverished officials.'[166]

In the Crimea under General Wrangel through 1920 the administration included approximately 10,000 bureaucrats – double the pre-1917 total for Taurida province. Living in dire want, because their wages covered no more than 10 per cent of their living expenses, married White officials with families cheated and stole to survive. At work bureaucrats did little more than smoke and drink tea, and within five months of arriving in the Crimea the White administration there collapsed. Even the censors did not prevent newspapers from reporting the chaos. In reaction by the autumn the civilian population awaited the Bolsheviks, while junior officers began planning to militarize and take over all civilian life for the sake of order, like the Bolsheviks were doing:[167] 'In the White south the worst aspects of Russian bureaucracy reached their apotheosis.'[168]

CHAPTER EIGHT

The Western Ukrainian National Republic, November 1918 to October 1920

With the collapse of Austria-Hungary the Polish Liquidation Commission in Cracow claimed authority over the entire province of Galicia. On 29 October 1918 it ordered officials there not to obey the orders of any 'foreign authority if they were contrary to the national interest.' In its last official act, however, the Habsburg monarchy on 31 October denied the Liquidation Commission any authority over the predominantly Ukrainian eastern Galicia (western Ukraine) and instructed its governor to appoint Ukrainians to all government posts there as soon as possible. The instruction was telegraphed to Cracow that evening, but the Liquidation Commission did not forward it to Lviv (Lwów, Lemberg).[1] On the afternoon of 1 November in Lviv the last Habsburg governor handed his authority over to his deputy, Volodymyr Detsykevych, who in turn, gave it to Ukrainian leaders who, with approximately 3,500 soldiers, had seized power that morning in all but two key cities in Galicia and then proclaimed the Western Ukrainian National Republic (ZUNR).[2] Local Polish political activists in Lviv took up arms against the new republic before the independent Polish government had been formed, without the permission of the Liquidation Commission. They found the city's Polish inhabitants unwilling to fight.[3] By 22 November, however, Poles controlled the city thanks to reinforcements from Poland that could arrive because Ukrainian troops had failed to hold Przemysl (Ukr: Peremyshl). By 13 November, as a result, the Poles controlled not only that city's huge army depot, but its strategic railway bridge over the San River that linked Cracow and Lviv.

In November 1918 Ukrainian national leaders claimed sovereignty over fifty-two eastern Galician districts (*povit, powiat, bezirk*) and approximately six million people. In fact, with the loss of Lviv, Przemysl, and their environs the ZUNR controlled forty districts, which in 1910 had just under four million people and was about as big as the Irish Republic (see Tables 12 and 13, Map 3). Fifteen per cent of this area's urban population was Ukrainian-speaking. Just how many people remained there in 1919 is not known. Eastern Galicia was on the front line, after four years of war its agriculture was in ruins, and it is estimated that by 1916 flight and death had reduced the population by at least 500,000.[4] Poland conquered the ZUNR in July 1919, after an eight-month war. Before western Ukraine was incorporated into Poland as *Malopolska Wschodnia,* it was briefly ruled by the Bolsheviks as the Galician Soviet Socialist Republic.

The Social and Institutional Background

In 1910 Ukrainian- and Polish-speakers made up respectively 27 and 34 per cent of eastern Galicia's urban population; an estimated 3 per cent of Polish-speakers were not Roman Catholics, and 3 per cent of the Uniates (Greek Catholics) were not Ukrainian-speakers. Thirty-eight per cent of the urban population were Jews. During the preceding twenty years Ukrainian-speaking Uniates had the fastest rate of urbanization, doubling between 1880 and 1900. In 1900 in eastern Galicia 53 per cent of the Polish urban population lived in towns with 10,000 or more people, while 53 per cent of the Ukrainian urban population lived in towns with 3,000 to 10,000 people. In the decades leading up to the First World War the Ukrainian proportion of the population of cities with 10,000 or more was increasing, while that of Poles and Jews was decreasing.[5]

With approximately one-fifth the number of Ukrainians as in the tsarist Ukrainian provinces, eastern Galicia had almost three times as many published titles in Ukrainian: forty-two newspapers and journals were published in 1910 in eastern Galicia, 63 per cent of them in Lviv. During the eight months of ZUNR statehood, sixty Ukrainian-language newspapers and journals appeared in twenty-four towns, with 30 per cent of them published in the capital, Stanyslaviv (today Ivano-Frankivsk). Whether the western Ukrainian-language press reached more people than the eastern Ukrainian-language press is unclear as only seven ZUNR titles appeared regularly for the duration of its existence.[6]

Western Ukrainians arguably had more experience with government and administration because they interacted with a bigger, more effective, and possibly less corrupt bureaucracy than their eastern co-nationals did. Against an estimated average per capita distribution of central government bureaucrats to total population in tsarist Ukraine of 1:1,642

(1:234 in urban centres), Galicia averaged 1:1,100.[7] At the turn of the century the border town of Pidvolochyske, for example, with approximately 5,500 inhabitants (8% Ukrainians), had eighty government employees (excluding teachers), of whom five were policemen and eight were night watchmen. With twenty-eight clerks (or secretaries), four judges, and four lawyers, the ratio of administrators to population averaged 1:196.[8] On the other hand, although Galician Ukrainians had more interaction with government, fewer of them worked in it. Declared Ukrainians comprised on average no more than 20 per cent of the region's administrative and white collar personnel. To a great degree this was because of discrimination. Polish superiors transferred declared Ukrainian subordinates out of eastern Galicia whenever possible. As noted later by Stanyslav Ozinkevych, who had served in pre-war Galicia before working for the ZUNR, the Poles denied Ukrainian patriots promotion and in their dossiers classified them as 'dangerous radicals' who had to be watched.[9] Nonetheless, although there probably were fewer declared Ukrainians who were government administrators in western than in eastern Ukraine, they were organized in a national unit when, in March 1918, lawyers formed a union of Ukrainian Government and Private Sector Administrators. As of 1917 eastern Ukrainians not only hired western Ukrainian refugees residing in Kyiv as administrators but also specifically invited them to work as bureaucrats in the Ukrainian republic's westernmost provinces – where they were particularly valuable because they knew German.[10]

Two months after taking power the ZUNR's prime minister declared that although most Polish administrators had quit, the remaining Ukrainian personnel had almost the entire administration functioning. In a region through which the front had rolled back and forth the government was able to prosecute and arrest lawbreakers and to round up enemies. Recruits and mail within its territory got to where they were supposed to go, as did the millions of returning prisoners of war moving both east and west. Rents and internal taxes had stopped being paid during the war, but with income from export taxes, left-over Austrian government and army funds, and subsidies from Kyiv, the ZUNR apparently could pay its officials regularly on the first of each month. Compared with independent Poland (see Chapter 9), Hungary, and Rumania, observed one former minister, the ZUNR 'was an oasis of order.'[11] Zakhar Skvarko, an official in the Kolomyia area, did not agree. He claimed that because political leaders had illusions about Polish willingness to listen to U.S. President Woodrow Wilson and the Versailles Treaty, they had failed to act decisively during their first two months in power, during which time they not only lost Lviv but let the country fall into chaos. Very critical of the young socialists who had occupied government positions, Skvarko wrote that what emerged from independence by 1919 was a series of local republics run by local military officers independent of civilian and central control. Under them shirkers, incompetents, and careerists took government jobs and filled offices while the army desperately needed men. Instead of state building these people engaged in demagogy and socialist agitation.[12]

Polish memoirists, for the most part, were people with little if any sympathy for Ukrainian national aspirations in what they considered to be a part of Poland. They note a dire lack of qualified personnel and describe a country on the verge of collapse with corruption rife. Ruled 'by bayonet, cudgel, and axe' by June 1919 all nationalities eagerly awaited the Polish army.[13] A Polish judge from Zhydachiv, the district neighbouring Bibrka to the south, labelled the town's Ukrainian council 'a gang in the worst sense of the term.' Ukrainian rule for him represented seven horrific months of police terror in conditions of 'Bolshevik-style anarchy.'[14] The Roman Catholic Archbishop of Lviv claimed anti-Polish violence was prevalent within the ZUNR in a report that he submitted to the Polish Foreign Ministry in early 1920, based on affidavits compiled by his priests in the wake of Polish victory.[15]

Evidence suggests that there is truth to both sides. While the ZUNR implemented some policies and experienced less internal violence and land seizures than was the case in eastern Ukraine, its ability to govern weakened and the role of the army expanded as war raged on. In his above-mentioned report, for instance, unlike the lay accounts, the archbishop stressed that in his opinion the violence was neither sporadic nor spontaneous, but planned and organized by the government. This implies that the ZUNR had the requisite people and structures in place. During the first months of the ZUNR's existence, in the town of Zolochiv life went on normally and the administration functioned. The district of Bibrka is cited as a model where neither Poles nor Jews complained. In the Myklashiv area enough taxes were collected to pay teachers but not administrators.[16] Between February and April 1919 the government could organize, collect, and collate reports on public health from forty-five western Ukrainian districts including those occupied by the Poles.[17] The government did not decree total control of the economy until the middle of April, and then it allotted fifty armed soldiers to all local food supply committees. The detachments were to accompany officials on their rounds to ensure that quotas and deliveries were observed and prevent the arbitrary requisitioning by local commanders that had been occurring before. How the state monopoly and fixed prices worked in practice remains unstudied. A reporter, pained by the sight of starving women and children begging on city streets, asked why this was so – as between January and March 1919 the ZUNR had received 426 railway wagonloads of foodstuffs from eastern Ukraine.[18] Polish lists of Ukrainian army supplies that the ZUNR had managed to assemble and stockpile in Ternopil, made after it had lost the city in May 1919, also point to a functioning governmental machine. It noted that there were as many as 2,000 fully loaded railway wagons, fifty locomotives, and ninety-two artillery pieces.[19]

Inspectors travelled the provinces and submitted reports about the war-related destruction that the new government had to cope with already in early 1919. Pidhaitsi district by then had been 'totally destroyed' and needed, but was not getting, twenty-five railway wagonloads of grain a month. Bibrka district had three empty pharmacies, one hospital requisitioned by the army, and no doctors, medics, nurses, or veterinarians. The commissar described the situation as 'catastrophic.' In the Brody area near the front eighteen villages had been razed and the survivors, living in fifteen or twenty shacks, were starving. Nineteen villages had been totally destroyed in Zboriv district. In one, Ditkivka, 805 people were living in dugouts.[20] By April 1919 complaints about breakdown appear. Theft of anything that could be removed from the railway system was rampant, as was arbitrary requisitioning by the army. The citizens of Drohobych complained of corrupt gendarmes, hunger, empty shelves, and Polish activists, of whom some who were former officials and still getting paid, openly agitating against Ukrainian independence.[21]

Some link the ZUNR's administrative accomplishments to the fact that before the First World War more educated Ukrainians under Austrian than under Russian rule were able to participate in numerous legal non-government organizations. Thus, the ZUNR functioned tolerably well because it supposedly enjoyed the advantage of having more Ukrainian-speaking Ukrainians per capita who were familiar with organizational and administrative practice than did any eastern Ukrainian government. No one has examined this claim in detail, but a preliminary review of the data on co-operatives suggests that their role as non-government training agencies should not be exaggerated. In all of Austrian Galicia before the war there were almost 3,500 co-ops of all nationalities, with a total membership of approximately 1.5 million. Of these, 550 in eastern

Galicia with 180,000 members were organized into the Ukrainian-led Regional Inspection Union. Assuming a household of five per member, it would mean that approximately 25 per cent of eastern Galicia's Ukrainian population was involved with the co-op movement. However, Ukrainian co-ops were smaller and poorer than Jewish or Polish co-ops. Galician Ukrainian co-op administrators, unlike their counterparts in tsarist Ukraine, were all part-timers. Students were reluctant to join. The work was tedious, paid little, and during the war the Galician Ukrainian co-op movement collapsed.[22]

Critical eyewitness accounts indicate that the role of national patriotism should not be overestimated either. Ukrainian bureaucrats threatened to go on strike unless they were paid, for example, lamented Sambir's district commissar. He also complained that he saw too many educated people hedging their bets, watching their backsides, and lining their pockets because they feared for the future.[23] Among officials there was corruption. A Polish report from Ternopil district claimed that the ZUNR already within weeks of its establishment had no moral authority and that, as a rule, officials sought only to make as much as possible because they did not think the country would last long; in weeks, allegedly, corrupt bureaucrats could make millions. Similar claims were made by a newly arrived Polish governor in August 1919, who remarked that Ukrainians disliked the term 'commissar' because it reminded them of bureaucrats who had used their public office for their private gain.[24] Another Polish eyewitness claimed that half-educated Ukrainian priests (referred to obliquely as those '*przy wielkiem oltarzu*'), and not the Jews, were the major speculators in goods. Paying less than one crown for a litre of oil in Boryslav, they sold it for 14 crowns in Berezhany.[25] Because only co-ops could legally buy petroleum, at 15,000 crowns per cistern, Jews would pay the co-op agents up to 100,000 crowns for their government voucher, for example. They, in turn, could sell the load for up to 300,000 crowns. Consequently, although government records show that all co-ops had oil, in reality villages had little if any.[26] A report on bureaucrats noted that they had inherited the faults of their Polish and Austrian predecessors while losing their earlier work habits and respect for superiors. In response, a letter begged readers to understand that bureaucrats were themselves poverty stricken. In a country where two meals in a restaurant cost 600 crowns, clerks made only 500 hryvnia a month. A later article noted nothing could be done without bribes and that in this field western Ukrainians outdid the Russians.[27]

Ukrainian peasants by 1914 belonged to national organizations and voted for national political parties;[28] yet, the initial enthusiasm that many of them had for the new state must not be seen in isolation from the disillusionment provoked by high taxation, fixed official prices, state monopolies, requisitions, conscription, corruption, and arbitrary district military commandants. Volunteers were few and leaders were shocked when they learned how many peasants were dodging the draft and deserting. Police took bribes and lost control over the flood of deserters or travelling Polish emissaries who went about openly agitating against the government and organizing opposition to it. Only in the territories that had experienced Polish rule and were then liberated in June 1919 did the army see tens of thousands of men more than eager to join.[29] The poor and landless did not seize land following the establishment of the ZUNR, but it is unlikely that this rural social stability was linked to national loyalty. Western Ukrainian leaders like the Poles and Czechs but unlike the Rada diffused radical proclivities and a massive rural upheaval by passing a Land Reform Bill in April 1919, promising land redistribution after the war ended. Announced on 8 May, peasants could have heard about it before the ZUNR fell two months later and have been convinced to wait. In the spring of 1918 small Communist groups had begun organizing soviets, strikes, and land seizures – but what percentage of these occurred in the ZUNR as opposed to in Polish-occupied territory, where disturbances could just as well have been nationally rather than socially motivated, is not known. Only in 1920 did discontent among the poor and landless produce considerable violence and support for the Bolsheviks. But by then like Polish peasants after experiencing Bolshevism, Ukrainian peasants concluded that Polish rule was the lesser evil.[30]

The ZUNR's relative internal stability and administrative accomplishments might be more reasonably linked to mundane realities. Like their Czech, Irish, and Polish counterparts (see Chapter 9), on the eve of the First World War the overwhelming majority of educated declared Ukrainians were loyalists.[31] But when national leaders decided to declare independence, they based their government on centrally appointed full-time staff – not on public organizations. Most of the political leaders, additionally, were professionals rather than humanist intellectuals. Because they took for granted what their Marxist-inclined countrymen to the east regarded as the 'bourgeois-nationalist' nature of their state, western Ukrainian leaders directed their supporters into government rather than into public organizations. They created government jobs by establishing state monopolies. Their reformist moderation, additionally, made their government appear less threatening to conservatives, both Ukrainian and non-Ukrainian, than the Central Rada and Directory governments to the east, whose radicalism tended to alienate this group. Nor were Galician Ukrainians forced to postpone creating an administration to placate strong anti-independence centralist interests, as were their Kyivan counterparts (see Chapter 3). Western Ukraine's organizational successes might also be related to its population distribution (see Table 13). Specifically, by 1917 the upheavals of the war had concentrated at least half of the remaining population in what would be the ZUNR's thirty-three eastern districts into thirteen towns and their suburbs.[32] Administrative control, consequently, was simpler than if these people had been dispersed in villages. While nominally a republic, finally, numerous references in memoirs suggest that in reality the ZUNR was from its origins a military dictatorship – which would explain why basic functions related to the army were carried out.

The latter point is confirmed not only by those Polish eyewitnesses who wrote about an insufferable police dictatorship, but by eastern Ukrainian officials themselves. From their perspective strict martial law in the ZUNR was commendable and understandable in time of war. Two Jewish ministers from the Directory in western Ukraine in 1919 were struck by how 'European' was its capital, Stanyslaviv. Avraham Revutsky described the ZUNR as 'a real government' whose authority was manifest and whose only flaw was that it 'governed too much.' He described an order strictly enforced by local commandants with tremendous power who, for example, could control each inhabitant's every step by a system of passes which were required for even the shortest journey. Solomon Goldelman attributed these rules to Austrian practices.[33] Similarly, a report on the ZUNR written for the Directory in August 1919 noted the profound Austrian influence; that May, it pointed out, just before its collapse and despite the disastrous situation on the front, the civilian administration and the police were functioning.[34]

Who Administered?

To replace the imperial governors the ZUNR's first interior minister on his second day in office spent five hours on the telephone imploring acquaintances to take administrative jobs. However, it was not the central leaders who created the bureaucracy. They only appointed or approved previously elected governors (*povitovi komisari*) and informed all towns in eastern Galicia that they had taken power. On the spot it was the commissar's responsibility to compile lists of those eligible to hold offices, and in case of emergency the commissar could appoint all officials. The ZUNR's central administration was in place by January 1919, but it was built rather from the bottom up than from the top down. In short as national leaders in towns and villages learned that the ZUNR had been proclaimed, they began organizing as best they could with whatever resources they had. On one level organizers had to deal with 'ambitious romantics' – 'patriots' who refused to do their normal jobs well and sought instead leading positions for which they were not competent. On another local leaders had the benefit of selfless patriots like the unknown caretaker of the important railway station at Halych. When the rest of the staff had refused to recognize the ZUNR, this man volunteered to take charge of the junction. He worked non-stop for ninety-six hours successfully routing troop-trains until relief arrived from another town.[35] In his memoirs the interior minister identified pre-war 'Muscophiles' as another unexpected source of competent officials: 'the administration's best reserve [of personnel].'[36]

Polish and Ukrainian accounts claim that few Polish officials remained in Ukrainian service; however, the contemporary records suggest that many did. An eastern Ukrainian newspaper reported that although Jews worked for the ZUNR, initially all urban Polish officials went on strike. By the end of January 1919, once the central government had restored the bureaucracy, however, rank-and-file Polish bureaucrats who wanted to work were complaining about their leaders who wanted them to strike against the government and/or sabotage it.[37] Evidence from twenty towns, each with between fifty and a hundred officials, indicates that most or all of the Polish administrators in fourteen (70%) of them remained at their desks at least until December 1918.[38] In the town of Sniatyn the Polish bureaucrats expressed their willingness to serve, only not in executive positions.[39] How many Poles actually were dismissed after January 1919 is not known. In the days after taking power the new government informed all officials twice that they had to swear loyalty to keep their jobs, and a month later, it circulated an official oath. The circular was dated 29 December with a 1 January deadline, and the instructions implied that there still were officials who had not sworn loyalty. This initiative was perhaps in response to the new Polish government's demand, on 22 November, for loyalty oaths from all of its officials (see Chapter 9) and the fear of mass resignations that might have sparked in the ZUNR.[40] No one was to be forced to swear loyalty, and lists of those who refused to do so were to be forwarded to the capital where a commission decided who could be rehired. In March 1919 the government specified that officials had to be citizens and pass a competency test and that those hired from then on had to know Ukrainian. In May 1919 it asked for lists of all released bureaucrats who had chosen to become citizens – which suggests a willingness to hire Poles.[41]

Administrators in eastern Galicia as of 1 November 1918, like those in Bohemia, had been ordered by the last representative of the last authority to work for the new national government, and it was up to that government who it would fire or hire. Poles in eastern Galicia, nonetheless, ignorant of this instruction, could consequently refuse to work for the ZUNR on the grounds that it was 'illegitimate.'[42] In Lviv itself, in Ukrainian-controlled sections, Polish administrators voted not to go to work until they heard from Warsaw.[43] The Liquidation Commission, for its part, ordered all Polish officials under the ZUNR to remain at their jobs and act officially only insofar as their behaviour was in the Polish interest. It specified that no Polish officials would be punished for working for the Ukrainian government if they were forced to do so. To make the choice between interests and principles easier, the Commission promised that it would try and pay all Polish bureaucrats in Ukrainian territory and that they would not lose seniority.[44] Yet, on the other hand, the Commission also began talks with the ZUNR. This willingness to come to terms with the new national state reflected the mood in Poland and the reluctance of the country's leader General Józef Pilsudski, for practical as well as principled reasons, to commit troops to war on his eastern border that November. It was the right-wing Polish National Democrats who finally forced Pilsudski to send troops against the ZUNR on 14 November – and not without resorting to unconscionable deceit.[45]

Just when provincial Polish officials learned of these various official decrees, and how they influenced behaviour in early November 1918, is yet to be fully studied. Initial work reveals as many attempts to compromise with as to oppose the new regime. In Berezhany Polish bureaucrats who came to work on Monday, 2 November, refused Ukrainians who requested them to remain at their desks. In other towns Polish leaders called for calm, cooperation in the interests of order, and waited for the decisions of the Paris Peace Council. In response to those people who at meetings said that they had to work for the new government because they needed the money and that it would be impossible to borrow from the Jews, who were not lending to Poles because of the recent pogrom in Lviv, organizers replied that they were prepared to raise a help fund by mortgaging their personal possessions. More substantially, for almost six months the director of the Berezhany Credit Union arranged to pay all striking Polish officials – until he was arrested. Polish officers also managed to give the town's Polish activists their demobilized Austrian regiment's pay chest, unknown to the Ukrainians, to augment their strike fund. Polish activists coordinated their activities through their Polish National Committee, which not only arranged regular contact with officials from the Liquidation Commission, but organized a fund to collect and distribute money to bureaucrats who by December 1918 refused to work for the ZUNR. They arranged loans from Polish banks in Poland – even with the assistance of the Ukrainian government. Local Jews donated the sizable amount of almost 200,000 crowns to support Polish bureaucrats who refused to work for the ZUNR. Clandestine money for striking Poles also came from Cracow.[46] Significantly, not all appear to have benefited from these funds, as in January 1919 those who were suffering the most were beginning to organize and were trying to convince their fellows to join them and work for the ZUNR.[47] In Boryslav in May a group of leading Ukrainian citizens complained that the government was continuing to pay Polish bureaucrats that it had dismissed for refusing to swear loyalty and had left them in their subsidized residences. They wanted the government to deport any Poles not working 'in our institutions' together with their families.[48]

Sambir was a town where the majority of Polish bureaucrats resigned. Yet, a few days later, the former mayor visited the new mayor and offered his services as an adviser. The Ukrainian gladly accepted and gave him a desk in his office. Within days the Pole was threatened by local Polish activists and so he stopped coming in.[49] Writing in 1919 in Lviv, a Polish eyewitness who considered Detsykevych to be one of a group that no one could identify as either Polish or Ukrainian provided a valuable insight into how events might have transpired had the Ukrainians held on to power: he complained that the number of people with uncertain national affinities would increase and they would abruptly reveal themselves as Ukrainians.[50]

Two extended contemporary Polish accounts describe how most Poles initially worked for the ZUNR on the basis of local agreements that recognized Ukrainian rule de facto and not de jure. One account from Ternopil cites common interest in local order as a motive for cooperation that was cut short by the central government's request for oaths of loyalty and its threat to dismiss without pay all who refused to take them. Another, from Stanyslaviv, claims that after Ukrainian leaders saw that they could not control the population they approached the Poles who had resigned and asked them to continue at their jobs. A resulting complicated local power-sharing arrangement collapsed after Lviv fell to the Poles, and the Ukrainian army began to override civilian officials in response. In reaction to what they regarded as anti-Polish behaviour provoked by the army – including requisitions and termination of pay from Cracow – by June 1919 the town's Polish bureaucrats had quit their jobs.[51] In the Myklashiv area local Polish organizations included the Ukrainian state symbol on their stamps, and Poles continued to work for the Tax Department until they were forced to take the oath in February. The local commissar did not know what to do because if the Poles departed only one Ukrainian would be left in the department. The district was near the front and all the other Poles had refused to swear the oath because they expected the Polish army to shortly occupy it. In Peremyshliany the commissar resolved the dilemma with his local Polish doctor, who had nothing against Ukrainian independence, by keeping him as a part-time official and thus free of the need to take the oath of loyalty.[52]

Some local Ukrainian officials arrested those advocating disobedience as a rule, but then released them after a few days, and in some towns, they allowed Poles to emigrate if they chose to do so. Gendarmes did begin arresting Poles en masse in late November 1918 in the wake of military defeats, and again in May 1919 after the government discovered secret Polish organizations plotting its overthrow.[53]

Besides Poles and Ukrainians the Uniate Church, which in 1901 had 2,200 priests, represented a third source of officials. Throughout the nineteenth century peasants normally trusted priests as their spokesmen, and many priests had gained administrative experience as organizers of reading clubs, sobriety societies, and co-operatives. This active involvement in secular affairs, encouraged initially by the edicts of Emperor Joseph II, was reaffirmed by the Pope in 1891 and by the Uniate Metropolitan in 1901. Although in 1914 priests comprised only 20 per cent of the Ukrainian delegates to the Vienna parliament, for instance, until 1891 they had averaged at least half of the delegates. By 1900 even those who disagreed with the church regarded the participation of priests in political life and public office as normal. Secular western Ukrainian political leaders were cool towards the Uniate Church in the decade before the First World War, but in 1918 the Metropolitan and all the bishops formally declared their support for the ZUNR.[54] Priests, in short, worked as administrative and elective officials.[55]

Educated secular Jews, a minority within the Jewish community that made up approximately 12 per cent of the population of eastern Galicia and approximately 42 per cent of its pre-war urban population, also worked as ZUNR administrators. Jews made up approximately 14 per cent of the provincial bureaucracy before the First World War and by 1918 had little sympathy for the Poles, who during the Russian occupation had assiduously helped tsarist bureaucrats dismiss them from their jobs.[56] Some of the Jews who remained resigned rather than work for the ZUNR, but others eagerly took up their old jobs for the new government and some even served as provincial governors.[57] One Polish judge at the time claimed that it was only thanks to its Jewish employees that the ZUNR could function at all. He added that they encouraged the 'more cowardly' among Polish officials to work for the Ukrainian government. A situation report from the Polish National Organization in Ternopil noted that the Jews supported the Ukrainian government en masse. Jews occupying high government positions, it claimed, were following a policy to implement decisions in favour of Ukrainians at the expense of Poles and they were 'more Ukrainian than the Ukrainians themselves would wish.'[58] The Directory's minister for Jewish affairs claimed that by March 1919 the ZUNR was excluding Jews from government positions because their leaders persisted in formally maintaining Jewish political neutrality.[59]

Jews played a key role as railway employees under the ZUNR, made voluntary contributions to the government, and as private traders ran the economy despite a declared state monopoly on trade. Jews were the only people in the ZUNR who had the capital, knowledge, and contacts necessary for domestic and foreign trade, and Ukrainians, formally in charge of the economy, had little choice but to turn a blind eye while Jews continued doing what they had been doing before. A newly arrived Polish governor of Rohatyn district in August 1919 reported that under the ZUNR Ukrainians had good economic and political relations with Jews: 'Through them and with their help officials made fortunes of hundreds of thousands.' Only in the last weeks of the war did ragged retreating Ukrainian troops loot Jewish homes.[60] Polish police, meanwhile, reported in June 1919 that many had sworn loyalty to and did work in the government. That same month an anonymous report from a Bolshevik eyewitness related that 'all Jews' were unambiguously pro-Ukrainian primarily thanks to pogroms committed by Polish troops during the last weeks of their offensive against the ZUNR. The Polish interior minister, conversely, reported that Jewish loyalty began to shift to the Poles with the fortunes of war.[61]

The records of the inventory-accounting section of the ZUNR's Military Secretariat provide not only a valuable insight into the role of Jews in the government's bureaucracy but also into the role of women. Deciding in April 1919 to recruit women to handle the increasing workloads, the number of staff in the section expanded to a total of twenty-four by the end of that month; of that number, sixteen were women and thirteen of the women were Jewish. All the hired women either had previous clerical experience or had completed specialized secretarial training, and all of them knew three languages: Polish, Ukrainian, and German. All the Jewish women wrote their application letters in Ukrainian. Particularly impressive were the qualifications of Josefina Erder, aged twenty. A graduate from Vienna, she worked for the eastern Galician Jewish National Council in 1919, and besides the languages all the other women knew, she also knew Hebrew and English. Furthermore, female staff members were quite prepared to stand up for their rights. Four secretaries in the ZUNR president's office, for example, complained in April 1919 that the officers' mess had begun charging them for meals that they hitherto had had for free. In their letter they pointed out that under Austrian rule female staff did not pay for meals and that since they only earned 800 hryvnia a month, they could not afford to pay almost 300 for meals. Faced with the prospect of having to eat in the non-commissioned officers' mess, they explained: 'we are intelligent girls and women and should not be forced to eat with chauffeurs and the like in the NCOs' mess.'[62]

Among the ZUNR's final instructions was an order, issued on the day the Entente sanctioned Poland's occupation of eastern Galicia, depriving all Ukrainian officials who worked for the Polish government of their Ukrainian citizenship and allowing any 'Ukrainian agent' to execute Polish bureaucrats attempting to exercise authority on Ukrainian territory.[63] In any case, by the time of the Bolshevik invasion in July 1920, Warsaw had replaced almost all former ZUNR bureaucrats in eastern Galicia with Poles – most of whom then fled the Bolsheviks. As a subsection head in the Chortkiv district town council, one who stayed, S. Wiehardt, apparently managed to keep his entire pre-Bolshevik Polish staff at their jobs and to sabotage Bolshevik policies – and this despite the fact that the first Bolshevik decrees in western Ukrainian lands implicitly included administrators among the 'agents of Polish rule' that were supposed to be arrested on sight.

The Galician Soviet Socialist Republic

The Galician Soviet Socialist Republic, during its two-month existence (July and August 1920), by all accounts, was plagued by a shortage of personnel.[64] Published Ukrainian memoir literature normally does not mention former ZUNR officials and notes that local educated Ukrainians either went to work for the Bolsheviks because they were conscripted or because they feared the consequences of Poles and Jews occupying all administrative positions. Exemption from requisitioning, pay, and rations were also persuasive. Bolshevik reports refer to hate of Petliura because of his alliance with Poland, which involved surrendering the ZUNR, as a reason western Ukrainians supported them. Just how many Ukrainian employees worked for the Bolsheviks remains to be determined. The district revkom in Borshchiv, for example, had over 150 full-time staff, and they could not all have been non-Ukrainians. All revkoms had to be one-half Ukrainian, one-quarter Jewish, and one-quarter Polish in composition, but whether this rule also applied to full-time bureaucrats is not known. What tended to happen was that the nationality of the heads determined which group had more of its nationals in the government's twelve ministries and which language they used. Borys Kolodii, a clerk in the War Commissariat, described how each of the staff members would distribute their positions to their co-nationals and then impose either Polish or Ukrainian as the de facto office language. By its end, the republic's education, war, and trade and manufacturing ministerial staffs, and its district military commanders, were mostly Polish Jews who functioned in Polish. Moscow, meanwhile, had allocated Soviet Galicia to Communist Poland as a province.[65]

Incomplete personnel lists suggest that Ukrainians were predominant in the revkom staffs. Nationality quotas perhaps explain why persons who might otherwise have been shot were left at their positions. Teodor Kobyloniak, for example, six days after being hired as secretary of a village revkom, was denounced by the local commissar to the secret police for being 'indifferent to Soviet rule.' Arrested, investigated, and then released, it emerged that after deserting from the ZUNR army, where he had served as a quartermaster clerk, and returning home after an absence of five years, he hid from the Poles and then volunteered for his job when the Red Army arrived. In his police statement Kobyloniak claimed that as the son of a poor peasant he was pro-Soviet and that as a simple soldier he was not responsible for the politics of the ZUNR army.[66] Some office workers, as might be imagined, attempted to covertly sabotage what they could. Many apparently spent their time translating back and forth between Russian, Ukrainian, Polish, and Yiddish, and copying reports and orders – for which they got little, if any, rations, and because of circumstances, probably no pay. In theory, in August 1920 lower middle-level bureaucrats in villages and small towns were supposed to get between 2,000 and 4,000 roubles a month, and central staff in bigger towns between 4,000 and 6,000. By that December pay had risen by an average of 2,000 to 3,000 roubles a month.[67]

Insight into the workings of the Soviet system, and the plight of its officials, is provided by the secret police investigation of two of Galicia's central revkom (*HalRevKom*) employees, Mykhailo Kapusta and Lonhyn Horbachevsky, who probably organized a protest against unfair rationing three weeks before the collapse of the Galician Republic. Exasperated by bad food at Ternopil's First Soviet Cafeteria, which was supposed to cater to all the HalRevKom's employees but left them so hungry that they could not stand up at work, they organized a meeting and wrote a petition signed by approximately thirty co-workers which they sent to the Workers and Peasants Inspectorate. What particularly infuriated these employees was the existence of a second cafeteria where 'some ate better,' although according to the head of the local Food Supply Committee the second cafeteria got no more rations than the first: 'The satiated have no right to accuse hungry co-workers of sabotage and counter-revolution. Communists must suffer like everyone else in the name of the proletarian revolution. Down with privilege. Down with the Soviet bourgeoisie. All are equal before the Revolution.' The organizers pointedly asked in their petition that if the second cafeteria was Soviet why was it closed to some employees, or if it was private how did it obtain items confiscated by the government? The situation was manifestly unjust, and there was very little that was 'communist' about those who organized or ate at the special cafeteria – which they labelled 'soviet bourgeois (*sov burzh*).' They had to be exposed and punished. Arrested for their efforts Kapusta and Horbachevsky, it turned out, both had higher education and one had Communist sympathies. In their statements both denied knowledge of the anti-Soviet parts of the petition when they signed it and said that had they read it, they would not have signed. The dossier does not contain statements concerning the third alleged organizer, while the bottom page of the petition with the thirty signatures is missing.[68]

Pay lists including 411 staff members in eleven revkoms, the Central Committee, and lists of officials in forty-eight villages include no more than a dozen Jewish names and a few Polish names. The highest percentage of non-Ukrainians were perhaps in the Ternopil province's revkom and in the HalRevKom's Food Supply Committee, where of the 144 employees fourteen were Jews and four were Poles. Co-op personnel avoided employment in Soviet food procurement organs,[69] and when the Poles returned to western Ukraine in October they arrested such persons as 'Bolshevik collaborators.'[70]

CHAPTER NINE

Bureaucrats in Other New European Governments

Acting in the name of direct democracy and the oppressed, the Bolsheviks, like the Jacobins, ended up creating a bureaucracy of unprecedented size around a core of pre-revolutionary functionaries. But since neither group represented a national minority or a national liberation movement within an empire their experiences with bureaucrats might sooner be contrasted with than compared to events in Ukrainian lands. Better comparative insight into the relationship between new governments and bureaucrats in Ukraine should be sought among other stateless nations whose leaders sought independence between 1914 and 1922. What events in Czechoslovakia, Ireland, and Poland suggest is that except perhaps in the case of Germans in Poland nationalism and declared nationality were not as decisive as some later claimed in deciding whether or not former imperial officials worked for new national governments. Rather, nationalism and declared nationality became decisive after new governments had established their rule and nationalists then made nationality a key criterion of selection.

Czechoslovakia

In Moravia, Silesia, and Bohemia, all parts of the Habsburg Empire before 1914, declared Germans held almost all of the high administrative positions, while declared Czechs held the lower ones. In Bohemia, where Czechs were 63 per cent of the population, they made up 95 per cent of the provincial bureaucracy. Czechs also staffed administrative offices in Vienna, Bosnia, and Galicia. Able to make careers within imperial ministries Czech officials were not well disposed towards Czech nationalist politicians, and their sons tended to become Germanophiles.

Slovakia was administered from Budapest. In 1900 no more than 500 of Hungary's 54,000 government employees (excluding teachers) were Slovak-speakers, while in 1919 no more than seventy-five of approximately 6,000 officials in Slovakia were declared Slovaks.[1]

Czech national leaders declared independence in October 1918, in agreement with Austrian civilian officials. But despite Czechs' reputation for being the emperor's least loyal subjects, until that autumn among Czechs separatists were a minority. Although their loyalty to Vienna was tempered by wartime measures such as the retraction of the right to use the Czech language in administration and the dismissal of Czech administrators, this must be seen against the background of the attempt by the military to abolish civil administration in the empire's Slav provinces, where the German governors of Bohemia and Moravia took the Czech side.[2] The all-party centre-right National Committee was accepted by Czech officials as the new national government, but their decision was arguably determined as much by its legality as by nationality because the last Austrian governor had ordered all bureaucrats to work with the committee. On the day after independence the Czech government announced that it would retain all officials and assured a delegation of bureaucrats' representatives, who had come to declare their readiness to serve, that for the moment they could continue working without an oath of loyalty, although it had also been prepared to dismiss officials considered to be too anti-nationalist. Radically inclined local national committees, which had already begun supervising former bureaucrats, were dismissing them and taking over their functions. Within a week of declaring independence, however, central leaders condemned this activity. Fearful of Bolshevism domestically, and eager to impress the Entente with their country's internal stability, they ordered the local committees to dissolve. In response to radical critics, who complained that even Austria had not dared to repress the local nationalist committees, the government announced that it would only consider staff dismissals in exceptional circumstances. In practice, it shifted hated officials elsewhere, and those who could not speak Czech to German-speaking areas. Within five weeks the local councils had disappeared.

The Czechs had many trained and disciplined troops abroad, but because they did not begin arriving home in significant numbers until January 1919, when they took power national leaders could count only on a volunteer militia and a handful of Czech soldiers in Prague. These sufficed to stop a counter-coup led by loyalist officers on the day after independence. As the independence proclamation was disseminated,

Czech troops throughout the country declared their support and disarmed their German counterparts. In the countryside, faced with a volatile landless peasantry, national leaders pre-empted rural revolution by sequestering all estates in November 1918 and then passing a Land Reform Bill in April 1919. In cities hunger and inflation led to serious strikes but until 1921 there was no Communist Party to organize them, while in December 1920 the socialists refused to support an attempt by radical leftists to bring down the government by a general strike.[3]

In Slovakia national leaders fearing continued subordination to Hungary decided to join Czecho-Slovakia. From a legal point of view Slovakia remained part of Hungary until June 1920 but, in practice, it came under Prague's control in January 1919. Although the new government wanted Hungarian officials to continue working, many left the country while those who remained ignored or sabotaged the new government. Only during the summer of 1919 after experiencing two months of Bolshevik rule, as part of the Hungarian Soviet Republic, did remaining former Hungarian and Hungarian-speaking Slovak officials change their minds and decide to work for, or least not oppose, a Czechoslovakian government that they now regarded as the lesser evil. During the interim, in a controversial move, a Czechophile centralist Slovak leader holding the position of Prague's minister for Slovakia and accused of pandering to Czech anti-Catholic prejudices, began to fill the local government offices with imported Czechs, instead of employing untrained Catholic Slovaks. By 1921 these 'imported Czechs' comprised 36 per cent of the region's administrators and postal personnel, while Slovaks made up 43 per cent, and Hungarians and Germans 18 per cent. In Silesia Germans comprised 40 per cent of the population, and German officials there refused to accept Prague's administrative authority, swore allegiance to republican Austria, and until the end of December 1921 worked alongside invited Austrian officials. Then with the agreement of the Entente the Czechs militarily occupied the province and expelled Austrian officials. German clerks still remained at their jobs until 1926 when 33,000 of them were dismissed; a decision to reduce government spending led to ministries releasing their non-Czech-speaking German employees first.[4]

Ireland

In English-ruled Ireland Roman Catholics could work for the British government from 1829 on, but only after 1870 were they allowed to enter the domestic civil service. Those who imagined that there were more officials than citizens in Ireland at the turn of the century were not pleased at the results of this change and bemoaned the proliferation of people who saw the secure small salary of the minor official as life's best prize: 'Some day a man ... will point out that the rigorous exclusion from official appointments is the best thing that could possibly happen to any section of the community. Those who have no hope, absolutely no hope at all ... of getting official positions will be obliged to turn to and work at something useful ... Having secured wealth and developed character, they will rule the rest of the country and reduce the official class to ... their proper position, making them hewers of wood and drawers of water.' While recognizing the importance of administration, the author noted that men with timid office souls did not make nations great: 'The more general the desire for office becomes, the smaller is the chance of national glory.'[5] Nationalists were uneasy about the increasing numbers of educated Catholics entering the professions – including the civil service. On the one hand, they hoped that educated Irish Catholics would 'swamp' local British Protestant-dominated offices, and they were quick to condemn perceived discrimination in employment. Yet at the same time they were uneasy about the consequences of mobility and deplored how the drive for 'respectability' led Catholics towards English culture, norms, and aspirations and away from Irish nationalism. Respectability, as one put it, was 'the root of all evil' because it was a desire that discouraged pride in Ireland.[6] Nonetheless, by 1900 a well-developed system of primary education and net of non-government nationalist organizations did produce educated Irishmen able to take government exams, while a Land Reform Bill passed in 1903 ensured that the nationally conscious Irish peasantry would be socially conservative. By 1914 almost 75 per cent of the peasantry in Ireland owned their own land, and Irish Catholics comprised 60 per cent of the island's nearly 27,000 government employees (of which 20,000 were postal workers).

Nationalists claimed that loyal mobile Catholics could not have both English accents and Irish autonomy (Home Rule), and were becoming 'West Britons.' Nonetheless, after 1880, Irish bureaucrats, like the educated in general, had reason to believe that union with Britain and their work as administrators benefited their country. Because London thought that nationalism could be neutralized by wide-ranging reforms, the decades before the First World War saw important, generally beneficial measures enacted in Ireland related to local government, land reform, education, health, and welfare. Still, there were, to be sure, grounds for that generation of educated Irishmen to be dissatisfied with their lot.

In a society where in 1900 the state was the biggest employer, perceived discrimination and blocked mobility at work among junior government employees could reinforce existing nationalist convictions or even incline the uncommitted to reject the empire loyalism of their fathers in favour of modern Irish nationalism.[7] Irish society was not, however, divided between those who did and those who did not consider themselves Irish. Some nationalists may not have liked the 'West Briton,' but the committed of this temperament did ultimately side with the moderate nationalist majority seeking autonomy legally, rather than with the small militant republican separatist minority. Perhaps because so many Irish nationalists were bureaucrats themselves, they were aware of the importance of administration.[8] One of them, Arthur Griffith, had actually prepared a detailed organizational blueprint for independence in his *The Resurrection of Hungary: A Parallel for Ireland* (1904). This best-seller argued that instead of working to send elected representatives to the central authority in London, Irish patriots should direct their energies to creating a parallel civil authority in Ireland.

In the spring of 1916 the republicans, who had attempted to take power in Dublin by force and declare independence, enjoyed little popular support and were defeated. The British prime minister's meeting with the captured ringleaders in the immediate aftermath, followed by his speech promising immediate Home Rule, however, swung Irish Catholics behind the republican cause. Seven days of fighting, they concluded, had achieved what decades of talking had failed to do. The republicans' newly acquired Irish Catholic support was reinforced by the threat of conscription, which resulted in a landslide victory for them (by the Sinn Fein party) in the 1918 parliamentary elections. Meeting in Dublin rather than taking their seats in London, members in January 1919 created an Irish parliament, declared independence, and appointed Arthur Griffith to create a bureaucracy.

After winning municipal elections in April 1919 the republican government controlled almost all local councils, and in September 1920 these councils formally broke their ties with London. Preoccupied with the Paris Peace Conference, India, and Egypt, British political leaders initially ignored the Irish, thinking that the republican government would collapse of its own incompetence. London finally did declare the republic illegal in September 1919 and imposed martial law. But Prime Minister Lloyd George refused to permit the introduction of a system of identification cards and passports, which meant that the Irish could come and go as they willed. Republican couriers and leaders rode their bicycles around Dublin and went about their business in broad daylight. Republicans intimidated loyalist imperial administrative personnel, but made it known that they assassinated only political personnel. Their primary target was the local police, the 9,000-strong Royal Irish Constabulary, which until 1920 was composed entirely of Irishmen. In the countryside there were instances of landlords forced to sell land and of soldiers of the Irish Republican Army (IRA) arresting Irish local radicals. Overall, however, peasants were passive thanks more to the pre-war land reform and the workings of a scrupulously fair Land Commission than to their recently acquired sense of nationality. Republican leaders could direct their cadres and attention to fighting the British and running the parallel administrative bureaucracy which by and large the population accepted.[9] According to one story, two prisoners held in custody by republican police on a remote island refused to be rescued by British police on the grounds that they were prisoners of the Irish Republic.[10]

Former Sinn Fein leaders who became senior government officials in Ireland scrupulously kept party positions and activities apart from government functions and did not transfer party members en masse from Sinn Fein into the civil administration. By 1920 republicans were running clandestine central ministries with 2,000 part-time and 300 paid full-time staff parallel to the education, taxation, and postal systems which republican leaders decided to leave alone. The National Land Bank, land tribunals, and courts provided a core of alternative services to the population through to 1922, but had too few people to be as effective as some later claimed they were.[11] Like the peasants, the educated Irish in 1919–21 arguably supported the state-building efforts of what three years earlier had been a despised fringe group less because of national loyalty than the threat of conscription. Nor were the majority of people prepared to break the law. It was important that the republicans therefore impress all concerned that their rule would not result in violence or anarchy and that it could provide services with due regard to property. By 1920, however, this attempt to use effective administration to win support from a populace that, like most people everywhere, preferred 'beating the system' to plotting rebellion was collapsing. While most of the middle- and lower-level staff in British offices appear to have sympathized with the Irish Republic, they nonetheless continued to work formally for London. How many simply did little or 'worked to rule' as opposed to actively passing on information to republicans is not known. No more than 900 officials (3% of the pre-war total) decided to openly work for the republic, and between 1916 and 1921 no more than 400 administrators were discharged for disloyalty.[12] Few Irish Catholic bureaucrats openly declared themselves or worked for the republic before the legal transfer of power. By hedging their bets the majority probably did help cripple the official and legal administration; however, they also contributed to bringing the republic's unofficial administration to the verge of collapse by late 1920. Thus, it could be argued that by withholding their services Irish Catholic bureaucrats weakened the attempt at independence.

Although hard-liners in Downing Street pursued a policy of repression, moderates had assigned top bureaucrats sympathetic with moderate Irish nationalism to Dublin to begin preparing the transfer of functions even before the passing of the Government of Ireland Act (1920), which provided for the legal transfer of the British administration to the republican government. Thus, when a year later London finally recognized southern Ireland as a 'Free State' within the British Empire, some 20,000 government employees who worked for the British government during the war could begin working for the Irish Republic less because it was Irish than because it was a legal successor government. Fewer than 1,000 officials, 'sticky old Irish officials with cold feet ... but jealous of their colleagues and care for their salaries,' retired or resigned.[13] Another group of officials who either would not or could not learn Gaelic resigned after the new government made knowledge of Gaelic compulsory for all of its employees. Although the terms of the Government of Ireland Act were rejected by some republicans, who fought a civil war over them, they were arguably important in keeping bureaucrats in Ireland at their desks after 1921. London did not resort to declaring Ireland a Crown colony, but neither did it recognize the Irish Republic as an independent government born of nationalist revolution. In strictly legal terms the republican government was a temporary executive committee that had been allotted de facto administrative functions for one year. Ireland got autonomy within the empire. Although galling to the republicans, this terminology gave their new government legitimacy in the eyes of bureaucrats. Able to count on their bureaucrats, the new leaders did not have to turn Ireland into a military dictatorship to stay in power.[14] Finally, the new national state did not hire women as administrators; women were an insignificant minority in the bureaucracy in Ireland both before and after 1922.[15]

Polish Officials and Imperial States

Before 1918 the three empires ruling Polish lands decided if and where Poles could work as government employees. In German Poland, where after 1848 the government had preferred not to hire Poles as clerks, Poles comprised no more than 10 per cent of the local administration, and in 1900 they occupied only the lowest administrative positions. In July 1918 Polish nationalists in German-ruled Poland established a conspiratorial organization, with the explicit purpose of preparing their members to take over government offices, and began planning to ensure that public organizations would be subordinated to the government after independence.[16] At this time Russian- and Austrian-ruled Poland, by contrast, had many Polish-born employees who had but few qualms about serving imperial powers. The nationalist literati, who acted as a national moral police force, freely denouncing 'treason' and 'betrayal' among their countrymen where they saw it, were ambivalent concerning the average administrator and hesitant to judge him.[17] Polish political leaders were divided over whether their countrymen should work for imperial governments, with socialists and liberals opposed and Free Masons, nationalists, and conservatives in favour.[18] Those opposed did not struggle with the dilemma of 'respectability' and assimilation, like the Irish, nor did they take their censure as far as assassination. Middle- and lower-level Polish Catholic government administrators were among the approximately 3,000 men killed by Polish assassination squads between 1905 and 1908 in Russian Poland.[19] The Polish Socialist Party (PPS), however, the major organizer of the squads in the region, never explicitly targeted such people. Their targets were institutions and persons 'detrimental' to them and the revolution, they declared, and comprised primarily soldiers, policemen, and high officials identified by function not nationality.[20] Polish Masons were established in German and Russian Poland. Opposed to the right-wing nationalist National Democrats (*ND* or *endecy*), they had influence on the administration and appointments there during the First World War, and members in the first Polish governments. Freemasonry was very weak in Galicia and had no Ukrainian members there.[21]

Throughout the tsarist empire in 1900 approximately 13,000 Poles were working in government and zemstvo/duma administrative capacities. In Russian Poland their numbers slowly declined from approximately 80 per cent of the local government bureaucracy at the beginning of the nineteenth century to 60 per cent by the end of it.[22] Many were second- and third-generation officials and as corrupt as their Russian counterparts. One accepted method of advancement was to denounce one's fellows as nationalist sympathizers. During the 1840s and 1850s impoverished educated gentry, with no other employment, considered themselves fortunate if they were among the few hired by the government – whose employees swelled from approximately 8,500 in 1828 to 15,000 by 1862. Another option for such people was to become one of the thousands of private estate administrators who could get work without contacts or education. But from the 1850s this option faded as landowners began dismissing officials in both Russian and Austrian Poland.[23]

Tsarist secret police reports suggest that between 1831 and 1914 the number of Polish Catholic officials who were active in anti-Russian groups declined. Some supported the 1831 uprising, but even those who publically declared themselves for the revolutionary government were later rehired if they had not taken up arms. Information on 1,328 persons arrested for participation in anti-Russian conspiratorial organizations between 1835 and 1846 shows that 20 per cent of them were government administrators – less than 3 per cent of all officials.[24] During the 1863 uprising foreign observers thought that all Polish officials supported it, while the Russians praised Polish employees of the Russian quartermaster's corps for their loyalty. Police reports indicate that approximately 20 per cent of mayors supported the uprising while 30 per cent opposed it.[25] In each of three staff reviews done in 1865, 1866, and 1867 the police identified between 5 and 10 per cent of the estimated 11,000 officials working in the ten Polish provinces as disloyal (*neblagonadezhni*). As they had done thirty years earlier the police dismissed only those who had actually fought in 1863. In one instance, of 444 individuals identified as disloyal, only 121 were actually tried. It would appear that, as Max Weber assumed, the overwhelming majority of Polish officials like their Irish and Czech counterparts were more inclined to accommodate with than oppose foreign rule. The reality for the majority in 1863 was perhaps best expressed by those who made special two-sided plaques for their town halls – a white eagle on one side to be displayed when revolutionary forces appeared and a double-headed black eagle on the other to show to tsarist troops.[26] A Mr Krukowski, who served as the secretary of the Warsaw Revolutionary Committee in 1863, appears again in 1871 as a holder of a tsarist commendation and editor of an official government provincial newspaper. The insurgent Wladyslaw Christofor not only held a job on a local government commission afterwards, but also was awarded the Suppression of the Polish Rebellion medal.[27]

Even a 3 to 5 per cent disloyalty rate seemed to be excessive for the secret police, however, who reported that all Polish employees were closet patriots kept at their desks only by fear and poverty. Polish officials passively resisted Russification measures, they claimed, refused promotion outside Polish lands, and governors in some provinces personally chose to correspond directly with the capital because they mistrusted their Polish subordinates.[28] In response to such charges of group disloyalty, loyalist Poles pointed out that there were fewer Polish Catholic officials active in nationalist groups than there were Russian Orthodox officials in socialist or anarchist groups. Moderate governors and Interior Ministry officials, for their part, argued that given the general shortage of administrators there was little choice but to retain as many Poles as possible and that not hiring the surplus of Russian-speaking Polish graduates produced yearly by secondary schools would alienate and radicalize them.[29]

In the ten Polish provinces of the Russian Empire, at the beginning of the twentieth century Poles who were employed faced secret promotion restrictions, but whether professional frustration overcame the modest benefits of holding a job in hard times and motivated a significant number to turn to nationalism is not known. Some administrators did join ND sponsored organizations before they became legal in 1905, but few actually joined the party.[30] Before 1919 perhaps as many as 3 per cent of ND members were government administrators.[31] During the 1905 revolution some Polish functionaries publically demanded the right to use Polish in government offices and were supported in the Duma by the ND. These same officials opposed separatism, however, and in 1915 most fled with the Russian army. They remained behind the lines without work, on full pay, until 1917 when the Provisional Government formally abolished the Russian administration of Poland and reassigned them to jobs in Ukraine and Russia. Those who remained in Poland worked for the Germans.[32]

After 1863 Russian conservatives usually won the hiring debates with the result that, overall, the number of Poles in service in the Polish provinces declined. In 1905 moderates were led by the newly apponted Minister of the Interior Sviatopolk-Mirsky and Prime Minister Witte. They convinced ministry heads and the tsar to support a request, made by the Polish loyalists Adam Krasinski and Wlodzimierz Spasowicz in 1904, to hire more Poles as government officials. The ensuing decree promised to introduce Polish as an official language, cancelled the perks and extra pay for declared Russians who took administrative positions in the Polish provinces, and implicitly instructed local officials to hire more Poles. The document went on to identify declared Russian officials who were earning extra pay in Polish provinces as a group responsible for bad government. Interested in maintaining tensions, these officials misrepresented the true situation of the country in their reports to maintain their own incomes and well-being. Resistance to liberal reforms persisted, however, and few of the announced changes were implemented. The Polish language was permitted only in private organizations, secret restrictions excluding Poles from specific higher government positions remained in force, and Russians still got preference in promotion. Despite support from the governors general of the western regions and ministers of justice and the interior, after 1907 the number of Poles in government jobs in the Polish provinces increased only marginally in the years up to the First World War.[33]

Some historians take foreign and 'hard-line' Russian police opinion as proof that Poles in foreign government service were national patriots. Those who note loyalist and moderate Russian opinion to the contrary claim that most rank-and-file Polish-speaking tsarist Catholic officials in the decades before the war had little interest in anything beyond their own homes and offices. The small number of arrested, the gap between high prices and low wages, the overall moral climate, and the Irish case, add credence to this latter view. Extremely low wages during the 1840s and 1850s, for instance, embittered Polish clerks in Russian Poland, but few job prospects outside government and a pay increase in 1861 played their role in keeping most Polish bureaucrats passive during the 1863 uprising. Prevailing attitudes also suggest that later nationalist and contemporary police characterizations of every Polish official as a clandestine patriotic saboteur are exaggerated. A widely circulated document among Poles in 1863 was a broadsheet titled 'The Polish Catechism.'[34] Purportedly written by a revolutionary, it contained ideas found in Adam Mickiewicz's *Konrad Wallenrod* (1828; a Russian translation came out in 1832) – a controversial work that, in the manner of Machiavelli, condones behaviour normally considered reprehensible and immoral if done in the name of national patriotism.[35] Among other instructions the 'Catechism' called on educated Poles to serve in the Russian government, with the express purpose of sabotaging its plans and activities: 'Strive by all means to make a fortune at the expense of the Russian treasury; this is no sin and no crime because, robbing Russia, you disable the enemy and enrich your own country. The Holy Church will pardon you.' Poles, it continued, should aspire to rise in the government, but only as far as trusted assistants to top ministers because as such they would avoid dismissal resulting either from loss of favour or failed implementation and be able to serve Poland that much longer: 'Strive to obtain an important post, and when you have the power, protect your brethren and give them good places too. All means are legitimate for this purpose, even if they appear base to others; remember this is all done for your country's sake, and thus your baseness will be looked upon as a great sacrifice by your countrymen ... When we [Poles] shall thus occupy all the important posts in Russia, she will herself become our tributary.'

This particular document has since been dismissed as a tsarist police forgery, and not all Polish contemporaries considered the behaviour that it advocated acceptable. Oskar Awejde, a lawyer by profession and one of the uprising's top leaders, as a prisoner condemned the 'Catechism' as a foul calumny intended to compromise the revolution in the public eye.[36] An English observer, who thought the 'Catechism' genuine, also felt obliged to write that there were many men 'of high honour' in public service in the Polish provinces 'who would not sully their reputation by any such combination of perfidy and self-interest.'[37] When in 1897 Poles planned to officially raise statues to Adam Mickiewicz in Warsaw, Cracow, and Lviv, the Ukrainian writer Ivan Franko, in an article published in German in Vienna that year, claimed that Mickiewicz had glorified treason as heroism in almost all of his works. This provoked a storm of protest from Polish literati, who in response emphatically proclaimed how loyal all Poles were to their monarchs.[38] The Polish social elite behaved according to circumstances – attending tsarist functions during 'liberal' times and declining on grounds of ill health during 'hard' times. Persons like Father Michal Radziwill of Warsaw, who chaired the committee in charge of erecting Mickiewicz's statue, must not be forgotten. As head of the city's charitable committee he denounced nationalists and removed books – including Polish classics – disliked by tsarist officials from the twenty-three public libraries under his supervision.[39] Antoni Wrotkowski, in charge of Warsaw's welcoming committee for the tsar in 1897, later played a key role in shutting down an underground Polish-language school system.

Nationalist opposition to empire before 1914 involved few people, and the most powerful opposition organization, the PPS, was a marginal group. Turn-of-the-century data from five imperial districts in Radom and Kielce provinces indicate that between 3,000 and 4,000 of their 300,000 Polish inhabitants were white collar workers, among whom were the 60 to 70 per cent of government employees who were Polish. As the strongest local party the PPS had 8,237 members and sympathizers, among whom were 200 'intellectuals' – eighty in Radom and 120 in Kielce. Together with an unknown number of professionals who belonged to or sympathized with the loyalist National Democrats, it is unlikely that more than 10 per cent of all white collar workers in the tsarist Polish provinces were politically committed to any Polish organizations. The most committed nationalists appear to have been among the 1,271 high school students of whom 35 per cent belonged to an organization. The government would have had reason to doubt the loyalties of no more than 3 per cent of the population at most.[40]

In Austria-Hungary by 1900, in the province of Galicia approximately 70 per cent (10,000 persons) of the government bureaucracy were declared Poles. Working for a government that granted their language official status in the province and set no internal barriers to their advancement, as in the Russian and German empires, Galician Polish officials had every reason to be loyal to Vienna, a loyalty reinforced by few job prospects outside government. On the eve of the Great War, emigre Polish socialist literati criticized them for servility, and some astute academics noted a distinct lack of professionalism. 'Until recently' one of their faults was a 'certain nervousness in dealing with interested parties like some sort of intruders.' Habsburg Polish officials would chase the public from their offices, while with peasants their behaviour would become 'coarsely barbaric.' These men 'could not come to see themselves as state functionaries obliged to calm and correct treatment of their fellow citizens.'[41]

In 1914 Polish conservatives opposed collaboration with the Russians, while the ND split on the issue. Poles were not arrested en masse during the first occupation of Galicia, but the remaining pro-Russian National Democrats were soon disillusioned. The tsarist authorities imported Russians and Poles from Russia as administrators and used Galician Poles only as translators and lower-level clerks 'without rights of state service.' How many officials remained behind Russian lines remains unknown. Among them were men who took advantage of Russian laws excluding Jews from government jobs to help their new employers fire their Jewish colleagues. It is also unknown how many of these Poles later fled with the Russians.[42] During this first occupation local Ukrainian administrators were not paid – but whether this was because they refused to work or were fired is unclear.[43] The returning Austrian forces placed Galicia under military rule, and until the emperor issued a decree forbidding doing so, the military dismissed an unknown number of Poles for collaboration with the Russians. During the second Russian occupation of eastern Galicia, the Russian Provisional Government began staffing its newly acquired Ukrainian lands with Ukrainians.

In his memoirs, published during the 1930s, one former western Galician Polish administrator claimed that the majority of his co-workers were patriots, who within the limits of their office furthered the national cause as best they could. To a great degree, he claimed, it was thanks to the combined informal and surreptitious activities of these administrators that nationalists were not repressed and their movement became as strong as it did. Other Poles who criticized men like himself, he wrote, did so from ignorance of their activity which by its nature had to be covert. Besides giving examples of his personal patriotic initiatives, which included mitigating the effects of requisitioning and diverting Polish money from Austrian war loans to the nationalist cause, he cited examples from pre-war police documents in his possession of similar pro-national initiatives by other Polish officials.[44]

Polish Officials and the Polish State

Between 1915 and 1918 Germany controlled the seven northern provinces of formerly Russian Poland via a military governor general, with an administrative staffed of approximately 13,000 imported German officials.[45] Alongside these functioned volunteer Polish civilian organizations in twenty-one cities that enjoyed urban self-government and two centralized parallel networks of various kinds of all-party councils and commissions run by either the left-wing National Central Committee (*Centralny Komitet Narodowy*) or the rival right-wing Inter-party Political Circle (*Miedzypartyjne Kolo Polityczne*). How many administrators were among the thousands of educated Poles who fled with the Russian army and how many remained is not known. In January 1917 Berlin agreed to the formation of a Provisional National Council (*Tymczasowa Rada Stanu*). Only the council's ministries of justice and education were headed by Poles initially but it also included a commission in charge of educating future administrators which by the end of 1918 was running courses for almost 2,000 students.[46] In May 1918 the Germans allowed national leaders, among whom were Masons, to take over all ministries, and by that November a Regency Council (*Rada Regencyjna*) had drawn up an administrative plan for Polish independence and begun organizing Polish railwaymen as well as staffing eight ministries – whose personnel now received on-the-job instructions from their German counterparts. Austria took over the southern provinces of Russian Poland in 1915. It manned its civil administration with remaining tsarist administrators who swore loyalty, imported Galician Polish officials, and also established an administrative school locally to train new administrators. Behind the front lines, the region enjoyed administrative stability, and no events tested Polish officials' corporate unity which they demonstrated in two collective protests. Learning from Austrian Foreign Minister Czernin of a proposal by to gradually dismiss all Polish officials in Austrian-controlled formerly Russian Poland, they effectively forestalled the measure in February 1918 by voting to resign en masse – while ensuring through Polish parliamentary deputies in Vienna that their resignations be rejected so that they could not be replaced by non-Poles. In March Polish administrators in Galicia took part in a one-day general strike protesting the Treaty of Brest-Litovsk.[47] Although the treaty tested Poles' loyalty, their allegiance to Austria never broke, as a new foreign minister stopped ratification of the treaty and abrogated the secret territorial clauses that had riled the Poles.

Depending on how one defines an independent national government, a Polish government can be said to have been formed either on 7 October or on 11, 14, or 18 November, 1918. On 22 November it declared that all officials had to swear allegiance to it. While in the short-lived Tarnobrzeg Republic all pre-war administrators were fired, in the rest of the country, apparently, the same Polish officials who had worked for imperial governments then worked for the new national government. There are references to those indifferent to independence leaving voluntarily or being fired by their more patriotic former colleagues.[48] But what happened during the first year of independence throughout Poland, when it verged on collapse, has yet to be examined thoroughly – in particular the relationship between the new government and the various wartime local all-party organizations mentioned above. Did their members peaceably dissolve their various councils and join the new administration, or did they have to be dismissed, as in Czechoslovakia? Also unknown is whether there was a massive influx of party members into the government bureaucracy.

In western Galicia the Polish Liquidation Commission's chief of administration noted that many officials were fired and that there was a subsequent shortage of staff – without mentioning nationality. In Polish-controlled regions of eastern Galicia he implied that most officials remained at their jobs.[49] At least one local western Galician leader is on record for doubting the loyalty of local former imperial officials, noting that they were totally discredited because they had implemented hated wartime measures and would have to be carefully controlled until they could be completely replaced. In 1919 in all of Poland 42 per cent of government employees were former Austrian officials and 38 per cent were from formerly Russian Poland.[50] Incomplete figures for Lublin province indicate that half of its government personnel were pre-war officials.[51] Among government employees, it should be noted, were Jews and

Ukrainians, some of whom, as indicated in a report from Biala district (east of Cracow), remained at their jobs into January 1919; of the nine Jews and twenty Ukrainians, apparently all but five of the Ukrainians were either loyal or apolitical.[52] Approximately 65 per cent of Poland's 28,000 officials employed in 1923 were known to have joined the new administration in 1918. That figure (18,200) corresponds roughly with the total number of Polish officials in Austrian, Russian, and German imperial service before the war.

In formerly German Poland all but some 20,000 German officials had left by December 1918. Polish leaders in Warsaw wanted those officials who remained to continue working and, to that end, signed an agreement with Germany – which also wanted the officials to stay. The officials themselves wanted to leave, and the local Polish leaders who disliked having Warsaw send them officials from outside their region wanted them to go. Offered employment on the same terms as Polish officials, the Germans mistrusted the government and told German interviewers that they refused to learn Polish and that working in Poland would be against their conscience. Until April 1920, when Germany refused to extend the treaty that allowed them to work in Poland, most Germans in Poland appear to have remained at their desks and worked alongside newly arrived Poles. After April 1920 most of the remaining Germans left, and Warsaw began replacing them en masse with former Galician officials.[53]

Undoubtedly some Polish officials were patriots motivated by ideals and patriotism, and they worked diligently. But evidence points to interests playing as important a role in bureaucrats' behaviour as Weber postulated they would. After declaring independence ministers discovered that alongside a shortage of skilled administrators they had a surplus of applicants for government jobs which gave some prospect of certainty in uncertain times. Corruption was rife. Bending to pressure from party leaders and friends to hire their sometimes titled, sometimes unqualified, and almost inevitably unemployed proteges, however, ministers transformed the problem of shortages of qualified staff into problems of incompetency and overstaffing: 'Except for the ministries of agriculture, justice, and labour, where there are some professionals at all levels – dilettantish, doctrinaire behaviour and ignorance predominate everywhere else.' Conservative Galician Poles complained that 'Bolshevized' Warsaw ministers preferred to hire people whose intelligence was uncorrupted by learning.[54] A British military adviser in 1919 wrote: 'My opinion of the Polish administration is such that I wonder at nothing they do.' The only public organization that worked was the fire brigade, and 'they are all Bolsheviks.'[55]

There are no detailed studies of Polish prices and wages between 1918 and 1920. In general, inflation and devaluation coexisted in Poland as they did in the rest of Europe. Unlike in Ukraine, however, Polish officials were paid on average less than urban workers were – but at least they did get paid.[56] In mid-1919 (when Poland had more than 700,000 unemployed), besides a salary, status, and perks, an office job also offered the possibility of avoiding the draft and extra income through graft.[57] In government Land Commission offices, for instance, there were two boxes on a table: one with a red cross and the other unmarked. Protocol required supplicants to ostentatiously drop donations into each box – putting more of a preferably foreign currency into the unmarked one.[58]

Within the first months of its establishment, popular condemnations of and lamentations about the new bureaucrats were heard in Poland's parliament. In February 1919 Wincenty Witos, leader of the Polish People's Party (PSL, also translated as the Polish Peasant(s) Party), echoed popular calls for the government to purge non-Poles from its bureaucracy. Yet Witos also complained that many administrators were working as if nothing had changed and that despite fierce shows of loyalty many had not given any indications of patriotism before independence. These same people 'only a few weeks ago, when it was by no means clear whether or not there would be an independent Poland, were forbidding their subordinates to speak Polish! If the regulation of our lives and future is to depend on such people then we must raise serious doubts about the future.' Going on to condemn Czechs who worked as government and estate administrators in particular, Witos asked whether there were no Poles to take their place: 'Everybody [each senior bureaucrat and landowner] has his own Benji [Benjamins – being an allusion to Jews], and there are those for whom these Benjis are Czechs [rather than Jews].'[59] Massive complaints in March 1920 led the Polish parliament to call for a review of the bureaucracy in the northwest. In response to a delegate's vigorous condemnation of the region's local officialdom, made four months later, the parliament established a special investigatory committee.[60] The director of Poland's National Bank remarked that only in 1921 was the bureaucracy able to administer daily civilian affairs and collect taxes.[61]

The best qualified Galician Poles were appalled by the new bureaucracy and often refused to transfer to Warsaw because they disliked the prospect of working under locals who they felt were unqualified.

Those who did go tended to be the least qualified, and critical observers blamed these 'half-educated elements' from a country 'noted for bad organization' for Poland's chaotic administration.[62] Polish leaders from the formerly Russian territories, meanwhile, echoing the long-standing prejudice of the Warsaw literati who did not consider Galician Poles to be 'real Poles,' looked down on them as bureaucratized renegades. This condescending contempt is captured in President Ignacy Paderewski's expressed amazement that a Galician Polish leader he had just met could speak Polish well.[63] Former Russian Poles, exploiting the stereotype of former Galician Polish officials as nationally indifferent unpatriotic automatons, convinced the Polish government to begin firing them first when the zloty collapsed in 1926, and the need to cut costs forced the government to dismiss employees.[64]

The behaviour of Polish officials in 1831 and 1863, complaints voiced in the Polish parliament, and the preoccupation of the nationalist literati with themes of national treason and betrayal remind us that anxious Polish-born imperial bureaucrats, faced with penury in 1918 and 1919, like most administrators elsewhere, followed their interests. Censured, if not shunned by nationalist literati activists, as late as 1936 administrators still felt stigmatized and were unable to discuss their past without obfuscation or apologetics: 'We all understand that among us Poles in the Galician administration there were those who admitted they were Polish yet obviously followed another line at work ... But for a few exceptions, I know of no incident where one of our friends went along the other line (*innej linji*). But that can happen. In such a difficult and complicated situation it is always possible to lose one's way ... If there were such moments, then I am convinced that these were exceptional, and more important, merely breaks of temporary disorientation resulting from misunderstandings.'[65]

Galician Polish bureaucrats were men who, during the war years to prove their loyalty to a sceptical Austrian military, incurred civilian wrath by the zealous enforcement of requisitions and work duties.[66] In short, it would not have surprised Weber if a good number of Polish officials after November 1918 were more interested in the new Polish national state as a new employer than as a new patria – a case of interests coinciding with principles. When the new national government's monopoly was challenged fifteen months after independence by another employer, in the form of a Bolshevik government which occupied the northeastern part of the new state for three weeks in July and August 1920, literate educated clerks, just like the overwhelming majority of Polish men in

Lviv in November 1919, and illiterate uneducated peasants alike did not behave as national leaders thought they should have. Their behaviour revealed that national loyalties were still brittle – just as they were further east – and that professional interests can trump principles.

Polish nationalists had begun to disseminate national ideas among the peasants in formerly Russian and Austrian Poland at the turn of the century and by the outbreak of the First World War had succeeded in mobilizing primarily the wealthier and the literate.[67] Wartime requisitions by German- and/or Russian-speaking troops helped turn the illiterate and poorer peasantry towards the Polish cause, but like in formerly tsarist Ukraine, conscription, fixed prices, shortages, and requisitions imposed by the new Polish state were just as crucial in tempering that patriotism. Peasants refused to pay taxes. Radical socialist, anti-Semitic, and anti-Polish agitation provoked them to violence, and deserters and demobilized soldiers both encouraged and armed them. Conscription was introduced in Poland in March 1919, but peasants helped conscripts flee and draft evasion rates averaged 50 per cent. In response, the government declared a State of Emergency in April 1919 that lasted until May 1921.[68] That August, in addition, with Bolshevik armies marching towards Warsaw, the government passed a long-awaited Land Reform Bill and appointed Witos premier. These initiatives localized and neutralized anti-state violence in 1920. Nonetheless, a considerable number of the poor and landless still supported the Bolsheviks, and draft evasion in Poland remained high that summer. Unlike in Ukraine, however, Polish leaders had loyal troops who could disarm civilians and quell violence before it spread. Also, they established clear lines of authority that subordinated local military commanders to governors and gave the latter control of local troops and gendarmes – thus minimizing the conflicts of authority that plagued local Ukrainian administration.[69]

In 1920, arriving in the wake of the Red Army, 5,700 Polish Communists apparently found enough educated secular Jews, workers, and local left-wing sympathizers in the territories they occupied, as well as middle- and lower-level local Polish professionals, to staff approximately 150 revkoms. Decrees announced that no one was allowed to leave their job and that those who obeyed orders would be safe.[70] There is no mention in the literature of a shortage of personnel or of sabotage by Poles in the Bolshevik administration. Local Polish Socialist Party members, in particular, disregarding party instructions to the contrary, actively participated in the establishment of Bolshevik rule in Poland. Poles later arrested because they worked for the Bolsheviks explained that they did so because of the status and relatively good pay. Some said that they had joined to avoid arrest; others explained that they had feigned loyalty in order to sabotage from within or to prevent foreign Bolshevik appointees from taking over local affairs. It is not known how many of these people had been administrators previously but, reminiscent of pre-war conservative and nationalist arguments, one of them claimed that by working for the Bolsheviks he had hoped to make their regime bearable. Intellectuals were obliged to take government jobs, he said, so that Poland would not become worse off than Russia, where 'vulgar hooligans' had dismissed the 'intelligentsia' and taken over the running of the country. After the war the Polish government arrested and/or executed by court martial hundreds of all nationalities as Bolshevik collaborators, but conducted no investigations on previous imperial employees. The moderate left complained that local right-wing activists and Catholic priests had used the opportunity to avenge themselves on anyone critical of them. The records of the PPS inquiry into its members' activities under Bolshevik rule have disappeared.[71]

When Poland took over Volyn and Podillia provinces in August 1919, the government dismissed almost all former Ukrainian officials, as they refused to swear loyalty, and replaced them with Galician Poles. All dismissals were ordered verbally, and when employees asked for written documents Polish commissars replied that they were not Bolsheviks and saw no need to waste time and paper on their orders. The unemployed former ZUNR officials were not allowed to go to the UNR.[72] Formally subject to a separate Volynian Civilian Board (*Zarzad Cywilny Wolynia*) local officials initially included Russian former tsarist employees who had not fled with the Bolsheviks, hoping that these two provinces would become part of a postwar democratic Russia.[73] Presumably the NDs played a key role in regional appointments and chose according to party criteria. This might explain why the head of the Volyn board's press section described the new Polish officials not as the apolitical officials of pre-war times but as rabid nationalists. Imbued with ND-inspired hatred of non-Poles, their anti-Ukrainian attitudes impeded integration.[74] As of 1923 the 5 to 10 per cent of Volyn province's administrators who were not Polish worked only at the lower levels.[75]

Occupied ZUNR territories, renamed *Malopolska wschodnia,* were initially under the supervision of a fifteen-member council residing in Cracow and headed by Kazimierz Galecki who, in order to win their loyalty, called on troops and administrators to be fair to the populace. Galecki distinguished, however, between 'Ukrainian agitators' and 'peaceful citizens of the Rus'nationality' which, in practice, gave officials and troops licence to do as they saw fit with the former. That normally resulted in mass arrests, beatings, requisitions, and summary executions. According to one Ukrainian report from the Drohobych area, Polish rule hardly represented law and administrative order: 'medieval times have returned; serfdom is revived, but worse than it was before.' Although this particular report dates from the summer of 1919, similar accounts continued to emerge well after the war ended.[76]

Article 26 of the November 1919 Statute on Eastern Galicia obliged Poland to staff the administration with locally born persons irrespective of language or religion in proportion to each nationality's share of the total population, and Article 40 forbade punishing any inhabitants of the province for their political loyalties between 1914 and 1920. A declared amnesty in November 1919 was never implemented. A petition to the Seym (parliament) for amnesty, and to allow all former employees to be hired, was criticized. Although Polish socialists in Warsaw wanted former eastern Galicia under military rule and were not averse to rehiring Ukrainian administrators, leaders in Lviv, dominated by the ND, placed the territory under a Polish-staffed civilian administration which they controlled.[77] In March 1919 they began mass dismissals of Ukrainians from government jobs in Lviv – although those same Ukrainians had all returned to work a month earlier, after the Poles took the city. In June, despite instructions from Warsaw to treat Ukrainians according to the norms of international law, local leaders ordered the police to begin compiling lists of former ZUNR administrators and the army to begin interning them.[78] Thus, while Warsaw politicians were negotiating with Germany to retain German officials in its western provinces, Polish politicians in western Ukraine were replacing Ukrainians and Jews with Poles who had served there before 1918. Before the end of the war with the ZUNR, eastern Galician Polish leaders had already dismissed and arrested between 7,000 and 8,000 Ukrainian government employees in the regions they had occupied. At the lowest levels, in the absence of a Polish candidate, Poles retained former ZUNR officials who swore loyalty and then paid them in worthless Ukrainian currency – while paying Poles in the still valid Austrian crowns.[79] Ukrainian officials who refused to take the oath of allegiance, because it included reference not only to the Polish state but to the Polish nation, were forced to do so. After the government changed the wording of the oath in December 1919 many former ZUNR employees who applied for jobs were rejected on what they considered were arbitrary and illegal grounds.[80] Those who were prepared to take the reworded oath to get work found that they first had to be vetted by 'rehabilitation committees' established in November 1919 – that apparently functioned independently of the central government and contrary to official policy. Organized by local ND and PPS activists these committees systematically rejected applicants either on the grounds of disloyalty or administrative technicalities. Particularly hard hit were Ukrainian railway and post office personnel. If a central minister overruled their decision and hired a Ukrainian, committees would threaten to call out all the local Polish employees on strike. Lviv authorities would also transfer provincial administrators to Lviv or further west and replace them with Poles recruited from former western Galicia.[81] During the first months of their occupation the Poles did not work according to clearly defined criteria of selection applicable to all prospective candidates. The local Polish teachers' organization decided in May 1919 to reinstall any teachers, Ukrainian or Polish, who in front of a commission stated that they had committed no acts of violence against Poles and had taken the ZUNR oath only to enable their families to survive materially. The instructions on rehiring that the Polish central government issued in December 1921 were broader and open to abuse. They forbade hiring anyone who had been involved in 'activities directed against the Polish state.'[82]

Incomplete figures indicate that between December 1919 and March 1920 of 3,200 applicants 79 per cent were accepted by the Polish government. In 1921 Ukrainians comprised 17 per cent of western Ukraine's almost 26,000 government employees (excluding teachers).[83] This was approximately the same proportion as before the war, but since this territory's bureaucracy had almost 10,000 more administrators in 1921 than in 1914 actually more Ukrainians worked for the government under Poland than under Austria. Whether these figures would have been higher if not for the discrimination is unclear.

Polish leaders excluded Jews from government employment both before and after they ratified the Minorities Treaty which stipulated the right of all citizens to apply for jobs.[84] The two Jewish members on the Government Commission for the Reinstatement of Dismissed Galician Officials resigned, protesting its reluctance to consider evidence favourable to Jews.[85] By 1921 no more than 2 per cent of all Poland's administrators were Jewish, and of these almost 90 per cent worked in western Ukraine, as municipal rather than central ministerial officials; from 14 per cent of all administrators in pre-war eastern Galicia, the Jewish share within the same area had declined to approximately 8 per cent in 1921.[86]

Conclusion

> ODESA PARTY MEMBERSHIP COMMITTEE CHAIRMAN: And one final question. Weren't you the fiddler at Makhno's wedding?
>
> ISAAK MOISEIEVYCH: Yes. But I can explain ...
>
> CHAIRMAN: Never mind. We cannot accept your application for membership.
>
> ISAAK'S WIFE (at home): But Isaak, you should have lied. Who can know? It was so long ago.
>
> ISAAK: And how could I lie if all the committee members were guests at the wedding!
>
> Soviet joke from the 1920s

Mykhailo Hrushevsky wrote in 1918 that he had cried when he reflected on how his nation's abilities in the arts contrasted with its inabilities in social and political affairs, and he claimed that it could not produce enough practical people able to organize and administer.[1] This idea also figures in other accounts of the revolutionary years. Yet, throughout the period, reports from all sides complained as often, if not more, about too many people of the wrong kind than of too few people in government offices. National leaders complained of Bolsheviks, Russian extremists, and Jews. Bolsheviks complained of 'Petliurites,' the petite bourgeoisie, and Jews. Whites complained of 'Petliurites' and Bolsheviks. The evidence examined for this book does not conclusively disprove Hrushevsky's opinion or that the lack of administrators was a key reason why national governments failed to maintain independence. However, it does seriously question this claim. It notes that there were officials of the new Ukrainian governments who had been imperial officials and who sometimes could implement some policies, an accomplishment that, in light of the upheavals of the time, should not be ignored. Nor was the White regime more administratively efficient because it presumably included more tsarist officials than other governments – although that has yet to be demonstrated. However supposedly 'underdeveloped' or 'incomplete' Ukrainian society might have been, it did have a pool of educated men and women who could be administrators, and while national leaders did sometimes fail to take advantage of opportunities, they did understand the importance of bureaucracy and bureaucrats and tried to mobilize the resources that were at their disposal. In this broader context, Osyp Nazaruk appears to have been closer to the truth when he observed that the main problem with the Ukrainian governments during the revolutionary years was not a shortage of educated men or those with administrative skill, but of competent political leaders – arguably much as was the case in 2004 to 2009.

Ukraine was no Slovakia, where in 1919 national leaders had seventy-five Slovak-speaking Slovaks with government administrative experience. At the beginning of the twentieth century in the Ukrainian provinces of the Russian Empire, approximately 60,000 people worked as administrators in government and private organizations. Of these approximately half declared their first language to be Ukrainian. This latter figure included anywhere between 10,000 and 15,000 government, co-op, and zemstvo/duma administrators. As of 1917 the total number of administrators had increased because of the war. There are no data on administrators in 1917 but they were part of the almost half-million people in the Ukrainian provinces who were working in non-industrial non-military institutions that year.

There are no detailed statistics for the war years, but what the examined evidence points to is that at the time there was an available pool of able administrators in Ukraine sufficiently competent in Ukrainian to work as bureaucrats in the independent national governments, and that many of them did so. There were also Ukrainian-born Russians, Poles, and secular Jews who were employed as government officials. Most Bolshevik government administrators, on the other hand, were either declared Russians or secular Jews, and of them many were from Russia, not Ukraine, and thus ignorant of the country and its language. While secular Jews worked as civil servants in all of the governments, except that of the Whites, probably more Jews worked for the Bolsheviks than for any of the national governments.

Dmytro Krainsky attributed patriotism and zeal to the UNR's new Ukrainian employees, but there is too little evidence about them, and their non-Ukrainian co-workers, to permit generalizations about how their professional interests related to the prospect of an autonomous and then independent Ukraine. Although in 1911 Leonid Karchevsky complained that 'it was hard for a native Russian man' to get a job in Podillia province because of Polish office cabals, there is nothing to suggest a 'bureaucratic nationalism' among 'Little Russian'/Ukrainian officials during the early 1900s. At most it might be argued that insofar as they shared a vocational dissatisfaction with their Russian co-workers, Ukrainians as a group were potentially receptive to a national message.

Loyalties were not determined by language use or identity only. From the point of view of political leaders who needed service personnel, it was rational to offer employment to all who swore loyalty. People faced with destitution cannot be too particular about who they work for or what they do. And the longer a government survived and was able to provide a modicum of services, the more people began working for and identifying with it. Some might label this symbiosis 'opportunism' or a product of 'political immaturity' but that is how people behave. At the time, at least one individual is on record for protesting against frequent condemnation of 'opportunists' and pointing out that this was destructive of Ukrainian state building.[2] Insofar as bureaucrats' professional inclinations are towards inertia rather than subversion, it was rational for them to work for all comers. As noted in Chapter 3, Ukraine's administrators' unions supported independence. A minority, composed of extremist declared Russians, Russian left Socialist Revolutionariess, Mensheviks, and Bolsheviks, did oppose Ukrainian statehood. But, not all Russian-speakers or Russian-speaking clerks were extremists or members of these political parties. There was no Russian territorial 'creole nationalism,' and most of Ukraine's Russians supported Ukrainian autonomy in 1917. Russian-speakers who accepted Ukrainian independence as a lesser evil to Bolshevism saw practical territorial reasons to support it. Professional and material interests also motivated ethnic Ukrainians indifferent to the national movement, and indifferent non-Ukrainians, to keep doing their old jobs in the new Ukrainian polity.

Planned sabotage existed, but is difficult to prove and to distinguish it from sloth, malfeasance, inefficiency due to committee as opposed to directorial decision making, or corruption. There was also personal intra-ministerial resistance to commands from Ukrainian ministers in Kyiv, but known examples of this are limited to cultural/linguistic issues. If between 1917 and 1921 officials as individuals interested in survival and in keeping their jobs found it difficult to determine which group and/or party in which city represented a government employer that had come to stay, their hesitations and vacillations cannot be arbitrarily labelled as a betrayal of the new Ukrainian state. One national activist and later minister complained that between 1917 and 1919 not as much as one russified 'Little Russian' in Katerynoslav joined the ranks of 'our Ukrainian intelligentsia.'[3] This was probably true, but 'our Ukrainian intelligentsia' was not coterminous with the national state and its governments.

This book has argued that national governments had competent staff, among which a core comprised former tsarist officials, and not all of them were 'anti-Ukrainian' or politicized neophytes. There were people who confirm Hrushevksy's assertion. In September 1918 Ievfymii Kysil, who had just graduated from teachers' college, applied for a job as a county secretary; he admitted in his application that he was not familiar with office work but hoped that he would quickly learn.[4] In October 1919 Mykola Morhach applied to the Directory's Ministry of Labour, explaining that he was a Social Democratic Party activist, had completed an urban primary school, and then continued with a program of self-education: 'thanks to which [he wrote in the third person] he had mastered a knowledge of Marxism and the dialectical method of thought.'[5]

Officials like those whose careers have been traced in this book would have taken exception to Hrushevsky's opinions. Makar Mokrytsky was employed throughout the entire period, appearing for the last time in 1921 in the records of the Liquidation Commission overseeing the reduction of the Directory's administrative staff in the Polish city of Tarnow; that September he resigned. Apollin Marshynsky became finance minister of the Directory's government-in-exile; he resigned in 1921 and emigrated to Czechslovakia. Alongside Marshynsky and Roman Trofymenko were men like Hryhorii Ziatkevych, Volodymyr Kol, and Polish-born Roman Catholic Vladimir Dzuvaltovsky-Gintovt, who also began their careers before the revolution and remained employed through all the regimes up to and including the Directory.[6] Nor should historians overlook Russians, like Sergei Shtern, who were prepared to support a Ukrainian regime that could maintain order on the grounds of administrative rationality. Alexei Tatishchev was not particularly enthused by Ukrainian independence, but he was prepared to work, in Ukrainian, for the Hetman; he ended his career working in General Wrangel's Land Ministry in southern Ukraine. Krainsky did not think that the Central Rada provided any kind of administrative rationality, yet he did work for it, and the Hetman, and admitted that Ukraine under the Rada was better off and suffered less than did Russia under the Bolsheviks. The Kyivan Jewish lawyer Goldenveizer also worked for all the regimes that controlled the capital until October 1919. Finally, no less significant were non-party declared Ukrainian Soviet officials like Fedir Kyrychuk; competent and devoted, Kyrychuk considered himself an honest, hard-working, self-made man who did his part building Bolshevik Ukraine in his native Volyn province. A collection of sixty-three Directory personnel files from the General Affairs Department of its Ministry of Economics, compiled in exile in 1921, shows that thirty-one of the individuals had pre-1917 clerical experience, and thirty-seven had completed secondary or higher education.[7]

Undoubtedly, present among national government bureaucrats were those who were motivated by principles rather than interests. There were presumably others who like Fedir Tykhonevych, who was a graduate of St Petersburg's polytechnic; in January 1918 he took a job with the Rada's Ministry of Internal Affairs, remained for only two months after the Hetman took power, and then applied for a job again to the Directory, explaining that he had quit when 'the course of the Hetman's politics became clear.' The loyalties of Mykhailo Morshchelivsky Korb-Stetsky were beyond question. Working in the Food Supply Ministry under the Rada, the Hetman, and then the Directory, he fled Kyiv when the Bolsheviks arrived and found his way to Serbia. He managed to return to Ukraine, in May 1920, from where he had to flee the oncoming Bolsheviks again, joining the Directory-in-exile that August in Tarnow, 'without clothes or money,' where he begged for, and got, a government job again.[8]

However, most of the bureaucrats who stayed at their jobs as Ukraine's regimes came and went were presumably more concerned with their professional interests, and to survive they prudently remained 'uncommitted.' Where individuals did commit, family members could often be on an opposite side – with each side discreetly helping the other when 'theirs' was in power; and keeping out of sight when it wasn't. This practice appears to have been widespread, and Ukrainian newspapers from 1919 contain complaints from irate citizens about people who remained at their jobs regardless of who ruled.[9] Multiple shifting loyalties found reflection in a popular song: '*Ia na bochtsi sydzhu / Pid bochkoiu kachka / Mii cholovik bolshevyk / A ia haidamachka*' (I am sitting on a barrel / Under the barrel is a duck / My husband is a Bolshevik / But I'm for the Otamans).'[10] Did they necessarily undermine state building? Such people played their role in creating an organizational continuity that made life possible. Working administrators, more numerous the lower the level, must be placed among those unknown numbers of people who tacitly supported each regime and did what they could at their jobs, but not zealously, so that representatives of the next regime would not shoot them when they came to power.

These were men like Matvei Davydovych and Semen Burlaka, in Okhtyrka district in Kharkiv province, who had taken up their minor posts well before the revolution and were still there when General Denikin controlled their territory.[11] Oleksander Sheptytsky, Evdokhii Kondriv, and Evstakhii Iakosyshyn all worked as local secretaries in Ushytsia disrict before 1914, and they were still at their desks in the autumn of 1919. In Kyiv province in 1919, purportedly, the same people held the same posts they had in 1917.[12] Luka Kyzyma, from Poltava province, worked as a district secretary, until he was appointed local military commandant by the Hetman; he also worked for the Bolsheviks, the Directory, the borotbists, and for a time, as a secret agent in Denikin's regime. Arrested by Colonel Makogon, when he worked for the Hetman, Kyzyma managed to escape, and then a year later, it was Kyzyma who recognized Makogon in Kamianets and revealed his identity, obliging him to flee. The Bolsheviks arrested Vasyl Korenchuk for three months for alleged links to the Directory. One of his statements, albeit made under duress, probably summarized the views of many: 'I was always apolitical and never joined [any political organization] and only followed orders [as would] any junior official.' After his release in December 1920, Korenchuk was allowed to take up his previous job as secretary. Not so fortunate were Kyryl Kuzmenko, Vasyl Klokosos, Oleksandra Kuzminsky, Fedir Borodenko, Zotyk Koroliuk, and Andrii Rozhko: Arrested in 1921 by the Bolsheviks for alleged membership in an anti-Bolshevik Directory plot, they were all either shot or jailed.[13]

National governments seem to have recruited few secular Jews or women in their central offices for any jobs beyond typist, but this was not necessarily the case in provincial offices. Jews apparently continued to work in the Ukrainian State even though they were formally forbidden to do so. In Sumy in Kharkiv province Zinaida Kramarenko finished high school in 1916; she could type in both Ukrainian and Russian, and from June 1917 she worked as an assistant clerk at city hall, quitting in September 1918, and that October she applied for a job in the Hetman's Ministry of Internal Affairs. In a collection of forty-eight personnel forms from the Directory's Land Ministry, filled out in 1920, we find twenty-two-year-old Nastia Velychko; illiterate, from a village in Volyn province, in 1917 she joined the Rada's War Ministry as a courier and was still delivering for the Directory in 1920. Nineteen-year-old Hanna Volodkivska was from a village in Podillia province; in 1917 she was still in school, but able to write and type she then worked as a secretary for the Land Ministry. Joseph Lyzik, aged nineteen, was a Jewish student who worked as an office clerk. Meanwhile, another Jewish student, having finished a course in Ukrainian studies in Kyiv in 1917, explained in his 1919 application letter to the Directory's Ministry of Justice that he wanted 'to work for the benefit of the Ukrainian National Republic.' Before joining the Directory's Land Ministry Edward Klepatsky worked for the Podillia zemstvo; born in Viatka, Russia, he was a Catholic Pole and a graduate of Warsaw's Veterinary College. Zina Martyniukivna, aged twenty-three, was born in a small town in Kyiv province. After finishing secondary school she worked in a bank and in 1917 in the Political Department of the Rada's Ministry of the Interior; involved in the street-fighting against the invading Bolsheviks in 1918, she also served as nurse before joining the Land Ministry.[14]

Eighty-nine people were working in the central offices of Kharkiv province's governor in March 1917. Where they were four years later is not known, nor is it known whether any personnel lists from those years from other provinces have survived that would tell us about their colleagues. The random samples examined here suggest that personnel turnover was significant and mostly due to mundane factors like retirements, promotions, transfers, and resignations rather than political purges. And while there is evidence of strong continuity of cadres between the tsarist and national governments, there is less about personnel carryover between the national and Bolshevik regimes. Perhaps most pre-1917 civil servants who were still employed in 1922, like Panas Myrny, worked for all of the regimes. Nevertheless, the continuity between non-Bolshevik and Bolshevik governments is more difficult to trace than that between the national governments. Besides the noted problem of destruction of records, the sheer size of the post-1921 government machine compared with its 1917 precursor meant that even had there been considerable continuity, the older staff would have been overwhelmed numerically by the new staff.

Those who survived may not have been heroic but they provided the backdrop to the more dramatic events. In light of the circumstances, by 1919 finding money and objects to trade for food could in any case take up as much time as professional duties.[15] Activists, idealists, and political leaders may not have liked such people but they had to influence, control, and/or exploit them. How well they did this was determined by the activists' and leaders' beliefs, skill, ingenuity, and dexterity in accommodating their interests.

National leaders did not organize an administrative bureaucracy before July 1917 because they could not: They did not organize a bureaucracy because they chose not to do so. They focused on forming coalitions with non-Ukrainian parties, a move that Hrushevsky later admitted was wrong.[16] Within offices, meanwhile, it appears that unions and committees dominated – and how this phenomenon related to the national movement is unknown. Eastern Ukrainian leaders, who agreed about attaining statehood democratically, legally, and peacefully, differed not over the need for administration but over whether it should be centralized and based on elected or on appointed officials. The two major political parties that dominated policy making in the Central Rada, the Social Democrats and the Socialist Federalists, accepted the need for bureaucracy but did not try to take over local branches of tsarist ministries because they were political moderates. Like their moderate Russian counterparts, they too lay great store on the zemstvos and city dumas as the administrative foundation of the new federal order and minimized the need for central government administration. Four months after they claimed authority, national leaders did begin trying to administer through the institutions Petrograd had formally allotted them, but it was only in March 1918 that they made a concerted effort to centralize administration – an effort that arguably could have been made six months earlier. Members of the most influential political party, the Ukrainian Socialist Revolutionaries, thought that world revolution was imminent. These Marxist populists were deeply suspicious of bureaucrats and envisaged a state administered by locally elected part-timers in the Zemgor (Union of Towns and Union of Zemstvos), co-ops, and food supply and land committees, without full-time centrally appointed professionals working alongside them. Unlike Jacobin or Bolshevik leaders, they did not modify their views in the face of reality. There is no evidence of party plenipotentiaries sent to enforce central control over local officials. All three major Ukrainian political parties condemned each other. The SRs condemned the SD and SF attempts to rule through appointed officials as 'dictatorship,' while SD and SF leaders condemned SR 'democracy' as 'anarchy.' Former tsarist officials condemned committee control as chaos. Alongside committee rule in offices, this difference of opinion did not provide a propitious environment for sustained central-institution building and hindered the efforts of those who did show administrative aptitude during the vital first months of the Rada.[17] Unlike in Czechoslovakia, furthermore, 'localists' of all parties and nationalities in Ukraine on the grounds of democracy refused to obey the commands of 'centralists' to disband in early 1918.

The imperial government prior to 1917 was only beginning to establish full-time central officials below district level where administration as a tangible daily reality did not exist. Despite reforms full-time officials in small towns and village secretaries normally remained subject to their village and town councils and not to the *new* county council. Administration exasperated the educated experts but it muddled along well enough to provide recruits, legal decisions, and taxes up to 1914. After three years of de facto military rule in half of the country, the vertical lines of authority and horizontal ties between civilian officials that had begun to emerge in the decades before the First World War were disrupted, but accounts of administrative catastrophe should be judged in light of the preconceptions of the urban educated who made them. Wartime observers in some instances might have only expressed impatience and criticism of a muddling along not much worse than what peacetime observers had tolerated. Whatever the case, the attempts of the Provisional Government to re-establish that order, and the collapse in 1917 of its monopoly on violence, did not improve matters. In the short run, within this situation the oratorical abilities and personalities of outside activists and newly arrived officials became crucial in shaping loyalties and implementing central commands locally.[18]

In the long run, governments had to be able to keep civil servants on the spot to provide funding services and protection in return for taxes and recruits, or they would have to extract those taxes and recruits by force. National leaders complained that peasants refused to pay taxes and surrender recruits because they lacked national consciousness, while local inspectors' reports often noted mitigating circumstances unrelated to issues of loyalty or identity. One issue that influenced attitudes to all governments, and not just the Ukrainian one, was the understanding of democracy. As succinctly reported in December 1917 by the Rada's commissar in Berdychiv district, 'Every village understood the national interest in its own way, that is, according to its own interests. Thus, the frequent refusals to obey the authorities on the grounds that the order is "contrary to the people's will."'[19] However, given the frequency of unimplemented decisions at the district level and lower before the war, the ability of locals to subvert central rules and decrees, and the tendency of local officials to passivity, the above-noted 'refusal' can also be seen as a rationalization of the traditional response to government. Villagers were beginning to realize that they belonged to something called 'Rossiia' or 'Ukraine' or 'Malorossiia' before 1917, and prolonged association with and exposure to a 'Ukrainian government' would have made more of them patriotic and inclined to sacrifice for it. But national governments did not hold territories for long enough to repair and extend those vertical ties that existed before 1917 and thus finish dismantling the closed indirect corporate rule characteristic of the countryside that underlay peasant parochialism everywhere. Nonetheless, the Directory during the crucial year of 1919 apparently did succeed in getting at least as much, if not more, from its population than did the Bolsheviks from theirs. National issues played an ancillary role in administrative matters, but not the determining one.

Whereas some bureaucrats disliked the national governments and some sabotaged them, there is little evidence of conscious sabotage and none of organized opposition or strikes. Inactivity, meanwhile, is not only a consequence of intentional sabotage or of inadequate staff; unimplemented decisions can result from the inefficiencies and shortcomings characteristic of all bureaucracies. What existed in core territories claimed by national leaders was not 'no government' or 'anarchy' because of too few administrators. Rather, against a background of organizational chaos that began during the First World War, there existed a plethora of overstaffed, separate, uncoordinated elected administrations on all levels, probably based on personal loyalties, which were never all subordinated to central ministries. This decentralized, dispersed authority, meanwhile, was what activists and sympathizers of the powerful Ukrainian Party of Socialist Revolutionaries wanted because that is how they imagined their independent Ukraine. Based in the provinces, this party represented a movement that mistrusted centralized government. Early modern European and Bolshevik state-building efforts reveal that such informal personal or party ties can establish control in localities and that central plenipotentiaries with arbitrary powers can then tie such local structures to central organizations. But, even if national leaders did have such plenipotentiaries, they were not able to hold on to their territories for long enough to have been able to tie regions to the centre. Alternatively, commissars and plenipotentiaries as central party agents could cause local administrative confusion because they overrode non-party ministerial chains of authority and disrupted procedure – a problem characteristic of all governments and the manifestations of which in Ukraine are worthy of a separate study.

By September 1917 most city dumas and most zemstvos did recognize the Central Rada, and by that November they were joined by the civil servants' unions – which effectively gave the Rada what remained of the tsarist administrative structure. Those bureaucrats later did little to directly aid the Bolshevik occupation. Whether or not it is merely coincidental that the Bolsheviks formally declared war on the Rada only after the Russian bureaucrats' strike ended, is unknown. When in January 1918 Ukrainian SD leaders finally decided that bureaucratic centralization was imperative, they alienated the SR-controlled zemstvos and city dumas, whose members resisted the attempt to restrict their administrative autonomy as an attack on their democratic right of self-government. During the political conflict administrative-executive personnel were left either without instructions or with contradictory ones. Ministerial building was then cut short by the German occupation.

For all the Central Rada's differences with Petrograd over territory and jurisdictions before the Bolshevik conquest, these differences did not include the need to continue the war, supply the army and cities, and delay land reform until the Constituent Assembly convened, or any other non-national issue. It is difficult to see what would have changed, therefore, if the Land Committees and local ministry offices in 1917 had followed Kyiv's instead of Petrograd's orders. The Provisional Government formally devolved selected powers to Kyiv in August 1917, and central ministries began to work through the Rada's General Secretariat in December 1917. But how by the end of 1917 'Ukrainian' or Kyivan-controlled officials could have imposed hated policies without force is not evident. All governments had to get food and taxes from reluctant peasants and all, including the Rada, began with fixed prices, then moved to limited requisitions from wealthier peasants and fines, and then to the use of troops. Ironically, moreover, due to the success of the Rada's own propaganda, by the autumn of 1917 people identified those policies in Ukraine with Kyiv rather than with Petrograd. All national leaders faced the prospect of resorting to the same violence against their people that the Bolsheviks used against Russians after June 1918. And if they used less force because they would not, rather than because they could not, is worthy of inquiry – as is the degree to which peasant expropriations under the Ukrainian State can be considered government policy.

Critics accused the Central Rada of being hostile to administrators and ignorant of and indifferent to administration. They pointed out that while the Rada issued decrees to local officials instead of orders and information, Petrograd kept up a regular deluge of instructions. This seems irrelevant. The Rada's educational and cultural initiatives would have been more successful had officials loyal to it had been in charge of implementation. But, given the war, shortages, inflation, and administrative disruption, would the realization of cultural and/or linguistic measures have brought military success, stability, administrative order, clean streets, or lower prices? Obviously, it irked the Rada that inasmuch as government officials did anything in Ukrainian territories, in practice until the autumn of 1917 most acted as agents of a Petrograd ministry. But, the General Secretariat was formally in charge of the old tsarist bureaucracy between December 1917 and April 1918, and that bureaucracy had accepted its legitimacy – without the encouragement of a Ukrainian law analogous to Article 129 of the 1919 Weimar Constitution that guaranteed civil servants a job for life as a vested 'inviolable right.' The Rada did not oblige functionaries to swear loyalty. It never threatened officials with arrest or dismissal without pension or institute office police supervision.

State building during the period in question cannot be linked directly or exclusively to national identity or nation building or to the idea of an 'underdeveloped society.' Within the broader context, these issues appear secondary. First, the degree and intensity of state intervention that the war forced on all participants was unprecedented and caught leaders in all countries unprepared. All were pioneers, faced chaos, resistance, the threat of collapse, and all proceeded by trial and error. The crucial variable determining success was time, which French and British and Russian leaders had had, but Ukrainian leaders did not. Second, from 1914 onwards the Ukrainian provinces were a staging area for the front, and in accordance with tsarist practice, were under military rule. Local commanders had full authority over civilian officials, and they subverted vertical ministerial ties which resulted in administrative confusion. Third, the Rada inherited this organizational confusion as well as that generated by the Provisional Government; it did not incorporate the zemstvos, city dumas, and military-industrial committees into the government hierarchy, nor clearly define relations between these civilian organizations, ministries, and various commissars. Fourth, in early February 1918 the Rada enacted a law that limited civil servants' work-week to forty-five hours and allowed overtime only 'in exceptional circumstances and for a limited time'; thist confirmed the Provisional Government's practice and may have met pre-revolutionary desires, but whether it was justified in wartime is debatable.[20] Fifth, by the end of 1917 civilian authorities had lost the monopoly on violence; police and disciplined troops were few, and in a country with thousands of wandering amnestied criminals, armed deserters, and demobilized soldiers, any government would have had difficulty maintaining authority. The Bolshevik Russian invasion made the situation worse by forcing Ukrainian leaders to channel men who would have better served as police into the army.

Sixth, national leaders devoted their efforts for too long to what turned out to be the wrong kind of organization. Until September 1917 they fostered the hundreds of civil organizations that had sprung up after March of that year, which then, contrary to expectations, worked at cross-purposes to the central government, thereby intensifying administrative disruption in the country as a whole, though not necessarily within individual regions, towns, or villages. There order and well-being depended on things like proximity to railway lines, the number of outsiders, and particular personalities. This strong preference for non-government and/or elected administrators, reinforced by a concern with legitimacy, led the Rada to postpone the creation of a national bureaucracy separate from the imperial one. Instead, until 1918, leaders directed their talents, efforts, time, and people towards elected representative and non-government public organizations. Expanding the functions of co-operatives, for instance, out of both conviction and legal necessity, Ukrainian political leaders benefited from the services of co-ops, but effectively directed a pool of literate skilled people into the private sector when they might have otherwise gone into government offices. The urban literate who could administer were not limited to one employer, the state, which was the only organization that could coordinate activities on the national level; they could choose from the plethora of non-government agencies that national leaders encouraged and that sometimes paid higher wages.

For these reasons the disorder manifested under the Central Rada cannot be linked only to national issues. National leaders inherited the structural problems of the existing administrative system that included multiple agencies with ill-defined functions, overlapping jurisdictions, few if any offices at the county level, and military circumvention of civilian authority. These problems were intensified by ill-defined legislation and party differences over policies and differences over whether a bureaucracy should even exist, as well as quarrelling within offices between junior and senior civil servants over primacy, hiring, grievances, and assignments. A comparison of the national and White administrations does not support the notion that the former were inept because their personnel were allegedly inexperienced. The White government was perhaps staffed by more experienced former higher-level tsarist personnel than its rivals, yet it was no more adept at organizing its rear than they were. Finally, the degree of administrative collapse should not be exaggerated. Local implementation of routine decisions was haphazard even before 1914, and historians should consider that observers in wartime were likely to be less tolerant of shortcomings than they would have been in peacetime. Much more research is necessary from all regions before conclusive generalizations about state building and administration can be made about all of Ukraine during the revolutionary period. There is evidence that some municipalities, for example, all of which were independent of central ministries as of 1917, maintained some services.

By March 1917 shortages and inflation had hit civil servants hard, and to cope the Provisional Government would shortly begin rationing, requisitioning, allocating, and arranging direct purchase or barter between its officials and producers. These practices were later continued by all governments. To provide in face of breakdown and shortages, all political leaders had to make their bureaucracies larger and more intrusive as the economic situation worsened, which ironically, made the administrations similar to each other. One aspect of this convergence was the reproduction within all the post-tsarist governments of the less-desirable traits of the tsarist system such as passivity, theft, graft, corruption, favouritism, and nepotism. In face of the upheaval and violence that led civil servants to use their public trust for private gain in order to survive, it would have been amazing had old practices not reproduced themselves in the new institutions. The circumstances could force even individuals who may perhaps have had personal motivation to honestly work to resort to behaviour that they may have considered otherwise impermissible. Accordingly, the various post-tsarist states can be regarded less as 'new states' and more as 'successor states' to the tsarist order. Vynnychenko and other top Ukrainian leaders by all accounts worked professionally and incessantly. Like Lenin, Stalin, and Trotsky they too could adapt their behaviour and thinking to running, rather than opposing a government. But not all of their subordinates, regardless of nationality, as inspectors' reports reveal, shared their zeal or ability. The head of the Directory's counter-intelligence unit observed how, during its last weeks, too many of its officials for lack of supervision were either passive or spent all their time in bars.[21]

A comparison of the national and Bolshevik administrations reveals six major differences between them. First, Ukraine's Bolsheviks had more civil servants because they could import thousands from Russia, and they hired thousands more literate secular Jews and women than did any national government. Districts in 1914 that were run by approximately

1,000 civil servants, were hiring up to 1,400 officials each by 1922.[22] A second element had to do with time. In January 1919 Russia's new Bolshevik administration, set up from January 1918, after the civil servants' strike, was still in place. It worked badly but it had worked continuously through the previous twelve months. The national government bureaucracies in former tsarist Ukrainian provinces in January 1919 were being restructured for the third time in two years. Only in western Ukraine did the national government have the same administration throughout its eight-month existence. Third, Ukraine, unlike Russia, had a private sector offering alternative employment to the educated, sometimes with higher wages, throughout the revolutionary years. This meant that clerks in national governments were not tied to their desks by threat of either hunger or no similar alternative work. Staff shortages were born of circumstances, not issues of nationality. In Bolshevik Ukraine control via rations did threaten to break down totally in 1921 when food shortages seriously disrupted rationing and civil servants did begin leaving their offices en masse. But this no longer threatened the regime's survival. By that time the million-strong Red Army in Ukraine could ensure that the Directory's partisan forces would not re-establish the Ukrainian National Republic in place of the Ukrainian Soviet Socialist Republic.

There are enough examples of persons who were indifferent to Ukrainian concerns and who worked as bureaucrats for the national governments either from inertia, self-interest, or necessity to suggest that they probably represented a larger group. There is no evidence of organized resistance by this group, or of national leaders using force against recalcitrant officials, which in turn, kept what recalcitrance did exist minimal and isolated. And because national leaders did not take power with an ideological plan for total social control, they approached the problem of staffing as a short-term technical problem – which included getting rid of saboteurs. This was unlike the Bolsheviks, which leads to a fourth difference between them and national leaders. As advocates of state ownership and massive government employment in a country without a private sector, the Bolsheviks systematized hiring and vetting and transformed indifferent and even hostile educated individuals into dependent civil servants via wages and rations. Faced with mass organized bureaucratic opposition in 1917, the Bolsheviks could thwart this lethal strike by resorting to an expedient that Ukrainian leaders did not use: they hired previously excluded groups en masse, namely, secular Jews and women. Fifth, the Bolsheviks thought up two other expedients in the form of party plenipotentiaries and Revolutionary Military

Committees. The former were sent by Moscow, whenever and wherever necessary, with Cheka assistants, to cajole and enforce obedience. As far as we know, no national parties resorted to this kind of direct arbitrary control. Revkoms, for all their problems, meanwhile, created a clear focus of authority and, because they could expropriate and confiscate at will, had funds to pay staff during the first weeks of occupation. Thus, they avoided the problem faced by national governments of not being able to hire or retain staff because they had no money for wages – particularly during the first crucial weeks of rule in a newly taken territory. Revkoms could enforce authority, additionally, because they could either count on local unemployed workers organized in the paramilitary Red Guard, or later, the Russian Red Army. National officials had no equivalent organization and fewer troops. They did not trust their voluntary paramilitary Free Cossacks (*Vilne kozatsvo*), which in any case did not exist throughout Ukraine, and they attached them to the Ministry of War only in January 1918. The Central Rada and the Directory did declare martial law but because both regimes limited the scope of military commandants rather than giving them unconditional and unlimited authority over civilian officials, they only intensified administrative confusion and deadlock.

Sixth, Bolshevik leaders had few qualms about resorting to terror, while national leaders arguably did – disavowing or condemning terror when their officials or troops engaged in it. No one has yet found any order from any Ukrainian leader comparable to what Lenin told Rakovsky to do in a secret order of May 1919 – 'Shoot on sight without mercy for hiding rifles' – or to his July 1920 command to Bolshevik armies to sweep through each Ukrainian county twice to strip them of everything they could and shoot those who resisted.[23] While national governments assigned surveillance and spying tasks to their secret police and gendarmes, only the Bolsheviks held on to territory long enough to organize the people needed to do these tasks routinely in every settlement. A standard thirty-seven-point Cheka instruction list, from October 1918, detailed how in each province, alongside the existing provincial Cheka and its armed units, additional special regional groups with their own armed units had to be formed to fight 'counter-revolution.' They were to set up covert surveillance and informant networks, investigate, and arrest. They could kill with the permission of the provincial Cheka.[24] In his report submitted to the Directory, a Ukrainian prisoner of war who had travelled through 200 villages in Bolshevik-controlled Kyiv province during his escape in early 1920 wrote that the head of the Workers and

Peasants Inspectorate of the First Cavalry Army, a man named Latipov, had told him that he didn't care if 75 per cent of Ukraine's population died of hunger. If they didn't, they would be shot anyways. That would make the remaining 25 per cent obedient: 'We need Ukraine, not its people' The latter, allegedly, were Rakovsky's own words. A comrade Turkin revealed to a local Ukrainian Communist in the town of Pavoloch, in late 1920, that his food requisition unit would not stop at anything: 'We will burn down these damned Kyiv, Podillia, and Volyn provinces, not leaving one stone on top of another and let all know just what the Communist Party is.'[25] Terror not only frightened people but apparently impressed them. This is suggested in a Directory commissar's report from June 1919 in Kamianets district, where he observed that people wanted a strong government that would use force to establish order and not merely appeal to people's conscience to obey.[26]

The use of force, the readiness to hire women and Jews en masse, and the ability to present former employees with the option of working or starving brought rank-and-file clerks into Bolshevik offices and kept them there. Faced with no pay, and without private 'strike funds,' Russians in Russia who chose not to flee had little choice but to make their peace with the Bolsheviks in January 1918. Within eight months the Bolsheviks had taken over the urban administration of all of central Russia. According to a White spy in a Moscow ministry, four months after taking power few people thought that the Bolsheviks would hold out, and although offices were filled with officials, no one was doing much work except those who were in charge of pay. It took another four months for officials to resign themselves to the reality of Bolshevik power and another four before Russians in general accepted Bolshevik power as state power.[27] As noted in Chapter 5, it took at least a year for Bolsheviks in Nizhnii Novogorod, about as far from Moscow as was Katerynoslav province from Kyiv, to take administrative control of the province to the county level. In Ukraine the Bolsheviks used the same measures they did in Russia regarding office personnel. They imported Russian workers and recruited Jews, women, and marginal, semi-literate ethnic Ukrainian peasants to staff their administration. In 1920 de facto centralization meant that almost 60 per cent of Bolshevik Ukraine's local soviet executive (*vykonkom*) staffs were directly subject to Moscow, not to Kharkiv. As suggested in Chapter 7, when the estimated proportion of declared Ukrainians who worked as officials in the first years of the Bolshevik regime is contrasted with the figures on literacy, Russians and Jews appear overrepresented because the new government was so huge that by 1922, when most literate-declared Ukrainians had accepted the Bolshevik regime, there were not enough of them to staff it.

Did these organizational differences account for Bolshevik victory, and was the Bolshevik administration in Ukraine more successful than national governments in providing functions, services, or in obtaining more food or recruits during the first months of rule in core territories? Arguably not. Even in 1921 Cheka reports suggest that the Bolsheviks had no more administrative control of Soviet Ukraine that year than the Rada had control of its provinces in 1917. Only from 1922 do these reports stop mentioning administrative chaos in their surveys of the bureaucracy and include mainly cases of individual ineptitude or corruption, or dissatisfaction caused by food shortages and staff malnutrition.[28] Additionally, the reports reviewed for this book do not suggest that when they did control core territories in 1918 and 1919 Bolshevik administrators got more recruits to the army and foodstuffs to cities from estimated totals at their disposition in percentage terms than had their Directory counterparts. Absolute Russian Bolshevik total numbers of recruits and amounts of food collected were higher than national totals because the Bolsheviks controlled a bigger core territory and thus more people. Once they established control over thirty Russian tsarist provinces, by December 1918, the Bolshevik government collected more food and soldiers from their sixty-five million subjects in absolute terms than Ukrainian leaders were able to get from a core territory that during the crucial year of 1919 never included more than three tsarist provinces and ten million people (see Maps 2 and 3).

In the crucial year of 1919 territory controlled by the Ukrainian government was smaller in size, population, and resources than Bolshevik-controlled territory, which meant that the longer war raged, the more resources the Bolsheviks would have. Ukraine's Bolsheviks were no more successful in imposing their control during the first months that they controlled a territory than were their rivals, and secret police reports on Ukraine's Bolshevik bureaucracy do not suggest that it was more 'efficient' than the national bureaucracy. No national government controlled a core territory for the whole twelve months that it took Russia's Bolsheviks to consolidate their control in Russia to the county level. It was the ability to procure more men and supplies in absolute terms, because they controlled more people and territory than the national governments, which accounts for the Bolshevik victory in Ukraine. Bureaucracies on all sides appear to have functioned equally badly regardless of how big they were or who was in them, making it difficult to construct a direct link between Bolshevik organizational particularities and the Bolshevik conquest of Ukraine. The deployment of plenipotentiaries who would appear and order 'change everything' was so frequent that they often ended up crossing each other at all levels and, at least in the short term, could produce more disruption than order.[29]

During the decisive year of 1919, on all sides, the shortage of arms and supplies, draft evasion, shirking, and desertion meant that only a small proportion of the total numbers in regular armies were front-line combat troops. This core averaged between 15,000 and 20,000 men who lived hand to mouth and fought in similarly desperate conditions.[30] Ukraine's Bolsheviks, however, could count on the Russian Red Army to augment their local force to levels that the two national governments could not match. Ukraine's Bolsheviks alone could not hold back the UNR offensive during the summer of 1919 because their Russian comrades were at that time seriously threatened by the Whites and by peasant revolts in Russia. They were able to destroy the UNR in November 1919 because the successful repulse of the White offensive in southern Ukraine and a lull in peasant resistance in southern and eastern Russia allowed Moscow to reinforce its western front. Thanks to their control of central Russia, the Bolsheviks could in absolute terms field more combat troops in Ukraine than could any of their rivals. In 1920 with all its thirty-six Russian provinces still under martial law, and tens of thousands of Red Army troops left there to fight anti-Bolshevik peasants, the Bolsheviks could still keep and supply one million troops in Ukraine. By 1920 there were 80,000 men in Ukraine doing nothing but expropriating food – to whom were seconded yet thousands more Red Army troops. No national government had an equivalent.[31] Nevertheless, one of the most effective tactics that Ukrainians used against the Bolsheviks in 1919–21 was to destroy the railway links between Ukraine and Russia to stop the transfer of troops from north to south.[32]

Nestor Makhno's Army, with anywhere between 10,000 and 40,000 men, was about as big as the regular forces of its opponents. Makhno refused on principle to establish a bureaucracy, and administration in his territory was done by soviets without Communist Party members. Apparently more successful in villages than towns, his Civilian Affairs commissions did keep a large army battle-worthy and ran hospitals, schools, a welfare system, and communications in a large territory for almost a year. In addition, the anecdote about Makhno's wedding directs our attention to the importance of contingency and multiple identities alongside interests in determining behaviour and loyalties. In 1919 Makhno signed successive agreements with every one of his rivals except the Whites.[33] After the revolutionary war all concerned minimized Makhno's appeal and regretted that they had been 'guests at the wedding.' If asked, all 'could explain.' But, like our unfortunate honest Jew, not all who admitted attending were forgiven. The malleable, indeterminate lines and identities defined by elites, which people had either ignored or adopted to survive, by 1922 had taken shape among them and hardened.

Western Ukrainian leaders decided from the first day of taking power to base their government on a central administration rather than on public organizations, and their efforts were not dissipated by a powerful Party of Socialist Revolutionaries opposed in principle to bureaucracy. The ZUNR was not plagued by multiple organizations with overlapping jurisdictions. A weak co-operative movement might have been beneficial to the ZUNR, as it meant that most if not all administrative jobs were in government offices. The ZUNR hired Jews and an unknown number of Polish officials. As far as can be determined, a number of Poles worked for the ZUNR for as long as they were not forced to take a loyalty oath. Some were intimidated by activists to resign, but local Poles knew that even if they did not work, the newly established Polish government, as well as local benefactors, would try to ensure that they got paid. Since the western Ukrainian bureaucracy does not seem to have been much worse than its Polish counterpart, it is doubtful that administrative matters played a key role in the victory of one side or the defeat of the other. Whatever the failings of the ZUNR's bureaucracy, they seem incidental to its collapse. That is more credibly explained by the loss of Przemysl and its railway bridge in November 1918, and the unlimited support and supplies that Poland got from France, particularly the 100,000-man Haller Army, which allowed Poland to militarily crush the ZUNR.[34]

This book has argued that all sides faced the same organizational and staffing problems and that all could establish some administrative control over territories that they held for longer than a few months. With the apparent exception of the Whites in the Crimea, the longer that a particular regime's control lasted, the more did that control incline people to obey and work for the regime. There is evidence that, for all the upheaval, civilian officials functioned in one way or another in core territories. Compared with their successful neighbours, Ukrainian leaders had much less time. Military fronts swung back and forth through Ukraine for four years. Groups could take and then lose power every few months or even weeks. New rulers were generally ready to keep the central and middle-level personnel and the existing local city, district, and village full-time administrators; nevertheless, turnover rates among these people due to non-political reasons appear to have been higher than they had been before 1914. Besides the changing staffs, office routines and procedures were radically changed when the Bolsheviks came – and were then changed back when they fled. All of this complicated continuity and implementation. Former professionals like Dmytro Krainsky understandably condemned administration by office committees, a phenomenon that did not exist in the ZUNR; however, it is necessary to balance Krainsky's opinion with that of someone who worked in such a committee – and there is no known source for such an opinion. Tens of thousands of wandering amnestied prisoners did not contribute to stability either. Krainsky, the director of provincial prisons, wrote in 1918: 'We knew these people and knew we were releasing them to pillage like wild animals from a locked cage.' When he asked one prisoner what he would do when released, the man smiled and drew his finger across his throat.[35]

Seemingly endless regime change made unpaid or poorly paid civil servants cynical and indifferent, while common people came to associate government more with violence and requisitions than with services or protection. Hrushevsky travelled from Kyiv to Kamianets and spoke with local SR activists in the wake of the Directory's retreat in February 1919. He observed that both the educated and the peasants in general had become apathetic and were withdrawing from public life. Morally exhausted and fearing death with the next regime change, people were disillusioned and leaving local politics to rabble-rousers. Their attitude towards government jobs, to public service in general, had become parasitical. Officials stole or wasted funds and sought to take, cut, and run as fast as they could.[36] Faced with endless attacks, people eventually stop calling the police or the army. They begin calling on their friends to form self-defence groups, or to make deals with the attacker. That is what happened in Ukraine.

From this perspective what is noteworthy about society and national government territory in Ukraine up to November 1919, as well as in Makhno's territory, is that within their core territories officials got some things done sometimes, perhaps as well as they might have before 1914. Alongside government agencies were informal and formal non-government organizations with their own bureaucracies. What remains to be studied is how these latter administrations worked, the relationship between the local leaders and central agents, and how this compared with analogous local-level links in Bolshevik-controlled territory. No less an important issue would be to uncover continuities from before the First World War and after 1917 with respect to the unwritten rules that determined how in order to survive people manoeuvred between formal rules and informal norms. Arguably, it was not as much 'administration' or officials that were absent in national or in Bolshevik Ukraine, as was central coordination.

Ukrainian leaders' initial decision in 1917 to base their autonomy on non-government social organizations, in hindsight, might be condemned as erroneous. By multiplying administrative organizations they contributed to the collapse of order that was already occurring, which was not in their interests since they were moderates and not revolutionaries. Yet, it might also be argued that since central control was collapsing in 1917 betting on non-government organizations was a reasonable choice. In either case, to invoke lack of personnel and administrative inability as reasons for failed independence is ahistorical, given the undeniable organizational accomplishments of each national government within its core territory. Central Rada leaders, it must be remembered, by January 1918 did accept the need for a centralized central bureaucracy.

Nor should historians uncritically accept claims made by Entente observers travelling with anti-Ukrainian White armies, or others, to the effect that Ukrainians 'lacked national consciousness' – until they have thoroughly considered the evidence to the contrary. Bolshevized Ukrainian soldiers did refuse to fight invading Latvian guards, Russian sailors, and Red Guards in December 1917 to January 1918; but then others, including Russian soldiers, refused to join the invading force, in light of which, the Bolsheviks disbanded all Ukrainian military organizations in Russia.[37] Most assuredly, Bolsheviks in Kryvyi Rih in March 1918 did not think Ukrainians were 'under-developed': 'We must extirpate (*vytriavliat*) the idea of an "independent Ukraine" by all possible means from the people's consciousness, which through inertia, might still smoulder among certain inconsequential groups as events have shown.'[38] White intelligence in the summer of 1919 labelled Ukrainian peasants unreliable soldiers because they were influenced by 'Petliurite propaganda' and supported independence; White officers demanded Russian draftees and wanted Ukrainian draftees sent to Russia. In early 1920 not more than 10 per cent of the Red Army in Soviet Ukraine was Ukrainian, and like their White counterparts, Red commanders wanted their Ukrainian recruits sent to Russia and demanded Russians whom they considered to be more loyal.[39] The next year Ukrainian Communists, in an internal party document, observed: 'Ukraine's population, including the very lowest, including a considerable portion of workers and urban dwellers who are linguistically Russified have come to see themselves as Ukrainians and distinctly contrast themselves both as a nation and a state to Russians and Russia.'[40]

What, finally, are we to make of Max Weber's hypothesis that professional interests or inertia trump identity and/or principles in determining loyalties? On the one hand, it would seem that the refusal of almost all Hungarian officials to work in the new Slovakia, and German officials to work for Poland, would refute it. Yet, despite this ostensible nationalism, both groups kept coming in to work, and the historical literature does not mention that either of them went on strike. Those Ukrainian, Czech, Irish, and Polish officials who supported their own new national states, or the Russian officials who eventually worked for the Bolsheviks, would seem to refute Weber, as they were also motivated by nationalism. So would the behaviour of those Ukrainians who worked for the Central Rada and the Directory but resigned rather than work for the Hetman. On the other hand, the fact that in Ireland, Bohemia, Poland, and Ukraine before the First World War, most 'native-born' administrators were indifferent if not hostile to their respective national-separatist movements, which they regarded as extremist, would support Weber's hypothesis – even though he never considered the relationship of national liberation to bureaucrat loyalties. The collapse of the imperial government they worked for obviously freed former employees from their duties. But, it should be remembered, the imperial Austrian government lent the successor Czech and Ukrainian national governments legitimacy by ordering its officials to work for them. Analogously, some 20,000 government employees who had hedged their bets and kept working for the British during the 'Irish wars' had no problems in working for the Irish Republic once London recognized it as a 'Free State.'

In Bolshevik Russia events neither prove nor disprove Weber. Officials there faced the threat of arrest at work and hunger following dismissal in conditions of privation and upheaval, factors that Weber never considered. Nor did Weber consider the possibility that politicians could free themselves from dependency on old regime bureaucrats by hiring en masse excluded groups, specifically in this case women and Jews, to do necessary administrative work. Officials did strike against the Bolsheviks, contrary to what Weber would have expected, but did tell their leaders in the winter of 1917 that they would refuse to work only for as long as the Provisional Government could pay them. This confirms the importance of inertia and material interests in determining behaviour. Thus, once the funds ran out, all Russian banks and factories had been nationalized, and raising private monies had become impossible, the strike ended and most former officials did go to work for the new government, as Weber postulated. If the Bolsheviks had not been willing to hire the previously excluded, or if individuals from previously excluded groups had refused to occupy empty desks in offices, the old regime bureaucrats' strike just might have unseated the Bolsheviks – in which case Russian events would have conclusively disproved Weber. Analogously, the refusal of some Polish officials to work for the ZUNR cannot be automatically attributed to national sympathies. Their behaviour cannot be judged apart from the financial support that they enjoyed from Cracow as well as their private strike fund. Moreover, unlike their Russian counterparts, their funds never ran out. Here again, in light of the contingencies determining the situation, Weber's generalization can neither be proven nor disproven.

The relationships between bureaucrats' loyalties, interests, and identities are not straightforward. Principles and interests could coincide. Officials without the luxury of a strike fund who chose not to, or could not flee new governments, had to balance principles and identity against the prospects of getting, however inadequate, salaries, benefits, rations, promotions, status, and opportunity for bribes and theft. While some on all sides avoided, worked for, or sabotaged their government, motivated by principles and identity, others kept their heads down and worried about their jobs rather than the about government they worked for. No one should be surprised if the latter were the majority in Ukraine – or anywhere else – nor assume that they necessarily weakened national state-building efforts.

APPENDIX 1

Tables

Table 1 Total and urban population, by province, 1897 and 1917

Province	Total 1897	Total 1917	Urban 1897	Urban 1917
Kyiv	3,527,208	4,439,185	431,508	1,139,000
Volyn	2,939 208	3,418,400	204,406	362,000
Podillia	2,984,615	3,873,900	204,773	355,000
Chernihiv	2,929,761	2,822,045	205,520	429,000
Poltava	2,766,938	3,873,900	264,292	450,000
Kharkiv	2,477,660	3,569,829	353,594	638,000
Katerynoslav	2,106,398	4,158,663	234,227	1,221,000
Kherson	3,094,815	3,528,900	765,800	1,148,000
Total	22,826,603	29,684,822	2,664,120	5,742,000

Sources: Gaponenko, Kabuzan, 'Materialy selskokhozaistvennykh perepisei 1916–1917 gg.,' 102, 114; Bruk, Kabuzan, 'Chislennost i rasselenie Ukrainskogo etnosa v XVIII – nachale XX v.,' 23–4. A 1919 census of unknown provenance gives the total population for that year as 30 million. DAKO, f. R142 op. 1 sprava 157.

Table 2 Number of Russian and Ukrainian journals and newspapers published in Ukraine, 1917–1920

Language	1917	1918	1919	1920
Russian	751	321	222	151
Ukrainian	106	218	173	73
Total	857	539	395	224

Sources: Leshchenko ed., *Kataloh dorevoliutsiinykh gazet,* 148–63, lists by town. Ihnatienko, *Ukrainska presa,* 70, lists by language. Rudy, *Hazetna periodyka,* lists 1,150 Russian, Ukrainian, and Jewish titles published in western and eastern Ukraine, 1917–20; of these, 382 were Bolshevik, 286 were in Ukrainian, 262 were dailies, and 21 saw only one edition. Ilinskii, ed., *Spisok povremennykh izdanii,* 243–9, 264–5, 272–5.

Table 3 Bolshevik newspapers published in Ukrainian and Russian in Ukraine, 1917–1920

Language	1917	1918	1919	1920
Russian	32	27	91	157
Ukrainian	3	2	24	46
Total	35	29	115	203

Sources: Leshchenko ed., *Kataloh dorevoliutsiinykh gazet,* 148–63, lists by town. Ihnatienko, *Ukrainska presa,* 70, lists by language. Rudy, *Hazetna periodyka,* lists 1,150 Russian Ukrainian and Jewish titles published in western and eastern Ukraine, 1917–20; of these, 382 were Bolshevik, 286 were in Ukrainian, 262 were dailies, and 21 saw only one edition. Ilinskii, ed., *Spisok povremennykh izdanii,* 243–9, 264–5, 272–5.

Table 4 Total and urban populations and estimated numbers of total and urban administrators, by province, in 1897

Province	Total population	Urban population	Estimated total admin	Estimated urban admin
Kyiv	3,527,208	431,508	2,424	1,991
Volyn	2,939,208	204,406	1,558	1,069
Podillia	2,984,615	204,773	1,508	991
Chernihiv	2,929,761	205,520	1,397	1,131
Poltava	2,766,938	264,292	1,320	1,256
Kharkiv	2,477,660	353,594	1,670	1,535
Katerynoslav	2,106,398	234,227	1,066	839
Kherson	3,094,815	765,800	2,572	2,577
Total	22,826,603	2,664,120	13,515	11, 389

Source: Obshchii svod po Imperii, I: 1, 9, 11; II: charts 20, 20a, 23.
Note: In cities at the imperial level 49% of census Category 1 were administrators while 40% were policemen and firefighters. Figures at the provincial level are not broken down in the published results. To determine provincial administrator totals, the imperial average was applied to the totals for the Ukrainian provinces. Figures for Kherson likely reflect an inapplicable average regional urban percentage. Odesa's large populations meant that policemen and firefighters probably comprised more than 40% and administrators less than 49% of census Category I in the province. Statistics on occupation are in the unpublished voters' lists for the 1917 Constituent Assembly elections. The 1916 and 1917 census have no data on occupation.

Table 5 Estimated administrators and auxiliary personnel in government, civic councils, and private organizations, by province, in 1897

Province	Government	City/rural councils	Private	Totals	Auxiliary gov't	Auxiliary council
Kyiv	2,424	824	7,190	10,438	941	761
Volyn	1,558	771	3,837	6,166	616	1,408
Podillia	1,508	748	4,546	6,802	596	691
Subtotal	5,490	2,343	15,573	23,406		
Chernihiv	1,397	756	3,837	5,990	552	697
Poltava	1,320	1,032	3,849	6,201	522	952
Kharkiv	1,670	1,274	4,171	7,115	388	1,176
Katerynoslav	1,066	802	3,601	5,469	422	741
Subtotal	5,453	3,866	15,458	24,775		
Kherson	2,572	1,201	6,611	10,384	987	1,109
Totals	13,515	7,408	37,642	58,565	5,024	7,535

Source: Obshchii svod po Imperii, I: 1, 9, 11; II: charts 20, 20a, 23.

Table 6 All and Ukrainian railway, communications, and legal personnel, by province, in 1897

Province	Railway		Communications		Legal	
	Total	Ukrainians	Total	Ukrainians	Total	Ukrainians
Kyiv	5,186	2,781	1,327	338	519	24
Volyn	3,806	3,032	723	163	297	24
Podillia	3,152	1,791	982	350	219	22
Chernihiv	4,570	2,632	591	233	218	72
Poltava	2,833	2,006	596	354	273	126
Kharkiv	8,678	4,019	1,117	361	348	86
Katerynoslav	12,577	3,717	1,085	236	173	18
Kherson	6,919	2,661	1,392	193	555	34
Totals	35,156	22,638	7,813	2,228	2,602	406

Source: Obshchii svod po Imperii, I: 1, 9, 11; II: charts 20, 20a, 23.
Note: In the census, Category 1 includes among the 43% listed as administrators an unspecified number of lawyers and judges; 17% were auxiliary personnel (caretakers, guards, couriers). In Category 13, 6% were administrators. In the fifty provinces west of the Urals 52% of Category 2 (*obshchestvennaia sluzhba*) were elected, full-time and part–time officials; 48% were auxiliaries. Subcategories are not indicated or divided according to language or gender for the provinces. *Pervaia vseobshchaia perepis,* charts 21, 22, vols. 8, 13, 16, 32, 33, 41, 46, 47, and 48. 'Civic councils' includes zemstvos, city duma, and village councils. Sadovsky, *Pratsia v SSSR.*

Table 7 Annual spending in small towns: Secretaries' salaries, as percentage of administrative budget and of total budget, total administrative budget and total budget, 1913–1917

	Salaries (roubles)	As % of admin. budget	As % of total budget	Total admin. budget (roubles)	Total budget (roubles)
1913	840	33	8	2,549	11,006
1914	1,140			2,754	13,591
1915	1,320			2,934	16,757
1916	1,920			3,690	29,757
1917	2,125	41	6	5,216	35,373

Source: TsDAVO, f. 1092 op. 4 sprava 83.
Note: Salaries of the mayor, his assistant, and the police are not included. Staff were all included into one group: 'the chief secretary and his assistants.' In 1918 the figures jump to 13,443, 30,863, and 78,071 roubles.

Table 8 Number of Jews and Ukrainians who declared themselves to be literate in Russian, total and urban, by province, 1897

	Jews		Ukrainians	
Province	Total	Urban	Total	Urban
Kyiv	99 341	41,934	323,421	3,548
Volyn	68,527	28,035	189,764	11,688
Podillia	72,830	25,782	251,471	13,467
Chernihiv	39,611	18,459	245,311	28,164
Poltava	44,362	32,002	364,649	38,789
Kharkiv	6,221	5,778	265,704	50,259
Katerynoslav	41,633	26,971	206,509	17,598
Kherson	112,201	84,083	221,466	36,393
Total	484,726	263,044	2,068,315	231,840

Source: Pervaia vseobshchaia perepis naseleniia Rossiiskoi imperii 1897 goda, chart no. 15, vols. 8, 13, 16, 32, 33, 41, 46, 47, and 48. Figures include ages 1–9 and 60+. TsDAVO, f. 1115 op. 1 sprava 48 nos. 110–11.
Note: The total number of Ukrainians and Jews able to read and write in Russian was 2,553,041, out of a total literate population of 3,477,591.

Table 9 Results of Duma elections (in per cent) in major cities, including garrisons

	All Ukrainian Parties	Jewish Parties	Kadets	Bolsheviks
Kyiv	26	8	25	6
Kreminchuh	17	14	13	?
Chernihiv	27	11	2	3
Vinnytsia	8	10	17	21
Zhytomir	8	12	33	15
Poltava	30	4	8	23
Kharkiv	4	7	11	9
Katerynoslav	9	9	15	20
Odesa	5	14	9	3
Average	15	11	15	13

Sources: Tereshchenko, *Politychna borotba na vyborakh,* 90–117; Boiko, 'Pidsumky munitsypalnoi kompanii 1917 dlia Ukrainskoho rukhu,' in Smolii, ed., *Tsentralna Rada,* I: 214–19; Guthier, 'Ukrainian Cities,' 162–64; O. Radkey, *The Agrarian Foes of Bolshevism,* 219, 243, 353; Chyrkova, 'Vybory do poltavskoi miskoi dumy 2 lypnia 1917r.,' 141.
Note: Listed cities are those with published returns from both elections. Russian Socialist Revolutionaries polled an estimated 35% of the votes cast.

Table 10 Total number of Bolshevik Revolutionary Military Committees (revkoms) in Bolshevik-controlled territory, 1918–1922

	Total	% of Total	% Excluding Siberia
All Bolshevik territory	31,358		
11 Siberian provinces	10,147	32	
32 Central Russian provinces	1,801	6	8
8 Ukrainian provinces (excluding Kherson, Crimea, and including Bessarabia)[a]	12,191	40	57

Sources: Bugai, *Chrezvychainye organy,* 86–87, 288–93; Rigby, *Lenin's Government,* 184–85.

[a] The Ukrainian total includes 422 revkoms from 1918, when they existed only as illegal underground cells. The Ukrainian total without this figure, 7,969, would represent 25.4% of the total number of revkoms, and 37.5% of the total excluding Siberia.

Table 11 Administrators in Ukraine in 1926: All, Ukrainians, Russians, and Jews

	n (%)	Men *n* (%)	Women *n* (%)
All administrators	126,155 (100)	100,725 (80)	25,430 (20)
Ukrainians	64,793 (51)	55,323 (55)	9,470 (37)
Russians	28,264 (22)	21,490 (21)	6,774 (27)
Jews	25,255 (20)	17,375 (17)	7,780 (31)

Sources: Vsesoiuznaia perepis naselennia 1926 g., vol. 28 Ukrainian SSR, chart IV, first six subgroups of Category VIII (*uchrezhdeniia*). This was a subcategory of *sluzhashchie* which lumped together 750,500 office workers and white-collar professionals with doctors, artists, cooks, guards, and servants. Of these, 84,000 were Russian immigrants posted from the Russian Republic (45% of all the Russians and 10% of the *sluzhashchie* total), 52% were Ukrainians, 17% were Jews. Olesevych et al., *Ukrainska liudnist S.S.S.R.* 79, Table XVI.

Table 12 Population in 1910 of districts later controlled by the ZUNR: Uniates, Roman Catholics, Jews, and total

District (*Povit*)	Uniates	Roman Catholics	Jews	Total
Lviv Area	4,74 8,000	145,700	77,300	701,900
Bibrka	61,500	16,600	10,200	88,500
Drohobych	102,200	37,600	29,600	171,700
Iavoriv	68,500	11,300	6,300	86,600
Rudky	49,000	21,500	6,400	77,200
Sambir	65,500	32,800	8,800	107,400
St Sambir	45,300	9,000	6,500	60,800
Zhovkva	82,800	16,900	9,500	109,700
Ternopil Area	980,400	439,800	188,300	1,612,100
Borshchiv	75,400	21,200	12,700	109,300
Brody	91,200	31,700	22,600	145,800
Berezhany	64,900	29,100	10,800	104,800
Buchach	77,300	43,500	17,500	138,300
Chortkiv	46,900	21,400	7,900	76,400
Husiatyn	58,800	26,800	11,300	96,900
Kaminka	70,000	28,400	14,700	11,500
Pidhaitsi	61,300	24,900	7,300	93,500
Peremyshliany	53,900	22,500	9,500	86,500
Skalat	48,300	35,100	12,600	96,000
Ternopil	76,100	46,200	19,700	142,100
Terebovlia	41,700	31,900	7,300	81,000
Zalishchyky	54,800	12,800	9,300	76,900
Zbarazh	43,600	22,600	5,300	71,500
Zboriv	42,800	11,700	6,200	60,700
Zolochiv	73,400	30,000	13,600	117,400
Stanyslaviv Area	1,104,100	201,800	188,400	1,506,000
Bohorodchany	58,000	3,600	7,500	69,500
Dolyna	86,300	12,300	12,800	113,800
Horodenka	70,000	11,800	10,100	91,900
Kalush	78,700	9,800	8,200	92,400
Kolomyia	77,300	22,200	23,900	124,500
Kosiv	71,500	4,000	9,700	85,200
Nadvirna	67,100	11,600	11,500	90,700
Pechenizhyn	40,900	1,700	4,200	46,800
Rohatyn	89,600	21,800	13,500	125,000
Skole	42,900	6,100	5,900	55,400
Stanyslaviv	91,000	35,300	29,800	157,400
Stryi	48,900	15,300	12,800	80,200
Sniatyn	70,700	7,200	10,200	88,600
Tovmach	84,800	20,700	9,700	115,500
Turka	68,800	5,200	11,700	85,800
Zhydachiv	63,000	13,200	6,900	83,300
Total	2,559,300	787,300	454,000	3,820,000

Sources: Gasowski, 'Struktura narodowosciowa ludnosci miejskiej w autonomicznej Galicji,' 91–105; Pilat, ed., *Wiadomosci statystyczne,* vol. 24, no. 3, pp. 23–4. Bujak, *Galicja,* I: 71, 131; Prusin, 'War and Nationality Conflict,' 38–9.

Table 13 Estimated urban population in ZUNR-controlled territory, by confession and total, 1910 and 1917

Town	Uniates	Roman Catholics	Jews	Total 1910	Total 1917
Lviv Area	13,810?	40,597?	33,517		88,871
Bobrka	1,779	1,330	2,502	5,628	
Drohobych	5,887	13,437	15,313	34,665	
Iavoriv	1,346	10,211	2,644	10,211	
Rudki			1,968	3,716	
Sambir	2,228	12,606	5,418	20,257	
St Sambir			1,827	4,931	
Zhovka	2,570	3,013	3,845	9,463	
Ternopil Area	31,331?	34,266?	74,993	162,917	
Borshchiv			1,263	4,765	
Brody	1,622	4,234	12,188	18,055	
Berezhany			4,582	12,717	
Buchach	4,121	2,369	7,777	14,286	138,000
Chortkiv	1,513	743	2,907	5,167	76,000
Husiatyn	1,264	1,230	3,288	5,799	
Kaminka	2,170	2,024	3,549	8,106	
Pidhaitsi	957	1,113	3,497	5,576	93,000
Peremyshliany			2,838	4,962	
Skalat	1,548	1,838	2,838		6,227
Ternopil	8,183	11,672	13,997	33,871	142,000
Terebovlia	3,726	3,202	2,088	9,075	81,000
Zalishchyky	1,103	904	3,382	5,438	
Zbarazh	4,080	2,598	3,291	9,983	
Zboriv	1,044	2,339	2,265	5,656	84,000
Zolochiv			5,243	13,234	
Stanyslaviv Area	33,003?	83,516?	85,018	208,269	
Bohorodchany			1,930	4,378	69,000
Dolyna	3,407	3,337	2,555	9,852	
Horodenka	1,332	5,650	4,210	11,223	
Kalush	1,501	2,787	4,363	8,653	
Kolomyia	5,421	18,306	18,930	42,676	124,000
Kosiv	478	2,107	2,950	5,536	85,000
Nadvirna	1,389	2,883	3,772	8,080	20,000
Pechenizhyn	536	4,351	1,777	6,667	46,000
Rohatyn	1,530	2,863	3,254	7,664	
Skole	1,362	1,932	3,099	6,425	
Stanyslaviv	3,986	13,996	15,213	33,328	158,000
Stryi	6,052	14,144	10,718	30,942	
Sniatyn	2,471	5,086	4,386	12,342	
Tovmach	1,708	1,907	2,082	5,719	110,000
Turka	1,830	4,167	4,887	10,911	
Zhydachiv			892	3,873	
Total	78,144?	158,379?	193,528	460,057	1,226,000?

Source: Gasowski, 'Struktura narodowosciowa ludnosci miejskiej w autonomicznej Galicji,' 91–105; Pilat, ed., *Wiadomosci statystyczne,* vol. 24, no. 3, pp. 23–4. Bujak, *Galicja,* I: 71, 131; Prusin, 'War and Nationality Conflict,' 38–9, 175. Unavailable to me at the time of writing were Prusin's sources and the totals for all of western Ukraine's towns.

Table 14 Population of Soviet Ukraine in 1920 by nationality, urban/rural place of residence, and literacy (incomplete)

	All counted *n* (%)	Ukrainians *n* (%)	Russians *n* (%)	Jews *n* (%)
All Ukraine	21,526,786	12,294,142 (73)	2,610,267 (15)	1,189,029 (7)
Rural	17,156,911			
Urban	4,361,595			
Literate	5,875,748	3,586,471 (29)	1,129,708 (43)	777,748 (65)
% of all literate		(61)	(19)	(13)
% of counted (16,963,312)	(35)	(21)	(7)	(5)
Kyiv (city total)	366,279	52,743 (14)	170,662 (47)	117,041 (32)
(literate total)	247,124	31,993 (13)	110,179 (45)	86,843 (35)
Kharkiv	269,924	57,366 (21)	136,466 (51)	55,474 (21)
Odesa	427,831	12,455 (3)	191,866 (49)	190,135 (44)
Poltava	76,648	44,222 (58)	7,666 (10)	21,747 (28)

Sources: Naselenie Ukrainy po dannymy perepisi 1920 goda. Statistika Ukrainy, no. 28 seriia 1. Demografiia tom 1. Vypusk 11 (Kharkiv, 1922) 2, 19, 22–3, 30, 31. *Naselenie Kievskoi gubernii po dannymy perepisi 1920 goda. Statistika Ukrainy.* Demografiia seriia 1 tom 1 vypusk 1 (Kharkiv, 1922) 20.

Note: Excludes Volyn province, four povits, and some volosts. Counted total includes 85% of population of tsarist Ukraine within 1917 borders. Urban population includes 617,301 people in small towns, counted as 'villages' in 1897. Estimated total was 25,621, 463 (20,886,682 rural; 4,726,501 urban – incl. 770,269 small towns). Only 16,963,312 of total counted indicated nationality. Highest number of declared Russians in Donetsk (885,471) and Odesa (436,984) provinces (51% of total). Highest number of Jews in Odesa (313,606) and Kyiv (321,401) provinces (53% of total). In reality the percentage total of Ukrainians was higher and of Russians was lower than indicated, as an unknown number of Ukrainians and Jews declared themselves as Russians. As more urban than rural residents could be counted, most of the 4 million excluded were Ukrainian. Enumerators in Kyiv and probably other towns both pressured Ukrainians to declare themselves Russians and/or subsequently changed forms to read 'Russian' where persons wrote 'Ukrainian.' *Chervonyi prapor* (Kyiv), 21, 22 March 1919.

APPENDIX 2

Provisional List of Administrators' Unions and Organizations (1917)

Petrograd

Ukrainska spilka sluzashchykh v uriadovykh pryvatnykh i hromadskyh instytutsiakh / Ukrainian Union of Employees in Government, Private, and Civil Institutions

Kyiv

1. *Sluzhashchii Kievskogo gubernskogo zemstva* / Kyiv Provincial Zemstvo Employees Union
2. *Soiuz viiskovykh uriadovtsiv* / Union of Military Officials
3. *Sluzhateli sudebnykh uchrezhdennia* / Union of Legal Office Employees
4. *Kievskii soiuz soiuzov pravitelsvennykh i obshchestvennykh organizatsii* / United Kyiv Union of Government and Civil Organizations
5. *Soiuz sluzhashchikh Kievskoi gorodskoi samoupravlenniia* / Union of Kyiv City Council Employees
6. *Profesiina spilka sluzhashchikh i sluzhytelei kazennykh i privatnykh ustanov Kyiva* / Professional Union of Government and Private Institution Employees of Kyiv
7. *Soiuz sluzhashchikh vyshchykh srednykh i nizshykh uchebnykh zaklad* / Union of Higher Middle and Lower School Employees
8. *Soiuz sluzhashchikh selskogo khozaistva* / Union of Agricultural Employees
9. *Soiuz sluzhashchikh grazhdanskikh pravitelsvennykh uchrezhdenii goroda Kieva* / Union of Government Office Employees in Kyiv
10. *Spilka spivrobitnykiv MVS* / Union of Interior Ministry Employees

Kharkiv

11. *Soiuz gorodskikh sluzhashchikh* / Union of City Employees
12. *Sluzhashchii gubernskoi prodovolchoi komiteta* / Union of Provincial Food Supply Committee Employees
13. *Soiuz obeidnanykh sluzhashchykh derzhavnykh hromadskykh i Pryvatnykh institutsiakh m. Kharkova* / Union of United Employees of Government Civil and Private Institutions of the City of Kharkiv
14. *Sluzhashchii iuzhnoho kraiu* / Union of Southern Region Employees
15. *Soiuz sluzhashchikh gorodskoi prodovolchoi komiteta* / Union of City Food Supply Committee Employees
16. *Kharkivskyi soiuz pravitelstvennykh sluzhashchikh* / Kharkiv Union of Government Office Employees
17. *Kharkivskii gubernskii komitet sluzhashchikh v pravitelsvennykh uchrezhdenniiakh ministerstva vnutrennykh del* / Kharkiv Committee of Interior Ministry Office Employees

Volyn/Podillia

18. *Soiuz sluzhashchikh v pravitelsvennykh i obshchesvennykh uchrezhdennia goroda Zhitomira i Volynskoi gubernii* / Union of Government and Civil Institution Employees in Zhytomir and Volyn Provinces
19. *Obednenniia nizhshykh sluzhashchikh v pravitelsvennykh i chastnykh uchrezhdenniiakh* / Union of Junior Government and Private Institution Employees (Zhytomir)
20. *Profesiinii soiuz prikazhchikov i sluzhashchikh gorodskoi dumy* / Professional Union of City Hall Clerks and Employees (Zhytomir)
21. *Professionalnyi soiuz sluzhashchykh* / Professional Union of Employees (Bratslav)

Other

22. *Ukrainskyi soiuz zemskykh robitnykiv na Katerynoslavi* / Ukrainian Union of Zemstvo Workers of Katerynoslav
23. *Ukrainska hromada pravnychykh pysariv* / Ukrainian Association of Legal Secretaries (Katerynoslav)
24. *Soiuz sluzhashchikh gorodskoi upravy* / Union of City Hall Employees (Poltava)

25. *Soiuz sluzhashchikh Poltavskoi kazennoi palaty i gubernskoi kaznachestva* / Union of Poltava Province Treasury and Finance Office Employees
26. *Soiuz sluzhashchikh v pravitelsvennykh i obshchestvennykh uchrezhdennia g. Chernigova* / Union of Government and Civil Institution Employees in Chernihiv
27. *Soiuz sluzhashchikh Starobilskoi gorodskoi dumy* / Union of Starobilsk City Hall Employees
28. *Soiuz sluzhashchikh v volosnykh i selskikh upravakh* / Union of County and Village Board Employees (Kupiansk)
29. *Soiuz kontorskikh i kantseliarnikh robotnikov g. Kupianska i uezda* / Union of Kupiansk City and District Desk and Office Workers

APPENDIX 3

Daily Life

Vlast sovetam / power to the soviets
zemlia kadetam / land to the kadets
dengi boshevikam/ money to the bolsheviks
shish [khui] muzhikam/ john henry for the peasants

Synelnikove village, Katerynoslav province, 1919[1]

Great events in cities involving the powerful, if they did influence lesser beings in the provinces, did not necessarily do so in the way the powerful desired. Nor are all people always driven by great aspirations. Accordingly, to have a better understanding of the conflicts between ideologies and rulers and ruled, it is important to pay attention to the complexities of responses to situations in the spaces below the societal heights. Perhaps the best recent study of this interrelationship during the Bolshevik Revolution is Ivan Narskii's account of how its horrors left an indelible scar on the Russians who lived through them, and account for some of the pathologies of Soviet society.[2]

In Ukraine, as might be imagined, life went on alongside the resistance, the disruptions, absurdities, and horrors, and people continued interacting with officials of one sort or another. Shortages of food, fuel, and goods, on the one hand, narrowed horizons as this forced people to spend more time thinking about how to obtain for their kin or community what was no longer easily obtainable, than about God or nation. This reflected and reinforced underlying social bonds. On the other hand, survival strategies to cope with the ordeals and whatever formal rules, officials, and institutions did function, often had to be imaginative and go beyond the tried and tested. 'The turbulence became a familiar and natural thing, almost a way of life; it was a new element within which the routines of everyday existence were conducted.'[3]

The demobilized soldier Ivan Iaroshenko noted the coming and going of regimes in his native Mirovaia (in Katerynoslav province) impassively. Arriving home from the front at the end of November 1917, he was happy to go back to work, and he noted on 8 December in his diary that there were rumours about the Bolsheviks dispersing the Russian Constituent Assembly. He did not mention the Central Rada. In his entry for 5 May 1918 we can read: 'worked, nothing new, the Hetman is in power.' While Hetman Skoropadsky issued many orders, Iaroshenko observed: 'no one listens' and there was 'nothing new.' Learning of the Hetman's fall, on 18 November, he awaited the new authorities and found the political situation confusing: 'They say the Hetman is a Kadet, Petliura a Republican, Mikhno [sic] an anarchist, the Russians are Bolsheviks, and everybody is against everybody else and they kill each other. It is horrible to watch this terrible history and I don't know when it will end.' His village declared itself Soviet on 22 January 1919, the same day that the Directory declared eastern and western Ukraine united into one Ukrainian National Republic, but everyone continued going to church and avoiding the draft – as they did when Mirovaia was under White rule. By November 1919, the village was under Makhno's control and 'the people had no trust in anyone and believe in nothing and no one.' The men avoided all call-ups and when one of Makhno's agitators appeared that November, the people paid no heed: 'they are so disillusioned they believe nothing that anyone says.' On 1 February 1920, the day Bolshevik troops again took his village, Iaroshenko wrote: 'Soviet power, nothing new, everything as it was.' During the summer of 1920, accordingly, the village still opposed requisitions while the men still avoided the draft. As head of the village executive committee, Iaroshenko, however, did note one change: 'everywhere Jews are in power and all of them demand grain and recruits.'[4]

If we had read Kyiv's *Iuzhnaia gazeta* on 17 or 20 December 1917, we would have learned in Kharkiv the postal and telegraph workers had just gone on strike against the occupying Bolshevik army, that in reply to a Bolshevik ultimatum the Rada had just sent its ultimatum threatening to declare war, and that Kyiv faced the imminent prospect of hunger. In the middle of all these columns, however, our sense of stability would have been reinforced by a big ad extolling the merits of Dr Gleea's *Stimulol*, which would stop us being nervous, flaccid, and irritable, and save us from premature impotence by imparting us with sexual energy. Customers had only to beware of phony substitutes. Dr Gleea's *Preparation* advertisement, which guaranteed all renewed sexual vigour in those troubled times, was carried by almost every major urban newspaper in Ukraine through to 1920. Nor did changes in government restrain Mr Alexander Liubov, resident of the town of Rzhyshchiv in Kyiv province, from earnestly seeing to his problems. Between 1909 and August 1918 he mailed seventy letters to his district head requesting him to take steps to stop 'hostile agitation' against him and bring the agitators to justice. A note from the commissar to the town's police chief dated March 1918 instructed him to inform Mr Liubov that he needed a doctor and not a commissar, and that his letters would in future find their way directly into the wastebasket, but this apparently had no effect. Had the commissar bothered to enquire further, he might have discovered that Mr Liubov had addressed over a hundred additional similar letters since 1905 to his predecessors demanding that legal action be initiated against officials who were persecuting him and besmirching his reputation throughout Kyiv province.[5] Clearly the 'big issues' of 1917 to 1921 did not concern everyone. A Rada agitator in Poltava province reported, in the autumn of 1917, that initially indifferent or hostile urban inhabitants had accepted the Rada's authority that August, but that in general, 'urban residents were mostly lazy citizens' who cared primarily about their private interests.[6]

One Tymish Brodsky similarly ignored changes of government. He was appointed an assistant county commissar by the Central Rada just before its demise, on 14 April 1918. Dismissed six days later by the new Hetman government, Brodsky did not think that regime change was a reason for him not to get paid, and, that same day, he wrote a letter to the new governor claiming that as a former official he was due half-pay. Since there was no record of his employment in the office, the reply came back, that it was impossible to make any decisions. After the new authorities discovered that Brodsky had worked no more than six days, they wrote that July telling him that there was no regulation about giving half-pay to former assistant commissars, and denied his request. Brodsky persisted. The last reference to him in the records is a letter from the provincial governor, dated 3 October, which noted that as he had a job in another district, he would definitely not get any half-pay.[7] Policemen in Kharkiv province also seem to have paid little heed to regime changes. As discovered in November 1919 by White intelligence, what they had routinely done until then to keep their jobs, successfully, with each incoming government was to explain that they were 'apolitical' and therefore reliable. Since the Whites were repulsed from eastern Ukraine the next month, local officers could not vet the police as ordered – and how they fared under the Bolsheviks is unknown.[8]

Eyewitnesses relate that normally opposing armies battled for control of towns and railway lines and left villages alone except to requisition.

Southwest of Katerynoslav, people living off-main roads, far from railroad stations, and without telegraph links could remain basically untouched by, and even ignorant of, events. Insofar as soldiers marched through occasionally, local inhabitants concluded that there was a war between cities, which as such, did not concern them. Their one political interest was to keep their land and maintain order. 'Whoever brings order will rule; we need nothing more.' The returned veterans who vaguely knew what Petliura (see Chapter 5) or the Bolsheviks represented, did not stay at home long, as they inevitably left to join one or other of the various armies, unless they were cripples. Although short of manufactured goods, such villages were well provisioned and once they saw that a passing detachment would not rob or requisition, they would usually provide it with food.[9] A village in Poltava province in 1920 refused a Red Army detachment wagons. It later heard that this happened to be a disciplined detachment and that a neighbouring village had supplied them with their needs with no problems or excesses. The villagers then had a meeting and sent a letter to the detachment apologizing for their earlier 'confusion': 'now that we know you are Red Army, that is, Soviet Power which we recognize, and not a bunch of commies [*a ne kommuna*] ... we have decided to give you as many wagons as you want.'[10]

Some villages declared themselves 'republics' and thus supposedly dissociated from surrounding events. If they were situated along railway lines they used their strategic location to highjack trains – of all governments.[11] Pereshash, a village 'republic' in Chernihiv province, considered itself to be subject to no group through to 1919. Organized on the initiative of its former owner, Volodymyr Korostovets, a liberal 'Little Russian' nobleman respected by the inhabitants because of his family's long-standing commitment to their well-being, the village even kept the Bolsheviks away. Faced with an army arrived to force them to submit to the nearest soviet, the owner called a meeting that declared itself the local soviet. That night, the inhabitants produced a document stating their intention to submit to the authority of a city soviet much further away than their nearest local one, Chernihiv, stamped it with a Soviet-looking stamp that they manufactured, and in the morning gave it to the Bolshevik commander. They were left alone thereafter and continued their affairs as before, although formally part of Bolshevik Ukraine.[12] In face of political uncertainty and no outside information, the inhabitants of the village of Napadiivka in Kyiv province, in September 1919, when it was under Directory control, preferred caution to commitment. Upon hearing of the imminent arrival of government inspectors to their village, the volost centre, they decorated the volost office with portraits of Shevchenko, Alexander III, and Lenin. Asked by the shocked inspectors why they had done so, they replied: 'If Ukraine wins, then we have Shevchenko; if Denikin, then we have His Imperial Majesty; and if the Bolsheviks win, then we have Lenin. Don't you see we are surrounded by three foes and we don't know which of them to serve and obey. If we had newspapers or information that told us what to do, then we would know whom to support and whom to serve.'[13]

Loyalties were not necessarily related to identity or class. Mainly Russian workers in the gunpowder factory in the northern town of Shostka, for example, were anti-Bolshevik. They took up arms in May 1918 and held out against a Bolshevik force for one week before being defeated. During that time, not only did they not get any help from Ukrainian-German forces, but they got no assistance either from the local Ukrainian village of Lokot. The peasants there were pro-Bolshevik although they were very rich – thanks to the good jobs they had at the powder factory.[14] Looking more closely at prosperous, yet pro-Bolshevik peasants, meanwhile, Bolshevik inspectors soon realized how things worked and why peasant congresses often passed all the resolutions put to them by local Communist party members. Referring to his observations in Volyn province, in June 1919, one such inspector observed: 'No one explains issues to peasants ... they assent to all the resolutions put to them, not understanding them, but knowing they will not be implemented any time soon.'[15]

Individual officials adapted to the times idiosyncratically. In southern Ukraine, the clerk of one of Makhno's armoured trains deliberately countersigned the orders of his commander illegibly because, he explained, no one knew who would be in power the next month and that a signature was evidence. 'Using it they can trace and hang.'[16] One enterprising former official established himself as a notary of sorts in Kamianets, under the Directory in the winter of 1919, where he issued 'certificates of loyalty'. Stamped with an old double-headed tsarist eagle seal, they confirmed that the bearer was known and 'loyal to the current government.'[17] The lone Bolshevik sympathizer in the Kaniv town Post Office, meanwhile, a comrade Kulikov, when he heard his party had taken power in Kyiv, decided that although his town was still under the Rada, he should help his cause, and so he promptly hung a sign in his office saying he would no longer accept Ukrainian money. The next day, distressed citizens took over 20,000 hryvni to the bank, the local merchants stopped accepting them, and the result was economic chaos. We do not know what happened afterwards, other than in his report the local commissar noted that tsarist police records indicated that comrade Kulikov had been an informer before 1917.[18] During the summer of 1920 the chairman of the Bolshevik Oleksandrivsk povit revkom decided to join Makhno. Before departing he requested a load of ammunition from his Bolshevik volost military committee, which he got, and then used to arm the detachment that he later organized.[19]

Makhno allowed all currencies on his territories, which ironically, gave the populace a sense of stability. Nonetheless, in November 1919, he decided it would be useful to have his own currency as well, so, via some old chums he arranged for Odesa counterfeiters to produce republican Russian roubles. The project collapsed after those involved discovered that they could not obtain the necessary ink. Regardless, Makhno's associates did print money-like receipts that they gave to those from whom they requisitioned goods. These were printed on plain paper with pictures and slogans, in Ukrainian, like: 'don't worry brother, Makhno has got money too. And we'll skin whoever doesn't take it' (*Oi hop, kuma ne zhurysia, v Makhna hroshi zavelysia. Khto ne budet hroshi brat, tomu shkuru budem drat*), or 'Makhno will see to whoever doesn't take this money' (*khto tykh hroshei ne bratyme, toho makhno dratyme*). Sometimes slogans were stamped on existing currencies. On Ukrainian karbovantsi they stamped 'for this money you can't even buy lice' (*za ti hroshi ne kupysh i voshi*).[20] Anyone visiting Makno's 'capital,' meanwhile, might have thought twice about just what 'anarchy' meant upon reading the following notice in the local newspaper, *Hulaipolskii nabat* (1 March 1919): 'Comrade Gorev, the postal, telegraph and telephone commissar has returned from his trip and has resumed his duties in his office in the Melenko buildiing. His hours are 9–3 daily except holidays.'

One of Makhno's lieutenants was Marusia Nikiforova. A hermaphrodite, Marusia had her male parts surgically removed in Paris, to where she had fled a prison sentence. She then joined the French Foreign Legion in 1914 and completed an officers' training course before returning to Ukraine. After gaining a reputation as one of Makhno's most vicious commanders, he put her in charge of his schools, hospitals, and nurseries. At one point she personally shot thirty-four men. She also had a weakness for sweets and would devour them in the cafes and bakeries that her troops expropriated.[21]

The innumerable armed groups that traversed Ukraine during the revolutionary years also had their idiosyncracies. On 21 February 1919, a six-hundred-strong unit of men belonging to no particular group or party rode into the town of Ivanhorod near Kamianets-Podilskyi and arrested the police. In the spring of 1919, a Bolshevik military inspector reported that a group that attacked his train outside of Kyiv carried blue and yellow national colours with the inscription: 'Long Live the Independent Ukrainian Soviet Republic. Foreigners Out.' After separating the Jewish party members from the non-Jews on the train, they explained that they were Bolsheviks fighting against Petliura, the Hetman, Communists, foreigners, and Jews, but then only shot the Jews.[22] In the village of Pushkari in central Ukraine, just after the Hetman had been deposed in December 1918, a man galloped to the volost office with a letter stamped with a red seal. He demanded fifty women for an Otaman Emichuk, to do his washing and cooking, and then galloped off. Faced with an ultimatum of delivering in three days or being shot, the men had a meeting, decided that they would not surrender their women, formed a militia, and began guarding their village around the clock. There is no record of whether the messenger returned to collect the women.[23] In the summer of 1921, when Bolshevik rule in Ukraine was still weak in the countryside and various partisan detachments still savagely murdered Bolshevik sympathizers and party members in villages, we have an example of one detachment galloping into a village near the town of Bratslav. The village was the volost centrer, and the group had apparently decided to destroy all the local records. When they arrived, however, the door was locked and they decided not to break in. Instead, they gave a speech to the assembled crowd, and then galloped off again – no doubt to the great relief of all those present.[24]

During the winter of 1917–18 Vera Urusova claimed that Katerynoslav's thieves had posted notices warning night watchmen that they risked death if they tried to deprive them of their livelihood by interfering with their activities. Under Bolshevik rule that spring, while walking on the street one day, she saw a mad- dog barking and scaring some schoolchildren. She ran to the local Bund office, and told its armed guards to shoot the dog. They refused saying that no natural phenomenon should be interfered with. Asking next a group of nearby soldiers to do something about the dog they replied: 'we are not political.'[25]

While historians frequently refer to a lack of authority and few officials, at least in 1917, popular opinion had the opposite view. Observing a mushrooming of committees and commissars, wits in Kharkiv composed the following ditty:

Iak respublyka nastala
sto nachalnykiv v nas stalo:
Atamany, komyssary,

komytetchikiv otary,
Podyvytsia, dobra liudy
V komytetakh khto povsiudy:
Arestanty, ta vory,
Holodravtsi brehuny.
Vsi v pravlenyiakh zasidaiut,
Tysiachi z vas poluchaiut ...[26]

When the Republic arose
We got a hundred directors
Otamans, commissars, and various committee men
Look, good people,
Who are in the various committees everywhere
Prisoners, bandits,
Cutthroats and liars
They All sit on boards
And take thousands from you.

In villages, in 1917, when communications still linked towns and villages, there was such massive support for the Rada that people wanted to pay taxes. In Troitska in Kyiv province in the autumn of 1917 peasants sent 40 roubles 'to our dear Ukraine for our common purpose.' They added that they would like the Central Rada to return some of the money for their 'election fund' but that it could keep the rest for use in whatever it had to.[27] Supporters of the Ukrainian Socialist Revolutionary party were no doubt pleased when the first issue of their paper *Vilne slovo* appeared in the summer of 1917. They were informed, right under the title, however, that the next issue could be delayed: 'Number 2 will be published when the editors have the time and money.' In 1918, under the Hetman, the editors of the Russian extreme-right Kyivan newspaper *Nasha Rodina* had difficulty financing their publication. To make ends meet they decided to stop printing anti-Semitic harangues and approached the city's rich Jews for subsidies.[28]

As the months passed, battles raged, and communications frayed, regimes came and went so quickly that not everyone knew exactly who ruled. Judgments about the outside governments and their officials began to vary wildly. In Poltava, people classified Makhno as 'Bolshevik, but not as much.'[29] In right-bank Ukraine in late 1919 a Bolshevik agent reported that while peasants reluctantly saw the Directory as a lesser evil, in general they favoured and supported Soviet power. 'But they fear

Soviet armies from Russia like the plague. They dream of "their own" [Ukrainian] Bolsheviks.' A similar report from Poltava province related that peasants there hated the Communists and considered Soviet power the best for them – as long as it did not include Jews, commissars, or ravaging troops. Having to go from office to office for eight days to get a permit to buy one pound of nails did nothing to ingratiate the Bolshevik regime with the peasants either. In the Uman region, pro-Bolshevik peasants thought Petliura would save them from the Communists and that Bolshevik Russia was a utopia because there were no Jews there. A Latvian in the region reported that peasants simply could not believe that Latvians or Russians or Poles could be Communists, as in their minds only Jews could be Communists.[30] An old peasant woman in a village between Proskuriv (today Khmelnytsky) and Kamianets-Podilskyi, whose name is not recorded, seems to have been satisfied with the Directory. After explaining to her interlocutor in November 1919 that God must be angry with the people to have given power to Jews (Bolsheviks), she regretted that just as things were getting better, thanks to 'Petliura's Ukraine,' they were changing again.[31] Not all were as well informed. In the same region that autumn, in reply to the question 'What's new?' another woman related: 'There was a Petlia [sic] here, and now there are some Tabachniki [troops belonging to Tiutiunnyk, one of Petliura's commanders] but we don't know what they want.'[32] In the summer of 1919 a conversation between a Jewish storekeeper on the outskirts of Kyiv and a recently arrived Russian for whom Kyiv was 'almost abroad,' and who had heard in 1917 that the 'honks' (*khokhly*) 'had declared some kind of independent Ukraine,' gives more insight into how common people viewed governments – and the relationship between violence and the state.[33] 'Who came after the Germans left?' asked the Russian: 'The Austrians, and how terrible it was,' replied the Jew. But 'what Austrians?' continued the Russian, you just said the Ukrainians came. 'They are the same – Austrians, Ukrainians, oh, how they beat us.' They continued:

> 'But how can Ukrainians come from Austria?'
> 'Petliura brought them.'
> 'Who is Petliura?'
> 'I don't know, he came from Austria.'
> 'But you must tell me.'
> 'I already did. He is a Red Ukrainian.'
> 'Where did he go?'

'He didn't go anywhere, he is in Vinnytsia and Zhlobyn, and he will come and will beat us again.'
'But don't the Bolsheviks beat you too?'
'They beat us, they beat us hard.'
'So there is no difference.'
'There is. The Bolsheviks beat everybody, Petliura only beats us.

In light of such evidence, it seems rather tenuous to directly link shifts in mass political support to political programs. Faced with the collapse of the Hetman, for instance,Ukrainian peasants who heard about it were no doubt influenced as much by Bolshevik promises as ignorance of life in Russia. No less important at the time was the widespread rumour that, once the Germans retreated, the English and French would return, together with their tsarist allies, and begin to shoot whoever had deserted in 1917. This predisposed men to support the Bolsheviks. Yet, just in case the Whites won, fearful for their lives, former soldiers enriched local counterfeiters as they rushed to buy phony medical-discharge certificates.[34]

Amid the upheavals, many still went out of their way to look their best. A contemporary resident of Makhno's capital tells us that this included all of his men: 'Often, during battles there were many horses standing outside Huliai-Pole's barbershop; these were Makhnovites gone for shaving and cutting, preening themselves and risking, for a haircut, to lose something more important – their heads.'[35] Some not only maintained their appearance but decided to change it. Pitrim Sorokin tells us that as news spread in Petrograd that the Bolsheviks had taken power, men with beards began to shave them off, while those without beards began to grow them. In Ukraine Mr Burdiushevsky from Balta, for instance, involved in various shady affairs while an official under Skoropadsky, decided to shave his huge Cossack-style mustache when he learned of the Hetman's fall. Those who knew him did not recognize him unless they stopped and looked at him for a few moments – which was presumably the desired reaction. Those who changed their facial appearance probably found it easier to survive General Denikin's occupation of Kyiv in the autumn of 1919, when police and informers, some with thick dossiers of photos, stood on corners and arrested whoever looked suspicious. Once the prisons were full, prisoners were sent to the city's finest hotel, the Hermitage.[36]

Others changed their name rather than their appearance and did so officially – which again, reveals that government wheels were turning.

Sometime during the war the common labourer Dmytro Bardak (meaning whorehouse), had joined the tsarist army. In 1917 he was a junior officer in the Ukrainian army and, that December, he had written a request to the Central Rada to change his 'offensive' surname to Dymetrenko. The letter took three weeks to get from Kharkiv to Kyiv, where for the next year it went from office to office, through all regime changes, until permission was finally granted in December 1918. The final letter informing the applicant of his successful application, however, dated January 1919, was apparently never sent, as it remains unsigned in the archives. Similarly left without a reply to his request to change his surname was Laiza Bezmozgyi (meaning no brains). In his case, Hetmanate officials did not know what to do, as his place of birth was no longer in Ukraine in 1918, but in Belarus.[37] While Fedor Bardakov and Laiza Bezmozgyi were waiting to hear about their requests, David Parshyvyi (meaning flea-infested) managed to have his desired surname, Davydiuk, legalized. Barukh Tarakan (cockroach), had presumably tried and failed before, as he wrote in his letter to Kyiv, that he hoped he could at last 'in independent Ukraine have the possibility of changing my surname' to Tarsky. A letter sent from Kyiv on 28 December 1918, to the local police chief in Bohopil, where Tarakan lived, asking him to hurry up with his report, is the last record we have of this case.[38] A Ukrainian peasant Andryi Svynarchuk (swinish) explained that, in the name of the reborn Ukrainian state, he as its faithful son, was taking the liberty to respectfully request its humane leader, the honourable hetman, to be allowed to change his name to 'Ukrainian' ('*Ukrainskyi*') 'because our Ukraine is an independent state.' An official in the Food Supply Ministry, Oleksander Volkov was less concerned about the connotations that surrounded his surname than the fact that it was Russian: 'Because of compulsory changing of surnames in Muscovy during the time of the autocracy that involved destroying Ukrainian names by adding the suffix "ov," my Ukrainian name was changed to a Russian one.' Regarding himself as a Ukrainian citizen with no wish to have a Russian-sounding name that gave him problems at work and in his private life, Oleksandr wanted to take a surname ending in 'enko' and gave the minister three suggestions from which to choose one.[39]

Still others adopted flexible attitudes to politics in the interests of survival. Vasyl Kulzhenko was a successful Ukrainian publisher who printed the Ukrainophobe newspaper *Kievlianin,* as well as currency and stamps for the Rada and Hetman, Bolshevik proclamations, and after 1921 he became chairman of the Soviet Ukrainian Union of Typographical

Workers. On the eve of the Hetman's fall, Kulzhenko's workers, who were all Bolsheviks, met daily and tried to decide whether or not they should support Petliura and the Ukrainian National Republic.[40] In the village of Sultanske an anonymous village secretary, a Rada army veteran, worked for all governments.[41] Polikarp Kyrychenko in Kyiv worked for the Bolsheviks, the Hetman, and then again the Bolsheviks. An A. Churuk in Starokonstantyniv also found employment with each government, as did a Dzygar in Chyhyryn: 'sufficiently pliable to hold his place as commissar under all regimes.'[42]

Skullduggery and bureaucratic absurdities did not end with the fall of the tsar. During the 1917 municipal elections in Ovruch, for instance, the local Russian extremists were number 5 on the list of parties. In another town they managed to steal a load of SR election posters with the well-known slogan 'Land and Peace.' As in that town the SRs happened to be number 5 on the list, thanks to their sleight of hand, the Ovruch extremists managed to win six of the twenty-seven seats on the council in their town – which was a lot for them in 1917. Concerned citizens in Novhorod-Volynskyi, meanwhile, caught out their crooks and submitted a complaint to the local prosecutor. Among the dirty tricks that they exposed was the election of a council member who was deaf and dumb, more votes than voters, and votes cast by imposters.[43] The massive influx into towns of undisciplined troops and the euphoria surrounding the collapse of the old order overturned prevailing conceptions of decorum and order. Half-naked soldiers from hospitals in Chernihiv took to living in the streets in the spring of 1917, where they fornicated in public with whatever women were willing. A high school principal one day, fed up at last, decided to confront these men and told them that they should be at the front. An altercation began, they beat him, and when a policeman arrived he charged and arrested the principal for assault and hooliganism. The judge subsequently found the high school principal guilty of disturbing the peace.[44] In October 1917 in Kharkiv one man decided to check whether his name was on the voters' list. At the provincial zemstvo office he was told to go to city hall, where he was then told that the section in question was in the local girls' high school. When he got there he was told that the man in charge would be there after 3 p.m. the next day, but upon arriving the next day, our supplicant was informed that the official's office hours ended at 3. When he came before 3 the following day he was told the office in question had moved to an unknown location.[45]

In Poltava, anyone entering the city in June 1918 would have found all its signs painted over with whitewash. This was not because owners opposed Ukrainianization, but because financially pressed city officials had placed a tax on words on signs.[46] During the winter of 1919, in Kamianets, townspeople found other creative ways to comply with the Directory's decree to Ukrainianize street signs. Some painted them over and replaced lettering with pictures. Others pasted over their permanent Russian-language metal sign with a Ukrainian-language paper sign, while others painted out only individual Russian letters. One reporter observed in the summer of 1920 that the only group in the city that had consistently advertised in Ukrainian were the Jews.[47] The year previous, there is on record a stereotypical situation. In Podillia province, the town of Solomna had grain but no sacks, so its mill could not grind flour. Ten kilometres up the road, the town of Sarny had no mill and no grain, but lots of sacks – and judging by the inspector's report, it seems that they never got together.[48] In the UNR, judges in 1919 had no law books except the old Tsarist Code. Accordingly, they sentenced severe offenders to exile in Siberia – whether this included a theoretically necessary sentence of exile is unknown. As the Directory had no jails when it was retreating, sentenced criminals were packed into a rear carriage of one of the government's trains.[49] When in April 1920 Directory forces occupied the town of Ananiv in Kherson province, the local commander apparently thought that everyone had at least some sense of decency as in his proclamation he instructed all escaped prisoners to immediately return to jail.[50]

Absurdist theatre also punctuated high politics. In Kharkiv in December 1917 the city branch of the Bolshevik party did not consider themselves part of Ukraine, did not recognize the twelve members of Ukraine's first Bolshevik government and only reluctantly allocated the People's Secretariat lodgings – in the city prison. The new 'ministers' spent their first night in power in cells from which they had to flee the next morning because of the filth, stench, and cold. Thereafter, because the new government had to share the only available office space with various other groups who were there first, all business had to be done when they were gone – at night. Local anti-Ukrainian Russian Bolsheviks that had gone to Moscow, meanwhile, were trying to convince Lenin that 'Ukraine' was not only a 'notion' but 'reactionary' and that he should dissolve the Kharkiv government.[51] During the last weeks of the Ukrainian state, in December 1918, the incoming leaders of the Directory had stopped with their army in Fastiv, where they decided the safest place to stay was the women's washroom in the town's railroad station. In the capital city, meanwhile, Directory activists had tea, sugar, canned food, and cognac delivered to them nightly by three Ukrainian SRs, who were chauffeurs in the Hetman's War Ministry, in ministry sedans. In return the drivers got 15,000 Russian roubles which they used to enjoy themselves and entertain the rest of the car-pool staff. At the same time, thanks to the lack of discipline at the city prison, jailed opposition leaders were in contact with their followers and able to freely follow events and issue their orders. Activists at liberty avoided arrest by staying with German soldiers who were German Social Democrat party members or sympathizers – and whose lodgings were not subject to Ukrainian law. Meanwhile, the local Red Cross mission had been taken over secretly by Bolsheviks, and they used its premises to recruit Red Army volunteers and channel fifty agents arriving daily from Moscow to Ukrainian towns. Local workers, for their part, were less interested in politics than prices. Those at Kyiv's railway yards did not support the UNR but they thought English and French armies were marching on Kyiv and hoped only that once they arrived prices would fall. The final absurdity is the secret police reports that identified these events, as they reveal a well-organized system functioning despite the virtual collapse of the government to which the system belonged.[52]

Not the least of bureaucratic-related misfortunes that accompanied regime change was time change. National authorities would decree that clocks either be set one hour back (Ukrainian time), or two hours back (central European time), while the Bolsheviks and the Whites would decree that they be reset one or two hours forward (Russian time). As some towns changed sides monthly the implications of not changing office hours, routines, or schedules could be profound– as for example if town officials would set their clocks as required, but officials at the train station forgot to. During their occupation of Kharkiv, in early 1919, the Bolsheviks decided to set clocks four hours fast to save energy. As a result, sunset in the Ukr.SSRoccurred at midnight.[53]

In the winter of 1919 the approximately 200 strong staff of the Letychiv *povit ispolkom* had to flee Directory troops and move to a nearby town, where, because there were not enough buildings for them, they had to sleep on their desks. To get a change of underwear, every week for the next six months, they paraded back and forth to Letychiv, where their families still lived, apparently untroubled by troops from either side.[54] In the detailed reports that ispolkoms had to submit to superiors, the comrades in Irkliv volost (in Kyiv province) had listed their own revkom as performing well during 1920. During their revkom's annual meeting, however, besides deciding on regular office hours and the need for extra staff, they also requested from Kyiv some leather or some shoes because, barefoot, their clerks could not come to work. Just how the committee managed to function 'well' in the absence of its barefoot clerks remains unexplained.[55] Seventy per cent of office workers in Zvenyhorod were also barefoot in February 1921, as was the 570-strong police force in nearby Uman, while 65,000 pairs of shoes were in warehouses in Kyiv, and factories there were manufacturing 12,000 pairs monthly as of September 1920.[56] In western Ukraine in August 1918, just after the Polish conquest, the occupying army in one unidentified town began requisitioning shoes without compensation. Inevitably, people stopped admitting they had any. Officers then began watching Ukrainian churches, noting who came to mass wearing shoes, and later sent detachments to their houses to take the shoes. After a few weeks, no one went to church any more.[57]

During the summer of 1919 in the town of Fastiv, a committed Communist was appalled to discover that only two of the town's twenty-two party members actually had a party identification card. Peasants in neighbouring villages had organized their own ispolkoms in complete disregard of the party, while all the members of the Committees of Poor Peasants were actually rich peasants. If that was not enough, he also noted in his report that after local party members had arrested and handed over former Directory officials to their local Cheka, the Cheka had released them. That same summer, in the Crimea, most of the Red Army were former Directory and Makhno troops and rich peasants while its Political Indoctrination section had only one party member.[58] In Skvit volost (in Kyiv province) of the sixty-seven who attended the Poor Peasants Committee Congress in May 1920, few seemed to be poor. Only one had no land or animals, only fourteen had no land, and only fifteen had no animals. Sixty-three were literate.[59] Worried about how the large number of Jews in their party was alienating local Ukrainians, one Bolshevik Party official in Ielysavethrad (today Kirovohrad) in March 1919 desperately wrote to his superiors requesting 'Orthodox' party workers. The party inspector in Kharkiv province in June 1919, appalled at how many 'anti-Bolshevik' clerks peopled its offices, reported that after the local Food Supply Committee had duly dismissed all of its 'anti-Bolshevik' clerks, it then rehired all of them again.[60]

Nor were military matters exempt from the ridiculous. During the summer of 1918 in an unnamed village, a German commander posted one soldier to guard an estate. If the guard was harmed, he told the villagers, he would order his divisional artillery to raze their village as well as those nearby. Terrified lest an outsider kill the soldier, the villagers delegated a group of their own men to guard him twenty-four hours a day. After a few weeks they tired of guarding the man and sent a delegation to German headquarters requesting a full detachment of troops for their village – which they did not get.[61] After the fall of the Hetman, Katerynoslav was not merely occupied successively by opposing forces, but simultaneously by all of them. For a few days, while Whites held the centre, the duma defended by the Jewish militia held the suburbs. Surrounding them were German troops who had declared themselves neutral, but fired at anyone approaching their positions. Surrounding the Germans were Petliura's Directory forces, which in turn, were surrounded by Makhno's Army and the Bolsheviks.

In early 1919 thousands of men in the First Bolshevik Army near Mozyr on the Prypiat River mutinied, killed their commissars, and began marching towards Ukrainian lines to surrender. When the soldiers of the small detachment holding the front saw a huge mass of troops advancing towards them, they thought it was an attack. As they withdrew, the advancing Reds began running to catch up with them. Terrified, the Ukrainians blew up the bridge that they had been guarding and fled. When later it emerged that these Red troops were actually surrendering, they had to be ferried across the river by boat.[62] A Bolshevik military unit near Bakhmut in 1919 sent a detachment into the town to requisition clothes and food from the wealthy. With no one to control them, they began requisitioning everything from everybody and among their trophies, disapprovingly reported by a party inspector, were apples, coffee, and women's underwear. The Bolshevik 14th Army, for its part, stationed in central Ukraine in May 1919, had not received any supplies for three months. Men were not only hungry but were reduced to walking barefoot and wearing women's sweaters. The latter article of clothing they likely obtained from the masses of women that swarmed around the army and presumably saw to various other needs as well. And this despite the fact that the army's quartermaster had tens of thousands of shoes and uniforms in his stores – 'a very suspicious situation,' noted the inspector. Among those to blame was the army's chief political officer, a Comrade Maizel, who 'had about as much communism in him as Denikin had liberalism' and who could be found evenings in his office dead drunk. Not wishing to conclude pessimistically, the inspector characterized the army as demoralized but nonetheless revolutionary in spirit.[63] In Zaporizhzha province in March 1922, Red Army soldiers who had decided to voice grievances to their local Workers and Peasants Inspectorate official would have been undoubtedly surprised to hear how Comrade Popovych explained to them the source of their problems: 'You see, that is what Communism and Soviet power gave you: you did not walk around in rags under the old regime, and now you do and are hungry to boot.'[64] Bolshevik situation reports from central Ukraine in the summer of 1919 describe how Red Army units would go on rampages declaring themselves against Communists, Jews, and Cheka agents, and shooting anyone they saw who belonged to any of these categories. In Podillia province the 4th Soviet Regiment issued a declaration asserting: 'When the Russian Communists came they brought with themselves Hetman officers and Black Hundreds [Russian extremists].' They went on to condemn the Jews and finished with the slogan: 'Long Live the Peasants and Workers Soviet.'[65]

In Kyiv, in January 1918, while the Bolshevik army was approaching and its agitators in the city were at work demoralizing troops and workers, various Ukrainian party activists were enjoying themselves in the city's bars and restaurants. Similarly in the spring of 1919, Petliura's head of counterintelligence observed that while Bolshevik armies were beating the hard-pressed Ukrainian army and closing on Vinnytsia and Kamianets, in those towns, streets, bars, and restaurants were overflowing with soldiers. Desperate for income the Directory's finance minister came up with a detailed luxury tax in July 1919, which his critics dismissed as absurd in a country lacking necessities and where no taxes could be collected in any case.[66] Not the least of the Directory's problems in supplying the army was that village clerks were not only often semiliterate, but that they were semiliterate in Russian and could not always understand written Ukrainian. Thus, in Podillia in 1919 an inspector reported how, when a local clerk got a telegram in Ukrainian requesting horses and clothing from villagers for the army, he read out the words including the punctuation as part of the text. Neither he nor the assembled could understand the telegram, as a result, they all had a good laugh, and the clerk excused his ignorance by saying he had never read a telegram, 'so sternly written,' like that before. As a result, the inspector continued, not only did the army go without, but the peasants concluded that the government was not using Ukrainian, but 'something from Galicia,' and were thus alienated both from the Directory and Ukrainian. He concluded his report noting the urgent need for courses for village clerks, where, among other things, they would be taught punctuation and short forms.[67]

Among the lunacies was a Bolshevik military unit including White Russians and Germans, fighting under a Ukrainian flag against the

Ukrainian National Republic. The explanation is simple. After the collapse of the ZUNR, the Galician army formally joined the Bolsheviks. By 1920, from its White Russian, German, and eastern Ukrainian prisoners of war, the Galician Ukrainians had formed two regiments to which they gave national blue-yellow flags and insignia. A Ukrainian Bolshevik in this unit was shocked to hear Galician Ukrainians calling Bolsheviks 'foreigners.' When he complained about Russians not giving commands in Ukrainian, he could not understand why in response his Galician Ukrainian officer told him not to mind. Nor did he understand why commissars did not order the mounted patrols that constantly drove around this unit in machine-gun trucks to open fire on them.[68] A second Bolshevik military unit formed of anti-Bolshevik eastern Ukrainians, the 361st Ukrainian Soviet Rifle Regiment, refused to fly red flags – which, they surreptitiously replaced with the national colours whenever they were issued. When it first marched into its base in Tiraspol flying blue-and-yellow flags and singing the Ukrainian national anthem, the local Bolsheviks ran away. While on border patrol they described themselves as 'Ukrainian Bolsheviks' to all comers.[69]

The small Ukrainian air force during the war also had problems. It faced the threat of its pilots flying into enemy territory and handing over their planes. A report from the 4th Squadron, stationed in a small town in northern Volyn in May 1919, reports that its commander, a certain Bogomolov, besides firing all the Ukrainian mechanics and replacing them with Russians, kept his own private female 'typist' – despite standing orders to the contrary. In addition, because he had given her an air force passenger railway wagon for living quarters, which she shared with her mother, the squadron's pilots had to live in a freight wagon. Bogomolov, moreover, seems to have lied about his credentials, as he did not know how to fly. Taking a new German Fokker up one day, he crashed, destroying the plane and his leg in the incident. The squadron's pilots suspected he was trying to repeat the feat of his friend, who some time earlier, had flown over to the Bolsheviks, given them his plane, and in return, been appointed assistant to the aviation commissar. According to the report, Bogomolov made no secret of the fact that he joined Ukraine's air force for the money and that he knew the Bolsheviks paid more – opinions shared by the Air Force's Inspector General Katenin, who was also a Russian.[70]

In Kharkiv in1921, because the activities of the police left much to be desired, Polina Vyshnevska and Nina Golovina were able to sponsor orgies on a regular basis at no. 4 Konotopska Street, and Comrade Soldatova, the laundry lady at Naberezhna no. 5, could calmly supply her best customers with home-brew – which she packaged between clean laundry sheets. Comrade Stetsko, who also brewed his own at home, sold and then drank his product, together with the local police and civilian officials, in their offices. Comrade Rifkin, meanwhile, had established a speak-easy/brothel in his rooms on Chernyshevsky Street. If someone had the right 'friends' he could enjoy some coffee and female company for the nominal sum of 20,000 roubles– when one pound of white bread cost 1,800 roubles.[71] In Bolshevik Ukraine in 1920 trains would arrive at stations with all their wagons duly sealed, weight noted, and with guards on the roof. When the doors were opened, these wagons were found to be empty.[72] Even the Cheka sometimes gave suspects the benefit of the doubt. Vadim Shcherbakivsky relates that in 1917, fearing for the worst, he had stockpiled some essential food items. Three years later an inspection of his lodgings revealed five pounds of flour and five-pound cone-shaped piles of pressed sugar. Without blinking, the head of the Poltava Zemstvo Museum explained that this was an exposition demonstrating 1916 zemstvo employees' rations. The Cheka commander accepted this.[73]

Amid the absurdities and chaos, were, of course, the horrors, of which the best documented are the anti-Jewish pogroms. Jews in towns like Cherkasy, Korsun, and Borzna, which changed hands monthly or even weekly, suffered at the hands of each successive occupant. In sworn affidavits doctors reported girls as young as ten gang-raped to death. After the Whites took Cherkasy in 1919, they began a three-day pogrom on 18 August. On 19 August, while it was raging at one end of town, the local tsarist sympathizers were feting their liberators at a ball at the other end of town with fireworks and an orchestra.[74] But all suffered and the sufferings left an indelible psychological imprint on those unfortunate enough to have had to live through them. Some were state-sponsored, others stemmed from the breakdown of government. These included not only rape, sadistic torture, extermination of specific target groups, and collective reprisals. Pigs and dogs ate bodies left on streets in sight of passers-by until someone got around to burying the remains. Between the Boh and Dnister rivers areas were so devastated by the spring of 1920 that they resembled the Western Front. In towns by the autumn of 1919 what commodities were available were astronomically expensive. Besides the shortage of food, there was a lack of fuel, which meant no hot water or heat or electricity. Hospitals were closed, doctors used herbs, and diseases, in particular typhus and syphilis, raged. In villages, no iron meant no horseshoes for the remaining horses, or for ploughs.

The 1919 harvest was unprecedented, but no one milled the contents of bursting silos because there were no buyers. Grain was milled only for moonshine, and drunkenness was endemic.[75] A Swiss officer commanding a Red Cross relief train arriving in early November 1919 was horrified by what he saw. This included witnessing the hotel maid removing used paper from the toilet bowl, washing it, and then placing it by the seat again for reuse.[76]

The break down of urban administration after six years of war meant that by 1920, as one journalist put it: 'All Ukraine is drowning in garbage and excrement.' In the spring of that year, Kamianets stored 12,000 barrels of garbage and excrement, while Vinnytsia and Zhmerynka stored 20,000 wagon loads each of filth. That October, in Kamianets-Podilskyi, the temporary capital, 80 to 100 barrels of waste had to be removed daily. But the authorities only had enough wagons and horses to remove no more than eight to ten barrels – with the results piled fence-high on the streets. Ever since the hospital lost its wagon, it had to dump its garbage and excrement on the street in front of it.[77] In some smaller towns by late 1919 the situation was even worse. In Khmilnyk, whose population of 25,000 was overwhelmingly Jewish, the poor lived two to three families per two to three rooms. Since there were no toilets or garbage pits, people threw excrement and garbage directly out of their windows and doors – or straight into the same local river that they used for drinking water. Those who did have a toilet of one sort or another, meanwhile, could only have it emptied if they were rich, since the one man who had a barrel, horse, and cart for waste, charged high removal rates. As the barrel was small and the roads bumpy, the cart's trail could be seen and smelled by all.[78] In Chortkiv, although hotels were full, they not only had a shortage of bedding, but no one to wash what they had which meant that they were soon all infested with bugs and lice. A shortage of fuel meant that by January 1919 water could not be pumped to the city's higher regions, where the main hospital and army barracks were located. Part of the barracks was turned into a prison, and as the main latrine in the middle of the courtyard was soon plugged, prisoners began relieving themselves in ever-widening circles around it. When it rained the courtyard turned into an unimaginable fetid swap of excrement. Since there was no running water, meanwhile, other indoor toilet drains were plugged. As gases built up from the accumulated excrement and garbage, the pressure resulted in occasional explosions that covered everything nearby in a brown sludge. One of the first places that this happened was in the bath and laundry rooms – which meant that prisoners no longer could wash themselves or their clothes. The medical officer inspecting wrote that what he saw reminded him of scenes from Dante's *Inferno* and that even an angel would emerge a Bolshevik from such a place.[79]

During the typhus epidemic in Makhno's hospitals, and others as well presumably, those who were too weak to chase the lice away were soon covered with a visible sheet of them, and as they groaned they were literally eaten alive.[80] In Poltava, people noticed that while typhus seemed to spread with the arrival of the Bolsheviks, no Bolsheviks appear to have died from it. The rumour soon spread that they sent men who had recovered, and were thus immune, around typhus wards in hospitals to collect the lice crawling over the living and the dead into bottles, which they then released among the 'bourgeoisie,' particularly at night in overcrowded railway wagons.[81] The other blight that ravaged the population from 1917 was alcoholism. Already that spring a journalist calling for repeal of prohibition listed some of its sorry consequences. In one village, the authorities had confiscated and poured a store of 80 proof grain spirits into the ground. It formed a huge mud lake and seeped under a steam boiler. Local inhabitants would shovel the mud into sacks and sell them at 10 roubles each to buyers who then somehow extracted half a bottle of liquor from their purchase. So much earth was dug and sold that the boiler collapsed and killed a number of scavengers who were underneath. Nevertheless, the digging selling bottling and drinking went on.[82]

In Kyiv in the spring of 1920 the population's main occupation was obtaining food and fuel, and the centre of life was the Jewish Market where tens of thousands converged daily to buy, sell, trade, and steal for ten to twelve hours daily. Near the university it was impossible to see the tram rails in the street because they were covered with garbage. Since there was no wheeled traffic, grass and bushes had begun growing on some streets. The Cheka executed anyone they pleased whenever they pleased, and people would find the mutilated, skinned corpses of victims in the street. Six high school teachers and ten students were shot by fleeing Bolsheviks 'for belonging to the Polish nation,' reported an eyewitness present at their funeral. While average employees could not live on their wages or rations even if they held two or three posts, Cheka agents lived well. They got their wages in still-valuable tsarist roubles and the belongings of their victims.[83]

A member of the official White Russian delegation in Poland in 1919–20 related: 'I was told by men of the volunteer armies that whole districts of Ukraine reminded one of a lunatic asylum.'[84] Yet, in that asylum, when the Directory's interior minister learned that a certain Mr Iushchyshyn, who was an official in the Press and Information Ministry, had made an obscene gesture to his permanent secretary when asked about how much money his ministry could expect for taking on a new function, he had him fired.[85] In Bolshevik-controlled Tarashcha in 1920 a wooden board cost 7,000 roubles – which was 1,000 more than an average clerk's monthly salary in a provincial town. This had serious implications for those who had to bury the dead. Since few could afford coffins, which cost anywhere from 20,000 roubles and up, many resorted to ripping boards off any available structure to make a box, thereby risking a beating, arrest, or summary execution. When officials did find boards, they could not find appropriate nails. As a result, until they gave up trying to put bodies into boxes, mourners would end up seeing the grizzly remains of the deceased at the bottom of the grave as the makeshift coffins would fall apart as soon as they hit the ground.[86]

In conclusion, we might leave the last word on daily life to Dmytro Matvienko, who reminds us that generalizations must be made carefully. A court clerk in Malyn before the war, and afterwards, under the Bolsheviks, a clerk in the town's police station, he was arrested in September 1920, but later released, on suspicion of sympathizing and conspiring with the government of the Ukrainian National Republic in -exile. In his reply to his interrogator, who had asked: 'How do you understand the Ukrainian question?' he had said: 'That is not an easy question to answer ('*Na etot vopros zatrudnilos* [*sic*] *otvetyt*).'[87]

APPENDIX 4

Prices and Wages

At the turn of the century, 25 to 35 roubles a month, the average wages of lower-level urban officials, equalled those of most workers, teachers, clerks, and actors. Middle-level officials, with 50 to 100 roubles a month, made as much as highly skilled workers like printers, while the highest officials earned up to 1,000 roubles a month. Pay was steady and those with rank (*chin*) got a pension, overtime, Christmas bonuses, and a 10 per cent raise every three years. The subject is unstudied but, by the turn of the century, for peasant families the badly paid government town job that brought status and covert perks for their sons at the bottom of the hierarchy was probably preferable to subsistence farming, emigration, or factory work. If they managed to attain a full-time middle-level position by the time they got married, they could survive economically at a period when average urban prices outside the capital, in kopeks per pound, averaged as follows: good meat, 10–14; sugar, 15: rye bread, 2–3; salt, 1–2.[1]

As yet there is no comprehensive history of prices and wages in Ukraine during the revolutionary years, however, scattered sources can provide an idea of what an average urban dweller and clerk had to cope with. As prices rose and supplies dwindled, staff spent less and less time in offices looking after business and more outside looking for food and fuel. And as gaps between wages and prices grew, so did incentives for corruption which damaged further already tattered public attitudes towards officials and government. Since corruption, in turn, impeded equitable rationing, black markets and co-operatives persisted as alternative organizations to government – and to total social collapse. Times were not only hard but confusing. Besides the currencies issued by the various governments, each of which as a rule, declared all others void within its territories when it arrived, people used locally issued coupons or stamps and, to avoid getting thoroughly cheated, had to follow the constantly changing exchange rates between all the different monies.

Already in the spring of 1917 the Kyiv province commissar was requesting the local zemstvo to provide twenty-four pairs of shoes for fifteen clerks on his staff who could not afford new ones – even if they had been able to find any to buy.[2] Middle-level officials that autumn were paid on average 300–400 roubles a month (12–16 per day) and lower-level personnel 150–200 roubles (6–8 per day). An office typist earning 150 roubles a monthly made about as much as an unskilled worker in Kyiv, 30–50 roubles more than a skilled worker in Kharkiv, twice as much as a university professor, and three times as much as a rural teacher – who usually had free housing and spent less on cheaper food.[3] As of November, wages were roughly the same in Ukraine and Russia for lower- and middle-level officials, but prices were lower in Ukraine. Between March and October 1917 average wages in Zvenyhorod had risen from 95 to 250 roubles a month for a secretary and from 95 to 235 for assistants, while those of typists remained at 75. Five months later, the Chyhyryn povit commissar pointed out that the absolute minimum he had to pay a secretary was 300, while a typist needed 150. The Chornobyl commissar said a living wage for a secretary was 600, while clerks should get 500. That March in Kyiv, clerks on the provincial commissar's staff earned between 140 and 170 roubles a month.[4]

By the end of 1917 in Kyiv, average wages for unskilled workers were 6.5 roubles a day and 11–12 roubles a day for skilled workers (300 per month). Average prices in kopeks per pound were: bread, 25; flour, 8; potatoes, 13; cabbage, 14; cottage cheese, 85. Butter cost 1.5 roubles and pork 1 rouble per pound. In central Ukraine, the price of one kilogram of flour ranged from 12 to 40 kopeks, and one kilogram of grain from 10 to 15 kopeks. In 1916 one pack of matches had risen to 50 kopeks from its 1914 price of 1 kopek.[5] In Katerynoslav, prices between 1914 and September 1917 had increased as follows, per pound: meat, 16 kopeks to 1 rouble 20; potatoes, 2 to 20 kopeks; soap, 11 kopeks to 1 rouble 10 kopeks; flour, 2 to 20 kopeks. Ten eggs had gone from 20 kopeks to 1 rouble 50, a suit from 50 to 300 roubles, a room from 15 to 60 roubles monthly, an apartment from 65 to 250 roubles, and 16 kilograms of coal or firewood from 19 kopeks to 1 rouble 50 kopeks.[6] In the town of Kupianka, east of Kharkiv, zemstvo clerks complained of impossible prices that same month and demanded wage increases to between 1,200 and 3,000 roubles a month, while doctors asked for 4,800.

In Zolotonosha, north of Chernihiv, advertisements for volost council clerks and secretaries that same month offered candidates between 600 and 1,800 karbovantsi monthly.[7]

Data from Kyiv suggest that married white-collar workers who owned their own dwellings could perhaps get by on their pay – depending on the size of their families and fuel costs. But not all officials everywhere actually got paid. The Provisional Government had managed to pay its officials in Russia through to December 1917 (see Chapter 6). Due to the breakdown in transportation, south-bound trains from Petrograd became infrequent in 1917 and, during that year, the State Bank was not always able to transport the monthly payroll to all of its Ukrainian affiliates. Inflation, devaluation, and hoarding since 1915, meanwhile, had emptied local banks and made them exceptionally dependent on the ever larger shipments of bills from Petrograd. Government workers, at least in Kyiv province, did get paid to the end of December and they appear to have been the only group of workers in that province that did not go on strike in 1917.[8] Towns that ran out of cash, like Zhytomir and Odesa, resorted to printing and using coupons in lieu of money. Worried about pay complaints, Ukrainian leaders after they took power requested funds from the Bolsheviks who, as of 1 (14) December, were still promising to deliver if the Central Rada recognized them. The day after the Bolsheviks announced that they would stop shipping cash, 4 (17) December, the Rada began negotiating credits directly with Petrograd and Kyivan bankers, and planning financial measures which included establishing a national currency.[9] Ten days later, faced with the Bolshevik takeover of Russian banks, the Rada hurriedly enacted a spate of financial legislation to raise cash. Consequently, whereas administrators in Kyiv got their December pay that January with funds raised by a levy imposed on all city businesses, presumably no one outside the capital got paid.[10]

Under the Hetman, higher government employees were well paid with perks, bonuses, supplements, allowances, and subsidies. High rents, rising prices, and devaluation made life difficult for married middle- and lower-level officials, however, who sometimes did not get paid at all, and who, until the autumn, when pay rates were changed, still got paid according to pre- 1914 rates, as no one had yet formally changed them.

After three months of relative stability under German occupation, in Kyiv prices increased in May 1918, just after the Rada fell. Ministries resorted not only to direct purchase from co-ops, but began issuing rations to employees, paying in kind, allowing leave to purchase goods in villages, and letting employees form departmental co-ops. Bread, potatoes, and pork doubled in price; butter and cottage cheese had tripled by December. Per pound prices were as follows: bread, 2 roubles 4 kopeks; potatoes, 15.6 roubles; butter, 9.2 roubles; pork, 4.9 roubles; cottage cheese, 3.5 roubles. Wages for workers in Ukraine had doubled by the end of 1918 from what they were a year earlier, and almost all Kyiv's registered population had ration cards.[11] In Volyn province that October prices, per kilogram, were: bread, 2–3 roubles; rye flour, 3 roubles; potatoes, 31 kopeks; butter, 25 roubles; pork,7 roubles. Three roubles bought 10 eggs.[12] In May 1918, in Katerynoslav, eggs cost 5 roubles per dozen, butter 4–5 roubles per kilogram, and men's leather slippers 300 roubles. Average prices per kilogram in the countryside were as follows: flour, 40–50 kopeks; bread, 50–60 kopeks; potatoes, 20–30 kopeks; meat, 3–4 karbovantsi; butter, 8–9 karbovantsi; soap, 3 karbovantsi.

Differences between small towns and cities could be substantial. During the summer of 1918 prices in Poltava, per pound in karbovantsi, were as follows: meat, 1.8; butter, 9–12; pork fat, 4.5–6; bread, 5–25. The same items in Kharkiv cost, respectively: 2.6–3.5, 12–14, 9–12, and 2–2.5. Ten eggs cost as much as 100 roubles.[13] Between June and December 1918 the price of a horse in Katerynoslav province doubled from 1,000 to 2,000 roubles.[14] Makar Mokrytsky complained that he could not afford the 350 karbovantsi monthly rent demanded by a landlord for a three-room flat. Asking the ministry to requisition it for him and his family, he was told that only military personnel had the right to requisitioned quarters. Writing sometime during the summer of 1918 Dmytro Krainsky complained that he had not been paid for two months. Under the Rada, skilled and unskilled workers with jobs could make over 1,000 roubles monthly, he wrote, while although lower-level government officials made less than workers, they nevertheless got more pay than higher officials. Whereas a peasant woman could afford 8 roubles for a bowl of soup in town, clerks and the educated in general could not pay more than 3 roubles 50 kopeks.[15]

Detailed figures from the time do not always confirm Krainsky's claims; however, in general, they do confirm that clerks were among the worse-off inhabitants. Whereas Krainsky claimed that the unskilled could earn as much as 30 roubles a day, presumably in Chernihiv, other sources indicate that in Kyiv wages for unskilled labourers in 1918 were, on average, 8 roubles a day. Lower-level married government clerks and rank-and-file policemen in the capital, whose income averaged at most between 200 and 250 roubles monthly (8–10.5 roubles a day) during the first months of the Hetman's rule, could perhaps afford the basics – if they paid no rent and got paid. At 400–500 roubles a month (16.5–21 per day), middle-level secretaries and typists in Kyiv made slightly more than skilled workers. In Kyiv, a police secretary could make 700 karbovantsi a month by the fall of 1918. Provincial police chiefs earned 750, procurators and governors 1,000 a month. A collectively signed letter from the employees of the Kyiv governor's office reveals that in May 1918 their average wages of between 140 and 200 karbovantsi a month left them hungry, wearing rags, and their families in a 'tragic' situation. Pay was doubled by the autumn, which could cover costs in the provinces, but not in Kyiv, thus employees' letters again began arriving to the Interior Ministry describing destitution.[16] Lower- and middle-level zemstvo clerks in central Ukraine complained that their 125–170 monthly wages (5–7 daily) were out of line with prices and inflation and that they could not shift to private sector employment since jobs there had been taken by other unemployed educated people.[17] Kyiv district zemstvo staff complained of malnutrition and of having to go and look for food and fuel during working hours. They submitted a request for a pay increase with a chart illustrating how prices in Kyiv in October 1918 were twenty-six times higher than they were in July1914. A list of eighty-eight everyday items showed that what cost 235 roubles at the beginning of the war had increased to 6,314 near its end. They also pointed out that one person needed 407 roubles a month to survive – which was more than the 1914 salaries of 200–300 roubles, the rate at which most of them were still being paid.[18] How Vonifat Kryvosheia, a secretary who had worked in the Kaniv povit office since 1902, could support his family of eight on his monthly pay of 125 karbovantsi, or how Terentyi Smetana in the Podillia governor's office supported his family of twelve on 425 karbovantsi in September 1918 is anyone's guess.[19]

Those who staffed the Directory's administration in Volyn and Podillia provinces in 1919, if they actually did get paid, got more than they did the previous year. Alongside their formal monthly salary of 400–500 karbovantsi, urban middle-level secretaries in central ministries got a hardship allowance, bonuses, and a per diem that could raise a monthly wage into the thousands. Thus, for the period June to December, a level 3 secretary, who formally received 500 karbovantsi per month, in fact got 5,543. In the autumn of 1919, Hryhory Demus, a clerk in the Press and Information Ministry, was formally paid 700 karbovantsi but, in fact, he got 9,730 karbovantsi for a month's work; Arsen Uzbek got 12,048, and the courier M. Furman, formally paid 1,000, in fact, got 6,571. Makar

Mokrytsky, in October 1919, was paid 7,556 a month. Village clerks in Volyn province averaged 300 to 750 a month that year, while wages for local council staff ranged from 1,700 to 3,600 karbovantsi per month.[20] In Podillia province the total number of tax collectors had increased by July 1919 to ninety-three from eighty-eight. Their monthly pay had been increased from 375 to 525 that January, but by the summer when a pencil cost 12 karbovantsi, that was still too little to cover living costs, or to attract new employees.[21]

A table comparing prices and wages in 1917 Kyiv with those in 1919 Kamianets, drawn up by the employees of one office, shows that prices during those two years had increased astronomically while the average wages for clerks had only doubled. While estimated living expenses in 1917 Kyiv were 150 roubles a month, in the summer of 1919 in Kamianets they were 4,000. While in the summer of 1918 in Kyiv a pair of shoes and rent for one room with utilities cost 100 karbovantsi, two years later in Kamianets the same items cost 25,000 and 6,850 karbovantsi respectively. The price of a loaf of bread had risen from 1 to 250 karbovantsi. In Kyiv during the winter of 1919–20, a good meal in a good restaurant cost as much as a pound of bread or meat – 5 karbovantsi. Five karbovantsi, however, represented almost one day's pay for the lowest paid office couriers, and in Vynnitsia it could only buy a skimpy meal in a cheap cafe. Per pound, pork fat cost 15–18 karbovantsi; potatoes, 45–60 kopeks, and bottle of milk, 23 kopeks.[22] In Rivne, in Volyn province, prices in karbovantsi per pound were: bread, 18; potatoes, 3; meat, 7–9; and sugar, 15. One egg cost as much as 4 karbovantsi.[23] By the spring of 1919 one pound of bread in Directory-controlled Ukraine cost between 10 and 20 roubles, and one kilogram of flour was 19 roubles. At a time when town dwellers needed from 30 to 80 karbovantsi a day for subsistence alone, depending on where they lived, most bureaucrats perhaps could survive – if they got paid. In Vinnytsia a family of three to four persons needed approximately 1,000 karbovantsi monthly to meet living costs in January 1919. The government statistical office noted that prices on average almost tripled in Kamianets-Podilskyi between April and July, and concluded that a family of three with their own house needed 1,500 karbovantsi a month to survive. That June a lunch in the city cost 45–50 karbovantsi, and employees were getting rations as well as wages. By September average prices in good restaurants in Kamianets were as follows, in karbovantsi: lunch, 650; supper, 500; a sandwich, 200; a cup of coffee, 95. That autumn a commission claimed that officials in Podillia province needed at least 11,500 karbovantsi a month just to survive.[24] In

Rivne the employees' union claimed that the minimal survival wage had increased between April and May 1919 from 500 to 1,500 karbovantsi. That September the Labour Ministry's Statistics Department reported that average workers' wages had increased seven-fold from January to 2,615 karbovantsi per month and that the minimal needed for survival was 4,156 per month.[25]

In May 1920, the Directory set new pay rates for lower- and middle-level employees which ranged from 2,000 to 7,000 monthly plus benefits for those who were married with children. By then, food for an adult cost at least 200 karbovantsi a day, fourteen currencies were in use, and prices and pay rates fluctuated wildly. One hundred karbovantsi could buy 10 eggs or carrots, a pound of beef, four bottles of milk, a kilogram of white bread or cottage cheese, a pound of laundry soap, half a pound of coffee, or 20 pounds of potatoes. Anyone who could pay in pre-war roubles, then the strongest currency after the German reichsmark, paid three times less than the price in karbovantsi.[26]

The government supplemented pay throughout 1919, but in July the Kamianets branch of the Ministries Administrators Association announced that their members were suffering such hardship that they would go on strike and take other work if they did not get higher wages – something they apparently did not do. While in September the Kamianets municipal workers did go on strike after almost two months of negotiating over pay, that December, the central union, which had declared that its members could not work because of severe hardship, also called on them not to lose faith.[27] Three months earlier, it should be noted, the Office Employees Union of Kamianets petitioned the Interior Ministry for a grant of 3,700 karbovantsi to buy clothes for the winter. After three successive evacuations since 1917 their members were destitute and literally had nothing but the clothes they were wearing.[28] The economic situation was made worse not only by the circulation of at least a dozen currencies in territory controlled by the Directory, but by a dramatic increase in the number of local authorities that were printing their own money due to a shortage of species outside the major cities. Between 1918 and 1920 sixty-nine towns, of which thirty-one were in Volyn and Podillia, and eighty institutions including local banks, city halls, zemstvos, factories, and Jewish Kahals, printed not only various kinds of coupons and credit notes, but also roubles, hryvni, and karbovantsi.[29] In villages, pay rates presumably were related to provisioning and part-time work. Thus, in August 1919, the monthly pay for secretaries in two different villages in Kalynivka povit was 25 roubles in one and 1,000 roubles in the other.[30]

Western Ukrainians were subject to the same inflation and devaluation as their eastern countrymen. Between January and May 1919 in the Drohobych region, the price per unit of sugar rose from 1 to 23 crowns and of bread from 72 centares to 14 crowns. The cost of pork fat rose from 20 to 64 crowns; the price of flour quadrupled, of meat doubled, and of milk quintupled. In December 1918 railway workers, who were being paid 400 crowns monthly, were hungry nonetheless, while in April of that year the 100,000 inhabitants of Drohobych province faced starvation. Lower-level married clerks earned 800 crowns monthly.[31] Officials accordingly took bribes and expected 'fees.' In May 1919, to simply hand a passport to the necessary official for a stamp, the secretary would expect 200 crowns, which was 60 more than the cost of a kilogram of hard-to-find cooking fat.[32]

In Bolshevik territories government clerks were not much better off materially. During its first four months in office the Provisional Government paid Easter bonuses to all employees, increased wages for Post and Telegraph and State Control Commission workers, and in August, gave a raise to lower-level officials. The minimal wage for the lowest-level contract workers became 40 roubles a month, and 75 for full-time workers – plus benefits.[33] Just after coming to power in Russia the Bolsheviks declared that administrators' wages would range from between 275 and 675 roubles a month. By January the highest officials were earning as much as 800.[34] By June 1918 a family of four needed at least 927 roubles a month (37 a day) to cover basic living costs.[35] At the beginning of 1919 when lower-level officials made between 200 and 350 monthly (8–15.5 a day), a pound of sugar in Ufa cost 28 roubles. By Easter one kilogram of flour cost 250 roubles.[36] By the end of 1919, when in Moscow markets potatoes cost 45 roubles a pound and meat 800, even 1,500–2,000 roubles a month was not enough to live on. It sufficed for 3–4 days complained, an anonymous petitioner to Lenin, 'and for the remaining 27 days must the administrator sit and think about what's going on in Rus?'[37] In January 1919 in Petrograd, when a family needed an estimated 1,500 roubles monthly to survive, the average pay of government employees was between 600 and 700. If people had to go to hospital, they were not paid and the benefits they did get did not cover families. Bread cost 20–25 roubles a pound. By the end of the year the price of bread had risen to 230–250 roubles, and one egg cost 80 roubles. In October 1920, while pay had risen to 6,000 roubles a month, bread had risen to 1,200–1,500 a kilogram, and the estimated minimal for subsistence was 75,000–100,000 roubles a month.[38]

During the first eight months of Bolshevik rule administrators got the same pay and rations as everyone else, but they were exempted from conscription, forced labour, and expropriations. A 'class ration' system introduced in July 1918 formally discriminated against bureaucrats as non-manual workers and placed them in category 3. By 1919, through bribery, connections, cajolery, and arguing department and/or ministerial heads could successfully obtain category 1 rations for their underlings. A new 'armoured ration' system introduced in November of that year placed some officials into category 1, which was expanded through 1920 to include almost all ministerial employees. But since delivery was irregular, and heads often distributed first to friends and cronies, all except for party members on the highest rung of the twenty-seven-tier ranking system, had to resort to theft, speculation, and bribery to survive. Administrators would appropriate for themselves confiscated goods, or goods that they were supposed to ration, or they would sell some of their rations on the market at high prices – which, of course, did nothing to ingratiate them with a hostile populace who already considered them privileged, corrupt, and incompetent.[39] During the famine in the Ural region in 1920–21, officials stole relief supplies for themselves and sold places on evacuation trains to starving refugees. Secret police reports claim that officials worked as administrators only to get food and clothing and saw nothing wrong in anything they did to obtain these necessities.[40] In May 1920, a survey in Viatka revealed that rations covered no more than one-third of an average family's food. Forty per cent was bought on the black market and another 22 per cent was obtained through barter.[41]

In Bolshevik Chernihiv, in December 1918, a single clerk renting one room and with a salary of 800 roubles a month, who paid 9 roubles daily for meals at his cafeteria, wrote in a letter to a newspaper that he was left with 350 roubles after expenses, but wondered whether his salary would have been enough for someone with a family to support. In reply, the editor wrote that the government could not afford to pay married workers more and that if it did local directors would then only hire single people.[42] In 1919 workers' wages averaged 300–350 roubles a month. That March newspapers reported that the minimal clerical wage in Kharkiv was insufficient for Kyiv, where the lowest paid earned less than 500 roubles a month (21 per day) and that the minimum wage for the capital would be raised to 1,873 roubles per month. That same month rationing was implemented – with higher officials getting the highest rations. By July a government commission raised the monthly salaries of the lowest administrators to between 1,700 and 2,900 roubles after learning that subsistence for a grown man averaged 2,200 monthly. Higher-level officials earned 2,300–4,000. Six months later, lunch at a public cafeteria cost 629 roubles for one person, while the average worker's wage had risen to 3,000 roubles a month, and the average clerk's wage to between 3,700 and 4,400. The estimated amount needed for daily subsistence rose from between 1,000 and 1,100 that April and to between 1,180 and 1,290 that May.

In Kharkiv, in 1919, Polish bank clerks estimated that they needed at least 95 roubles a day or 3,000 roubles a month to survive. In Kyiv in July 1920, prices had risen to anywhere between two and four times what they were in May 1919. One pencil cost 100 roubles and a bottle of ink 300.[43] In roubles per pound that month, white bread cost 38; salt, 48; cream, 35; butter, 120; sugar, 55; sausage, 60–80; potatoes, 8; and cottage cheese, 35.[44] On average, on the free-urban market, the price of bread averaged 25 roubles per kilogram, flour between 15 and 40 roubles per kilogram (depending on the quality), a pair of boots 2,000–5,000, and pork fat, 250–300 roubles per kilogram. By the end of 1920, wages had risen on average ten-fold while prices had risen anywhere from 50- to 100-fold. A full-time typist in a Food Supply Committee office was earning, on average, 2,400 Soviet roubles a month (100 per day). In Berdychiv, immediately after the Bolshevik takeover in October 1919, an agent reported, goods disappeared from shops and prices rose astronomically. Bread that cost 15 Kerensky roubles had risen to 60 Soviet roubles, butter rose from 100 to 400 roubles a pound, and the price of a pair of gloves went from 150 to 800 roubles. Since merchants either refused Soviet roubles or offered a low exchange rate, Bolshevik office employees could not buy very much.[45] In Zolotonosh (in Poltava province), in the summer of 1919, clerks earned an average of 600–700 roubles a month, and most went to work barefoot because when shoes did become available they were unaffordable. Local peasants for their part refused to sell for money and only traded food for commodities.[46]

In Hostomel, just north of Kyiv, in July 1920, five months after the town was retaken from the Directory, three volost office clerks protested that they had not received their rations for that entire period and that for their 4,000 karbovantsi monthly pay, all they could buy was seven boxes of matches. Like their counterparts in Directory territory, who said that they could not continue working for the miserable wages that they were being paid, the Bolshevik clerks wrote that unless they got at least 160 kilograms of flour each they would resign.[47] In August 1920, in Kyiv, average monthly salaries for senior high school teachers and high school accountants were 6,000– 6,700. To survive, city teachers formed co-ops, made direct agreements with rural co-ops, and traded books for food. In one such contract we see that in return for 617 copies of an almanac/calendar valued at 75 roubles each, the teachers got 1,848 eggs – which indicates that one egg cost at least 25 roubles – up from 2 roubles in May 1918. In August 1918, the average cost of a novel in Kyiv was less than 5 roubles. In another contract, the co-op exchanged 13 books (3,500 copies) for 328 kilograms of flour, 164 of sugar, 164 of groats, and 5 of pork fat. As one inspector noted in October 1920, 5,000–6,000 roubles monthly and a 10- 15-pound bread ration were not enough to live on and, not surprisingly, officials were corrupt, took bribes, and spent more time trying to supplement their wages than doing their work.[48]

In December 1921, the lowest monthly wage was 3,026 roubles, department heads made 13,000, and middle-level officials averaged 4,000–5,000. Washerwomen earned 1,750 roubles a month; carpenters, 4,000; and department directors and office heads 6,400.[49] Depending on location and quality, one kilogram of bread cost 1,000 roubles or more; a pair of boots, 70,000; and flour, as much as 1,250 per kilogram. In Poltava, in 1921, one kilogram of sugar sold for 112,000 roubles and one kilogram of rye bread for 16,000. In Kharkiv, a pound of soap cost as much as 5,000 roubles. The 'bagmen' who could supply urban markets thanks to regional price differences in 1920 paid, on average, bribes of 2,000–4,000 roubles to policemen to allow them to pass – more if a superior was present.[50] In Katerynoslav province, the price of a cow that in October 1918 had cost 1,000 roubles, by January 1922 had risen to 9 million roubles.[51]

A former secretary/translator, who had worked for military intelligence in the Commissariat of War, recollected that during the summer of 1919 in Kyiv, depending on overtime, she had earned between 10,000 and 15,000 Soviet roubles a month (400–600 per day). Besides wages and a daily unappetizing meal at a government cafeteria, this middle-level employee also got, when available, one pound of bread daily, and three pounds monthly of sugar, coffee, and cacao. A take-out lunch from a government employees' cafeteria cost 50 roubles. She also had perks such as access to confiscated and/or contraband goods – which individuals exploited according to their individual conscience. On the free market, the price of a pound of bread had jumped to 150 roubles.[52] Such middle-level Bolshevik administrators complained they were undernourished, and when their rations were not delivered and their cafeterias did not work – they starved.

It is difficult to determine whether Soviet employees were better off materially than their Directory counterparts. Unlike their Bolshevik counterparts, Directory employees unsympathetic towards the Ukrainian cause at least did not work in conditions of terror and, on the free market, their Ukrainian karbovantsi were worth more than Soviet roubles, which merchants often refused to accept even in Bolshevik-ruled zones. During the autumn of 1920 the preferred currency in Kyiv province was tsarist roubles. In Volyn province 1 karbovanets equalled 10 Soviet roubles.

Finally, while the Whites in their territories accepted lower-level personnel who had worked for the Bolsheviks, they paid them less, relative to prices and inflation, than did the Bolsheviks. In August 1919 in Poltava, the city paid administrators 500 roubles a month (21 per day). White bread cost 10 roubles a loaf; one cabbage, 5–7 roubles; one chicken, 50–60 roubles; and a pair of boots was 1,000 roubles or more. A forged passport with the district police chief's signature cost 1,000 roubles in Kharkiv. One pound of cottage cheese cost 8–9 roubles, one pound of sugar was 20–25 roubles.[53] In Kyiv that September, middle-level pay ranged from 450 to 1,000 roubles monthly with a bonus for the married. Prices were as follows, in roubles per pound: white bread, 20–50; butter, 225–280; cottage cheese, 50–60; meat, 100–120; and potatoes, 10–12. Two months later, as the new government established itself, butter dropped to 160–220, meat to 35–50, and potatoes to 8–9. Prices that summer were similar to those in Kharkiv, and tended to fall there as well. Inhabitants, nonetheless, were malnourished because either they had no work or were paid little. Mines in the Kharkiv region producing much-needed coal for trains, were staffed mostly by forced labour.[54] In the Crimea, in 1920, the monthly cost of minimal expenses for a family of three rose from 23,000 roubles in March to 535,000 by September, while wages covered no more than 30 per cent of that at best. Prostitutes only took Turkish lire. People fleeing to Turkey discovered that there was no toilet paper on the ships, and thus refugees found a use for their White roubles as toilet paper.[55]

In a letter to the editor, speaking for those few individuals who had worked for all the governments that had passed through the country since 1917 and were apolitical, one bureaucrat wrote that the Red Terror had been so horrific that those who survived were only a shadow of their former selves. No one could have possibly accumulated any wealth during the upheaval of the previous months except the most inhuman and cruel speculators. He begged the White government for food, clothes, and pay.[56] As far as can be determined his position was much like that of employees in all of the governments in Ukraine during the revolutionary years.

Notes

Introduction

1 Of the major groups at the time the Ukrainian Communists are the least studied. The most recent work does not examine their influence on the local level: see Ohienko, *Diialnist Ukrainskikh natsional-kommunistiv.*

2 Dates in Tronko, ed., *Istoriia mist i sil Ukrainskoi RSR,* 26 vols.

3 Easter, *Reconstructing the State,* 84; Yaney, *The Urge to Mobilize,* 478, 498, 503; Rigby, *Lenin's Government.* Mann, 'The Autonomous Power of the State,' 112, summarizes the opposing claim that such networks impede state building.

4 Roth, Wittich, eds., *Max Weber,* I: 1207. Weber implicitly linked Protestantism and bureaucracy in this essay.

5 Some councils were more successful at keeping municipal services running than others. There are studies of individual cities but no overall synthesis. See Hospodarenko, Diialnist mistsevykh orhaniv vlady; Plaskyi, 'Miske hromadske samovriaduvannia.'

6 Roth, Wittich, eds., *Max Weber,* I: 224, 264–6, 988–9. Weber wrote these lines between 1913 and 1919 and knew about the German revolution. In his view the Bolsheviks had established a military dictatorship and were threatening officials with starvation to force them to work. 'However, in the long term the state machinery and economy cannot be run in this way.' This seems to contradict his idea of bureaucratic inertia. Weber died in 1920 and never thought out the implications of Russian events for his theory. Eldridge, ed., *Max Weber: The interpretation of Social Reality,* 216.

7 Soemardjian, 'Bureaucratic Organization in a Time of Revolution;' LaPalombara ed., *Bureaucracy and Political Development, passim;* Braibanti et al., *Asian Bureaucratic Systems;* Riggs, 'Modernity and Bureaucracy.'

8 Antoshkin, *Professionalnoe dvizhenie sluzhashchikh 1917–1924* gg.; Serebrianskii, *Ot Kerenshchiny k proletarskoi diktature;* Melgunov, *Kak bolsheviki zakhvatili vlast;* Iroshnikov, *Sozdanie sovetskogo tsentralnogo gosudarstvennogo apparata;* Iroshnikov, *Predsedatel soveta narodnykh komissarov;* Rigby, *Lenin's Government; Sovnarkom 1917–1922;* Orlovsky 'State Building in the Civil War Era: The Role of the Lower Middle Strata,' in Koenker et al., eds., *Party, State, and Society in the Russian Civil War,* 180–209; Pipes, *The Russian Revolution,* 526–9; Pipes, *Russia under the Bolshevik Regime;* Gimpelson, *Sovetskie upravlentsy 1917–1920 gg.;* Smirnova, 'Byvshie liudi' Sovetskoi Rossii'; Easter, *Reconstructing.* On the Whites see: Buldakov, *Beloe dvizhenie na iuge Rossii;* Medvedev, *Politiko-iuridicheskaia sushchnost interventsii i gosudarstvenno-pravovaia organizatsiia belogo dvizneniia;* Karpenko, *Belye generaly.*

9 Kolesnikov, *Professionalnoe dvizheniia i kontrrevoliutsiia;* Kolesnikov, *Rabochee i professionalnoe dvizhenie; Profsoiuzy posle oktiabria na Ukraine;* Kreizel, *Professionalnoe dvizhenie i Avstro-germanskaia okkupatsiia.* Korolivskii, ed., *Podgotovka velikoi oktiabrskoi sotsialisticheskoi revoliutsii na Ukraine,* contains documents related to every union and social group except state bureaucrats.

10 Rybalka, *Rozhrom burzhuazno-natsionalistychnoi dyrektorii na Ukraini,* 182; Korolivskii et al., *Pobeda sovetskoi vlasti na Ukraine,* 453–65. Skaba et al., *Ukrainska RSR v period hromadianskoi viiny 1917–1920.* English-language historiography does not dwell on administration. Adams, *The Bolsheviks,* is a rare book that does mention administrative problems in Bolshevik Ukraine.

11 Myronenko, *Svitoch ukrainskoi derzhavnosti;* Andrusyshyn, *U poshukakh sotsialnoi rivnovahy* examines the Ministry of Labour under all Ukrainian governments. On the Hetmanate, Doroshenko, *Istoriia Ukrainy 1917–1923 rr,* provides the most detail available in pre-1991 literature on local administration. More recent studies of the bureaucracy are Iarymenko, *Administrativa reforma,* and Vyshnevsky, ed., *Naukovo-dokumentalna zbirka.* Lozovy, *Vnutrishnia ta zovnishnia polityka Dyrektorii* has examined aspects of administration in the UNR. The most detailed modern work on western Ukraine is by O. Pavlyshyn, 'Orhanizatsiia tsyvilnoi vlady ZUNR u povitakh Halychyny.' A number of post-1991 doctoral dissertations either mention administration and bureaucracy or are devoted to a particular ministry and its ability to implement policies locally. Two provide detailed overviews: Lebedeva, *Stvorennia uriadu Ukrainskoi Narodnoi Respubliky,* and Kharchenko, *Stanovlennia mistsevykh orhaniv vykonavchoi vlady ... v Ukrainskyi derzhavi.*

12 Vynnychenko, *Vidrodzhennia natsii,* I: 256; II: 108. Similar opinion was expressed in Kyivan Ukrainian newspapers in May 1920. Lisevych, *U vidblysku,* 49.

13 Hupka, *Z czasow wielkiej wojny*, 341.

14 Khrystiuk, *Zamitky i materialy do istorii Ukrainskoi revoliutsii*, II: 134–6; Shapoval, *Velyka revoliutsiia i Ukrainska vyzvolna prohrama*, 14–18, 240–1; Hryhoriiv, *Spohady 'ruiinnyka,'* 87–9, 178–83; Mazepa, *Ukraina v ohni i buri revoliutsii*, II: 149, III: 114–16; Martos, *Vyzvolnyi zdvyh Ukrainy*, 60–73; Makukh, *Na narodni sluzhbi*, 233. Pipes, *The Formation of the Soviet Union*, 149.

15 Subtelny, *Ukraine*, 354, and Zaitsev et al., *Istoriia Ukrainy*, 250, represent the majority view. Hrytsak, *Narys istorii Ukrainy*, 116, supports Doroshenko's interpretation.

16 Doroshenko, *Istoriia Ukrainy 1917–1923 rr*, I: 78, 127; II: 103; Doroshenko, *Moi spomyny pro nedavne mynule (1914–1920)*, 256–7.

17 Hryhoriiv, 'Zlochynstva politychnoi bezhramotnosty.' He did not pursue this theme in his *Spomyny*. Borys Martos, *Oskilko i Bolbochan*, 34, makes a similar observation when complaining about people who worked for the Directory only because they sought refuge from the Bolsheviks.

18 Shtern, *V ogne grazhdanskoi voiny*, 172, 174, 180.

19 Nazaruk, *Rik na velykyi Ukraini*, 267–8, 368; Kobets, *Zapysky*, 396–7.

20 The Statistics Department of the Ministry of Labour, formed March 1919 with a staff of four, compiled some figures on workers' wages. Some statistics from the Food Supply Ministry also exist. TsDAVO, f. 3305 op.1 sprava 19; f. 2198 op.1 sprava 159. *Zbirnyk statystychnykh vidomostei po narodnem hospodarstva Ukrainy* (Kyiv, 1919) only goes to 1916.

21 DAKO, f. R2976 op.1 sprava 24.

22 Kriezel, *Iz istorii profdvizheniia*, 1.

23 TsDAHO, f. 1 op. 20 sprava 300 nos. 16, 19, 58, 62, 158.

24 Chekanovsky, 'Ohliad mizhnarodnoi polityky,' *Volia Tyzhnevyk*, vol. 1 no. 9 (Feb. 1920), 436. The Directory's agriculture minister was appalled by this development which, he said, taught people it was possible to live without government. Kovalevsky, 'Problemy,' *Volia*, vol. 1 no. 11 (March 1920), 518.

25 Dotsenko, *Litopys Ukrainskoi revoliutsii.*, vol. 2, bk. 4, p. 326.

26 *Trybuna*, 21 Jan. 1919.

27 Makhno, *Russkaia revoliutsiia*, 20, 45–7, 70–3, 92. The anarchists and their supporters dominated the local soviets, unions, and all-party committees (*obschestvennyi komitet*). Makhno does not mention full-time clerks in his memoirs. He considered national leaders to be insufficiently radical socially and too anti-Russian (98–9, 113).

28 Cited in Nikolaev, ed., *A. Vetlugin. Sochineniia*, 102; cited in Chop, *Makhnovsky rukh*, 94.

29 Belenkin *Avantiuristy velikoi smuty*, 196.

30 Danilov, ed., *Nestor Makhno*, 129, 791.

31 Belash, *Dorogi,* 352–60. 'Makhnovsky rukh,' 119. Published protocols of the Military Council from December 1919 in Danilov, ed., *Nestor Makhno,* 279–86.

32 The Ethnographic Institute of the Academy of Sciences during the 1920s did not collect oral histories of the revolution from peasants. There is however a valuable compilation by M. Levchenko: *Opovidannia selian za chasy hromadianskoi viiny na Vkraiini* (Kyiv, 1926).

1 Ukrainians and Government Bureaucracy before 1917

1 Statistics on occupation are in the unpublished voters' lists for the 1917 Constituent Assembly elections. There are no 1916 and 1917 census data on occupation. Gaponenko, Kabuzan, 'Materialy selskokhozaistvennykh perepisei 1916–1917 gg.,' 102, 114; Bruk, Kabuzan, 'Chislennost i rasselenie Ukrainskogo etnosa v. XVIII–nachale XX v.,' 23–4. A 1919 census of unknown provenance gives the total population for that year as 30 million. DAKO, f. R142 op. 1 sprava 157. All tables mentioned in this book are to be found in Appendix 1.

2 Rogger, *Russia in the Age of Modernisation and Revolution,* 126; P. Tronko, ed., *Istoriia mist i sil Ukrainy* passim. Guthier, 'The Roots of Popular Ukrainian Nationalism,' 147.

3 Sukhov, *Ekonomichna heohrafiia Ukrainy,* 142, 151.

4 Ivanov, *Uezdnaia Rossiia,* 13, 59.

5 Semenov-Tian-Shanskii, *Gorod i derevnia,* 76. Official categories remained in force to 1917. Tsarist policy fostered food processing and light finishing in small towns because the raw materials were close by. Landowners who built manufacturing concerns in small towns got tax exemptions.

6 Ryndzionskii, *Krestiane i gorod,* 151, 156, 171, 176, 230. This book examines the entire USSR and includes the three southern Ukrainian provinces with two Russian ones into its 'southern region' –for which it lists 395 urban-type settlements legally classified as villages. I know of no similar work devoted exclusively to the Ukrainian provinces.

7 Ialansky, Verovka, *Nestor i Halyna,* 26–34.

8 Iaroshevich, ed., *Ves Iugo-Zapadnyi krai: Spravochnaia Kniga,* 618–27. Ostapenko, *Ekonomichna heohrafiia Ukrainy,* 205. Uman's population was 46,572. The next largest town was Talne with 9,000. The third and fourth largest settlements were the 'villages' Kameneche (pop. 4,285) and Mankivka (pop. 4,156).

9 Ostapenko, *Ekonomichna heohrafiia Ukrainy,* 205–6. Ostapenko gives the total population on the eve of the revolution as 38 million.

10 *Obshchii svod po Imperii rezultatov razrabotki dannykh perepisi 1897 g. po Imperii,* vol. I (SPB 1905); *prilozhenie,* chart no. 6; Kurman, Lebedinskii, *Naselenie bolshogo sotsialisticheskogo goroda,* 122; Vikul, 'Liudnist mista Kyiva,' 226.

11 Krawchenko, *Social Change and National Consciousness,* 11; Shapoval, *Misto i selo,* 10; Khrystiuk, *Zamitky i materialy,* I: 89.

12 Fedor, *Patterns,* 140, 152; Krukhliak, 'Torhovelna burzhuaziia v Ukraini (60-ti roky XIX st. – 1914 r.),' 72–7.

13 Mochalova, ed., 'Vladimir Vernadskii: Volnoe,' 86.

14 Porsh, 'P. Struve v Ukrainskii spravi,' 333–41, abridged in: M. Hordienko [pseud.], 'Kapitalizm i russkaia kultura na Ukraine,' *Ukrainskaia zhizn* 9 (1912) 16–32, 20–8. His argument was written in response to P.B. Struve, who claimed that in Ukraine 'capitalism would speak Russian': 'Obshcherusskaia kultura i ukrainskii partikularizm,' *Russkaia mysl* (Jan. 1912) 65–86.

15 *Goroda Rossii,* 410–13, 574–8; TsDAVO, f. 1092 op. 5 sprava 8 no. 4.

16 Sukhov, *Ekonomichna heohrafiia Ukrainy,* 103–4, 151, 167–73; *Bolshaia entsiklopediia,* XVI: 490–1. Maps of railway and telegraph lines are in P.P. Semenov, ed., *Polnoe geograficheskoe opisanie nashego otechestva,* 19 vols. Ostapenko claims Ukraine had almost 19,000 km of track – approximately as much as Italy. *Ekonomichna heohrafiia Ukrainy,* 186–8.

17 Leshchenko, ed., *Kataloh dorevoliutsiinykh gazet,* 148–63, lists pre-revolutionary newspapers by town. Ihantienko, *Ukrainska presa,* 70, lists according to language; his totals include a few publications that saw only one or two issues and exclude imported titles, while it is unclear if he includes or excludes Bolshevik publications in his totals. Rudy, *Hazetna periodyka,* lists 1,150 Russian, Ukrainian, and Jewish titles published in western and eastern Ukraine between 1917 and 1920; of these, 381 were Bolshevik, 286 were in Ukrainian, 262 were dailies, and 21 saw only one edition.

18 Ilinskii, ed., *Spisok povremennykh izdanii,* 243–9, 264–5, 272–5; titles are listed by province. Someone in Kyiv supposedly ignored a chance to buy a new press in August from the American manufacturer in Petrograd. *Nova Rada,* 21 Dec. 1917 (3 Jan. 1918).

19 Loka, ed., *Prasa Polska w latach 1864–1918,* 89; Loka, *Prasa w latach 1918–1939,* 406, 432.

20 Skachkov, ed., *Periodychni vydannia URSR,* 312–560; these totals differ from Ihnatienko's and are probably more reliable.

21 Velychenko, 'The Bureaucracy, Police, and Army in Twentieth-Century Ukraine,' 69, 73.

22 Zyrianov, 'Sotsialnaia struktura mestnogo upravlenniia kapitalisticheskoi Rossii (1861–1914),' 248, 276; Matkhanova, 'Formalnaia i neformalnaia ierarkhiia,' 160; Guadin, *Ruling Peasants.*

23 Ivanov, *Uezdnaia,* 44. The mayor and the chairman of the local zemstvo and assembly of gentry were elected.

24 *Obshchii svod po Imperii,* I: 1, 9, and 11; II: charts 20, 20a, and 23. Category 1 includes among the 43% listed as administrators an unspecified number of lawyers and judges; 17% were auxiliary personnel (caretakers, guards, couriers). In Category 13, 6% were administrators. In the fifty provinces west of the Urals 52% of Category 2 (*obshchestvennaia sluzhba*) employees were elected, full-time and part-time officials, while 48% were auxiliary employees like janitors or guards paid by the state but not administrators. Subcategories for the provinces are not indicated or divided according to language or gender. *Pervaia vseobshchaia perepis,* chart nos. 21, 22, vols. 8, 13, 16, 32, 33, 41, 46, 47, and 48. 'Civil councils' includes zemstvos, city duma, and village councils. Sadovsky, *Pratsia v SSSR.*

25 Pomeranz, 'Justice from the Underground,' 319–40. Though condemned by the legal profession, common people used their services extensively in cities and towns.

26 Efremov, ed., *Rossia v mirovoi voine 1914–1918 goda,* 24, 25; Sudavtsov, *Zemskoe i gorodskoe samoupravlenie,* 39.

27 Anifimov, Korelin, eds., *Rossiia 1913 god.: Statistiko-dokumentalny spravochnik,* 265. Ostapenko, *Ekonomichna heohrafiia Ukrainy,* 201; he gives a total of 33,600 officials and 66,000 county (*volost*) secretaries, but no sources. By 1906 the total number of railway employees had tripled – to over 14,000. Bohatchuk, 'Sotsialne stanovyshche zaliznychnykiv Ukrainy,' 91.

28 Guthier, 'Ukrainian Cities during the Revolution and the Interwar Era,' 160; *Pervaia vseobshchaia perepis,* vol. 18, chart XXI. Iarmysh, ed., *Istoriia mista Kharkova,* 7, 128, 152.

29 Totals include only credit and consumers' co-ops. Vytanovych, *Istoriia Ukrainskoho kooperatyvnoho rukhu,* 113, 184, 220, 235, 329.

30 Sadovsky, *Pratsia,* 13; Korolivsky et al., *Pobeda,* 35; Gaponenko, *Rabochii klass Rossii v 1917 godu,* 444.

31 Koenker, ed., *Tret'ya Vserossiiskaya Konferentsiya Professionalnykh Soyuzov,* xii.

32 Volin, *Deiatelnost menshevikov v profsoiuzakh pri sovetskoi vlasti,* 61.

33 Gaudin, *Ruling Peasants,* 208. Charts and figures on Tambov were kindly given to me by V.V. Kanishchev: 'Gorodskie srednie sloi v period formirovannia osnov sovetskogo obshchestva: Oktiabr 1917–1920 gg. (Po materialam tsentra Rossii).'

34 Gorianov, *Ustavy o voinskoi povinnosti ... dopolnennye vsemi pozdneishimi uzakoneniiami po 1 iunia 1913 g.,* 12th ed., Appendix 7; Golovin, *The Russian Army in World War I,* 26, 62, 71–3, 203.

35 Cited in Sanborn, 'Drafting the Nation,' 98. The practice was also widespread in Kharkiv province. TsDAVO, f. 2 op. 2 sprava 293 no. 136.
36 TsDAVO, f. 1092 op. 4 sprava 83. Wages of the mayor and his assistant and the police are not included. Staff were all included into one group: 'the chief secretary and his assistants.' In 1918 the figures jump to 13,443, 30,863, and 78,071.
37 Emmons, ed., *Time of Troubles: The Diary of Iurii Valdimirovich Got'e,* 32; Golovin, *The Russian Army,* 62, 112–17.
38 *Pervaia vseobshchaia perepis naseleniia Rossiiskoi imperii 1897 g.,* chart no. 15, vols. 8, 13, 16, 32, 33, 41, 46, 47, and 48. Figures include ages 1–9 and 60+. TsDAVO, f. 1115 op. 1 sprava 48 nos. 110–11.
39 Chubinsky, 'Dva slova o selskom uchilishche voobshche,' 54–9.
40 Golubov, Lokhmatova, 'Reformirovanie obshchestva i sudby liudei: popytki analiza psykhologicheskikh aspekotov preobrazovanii serediny XIX veka,' 77–8.
41 The total number of pupils in Katerynoslav province increased from 46,650 in 1891 to 108,703 in 1897. Kohtiants, 'Tserkovno-parafiialni shkoly u Katerynoslavskii eparkhii v 1884–1916 rokakh,' 396. Prysiazhniuk, *Ukrainske selianstvo,* 71. Velychenko, 'Identities Loyalties and Service in Imperial Russia: Who Administered the Borderlands?' 199–204.
42 Eklof, *Russian Peasant Schools,* 292, 452; Borysenko, *Borotba demokratychnykh syl za narodnu osvitu,* 47.
43 [Anon], 'Na Ukraine,' *Izvestiia* (6 Jan. to 24 Dec.) 1917; here and elsewhere throughout this book, my translation, unless otherwise stated, for quoted material not published in English.
44 Chykalenko, *Shchodennyk (1907–1917),* 383; Livytska, *Na hrani dvokh epokh,* 330. In provincial towns Jews normally spoke Ukrainian.
45 *Rada,* 24 March (10 April) 1914.
46 *Rada,* 4 (17) May 1914.
47 Velychenko, 'Identities Loyalties and Service,' 205, 209.
48 Chykalenko, *Shchodennyk,* 290; *Rada,* 10 June 1914.
49 TsDAVO, f. 4439 op.1 sprava 4 nos. 14–16. In his undated memoirs, probably written in the 1920s, Marshynsky focused on the trip to Galicia in 1889 and on his arrest. TsDAVO, f. 4439 op.1 sprava 1.
50 TsDAVO, f. 2198 op. 2 sprava 131.
51 TsDAVO, f. 1092 op. 1 sprava 3; f. 1276 op. 1 sprava 140. DASBU, f. FP74554 vol. 13 nos. 100–1; FP 73878, vol. 2 nos. 64–120.
52 TsDAVO, f. 1092c op. 4 sprava 153; the form is in Ukrainian. DAKO, f. 1239 op. 196 sprava 21 no. 12.
53 Skoropadsky, *Spohady,* 12. Drahomanov pointed out that educated 'Little Russians' were bilingual and eagerly bought the few Ukrainian publications

that went beyond 'ethnographic patriotism'and dealt with current issues. See Dei, Zasenko, Lysenko, eds., *Mykhailo Petrovych Drahomanov,* I: 138, 308; II: 401–2.

54 Kulikov, *Biurokraticheskaia elita,* 12–13, 436–43.

55 DAKO, f. 1239 op. 196 sprava 21 nos. 58, 60, 69.

56 *Sputnik chinovnika,* no. 19 (1913) 11. DIA, f. 274 op. 1 sprava 3005, 3159; op. 4 sprava 251.

57 *Sputnik chinovnika,* no. 5 (1913); no. 82–9 (1914) 8.

58 Ibid., no. 3 (1912) 29.

59 Ibid., no. 20 (1913).

60 Ibid., no. 33 (1914) 16–17.

61 Ibid., no. 9 (1913) 20–2; no. 14 (1913) 15.

62 Ibid., no. 6 (1911); no. 23 (1912); no. 32 (1913). On the eve of the war, policy was beginning to change. While the Ministry of Education continued to forbid teachers to form or join any organizations, the Land Ministry was encouraging its employees to do so in the hope that they would thereby improve their knowledge and skills. Ibid., no. 6 (1914).

63 Ibid., no. 22 (1912) 18–20; no. 4 (1913) 23.

64 Ibid., no. 14 (1911) 27–30.

65 Ibid., no. 21 (1912) 22; no. 10 (1911) 20–3; no. 12 (1911) 15–20.

66 Ibid., no. 25 (1912) 1–13.

67 Ibid., no. 18 (1911) 21.

68 Ibid., no. 20 (1912) 1–6. In 1914 village secretaries began publishing their own journal, *Volostnoi pisar.* They wanted to be full-time officials with pensions rather than elected council personnel.

69 DAKO, f. 2 op. 79 sprava 37 nos. 85, 205–231, 382; sprava 202 nos. 79–80. All applications in the sample were rejected. Replies were sent out within days unless the application was sent for police vetting which could take up to four months. The governor's assistant secretary sent replies to the applicant's local police chief rather than to the applicant.

70 DIA, f. 442 op. 641 sprava 23 nos. 101, 178, 226–31; op. 640 sprava 23 nos. 199–201 and passim.

71 Cited in Peroutka, *Budovani statu,* I: 135.

72 DAHO, f. 5 op. 1 sprava 21 nos. 105–6. Doroshenko, *Istoriia Ukrainy 1917–21,* I: 270–1.

73 Tatishchev, *Zemli i liudi,* 16, 305.

74 Cited in Lototsky, *Storinky mynuloho,* III: 127.

75 Rusova, 'Moi spomyny,' *Za sto let,* bk. 3 (1928): 177; Lototsky, *Storinky mynuloho,* II: 16.

76 Velychenko, 'Local Officialdom and National Movements in Imperial Russia,' 74–85.

77 Antonenko-Davydovych, *Tvory,* II: 514, 534–5.

78 DAKO, f. 1239 op. 196, sprava 21 nos. 15, 48, 77.

79 DIA, f. 442 op. 642 sprava 27 nos. 18–22.

80 Miller, *Ukrainskii vopros;* Chykalenko, *Shchodennyk,* 115, 254.

81 Ostrovskii, *Kto stoial za spinoi Stalina,* 530–74; Pyvovar, 'Truzheniki na polzu obruseniia kraia,' 69. Between 1907 and 1917 the police registered the names of two million people who had come to their attention. Except for parts of letter A the catalogue survived the revolution and is now in the Russian State Archive. It could be used to identify links between Ukrainians in the administration and in the national movement. Baiguzin, ed., *Gosudarstvennaia bozopastnost Rossii,* 107.

82 DIA, f. 442 op. 641 sprava 23 nos. 32–4. In Perm his Polish enemy: 'staralsia menia kak russkago unizhit i vovse izbavitsia.'

83 Velychenko, 'Local Officialdom.'

84 Iurkevich, *Minuvshee prokhodit predo mnoiu,* 7.

85 Chykalenko, *Shchodennyk,* 382; Doroshenko, *Moi spomyny pro davne minule,* 141. Although both men note the success of the provincial Prosvita, Chykalenko does not mention Doroshenko and Doroshenko does not mention Iavornytsky.

86 *Trybuna,* 26 Dec. 1918.

87 Korsunsky 'Panas Iakovych Rudchenko (Panas Myrnyi) iak sluzhbovets, hromadianyn i liudyna,' 236–56; Panas Myrnyi, *Zibrannia tvoriv,* VII: 323. TsDAVO, f. 2199 op. 5 sprava 195 no. 2. Between his resignation and application he had been in the army.

88 Doroshenko, 'Ukrainskyi rukh 1890-ykh rokiv v osvitlenni Avstriiskoho konsula v Kyivi,' 63–4. Naumov, *Ukrainsky politychny rukh,* 223–31, provides dozens of names of national activists holding clerical positions in government and non-government offices throughout left-bank Ukraine before the war. See also Kasianov, *Ukrainska intelihentsiia,* 49–50.

89 Shevchenko, ed., *Ukrainski politychni partii,* 30; Chykalenko, *Shchodennyk,* 379–81. The named delegate was not the future Hetman. At the same time rural activists circulated a petition signed by 200 peasants condemning Rodzianko, the Ukrainian-born chairman of the Duma, for claiming Ukrainians did not want Ukrainian used in schools.

90 Hermaize, ed., 'Materialy do istorii Ukrainskoho rukhu za svitovoi viiny,' 292.

91 Geifman, *Thou Shalt Kill: Revolutionary Terrorism in Russia,* 21; Holubovsky, Kulyk, *Ukrainskyi politychnyi rukh,* 79–81.

92 Predislovii, Stepansky, eds., *Professionalnoe dvizhenie sluzhashchikh Ukrainy,* 145.

93 Prykhodko, *Pid sontsem Podillia,* 67–8, 130, 157–60, 196–7, 246.

94 Halahan, *Z moikh spomyniv,* I: 198.

95 In 1905–07, 84% of a total of 222,488 members belonged to an extreme-right group. I.N. Kiselev et al., 'Politicheskie partii v Rossii v 1905–1907 gg.: chislennost, sostav, razmeshchenie,' *Istoriia SSSR,* no. 4 (1990) 77–8. There were 8,631 Kadets, 7,857 Octobrists, and an estimated 2,000 belonged to Ukrainian national parties. Donchenko, *Liberalni parti,* 82–5. In 1917 total party membership in Ukraine was at least 214,500 – not including Ukrainian members in the Russian PSR (all-Russian, 500,000), Zionists (all-Russian, 28,000), and Kadets (all-Russian, 60,000), which are not known. Among the other parties were the following numbers: Bolsheviks, 50,000; Mensheviks, 30,000; UPSR, 75,000; USDP, 40,000; Bund, 11,000; Russian extremists, 8,500. Naiman, *Ievreiski partii ta ob'eidnannia Ukrainy,* 46; Shelokhaev, ed., *Politicheskie partii Rossii konets XIX – pervaia tret XX veka;* Spirin, *Krusheniie pomeshchichykh i burzhuaznykh partii v Rossii,* 300–1; Kirianov, 'Chislennost i sostav pravykh partii v Rossii v 1914–1917 gg.,' in Smirnov, et al., *Rossiia i pervaiai mirovaia voina,* 219–21.

96 No more than 5% of Bolsheviks and 7.5% of PSR members were employees (*sluzhashchie*) – this included the private sector as well as government personnel. Brovin, 'K voprosu ob izuchenii sostava bolshevistskoi partii nakanune i v period revoliutsii,' in Rodionov et al., eds., *Revoliutsiia 1905–07 godov v Rossii,* 175; Erofeev, 'K voprosu o chislennosti i sostave partii eserov nakanune pervoi rossiiskoi revoliutsii,' in Gusev, ed., *Neproletarskie partii Rossii v trekh revoliutsiakh,* 126–30; Leonov, *Partiia sotsialistov-revoliutsionerov v 1905–1907 gg.,* 59–67. See also Hildermeier, *The Russian Socialist Revolutionary Party before the First World War,* 278.

97 Shelokhaev, *Kadety-glavnaia partiia liberalnoi burzhuazii v borbe s revoliutsiei,* 67–9, and *Partiia oktiabristov v period pervoi rossiiskoi revoliutsii,* 43–5; Emmons, *The Formation of Political Parties: The First National Elections in Russia,* 177, 217.

98 Sidorov, 'Mobilizatsiia reaktsii v 1906,' 162; Emmons, *Formation of Political Parties,* 184. From January 1906 superiors decided whether subordinates' could join political organizations.

99 Samartsev, 'Chornosotentsi na Ukraini (1905–1917 rr.),' 94; Stepanov, *Chernaia sotnia v Rossii,* 114–15.

100 Kirianov, 'Krainie pravye partii i obshchestvo,' in Kirianov, Shevyrin, eds., *Politicheskie partii i obshchestvo v Rossii,* 173–7; Emmons, *Formation of Political Parties,* 190–1.

101 Stepanov, 'Chislesnnost i sostav pravykh partii v Rossii v 1914–1917 gg.,' in Smirnov et al., *Rossiia i pervaia mirovaia voina,* 219–21.

102 Kirianov, 'Pravye v 1915–fevrale 1917 po perliustrirovannym Departmentom politsii pismam,' 182.

103 Smith, 'Political Freemasonry in Russia, 1906–1918: A Discussion of the Sources,' 167–8. Startsev, *Russkoe politicheskoe masonstvo nachala XX veka,* 161–5. The extent of Masonic influence is disputed.

104 Nikovsky 'Masonstvo v Rossii pered revoliutsieiu i na pochatku viiny,' 156, 159; Kryzhanovska, *Taemni orhanizatsii v hromadsko-politychnomu zhytti Ukrainy,* 94–101; Bilokin, 'Masony i Ukraina,' 188–97; Hass, *Loza i Polityka: Masoneria Rosyjska,* 279–85. Ukrainian Masons also split between federalists and separatists in January 1918. Kryzhanovska, 117–23, and Bilokin, 188–9, list Ukrainian masons.

105 *Rada,* 10 Jan. 1914.

106 Approximately half of the urban population could vote and of those anywhere between 40% and 60% actually did. Listed cities on the chart are those with published returns from both elections. Russian PSR candidates polled an estimated 35% of the vote. There is no comprehensive study of the 1917 elections in Ukraine and, because parties combined into blocs, return summaries are difficult to collate and compare. Tereshchenko, *Politychna borotba na vyborakh do miskykh dum Ukrainy,* 90–117; Boiko, 'Pidsumky munitsypalnoi kompanii 1917 dlia Ukrainskoho rukhu,'; Smolii, ed., *Tsentralna Rada i Ukrainskyi derzhavotvorchyi protses,* I: 214–19; Guthier, 'Ukrainian Cities,' 162–4; Radkey, *The Agrarian Foes of Bolshevism,* 243; Chyrkova, ' Vybory do poltavskoi miskoi dumy 2 lypnia 1917r.,' 141.

107 *ARR,* VI: 181. The June Kadet party conference accepted federalism in principle – a position later rejected by its central committee. Donchenko, *Liberalni parti,* 258.

108 Unlike the vacuous obfuscation of Lenin and Stalin about national self-determination that all could interpret as they wished, the centralist, pro-Russian anti-Ukrainian views of key local leaders like Evgeniia Bosh, G. Piatakov, E. Preobrazhanskii, and A. Kollontai were explicit. Lenin's rival Pavel Axelrod in 1910 had called the Bolsheviks 'a gang of Black Hundreds and criminals in the Social Democratic movement.' Cited in Frenkin, *Zakhvat vlasti,* 73, 113–14.

109 Miliukov wrote: 'In the Kyiv group it is difficult to determine where the Kadets end and the Ukrainians begin.' Manilov et al., *1917 god na Kyivshchine,* 147, 156, 198; Mikhutina, *Ukrainskii vopros,* 133–4.

110 Radkey, *Agrarian Foes,* 219, 353.

111 Ibid., 179.

112 TsDAVO, f. 1115 op. 46 and 48. In 12 of these reports, which are particularly analytical and well written, only one, from Olhopil, notes anti-Ukrainian sentiment. In towns where they constituted a high proportion of the population, Jews could make up as much as 50% of council members, as in Berdychiv and Skvyr. But they were divided between Bundists, Zionists, and Traditionalists, who were subdivided among themselves. Significantly, the Ukrainian reports noted this. Analogously, an elected 'Ukrainian' member did not necessarily belong to a national party.

113 Radkey, *Russia Goes to the Polls,* 149; Radkey gives no separate urban totals.

114 Manilov et al., *1917 god na Kyivshchine,* 415. Polish and Jewish parties supported autonomy and split over Ukrainian independence. The Kadets and Russian SR members opposed independence .

115 Volin, *Mensheviki na Ukraine,* 28–30, 42, 66–7, 73; Volin, *Deiatelnost Menshevikov v profsoiuzakh,* 61–4. In the spring of 1918 Russian Mensheviks had decided to support the Bolsheviks, and that December so did Ukraine's Mensheviks in Kharkiv. The majority in non-Bolshevik Ukraine decided on 'neutrality.' This involved directing union activity to economic issues and refraining from calls to overthrow either the Hetman or the Directory or the Kharkiv Bolsheviks.

2 Bureaucracy, Law, and Political Parties in Ukrainian Thought

1 [Bezborodko], 'Zapiska kniaza Bezborodki o potrebnostiakh imperii Rossiiskoi,' 297–300; [Kochubei], 'Zapiska V. I. Kochubeia o polozhenii Imperii i o merakh k prekrashcheniiu bezporiadkov i vvedenii luchshago ustroistva v raznyia otrasli, pravitelstvo sostavliaiushchiia,' 5–26.

2 Perkin, *The Rise of Professional Society,* 228.

3 Shevchenko stated this explicitly in his 1847 introduction to an unpublished edition of the *Kobzar.* The essay was published in 1886 and again in 1906. Taras Shevchenko, *Povne zibrannia tvoriv* (1881), VI: 315, 557.

4 Petrov, 'Teoria "kulturnytstva" v Kulishevomu lystuvannia r. 1856–57,' 149–63.

5 Chornopysky, ed., *Ivan Nechui-Levytsky. Ukrainstvo na literaturnykh pozvakh z Moskovshchynoiu,* 150.

6 Proudhon, *General Idea of Revolution in the Nineteenth Century,* 293–4; original emphasis.

7 Drahomanov, 'Peredne slovo [do "Hromady"],' in Mishchuk, ed., *M.P. Drahomanov. Vybrane,* 293, 296–8, 301, 318–21.

8 Korniichuk, ed., *S.A. Podolynsky,* 74–8. A similar account was in F. Volkhovsky, *Pravdyve slovo khliboroba do svoikh zemliakiv.*

9 Ivan Franko, *Zibrannia tvoriv,* 45: 52, 139, 452. Khrystiuk, *Zamitky,* III: 97.

10 Holovko, *Iakyi derzhavnyi lad musyt buty;* Pilch, *Choho nas Ukraintsiv ... prozvaly burzhuiamy;* Boiko, *Zemstvo i narodna uprava;* Hryhoriev-Nash, *Iakoi respubliky treba bidnym liudam;* Zahirnia, *Pro derzhavnyi lad.*

11 Verstiuk et al., *Ukrainskyi natsionalnyi rukh,* 161–2; Lozytsky, ed., *Vynnychenko,* 39, 206.

12 Cited in Atoian, *Volia k pravu,* 103.

13 Chop, 'Makhnovsky rukh v Ukraine 1917–21 rr.,' 41–59.

14 Belash, *Dorogi,* 225, 325–6. Proclamations declared that central councils of unions would 'establish the necessary technical offices' and that the task of uniting regions 'will emerge by itself (*ustanovitsia*).' TsDAHO, f. 1 op. 20 sprava 328 no. 27.

15 Lavrov, 'Gosudarstvennyi element v budushchem obshchestve,' *Vpered* (1876), IV: 63, 75–7, 118–20. Lavrov witnessed the Paris Commune which he thought proved that anybody could administer.

16 Church, *Revolution and Red Tape,* 47.

17 Into the 1860s village schools were normally next door to the local administrative office. Children regularly saw supplicants grovelling, secretaries beating and/or swearing at them, and drew their own conclusions about the nature of 'administration.' Chubinsky, 'Dva slova.' Secretaries in Russia tended to be urban outsiders rather than native villagers and held their post for an average of three to four years. The situation in Ukraine is unstudied. Guadin, *Ruling Peasants,* 69–73.

18 The politics of bureaucracy should not be confused with electoral politics which peasants had mastered well. Displeased with the *volost,* whose administrative borders did not correspond to village borders and most of whose functions duplicated village or *povit* functions, heads of households normally avoided volost affairs and as officials normally did as little as possible so as not to he held to account by their neighbours when they relinquished their positions. They continued using avoidance tactics after 1917 such as intentionally electing rogues and criminals as representatives. They reasoned that the best way to peacefully rid themselves of undesirables was to send them off in official capacities to various assemblies and conventions where they would be far away from the village for as long as possible. During the revolution the practice had an added benefit since elected officials were usually the first to be imprisoned by incoming soldiers. Korostovetz, *Seed and Harvest,* 97–8. Gaudin, *Ruling Peasants,* 73–84. Mykhailiuk, *Selianstvo Ukrainy,* devotes some attention to peasant attitudes to authority but tends to assume that generalizations derived from Russian peasant experience are applicable to Ukrainian peasants – which was not necessarily so.

19 Mikulina, *Ukrainskii vopros,* 90–1.
20 *Hromadianyn,* 31 July (13 Aug.) 1917.
21 *Khto taki sotsialisty-revoliutsionery i choho vony domohaiutsia?*
22 Shevchenko, ed., *Ukrainski politychni partii,* 271–2, 279; Carr, ed., *Bukharin and Preobrazhansky: The ABC of Communism,* 231, 235–7. In 1919 Lavrov's sympathetic account of the Paris Commune was republished and the last volume of his collected works appeared in 1920.
23 Drahomanov, *Volnyi souiz–vilna spilka: Opyt Ukrainskoi politiko-sotsialnoi programmy,* 126–7, 153, 172.
24 Iavorenko, *Choho nam treba;* Dolenko, *Khto narodovi vorokh,* anon, *Demokratychna respublika,* 21–3. Kolesnyk, Mohylnyi, *Ukrainski liberalno-demokratychni partii,* 205–9, 213, 220. At the time, the Ukrainian Revolutionary Party, Ukrainian Democratic Party and Ukrainian Democratic Revolutionary Party were 'moderate.'
25 Shevchenko, *Ukrainski politychni partii,* 40, 72, 84, 90–7, 120, 179. Verstiuk, ed., *Ukrainskyi natsionalnyi rukh,* 504. The SF's in June 1917 saw finance, industry, communications, agriculture, justice, culture, and labour as local Ukrainian jurisdictions.
26 Shevchenko, *Ukrainski politychni partii,* 136, 150,
27 Stetsiuk, *Stanislav Dnistriansky iak konstytutsionalist,* 59–64.
28 Shevchenko, *Ukrainski politychni partii,* 25. 'Biurokratiia i polityka,' *Dilo* (18 March 1910). This article was anonymous but the editor, Volodymyr Bachynsky, or Iulian Romanchuk, just elected vice-president of the Austrian parliament, could have written it. Both were leading National Democrats.
29 Khrytsiuk, *Zamitky,* I: 123; Tanin-Lvov, ed., 'Pamiatnaia zapiska.'
30 Baehr, Wells, eds., *The Russian Revolution: Max Weber,* 254, 262.
31 Max Weber, I: 267–69. II: 1393, 1399, 1408, 1417–19. In 1918 Weber visited Kyiv as a member of an official delegation. Shapoval, 'Hetmanshchyna i dyrektoriia: Uryvky iz spomyniv,' *Vitchyzna*–nos. 11–12 (1995) 140.
32 Demydenko, ed., *Velykyi ukrainets,* 70, 112, 129–30, 142–3, 168–70. On the legal control of bureaucracy in practice see Myronenko, *Svitoch,* 222.
33 Kulikov, *Biurokraticheskaia elita,* 56–68, 394. Two hundred million came from the tsar's personal account. Shevyrin, *Zemskii,* 35–7. Tsarist ministers opposed to the independence of the Zemgor that same year expressed alarm at how big it had become and its usurpation of government functions.
34 Rosenberg, 'Social Mediation and State Control,' *Social History,* no. 2 (May 1994) 175–9; Wartenweiler, *Civil Society and Academic Debate in Russia,* 118–26; Holquist, *Making War, Forging Revolution,* 44–5.
35 Weber, II: 1402
36 Vynnychenko, *Vidrodzhennia,* II: 107–9.

37 Doroshenko, *Istoriia,* I: 127. At an all-party meeting with the Hetman's representatives in April 1918, it emerged that the SRs and SDs were split over the issue of cooperation. Vynnychenko was the most outspoken in favour of participation within the new government. Hrushevsky and Petliura opposed it. Zaitsev, 'Zhmut spohadiv.'

38 Khrystiuk, *Zamitky,* IV: 53, 76. Hryhoriiv, in *Vchimosia panuvaty* (1919) did not condemn the elective principle but now emphasized that only the knowledgeable and educated could administer.

39 Shevchenko, ed., *Ukrainski politychni partii,* 25, 42, 98–9, 121, 151–3. Strilets, 120. *Nova Rada* (27 June 1917). Even the conservative Agriculturalist Party envisaged an expansion rather than a reduction of government duties (Strilets, 136).

40 Bowman, ed., *Edward Bellamy Abroad,* 71–2, 494, 512, 514. The book also saw three Yiddish printings – one published in Berdychiv. A Ukrainian edition appeared in 1932.

41 Myronenko, *Svitoch,* 191–8; Verstiuk, II: 307–9. Regulations limiting electricity were published in *Narodnia volia* (15/28 Dec. 1917). On 24 Jan. 1918 (*Kievskaia mysl*) the Rada announced its intention to create one organ controlling the entire economy.

42 Sidak, *Natsionalni spetssluzhby v period Ukrainskoi revoliutsii,* 133, 140; Sidak, ed., *Rozvidka i kontrrozvidka Ukrainy,* 31–3, 52–3, 65.

43 Andrusyshyn, 'Problemy okhorony pratsi,' 16. TsDAVO, f. 1092c op. 2 sprava 392 nos. 20, 35. The decree was not actually written until three months later, when the Directory had been thrown back into Podillia and Volyn provinces. In the draft version the reference to circulating the decree by telegraph was crossed out and replaced with the word 'messenger.'

44 Hrushevsky, 'Ukrainska partiia sotsiialistiv-revolitsioneriv ta ii zavdannia,' 20.

45 Shapoval, *Revoliutsiinyi sotsializm na Ukraini,* 213

46 Nazaruk, *Rik,* 198; Doroshenko, *Spomyny,* 259, 352.

47 Andrievsky, *Z Mynuloho,* II pt. 2: 218.

48 Nazaruk, 214, 313.

49 Summarized in Easter, *Reconstructing,* 3–17.

3 The Central Rada, March 1917 to April 1918

1 Myronenko, *Svitoch,* 98–105.

2 For printed instructions on how to organize local co-op. and peasants' union groups see Verstiuk, ed., *Ukraiinska tsentralna rada,* I: 55, 303. *Kyivska zemska hazeta,* 14, 30 Sept. 1917. A. Savitsky, *Silsko-hospodarska*

kooperatsia: Praktychnyi poradnyk. P. Kolokolnikov, *Professionalnoe dvizhenie v Rossii. Organizatsiia soiuzov.*

3 Petriv, *Spomyny,* I: 148. TsDAVO, f. 1115 op. 1 sprava 42 no. 17.

4 TsDAVO, f. 1434 op. 1 sprava 4 nos. 70–100 contains a series of telegrams of this sort that Vynnychenko and district commissars sent each other in August and September 1917.

5 Tynchenko, *Persha Ukrainsko-bolshevytska viina,* 138.

6 TsDAHO, f. 57 op. 2 sprava 221 no. 1.

7 Verstiuk, ed., *Ukrainska tsentralna rada,* II: 168–9.

8 Gill, *Peasants and Government in the Russian Revolution,* passim.

9 TsDAHO, f. 5 op. 1 sprava 21 no. 10, 15v, 19–20, 29, 77. Krainsky was born in Poltava province. He considered himself a 'Little Russian' and supported autonomy, not independence. A Kadet sympathizer he travelled Ukraine extensively in 1917 and claims his account is representative of the situation in provincial towns.

10 Shcherbakov, 'Zhovtnevyi period na chernihivshchyni,' 299–300; Doroshenko, *Istoriia,* I: 60. *Nova Rada,* 26 April (6 May) 1917.

11 Verstiuk, ed., *Ukrainska tsentralna rada,* II: 168–9.

12 Gerasimenko, 'Obshchestvennye ispolnitelnye komitety v revoliutsii 1917 g.,' in P.V. Volobuev et al., *1917 god v sudbakh Rossii i mira: Fevralskaia revoliutsiia,* 155; Oloviannikov, 'Provintsiia 1917 g. Narodnaia vlast v Kurskoi gubernii,' in ibid., 367– 71.

13 Verstiuk, ed., *Ukraiinska tsentralna rada,* I: 40, 85.

14 Specifically, O. Lototsky, M. Slavynsky, and P. Stebnytsky. Strilets, *Ukrainska ... partiia,* 85–6.

15 Hrushevsky, 'Spomyny,' *Kyiv* 8 (1989) 131; 'Shcho Vono,' 47. Written 19 June.

16 Hrushevsky, 'Spomyny,' *Kyiv* 10 (1989) 152.

17 Khrystiuk, *Zamitky,* I: 136; II: 116.

18 Hryhoriiv, *Spohady,* 113–23, 206.

19 Verstiuk et al., *Ukrainskyi natsionalno-vyzvolnyi rukh,* 455; see also 365–7, 396–401, 491–5, 526–7, 605–6.

20 Surovtsova, *Spohady,* 65.

21 Goldelman, *Lysty zhydivskoho sotsial-demokrata,* 20. Goldelman, a Zionist who worked in the zemstvo before the war and was a minister in the Directory, made these remarks in March 1919.

22 [Anon.] 'Na Ukraine,' *Izvestiia* (24 Dec. 1917/6 Jan. 1918). He earlier disparages the newly educated as 'bourgeois' whose greatest ambition was to adopt the manners and ways of tsarist officialdom – cf. Chapter 1.

23 Lebedeva, 'Stvorennia uriadu,' 124–5.

24 Khrystiuk, II: 186; Manilov, *1917 god*, 128. Skoropadsky, *Spohady*, 95–6. Disbanded by the Hetman, the commissars later supported the Directory. See also Khrystiuk, *Zamitky*, II: 185; Myronenko, *Svitoch*, 195–8, 229.

25 Hrushevksky, 'Spomyny,' *Kyiv*10 (1989) 132–3. Khrystiuk, I: 77, identifies himself, Hrushevsky, and Vynnychenko as the initiators of the idea to create a Secretariat as a territorial administrative organ, and the SFs and SDs as opponents. He claims that had he, as co-author, included the word 'administration' in the 'Declaration,' the Rada would have split.

26 Verstiuk, ed., *Ukraiinska tsentralna rada,* I: 105, 120, 158.

27 Hrushevsky, 'Spomyny,' *Kyiv* 10 (1989): 137–8; Doroshenko, *Istoriia,* I: 127, 140.

28 Verstiuk et al., *Ukrainskyi natsionalnyi rukh,* 163–4.

29 Verstiuk, ed., *Ukrainska tsentralna rada,* I: 181. Petrograd's initial statement of recognition contained no. references to specific ministries or functions

30 Verstiuk et al., *Ukrainskyi natsionalnyi rukh,* 787–9. *Iuzhnaia kopeika,* 13 Oct. 1917.

31 TsDAVO, f. 1327 op. 1 sprava 42 no. 51.

32 Sidak, ed., *Vyzvolni zmahannia,* 64–6, 100.

33 *Selianska dumka,* 9 Dec. 1917.

34 The Ukrainian National Council in Petrograd suggested provincial-level candidates to the Provisional Government. At the local level local councils dismissed commissars they disliked. Verstiuk et al., *Ukrainskyi natsionalnyi rukh,* 266.

35 Myronenko, *Svitoch,* 59. Hrushevsky , 'Spomyny,' *Kyiv* 11 (1989): 150. Khrystiuk makes no reference to such intitiatives, see I: 96; 114; II: 13, 16, 121. Doroshenko, *Istoriia,* I: 140, claims no such initiatives were ever taken.

36 Verstiuk, ed., *Ukrainska tsentralna rada,* I: 343.

37 *Nova Rada,* 26 Nov. 1917. Kobets, *Zapysky,* 396.

38 Verstiuk, ed., *Ukrainska tsentralna rada,* I: 332, 342. Khrystiuk, I: 114–15; II: 15–16. Petrograd controlled communications, transportation and supply issues but retained the right in emergencies to issue orders to the land, education, and finance offices formally allotted to Kyiv. Startsev, *Russkoe,* 162–3 lists Freemasons in the central government.

39 Promised 21 September, the funds were sent into account no. 430926 in Kyiv, as confirmed by the Rada's commissioner in Petrograd. TsDAVO, f. 2241 op. 1 sprava 4, nos. 34–9, 93, 96, 100–2.

40 Any generalizations should also consider what bureaucrats did in provinces formally excluded from the Rada's jurisdiction, but whose populations and institutions declared that they recognized Kyiv as their political capital. These included 28 volosts in Bakhmut povit and the Huliai-Pole

soviet (in Katerynoslav province), the Kherson povit peasant soviet, and the Kharkiv provincial soviet and its provincial council. *Nova rada*, 12 Oct. 1917; *Narodnoe delo*, 1 Sept. 1917; *Russkaia zhyzn*, 13 Sept. 1917; *Narodna volia*, 24 Sept. 1917.

41 *ARR*, XII: 84

42 TsDAHO, f. 5 op. 1 sprava 21 nos. 32–3.

43 TsDAVO, f. 3778 op. 1 sprava 1 no. 63; f. 1327 op. 1 sprava 30.

44 Dates posted and received are on letters sent to the Rada in: TsDAVDO f. 1113 op. 1; f. 69 op. 1; f. 1216 op. 1 sprava 15. DAKO, f. R2796 op. 2 sprava 3, 4.

45 DAKO, f. 2796 op. 1 sprava 37 nos. 17–18.

46 Skoropadsky, *Spohady*, 202. They later surrendered these assets to the Hetman.

47 Cited in *Izvestiia*, 1 (13) Dec. 1917; cooperation also noted by a later eyewitness analysis: *Izvestiia*, 24 Dec. 1917 (6 Jan. 1918). Verstiuk, ed., I: 477. The League (*Iugo vostochnyi soiuz kazachikh voisk)* was formally subject to the Don Civic Council (*Donskoi grazhdanskyi soviet*) that claimed the mantle of the Provisional Government.

48 DAKO, f. R2976 op. 1 sprava 23. Radomysl had a union of government and non-government administrators.

49 DAKO, f. R2976 op. 1 sprava 24 no. 4.

50 *Izvestiia Nizhinskogo obshchestvennogo komiteta*, 23 July 1917.

51 Sidorov, ed., *Ekonomicheskoi polozhenie Rossii nakanune velikoi oktiabrskoi sotsialisticheskoi revoliutsii*, II: 361; Verstiuk et al., *Ukrainskyi natsionalnyi rukh*, 859; Myronenko, *Svitoch*, 207–8, 213, 216, 218.

52 Anfimov, 'Tsarska okhranka,' 209. *ARR*, XVIII: 10, 18–21.

53 *Tribuna gosudarstvennykh sluzashchikh*, no. 2, 1917. Antoshkin, *Professionalnoe*, 141–2, notes that pre-1917 officials in Ukraine were less militant than their Russian counterparts. It is unclear what he means in light of their organizational activism in 1917 and that Miretsky published his *Sputnik chinovnika* in Kyiv.

54 *Tribuna*, no. 1 (1917).

55 *Tribuna*, no. 4 (1917); *Iuzhnaia kopeika*, 1 March 1917. The article notes that Bolkhovsky povit had only one administrator.

56 TsDAHO, f. 5 op. 1 sprava 21 no. 19 v. *Nova Rada*, 23 July (5 Aug.) 1917. 449 respondents were pleased that the tsar had abdicated and 512 were happy that tsarist power had been destroyed; 704 supported the Provisional Government.

57 TsDAVO, f. 2199 op. 6 sprava 44 nos. 108–11.

58 TsDAVO, f. 3266 op. 1 sprava 3 nos. 3, 8, 10, 13–14; op. 2 sprava 2.

59 TsDAHO, f. 5 op. 1 sprava 21 nos. 59–60.

60 *Nova Rada,* 23 Aug. (5 Sept.), 26 May (8 June), 1917
61 *Zemske dilo,* 1 (14) and 7 (20) Nov. 1917; TsDAVO, f. 3164 op. 1 sprava 20 no. 87.
62 TsDAVO, f. 1092 op. 1 sprava 3; f. 1276 op. 1 sprava 140. DAKO, f. R2796 op. 2 sprava 5 nos. 1, 2, 18. These eleven constituted half of twenty-one officials given awards that May.
63 TsDAVO, f. 1327 op. 1 sprava 5 no. 17; f. 2199 op. 4 sprava 5 nos. 1–3.
64 DASBU, f. FP74554 vols. 7, 13; vol. 14 no. 100.
65 *Trudovaia Volyn,* 28 March (10April) 1918. An unknown number of Roman Catholic Poles worked as administrators, Verstiuk, ed., *Ukrainska tsentralna rada,* II: 235, 285. Appointments are listed in *Derzhavnyi vistnyk,* passim, April–May 1918. TsDAVO, f. 1115 op. 1 sprava 74 nos. 85–93, 104; f. 165 op. 1 sprava 53 nos. 14–53.
66 DAKO, f. R2797 sprava 133 no. 20. Having failed to pay the necessary fee, Lytvyn had to apply again. His second letter, sent when the Rada was in power, arrived when the Hetmanate was in power (sprava 70 no. 36).
67 TsDAVO, f. 1115 op. 1 sprava 42 no. 5; sprava 15 nos. 34, 38, 69. Of fifty-six applicants, seven mentioned hardship and six stated that they wanted to 'help Ukraine.'
68 *Borotba,* 6 (19) March; 18 March (3April), 1918. Myronenko, *Svitoch,* 188–98, 268, 274. Myronenko, *Svitoch,* 55, identifies sixteen permanent secretaries. *Vistnyk Rady Narodnykh Ministriv Ukrainskoi Respubliky,* 13 Jan. 1918.
69 *Derzhavnyi vistnyk,* passim, 1917; *Vistnyk rady narodnykh ministriv Ukrainskoi Respubliky,* passim, April 1918. While men candidates only had to pass a test for a government job, women candidates had to have at least secondary education.
70 Guthier, 'Ukrainian Cities,' 160. DIA, f. 721 op. 3 sprava 33.
71 TsDAVO, f 2198 op. 2 sprava 37 no. 42.
72 TsDAVO, f. 3305 op. 2 sprava 22.
73 DAKO, f. R2796 op. 1 sprava 52 nos. 23, 51–3, 62; f. R2797 op. 1 sprava 133 no. 30. Kucherenko also claimed that the city's Employment Office, where he worked, was controlled by the local Jews.
74 TsDAVO, f. 628 op. 1 sprava 29 no. 10; also Kamianets district, sprava 28.
75 Vytanovych, *Istoriia Ukrainskoho kooperatyvnoho rukhu,* 127, 193, 220, 235, 598; Dillon, 'The Rural Cooperative Movement,' Chapter 9.
76 See below Chapter 7
77 *Prilutskaia dumka,* 25 Aug. 1917; *Vilne slovo,* 21 and 28 June, 9 and 30 Aug., 4 Oct. 1917; *Vilna Ukraina,* 22 June 1917; *Hromadianyn,* 4 July 1917.
78 Mustafin, 'Samostoiatelnaia Ukraina. Pravlenie rady,' in Tiutiukin et al., *1917 god v sudbakh Rossii i mira: Oktiabrskaia revoliutsiia,* 193.

79 TsDAHO, f. 5 op. 1 sprava 21 nos. 32–3, 77–8.
80 *Narodnia volia*, 27 Dec. 1917 (14 Jan. 1918).
81 The first reference I found to this organization was in *Nova rada* and *Borotba* (24 Feb./9 March 1918). There is also reference there to a 'Tymchasovyi tsentralnyi komitet spivrobitnykiv uriadovykh ministerstva.' P. Stebnytsky, M. Korchynsky, and H. Holoskevych were possibly the people behind this initiative.
82 Vynnychenko, *Vidrodzhennia*, II: 113, 117, 307.
83 Chykalenko, *Uryvok*, 12. Mykola Mikhnovsky shared this opinion. Hryhoriiv, *Spohady*, 116–19. Only lesser know activists advocated immediate independence.
84 Hrushevsky, 'Spomyny,' *Kyiv* 11 (1989): 131–2.
85 *Holos naroda*, 13 (23) Sept. 1917. The Provisional Government declared an eight-hour work-day that October.
86 *Derzhavnyi vistnyk*, 24 April 1918. Because peasant-elected volost councils, by contrast, reduced wages on the grounds that office-work was not 'real work,' experienced officials were loath to work for them. Lozovy, *Ahrarna revoliutsiia*, 227–30.
87 Verstiuk, ed., *Ukrainska tsentralna rada*, I: 52. Whether or not either side knew that Petrograd did not require civilian officials to swear loyalty is unknown.
88 Verstiuk, ed., *Ukrainska tsentralna rada*, I: 318. *Nova Rada*, 3 (16) June; 18 (21) July; 4 (17) Oct., 1917.
89 Mashkin, 'Dvi ideii...,' 232–9. Kyiv province zemstvo officials recognized the Rada on 8 Nov. Three days later those of the Kharkiv Food Supply Committee did likewise. *Kievska zemska gazeta*, 5 Dec. 1917; *Nova Hromada*, 9/22 Dec. 1917.
90 Cf. Illustrations (Figure 2). Also, TsNB (starodruky) KL *689, 690. Kyivskaia mysl*, 1 (14) and 15 (28) Dec. 1917.
91 *Poltavskyi den*, 16 June, 7 and 20 July, 1917.
92 TsDAVO, f. 2199 op. 5 sprava 113 nos. 1–5.
93 Hrushevsky, *Na porozi*, 43.
94 Livytska, *Na hrani dvokh epokh*, 267–68. Chebotariv, commander of the Rada's forces in Kharkiv, was in Poltava in December 1917. He claimed Governor Livytsky did nothing but drink in the company of his officials – which at least may have left all under his authority favourably disposed towards the Rada. Sidak, ed., *Vyzvolni zmahannia*, 82.
95 TsDAHO, f 5 op. 1 sprava 21 nos. 76–7.
96 Verstiuk, ed., *Ukrainskyi natsionalny rukh*, 456.
97 How local institutions functioned is unstudied. Recent studies suggest that breakdown may not have been as widespread as thought: Hospodarenko, 'Zemske samovriaduvannia v novobuzkii volosti khersonskoho povitu

(1917–1919 rr.),' 56–60. The records of the Agrarian Section of the Food Supply Ministry on the south-western front, and those of the Kremenets povit Land Committee indicate that both institutions functioned through 1917 and into 1918. TsDAVO, f. 2145 op. 1 sprava 11; f. 2028 op. 1. Historians have quantified incidents of land seizures during the Rada's rule. They have yet to quantify then compare those figures with the number of land cases submitted to and acted upon by local land committees.

98 Tronko, ed., *Kyivshchyna*, 9. A request for troops to deal with Bolsheviks.

99 *ARR*, VI: 196. He does not mention that the Rada fired all lawyers who did not know Ukrainian. Skoropadsky, *Spohady*, 256.

100 *Narodnia volia*, 28 Nov. (15 Dec.) 1917. This paper was supported by the Ukrainian SRs and had a press run of 200,000.

101 *Chernigovskii krai*, 22 Nov. 1917. Krainsky does not mention this in his diary.

102 *Iuzhnaia kopeika*, 16 Dec. 1917; *Kievskaia mysl*, 1 and 14 Dec. 1917; *Slavianoserbsky khliborob*, 2 (19) Nov. 1917; *Nova Hromada*, 13 (26) Dec. 1917; *Narodna volia*, 8 (21) Nov. 1917.

103 *Narodnia volia*, 24 Oct (11 Nov.) 1917; *Nova Hromada*, 30 Dec. (12 Jan.) 1918.

104 TsDAHO, f. 5 op. 1 sprava 21 nos. 38, 44, 60. TsDAVO, f. 2199 op. 6 sprava 15 no. 1.

105 *Nova hromada*, 31 Dec. 1917 (13 Jan. 1918).

106 *Nova rada*, 24 Jan. (6 Feb.), 4 (17) Feb., 1918.

107 *Nova rada*, 24 Feb. (11 March) 1918.

108 *Nova rada*, 24 Jan. 1917; *Poslednie novosti*, 22 and 31 Jan. 1918.

109 P. Bachynsky, ed., *Dokumenty trahichnoi istorii Ukrainy*, 51.

110 Verstiuk, ed., *Ukrainska tsentralna rada*, I: 521.

111 Chykalenko, *Uryvok*, 33, mentions the town council, the courts, and the entire Russian 'intelligentsia.' Tynchenko, *Persha Ukrainsko-bilshovytska viina*, 255.

112 Reprinted in *Poslednie novosti*, 4 (17) Jan. 1918.

113 Hrynevych et al., *Istoriia*, 31n. *Narodnia volia*, 16 Feb. (3 March), 20 Feb. (5 March), 1918; *Nova rada*, 28 Jan. (5 Feb.); 23 Feb. (8March). *Kievskaia mysl*, 24 Feb. (9 March) 1918.

114 *Poslednie novosti*, 19 Feb. (4 March), 27 Feb. (7 March), 1918. An apologist admitted that the duma had ignored the Rada's prohibition of talks with the invading Bolsheviks. Considering itself neutral it had sent delegations to both sides. The one to the Rada was unable to find anyone to talk with, while the one to the Bolsheviks returned with an ultimatum of surrender on the morning of 26 January – which the duma could not deliver because by then the Rada had left the city. The duma subsequently protested at being treated by the Bolsheviks as merely one of their revkom economic administrative units. S.M., 'Gorodskaia duma,' 30–5.

115 *Iuzhnaia kopeika,* 25 Oct. 1917.

116 *Iuzhnaia kopeika,* 14 and 18 Nov. 1917; *Nova hromada,* 9 (22) Dec. 1917.

117 Shtern, *V ogne,* 174–5. Former member of the State Council V.I. Hurko, who considered a movement that made heroes of a traitor (Mazepa) and 'semi-literate folk-song writer' (Shevchenko) a bad joke, nonetheless, accepted that 'malorossiia,' as he called Ukraine, should have autonomy for practical administrative reasons. *ARR,* XV: 27–8.

118 Manilov, ed., 298. A constant theme in reports to Petrograd from June until September was that the countryside had remained peaceful primarily thanks to the efforts of the Rada. Verstiuk et al., *Ukrainskyi natsionalny rukh,* 393, 632, 857; Korolivsky, ed., *Pobeda Sovetskoi vlasti,* 234.

119 Mustafin, 'Samostoiatelnaia Ukraina. Pravlenie rady,', 390–2.

120 Chykalenko, *Uryvok,* 19.

121 Zhdanova, 'Problema federativnogo ustroistva,' 19.

122 *Kievskaia mysl,* 12 (25) Dec. 1917; *Iuzhnaia gazeta,* 4 Jan. 1918*; Iuznaia kopeika,* 16 Jan. 1918. The Kaluga Union was apparently part of the broader initiative organized by Moscow Kadets and right-wing Mensheviks, and what links they had to the Russian Radical Party is unknown. One activist supporting this initiative, which was linked to attempts to create an alternative opposition movement to the Bolsheviks, was the Russian co-op leader E. Kuskova. *Utro Rossii,* 28 Dec. 1917; *Russkie vedomostie,* 19 Feb. 1918. The Ukrainian-language *Nova Hromada,* 12 (25) Dec. 1917, added that *Soiuz* delegates protested at the recent return to Ukraine of historical artefacts from Petrograd museums.

123 *Kievlianin,* 23 Jan. (25 Feb.) 1918.

124 *Kievlianin,* 22 Aug. 1919.

125 Bilokin, 'Masony,' 193.

126 *Nova rada,* 24 Jan. and 20 Feb. 1918; *Narodnia volia,* 22 Jan. 1918. *Kyivskaia mysl,* 26 Nov. 1917. *Kyivskaia mysl,* 26 Nov. (9 Dec.) 1917 refers to an unnamed Moscow Black Hundred organization recognizing the Bolsheviks and supplying them with strike-breaking clerks for their offices.

127 Verstiuk, ed., *Ukrainska tsentralna rada,* I : 381, 391.

128 Manilov et al., *1917 god,* 351.

129 Verstiuk, ed., I: 404, 474, 489.

130 Manilov, 378.

131 Full text in *Kievskaia mysl,* 24 Nov. 1917. Reported in *Iuzhnaia kopeika,* 24 Nov. 1917. Verstiuk, ed., I: 476.

132 *Kievskaia mysl,* 1 Dec. 1917; *Chernigovskii krai,* 14 Dec. 1917.

133 *Kievskiia gorodskiia izvestiia,* no. 12 (1917) 46.

134 *Volynske zhyttia*, 22 Jan. 1918. TsDAVO, f. 2199 op. 6 sprava 44. This folder contains some of the Commission's records.

135 TsDAHO, f. 5 op. 1 sprava 21 nos. 33–4.

136 *Borotba*, 16 Feb. (1March) 1918.

137 Verstiuk, ed., *Ukrainska tsentralna rada*, II: 181; Myronenko, *Svitoch*, 118.

138 *Trudovaia Volyn*, 7 (20) March 1918. *Narodnia volia*, 25 March (5 April) 1918.

139 DAKO, f. R 2797 op. 1 sprava 127 no. 1. Of the eighteen who had served, three had returned and two had requested release.

140 *Vistnyk rady narodnykh ministriv Ukrainskoi narodnoi respubliky* (9 April 1918). DAKO, f. R2796 op. 2 sprava 3 no. 49. Samples of application letters from January through April 1918: DAKO, f. R2797 op. 1 sprava 133 nos. 1–69. TsDAHO, f. 5 op. 1 sprava 21 nos. 79–80.

141 Kossak, *The Blaze*, 163, 167, 180; Olesiuk, 'Kamianets – zolotyi vinets: Spomyny z 1918-1919 rr.,' 97; Tyrras, ed., *Letters*, 360.

142 Stavrovskii, 'Chernye gody, ili "Bestia Triumphalis" (1917–1922),' *Minuvshee Istoricheskii almanakh*, 14 (1993) 46. TsDAVO, f. 433 op. 1 sprava 1 nos. 27–42, 87.

143 *Rada*, 13 (26) March 1918; *Narodnia volia*, 9 (27) April; 13 (31) March, 1918.

144 Cited in Medrzecki, *Niemiecka interwencja militarna*, 134.

145 Tymoshchuk, *Okhronnyi apparat ukrainskoi derzhavy*, 66–9.

146 *Kyivskaia mysl*, 3 (16) April 1918.

147 *Narodnia volia*, 3 (16), 4 (17), 5 (18), and 7 (20) April, 1918. A captain in a Ukrainian regiment was so disgusted by illegal requisitioning that he sent a telegram about what he witnessed to the Rada. His superiors intercepted it and arrested him, charged him with drunkenness, beating subordinates, and attempting to murder his superior officer. Ibid., 1 (14) April.

148 DAKO, f. R2796 op. 1 sprava 52 nos. 69–70.

149 Doroshenko, *Istoriia*, I: 127, 140 198; II: 9–11. Doroshenko, *Moi spomyne*, 180. *ARR*, XII: 84.

150 *ARR*, I: 288.

151 Verstiuk, ed., *Ukrainska tsentralna Rada*, I: 247.

152 Kharchenko, Stannovlennia mistsevykh orhaniv, 45–6; *Kievskaia mysl*, 9 (22) March 1918.

153 Kharchenko, 'Stanovlenniia,' 108–23. *Kievskaia mysl*, 12 (25) Dec. 1917 contains a summary of a speech to the newly formed Ukrainian Union of Towns describing the desired relations.

154 Sorokina et al., *V.I. Vernadskii*, 72–5, 82.

4 The Ukrainian State, April to December 1918

1 Tymoshchuk, *Okhronnyi apparat,*76; Kharchenko, *Stanovlennia,* 78–84. All Ukrainian parties except the left SRs (*Borotbists*) allowed their members to participate in elected bodies and to hold lower-level government positions.

2 Skoropadsky, *Spohady,* 125. The earlier version is reprinted in *Hetman Pavlo Skoropadsky: Spomyny,* 76.

3 Cited in Medrzecki, *Niemiecka,* 207–8.

4 *Trybuna,* 19 Jan. 1919.

5 Mazepa, *Ukraina,* I: 53. Later in emigration, Vynnychenko accused the Hetman of totally restoring all pre-revolutionary personnel to office and thereby destroying Ukrainian independence. He claimed local officials consciously discredited independence because they went out of their way to ensure that the people identified the Ukrainian state with the hated requisitioning policies. Vynnychenko, *Vidrodzhennia,* III: 78–9, 100. This was not his opinion at the time.

6 Dragan, ed., *Luka Myshuha: Zbirnyk,* 55. High transit fees on commercial goods were the town's only source of income.

7 *Trybuna,* 29 Jan. 1919.

8 TsDAVO, f. 1216 op. 1 sprava 73 nos. 10–14, 40, 51,169. Three months after the original complaint had been received in Kyiv, an investigation reported the one of Jews in question was exiled and that the rest had either disappeared or were innocent. It contained no mention of either the governor or the police chief.

9 Kryshyna, 'Diialnist Nimetskoi viiskovoi administratsii,' 125–40.

10 Ibid., 249. Each povit that August was supposed to include 525 officials. *Derzhavny visnyk,* 2 and 17 Aug. 1918. If to these we add zemstvo and locally based central officials, the total would be approximately the same as in 1914, i.e., 1,000. TsDAVO, f. 543 op. 1 sprava 8 nos. 1-8. DAKO, f. R2794 op. 1 sprava 45 nos. 4–6. Zhvanko, 'Vnutrishnia polityka.' Surviving volost records reveal administrators able to compile lists of local prisoners of war that included their mailing addresses. TsDAVO, f. 1425 op. 1.

11 Verstiuk, ed., *Evhen Chykalenko,* 236; Skoropadsky, *Spohady,* 202, 224. The Bolsheviks in June 1919 ordered all instruments to be registered and requisitioned on pain of imprisonment. TsDAVO, f. 1738 op. 1 sprava 14 no. 112.

12 TsDAVO, f. 433 op. 1 sprava 52 no. 85; f. 1532 op. 3 sprava 9 nos. 55, 109.

13 DAKO, f. R2794 op. 1 sprava 4 no. 40.

14 Some had worked for the Rada and five were Ukrainian-born Germans. Doroshenko, *Istoriia,* II: 66–9, 86, 89–93, 98–102, 107, 260, 264–5; Doroshenko, *Spomyny,* 256–7; V. Levytsky, *Ukrainska derzhavna put,* 59–60, 70–81.

15 Skoropadsky, *Spohady*, 233. Ukrainian socialists, who were willing to cooperate, ultimately refused because the German commander, Gen. Groener, did not allow Skoropadsky to accept their conditions. Zaitsev, 'Zhmut spohadiv.'
16 Tatishchev, *Zemli i liudi*, 301.
17 Trubetskoi, 82, 98, 110. '*Vino vlasti udarila emu v golovu, i on stal podderzhivat samostiinost.*'
18 *Kievlianin*, 6 Sept. 1918; Anderson, ed., *Dnevnik P.N. Miliukova*, 72.
19 Andrusyshyn, *U poshukakh*, 65.
20 *Russkii golos*, 8 Nov. 1918. TsDAVO, f. 2199 op. 1 sprava 6 nos. 3–6.
21 TsDAVO, f. 2198 op. 2 sprava 74, 76, 82, 87.
22 *Golos Kieva*, 13 June 1918; DAKO, f. 1239 op. 196 sprava 21 nos. 12–185. Knowledge of Ukrainian, they also feared, might put some at a disadvantage in terms of promotion and thus create a bad office atmosphere.
23 Volkov, ed., *1918 god*, 287.
24 DAKO, f. R2797 op. 1 sprava 6 no. 21.
25 DAKO, f. R2797 op. 1 sprava 70 nos. 41, 74, 102, 163.
26 Zaitsev, 'Zhmut spohadiv pro V. Vynnychenka.' TsDAVO, f. 2199 op. 1 sprava 214 nos. 54–77; sprava 213 nos. 47–66; sprava 217 nos. 71–87. Of the twenty-three who left the Katernyslav offices in 1918, fourteen did so 'by own request.' The remainder were transferred. Ibid., nos. 59–61. These twenty-three are all included in the December 1918 list of employees.
27 Mikhailov, 'Getman i getmanshchina,' 69; Skoropadsky, *Spohady*, 201–2. Sidak, *Natsionalni spetzsluzhby*, 115.
28 Strilets, *Ukrainska . . . partiia*, 155.
29 TsDAVO, f. 433 op. 1 sprava 52 no. 55. Three of the four Podillia clerks had been working as clerks since 1906. DASBU, f. 73878 vol. 2.
30 TsDAVO, f. 1092c op. 2 sprava 312 nos. 19, 69, 112, 189.
31 TsDAVO, f. 2199 op. 6 sprava 11, nos. 6, 18, 57; op. 5 sprava 69. DAKO, f. R1239 op. 126 sprava 11 no. 35.
32 DAKO, f. R2797 op. 1 sprava 109 nos. 20, 94–6, 105; sprava 127 nos. 1–23, 30; sprava 46 nos. 39–45. Sixteen of those on the June 1918 list were on a Rada list compiled that March. TsDAVO, f. 538 op. 1 sprava 4 no. 116.
33 DAKO, f. R2794 op. 1 sprava 45 nos. 4–6; f. R2797 op. 1 sprava 27 nos. 14–17. Only three men were new. Of the original staff, two had died, one had retired, and one had disappeared. The Kyivan provincial governor appears to have begun dismissing village secretaries en masse in November. Ibid., sprava 7 nos. 17–34, 58–72. It is unknown if this was also done in other provinces.
34 DAKO, f. R2797 op. 1 sprava 26 nos. 6–10; sprava 23 nos. 13–16; op. 2 sprava 28 no. 46. These particular statistics list only those eligible for supplementary pay.

35 TsDAVO, f. 1425 op. 1 sprava 5 nos. 58–9, 60, 74. DAKO, f. R2797 op. 1 sprava 109 nos. 94–96.

36 Skoropadsky, *Spohady*, 158, 175, 241, 256–7, 292 . TsDAVO, f. 1092c op. 2 sprava 169 nos. 2, 75. The representative from the Directory's Political Department was suspicious claiming that although pay was the same everywhere, no other police chiefs hired Jews.

37 Trubetskoi, *Gody*, 91. DAKO, f. R2794 op. 1 sprava 4 no 10. That May he had a job in the Interior Ministry.

38 *Kievskaia zhyzn*, 22 Oct. (4 Nov.) 1918. DAKO, f. R2794 op. 1 passim; f. R2797 op. 1 sprava 70 no. 5.

39 Popov, ed., *Revoliutsiia na Ukraine po memuaram belykh*, 261; Gusev-Orenburgskii, ed., *Kniga o evreiskikh pogromakh*, 40. Postings listed in *Derzhavnyi vistnyk* include almost no Jewish names. TsDAVO, f. 1216 op. 1 sprava 70 nos. 161, 292.

40 DAKO, f. R2797 op. 1 sprava 6 no. 74. *Podolsky krai*, 22 Dec. 1918 (4 Jan. 1919).

41 Kharchenko, *Stanovlennia*, 90–192. TsDAVO, f. 73c op. 1 sprava 123 no. 101, is a letter from a Zvenyhorod duma member complaining about Isak Shlemov Konstantinovskii, who, although known by all concerned to be a crook with tens of thousands of unaccounted roubles in his account, nevertheless, always managed to have a position in the duma.

42 DAKO, f. R2797 op. 2 sprava 40 nos. 18, 35–6; sprava 40 nos. 63–8.

43 TsDAVO, f. 1530 op. 1 sprava 1 nos. 25, 49–59, 76.

44 Sidak, *Natsionalni spetssluzhby*, 94–5, 100; Tymoshchuk, 105, 333–5. DAKO, f. R2797 op. 1 sprava 8 no. 105, 129.

45 DAKO, f. R2794 op. 1 sprava 5 nos. 99–101. The Kyiv provincial governor explicitly instructed police and gendarme detachments not to use force. Troops were hired by private agents as punitive detachments against peasants but this was illegal. Kharchenko and Tymoshchuk both note that arbitrary violence against Ukrainian peasants was more often committed by local Austrian or German military units and returned landowners on their own initiative, than by the Hetman's government. Nonetheless, thousands of arrests, in Chernihiv province, presumably repeated elsewhere, also undoubtedly did their part to quell the rural violence. TsDAVO, f. 1216 op. 1 sprava 89 contains prisoners' files.

46 TsDAVO, f. 1216 op. 1 sprava 89 no. 189.

47 Skoropadsky, *Spohady*, 292. Antonov-Ovsienko, *Zapiski*, III: 12.

48 Kryzhanovska, *Taemni*, 101; Hass, *Loza i Polityka*, 286.

49 Anderson, ed., *Dnevnik*, 33, 102; Trubetskoi, *Gody*, 80, 116, 128; Doroshenko, *Istoriia*, II: 44–5. The German General Staff entertained discussions with

Miliukov because, unlike the Foreign Office which supported Ukrainian independence, they preferred a restored Russian Empire on Germany's eastern border.

50 Kryshyna, 'Diialnist,' 82, 88.

51 *Kievskaia mysl,* 25 Feb., 19 March, 8 (21) Sept. 1918. Ukrainian supporters saw no realistic alternative to the Hetman and thought that a state federated with Russia, but backed by the Entente thanks to its repayment of tsarist debts, was better than no state at all. Verstiuk, ed., *Evhen Chykalenko,* 103, 156.

52 Others saw a renewed Treaty of 1654 as the basis of a Ukrainian-Russian link. Khrytsiuk, *Ukrainska revolutsiia,* II: 107. Golitsyn thought Denikin should have accepted the reality of Ukraine and attacked Moscow not Kyiv in 1919. Golitsyn's memoirs were published when this book was in print. I am grateful to Ernest Gyidel for showing me his references from the Bekhmetev Archive (Columbia University) ms: 136, 167, 169, 204.

53 Sorokina, *Vernadskii,* 45, 72, 98. In 1931 the Hetman's minister of Church affairs wrote that Ukraine should be strong enough not to have to fear Russia, and Russia magnanimous enough (*velikodushiia*) not to try and destroy it. Zenkovskii, *Piat mesiatsev,* 155–8.

54 Shtern, *V ogne grazhdanskoi voiny,* 179–81, 184. Writing six months after falling from power, Skoropadsky claimed that this territorial loyalty reflected a wish for a decentralized Russia rather than the Ukrainian-Russian federation he envisaged. In any case, he thought such people were a minority among the Russians. *Spohady,* 15.

55 Tatishchev, *Zemli i liudi,* 304.

56 Mikhailov, 'Getman i getmanshchina,' 67–8; *ARR,* XV: 29, 32.

57 *ARR,* VIII: 167.

58 *Pridnepdrovskii krai,* 2 (15) Sept. 1918

59 *Utro,* 4 (17) Oct. 1918.

60 *Zhyttia Podillia,* 15 Dec. 1918; *Vozrozhdenie,* 25 Aug. (2 Sept.) 1918.

61 *Vilnyi holos,* 1 (14) June 1918.

62 *ARR,* XVIII: 145–6.

5 The Directory, December 1918 to November 1919

1 DASBU, f. 69270 vol. 31, pp. 2–5.

2 Serhiienko, ed., *Symon Petliura,* IV: 210.

3 TsDAVO, f. 1092 op. 2 sprava 74 no. 196; sprava 63 no. 6. Sidak, ed., *Vyzvolni zmahannia,* 27–33.

4 Stavrovskii, 'Chernye gody, ili "Bestia Triumphalis,"' 53.

5 TsDAVO, f. 4591 op. 1 sprava 6 no. 168.

6 Kulchytsky, *Shabli z pluhiv,* 188–9. Of these, twenty-seven commanded a total of almost 50,000 men and they tied down one million Bolshevik troops. The otamans have only begun to be studied. The only otaman known to have written memoirs, Liuty-Liutenko, does not mention civilian administration. Liuty-Liutenko, *Vohon z kholodnoho iaru,* 53.
7 Khrystiuk, *Zamitky,* III: 68, 81–3 104.
8 *Trybuna,* 26 Dec. 1918.
9 TsDAVO, f. 1509 op. 5 sprava 42. On 29 January in face of the Bolshevik advance all ministries were ordered to dismiss two-thirds of their personnel within seven days (f. 1092c op. 2 sprava 283 no. 46). That February another decree summarily dismissed all those who had remained in Bolshevik territory after the Directory fled Kyiv, but with three months pay (no. 47).
10 *Trybuna,* 21 and 26 Dec. 1918; *Ukraina,* 4 (17) Jan., 20 Jan. (2 Feb.) 1919; *Zhyttia Podillia,* 14 Jan. 1919. In a secret telegram of 19 January Vynnychenko ordered all ministers and department heads to inform him immediately of what they had done to carry out the earlier dismissal orders. TsDAVO, f. 3305 op. 1 sprava 2 nos. 3–4.
11 DASBU, f. 73878 vol. 15; *Slovo,* 12 Oct. 1920.
12 Doroshenko, *Spomyny,* 399; Lytvyn et al., *Uriady Ukrainy u XX st.,* 141, 194. Andrusyshyn, *Tserkva v Ukrainskyi Derzhavi,* 29, 38. Orders were repeatedly issued to compile lists of pro-Bolshevik officials, but I did not find such lists in the archives. TsDAVO, f. 1092 op. 1 sprava 10; op. 2 sprava 63 no. 41.
13 Vynnychenko, *Vidrodzhennia,* III: 265. He is supported by Chebotariv who noted White Russians in top positions in the Directory's Food Supply Ministry. Sidak, ed., *Vyzvolni zmahannia,* 47.
14 *ARR,* III: 236.
15 Andrievsky, *Z mynuloho,* II pt. 2, 7.
16 *Robitnycha hazeta,* 12 Sept. 1919. A decree by Petliura in October 1919 specified only dismissal for sedition. TsDAVO, f. 538 op. 1 sprava 64 no. 333.
17 Doroshenko, *Istoriia,* II: 67–8.
18 Hass, *Ambicje rachuby rzeczywistosc: Wolnomulartwo,* 176–7. Other Masons were inactive or had left the country. Hass, 289–90; Kryzhanovska, 102–4. The influence of a supposedly 8,000-strong organization of pro-independence Masons led by Petliura's Secretary, Mykola Myronovych, is disputed.
19 TsDAVO, f. 1092 op. 2 sprava 13 no. 44.
20 TsDAVO, f. 1092c op. 2 sprava 312 no. 203; op. 4 sprava 57 nos. 20–1. f. 543 op. 1 sprava 8 nos. 1–8.
21 TsDAVO, f. 2208c op. 2 sprava 8 nos. 11–15.
22 TsDAVO, f. 1509 op. 5 sprava 62.
23 TsDAVO, f. 1062 op. 1 sprava 6 nos. 242–9. While all provinces were represented in the ministry, half of the staff came from three regions: Kyiv

province (15), Poltava province (13), and eastern Galicia (14) (f. 1062 op. 1 sprava 18 no. 19).

24 TsDAVO, f. 2537 op. 2 sprava 158 nos. 30, 42–3; f. 538 op. 1 sprava 84 no. 88; sprava 118.

25 TsDAVO, f. 1092 op. 4 sprava 38 nos. 125, 380, 439, 453; f. 1092c op. 2 sprava 460 no. 16.

26 Sidak, *Natsionani spetssluzhby,* 130–1. TsDAVO, f. 1092 op. 5 sprava 1 nos. 11–21.

27 TsDAVO, f. 2537 op. 5 sprava 21 nos. 1–4, 26–9.

28 TsDAVO, f. 1092 op. 4 sprava 42 no. 27, 54; sprava 43 no. 80. The office was abolished that July but all the workers remained on the government payroll and got rises.

29 TsDAVO, f. 538 op. 1 sprava 84 no. 207–9; sprava 92 no 7. These reports from five povits in Podillia, simply say that within 24 hours the administration was in place – which would not have been possible without old staff resuming their duties. Ibid., f. 1092 op. 2 sprava 71 no. 80.

30 TsDAVO, f. 1092c op. 2 sprava 292 no. 2. Most also seem to have held jobs under the Directory before the Bolsheviks came.

31 *ARR,* VI: 262; *Volynskaia molva,* 6 Apr. 1919; *Volynske zhyttia,* 2 (15) Feb. 1919; *Slovo,* 31 Oct. (13 Nov.) 1919. Miliakova, ed., *Kniga,* 22. I have found only one instance of Directory officials, in this case nine army-lawyers, charged with treason who faced the death penalty because they worked fot the Bolsheviks. They were found not guilty. *Ukraina* (Kamianets), 7 Sept. 1919.

32 TsDAVO, f. 538 op. 1 sprava 4 nos. 116, 317; sprava 26 nos. 19–20, 225–8. The Vinnytsia list included only those with fifteen years' service or more.

33 DAKO, f. R2796 op. 1 sprava 51 no. 63. Of twenty povit commissars in Kyiv province in April 1918, only six had been at their jobs in November 1917. Ibid., no. 46.

34 TsDAVO, f. 1216 op. 1 sprava 129; f. 2198 op. 2 sprava 26 no. 4.

35 TsDAVO, f. 1530 op. 1 sprava 1 nos. 49–59; sprava 24 nos. 22–3, 48.

36 TsDAVO, f. 1113c op. 2 sprava 47; f. 1092c op. 2 sprava 140, 170 contain hundreds of application letters. A list of 288 central officials who staffed all levels between December 1918 and October 1919 has survived but not their personal files. TsDAVO, f. 1092 op. 1 sprava 2.

37 TsDAVO, f. 1509 op. 1 sprava 188, 189, 193, 192, 187. Ibid., sprava 191 nos. 21, 43.

38 *Ukraina,* 6 (19) Jan. 1919

39 Mazepa, *Ukraina,* II: 126, 49; *Ukraina,* 20 Jan. (2 Feb.), 28 Jan. (15 Feb.) 1919. *Hromadska dumka,* 3 June 1920.

40 Iablonovsky, *Vid vlady piatokh to dyktatury odnoho,* 61. The school was supposedly opened under the Rada in April 1918. *Slovo,* 18 Oct. 1920.

41 TsDAVO, f. 1113 op. 2, sprava 21, nos. 61, 68; sprava 22 no. 130; sprava 27 nos. 17–18; sprava 47 no. 3.
42 *Zhyttia Podillia*, 12 Feb. 1919
43 TsDAVO, f. 1276 op. 1 sprava 140; f. 1092c op. 2 sprava 35 nos. 9–10.
44 Kovalchuk, *Nevidoma viina*, 450. What lends his allegations credibility is that Makogon, in his report, begged his superiors to give him a front-line appointment. During his Cheka interrogation in 1920 the former head of the Directory's Labour Congress Secretariat, Iuryi Skuhar-Skvarsky, identified General Shaiblei in the Directory's Ministry of War as a White agent. Petliura apparently trusted him and ignored warnings about his true loyalties. DASBU, 69270 vol. 18 p. 25v.
45 TsDAVO, f. 528 op. 1 sprava 64 nos. 269, 308. The organization in question, Poali-Zion, recognized the Directory and functioned legally. The provincial governor instructed the povit commissar three weeks later, to punish those responsible. There is no record of Karbovsky being arrested or dismissed.
46 TsDAVO, f. 1092 op. 2 sprava 11 nos. 11–12; sprava 16 no. 40. *Respublykanski visti*, 23 Jan 1920; *Ukraina*, 15 (28) Jan. 1919; *Zhyttia Podillia*, 15 Feb., 4 and 7 April, 1919. *Robitnycha hazeta*, 22 Feb. 1919 published a long complaint by the Ukrainian administrators' association about former tsarist officers sabotaging the finance departments
47 Kossak, *The Blaze*, 244–5; Mikhutina, *Ukrainskii vopros*, 157.
48 Lozovyi, *Vnutrishnia ta zovnishnia polityka*, 140.
49 TsDAVO, f. 1092 op. 2 sprava 63 no. 68.
50 *Dnistrianska khvylia*, 24 Sept. 1919.
51 Gusev-Orenburgskii, *Kniga*, 131.
52 Bachynsky, ed., *Dokumenty*, 159; TsDAVO, f. 1902 op. 2 sprava 68 nos. 103–7.
53 *Zhyttia Podillia*, 21 Feb. 1919.
54 TsDAVO, f. 2198 op. 2 sprava 59.
55 TsDAVO, f. 1092c2 op. 2 sprava 56 no. 266; op. 1 sprava 4 nos. 1–7.
56 TsDAVO, f 1062 op. 1 sprava 7 nos. 11, 17, 21.
57 TsDAVO, f. 3305 op. 1 sprava 15 no. 11. There are no other documents about this case. Bezpalko termed the case 'characteristic.'
58 *Volynskaia molva*, 1 Jan. 1919.
59 *Podolskaia mysl*, 3 (16) Jan. 1919
60 *Kievskii den*, 16, 23, 26, and 29 May 1920. The 'Hromadsky komitet' was organized by Serhyi Efremov. Strilets, *Ukrainska ... partiia*, 213–14. A long article in *Slovo* (16 Oct. 1919) identifying Black Hundreds members, Bolsheviks, and criminals as threats did not mention Russians as a group. The SR/co-op newspaper *Trudova hromada* (29 June, 5 and 9 Sept., 1919) ran articles condemning 'experts' rather than 'Russians.'

61 *Slovo,* 5 Oct. 1919.

62 Miliakova, ed., *Kniga,* 175. TsDAHO, f. 1 op. 18 sprava 16 no. 50. In a letter to the Orgbureau written after his return to Moscow, Popov explained that the Bolsheviks could either destroy Ukrainian separatism by force, as they were doing, or destroy what produced it by creating a sovereign Soviet Ukrainian state which would have meant supporting the Ukrainian communists (borotbists). The opposite of what Lenin was doing (no. 59).

63 TsDAVO, f. 1092 op. 2 sprava 16 nos. 376, 380.

64 TsDAVO, f. 3305 op. 2 sprava 22, 25; sprava 6 no. 1. The Ministry of Press and Information 1919 payrolls list Jewish names, and Jews wrote application letters in Ukrainian. TsDAVO, f. 1113 op. 2 sprava 9–10. At least ten of the Ministry of Labour's 188 central staff members were Jewish (f. 1065 op. 4 sprava 3 nos. 26–42). Further research could reveal more Jewish clerks in volost and povit offices. TsDAVO, f. 1601 op. 1 sprava 7 no. 304. Personnel lists in the February and March issues of *Vistnyk* contain some Jewish names. *Vistnyk Ukrainskoi Narodnoi Respubliky,* 29 July 1919. *Vistnyk rady narodnykh ministriv Ukrainskoi respubliky,* April 1918, passim, lists considerable numbers of students released from military service.

65 Goldelman, *Lysty,* 52.

66 *ARR,* IV: 152–3, 155; VI: 262, 281. Verstiuk, ed., Evhen Chykalenko, 359–60.

67 Skoropadsky, *Spohady,* 254.

68 TsDAVO, f. 1092c2 op. 2 sprava 57 nos. 74, 191, 196; sprava 63 no. 6; f. 538 op. 1 sprava 84 no. 112. The village was the volost centre.

69 *Zhyttia Podillia,* 4 Apr. 1919.

70 TsDAVO, f. 1092c2 op. 2 sprava 57 no. 191; sprava 63 no. 6.

71 TsDAVO, f. 1113c op.1 sprava 16; op. 2 sprava 145 no. 2.

72 TsDAVO, f. 628 op. 1 sprava 29 no. 10, 31. Kovalchuk, *Nevidoma viina,* 362.

73 TsDAVO, f. 528 op1 sprava 84 no. 166.

74 TsDAVO, f. 1092 op. 2 sprava 62 nos. 56, 57, 14, 15; f. 543 op. 1 sprava 8 no. 25. In response, the local board requested the minister to reconsider his decision (no. 27).

75 TsDAVO, f. 538 sprava 89 nos. 8–9, 25–7.

76 TsDAVO, f. 538 op. 1 sprava 89 nos. 181–4, 202–4, 209–30.

77 Ibid., nos. 85–9.

78 TsDAVO, f. 1601 op. 1 sprava 7 no. 107; f. 538 op. 1 sprava 96 nos. 7–8.

79 TsDAVO, f. 1480 op.1 sprava 1 no. 294.

80 *Vistnyk Rady ministriv,* no. 5, 1919; *Ukraina,* 20 Jan. (2 Feb.) 1919. A government inspector noted that it was anyone's guess where grain requisitioned by the army, done contrary to regulations, ended up. TsDAVO, f. 1092 op. 1 sprava 7 nos. 25–32.

81 *Nash shliakh,* 22 May 1920. TsDAVO, f. 1902 op. 2 sprava 62 nos. 72, 73; f. 1075 op. 2 sprava 3 no. 82.
82 TsDAVO, f. 1062 op. 1 sprava 20, no. 3.
83 *Trudova hromada,* 7 Nov. 1919. Ushytsia povit. Implicit in this account is that locals either ignored, or did not even know martial law existed, as the author states that some officers, who in theory were supposed to be the single local authority, acted beyond their competence.
84 TsDAVO, f. 538 op. 1 sprava 116 nos. 23–4; f. 1113 op. 2 sprava 40–5.
85 TsDAVO, f. 3305 op. 1 sprava 11 nos. 9, 17, 29–30. Even as late as September 1919 Directory officials still had not legally defined rights and could be dismissed at will. An anonymous critic noted that dismissing officials in territory under enemy occupation was contrary to accepted international practice and undermined statebuilding. *Ukraina* (Kamianets), 23 Aug, 1919.
86 *Zhyttia Podillia,* 5 April 1919. Nazaruk, *Rik,* 92.
87 *Slovo,* 14 Oct. 1920.
88 *Vistnyk Ukrainskoi narodnoi respubliki,* 8 Aug. 1919.
89 *Zhyttia Podillia,* 30 March 1919.
90 *Narodnia volia,* 17 (30) Jan. 1919.
91 TsDAVO, f. 543 op. 1 sprava 64 nos. 26–8.
92 TsDAVO, f. 1092 op. 4 sprava 38 no. 514.
93 TsDAVO, f. 528 op. 1 sprava 41 nos. 125, 342. *Vistnyk Ukrainskoi narodnoi respubliky,* 10 Feb., 20 July, 21 Sept. 1919; *Ukraina,* 25 Feb. (12 March) 1919. Proposed solutions ranged from hiring only the wounded, to setting up commissions in government departments to vet the men – which implies that there were people to do it.
94 TsDAVO, f. 3305 op. 1 sprava 12 no. 12.
95 TsDAVO, f. 2299 op. 1 sprava 1 no. 19. Nazaruk, *Rik,* 88, 214, 248–9, 299, 313. Mazepa, 75n, and Dotsenko, 314, claimed that Nazaruk was biased and that he exaggerated. Chebotariv supports Nazaruk. In September the government declared that all able-bodied men in offices had to report for duty. *Robitnycha hazeta,* 30 Sept. 1920.
96 Sidak, ed., *Vyzvolni zmahannia,* 47, 95.
97 *Trudova hromada,* 31 Aug. 1919.
98 *Dnistrianska khvylia,* 8 Oct. 1919. The penalty for buying military-ware from soldiers went up from two to three weeks' imprisonment in 1915 to two to three months' in 1917. DAKO, f. R1718 op. 1 sprava 132 no.7; sprava 121 no. 261; sprava 122 nos. 56, 63, 69, 76, 78, 260.
99 Kovalchuk, *Nevidoma viina,* 478.
100 Nazaruk, *Rik,* 239, 313.
101 Ibid., 94–6.
102 Khrystiuk, *Zamitky,* IV: 14.

103 *Zhyttia Podillia,* 23 Jan. 1919. Analogous descriptions are also found in Bolshevik reports.

104 TsDAVO, f. 1092 op. 2 sprava 71 nos. 144–51.

105 Lisevych, *U vidblysku,* 49–51, 97–9. Voluntary organizations played their role, but the author does not explain why Ukrainians worked in voluntary organizations rather than in the government bureaucracy. Directory employees in Kyiv did not think they would be paid, but some were paid just before the Bolsheviks retook the city. Tronko, ed., *Kievshchina v gody grazhdanskoi voiny,* 153, 327; *ARR,* VI: 281.

106 TsDAHO, f. 1 op. 20 sprava 19 nos. 1–7. The names of those responsible are probably in the personnel lists of the Quartermaster General's Office. TsDAVO, f. 2299 op. 1 sprava 1 nos. 49–54; f. 2198 sprava 1 op. 216 nos. 118–21. The efficiency of the War Ministry is confirmed by Tatishchev who noted it contained many western Ukrainians. Tatishchev, *Zemli,* 312.

107 TsDAVO, f. 2198 op. 1 sprava 149. The pages in this folio all have three numbers and do not follow any order (sprava 216 nos. 156, 179, 212, 254).

108 TsDAVO, f. 2198 sprava 216 nos. 32, 58, 93, 165, 170, 179, 190–1, 252, 257, 291, 322. On the local level there also could be as many three different officials, plus a local army officer, responsible to different entities, alongside the Food Ministry agent, all giving different orders related to food supply. The Road Ministry, for instance, when it did not get food for its 400,000 employees west of the Dnipro, seized cargoes. TsDAVO, f. 2198 op. 1 sprava 87 nos. 36–8; sprava 150, 151, passim.

109 TsDAVO, f. 3305 op. 1 sprava 13 nos. 1–71, 78–179 (31 Jan. to 30 Nov.).

110 TsDAVO, f. 1062 op. 1 sprava 7 nos. 184, 246–9. These figures are from an inspection carried out in August and September 1919. Trains used only wood for fuel, and the main cause of mechanical failures was the acute lack of grease. Rail-movement situation reports for January 1919 suggest that functioning stock was used primarily for taking German troops home. TsDAHO, f. 57 op. 2 sprava 237 nos. 8–14.

111 TsDAVO, f. 1113 op. 1 sprava 27 nos. 9, 62.

112 Andrievsky, *Z Mynuloho,* II pt. 2: 162–74. Karpenko, ed., *Zakhidno Ukrainska Respublika,* III: 81, 89. Trade was brisk and corrupt officials could 'sell' an entire train of oil to speculators for as much as 40,000 Austrian crowns. *Trudova hromada,* 31 Aug. 1919.

113 TsDAHO, f. 43 op. 1 sprava 45 nos. 9–10. The agent also remarked that abroad the republic had its representatives in every country except Spain and Japan.

114 Miliakova, ed., *Kniga,* 31, 41, 94. Gusev-Orenburgskii, *Kniga,* 36, 41, 48. TsDAVO, f. 1092 op. 2 sprava 165 nos. 311, 312, 590. The commander initially refused a gift of 200,000 hryvnia from the Jews but then took 300,000 hryvnia as a contribution for the needs of his troops – all registered in the

official report. The officer himself gave a slightly different version of events in his unpublished memoirs. Finkelshtien, *Za dela ruk svoikh*, 108–23.

115 TsDAVO, f. 543 op. 1 sprava 28 nos. 14–18; f. 1062 op. 1 sprava 18, 22–4. His appeal was successful and the minister allotted him some funds, but the Directory would shortly collapse.

116 TsDAVO, f. 538 op. 1 sprava 64 nos. 373–4; f. 1092 op. 2 sprava 67 contains multiple copies of intradepartmental and centre-local correspondence that give an idea of things that were being done. Ibid., sprava 63 no 68; f. 119 op. 1 sprava 5 nos. 4, 40–4.

117 TsDAVO, f. 1092 op. 4 sprava 88 nos. 4, 24, 28. In 1919 Kamianets had a telegraph connection with 130 villages and towns. TsDAVO, f. 1062 op. 1 sprava 7, no. 235.

118 TsDAVO, f. 538 op. 1 sprava 26 nos. 188–254.

119 TsDAVO, f. 538, op. 1 sprava 89 no. 225. Another copy is in : f. 1092 op. 2 sprava 71 nos. 91–4. See sprava 17 for typed volost reports up to December 1918; sprava 24 contains handwritten reports from 1919.

120 TsDAVO, f. 528 op. 1 sprava 41 no. 263.

121 TsDAVO, f. 2299 op. 1 sprava 1 nos. 13, 23.

122 *Trudova Hromada*, 31 Aug. 1919. Not the least of the province's strengths was a centralized union organization approximately 6,000 strong.

123 TsDAVO, f. 1 op. 1 sprava 24, no. 4; sprava 27 nos. 9–12, 15–22.

124 TsDAVO, f. 1092 op. 2 sprava 71 nos. 144, 172, 188, 246; ibid., f. 538 op. 1 sprava 89 nos. 164–5, 202–4. *Zhyttia Podillia*, 2 Jan., 28 Feb., 3 April, 1919. Between October 1918 and August 1919 Proskuriv povit apparently paid approximately 1,500,000 karbovantsi in taxes and local officials claimed that they could have collected more had they more collectors. How much was actually paid in 1919 is not noted. TsDAVO, f. 543 op. 1 sprava 5 no. 9.

125 Andrusyshyn, 'Problemy okhorony pratsi,' 10–11, 14. TsDAVO, f. 1530 op. 1 sprava 1 no. 75; f. 1092 op. 6 sprava 1 no 21.

126 TsDAVO, f. 538 op. 1 sprava 84 no. 112.

127 TsDAVO, f. 1092c op. 2 sprava 56 nos. 67, 246–54; sprava 140 no. 45.

128 *Zhyttia Podillia*, 9 Feb. 1919; *Novyi shliakh*, 19 June 1920.

129 Dotsenko, *Litopys*, II pt. 5: 184–201. The Whites reluctantly tolerated Ukrainian schools as private institutions. The Bolsheviks recognized and funded them.

130 *Zhyttia Podillia*, 9March 1919.

131 Ibid., 5 and 23 Jan. 1919; TsDAVO, f. 1092 op. 2 sprava 71 no. 21; op. 5 sprava 8, nos. 5–14; sprava 358 op. 1 sprava 90 no. 43. Kovalchuk, *Nevidoma viina*, 363. TsDAHO, f. 1 op. 20 sprava 39 no. 88. All UNR conscription and desertion statistics have not yet been studied.

132 Makno, *Ukrainskaia revoliutsiia*, 174; Legiec, *Armia*, 15, 21, 25–7.

133 TsDAVO, f. 538 op. 1 sprava 84 nos. 8–33. While in Kamianets povit no more than 214 of an expected 5,750 eligible men actually appeared at mobilization points in June, in Mohyliv povit 2,000 appeared, and another 3,600 were collected by detachments sent into two other povits. Bratslav, Ushytsia, Haisinsk, Litynsk, and Letychiv povits reported good turnouts – if not initially, then after army units had arrived, threatened shirkers with punishment, and rounded up deserters. TsDAVO, f. 538 op. 1 sprava 89 nos. 220, 222, 229–30; sprava 94 nos. 7–12; sprava 97 nos. 1–2; sprava 94 nos. 7–8.

134 TsDAVO, f. 538 op. 1 sprava 84 nos. 142 , 166, 219–21, 252–3; f. 1 op. 1 sprava 27 no. 31, which contains a copy of the decree on soldiers' family benefits.

135 TsDAVO, f. 538 op. 1 sprava 41 no. 115.

136 Dotsenko, *Litopys*, II pt. 4: 248–9, claims that the peasantry donated voluntarily. Kovalevsky, *Pry dzerelakh*, and commissars' reports claimed that they refused. TsDAVO, f. 538 op. 1 sprava 89 nos. 63–5. The specific reference is to Kamianets povit in 1919.

137 Sidak, ed., *Vyzvolni zmahannia*, 49, 54–5.

138 TsDAVO, f. 538 op. 1 sprava 41 nos. 187–8, 200; sprava 84 nos. 190, 210.

139 TsDAVO, f. 1078 op. 1 sprava 75 nos. 60–115.

140 TsDAVO, f. 1092 op. 1 sprava 7; op. 2 sprava 13 no. 69; op. 5 sprava 8 no. 5. Lozovy, *Vnutrishnia*, 98–139, gives examples of administrative achievements but concludes that the administration verged on collapse.

141 There is heated debate on this issue. Skvarsky specified that pogroms resulted from the lack of government. DASBU, 69270 vol. 18, p. 22. One vital document on the subject is the minutes of a July 1919 meeting between Petliura and six prominent Jewish leaders. They express their loyalty but doubted Petliura's expressed intentions and point to Black Hundred extremists in the army and bureaucracy as agents of pogroms. Serhiichuk, *Symon Petliura i evreistvo*, 92–102. Two recent representative contributions from each side are by Serhiichuk, ibid., and Finklshtien, *Za dela.* Jewish eyewitness accounts normally exclude western Ukrainian troops from the pogromists. Of three accounts from Uman Ovruch, and Zhytomir that mention anti-Semitic civilian officials as provocateurs or participants, one specified that Ukrainian officials disseminated anti-Semitic slogans. Miliakova, ed., *Kniga*, 15, 23, 40, 90, 119. On Galician troops, see ibid., 243, 275.

142 Strilets, *Ukrainska ... partiia*, 237–8. The claim is confirmed by P.V., 'Volyn,' *Volia*, no. 11 (March 1920) 23; Dolnytsky, 'Shevchenkivske sviato v Bershadi na Velykyi Ukraini v 1920,' *Volia*, no. 5 (March 1923) 12; Mahalevsky, *Ostannyi akt tragedii*, 25.

143 *Trybuna*, 24 Dec. 1919. Cited in Dillon, 'The Rural Cooperative Movement,' Chapter 10. See also: *Biuleten informatsiinoho viddilu Ministerstva Zemelnykh sprav* (no. 18, 1919). In April 1920 the Hospodar Soiuz got a contract to transport released officials home. TsDAVO, f. 1113 op. 2 sprava 81 no. 10.

144 *Trudova hromada*, 25 Sept. 1919; TsDAVO, f. 1092c op. 2 sprava 56 no. 266.

145 *Trudova respublika*, Feb. 1919. Sometimes organizations existed only on paper, as their elected members were often activists in other groups or towns as well, and thus they had limited connection to the *Spilka* and/or to the SR party unit that they formally represented.

6 Bureaucrats and Bolsheviks in Russia

1 The Provisional Government also removed ministers for political reasons, and by November 1917 had replaced approximately half of permanent secretaries and department heads. The motivations for these latter changes were not examined in the only study devoted to the subject: Kulikov, 'Vremennoe pravitelstvo i vysshaia tsarskaia biurokratiia,' 78–80.

2 *Vestnik vremennago pravitelstva*, 14 (27) June 1917.

3 *Tribuna gosudarstvennykh sluzhashchikh* (1917): no. 2: 5; no. 3: 7; no. 5: 6; no. 7; no. 8.

4 Lenin, *Polnoe sobranie sochinenii*, 34: 305–16; 35: 159, 162–3, 195–6. *Leninskii Sbornik*, 11: 391–2.

5 Lenin, *Polnoe sobranie*, 35: 42.

6 Golub, ed., *Velikaia oktiabrskaia sotsialisticheskaia revoliutsiia. Entsiklopediia*, 450. No source is given for this figure. Nielson, Weil, eds., *Russkaia revoliutsiia glazami petrogradskogo chinovnika*, 28.

7 Korostovetz, *Seed and Harvest*, 301–7. To my knowledge no one has yet studied the union's records, '*Delo soiuza soiuzov sluzhashchykh gosudarstvennykh uchrezhdennii*,' in the Central FSB Archive in Moscow.

8 Korenevskaia, ed., *F.Ia. Rostovskii. Dnevnik*, 400. Tatishchev, *Zemli i liudi*, 271, 272–5. Rumour had it that Bolsheviks were hiring Germans en masse.

9 *Russkaia zhizn*, 24 Nov. 1917

10 *Kievskaia mysl*, 24 Dec. 1917 (6 Jan. 1918).

11 The head of the Postal and Telegraph Workers Union described events in detail in a speech – after which he was arrested: *Vestnik Vserossiisskago pochtovo-telegrafichnago souiza*, no. 16–20 December 7, 1918.

12 *Tribuna gosdarstvennykh sluzhashchikh*, no. 2 (1918) 16–17; *Kievskaia mysl*, 6 Dec. 1917.

13 Vladimirova, *God sluzhby*, 75–82, claims that the strike affected all the Russian provinces. Aronson, *Rossia v epokhu revoliutsii*, 212–15, 221–6. Fraiman, *Forpost sotsialisticheskoi revoliutsii*, 103–13; Iroshnikov, *Sozdanie*, 157–211; Antoshkin, *Professionalnoe dvizhenie sluzhashchikh*, 52–5, 99–112; Rigby, *Lenin's Government*, 40–52; Buldakov et al., *Borba za massy v trekh revoliutsiiakh v Rossii*, 174, 258–61; Mints, *Istoriia velikogo oktiabra*, III: 762–92. It is still not known whether Lenin actually had millions of German reichsmarks – which could have financed Bolshevik supporters before he nationalized the banks.

14 Neilsen, Weil, eds., *Russkaia revoliutsiia* , 20.

15 Lenin, *Polnoe*, 35: 374–75. In April 1921 the secret police was assigned the task of registering every single government employee. Baiguzin, ed., *Gosudarstvennaia bezopasnost Rossii*, 457.

16 Baiguzin, ed., *Gosudarstvennaia bezopasnost Rossii*, 344–6, 358–9, 387.

17 That February saw the first public declarations in Russia of former non-Bolsheviks who had decided to work for the new government in the name of Russian national interests. Hardeman, *Coming to Terms with the Soviet Regime*, 5.

18 Neilsen, Wier, eds., *Russkaia revoliutsiia*, 23. Political parties as well as non-party government and private administrators also organized passive anti-Bolshevik resistance. Kanishchev, '"Melkoburzhuaznaia kontrrevoliutsiia": soprotivlenie gorodskikh srednikh sloev stanovleniiu "diktatury proletariata,"' in Tiutiutkin, ed., *1917 god*, 179–80. Idem., 'Miatezhnyi obyvatel,' 172–3.

19 Senin, ed., '"Naskolko deshevo stala tsenitsia zhizn" Dnevnik bezhetskogo sviashchennika I.N. Postnikova,' no. 3: 31–47; no. 4:10–30; no. 5: 13–29.

20 *Iuzhnaia kopeika*, 8 (21) Dec. 1917. *Kievskaia mysl*, 8 (21) Dec. 1917; *Poslednie novosti*, 5 (18) Jan 1918.

21 Sudavtsov, *Zemskoe i gorodskoe samoupravlenie*, 572, 584, 628–9, claims that the strike ended at the end of December, when in fact it ended two months later. *Utro Rossii*, 8March (23 Feb.) 1918.

22 Kanishchev, 'Melkoburzhuaznaia kontrrevoliutsiia,' 174–87.

23 Narskii, *Zhizn*, 57.

24 Neilsen, Wier, eds., *Russkaia revoliutsiia*, 38, 49–50. Budnitskii, *Rosiisskie evrei*, 96.

25 Sudavtsov, 584, 602–3.

26 *ARR*, III: 147; VI: 306–9, 316, 328–30. Emigre accounts of accommodation are confirmed by archival evidence: Smirnova, '*Byvshie liudi*,' 91–108.

27 Borman, 'Moskva-1918,' 140; Kniazev, 'Iz zapisnoi knizhki,' 4 (1993) 99, 119; 5 (1994) 169, 174, 177, 185. Kniazev remarked in October, when White armies were marching towards Moscow, that officials had begun fleeing to Petrograd. They knew that if the Bolsheviks were defeated there would be

no sympathy for those who, thanks to their jobs, lived in expropriated flats or hotel rooms (1993: 117).

28 Baiguzin, *Gosudarstvennaia bezopastnost Rossii,* 395. Secret preparations for flight continued through 1919.

29 Okninskii, *Dva goda.*

30 Nielson, Wier, eds., *Russkaia revoliutsiia,* 25.

31 Fleer, 'Vremennoe pravitelstvo posle oktiabra,' 202–3, 208; Gindin, 'Kak Bolsheviki ovladeli gosbankom,' 224–37. Vernadskii notes that Ministry of Education personnel decided on 15 (25) November to end the strike when the Constituent Assembly met. Sorokina et al., *V.I. Vernadskii,* 40.

32 Senin, 'Naskolko deshevo,' no. 3: 38; no. 5: 25.

33 Miakotin, 'Iz nedalekago proshlago,' 205, 210; Lophukhin, 'Posle 25 oktiabra,' 14, 61–2; Korenevskaia, ed., *F. Ia Rostovskii,* 410, 429. Narskii, *Zhizn v katastrofe,* 469–71.

34 Okninskii, 33. Kanischev, Riazanov, 'Dekrety sovetskoi vlasti,' 165–8.

35 Cited in Budnitskii, *Rossiiskie evrei,* 97–8.

36 Budnitskii, 101. By 1923 the number of Jews in Petrograd had increased by three times their pre-revolutionary total, and in Moscow by ten times – to over 80,000. M. Altschuler, 'Russia and Her Jews: The Impact of the 1914 War,' *Wiener Library Journal,* no. 30–1 (1972–74) 12–14; Halevy, 'Jewish Students in Soviet Universities in the 1920s,' *Soviet Jewish Affairs,* no. 1 (1976) 56–70. Vietzblit, *Rukh Evreiskoi liudnosti,* 140.

37 Cited in Gitelman, *Jewish Nationality and Soviet Politics,* 115–116. Budnitskii, 93–4. Kniazev, 'Iz zapisnoi,' 5 (1994) 184, 186.

38 *ARR,* II: 102.

39 Rogalina, Telitsyn, 'Nu, polno mne zagadyvat,' 85; Kniazev, 'Iz zapisnoi knizhki,' 114.

40 *Tribuna,* no. 4 (1918) 9–10.

41 *Tribuna,* no. 19 (1918) 1–7.

42 *Tribuna,* no. 23–4 (1918).

43 *Tribuna* (1918) no. 25–6: 4–11, 35–7; no. 33: 6

44 *Tribuna* (1918) no. 34: 1–4; no. 35: 3–5.

45 A letter in *Tribuna,* no. 20 (1918) 7, praises the new relations, while another in no. 35, observes that everything in offices was as it had been before 1917.

46 Listed in Utgof, 'Ufimskoe gosudarstvennoe soveshchanie 1918 goda,' 18. Osipova, *Rossiiskoe krestianstvo,* 161.

47 Narskii, *Zhizn,* 301. Kniazev, 'Iz zapisnoi knizhki,' 5 (1994) 167.

48 Okninskii, *Dva goda,* 38, 171. One of the benefits of office work was that incoming newspapers provided the staff with paper for rolling cigarettes.

49 Bakhturina, Kozhevnikova, eds., *Gosudarstvennyi apparat Rossii v gody revoliutsii i grazhdanskoi voiny*, 51–2; Smirnova, 115–16; Brovkin, *Behind*, 134–42, 310; Gimpelson, 185–6; Maslov, *Rossiia posle chetyrekh let revoliutsii*, 85–92, 112–16.

50 Baiguzin, ed., *Gosudartsvennaia bezopastnost Rossii*, 341.

51 Mints, *Istoriia*, 771, 781. The Petrograd duma was the first that the Bolsheviks dissolved (16 Nov. [29 Dec.]) and apparently only 5% of its administrative staff were still working for it by July 1918. I am grateful to V. Kanishchev of Tambov University and his student N.V. Strekalova for figures on Voronezh province.

52 *Trudy tsentralnogo statisticheskogo upravleniia*, vol. 8, no. 2 (1922) 294, 301, 304. Figures are incomplete and include railway, postal, and telegraph personnel, as well as 20 830 doctors, artists, and teachers. There were in addition at least one million office staff in state-owned enterprises. *Trudy tsentralnogo statisticheskogo upravleniia*, vol. 8, no. 3 (1922) 206. Kniazev, 'Iz zapisnoi knizhki,' 99.

53 Figes, *Peasant Russia Civil War*, 225, 237–9. Lepeshkin, *Mestnye organy vlasti sovetskogo gosudarstva*, 62.

54 Figes, *A People's Tragedy*, 690.

55 Massive layoffs provided thousands of unemployed workers as recruits for what were initially called 'factory guards,' who were well paid and fed with army rations. The money came from industrialists. When owners realized that the guards were simply a Bolshevik army and tried to stop paying, they faced strikes or armed delegations in their offices. Frenkin, *Zakhvat vlasti*, 273–4, 355, 372–4. Brovkin, *Behind the Front Line*, 134–42; Gimpelson, *Sovetskie upravlentsy*, 127, 132, 134, 142; Okninskii, *Dva goda*, 45–55, describes his volost ispolkom office and co-workers.

56 Gimpelson, *Sovetskie upravlentsy*,, 135. Twenty-eight per cent identified their pre-1917 profession as 'sluzhashchie' but in 1919–1920 figures this term referred only to clerks in private and social organizations. The category 'state employees' identified in 1921, might also refer only to one's position at the time. Vladimirskii, *Sovety, ispolkomy i siezdy sovetov*, I: 14; II: 49, 58.

57 Narskii, *Zhizn*, 445.

58 Iroshnikov, *Predsedatel soveta narodnykh komissarov*, 341–45. None of the eighteen questions asked about gender. Before and after 1917 *sluzashchie* averaged 16% of new party members. Buldakov et al., *Borba*, 267.

59 Smirnova, '*Byvshie liudi*,' 98.

60 Church, *Revolution*, 82, 103.

61 Osipova, *Rossiiskoe krestianstvo*, 113–24, 216, 282, 301, 309, 313, 316, The success of the November draft is also explained by the support local left-wing PSR

leaders, who dominated local soviets and military commissions, for peace with Germany. Those against had resigned. The PSR was split, however. It split again in February 1919 and without its central co-ordination and leadership local anti-Bolshevik revolts that year could be quashed (151, 160, 296).

62 *Vosmoi siezd,* 188–91.

63 Easter, *Reconstructing,* 33–4, 75–8, 83–5, 90, 95. Yaney, *Urge to Mobilize,* 503–5.

64 It is unclear if there were 1,000–1,500 armed men per province or per region at the immediate disposition of the Cheka. Sakharov et al., *Obshchestvo i vlast,* 38–42.

65 Sanborn, 'Drafting the Nation,' 150–8, 339–40.

66 *ARR,* XII: 106. Landis, *Bandits and Partisans,* 34–5.

67 Baiguzin, ed., *Gosudarstvennaia bezopastnost Rossii,* 408–9.

7 Bureaucrats, Bolsheviks, and Whites in Ukraine

1 The Bolsheviks held nineteen of the forty seats in the Kharkiv city soviet executive in early December 1917, when they got it to drop its earlier support for Kyiv and align with Moscow. Iarmysh, ed., *Istoriia mista Kharkova,* 161. As of October 1917, Ukraine had 15,000 Red Guards. Moscow and Petrograd sent 31,000 Russian Red Guards into Ukraine before the Bolsheviks declared war on the Rada. They shipped arms and munitions to the major Ukrainian cities on 30 November (11 December). R. Wade, *Red Guards and Workers' Militias,* 270; Hrynevych, *Istoriia,* 49. Frenkin, *Zakhvat vlasti,* 339; Zdorov, *Ukrainskyi zhovten,* 152–3, 156. Zdorov writes that Ukraine had 240 soviets and that representatives of eighty-two attended the Kharkiv meeting.

2 Bachynsky, ed., *Dokumenty trahichnoi istorii,* 63. 'We never recognized the Ukrainian National Republic as totally soveriegn (*nezavisimaia*) but only as a more or less independent unit tied federally with the all-Russia workers-peasants republic.'

3 Korolivsky, *Pobeda,* 479–81; Babko et al., *Velikaia Oktiabrskaia sotsialisticheskaia revoliutsiia ... chast vtoraia,* 510, 523, 530, 790. Another 100 million roubles arrived 22 January, but thereafter, until its fall, Moscow supposedly sent nothing to its Ukrainian administration. Zdorov, *Ukrainskyi zhovten,* 179–80.

4 *Nova Rada,* 20 Feb. (5 March), 22 Feb. (7 March), 1918; *Poslednie novosti,* 31 Jan. (13 Feb.), 22 Feb. (4 March), 1918. Despite the official adoption of the new calendar as of 16 Feb. (OS), some newspapers still used both dates after 1 March (NS).

5 Babko et al., 697, 767, 807, 841, 884; Doroshenko, *Istoriia,* I: 294, 341; Bosh, *God borby,* 146. Kyivan Bolsheviks burned their personnel lists in June 1919. *ARR,* VI: 257. *Iuzhnaia kopeika,* 3 (16) Feb. 1918. The financial records of

the Rada's chancellery show that its staff did get its pay in advance. TsDAVO, f. 1115 op. 1 sprava 74 nos. 164, 165.

6 Zatonsky, 'Uryvky z spohadiv,' no. 4 (1929) 154–5. An estimated 12% of Antonov's army in January 1918 were Ukrainians. Tynchenko, *Persha Ukrainsko-bolshevytska viina*, 148. In Chernihiv, Dmytro Krainsky was struck by the clearly Russian physiognomy of the invading army. TsDAHO, f. 5 op. 1 sprava 21 no. 55.

7 Lenin, negotiating at Brest, tended to support Ukraine's Bolsheviks against the imported Russians when conflicts occurred. Zdorov, *Ukrainskyi zhoven*, 183–5.

8 TsDAHO, f. 5 op. 1 sprava 21 no. 60.

9 Mazepa, I: 45. Successive governments only replaced the heads. Kuras, ed., *Velykyi zhovten i hromadianska viina na Ukraini*, 503.

10 The Bolsheviks had to arrest 3,000 postal and telegraph employees. *Nova Hromada*, 15 (28) Dec. 1917. Hamretsky et al., *Triumfalnoe shestvie sovetskoi vlasti na Ukraine*, 110–11; Tymofiev, 'Pro borotbu radianskoi vlady za revoliutsiinu perebudovu,' 112–15. *Nova Hromada*, 13 (31) Jan. 1918; *Kievskaia mysl*, 30 Dec. 1917.

11 Babko et al., 878. The declaration appeared within days of the formation of a provincial commission to combat 'sabotage, speculation and administrative crimes' (830).

12 Tkachenko, 'Oleksandrivsk na zlami epoch,' 22–3.

13 TsDAVO, f. 1 op. 1 sprava 164 nos. 64, 92, 166.

14 DAKO, f. R1239 op. 124 sprava 3; f. R1048 op.1 sprava 17 no. 161.

15 TsDAVO, f. 538 op. 1 sprava 26 no. 418. Reports from six volosts in Podillia province note that most of their staffs did not work for the Bolsheviks. Ibid., f. 543 op. 1 sprava 28 nos. 1–13.

16 *Slavianoserbsky khliborob*, 2 (19) Nov. 1917; *Poslednie novosti*, 7 (20) Feb. 1917. DAKO, f. R2976 op. 1 sprava 24 no. 5. TsDAHO, f. 1 op. 20 sprava 17 nos. 33, 35.

17 *Trybuna*, 5 Feb. 1919; TsDAVO, f. 1092 op. 2 sprava 16 no. 78. f. 2207 op. 5. sprava 24 no. 3. TsDAVO, f. 2199 op. 1 sprava 163 nos. 1, 14; sprava 167 nos. 14, 36–8.

18 Tatishchev, *Zemli*, 321, 324.

19 *Borotba*, 12 and 18 Feb. 1919. Work could not begin until the Bolsheviks seized typewriters from stores. The records of the Food Supply Ministry do not suggest rampant uncontrolled corruption. There exists, however, a case filed by the Directory against a senior departmental accountant who on the eve of the Hetman's fall absconded with a sizable sum from the payroll. TsDAVO, f. 2198, op. 1. The court case is in sprava 38.

20 TsDAVO, f. 5 op. 1. TsDAHO, f. 5 op. 1 sprava 245 nos. 12 DAKO 13, 19. A list of 127 former UNR Interior Ministry personnel who continued working for the Bolsheviks is in TsDAVO, f. 2 op. 1 sprava 421 nos. 14–18.

21 TsDAVO, f. 539 op. 1 sprava 13 nos. 187–93; sprava 59 no. 142; sprava 60 nos. 40–1.

22 TsDAVO, f. 2 op. 1 sprava 406 no. 2; sprava 242 nos. 12–15, 25–31, 39–57. I was unable to locate the fourteen files listed in this report with the names of all 827 employees (no. 32).

23 TsDAHO, f. 57 op. 2 sprava 321 nos. 36, 38.

24 Khrystiuk, *Zamitky*, IV: 174.

25 *Chervonyi prapor*, 4 March 1919. All Postal and Telegraph personnel were fired on 29 March, and new hiring began two days later. On 2 April *Chervonyi prapor* reported that some former employees were rehired. On 12 April it reported that a Kyiv city regional Health Department head had fired employees for using Ukrainian.

26 DAKO, f. R1 op. 1 sprava 93 nos. 17–19; f. R102 op. 1 sprava 743 no. 22. TsDAVO, f. 1601 op. 1 sprava 7 nos. 75, 196, 164, 168, 176, 205, 215, 246. Applicants probably considered it prudent not to reveal that they had worked for the national governments if they had. TsDAVO, f. 2 op. 1 sprava 547 contains a collection of letters from individuals asking Rakovsky directly for jobs. They do not contain sufficient information about their authors to allow generalizations about them.

27 *Proletarska borotba*, 20 Nov. 1919.

28 Iu. Tiutiunnyk, *Zymovyi pokhid*, 44–5; Maistrenko, *Borotbism*, 118–22.

29 *Chervonyi prapor*, 28 Feb. 1919. TsDAHO, f. 57 op. 2 sprava 306 no. 86.

30 TsDAHO, f. 59 op. 1 sprava 552.

31 TsDAVO, f. 2 op. 1 sprava 635 no 16. Aleksandr Nefedov was Russian. Eight of the seventeen declared themselves Ukrainian.

32 TsDAHO, f. 1 op. 20 sprava 305 nos. 6, 27–9, 58, 66–8.

33 TsDAVO, f. 2 op. 1 sprava 631 nos. 6, 10. As of September, thirty-three of the province's 169 volosts were not under control at all, and in 26 people were passive but hostile. Only 26 of the counties did not have a phone-link to district capitals. Until the end of that year, Bolshevik control of villages usually ended when their troops left. During an undated meeting of Ukraine's Central Executive Committee leaders learned that even local military committees were infiltrated by UNR officers and Makhno sympathizers. Leaders decided to request 'an entire prepared apparatus (*tselyi riad gotovykh apparatov*) from Russia' – cryptically called 'the centre' – just as Dzerzhinskii had done with his Cheka. TsDAVO, f 2 op. 1 sprava 273 nos. 127–30.

34 TsDAHO, f. 1 op. 20 sprava 305 nos. 6, 27–9, 58, 66–8; op. 18 sprava 22 no. 45; op. 18 sprava 62 nos. 9, 30. TsDAVO, f. 2 op. 1 sprava 252 no. 19.

35 TsDAVO, f. 2 op. 1 sprava 241 no. 67. This report was written by two of the revkom's clerks, who were appalled.

36 TsDAVO, f. 2 op. 1 sprava 617 nos. 4–5, 70–1.

37 TsDAHO, f. 1 op. 20 sprava 16 no. 34. TsDAVO, f. 1 op. 1 sprava 183 no. 238; sprava 17 no. 37; f. 1113 op. 2 sprava 213 nos. 59–60; sprava 200 no. 4. Danilov, ed., *Nestor Makhno,* 132, 433, 438, 449. Kondufor, ed., *Ukraina v 1917–1921 gg.*, 187.

38 TsDAHO, f. 1 op. 20 sprava 21 nos. 14–15, 55–65.

39 TsDAHO, f. 1 op. 20 sprava 17 nos. 47, 125–8. The latter report contains no figures.

40 R. Budberg, 'Pod vlastiu bolshevikov,' 103–4, 135. Korolivsky et al., *Grazhdanskaia voina,* I: 633, 662, 721; I pt. 2: 75, 87, 113, 115, 117, 182, 189, 208, 283, 296, 360; II: 175. DAKO, f. R4395 op. 1 sprava 25 no. 50. TsDAHO, f. 1 op. 20 sprava 300 no. 21; sprava 21 no. 12. Of 4,173 men subject to call up in Ohtyrka povit, 2,429 reached the army. Of 342 former troopers, gunners, and machine-gunners called up, 156 went to the front (no. 25).

41 TsDAVO, f. 1 op. 20 sprava 16 no. 34; DAKO, f. R1 op.1 sprava 38 passim.

42 Revehuk, 'Lenin i borotba,' 63. TsDAHO, f. 5 op. 1 sprava 52 nos. 21, 116. Lenin himself set the target higher than recommended by his Ukrainian subordinates, in part, to lessen the burden on Russian peasants and thus neutralize their opposition to his regime. Nesterov, Zemzuilina, Zakharchenko, *U pokhodi,* 38, 44–7. In 1920 the squads managed to seize 40% of their quota.

43 Baiguzin, ed., *Gosudarstvennaia bezopastnost,* 342n; Lenin, *Polnoe,* 51: 245–6. Stalin was in charge of the operation, and Lenin specified that he could import thousands of Russian workers into each party cell in every military formation to ensure that the maximum amount of grain was taken from the peasants. For Lenin's requisition orders in Russia in 1918 see ibid., 50: 137, 143–8, 152. In theory, only 'the rich' (*kulak*) were subject to requisitioning. In practice, each local official decided who was 'rich.' Zakharchenko, Zemziukina Nesterov, *U pokhodi,* 87–8.

44 DAKO, f. R1 op. 1 sprava 261 nos. 112, 252, 320, 327, 364; sprava 283 nos. 5–11. Summarized party situation reports from Zvenyhorod povit early 1921 are in TsDAHO, f. 1 op. 1 sprava 282 nos. 53–83, 386–93. Each povit institution was allowed only 1,500 words per telegram daily, which officials claimed was insufficient (no. 241).

45 DAKO, f. R1049 op. 1 sprava 17 no. 401.

46 *ARR,* VI: 247, 253.

47 *ARR*, XV: 213.
48 *Kommunist* (Kyiv), 5June 1920; *Chervonyi stiah*, 6 June 1919. TsDAHO, f. 1 op. 20 sprava 21 no. 14; sprava 35 no. 119. *Borotba*, 14 Jan. 1920.
49 *ARR*, XX: 216, 220–30, 235. Poletika, *Vidennoe i perezhitoe*, 151. TsDAVO, f. 1 op. 1 sprava 33 no. 259.
50 *ARR*, VI: 256–7, 263. When the Whites took Kyiv in late 1919 they did nothing to former Soviet employees.
51 Lykho, 'Sovetskaia vlast na mestakh,' 138.
52 TsDAHO, f 5 op. 1 sprava 21 no. 60.
53 Danilov, ed., *Nestor Makhno*, 450, 457; Belosh, *Dorogi*, 382–3.
54 DAKO, f. R111 op. 1 sprava 8 nos. 4–6. TsDAHO, f. 1 op. 18 sprava 1 no. 4. The Bolshevik agent who reported this behaviour called it 'criminal.'
55 TsDAHO, f. 1 op. 20 sprava 300 no. 340–51.
56 TsDAVO, f. 2 op. 1 sprava 634 nos. 44–5.
57 TsDAVO, f. 3305 op. 1 sprava 14 no. 44.
58 DAKO, f. R1 op. 1 sprava 93 no. 90.
59 *Professionalnoe dvizhenie*, 4 July, 1 Aug. 1919.
60 *ARR*, XII: 108, 138.
61 DAKO, f. R3 op. 2 sprava 47; f. R4395 op. 1 sprava 25 no. 32; also, f. R1048 and R1049 op. 1. Correspondence between Chornobyl povit revkoms in March 1920 (DAKO, f. R4395 op. 1 sprava 25) contains very detailed instructions regarding conscription procedures and draft dodgers. Most local documents that year were written/printed on the back of old documents.
62 DAKO, f.R1 op. 1 sprava 16 no. 160; sprava 93 nos. 5–62, 78–81, 86. Of 161 revkoms in Zvenyhorod povit's seventeen volosts in 1920, sixty-three in seven volosts were functioning 'badly.'
63 Borysov, *Prodovolcha polityka na Ukraini*, 85–6. This assumes a five-day eight-hour work week for 1,976 incoming and 2,917 outgoing items. TsDAVO, f. 5 op. 1 sprava 116 no. 25.
64 DAKO, f. R1 op. 1 sprava 38 nos. 108, 118. TsDAVO, f. 1 op.2 sprava 152; sprava 146 no. 118.
65 TsDAHO, f. 1 op. 20 sprava 300 nos. 340–51; f. 1 op. 20 sprava 305 for reports from 1919 and 1920. The organization published an internal bulletin three or four times monthly from the spring of 1920. There are statistical reports of successful redress of grievances for individual regions but not for the entire country for the first years of Soviet rule. TsDAVO, f. 2c op. 2 sprava 66 nos. 13–18; f 1 op. 1 sprava 58 no. 34; f. 539 op. 1 sprava 13 no. 289. These compilations included instructions to lock the office at the end of the day and making the senior typist or section heads personally

responsible for administrative errors – an unwelcome prospect given the omnipresent Cheka.

66 TsDAVO, f. 2 op. 1 sprava 622 no. 57. Bilotserkva Povit Revkom decree no. 16. (Oct. 1920).

67 TsDAHO, f. 1 op. 20 sprava 646 nos. 5v, 32–3, 76v, 87v, 92, 48.

68 TsDAHO, f. 1 op. 39 no. 193.

69 TsDAHO, f. 1 op. 20 sprava 1308 no. 47. 'Otchet o polugodnichnoi deiatelnosti,' 318.

70 TsDAVO, f. 1113 op. 2 sprava 200 no. 3, 65. TsDAHO, f. 1 op. 20 sprava 643 nos. 2–20. 40–54, 65–75; sprava 646 nos. 90–110, 131v, 151–62. The one reported strike threat was from Kostiantynivka in Poltava province: ibid., f. 1 op. 20 sprava 642 nos. 84, 87, 173. Cheka situation reports were secret and issued in numbered copies to no more than twenty-one of the highest government leaders.

71 Vargatiuk, ed., *Bolshevistskie organizatsii Ukrainy*, 533. Four months later Bolshevik organizers in Kyiv reported that because of the pillaging and anti-Ukrainian pogroms by their Russian troops in Chernihiv and Kyiv that winter workers were not joining the Bolsheviks (651). Zdorov, *Ukrainskyi zhovten*, claims that Ukraine's Bolsheviks in 1917 were more assertive of their autonomy from Moscow than normally thought.

72 TsDAHO, f. 1 op. 1 sprava 7 no. 64. Lapchinskii, 'Gomelskoe soveshchanie,' 40. Bolshevik employees who had fled to Russia that spring were registered as refugees. The resolution of April 1918 referred to government departments and officials from 'German' or temporarily 'occupied provinces' and required that the final official document had to indicate that the Russian Republic did not surrender its rule (*verkhovenstvo*) in the 'occupied provinces.' A later resolution that November placing 'all regions on the southern and western borders of the RSFSR liberated from occupation' under the direct authority of the Russian Food Supply commissar had the note: 'not to be published.' TsDAHO, f. 57 op. 2 sprava 76 nos. 166, 179.

73 Iurchuk et al., *Komunistychna partiia Ukrainy v rezoliutsiiakh. Tom pershyi*, 70–1. TsDAHO, f. 1 op. 1 sprava 57 no. 3. Ukrainian Bolsheviks were displeased with their limited jurisdictions and got greater prerogatives for their republic in the Workers and Peasants Union Treaty of December 1920. The Communist Party of Ukraine (Bolshevik) had no national status and was merely a provincial organization of the Russian Communist Party.

74 Belosh, *Dorogi*, 171, 281–2. 'National' Bolshevik military formations were abolished in June 1919, but in January 1920 Bolshevik leaders declared that commissars and officers in Ukraine should be nationals or at least familiar with the country. In January 1921, 9% of the Red Army in Ukraine

were Ukrainians. Korolivsky et al., *Grazhdanskaia voina*, II: 675; Hrynevych, *Istoriia*, 163–5, 172, 245.

75 TsDAHO, f. 1 op. 20 sprava 300 no. 346. The *Otchet narodnoho komiteta vnutrennykh del USSR za 1920 god* made no mention either of the issue of subordination to Moscow in 1919, nor to the eighteen western Ukrainians in the Housing Ministry staff (340–51).

76 Buhai, *Chrezvychainye organy*, 86–7, 288–93. Likewise, local food supply commissars and Cheka personnel were subject only to their Moscow superiors. Rigby, *Lenin's Government*, 184–5.

77 Lenin, *Polnoe*, 51, 95–6. In the same note he ordered the thirty-four signatories to be put under surveillance and dispersed among other party workers. Someone from the Orgburo in the accompanying note labeled the request 'irresponsible politicking.' In Kharkiv, letter writers complained about the mass influx of Russians ignorant of the country and its language and a simultaneous impeding of Ukrainians from entering it and warned those Russians were provoking anti-Soviet uprisings. While Russian 'dregs' were given jobs, Ukrainians were not. If this continued, once the 'Ukrainian Red Army' had finished with Denikin they would have to chase out all the Russians. *Proletarska Pravda* (Kharkiv), 2, 6, and 7 Jan. 1920.

78 TsDAHO, f. 1 op. 20 sprava 20 nos. 1–3. M. Avdienko and O. Iaroshchenko.

79 Volyn, Zaporizhzhia (incl. Katerynoslav), Podillia, Kharkiv. My Soviet total excludes 902 doctors, nurses, artists, and teachers. *Trudy tsentralnogo statisticheskogo upravleniia*, vol. 8, no. 2 (1922) 296–300.

80 TsDAVO, f. 1 op. 2 sprava123 nos. 51, 53; sprava 152; sprava 146 nos. 52, 125, 140, 142, 151. The names of all Ukrainian provincial and povit vykonkom and Food Supply Ministry heads are in f. 340 op. 1 sprava 3011 nos. 3–15.

81 TsDAVO, f. 2 op. 2 sprava 73 nos. 37, 41–2.

82 TsDAVO, f. 5 op. 1 sprava 1121 nos. 8, 11. It also noted that because of the war Russians interested in bureaucracy as a phenomenon had lost contact with their foreign counterparts. The commission itself produced an impressive closely typed five-page description of its functions and a list of thirty-five questions that all government departments had to answer and return – which they evidently did. TsDAVO, f. 2 op. 2 sprava 73 nos. 12, 17–22; sprava 126.

83 *ARR*, VI: 237, 247.

84 *Izvestiia* (Kyiv), 5 and 20 March 1919.

85 *Radianska vlada*, 13 Feb. 1919. No more figures appear afterwards. Oliinyk, 'Diialnist partiinykh orhanizatsii po polipshenniu roboty derzhapparatu u vidbudovnyi period (1921–1925 rr.),' 66–7.

86 *Naselenie v gorodakh,* 40, 42, 44. 'Towns' were defined as settlements with 500 or more inhabitants.
87 *Trudy tsentralnogo statisticheskogo upravleniia,* vol. 8, no. 7 (1926) 177–8.
88 *Izvestiia ispolnitelnogo komiteta Kievskogo soveta rabochikh deputatov,* 27 Feb., 15 March, 1919. Administrators are specifically referred to only in the decree reorganizing the Justice Ministry.
89 These sometimes reached absurd proportions. In an order later rescinded by Moscow, the Poltava province party secretary in June 1919 ordered all city inhabitants other than employees, union, and party members to surrender within three days, on pain of arrest, almost all of their private effects. Among listed permitted items were ten matches per smoker, three plates and one spoon per person. TsDAVO, f. 1 op. 1 sprava 58 nos. 116–22.
90 *ARR,* IX: 199–220. The availability of personnel is confirmed by Bolshevik reports that describe city services as functioning within three days of their arrival. Tronko, ed., *Kievshchina,* 153.
91 Volkov-Muromets, *Iunost ot viazmy do feodosii,* 273–5, 301–2.
92 TsDAHO, f. 43 op. 1 sprava 54 no. 2. TsDAVO, f. 2 op. 1 sprava 241.
93 Pavliuchenkov, *Voennyi kommunizm,* 256, 259.
94 Amiantov et al., *V.I. Lenin: Neizvestnye dokumenty,* 307; *Vosmaia konferentsiia RKP(b) dekabr 1919 goda,* 189–90. The resolutions of the March 1919 Ukrainian Party Conference confirming these decisions do not mention personnel criteria at all.
95 Nathans, *Beyond the Pale,* 110, 272–4, 314–15. Pre-war informer lists published in the autumn of 1917 revealed that in Podillia and Volyn provinces during the previous decade as many as 30% were Jews – including a Mr Gitler. TsDIA f. 2233 op. 3 nos. 31, 33, 34. Of a sample of 210 from the years 1910 to 1917, forty were Jews.
96 Vietsblit, *Rukh Evreiskoi liudnosti,* 138–9, 155–75.
97 Goldelman, *Lysty,* 16, 33. A situation report from Kremenchuk in late 1919, where at least half the provincial party committee were secular Jews reported that the city's Jews, presumably the Zionists and religious Jews, did nothing to help the Communists. TsDAHO, f. 1 op. 18 sprava 28 no. 7.
98 Tkachenko, 'Oleksandrivsk,' 28.
99 M. Rafes, *Dva goda revoliutsii na Ukraine,* 164. TsDAVO, f. 340 op. 1 sprava 3006 no. 5; sprava 3018, no. 114.
100 TsDAVO, f. 2 op. 1 sprava 792 nos. 3–6. The document has no date.
101 Heifetz, ed., *The Slaughter of the Jews,* 312, 314, 316; see also, 297. While this witness relates that pogromists did not touch Russian Communists, another claims that they did (406). In May 1922 the proportion of Jews

in Ukraine's 236 strong Central Executive Committee had fallen to 16% from 27% while that of ethnic Ukrainian increased from 15% to 27%. Declared Russians increased from 42% to 49%. TsDAVO, f. 1 op. 2 sprava 507 no. 18.

102 Heifetz, 404. The revkom members are named in a UNR military intelligence report from mid-1920. TsDAVO, f. 4465 op. 1 sprava 2 nos. 4–5. In a report from 1919, the Jewish section of the party observed that only when they faced forced collectivization and requisitions did peasants become anti-Jewish, stop following Jewish Bolshevik leaders, and begin associating Jews with Communism. Lenin, *O Evreiskom voprose*, 59.

103 Pavliuchenkov, *Voennyi kommunizm v Rossii*, 254, 261. There is one town on record, Kaminsk in Katerynoslav province, as having no Jews at all in its Bolshevik administration. They feared that if they took jobs there they would all be killed when non-Bolshevik troops took the town. Miliakova, ed., *Kniga*, 406.

104 DASBU, f. 69270 vol. 32 p. 9v. The idea appears in a Jewish joke from the period which related that Trotskys made the revolution and the Bronsteins then paid for it.

105 TsDAVO, f. 1113 op. 2 sprava 213 no. 74; sprava 197 no. 184.

106 *Kommunist* (Kyiv), 3 April 1918; *Nachalo*, 31 July 1918. TsDAVO, f. 1 op. 1 sprava 164 no. 20.

107 Danilov, ed., *Nestor Makhno*, 132; also, 343, 433. Dzerzhinskii specifically demanded that Russia send complete revkoms to Ukraine.

108 Nazarenko et al., *V.I. Lenin pro Ukrainu*, II: 203, 229, 378.

109 Bevzo et al., *Ukrainska revoliutsiia i derzhavnist*, 195.

110 Chekonovsky, 'Ohliad mizhnarodnoi polityky,' *Volia: Tyzhnevyk*, vol. 2, no. 5 (1920) 227; Skaba et al., *Ukrainska RSR*, III: 33.

111 Skaba et al., *Ukrainska RSR*, III: 31–2; Vynnychenko, *Vidrodzhennia*, III: 316. Authors do not specify percentages of activists by nationality, but do note the reluctance of Ukrainian-born individuals to work in the requisition squads. Revehuk, 'Lenin i borotba,' 61; Mykhailychenko, 'Prodovolcha polityka,' 127–8.

112 Sidak, *Natsionalni spetssluzhby*, 124.

113 TsDAHO, f. 1 op. 20 sprava 300, sprava 340–51.

114 *Trudy*, vol. 8, no. 2, 296–300. TsDAHO, f. 1 op. 20 sprava 35 no. 119.

115 Kapustian, 'Ukrainskoe krestianstvo i vlast v pervye gody NEPA,' 171. H.T. Isyp et al., *Komitety nezamoznykh selian Ukrainy*, 112. TsDAVO, f. 1738 op. 1 sprava 46 no. 60, records how a Kyiv povit vykonkom on 5 July 1919, sent someone to replace an incompetent volost vykonkom. His task was to mobilize the local Committee of Poor Peasants to 're-elect' it by 29 July.

TsDAHO, f. 1 op. 20 sprava 35 no. 166. In May 1919 members were paid 300 roubles. TsDAVO, f. 2 op. 2 sprava 414 no 10.

116 Danilov, ed., *Nestor Makhno*, 440.

117 Hrebennikova, 'Komitety,' 187–8. Members included old widows who had joined unwittingly, hoping only for material assistance.

118 Kabanov, 'Vliianie voin i revoliutsii na krestianstsvo,' 143. TsDAHO, f. 1 op. 20 sprava 21 no. 7. On the purges, see DAKO, f. R1218 op. 1 sprava 3 nos. 15, 14, 38, 63, 105. Only 23% of the delegates to the first two Ukrainian Poor Peasants Congresses could speak Ukrainian. Nesterov, Zemzuilina, Zakharchenko, *U pokhodi*, 56.

119 TsDAVO, f. 1 op. 1 sprava 164, nos. 64, 300–7.

120 Bronnikov, 'Sozdanie sovetskoi intelligentsii iz raboche-krestianskoi mlodezhi v gody grazhdanskoi voiny,' 155, 158. TsDAVO, f. 1113 op. 2 sprava 213 nos. 59–60. Directory situation reports from the autumn of 1921 show that Communists in Kamianets had secret instructions to exclude Jews from higher positions.

121 DAKO, f. 4395 op. 1 sprava 32 nos. 13, 27, 37–8.

122 *Kommunist* (Kyiv), 15April 1920. *Izvestiia* (Chernihiv), 14 Dec. 1918. TsDAVO, f. 2 op. 1 sprava 141 no. 8.

123 TsDAHO, f. 5 op. 1 sprava 62 nos. 40, 82.

124 *Zhyttia Podillia*, 18 April 1919. Danilov, ed., *Nestor Makhno*, 346.

125 TsDAVO, f. 2. op. 1 sprava 636 nos. 8–9.

126 DASBU, f. 74760 vol. 12 pp. 42, 61; see also vol. 15. TsDAHO, f. 1 op. 20 sprava 642 nos. 355–61.

127 TsDAHO, f. 1 op. 20 sprava 224 nos. 6, 17; sprava 30 no. 41; sprava 19 nos. 52–4; f. 5 op. 5 sprava 240 no. 76; sprava 241 nos. 54–5. TsDAVO, f. 539 op. 1 sprava 74 no. 17.

128 TsDAVO, f. 2 op. 1 sprava 241 nos. 107–9.

129 *Kommunist* (Kyiv), 18 June 1919; *Izvestiia*, 10 July. TsDAVO, f . 1738 op. 1 sprava 46 no. 41.

130 *Kommunist* (Kyiv), 26 March, 3 and 15 April, 19 June. M. Lebedynets, M. Rafes, A. Kheifets, and a 'Vrena' comprised the tribunal which was attached to the provincial party committee headed by A. Bubnov.

131 Ibid., 27 April.

132 *Chervonyi stiakh*, 29 July, 3 Aug., 1919.

133 Tronko, ed., *Kievshchina*, 176–7.

134 TsDAVO, f. 1 op. 1 sprava 165 no. 181.

135 *Borotba*, 14 (17) March 1918.

136 *Izvestiia* (Kyiv)., 3 April 1919. The names of those identified and dismissed as 'enemies' appeared on a 'Black Board,' e.g., on 12 July.

137 *Radianska vlada*, 5 Feb. 1920.
138 TsDAVO, f. 2 op. 1 sprava 447 nos. 1–3.
139 TsDAVO, f. 340 op. 1 sprava 2979 nos. 108, 114; sprava 2980 nos. 7–9; sprava 2983 nos. 1, 38, 44, 190; f. 539 op. 1 sprava 75 no. 80. For its activities in Kherson autumn 1920 see Rubach et al., *Radianske budivnytsvo na Ukraini v roky hromadianskoi viiny*, 848, 856.
140 Rubach et al., *Radianske*, 240, 322, 374, 833.
141 Vasiliev et al., *Politychni represii na Podilli*, 41. Five were Jews, sixw were declared Russians. Of the 430, 140 were cleaners working in hotels run by the committee. TsDAVO, f. 1 op. 1 sprava 164; f. 1 op. 2 sprava 340 no. 81.
142 *Nash shliakh*, 22 May 1920.
143 *Chervonyi stiakh*, 29 July 1919. *Vilna Ukraina*, 18 May 1919. TsDAHO, f. 1 op. 20 sprava 305 no. 57.
144 Andrusyshyn, *U poshukakh*, 98. DASBU f. 69270 vol. 32 p. 82.
145 TsDAVO, f. 2 op. 1 sprava 608 no. 6.
146 TsDAVO, f. 1 op. 2 sprava 470 nos. 1–60; sprava 466 nos. 16–50. TsDAVO, f. 1 op. 1 sprava 190 nos. 1–32; op. 2 sprava 507 no 18. See also TsDAVO, f. 1 op. 1 sprava 152, 153, 154; f. 340 op. 1 sprava 3006. Vynnychenko sympathized with national communism and in 1920 travelled to Ukraine. Disillusioned, he refused to accept a ministerial position. Vynnychenko was married to a Jew and was a judeophile, yet, in conversation after his return, he expressed shock at the predominance of Jews in Kharkiv bureaus and said that as a minister he could hardly carry-out Ukrainian policies with non-Ukrainian personnel. He made no mention of Jews in his later published article which condemns Bolshevism for its centralization, militarization, and Russification. Verstiuk, ed., *Evhen Chykalenko*, 449, 476–84.
147 TsDAVO, f. 1. op. 2 sprava 340 no. 81; f. 340 op. 1 sprava 3011 nos. 9–15; f. 539 op. 1 sprava 13 nos. 187–9; f. 340 op. 1, sprava 3018 nos. 15–216; sprava 3006. Some Soviet forms included place of birth and language. Not many Bolshevik Jews sympathized with Ukrainian national aspirations.
148 It would in theory be possible to determine this because in 1921 the Cheka began registering all government employees who had previously worked for its rival governments. Baiguzin, ed., *Gosudarstvennaia*, 457; Lykho, 'Sovetskaia vlast na mestakh,' 188.
149 Babii, *Ukrainska radianska derzhava*, 101; Maistrenko, *Istoriia moho pokolinnia*, 183. Of Kyiv city employees and workers 41 % were Ukrainian by nationality, 19% used Ukrainian as their first language, 36% were Russian but 62% were Russian-speakers. In Uman , 10% (609) of all workers and public employees were Russians, and 58% (3,706) were Ukrainian; 17% were Russian-speakers and 58% Ukrainian-speakers. Jews comprised

29% (1,848) of the total workforce and 81% (1,489) of them considered Yiddish their first language. The total number of workers here (6,423), excludes 4,234 sugar refinery workers who were not classified by language use. DAKO, f. R708 op. 1 sprava 675 nos. 7, 315.

150 *Naselennia v mistakh Ukrainy*, 49–50, 62–70, 107-09. *Statistyka Truda. Statistyka Ukrainy.* seriia X, tom 1 vyp. 4 no. 58 (Kharkiv, 1925) 2. Of 334,481 government employees, 136,615 were artists, medical personnel, guards, police, firemen, teachers, technical personnel, and retail clerks. The urban industrial proletariat numbered 107,114. The urban population was just over five million, about the same as in 1917: Ukrainians averaged 43%, Russians 27%, and Jews 17%.

151 *Vsesoiuznaia perepis naselennia 1926 g.*, vol. 28, Ukrainian SSR, Chart IV, first six sub-groups of Category VIII *(uchrezhdeniia).* This was a sub-category of *sluzhashchie* which lumped together 750,500 office workers and white-collar professionals with doctors, artists, cooks, guards, and servants. Of these, 84,000 were Russian immigrants posted from the Russian Republic (45% of all the Russians and 10% of the *sluzhashchie* total), 52% were Ukrainians, 17% Jews. Olesevych et al., *Ukrainska liudnist S.S.S.R.*, 79, Table XVI.

152 Pyrih, et al, 'Do istorii mizhnatsionalnykh protsesiv na Ukraini,' 101.

153 Ulianovsky, ed., 'Memuary,' 158, 180.

154 *Golos iuga*, 9 and 29 Aug. 1919. Mironenko et al., *Zhurnal zasedanii*, 537, 811.

155 TsDAHO, f. 1 op. 20 sprava 39 nos. 16, 23, 44. Lawyers in Kyiv established a disciplinary tribunal to determine which of their fellows 'behaved unethically' under Bolshevik rule. *Kievskaia zhizn*, 17 (30) Sept. 1919. TsDAVO, f. 1539 op. 1 sprava 55 no. 19; f. 1682 op. 1 sprava 1 nos. 27, 57 on Bolshevik personnel in Kharkiv province.

156 Smirnova, 'Sotsialnyi portret'; Butakov, *Beloe dvizhenie na iuge Rossii*, 137–40, 165–6; Medvedev, *Politiko-iuridicheskaia sushchnost*, 102–78; Korolivsky et al., *Grazhdanskaia voina*, II: 446.

157 Karpenko, *Belye generaly*, 214.

158 Tatishchev, *Zemli*, 329.

159 *Kievlianin*, 22 Aug. 1919.

160 TsDAVO, f. 1742 op. 4 sprava 7.

161 The core of Denikin's territory were Stavropol and Chornomorsk provinces in Russia. Karpenko, *Belye generaly*, 210–14, 249–51, 281–7.

162 Tatishchev, *Zemli*, 331; Karpenko, 298, 304–5.

163 TsDAHO, f. 1 op. 18 sprava 16 nos. 31v, 55.

164 Tsvetkov, *Belye Armii*, 14, 27, 38. German settlers were the best source of recruits. A surge in rural recruitment in central Ukraine in the autumn of 1920 coincided with Makhno's short-lived alliance with General Wrangel.

165 TsDAVO, f. 2155 op. 1 sprava 30–1; sprava 33 nos. 56–8, 71, 108–10; f. 294 op. 1 sprava 66. Ulianovsky, ed., 'Vadim Shcherbakivsky: Memuary,' 107.

166 Sokolov, *Pravlenie*, 182.

167 Karpenko, *Belye generaly*, 348–54, 359, 392.

168 Ibid., 419.

8 The Western Ukrainian National Republic, November 1918 to October 1920

1 Klimecki, 'Polskie struktury panstwowe w bylym zaborze austriackim. Administracja i wojsko,' in Ajnenkiel, ed., *Rok 1918*, 119; Levytsky, *Velykyi zryv*, 134–5.

2 Within three weeks returned demobilized regulars had increased the total number of troops at the disposition of the new government to roughly 6,000. Chubaty, 'Derzhavnyi lad na Zakhidnyi oblasti,' in Luzhnytsky, Padokh, eds., *U Poshukakh istorychnoi pravdy*, 18; Lytvyn, *Ukrainsko-polska viina*, 44, 74.

3 Krysiak, 30, 136–41; Milinski, *Pulkownik*, 83, 112, 127. Of the city's approximate 100,000 Roman Catholics and 18,000 Polish Greek Catholics, 1,502 volunteered to fight the Ukrainians during the first weeks of November. Of these, 474 were accepted for front-line duty. In mid-November Polish forces listed 3,354 men drawing rations and 1,884 on the front line. Leaders relied on some troops who happened to be in the city and on inexperienced, enthusiastic, teenagers. By chance, an earlier planned congress of Polish youth organizations had brought hundreds of student activists to Lviv just before the coup. In Peremyshl, Ukrainians negotiated with Polish leaders rather than arresting them and failed to blow up the bridge when they could have.

4 Shankovsky, *Ukrainska halytska armiia*, 19–22; Makarchuk, *Ukrainska respublika Halychan*, 134–7. How many of each national group was included in this total is unknown.

5 Austrian census figures classified by religion and language use. Gasowski, 'Struktura narodowosciowa ludnosci miejskiej w autonomicznej Galicji,' 91–105; Pilat, ed., *Wiadomosci statystyczne*, vol. 24, no. 3, pp. 23–4.

6 Misilo, 'Prasa Zachodno-ukrainskiej Republiki Ludowej,' 53–76.

7 Bujak, *Galicja*, I: 71, 131; Ihnatowicz, 'Urzednicy galicyjscy w dobie autonomii,' *Spoleczenstwo polskie XVIII i XIX wieku*, VI (1974) 211. The lowest two categories of officials, which included local post office clerks and guards, comprised 12,700 of the 19,000 officials in all Galicia.

8 For consistent comparisons, judges and lawyers must be included in Galician figures because they are included in tsarist figures. The opening of an Emigration Office in town led to a sharp decline in Ukrainians after 1900. Hoff, 'Podwoloczynska w XIX i pierwszej polowie XX wieku,' 82–3.

9 Pavlyshyn, 'Derzhavne budivnytstvo ZUNR-ZOUNR: Problema natsionalnykh kadriv,' in V. Smolyi, ed., *Tsentralna Rada*, I: 98. TsDAVO, f. 2192 op. 1 sprava 6 nos. 304–6. While Polish conservatives were inclined to co-operate with Ukrainians before the war, the anti-Ukrainian Polish National Democrats (ND or *endecja*) dominated eastern Galician politics during those years. Insofar as nationalism is a theory that calls for cultural and political borders to coincide, Poles who wanted a Polish national state to include Ukrainian lands were, strictly speaking, not 'nationalists' but 'imperialists' or 'expansionists.' The Polish-Ukrainian ethnic border then ran along the San River. Poles justified their claims in historical not ethnic terms.

10 Olesiuk, ' Kamianets,' 95.

11 *Vpered* (Lviv), 26 Jan. 1919. Makukh, *Na narodni sluzhbi*, 228–30, 24; Tsehelsky, *Vid legend do pravdy*, 54–5, 86–9, 111, 126, 174, 209; Chaikovsky, *Chorni riadky*, 18–62.

12 'Derzhavnyi instinkt i metody budivnytsva Ukrainskoi derzhavy,' *Hromadska dumka [Dilo]*, 19–24 July 1920. Skvarka was a National Democrat.

13 Hunczak, ed., *Ukraine and Poland in Documents*, 99, 201–3.

14 Orski, *W zachodniej 'respublice' Ukrainskiej*, 21, 42. An activist who labelled the methods that Ukrainian police used to contain his organization's anti-governmental sabotage and diversion 'terrorism,' also admits that it effectively neutralized its activities in towns and restricted it to organizing in Polish villages. Warezak, 'Polska Organizacja Wojskowa w okregu Tarnopolskim (1918-1919),' 400, 404, 406.

15 Wolczynski, ed., *Nieznana korespondencja arcybiskupow metropolitow Lwowskich Jozefa Bilczewskiego z Andrzejem Szeptyckim*, 164.

16 Shukhevych, *Spomyny*, I: 89–90; Potopnyk, *Pohliadom u mynule*, 112. TsDAVO, f. 3982 op. 1 sprava 11 nos. 7–8.

17 TsDAVO, f. 3982 op. 1 sprava 2.

18 *Zhyttia Podillia*, 30 March 1919.

19 Milinski, *Pulkownik*, 221n.

20 TsDAVO, f. 3982 op. 1 sprava 12 no. 14; sprava 13 nos. 31, 121–2. Karpenko, ed., *Zakhidno-Ukrainska Narodna Respublika*, III: 88, 131–2.

21 Karpenko, ed., *Zakhidno-Ukrainska Narodna Respublika*, II: 375–6, 386–9.

22 Inglot, ed., *Zarys historii Polskiego ruchu spoldzielczego*, I pt. 1: 214–17; Vytanovych, *Istoriia*, 158, 329. Roughly 126,000 Ukrainians also belonged to either one of the 400 state-funded credit unions or the 106 pro-Russian co-ops. All co-ops were open to all nationalities and sometimes belonged to regional unions of other nationalities.

23 Chaikovsky, *Chorni riadky*, 82–2, 114.

24 Przenioslo, *Narodziny*, 188. Karpenko, ed., *Zakhidno-Ukrainska Narodna Respublika* , III: 154–5. Orski reports that peasants not only complained about bribery but also believed that ZUNR officials were paid excessively high wages. *W zachodniej 'respublice,'* 32.

25 Mykytiuk, ed., *Ukrainska halytska armiia*, IV: 41.

26 Birchak, 'Sotsialisty derzhavnymy budivnychymy' no. 11: 792-93; Wiszniewski, *Brzezany i kresy poludniowo-wschodnie rzeczypospolitej Polskiej*, 65–8.

27 *Narod*, 3, 6, and 14 May 1919. Semen Vityk, a Social Democrat in charge of the Petroleum Commission, insisted that he do everything himself and thus had few office workers. Birchak, 'Sotsialisty,' no. 9: 658–62.

28 The loyalties of tens of thousands of Polish-speaking Uniates and Ukrainian-speaking Catholics have not been studied. Memoir literature often refers to fathers, daughters, sons, brothers, and sisters supporting opposite sides during the war. Although both churches had long fought each other over souls, bishops had also promoted mutual respect and urged their priests to put 'God before Caesar' in national matters. Thus, in villages, priests and laity would formally attend each other's feasts. This stopped in the decade before the war, when both churches explicitly identified themselves with two national political parties: the right-wing Polish National Democrat party in the case of the Roman Catholics and the centre-left Ukrainian National Democratic party in the case of the Uniates. Osadczy, 'Stosunki miedzyobrzadkowe a kwestia narodowa w Galicji wschodniej,' 69–102; Osadczy, 'Kler katolicki obu obrzadkow wobec Polsko-Ruskiej rywalizacji w Galicji wschodniej w XIX i XX wieku,' 86–90.

29 Krotofil, *Ukrainska armia*, 59n, 73, 215. Karpenko, ed., *Zakhidno-Ukrainska Narodna Respublika*, I: 375–7, 387–8. At government meetings in May officials learned that even bed linen destined for hospitals was being stolen. Polish intelligence reports attribute this new-found spirit to Bolshevik propaganda which convinced peasant-soldiers that they were fighting a class war, not a national war against Poland. Krotofil, 217.

30 Szczepanski, *Spoleczenstwo Polski w Walce z najazdem Bolszewickim 1920 roku*, 82, 282, 466, 468. Polish peasants identified Polish independence with serfdom and rule by landlords; in eastern Galicia this predisposed them to support the ZUNR. Shukhevych, *Spomyny*, I: 116.

31 Evhen Petrushevych, head of the Ukrainian parliamentary delegation in Vienna before he became the ZUNR president, refused to support an initiative taken in April 1918 to form a military unit to fight with the Entente, as the Czechs and Poles had done; he said it would be dishonourable. Levytsky, *Velykyi zryv*, 53.

32 Prusin, 'War and Nationality Conflict in Eastern Galicia, 1914–1920,' 38–9, 175.

33 Revutsky, *Wrenching Times*, 241.
34 TsDAVO, f. 1092 op. 2 sprava 6 no. 106.
35 Birchak, 'Drohobytska,' *Vistnyk* no. 9 (1931) 1005–9.
36 Tsehelsky, *Vid legend do pravdy*, 87. Before the war these Russophiles or 'Old Ruthenians' were a politically pro-Russian group that competed with Ukrainian national leaders for the political leadership of the eastern Galician peasants.
37 *Respublikanski visti*, 20 and 30 Jan. 1919.
38 Pavlyshyn ' Orhanizatsiia tsyvilnoi vlady ZUNR u povitakh Halychyny,' 147–8; Sonevetska et al., *Istorychno-memuarnyi zbirnyk Chortkivskoi okruhy*, 525–6. Almost all 15,000 Polish teachers in eastern Galicia swore loyalty to the ZUNR – some were urged to do so by Polish activists in the interests of 'Polishness.' Lukomski et al., *Wojna Polsko-Ukrainska*, 101. Of three Polish newspapers in Stanyslaviv, the capital, one (*Glos prawdy*) was pro-ZUNR and a second (*Informator*) was neutral. Misilo, 'Prasa,' 72–3.
39 Mykytiuk, *Ukrainska halytska armiia*, III: 111.
40 Karpenko, ed., *Zakhidno-Ukrainska Narodna Respublika*, I: 3, 39, 136–7. Tyshchyk, *Zakhidno Ukrainska Narodna Respublika*, 242–3.
41 Karpenko, ed., *Zakhidno-Ukrainska Narodna Respublika*, I: 289, 338. As of 8 April all belonging to a social group, '*hromada*,' in the ZUNR were considered to be citizens of the UNR unless they formally notified the government by 20 May that they were citizens of another country (335).
42 Most eyewitness accounts ignore the legal issue and justify refusal to work in terms of patriotic loyalty. More balanced accounts relate that others deferred decisions until they heard from the Liquidation Commission – which they regarded as the legal government. It must also be noted that after two Russian occupations, it is unclear how many pre-1915 officials were still working in 1918. Orski, 18, 28; Wiszniewski, *Brzezany i kresy poludniowowschodnie rzeczypospolitej polskiej*, 77.
43 Krysiak, *Z dni grozy w lwowie*, 36.
44 Przenioslo, ed., *Narodziny*, 177. There are numerous versions of the document. This version is undated. The version cited by Klimecki, cf. no. 33, is dated 29 October.
45 Kuzma, *Lystopadovi dni.*, 325–35. Anti-Ukrainian Poles hoped to win support for their war against the ZUNR from their reluctant countrymen by spreading false reports about Ukrainian atrocities – as later admitted by Lviv's Polish commander Czeslaw Maczynski. Boleslaw Eustachiewicz claimed before a mass audience in Warsaw that he had witnessed Ukrainian atrocities in Lviv that November although he had left the city on 25 October – before the Ukrainians took power. A local Polish official is on record in a Ukrainian

newspaper as expressing amazement at what peaceful and orderly fashion Ukrainians had taken over power. Pavlyshyn, 'Polske naselennia,' 209.

46 Kuzma, *Lystopadovi dni*, 113; *Vpered*, 2 July 1920; Przynioslo, *Narodziny*, 181–4, Wiszniewski, *Brzezany I kresy*, 59–60, 72, 78–80. Pavlyshyn, 'Polske naselennia,' 213, 220, 221. The first to announce monetary support for officials who refused to work was the Polish Committee in Stanyslaviv on 20 November. In one office Ukrainians refused to retain Poles who said they would work if they did not have to take the oath. Orski, *W zachodniej*, 36. The author does not indicate if this was organized by the Liquidation Commission.

47 Orski, 28.

48 Karpenko, ed., 387–8.

49 Chaikovksy, 19.

50 Krysiak, *Z dni grozy w lwowie*, 36–7.

51 Prznioslo, ed., *Narodziny*, 184–5, 195–6; Adamczyk, 'Zachidnoukrainska Republika Ludowa,' Mankowski, ed., *Niepodleglosc Polski*, 193; Kuzma, *Lystopadovi dni 1918 r.*, 247.

52 TsDAVO, f. 3982 op. 1 sprava 11 no. 8; sprava 12 no. 15.

53 The major anti-Ukrainian group was the Polish Military Organization (PWO) which in February 1919 numbered approximately 2,900. Pavlyshyn, 'Polske naseleniia,' 227; Pavlyshyn , 'Orhanizatsiia,' 167; 'Ukrainski uriadovtsi pered sudom,' *Vpered*, 5, 10, and 11 July 1920. Estimates of the number of interned Poles range from 2,000 to between 3,000 and 25,000. Pavlyshyn, 'Polske naseleniia,' 235; Lukomski et al., 96.

54 Kachor, 'Rolia dukhovenstva i tserkvy v ekonomichnomu vidrozhenni zakhidnoi Ukrainy,' in Baran, Gerus, eds., *Zbirnyk tysiacholittia khrystianstva v Ukraini*, 103–9; Krochmal, 'Przemiany wewnetrze w kosciele Greckokatolickim w Galicji w drugiej polowie XIX wieku,' 69–74. A. Kolodny et al., *Istoriia relihii v Ukraini* IV: 401, 421.

55 A partial list in Mykytiuk, ed., *Ukrainska halytska armiia*, I: 306–7.

56 By the end of the Russian occupation thirteen Jewish administrators and fifty-five other employees of an original 700 in the region remained at their jobs, and these were fired when the Austrians returned. Prusin, 'War and Nationality Conflict,' 125, 165, 170.

57 Mahler, 'Jews in Public Service and the Liberal Professions,' 305; Wrobel, 'Barucha Mikcha Galicyjskie wspomnienia wojenne 1914–1920,' 96.

58 Wiszniewski, *Brzezany*, 111. Orski, *W zachodniej*, 16, 29. Orski was decidedly anti-Ukrainian and did not approve of Jewish behaviour. It is unclear if he was referring to the entire country or only to his own town. Zhydachiv, Przenioslo, eds. *Narodziny*, 187, 190.

59 Revutsky, *Wrenching Times*, 242. The Jewish National Council's decision to formally recognize the ZUNR in May 1919 came too late to influence events. Hon, '"Ievreiska vulytsia" Zakhidnoukrainskoi narodnoi respubliki,' 258.

60 Goldelman, *Lysty*, 28. Karpenko, ed., *Zakhidno-Ukrainska Narodna Respublika*, III: 153.

61 Adamczyk, 'Zachidnoukrainska Republika Ludowa 1918–1919,' 194; Klimecki, *Polsko-Ukrainska wojna o Lwow i Galicje wschodnia*, 112; Pohrebynska, Hon, *Evreii v zakhidnoukrainskyi narodnyi respublitsi*, 46. Sobczak, *Stosunek narodowej demokracji do kwestii Zydowskiej w Polsce*, 86–9. TsDAVO, f. 1 op. 1 sprava 124 no. 57v.

62 With the collapse of the ZUNR that May, the section dismissed all its employees. TsDAVO, f. 2192 op. 2 sprava 9 nos. 23–5, 52–5, 79, 90; sprava 13 no. 2. Three of the four signatures are legible: Lydia Hryhorovych, Halyna Mandzyi, and Teodoziia Hiushkevych. TsDAVO, f. 2192 op. 1 sprava 6 no. 117.

63 Hunczak, ed., *Ukraine and Poland in Documents*, vol. 2, p. 131.

64 Tyshchyk, *Halytska*, 70, 164, 181. In western Ukraine, unlike in Poland, the Bolsheviks sent poor Polish peasants to the army instead of giving them land. Szczepanski, 347.

65 Kolodyi, *Halytska*, 8, 10, 12–16. Ukrainian Communists within the Galician republic who wanted it to be part of Soviet Ukraine were a minority. For party discussion concerning its status see TsDAVO, f. 2 op. 1 sprava 124 nos. 3, 21–5. Contemporary reports claimed that the Poles Litwinowicz, Gubert, and Sawka dominated the revkom. Most Poles were from tsarist Russian Poland, were as anti-Ukrainian as their Russian comrades, and wanted western Ukraine annexed to a Communist Poland. Whereas Ukrainians had to follow the three official languages regulation in their work, the Poles and Jews ignored it without censure and used only Polish. *Ukrainska Dumka*, 13, 14, 17, 19, and 20 Oct. 1920.

66 TsDAVO, f. 2997 op. 1 sprava 98.

67 TsDAVO, f. 2189 op. 1 sprava 2 nos. 1–2; sprava 31 nos. 25, 28; sprava 9 nos. 1–2.

68 TsDAVO, f. 2997 op. 1 sprava 66 nos. 6–11.

69 TsDAVO, f. 2189 op. 1 sprava 33; op. 2 sprava 4. Today the personnel lists of the various Galician governments are all in different cities and would be difficult to compare with each other.

70 Tyshchyk, *Halytska*, 168–9; Sonevetska et al., *Istorychno-memuarnyi zbirnyk*, 295, 532; Hirniak, *Ostanyi akt*, 225–6, 235–6.

9 Bureaucrats in Other New European Governments

1 Hantsch, *Die Nationalitatenfrage im alten Osterreich*, 25–35, 116–17; Culen, *Cesi a Slovaci v statnych sluzbach CSR*, 19–21. The pre-war census recorded language use not national identity, and ignored bilingualism. National affiliation should be linked to the level of education and whether place of residence was urban or rural, as well as to language use.

2 Zeman, *The Break-up of the Habsburg Empire*, 50–7. As of 1918 Czech and German Masons began to cooperate for the first time, but, like Austrian Masons, they do not appear to have played a significant role in events or staffing. Hass, *Ambicje*, 140–1.

3 Opocensky, *The Collapse of the Austro-Hungarian Monarchy and the Rise of the Czechoslovak State*; Shmeral, *Obrazovanie chekhoslovatskoi respubliki*, 136–66, 202–39.

4 Bakke, *Doomed to Failure? The Czechoslovak Nation Project and the Slovak Autonomist Reaction*, 408–11; Glaser, *Czecho-slovakia A Critical History*, 17–29; Wiskemann, *Czechs and Germans*, 126.

5 Birmingham [pseud. J. O. Hannay], *Irishmen All*, 25, 27.

6 Paseta, *Before the Revolution: Nationalism, Social Change and Ireland's Catholic Elite*, 94–7, 119–34. Part of the nationalist argument was that the British educational system contributed to Irish backwardness because it was geared to producing clerks rather than technicians.

7 Hutchinson, *The Dynamics of Cultural Nationalism*, 262–79.

8 Garvin, 'Great Hatred, Little Room: Social Background and Political Sentiment among Revolutionary Activists in Ireland 1890–1920,' in Boyce, ed., *The Revolution in Ireland*, 104–5.

9 McColgen, *British Policy and the Irish Administration*, 70; McBride, *The Greening of Dublin Castle*, 21–2, 190, 262, 276, 287, 302–9. Fitzpatrick, 'The Geography of Irish Nationalism, 1910–1921,' in Philpin, ed., *Nationalism and Popular Protest in Ireland*, 403–40; Jeffery, 'British Security Policy in Ireland,' in Collins ed., *Nationalism and Unionism: Conflict in Ireland*, 163–75.

10 Macardle, *The Irish Republic*, 349–50.

11 Mitchell, *Revolutionary Government in Ireland*; Laffan, *The Resurrection of Ireland*, 305–8, 320, 321; Hopkinson, *The Irish War of Independence*, 43–5.

12 McBride, *The Greening of Dublin Castle*, 218, 262, 275

13 Cited in Mitchell, *Revolutionary Government*, 203.

14 McColgan, *British Policy*, 32, 100, 132–6.

15 Correspondence with Mary E. Daly, University College Dublin, Sept. 2002.

16 Bardach, ed., *Historiia panstwa i prawa Polski*, IV: 533, 551; Dworecki, 'Ksztaltowanie sie polskich struktur panstwowych w bylym zaborze pruskim,' in Ajnenkiel, ed., *Rok 1918: Odrodzona Polska w Europie*, 83–5.

17 Micinska, *Zdrada. Corka Nocy. Pojecie zdrady narodowej,* 168–75.

18 Chwalba, *Polacy w sluzbie moskali,* 74–87. Stanislaw Krzeminski and Jozef Potocki opposed collaborating; Erazm Piltz and Zygmunt Wielopolski argued in favour.

19 Geifman, *Thou Shalt Kill,* 25–7.

20 Tych, ed., *PPS-Lewica 1906–1918: Materialy i dokumenty,* I: 14; Pobog-Malinowski, *Jozef Pilsudski,* II: 325, 405–6, 427, 506–7. Geifman, *Thou Shalt Kill,* using Russian police archives, refers to a Polish terrorist organization uncovered by police before it could realize its objective of assassinating 'traitors' – a category that could have included Polish Catholic officials. Polish sources contain no references to the *Zwiazek robotniczy narodowy.*

21 Chajn, *Polskie wolnomularstwo,* 100–2, 118–23, 130, 175; Hass, *Masoneria Polska XX wieku,* 32, 51–5; Hass, *Ambicje,* 153–4.

22 Hantsch, *Die Nationalitatenfrage,* Chapter 1.

23 Gorizontow, 'Aparat urzednicy Krolewstwa Polskiego w okresie rzadow Paszkiewicza,' 45–6, 49, 50–2, 56; Rzepniewska, 'Wiejscy oficialisci,' in Kula, ed., *Spoleczenstwo krolewstwa polskiego,* I: 228–34.

24 Berghauzen, 'Z badan nad skladem spolecznym i ideologia organizacji spiskowych w Krolestwie Polskim w latach 1835–1846,' in Kieniewicz et al., *Z epoki Mickiewicza,* 165–8. Between 1833 and 1862 4,037 persons were arrested – approximately 0.5% of Russian Poland's total population; 6% were priests, and 6% were private estate administrators.

25 Caban, 'Urzednicy administracji panstwowej a powstanie styczniowe,' in Czepulis-Rastenis, ed., *Inteligencja Polska XIX i XX wieku,* 170.

26 Chwalba, *Polacy w sluzbie moskali,* 17–19; Day, *The Russian Government in Poland,* 169; Kieniewicz, *Powstanie styczniowe,* 554.

27 Kozlowski, 'Urzednicy polscy Krolestwie Kongresowym po powstaniu styczniowym (do 1880 r.),' in Szwarc, Wieczorkiewicz, eds., *Unifikacja za wszelka cen,* 79, 81–2.

28 Wiech, Caban, eds., *Sytuacja polityczna Krolewstwa Polskiego s swietle tajnych raportow naczelnikow warszawskiego okregu zandarmerii* , 181, 290.

29 Wiech, *Spoleczenstwo krolestwa polskiego w oczach carskiej policiji politycznej,* 227, 239, 244–5. Czepulis-Rastenis, *'Klasa umyslowa': Inteligencja Krolestwa Polskiego,* 71.

30 Sadowski, *Polska inteligencja prowincjonalna i jej ideowe dylematy,* 78–87; Chwalba, *Polacy w sluzbie,* 64–74, 244; Nikharadze, 'The World of Imperial Provincial Bureaucracy: Russian Poland, 1870–1904,' 40, 76.

31 Kozicki, *Historia ligi narodowej,* 569–88, lists approximately 700 party members. Of the roughly 600 identified by occupation and who joined before 1919, eighteen were administrators. ND leaders before the war intentionally kept their party small, and its influence cannot be judged in terms of its

size – 500 in Prussian Poland in 1911. Their preferred method of organizing sympathizers was to recruit them into ostensibly non-political 'front groups' whose combined memberships were in the thousands. Marczewski, *Narodowa Demokracja w poznanskiem*, 323.

32 Latawiec, 'Ewakuacja cywilnej administracji ... latem 1915,' 168, notes that sixteen of 160 office staffers at the district level remained behind in Lublin province. Polish Russophile sentiment was strong until the Bolshevik revolution. Hupka, *Z czasow, wielkiej wojny*, 155, 189, 268. Bobrzynski, *Wskrzeszenie panstwa Polskiego*, I: 145.

33 Chwalba, *Polacy*, 35–7, 126–44, 238; Jaszkiewicz, *Carat i sprawy Polskie*, 61–7.

34 Full English translation in Day, *Russian Government in Poland*, 9–13.There is no known original Polish version of the text. Polish translations were later made from an alleged Russian translation that first appeared in correspondence to the Russian governor general in March 1863.

35 The government banned the book in 1834. It was republished abroad, but those Poles who could read preferred to read Mickiewicz's other better known works. Kopczynski, *Mickiewicz i jego czytelnicy*.

36 Kieniewicz, *Powstanie styczNowie*, 754; Libera, ed., *'Konrad Wallenrod' Adama Mickiewicza*, 71.

37 Day, *Russian Government in Poland*, 7.

38 Micinska, *Zdrada*, 210; Kuplowski, ed., *Iwan Franko O literaturze polskiej*, 70–3.

39 Chimiak, *Gubernatorzy Rosyjscy w krolestwie polskim*, 193, 208, 231, 251; Heflich, 'Walka o czytelnie Warsawskiego Towarzystwa Dobroczynosci,' 343–8.

40 Pajak, *Konspiracyjne zycie polityczne w Staropolskim Okregu Przemyslowym*, 33–5, 41–2, 72–3, 136–8, 179, 196, 231–6. The ND, legal after 1905, had thirty-one 'circles' (*kolo*) in the region. If we assume an average membership of twelve per circle this would mean a total of between 300 and 400 ND members.

41 See n13 above; Homola, ed., *Pamietniki urzednikow galicyjskich*, 20–1. Bujak, *Galicya*, 185.

42 *Galitsiia: Vremennyi voennyi general-gubernator.* Prilozhenie 1, 7–17; Bobrzynski, *Wskrzeszenie panstwa Polskiego*, I: 18–19, 42–5, 77. Petrovych, *Halychyna*, 114.

43 Birchak, 'Drohobytska Epopeia,' no. 7-8, (1931) 618.

44 Spiss, *Ze Wspomnien C.K. Urzednika Politycznego*, 19, 59–60, 81–2, 97–103. In response to Austrian arguments that Polish independence would mean serfdom for peasants, Polish priests in their sermons claimed that only a Polish administration would give peasants' justice.

45 E.R. Burke, 'Polish Policy of the Central Powers during the World War,' Ph.D. Dissertation (University of Chicago, 1936) 60.

46 Suleja, *Tymczasowa Rada Stany*, 172–8.

47 Lewandowski, *Krolestwo Polskie pod okupacja austriacka*, 26, 98, 112, 118; Lewandowski, 'Budowa panstwa polskiego przed listopadem 1918 roku,' in Mankowski, ed., *Niepodleglosc Polski*, 17; Lewandowski, 24; Pajewski, *Odbudowa panstwa polskiego*, 90, 236. By chance, a Pole was on duty when Czernin's telegram about the treaty arrived in Vienna and he made its terms known.

48 Spiss, *Ze wspomnien*, 104

49 Lasocki, *Wspomnienia szefa administracji*, 14, 67.

50 Przenioslo, ed., *Narodziny*, 25. Zarnowski, *Struktura spoleczna inteligencji w Polsce*, 207.

51 Kozyra, 'Urzad wojewodzki w Lublinie,' 141, 154. In February 1920 at least twenty-five of the province's sixty officials had worked either for the tsar or the emperor.

52 Przenioslo, ed., *Narodziny*, 147–9.

53 Wojciechowski, *Powrot Pomorza do Polski*, 145, 176–8; Stazewski, 'Problem pozostania urzednikow niemieckich w Wielkopolsce i na Pomorzu w latach 1919–1920,' 59–81.

54 Bobrzynski, *Wskrzeszenie*, II: 128–33; Hupka, *Z czasow*, 415–16, 419, 404.

55 Cited in N. Stone, 'An Englishman in Old Poland,' *The Spectator*, 11 July (1987) 15.

56 Zarnowski, *Struktura spoleczna inteligencji*, 183–5.

57 Landau, Tomaszewski, *Gospodarka Polski miedzywojennej 1918–1939*, I: 117, 122, 124–6.

58 Korostowetz, 68.

59 *Piast*, 2 March (1919) 9.

60 Borzyszkowski, Hauser, *Sejm Rzeczypospolitej o Pomorzu 1920 roku*, 6.

61 Karpinski, *Pamietnik dziesieciolecia*, 260.

62 Korostowetz, *The Rebirth of Poland*, 29, 51.

63 Micinska, *Zdrada: Corka Nocy*, 166, 173, 188–90.

64 Spiss, *Ze wspomnien*, 4.

65 Ibid., 104–5.

66 Lasocki, 15. This reference does not specify nationality. It is at odds with Spiss's assertion that one reason that people supported independence was because Polish administrators had helped soften the effects of wartime requisitioning. Spiss, 94–5.

67 Molenda, *Chlopi Narod Niepodleglosc*, 216–66, 355–7.

68 Przenioslo, ed., *Narodziny*, 141–6, 149–50, 166–7, 219–25. Krotofil, *Ukrainska armia*, 59n3. Szczepanski, *Spoleczenstwo Polski*, 144, 233, 282.

69 Kania, *W cieniu Orlat Lwowskich*, 237-41.

70 Szczepanski, *Spoleczenstwo Polski*, 311, 328–32; decrees are reproduced at 315. Brzoz, Rolinski, eds., *Rok 1920*, Appendix.

71 Szczepanski, 368–9, 388, 417. In Belorussian lands Orthodox administrators and peasants willingly staffed Bolshevik offices (395–6).

72 *Robitnycha gazeta*, 20 Sept. 1919. TsDAVDO, f. 1113c op. 2 sprava 74 no. 23.

73 Szczepanski, 136; Chwalba, *Polacy*, 244; Chekanovsky, 'Ohliad mizhnarodnoi polityky,' *Volia. Tyzhnevyk*, vol. 1, no. 10 (1920) 501; Zielinska, 'Postawy mieszkancow Wolynia w czasie wojny polsko-bolszewickiej,' in Kolodziejczyk, ed., *Spoleczenstwo polskie w dobie I wojny swiatowej i wojny polsko-bolszewickiej*, 278–9.

74 Stempowski, 'Ukraina (1919–1920),' 85; Hunczak, ed., I: 200. During the Austrian occupation Vienna refused Ukrainian demands to send Ukrainian administrators from Galicia to Volyn and instead sent Polish officials.

75 Medrzecki, *Wojewodztwo wolynskie 1921–1939*, 22, 25, 121. Local landowners who had staffed the administration before 1921 resigned en masse afterwards in protest at Warsaw's land policy.

76 The council published a newsletter: *Dziennik Rozporzadzen Generalnego Delegata Rzadu dla Galicyi*. Karpenko, ed., *Zakhidno-Ukrainska Respublika*, III: 11, 32–6, 107–18, 132, 159–62. See also *Krivava knyha Chastyna II: Ukrainska Halychyna pid okupatsieiu Polshchi*.

77 *Vpered* (Lviv), 13 March 1919. *Nash Shliakh*, 10 July 1920.

78 Klimecki, 'Polskie struktury panstwowe w bylym zaborze austriackim. Administracja i wojsko,' 126–7. Instructions to local governors issued in May 1919 on the treatment of Ukrainians made no mention of leaving administrators at their posts until further notice. Hunczak, ed., I: 131.

79 Polish troops paid Ukrainian civilian employees in Ukrainian money and Poles in Polish money. Hupka, *Z czasow*, 428.

80 Megas, *Tragediia Halytskoi Ukrainy*, 166, 220. The first oath is reproduced at 140. *Krivava knyha Chastyna I: Materiialy do Polskoi invazii na Ukrainski zemli Skhidnoi Halychyny*, 85–6; *Krivava knyha: Chastyna II*, 12–15, 135. The second volume does not mention forcing oaths. Szczepanski, *Spoleczenstwo Polski*, 468. By 1920 the Poles had interned approximately 25,000 Ukrainians. Lukomski et al., *Wojna*, 100. Ukrainians claimed there were 250,000. *Krivava knyha: Chastyna I*, 5.

81 Ukrainian newspapers closely followed government hiring throughout 1920 in the wake of the Ukrainian-Polish alliance. *Vpered*, 14, 16, and 23 Jan.; 4 and 19 Feb.; 6 June; 11 and 13 Aug; *Zemlia i volia*, 13 June 1920.

82 Lukomski, *Wojna*, 101; *Dziennik Ludowy*, 28 Dec. 1921.

83 Dudiak, 'Dynamika natsionalnoho skladu sluzhbovtsiv administratyvnykh organiv skhidnoi Halychyny u mizhvoiennyi period,' 367–8.

84 Ibid., 254, 259; *American Jewish Yearbook*, vol. 22 (1920–1921) (Philadelphia, 1920) vol. 21: 252; vol. 23: 186.

85 Ibid, 22: 244, 260.

86 While the major leaders supported equal hiring in principle, rank-and-file politicians publically drew attention pro-German, pro-Austrian, or Bolshevik Jews. Lewin, *A History of Polish Jewry*, 105–9, 126–7, 189. Mahler, 'Jews in Public Service,' 301–7; Dudiak, 'Dynamika,' 368.

Conclusion

1 Demydenko, ed., *Velykyi ukrainets*, 157.
2 *Narodnia volia*, 25 March (7 April) 1918.
3 Mazepa, *Ukraina v ohni i buri revoliutsii*, I: 18.
4 TsDAVO, f. 1530 op.1 sprava 1 no. 67.
5 TsDAVO, f. 3305 op.2 sprava 10 no. 2.
6 TsDAVO, f. 1092 op. 3 sprava 273 no. 23; f. 2198 op. 2 sprava 37, 47, 56.
7 TsDAVO, f. 3305 op. 1 sprava 17; the sample included eleven women.
8 TsDAVO, f. 3305 op. 1 sprava 20; the writing in the original is indistinct, and my rendering of Kolb-Stetskyi's name may be incorrect. TsDAVO, f. 1092 op. 2 sprava 362 no. 9.
9 *Zhyttia Podillia*, 18 April 1919.
10 Cited in Kulchytsky, *Shabli*, 213n3.
11 TsDAVO, f. 2155 op. 1 sprava 33 no. 307.
12 TsDAVO, f. 543 op. 1,sprava 28 nos. 1–13. Two of them began working in 1904 and 1905. *Vpered* (Kyiv), 27 Feb. 1919.
13 Kovalchuk, *Nevidoma viina*, 460. DASBU, f. FP74554 vols. 7, 13, 14. They belonged to the so-called *Kozacha Rada*. DASBU, f. FP73878 vol. 2 no. 43.
14 TsDAVO, f. 1062 op. 2 sprava 60; f. 2208 op. 4 sprava 9 no. 44. DAKO, f. R2797 op. 1 sprava 133 no. 132.
15 Poletika, *Videnno*e, 91, 161.
16 Hrushevsky, 'Spomyny,' *Kyiv*, no. 10 (1989) 122. This reluctance is curious in view ofthe attempt of Generals Alexiev and Dukhonin to prevent the dissolution of the army by agreeing to its Ukrainianization.
17 Khrystiuk, *Zamitky*, IV: 147–50, 172.
18 Cf chap.1, DASBU, f. FP69270 vol. 31, pp. 7–8.
19 TsDAVO, f. 2796 op. 1 sprava 16 no. 30.
20 TsDAVO, f. 528 op. 1 sprava 41 no. 294.
21 Sidak, ed., *Vyzvolni zmahannia*, 49.
22 TsDAVO, f. 1 op. 2 sprava 126, nos. 44–5. These figures were compiled by the commission assigned to reduce the size of the Soviet bureaucracy. Its pre-1917 total included police and guards, while its 1921 total of 1,351 did not include either them or the administrative staffs of the local Soviet Land, Health, and Education ministries.

23 TsDAVO, f. 2 op. 1 sprava 232 no. 201. This original telegram has a marginal note indicating that it was received in code. The published version does not mention this. Lenin, *Polnoe Sobranie Sochinennia,* 50: 324; 51: 245–6.

24 Sakharov et al., *Obshchestvo i vlast,* 81–8.

25 TsDAVO, f. 1113 op. 2 sprava 200 no. 4.

26 TsDAVO, f. 1092 op. 2 sprava 76 no. 199. TsDAHO, f. 8 op. 1 sprava 40 no. 61.

27 Borman, 'Moskva – 1918,' 140–2.

28 TsDAHO, f. 1 op. 20 sprava 1276 and 1308 no. 54. Bread prices had fallen from 900,000 roubles for a pound of white bread in March, to 125,000 roubles in May. Starvation and cannibalism existed in rural Zaporizhzhia province into 1923 (nos. 71, 67).

29 Adams, *The Bolsheviks,* 329–31, 339.

30 Kovalchuk, *Nevidoma viina,* 47, 82, 95, 99; Legiec, *Armia,* 22–3; Shankovsky, *Ukrainska,* 58, 168, 194, 199–202. Shankovsky had no access to reliable Soviet figures. In the Red Army only the commissars, who had the authority to shoot to kill at their discretion were well armed, clothed, and fed – which resulted in intense dissatisfaction among the rank and file. TsDAHO, f. 1 op. 20 sprava 39 no. 8; sprava 20 nos. 58–60 contains a complaint by mobilized Bolshevik sympathizers about their horrible conditions of service in 1919. While Ukrainian troops were perhaps more seriously handicapped by shortages of supplies than were their enemies, this was balanced by the latter's need to divert troops to fight strong partisan forces.

31 Martyniuk, *Selianstvo Ukrainy,* 236, 238. Alongside regular troops the Bolsheviks had special Cheka troops whose numbers had risen from 11,000 in December 1918 to 68,000 by December 1920. Baiguzin, ed., *Gosudarsvennaia bezopastnost Rossii,* 361, 380.

32 Osipova, *Rossiiskoe krestianstvo,* 322. *Trudova hromada,* 2 May 1919. TsDAVO, f. 2 op. 2 sprava 293 no. 152.

33 Like the others who sought by association to garner some of Makhno's immense popularity General Wrangel also attempted to come to terms. Although refused, however, he pretended that he did have an alliance. White propaganda disseminated the lie, and Wrangel thus enjoyed a sudden flood of Ukrainian peasants into his army in the autumn of 1919. Makhno's attitude towards the Whites was ambiguous as he executed some of his commanders who allied with them but not others. Verstiuk, *Makhnovshchyna,* 258–9.

34 Because it was well supplied it did not requisition, which won them the support of Ukrainian peasants who bitterly condemned the requisitioning of the Ukrainian army and non-Haller Polish forces. TsDAHO, f. 9 op. 1 sprava 28 nos. 22–3.

35 TsDAHO, f. 5 op. 1 sprava 21 no. 94; he also noted that a number of his former prisoners became Bolshevik committee chairmen.

36 *Zhyttia Podillia,* 8 March 1919.

37 Frenkin, *Zakhvat vlasti,* 339–41.

38 Originally published in *Izvestiia Iuga* in an article supporting the short-lived Rih Republic: TsDAHO, f. 5 op. 1 sprava 258 nos. 237–41.

39 Tsvetkov, *Belye armii,* 51–2; Hrynevych, *Istoriia,* 245–7.

40 The *Vzgliad na polozheniia na Ukraine* was printed by the Kyiv branch of the Ukrainian Communist Party in connection with the party's bid for Comintern membership; TsDAVO, f. 2 op. 1 sprava 564 nos. 32–3.

Appendix 3 Daily Life

1 Danilov, ed., *Nestor Makhno,* 775.

2 Narskii, *Zhizn v katastrofe: Budni naseleniia Urala.*

3 Kravchenko, *I Chose Freedom,* 23.

4 Boiko et al., *Dzherela,* V bk. 1, pt. 1: 276, 282, 287, 292.

5 DAKO, f. 2794 op. 1 sprava 45 nos. 125, 136; f. 2797 op. 1 sprava 98 no. 79.

6 TsDAVO, f. 1115 op.1 sprava 46 no. 14, 62 (based on personal observations in the 28 towns of Lebedivka povit).

7 DAKO, f. 2797 op. 1 sprava 127 nos. 7, 9, 11, 33, 77.

8 TsDAVO, f. 1682 op. 1 sprava 1 no. 57.

9 Volkov, ed., *1918 god na Ukraine,* 273–4.

10 Pavliuchenkov, *Voennyi kommunizm,* 124. As of 1919 peasants normally sympathized with soviets and Bolshevism which they identified with the slogans of 1917, and did not link with Communists, who they identified with terror, requisitions, and collective farms.

11 Dotsenko, *Litopys Ukrainskoi revoliutsii,* II, bk. 4: 326.

12 Kostorovetz, *Seed and Harvest,* 316–37.

13 Kovalchuk, *Nevidoma viina 1919 roku,* 363.

14 *Narodnia volia,* 17 April 1918.

15 TsDAVO, f. 1 op. 20 sprava 21 no. 53.

16 Danilov, ed., *Nestor Makhno,* 796.

17 *Zhyttia Podillia,* 9 Feb. 1919.

18 DAKO, f. R2976 op. 1 sprava 24 no. 6.

19 Danilov, ed., *Nestor Makhno,* 442.

20 Chop, 'Makhnovsky rukh,' 119. Belash and Belash, *Dorogi Nestora Makhno,* 466.

21 Belenkin, *Avantiuristy velikoi smuty,* 187–215.

22 Danilov, ed., *Nestor Makhno,* 133.

23 *Pridneprovskii krai*, 27 Nov. (10 Dec.) 1918
24 TsDAVO, f. 1 op. 20 sprava 642 no. 210v.
25 Tyrras, ed., *Letters*, 299, 337.
26 *Narodne slovo*, 12 (27) Sept. 1917.
27 TsDAVO, f. 1434 op. 1 sprava 4 no. 8.
28 TsDAHO, f. 5 op. 1 sprava 258 no 8. From an unsigned report by the Directory Investigative Committee that examined former Hetmanate officials.
29 Ulianovsky, ed., 'Memuary,' 120.
30 TsDAHO, f. 1 op. 18 sprava 16 nos. 50, 55v, 83; sprava 26 16, 35.
31 Dotsenko, *Litopys*, II, pt. 4: 324.
32 Cited in Sidak, ed., *Vyzvolni zmahannia*, 35. Tobacco is *tiutiun* in Ukrainian, *tabak* in Russian.
33 Volkov-Muromets, *Iunost ot Viazmy do Feodosii*, 216, 271–2. 'Ukrainians from Austria' refers to the Austrian-uniformed western Ukrainian troops in the Directory's army.
34 *ARR*, XVIII: 150–1.
35 Belash, *Dorogi*, 410.
36 TsDAHO, f. 1 op. 20 sprava 39 no. 52. Prisoners did not enjoy their stay long as they were usually shot within three days.
37 TsDAVO, f. 2207 op. 5 sprava 10; f. 2208c op. 6 sprava 6.
38 *Promin*, 22 Feb. 1919. TsDAVO, f. 2207 pt. 5; f. 2207 op. 5 sprava 8.
39 TsDAVO, f. 2208c op. 6 sprava 34; sprava 35.
40 Poletika, *Videnno*e, 197. TsDAVO, f. 1216 op. 1 sprava 71 no. 240.
41 Chykalenko, *Uryvky z spohadiv z rokiv 1919–1920*, 56.
42 Heifetz, ed., *The Slaughter of the Jews*, 274; Kossak, *The Blaze*, 270; 'Bytovoi dokument,' *Na chuzhoi storone*, VII (1924) 185.
43 TsDAVO, f. 1115 op. 1 sprava 48 nos. 148, 150, 152.
44 TsDAHO, f. 5 op. 1 sprava 21 no. 20.
45 *Russkaia zhizn*, 21 Oct. 1917.
46 *Vilnyi holos*, 1 (19) June 1918.
47 *Zhyttia Podillia*, 9 Feb. 1919; *Novyi shliakh*, 19 June 1920.
48 TsDAVO, f. 538 op. 1 sprava 89 no. 191. The problem appears to have been distributing the millions of sacks that were in the country rather than an actual shortage. As of December 1918 there were five million in a depot in Poltava. TsDAVO, f. 2198 op. 1 sprava no. 148.
49 Sidak, ed., *Vyzvolni zmahannia*, 53.
50 TsDAHO, f. 1 op. 20 sprava 328 no. 140.
51 Zdorov, *Ukrainskyi zhovten*, 158–9.
52 TsDAVO, f. 1216 op 1 sprava 71 nos. 145, 219, 245, 293.
53 Tatishchev, *Zemli*, 327.

54 TsDAVO, f. 59 op. 1 sprava 552 no. 9.
55 DAKO, f. R1 op. 1 sprava 93 nos. 5–6, 131.
56 DAKO, f. R1 op. 1 sprava 284, no. 23; sprava 285 no 9; f. R111 op. 1 sprava 61 no. 342.
57 TsDAVO, f. 2192 op. 1 sprava 6 no. 115.
58 TsDAHO, f. 1 op. 20 sprava 21 nos. 142, 166.
59 DAKO, f. R1 op. 1 sprava 93 no. 10.
60 TsDAHO, f. 1 op. 20 sprava 21 no. 14.
61 Nazhivin, *Zapiski o revoliutsii,* 157. Golitsyn gives another variant in his memoirs – written during the 1940s (214). There, the fearful peasants from a village near Kharkiv sent a delegation to the military asking them to remove the sentry and promising in the future to ignore agitators telling them to refuse requisitions. I am grateful to Ernest Gyidel for access to his copy of the memoirs.
62 Verstiuk, ed., *Evhen Chykalenko,* 57.
63 TsDAHO, f. 1 op. 20 sprava 17 no. 167; sprava 19 nos. 42–3.
64 TsDAHO, f. 1 op. 20 sprava 1308 no. 40.
65 TsDAVO, f. 2 op. 1 sprava 252, nos. 33v, 35, 36, 38v; sprava 241 no. 84,
66 Sidak, ed., *Vyzvolni zmahannia,* 47, 95; Vynnychenko, *Vidrodzhennia,* III: 355–6.
67 TsDAVO, f. 538 op. 1 sprava 116 no. 16. The clerk referred to the telegram as 'kruto napysanno.'
68 Sosiura, *Tretia rota,* 181–3.
69 Mazepa, *Ukraina,* II: 221.
70 TsDAHO, f. 269 op. 1 sprava 39 no. 24.
71 TsDAHO, f. 1 op. 20 sprava 643 nos. 12–15, 60.
72 Pavliuchenkov, *Voennyi kommunizm.*
73 Ulianovsky, ed., 'Memuary,' 150.
74 Miliakova, ed., *Kniga pogromov,* 223, 229, 285, 353–6.
75 Mazepa, *Ukraina,* II: 228. Verstiuk, ed., *Evhen Chykalenko,* 220–21. A train trip from Kharkiv to Kyiv that took 16 hours in 1914 took 16 days in 1919.
76 Mykytiuk, ed., *Ukrainska halytska armiia,* II: 218. Major Ernest Leder's report was originally published in *Revue Internationale de la Croix Rouge,* no. 13 (1920).
77 *Den* (Kyiv), 23 May 1920; *Slovo,* 14 Oct. 1920.
78 TsDAVO, f. 1092 op. 2 sprava 165 nos. 312–17. To deal with the situation in the absence of funding, the Directory commissar begged the local rich Jews to pay for cleaning – which they refused to do until he arrested some of their representatives, publically beat them in front of the town hall, and then threatened to jail all the representatives as traitors unless they contributed.

79 TsDAVO, f. 3982 op. 1 sprava 2 no. 32.
80 Danilov, ed., *Nestor Makhno*, 796.
81 Ulianovsky, ed., 'Memuary,' 111.
82 *Nova Rada*, 27 March (9 April) 1917.
83 Verstiuk, ed., *Evhen Chykalenko*, 377.
84 Korostowetz, *The Rebirth of Poland*, 218.
85 TsDAVO, f. 1092 op. 2 sprava 73 no. 80. While saying 'this is what you'll get,' he raised his fist with his thumb between his index and forefinger.
86 DAKO, f. R1 op. 1 sprava 283 no. 31.
87 DASBU, f. 73878 vol. 2, 10v.

Appendix 4 Prices and Wages

1 *Goroda Rossii v 1904 goda*, (1906) 450–1.
2 TsDAVO, f. 1716 op. 2 sprava 42 nos. 23, 24.
3 Myronenko, *Svitoch*, 67–8; Reent, 'Kryzovi tendentsii,' *Visnyk APSV*, 95. Iroshnikov, *Sozdanie*, 255–6. Myronenko does not specify if he is referring only to the Rada's employees or all government employees in Ukraine. My figures assume a six-day work-week.
4 DAKO, f. R2796 op. 2 sprava 3 nos. 13, 20, 28, 44, 47; sprava 5 no. 1.
5 All figures are rounded off. *Statisticheskii biulleten po gorodu Kyiva*, 2–8, 9, 11. Prices were 20%–50% lower in nearby villages. Reent, 'Kryzovi tendentsii,' 91–2; Sudavtsov, *Zemskoe i gorodskoe samoupravlenie*, 177.
6 *Tribuna gosudarstvennykh sluzashchikh*, no. 8 (1917) 15–16. An irrate citizen in Kyiv, meanwhile, circulated a poster in which he attributed price differences between the capital and the province as speculation. A certain Mr Rubinstein smuggled butter that cost 4–5 roubles per pound in Volyn, to Kyiv in railway baggage, where, corrupt officials in city dairies then sold it at 15–16 roubles per pound. Mr Rubinstien supposedly smuggled almost 5,000 kilos monthly into the capital. DAKO, f. R2796 op. 1 sprava 37 no. 7.
7 *Vilne slovo*, 4 Oct. 1917; *Holos naroda*, 4 Oct. 1917.
8 A Union of Office Workers Unions in Ukraine, including government administrators, was formed 10 (27) Dec. Manilov et al., *1917 god*, 410. Manilov mentions every strike in the city.
9 The last shipment arrived mid-November. Verstiuk, ed., *Ukrainska Tsentralna Rada*, I: 434, 446, 457, 499, 517, 577n375. Babko et al., *Velikaia oktiabrskaia sotsialisticheskaia revoiliutsiia ... Chast vtoraia*, 405.
10 Kovanko, 'Biudget mista Kyiva,' 38–9; Dmitrienko, Lysenko, 'Natsionalna valiuta Ukrainy,' 27–8; Verstiuk, ed., *Ukrainska Tsentralna Rada*, II: 39–46, 51, 57. DAKO, f. R2796 op 2 sprava 3. Whether Ukrainian leaders used

any of the money they got from France or Britain that winter to pay wages is unknown. In late December France and Britain agreed to support the Rada and gave it money, but did not recognize Ukrainian independence. Although the Rada had decided to negotiate with the Germans on 9 (22) December, it assured the Entente that it preferred an alliance with them – on condition they recognize Ukraine. Opponents of the German alliance, including Petliura, with French backing planned a coup for 15 (28) January. G.H. Soutou ed., *Recherches sur la France et le Probleme des Nationalities pendant la Primiere Guerre mondiale* (Paris, 1995) 127, 136–9; Khrystiuk, II: 92.

11 *Statisticheskii Biulleten*, 2–8, 9, 11. TsDAVO, f. 2199 op. 6 sprava 11 passim.

12 *Volynska narodna hazeta*, 17 Dec. 1918.

13 Nesvitsky, *Poltava ... 1917–1920*, 57–60.

14 Boiko et al., *Memuary*, V bk. 1 pt. 1: 279, 286.

15 TsDAHO, f. 5 op. 1 sprava 21 nos. 78–9.

16 DAKO, f. 2797 op. 1 sprava 109 nos. 18–20, 68; sprava 110 nos. 29–30, 90.

17 Andrusyshyn, *U poshukakh*, 47, 69; Tymoshchuk, *Okhronnyi apparat*, 115–18, 261, 347, 356; Tyrras, ed., *Letters*, 378. *Derzhavnyi Vistnyk*, 24 May 1918: *Vistnyk Oleksandrivskoho povitovoho zemstva*, 16 Aug. 1918. *Vozrozhdenie*, 1 (18) July, 6 (19) Sept., reported that government and zemstvo officials in the Kharkiv region were not getting paid.

18 DAKO, f. 1239 op. 126 sprava 11 nos. 3, 14–15, 17; f. 2794 op. 1 sprava 41 nos. 147–8. The lowest pay rate was 90 monthly for a volost council clerk. The highest increases were for kerosene (110 times more expensive) and cloth (180 times more expensive).

19 DAKO, f. R2797 op. 2 sprava 28 no. 68; TsDAVO, f. 538 op. 1 sprava 4 no. 320.

20 TsDAVO, f. 1113 op. 2 sprava 9, nos. 51, 24, 38, 67; f. 1092 op. 1 sprava 3; f. 1092c op. 2 sprava 227; f. 543 op. 1 sprava 6 no. 13, sprava 28 nos. 1–13.

21 TsDAVO f. 1509 op. 1 sprava 88 nos. 20, 43, 76; f. 2199 op. 1 sprava 163 nos. 7–14. The department was supposed to have 120 staff members as of August 1919.

22 TsDAVO, f. 1092c op. 2 sprava 392 nos. 81–2; op. 4 sprava 42 nos. 53–7. *Trybuna*, 24 Dec. 1918; *Vistnyk Ukrainskoi Narodnoi Respubliky*, 12 Feb. 1919.

23 *Vilna Ukraina*, 18 May 1919.

24 TsDAVO, f. 538 op. 1 sprava 26 no. 236; f. 1092 op. 2 sprava 13 no. 73; f. 1092c op. 2 sprava 47 no. 25; op 6 sprava 2 nos. 65–6: f. 1509 op. 5 sprava 49 no. 15.

25 TsDAVO, f. 3305 op. 1 sprava 2 nos. 3–4; sprava 19 no. 21.

26 *Kyivskyi den*, 6 June 1920; Lisevych, *U vidblysku*, 108, 110–11. Reent, 'Kryzovi tendentsii u silskomu hospodarstvi,' 91–2; Sudavtsov, *Zemskoe i gorodskoe*

samoupravlenie, 177; Andrusyshyn, *Tserkva v ukrainskyi derzhavi,* 32–3, 36. Lisevych, 107.

27 Mykytiuk, *Ukrainska halytska armiia,* II: 218; *Nash shliakh,* 11 Dec. 1919. TsDAVO, f. 1092c op. 2 sprava 76 no. 230; f. 528 op. 1 sprava 41 no. 281. The Union of Interior Ministry Officials (*Spilka spivrobitnykiv MVS*) formed under the Rada and dissolved by the Hetman, reformed in January 1919 and the next month, together with its counterparts in the finance and post and telegraph ministries, formed a single union for employees in the Directory's twelve ministries. The *Tymchasova komitet rady spivrobitnykiv tsentralnykh derzhavnykh ustanov* is mentioned in *Vilna Ukraina* (Rivne, 1919) 17. TsDAVO, f. 3092 op. 2 sprava 16 no. 110.

28 TsDAVO, f. 1092 op. 2 sprava 111 no. 7. Their request was granted ten days later. The union was formed and duly registered its charter in March 1919. TsDAVO, f. 528 op. 1 sprava 41 nos. 56–60.

29 Trembitsky, 'Hroshi na Volyni 1917–1920,' *Litopys Volyni,* no. 10–11 (1972) 58–65. Seven towns in western Ukraine and apparently only three in Kyiv province and two in Taurida province printed their own currencies. *Nash shliakh* printed regular currency conversion charts for readers in 1919–20.

30 TsDAVO, f. 1 op. 1 sprava 24 nos. 4, 7.

31 Mykytiuk, *Ukrainska halytska armiia,* II: 28; Birchak, 'Sotsialisty derzhavnymy budivnychymy,' *Vistnyk,* no. 11 (1935) 793; Makarchuk, 142–4.

32 Goldelman, *Lysty* 28; Revutsky, *Wrenching Times in Ukraine,* 241–2; Karpenko, ed., *Zakhidno-Ukrainska narodna respublika,* 367.

33 Kozlov, Mironenko, eds., *Arkhiv noveishei istorii Rossii,* VII: 203; IX: 254, 268.

34 *Tribuna,* no. 1 (1918); Iroshnikov, *Sozdanie,* 255–6.

35 *Tribuna,* no. 23–4.

36 Narskii, *Zhizn,* 252.

37 Livshin et al., *Pisma vo vlast 1917–1927,* 147, 148.

38 Kniazev, 'Iz zapisnoi knizhki,' *Russkoe proshloe,* 5 (1994) 148, 158–9, 175–6, 186–7. In December 1919 the author calculated that one day's food for a family, which had cost 93 kopeks before the war, had risen to cost roubles.

39 Livshin, 182; Borrero, *Hungry Moscow,* 123–7; Borisenko, *Dokumenty o deialnosti Tsentralnoi Komissii po snabzheniiu,* 130; *ARR,* II: 102–3.

40 Narskii, *Zhizn,* 475.

41 Ibid., 544.

42 *Izvestiia Chernigovskogo gubernskogo ... komiteta,* 28 Dec. 1918.

43 May 1918 prices in Kyiv, TsDAHO, f. 5 op. 1 sprava 52 nos. 9, 106; *Kommunist* (Kyiv), 28 March, 28 June, 1919; *Izvestiia* (Kyiv), 15, 22 March, 19 May, 1919; TsDAVO, f. 539 op. 1 sprava 35 nos. 37–9, 62, 66; f. 2 op. 1 sprava 422 no. 21. Department heads in Kharkiv during the spring of 1919 earned 1,000

roubles monthly; secretaries and clerks between 600 and 900. TsDAHO, f. 41 op. 1 sprava 34 no. 20. DAKO, f. R114 op. 1 sprava 18 no. 251.

44 *Nachalo,* 16 July 1920. A price list from the previous year suggests that prices jumped that May–June and then remained stable. *Chervonyi stiakh,* 18 July 1919. Eggs cost 6 karbovantsi each while one pickle cost 10–15 karbovantsi.

45 TsDAHO, f. 1 op. 18 sprava 32 no 9.

46 *Chervonyi Stiakh,* 21 July 1919.

47 DAKO, f. R1049 op. 1 sprava 17 no. 183. As subsequent signatures on documents are illegible it is impossible to determine if these three men actually left. If they did, others apparently took their place as all documents from the volost office were countersigned by secretaries.

48 DAKO, f. R1 op. 1 sprava 38 nos.164–5; DASBU, f. 73788 vol. 15 nos. 30, 63, 116–18, 193.

49 TsDAVO, f. 1 op. 1 sprava 190 nos. 7–13; op. 2 sprava 146 nos. 152, 179–84. In the five months since July, wages had risen by 3,000 roubles for the highest officials and by 1,000 roubles for the lowest paid.

50 Isakov, 'Spivvidnoshennia tsin ta realnykh dokhodiv hromadian,' 145, 150–8. TsDAVO, f. 1 op. 20 sprava 643 no. 12. In Kharkiv in March 1921 white bread cost 1,800 roubles per pound. In 1919 one Soviet rouble was worth 20 Kerensky kopeks. The Bolsheviks sometimes paid in Soviet roubles, but accepted only Ukrainian money for taxes, levies, fines, and duties. *Nash shliakh,* 22 May 1920.

51 Boiko et al., *Dzherela,* V: bk. 1 pt. 1, 286, 297.

52 The author wrote from memory in the diaspora. The archival evidence suggests her salary was probably 1,000–1,500 roubles and that bread cost 15 roubles. Gaug, 'Na sluzhbe v bolshevikov,' 203, 220–1; Davydov, *Nelegalnoe snabzheniia naselenia i vlast,* 97, 290. Between March and July 1919 prices had more than quadrupled and the Soviet ruble had fallen to less than a fifth of its earlier worth in Bolshevik Ukraine.

53 *Golos iuga,* 13 Aug. 1919. TsDAHO, f. 1 op. 18 sprava 16 nos. 15, 32, 49. Poltava administrators demanded higher pay throughout the autumn. In November they refused to strike after rejecting the city's final pay offer because they felt that under the circumstances they should not. *Golos iuga,* 10 Nov. 1919. While prices rose thirty-fold during 1919, wages increased no more than five-fold.

54 *Kievskaia zhizn,* 1 (14) Sept., 10 (23) Nov. 1919. *Kievskie gubernskie vedomosti,* 21 Sept. 1919.

55 Karpenko, Belye generaly, 391, 409.

56 *Kievlianin,* 22 Aug. 1919.

Bibliography

Primary Sources

Archives

TsDAVO (Tsentralnyi derzhavnyi arkhiv vyshchykh orhaniv vlady ta upravlinnia Ukrainy)
Fonds : Central Rada (433, 1113, 1115, 1716, 1062, 1063, 1327, 1425, 2028, 2199, 2207, 2241, 3305, 3266, 3778). Ukrainian State (433, 1216, 1276, 1425, 1530, 1532, 2199, 2207, 2208, 3164). Ukrainian National Republic (119, 538, 543, 628, 1062, 1063, 1078, 1092, 1425, 1509, 1601, 2198, 2299, 2537, 3305, 4439, 4591). The Whites (897, 1682, 1742, 2155, 3699). Bolshevik Ukraine (1, 2, 5, 340, 539, 1078, 1738). Western Ukraine (2189, 2192, 2299, 2997, 3982).

TsDAHO (Tsentralnyi derzhavny arkhiv hromadskykh obiednan Ukrainy)
Fonds: Bolshevik Ukraine (1, 5, 8, 9, 43, 57, 59, 120, 269).

DASBU (Derzhavnyi arkhiv Sluzhby Bezpeky Ukrainy)
Fonds: Soviet Ukraine (FP 69270, FP73788, FP73878, FP 74554, FP 74760).

DAKO (Derzhavnyi arkhiv Kyivskoi oblasti)
Fonds: All governments (2, 1239, R1, R3, R5, R102, R111, R114, R708, R1048, R1049, R1218, R2794, R2796, R2797, R4395).

DIA (Tsentralnyi derzhvanyi istorychnyi arkhiv)
Fonds: – Tsarist Ukraine (H274, 442, 721, 2233).

Newspapers

Borotba (Kyiv, 1917)
Chernigovskii krai (Chernihiv, 1917)
Chervonyi prapor / Chervonyi stiah (Kyiv, 1919)
Derzhavnyi vistnyk (Kyiv, 1918)
Dnistrianska khvylia (Mohyliv, 1919)
Dziennik Ludowy (Lviv, 1918–20)
Golos iuga (Poltava, 1919)
Golos naroda (Kupiansk, 1917)
Hromadianyn (Zhytomir, 1917)
Iuzhnaia kopeika (Kyiv, 1917–19)
Iuzhnyi krai (Kharkiv, 1917)
Izvestiia Chernigovskogo gubernskogo i Pochepskogo uezdnogo ispolnitelnogo komiteta (Chernihiv, 1918)
Izvestiia ispolnitelnogo komiteta Kievskogo soveta rabochikh deputatov (Kyiv, 1919–20)
Izvestiia (Moscow, 1917)
Izvestiia Nezhinskogo obshchestvenogo komiteta (Nizhyn, 1917)
Kievlianin (Kyiv, 1917–19)
Kievskaia mysl (Kyiv, 1917–20)
Kievskaia zhizn (Kyiv, 1919)
Kievskii den (Kyiv, 1920)
Kievskii gubernialni visti (Kyiv, 1917)
Kyivska zemska hazeta (Kyiv, 1917)
Kommunist (Kyiv, 1919–20)
Molva (Kyiv, 1919)
Nachalo (Kyiv, 1919)
Narod (Stanislaviv, 1919)
Narodnaia gazeta (Kyiv, 1919)
Narodnaia zhizn (Katerynoslav, 1917)
Narodnia volia (Kyiv, 1917–19)
Nash shliakh (Kamianets-Podilskyi, 1919)
Nova Hromada (Kharkiv, 1917)
Nova Rada (Kyiv, 1917, 1918)
Podolskaia mysl (Kamianets-Podilskyi, 1919)
Podolskyi krai (Kamianets-Podilskyi, 1919)
Poltavskii den (Poltava, 1917)
Poslednie novosti (Kyiv, 1918–19)
Pridneprovskii krai (Katerynoslav, 1918)
Professionalnoe dvizhenie (Kyiv, 1919)
Prylutska dumka (Pryluky, 1917)

Rada (Kyiv, 1910-14)
Radianska vlada (Poltava, 1920)
Respublikanski visti (Vinnytsia, 1919)
*Robitnycha hazeta (*Kyiv, 1917–19)
Russkaia zhizn (Kharkiv, 1917–18)
Russkii golos (Kyiv, 1918)
Selianska dumka (Berdychiv, 1917)
Slavianoserbsky khliborob (Luhansk, 1917)
Slovo (Kyiv, 1919)
Trudovaia Volyn (Zhytomir, 1917)
Trybuna (Kyiv, 1918–19)
Ukraina (Kyiv, 1919)
Ukrainska Dumka / Hromadska dumka (Lviv, 1920)
Utro Rossii (Moscow, 1917, 1918)
Vilne slovo (Zolotonosh, 1917)
Vestnik Volynskago gubernsksogo komissara (Zhytomir, 1917)
*Vestnik vremennago pravitelsva (*Petrograd, 1917)
Vestnik Vserossiisskago pochtovo-telegrafichnago souiza (St Petersburg, 1917–18)
Vilna Ukraina (Rivne, 1919)
Vilnyi holos (Poltava, 1918)
Vistnyk Oleksandrivskoho povitovoho zemstva (Zaporizhzhia, 1918)
Vistnyk rady narodnykh ministriv Ukrainskoi Respubliky (Kyiv, 1918)
Vistnyk Ukrainskoi Narodnoi Respubliky (Kyiv and Kamianets, 1919)
Volia. Tyzhnevyk (Vienna, 1918–21)
Volyn (Zhytomir, 1918)
Volynska narodna hazeta (Zhytomir, 1918)
Volynskaia molva (Zhytomir, 1918)
Volynske zhyttia (Zhytomir, 1918)
Vozrozhdenie (Kharkiv, 1918)
Vpered (Lviv, Kyiv, 1919–22)
Zemske dilo (Kharkiv, 1917)
Zemlia i volia (Lviv, 1921–22)
Zhyttia Podillia (Kamianets-Podilskyi, 1918–19)

Memoirs, Pamphlets, and Document Collections

Amiantov, Iu.N., et al. *V.I. Lenin: Neizvestnye dokumenty 1891–1922*. Moscow, 1999.
Anderson, K.M., ed. *Dnevnik P.N. Miliukova 1918–21*. Moscow, 2005.
Andrievsky, V. *Z Mynuloho*. 2 vols. Berlin, 1921–23.
Anifimov, A.M., Korelin A.P., eds. *Rossiia 1913 god.: Statistiko-dokumentalny spravochnik*. St Petersburg, 1995.

Anfimov, A.M. 'Tsarskaia okhranka o politicheskom polozhenii v strane v kontse 1916 g. *Istoricheskii arkhiv*, nos. 1–3 (Jan.–Feb. 1960) 203–9.

Anon. *Demokratychna respublika.* Kyiv, 1905.

Anon. *Iak i dlia choho treba orhanizuvatysia.* Poltava, 1917.

Anon. *Iakoho ladu nam treba.* Kyiv, 1917.

Antonenko-Davydovych, B. *Tvory v dvokh tomakh.* 2 vols. Kyiv, 1999.

Arkhiv Russkoi Revoliutsii (*ARR*). 22 vols. Berlin, 1921–37.

Bachynsky, P., ed. *Dokumenty trahichnoi istorii Ukrainy (1917–1927 rr).* Kyiv, 1999.

Belash, A.V., Belash, V.F. *Dorogi Nestora Makhna.* Kyiv, 1993.

[Bezborodko A.]. 'Zapiska kniaza Bezborodki o potrebnostiakh imperii Rossiiskoi.' *Russkii arkhiv* 1877, bk. 1.

Bilinkis, L. 'Hromadianska viina na Ukraini ta Evreii: Fragmenty.' *Khronika 2000,* 21–2 (1998) 234–51.

Birchak, V. 'Drohobytska Epopeia.' *Literaturno-naukovyi vistnyk*, vol. 106, nos. 7–8 (1931) 613–24; no. 9 1003-1010.

– 'Sotsialisty derzhavnymy budivnychymy.' *Vistnyk*, no. 9 (1935) 658–62; no. 11 787–97.

Bobrzynski, M. *Wskrzeszenie panstwa Polskiego.* Cracow, 1925.

Boiko, A., et al. *Dzherela z istorii Pivdennoi Ukrainy*, vol. 5, bks. 1–2, *Memuary ta shchodennyky, chastyna 1.* Zaporizhzhia, 2005.

Boiko, V. *Zemstvo i narodni upravy.* Kyiv, 1917.

Borisenko, B.I. *Dokumenty o deialnosti Tsentralnoi Komissii po snabzheniiu … kak istoricheskii istochnik.* Moscow, 1985.

Borman, A.A. 'Moskva – 1918 (Iz zapisok seretnogo agenta v Kremle).' *Russkoe proshloe,* 1 (1991) 115–49.

Bosh, E. *God borby.* Moscow, 1925.

Brzoza, C., Rolinski, A., eds. *Bij Bolszewika! Rok 1920 w przekazie historycznym i literackim.* Cracow, 1990.

Budberg, R.Iu. 'Pod vlastiu bolshevikov v Kieve.' *Na chuzhoi storone,* no. 4 (1924) 101–34.

Bujak, F. *Galicja.* Lwow, 1908.

Carr, E.H., ed. *Bukharin and Preobrazhansky: The ABC of Communism.* London, 1970.

Chaikovsky, A. *Chorni riadky.* Lviv, 1930.

Chornopysky, M., ed. *Ivan Nechui-Levytsky: Ukrainstvo na literaturnykh pozvakh z Moskovshchynoiu.* Lviv, 1998.

Chubaty, M. 'Derzhavnyi lad na Zakhidnyi oblasti Ukrainskoi Narodnoi Respubliky.' In H. Luzhnytsky, Ia. Padokh, eds., *U Poshukakh istorychnoi pravdy.* New York, 1987.

Chubinsky, P. 'Dva slova o selskom uchilishsche voobshche i ob uchilishche dlia selskikh uchitelei.' *Osnova,* no. 4 (1862) 54–61.

Chykalenko, Ie. *Shchodennyk (1907–1917).* Lviv, 1931.
– *Uryvok z moiikh spomyniv za 1917 r.* Prague, 1932.
Danilov, V., et al. *Nestor Makhno: Krestianskoe dvizhenie na Ukraine 1918–1921. Dokumenty i materialy.* Moscow, 2006.
Dei, O., Zasenko, O., Lysenko, O., eds. *Mykhailo Petrovych Drahomanov: Literaturno-publitsystychni pratsi u dvokh tomakh.* Kyiv, 1970.
Demydenko, A.I., ed. *Velykyi Ukrainets.* Kyiv, 1992.
Dolenko, M. [pseud. M. Hrinchenko]. *Khto narodovi voroh.* Lviv, 1905; repr. Kyiv, 1917.
Doroshenko, D. 'Ukrainskyi rukh 1890-ykh rokiv v osvitlenni Avstriiskoho konsula v Kievi.' *Z Mynuloho. Zbirnyk.* Warsaw, 1938, vol. 1: 62–5.
– *Moi spomyny pro davne mynule: 1901–1914 roky.* Winnipeg, 1949.
– *Istoriia Ukrainy 1917–1923 rr.* 2nd ed. New York, 1954.
– *Moi spomyny pro nedavne mynule (1914–1920).* 2nd ed. Munich, 1969.
Dotsenko, O. *Litopys Ukrainskoi revoliutsii: Materialy i dokumenty do istorii Ukrainskoi revoliutsii.* Reprint ed. Philadelphia, 1988 [1923].
Dragan, A., ed. *Luka Myshuha: Zbirnyk.* Jersey City, 1973.
Drahomanov, M. *Volnyi souiz – vilna spilka: Opyt Ukrainskoi politiko-sotsialnoi programmy.* Trans. T. Andrusiak, *Shliakh do Svobody.* Lviv, 1998.
Emmons, T., ed. *Time of Troubles: The Diary of Iurii Valdimirovich Got'e.* Princeton, 1989.
Fleer, M. 'Vremennoe pravitelstvo posle oktiabra.' *Krasnyi arkhiv,* vol. 6 (1924) 195–221.
Franko, I. *Zibrannia tvoriv u piatdesiaty tomakh.* Kyiv, 1986.
Galitisiia. Vremennyi voennyi general-gubernator. Otchet kantseliarii voennogo general-gubernatora Galitsii v period vremen s 28 avgusta 1914 po 1 iulia 1915 goda. Kyiv, 1916.
Gaug, K. 'Na sluzhbe v bolshevikov.' *Beloe delo,* vol. 2 (1927) 202–31.
Goldelman, S. *Lysty zhydivskoho sotsial-demokrata pro Ukrainu.* Vienna, 1921.
Gorianov, S.M. *Ustavy o voinskoi povinnosti ... dopolnennye vsemi pozdneishimi uzakoneniiami po 1 iunia 1913 g.* 12th ed. St Petersburg, 1913.
Goroda Rossii v 1910. St Petersburg, 1914.
Gusev-Orenburgskii, O., ed. *Kniga o evreiskikh pogromakh.* Petersburg and Berlin, 1921.
Halahan, M. *Z moikh spomyniv.* Lviv, 1930.
Heifetz, E., ed. *The Slaughter of the Jews in the Ukraine in 1919.* New York, 1921.
Hermaize, O., ed. 'Materialy do istorii Ukrainskoho rukhu za svitovoi viiny.' *Ukrainskyi arkheohrafichnyi zbirnyk,* vol.1 (1926).
Hirniak, N. *Ostannyi akt trahedii Ukrainskoi Halytskoi Armii* np, 1959.
Holovko, N. *Iakyi derzhavnyi lad musyt buty.* Kyiv, 1917.

Homola, I., ed. *Pamietniki urzednikow galicyjskich.* Cracow, 1978.
Hrushevsky, M. *Na porozi novoi Ukrainy.* Kyiv, 1918.
Hunczak, T., ed. *Ukraine and Poland in Documents. 1918–1922.* New York, 1983.
Hupka, J. *Z czasow Wielkiej Wojny.* 2nd ed. Lviv, 1937.
Hrushevsky, M. 'Ukrainska partiia sotsiialistiv-revoliutsioneriv ta ii zavdannia.' *Boritesia – Poborete,* no. 1 (1920) 1–54.
– 'Shcho Vono.' Reprinted in *Ukrainskyi istoryk,* vol. 39 nos. 1–4 (2002) 46–8 [1917].
– 'Spomyny.' *Kyiv,* no. 8 (1989) 103–54; no. 9, 108–49; no. 10, 122–58; no. 11, 113–55.
Hryhoriev-nash [pseud. M. Hryhoriiv]. *Iakoi respubliky treba bidnym liudam.* Kyiv, 1917.
– *Vchimosia panuvaty.* Kyiv, 1919.
– 'Zlochynstva politychnoi bezhramotnosty.' *Nova Ukraina,* no. 12 (1922).
Hryhoriiv, M. *Spohady 'ruiinnyka.'* Lviv, 1938.
Iaroshevich, A.I., ed. *Ves Iugo-Zapadnyi krai: Spravochnaia i adresnaia kniga po Kievskoi, Volynskoi i Podolskoi guberniiam.* Kyiv, 1914.
Iavorenko, L. *Choho nam treba.* Lviv, 1905.
Ilinskii, L.K., ed. *Spisok povremennykh izdanii.* Petrograd, 1922.
Isyp, H.T., et al. *Komitety nezamoznykh selian Ukrainy (1920–1933). Zbirnyk dokumentiv i materialiv.* Kyiv, 1968.
Iurchuk V.I., et al. *Komunistychna partiia Ukrainy v rezoliutsiiakh i rishenniakh ziizdiv, konferentsii i plenumiv Ts. K. Tom pershyi 1918–1941.* Kyiv, 1976.
Iurkevich, Iu. *Minuvshee prokhodit predo mnoiu.* Moscow, 2000.
Karpenko, O., ed. *Zakhidno-Ukrainska Narodna Respublika 1918–1923.* 3 vols. Lviv, 2001.
Khrystiuk, P. *Zamitky i materialy do istorii Ukrainskoi revoliutsii 1917–20.* Reprint ed. New York, 1969 [1921].
Khto taki sotsialisty-revoliutsionery i choho vony domohaiutsia? Kyiv, 1917.
Kniazev, G.A. 'Iz zapisnoi knizhki Russkogo intelligenta za vremia voiny i revoliutsii (1918 g.).' *Russkoe proshloe,* no. 4 (1993) 35–150; no. 5 (1994) 148–242.
Kobets, O. [Varavva, O.]. *Zapysky Polonenoho.* Munich, 1959.
Koenker, D., ed. *Tret'ya Vserossiiskaya Konferentsiya Professionalnykh Soyuzov 3–11 Iyulya (20–28) Iyunaya st.st.) 1917 goda: Stenograficheskii otchet.* Reprint ed. New York, 1982 [1927].
[Kochubei V.I.]. 'Zapiska V. I. Kochubeia o polozhenii Imperii i o merakh k prekrashcheniiu bezporiadkov i vvedenii luchshago ustroistva v raznyia otrasli, pravitelstvo sostavliaiushchiia.' *Sbornik imperatorskago Russkago istoricheskago obshchestva,* 90 (1894) 5–26.
Kolodyi, B. *Halytska sotsialistychna radianska respublika: Spomyny z 1920 roku.* Lviv, 1932.

Korniichuk, L., ed. *S.A. Podolynsky: Vybrani tovry*. Kyiv, 2000.

Korolivsky, S.M., et al. *Grazhdanskaia voina na Ukraine*. 3 vols. Kyiv, 1967.

Korostovetz, V. *Seed and Harvest*. London, 1923.

Korostowetz, W.S. *The Rebirth of Poland*. London, 1928.

Korsunsky, M. 'Panas Iakovych Rudchenko (Panas Myrnyi) iak sluzhbovets, hromadianyn i liudyna ... (Z vlasnykh spomyniv).' *Chervonyi shliakh*, nos. 7–8 (1927) 236–56.

Kossak, S. *The Blaze*. New York, 1927.

Kovalevsky, M. *Pry dzherelakh borotby*. Innsbruck, 1960.

Kozlov V.A., Mironenko, C.V., eds. *Arkhiv noveishei istorii Rossii: Sektsiia 'publikatsii.'* 9 vols. Moscow 2001–.

Kravchenko, V. *I Chose Freedom*. New York, 1946.

Krivava knyha Chastyna I. Materiialy do Polskoi invazii na Ukrainski zemli Skhidnoi Halychyny 1918/1919 roku. Vienna, 1919.

Krivava knyha Chastyna II. Ukrainska Halychyna pid okupatsieiu Polshchi v rr. 1918–1920. Vienna, 1921.

Krysiak, F.S. *W dni grozy we Lwowie*. 2nd ed. Rzeszow, 2003.

Kuplowski, M., ed. *Iwan Franko o literaturze polskiej*. Rzeszow, 1979.

Kuzma, O. *Lystopadovi dni 1918 r*. 2nd ed. New York, 1960.

Lapchinskii, G. 'Gomelskoe soveshchenie: Vospominaniia.' *Litopys revoliutsii*, no. 6 (1926) 36–50.

Lasocki, Z. *Wspomnienia szefa administracji P.K.L. K.Rz*. Cracow, 1931.

Lavrov, P.I. 'Gosudarstvennyi element v budushchem obshchestve.' *Vpered*, vol. 4 (1876).

Lenin, V.I. *Polnoe sobranie sochinenii*. 55 vols. Moscow, 1959–65.

Leninskii Sbornik. 40 vols. Moscow, 1924–85.

Levytsky, K. *Velykyi zryv*. Lviv, 1931.

Levytsky, V. *Ukrainska derzhavna put*. Lviv, 1933.

Lisevych, I. *U vidblysku polskykh bahnetiv: Zhyttia Kieva pid chas perebuvannia v nomu polskykh viisk (traven-cherven 1920 r.)*. Kyiv, 2002.

Livshin, A.I., et al. *Pisma vo vlast 1917–1927*. Moscow, 1998.

Livytska, M. *Na hrani dvokh epoch*. New York, 1972.

Lophukhin, V.B. 'Posle 25 oktiabra.' *Minuvshee*, vol. 1 (1986) 9–98.

Lototsky, O. *Storinky mynuloho*. 3 vols. Warsaw, 1932–34.

Lozytsky, V., ed. *Vynnychenko i Ukrainska sotsial demokratiia*. Kyiv, 2008.

Lykho, P.S. 'Sovetskaia vlast na mestakh: Robota kommunistychnoi partii Chornuskoho raionu na Poltavshchyni (1921–1941). *Ukrainskyi zbirnyk*, 8 (1957) 99–172.

Mahalevsky, Iu. *Ostannyi akt tragedii*. Lviv, 1928.

Maistrenko, I. *Istoriia moho pokolinnia*. Edmonton, 1985.

Makhno, N. *Russkaia revoliutsiia na Ukraine (ot marta 1917g. po aprel 1918 god.)* Paris, 1929.

– *Ukrainskaia revoliutsiia (iul-dekabr 1918 g.).* Paris, 1937.
Makukh, I. *Na narodni sluzhbi.* Detroit, 1958.
Manilov, V., et al. *1917 god na Kievshchine. Khronika sobytii.* Kyiv, 1928.
Martos, B. *Vyzvolnyi zdvyh Ukrainy.* New York, 1989.
– *Oskilko i Bolbochan.* Munich, 1958.
Maslov, S.S. *Rossiia posle chetyrekh let revoliutsii.* Paris, 1922.
Mazepa, I. *Ukraina v ohni i buri revoliutsii 1917–21.* Munich, 1951.
Megas, O. *Tragediia Halytskoi Ukrainy.* Winnipeg, 1920.
Melgunov, S. *Kak Bolsheviki zakhvatili vlast.* Paris, 1953.
Miakotin, V. 'Iz nedalekago proshlago.' *Na chuzhoi storone,* 11 (1925) 205–36.
Miliakova, L.B. *Kniga pogromov. Pogromy na Ukraine... v period Grazhdanskoi voiny 1918–1922 gg.: Sbornik dokumentov.* Moscow, 2007.
Mironenko, S.A., et al. *Zhurnaly zasedanii Osobogo soveshchaniia pri Glavnokomanduiushchem Vooruzhennymi Silami na Iuge Rossii A.I. Denikine.* Moscow, 2008.
Mishchuk, R.S., ed. *M.P. Drahomanov: Vybrane.* Kyiv, 1991.
Mochalova, I., ed. 'Vladimir Vernadskii: Volnoe.' *Rodina,* no. 8 (1999) 85–7.
Myrny, P. *Zibrannia tvoriv u semy tomakh.* Kyiv, 1971.
Naselennia v mistakh Ukrainy za dannymy vsesoiuznoho miskoho perepisu 15 bereznia 1923. Kharkiv, 1925.
Nazarenko, I.D., et al. *V.I. Lenin pro Ukrainu.* Kyiv, 1969.
Nazaruk, O. *Rik na velykyi Ukraini.* Vienna, 1920.
Nazhivin, I. *Zapiski o revoliutsii.* Vienna, 1921.
Nielson, J.P., Weil, B. eds. *Russkaia revoliutsiia glazami petrogradskogo chinovnika: Dnevnik 1917–1918 gg.* Oslo, 1986.
Nikolaev, D.D., ed. *A. Vetlugin. Sochineniia.* Moscow, 2000.
Nikovsky, A. 'Masonstvo v Rossii pered revoliutsieiu i na pochatku viiny.' *Geneza,* vol. 1, no. 4 (1996) 149–60.
Obshchii svod po Imperii rezultatov razrabotki dannykh perepisi 1897 g. po Imperii. vols. 1 and 2. St Petersburg, 1905.
Okninskii, A.L. *Dva goda sredi krestian.* Riga, 1936.
Olesevych, T., et al. *Ukrainska liudnist S.S.S.R.* Warsaw, 1931.
Olesiuk, T. 'Kamianets – zolotyi vinets. Spomyny z 1918-1919 rr.' *Pamiatky Ukrainy,* nos. 3–4 (2002) 91–109.
Orski, S. *W zachodniej 'respublice' Ukrainskiej.* Lwow, 1919.
'Otchet o polugodnicheskoi deiatelnosti (ianvar-iun 1922 godu).' *Z arkhiviv VUChK, GPU, NKVD, KGB,* vols. 1–2, nos. 4–5 (1997) 317–84.
Pervaia vseobshchaia perepis naseleniia Rossiiskoi imperii 1897 goda. St Petersburg, 1897–1905.
Petriv V. *Spomyny z chasiv Ukrainskoi revoliutsii (1917–1921).* 4 vols. Lviv, 1927–31.

Petrovych, I. *Halychyna pid Rosiiskoi okupatsii: Serpen 1914 cherven 1915.* Lviv, 1917.

Pilat, T., ed. *Wiadomosci statystyczne o stosunkach krajowych.* vol. 24 Lviv, 1912.

Pilch, O. *Choho nas Ukraintsiv katsapy-bolshevyky prozvaly burzhuiamy?* Kyiv, 1917.

Poletika, N.P. *Videnoe i perezhitoe.* Tel Aviv, 1982.

Popov, N., ed. *Revoliutsiia na Ukraine po memuaram belykh.* Moscow, 1930.

Porsh, M. 'P. Struve v Ukrainskii spravi.' *Literaturno-naukovyi vistnyk,* 58 (May 1912) 333–41.

Potopnyk, M. *Pohliadom u mynule.* Pine Brook, NJ, 1990.

Proudhon, P. *General Idea of the Revolution in the Nineteenth Century.* Trans. J. Robinson. London, 1923.

Prykhodko, V. *Pid sontsem Podillia.* Lviv, 1931.

Przenioslo, M., ed. *Narodziny niepodleglosci w Galicji (1918–1919).* Kielce, 2007.

Pyrih, R.Ia., et al. 'Do istorii mizhnatsionalnykh protsesiv na Ukraini.' *Ukrainsky istorychnyi zhurnal,* no. 1 (1991) 99–112.

Rafes, M. *Dva goda revoliutsii na Ukraine.* Moscow, 1920.

Revutsky, A. *Wrenching Times in Ukraine.* Trans. S. Revutsky, M. Kantorowitz. St John's, NL, 1998.

Rogalina, N.L., Telitsyn V.L. 'Nu, polno mne zagadyvat o khode istorii.' *Otechestvennaia istoriia,* no. 3 (1997) 76–95.

Rusova, S. 'Moi spomyny.' *Za sto let.* bk. 3. Kyiv, 1928.

Sadovsky, V. *Pratsia v SSSR.* Warsaw, 1932.

Sakharov, A.N., Kulakov, A.A., et al. *Obshchestvo i vlast. Rossiiskaia provintsiia,* vol. 1, *1917– seredina 30-kh godov.* Moscow, 2002.

Semenov, P.P., ed. *Polnoe geograficheskoe opisanie nashego otechestva.* 19 vols. St Petersburg, 1899–1914.

Senin, S., ed. '"Naskolko deshevo stala tsenitsia zhizn": Dnevnik Bezhetskogo sviashchennika I.N. Postnikova.' *Istochnik,* no. 3 (1996) 31–57; no. 4: 10–30; no. 5: 13–29.

Shapoval, M. *Revoliutsiinyi sotsializm na Ukraini.* Vienna, 1921.

– *Velyka revoliutsiia i Ukrainska vyzvolna prohrama.* Prague, 1928.

– 'Hetmanshchyna i Dyrektoriia: Uryvky iz spomyniv.' *Vitchyzna,* nos. 11–12 (1995) 131–41.

Shevchenko, T. *Povne zibrannia tvoriv u shesty tomakh.* Kyiv, 1964.

Shevchenko, V., ed. *Ukrainski politychni partii kintsia XIX – pochatku XX stolittia.* Kyiv, 1993.

Shtern, S. *V ogne grazhdanskoi voiny.* Berlin, 1922.

Shukhevych, S. *Spomyny.* 5 vols. Lviv, 1929.

Sidak, V., ed. *Vyzvolni zmahannia ochyma kontrrozvidnyka (dokumentalna spadshchyna Mykoly Chebotariva).* Kyiv, 2003.

Skoropadsky, P. *Spohady: kinets 1917 – hruden 1918.* Kyiv, 1995.
Sokolov, K.N. *Pravlenie generala Denikina (iz vospomianii).* Sofia, 1921.
Sorokina, M.Iu, et al. *V.I. Vernadskii: Dnevniki 1917–1921.* Kyiv, 1994.
Sosiura, V. *Tretia rota.* Kyiv, 1988.
Spiss, T. *Ze Wspomnien C.K. Urzednika Politycznego.* Rzeszow, 1936.
Sputnik chinovnika. Kyiv, 1911–14.
Statisticheskii biulleten po gorode Kieva. vol. 4. *Ekonomicheskaia statistika.* Kyiv, 1920.
Stavrovskii, S.N. 'Chernye gody, ili "Bestia Triumphalis" (1917–1922).' *Minuvshee Istoricheskii almanakh,* vol. 14 (1993) 7–98.
Stazewski, M. 'Problem pozostania urzednikow niemieckich w Wielkopolsce i na Pomorzu w latach 1919–1920.' *Studia Historica Slavo-Germanica,* vol. 21 (1996) 59–81.
Surovtsova, N. *Spohady.* Kyiv, 1996.
Tanin-Lvov, A.A., ed. 'Pamiatnaia zapiska ob oblastnom upravlennii v Ukrainskikh guberniiakh.' *Istoricheskii arkhiv,* 2 (1997) 35–42.
Tatishchev, A.A. *Zemli i liudi: V gushche pereselencheskogo dvizheniia (1906–1921).* Moscow, 2001.
Tiutiunnyk, Iu. *Zymovyi pokhid 1919–1920.* Warsaw, 1923.
Tkachenko, V. Oleksandrivsk na zlami epokh: dokumenty i materialy.' *Pivdenna Ukraina XVII–XIX stolitta,* 1 (1998) 7–16.
Tronko, P.T., ed. *Kievshchina v gody grazhdanskoi voiny i inostrannoi voennoi interventsii (1918–1920 gg.).* Kyiv, 1962.
Tribuna gosudarstvennykh sluzashchikh. Petrograd, 1917–19.
Trubetskoi, G.N. *Gody smute i nadezhde.* Montreal, 1981.
Trudy tsentralnogo statisticheskogo upravleniia. 35 vols. Moscow, 1920–27.
Tsehelsky, L. *Vid legend do pravdy.* New York, 1960.
Tych, F. , ed. *PPS-Lewica 1906–1918: Materialy i dokumenty.* Warsaw, 1961.
Tyrras, N., ed. *Letters of Life in an Aristocratic Russian Household before and after the Revolution.* Lewiston, NY, 2000.
Ulianovsky, V., ed. 'Vadim Shcherbakivsky: Memuary.' *Pamiatky Ukrainy,* no. 4 (2007) 22–194.
Utgof, V.L. 'Ufimskoe gosudarstvennoe soveshchanie 1918 goda.' *Byloe,* 16 (1921) 15–41.
Vargatiuk, P.L., ed. *Bolshevistskie organizatsii Ukrainy: organizatsionno-partiinaia deiatelnost (mart 1917 – iul 1918 g.).* Kyiv, 1990.
Vasiliev, V., et al. *Politychni represii na Podilli.* Vinnytsia, 1999.
Veitsblit, I.I. *Rukh Evreiskoi liudnosti na Ukraini periodu 1897–1926 rokiv.* Kharkiv, 1930.
Verstiuk, V., ed. *Ukraiinska tsentralna rada: Dokumenty i materiialy u dvokh tomakh.* Kyiv, 1996.

Verstiuk V., Antonovych, M., eds. *Evhen Chykalenko: Shchodennyk 1919–1920.* Kyiv and New York, 2005.

Verstiuk, V., et al. *Ukrainskyi natsionalno-vyszvolnyi rukh berezen-lystopad 1917 roku: Dokumenty i materialy.* Kyiv, 2003.

Vladimirskii, M. *Sovety, ispolkomy i siezdy sovetov.* Moscow, 1920.

Volin, S. *Deiatelnost menshevikov v profsoiuzakh pri sovetskoi vlasti*. Inter-University Project on the History of the Menshevik Movement. New York, 1962.

– *Mensheviki na Ukraine (1917–1921).* Benson, VT, 1990.

Volkov, S.V., ed. *1918 god na Ukraine.* Moscow, 2001.

Volkov-Muromets, N.V. *Iunost ot viazmy do feodosii (1902–1920).* Paris, 1983.

Vosmaia konferentsiia RKP(b) dekabr 1919 goda. Protokoly. Moscow, 1961.

Vosmoi sezd RKP/b/ mart 1919 goda: Protokoly. Moscow, 1959.

Vsesoiuznaia perepis naselennia 1926 g. Moscow, 1930.

Vynnychenko, V. *Vidrodzhennia natsii.* 3 vols. Vienna, 1920.

Warezak, J. 'Polska Organizacja Wojskowa w okregu Tarnopolskim (1918–1919).' *Niepodleglosc,* vol. 14, no. 3 (1936) 393–413.

Wiech, S., Caban, W., eds. *Sytuacja polityczna Krolewstwa Polskiego s swietle tajnych raportow naczelnikow warszawskiego okregu zandarmerii z lat 1867–1872 i 1878.* Kielce, 1999.

Wiszniewski, S. *Brzezany i kresy poludniowo – wschodnie Rzeczypospolitej Polskiej w wojnie Ukrainsko-Polskiej 1918–1919.* Lviv, 1935.

Wojciechowski, M. *Powrot Pomorza do Polski 1918–1920.* Warsaw, 1981.

Wolcznski, J., ed. *Nieznana korespondencja arcybiskupow metropolitow Lwowskich Jozefa Bilczewskiego z Andrzejem Szeptyckim w czasie wojny Polsko-Ukrainskiej 1918–1919.* Lwow and Cracow, 1997.

Zahirnia M. [pseud. M. Hrinchenko]. *Pro derzhavnyi lad u vsiakykh narodiv.* Kyiv, 1917.

Zatonsky, V. 'Uryvky z spohadiv pro Ukrainsku revoliutsiiu.' *Litopys revoliutsii,* (1929) no. 4: 139–72; no. 5: 115–41.

Zenkovskii, V. *Piat mesiatsev u vlasti: Vospominaniia.* Moscow, 1995.

Secondary Sources

General

Bowman, S.E., ed. *Edward Bellamy Abroad.* New York, 1962.

Braibanti, R., et al. *Asian Bureaucratic Systems Emergent from the British Imperial Tradition.* Durham, NC, 1966.

Church, C.H. *Revolution and Red Tape: The French Ministerial Bureaucracy 1770–1850.* Oxford, 1981.

Eldridge, J.E.T., ed. *Max Weber: The Interpretation of Social Reality*. London, 1971.
LaPalombara, J.G., ed. *Bureaucracy and Political Development*. Princeton, 1963.
Mann, M. 'The Autonomous Power of the State.' In J. Hall, ed., *States in History*. Oxford, 1986, 109–36.
Perkin, H. *The Rise of Professional Society: England since 1880*. London, 1989.
Riggs, F. 'Modernity and Bureaucracy.' *Public Administration Review*, no. 4 (July–Aug. 1997) 347–53.
Roth, G., Wittich, C., eds. *Max Weber: Economics and Society*. Berkeley, 1978.
Soemardjian, S. 'Bureaucratic Organization in a Time of Revolution.' *Administrative Science Quarterly*, no. 2 (Sept. 1957) 182–99.

Central and Eastern Ukraine, Russia

Adams, A. *The Bolsheviks in the Ukraine: The Second Campaign, 1918–1919*. New Haven, 1963.
Andrusyshyn, B. *U poshukakh sotsialnoi rivnovahy*. Kyiv, 1995.
– *Tserkva v ukrainskyi derzhavi 1917–1920 rr.* Kyiv, 1997.
– 'Problemy okhorony pratsi ta sotsialnoho zabezpechennia, borotba z bezrobittiam za doby Dyrektorii UNR.' *Visnyk Akademii pratsi i sotsialnykh vidnosyn Federatsii profspilok Ukrainy*, no. 2 (2003) 8–13.
Antoshkin, D. *Professionalnoe dvizhenie sluzhashchikh 1917–1924* gg. Moscow, 1927.
Aronson, G. *Rossiia v epokhu revoliutsii*. New York, 1966.
Atoian, O.N. *Volia k pravu: Issledovannia makhnovshchiny i narodnago pravosoznaniia*. Luhansk, 2003.
Babii, B.M. *Ukrainska radianska derzhava 1921–1925*. Kyiv, 1961.
Babko, Iu.V., et al. *Velikaia oktiabrskaia sotsialisticheskaia revoiliutsiia i pobeda sovetskoi vlasti na Ukraine. Khronika vazhneishikh istoriko-parteinykh i revoliutsionnykh sobytii v dvukh chastiakh. Chast vtoraia*. Kyiv, 1982.
Baehr, P., Wells, G.C., eds. *The Russian Revolution: Max Weber*. Cambridge, 1995.
Baiguzin, R.N. *Gosudarstvennaia bezopasnost Rossii: istoriia i sovremennost*. Moscow, 2004.
Bakhturina, A.Iu., Kozhevnikova, G.V., eds. *Gosudarstvennyi apparat Rossii v gody revoliutsii i grazhdanskoi voiny*. Moscow, 1998.
Belenkin, B. *Avantiuristy velikoi smuty*. Moscow, 2001.
Bevzo, T.A., et al. *Ukrainska revoliutsiia i derzhavnist 1917–1920 rr.* Kyiv, 1998.
Bilokin, S. 'Masony i Ukraina.' *Pamiatky Ukrainy*, 2 (2002) 181–97.
Bohatchuk, S. 'Sotsialne stanovyshche zaliznychnykiv Ukrainy.' *Ukrainskyi istorychnyi zbirnyk 2000*. Kyiv, 2002, 89–95.
Borrero, M. *Hungry Moscow: Scarcity and Urban Society in the Russian Civil War 1917–1921*. New York, 2003.

Borysenko, V.I. *Borotba demokratychnykh syl za narodnu osvitu na Ukraini v 60–90kh rokakh XIX st.* Kyiv, 1980.

Borysov, V.I. *Prodovolcha polityka na Ukraini 1917–1920.* Luhansk, 1991.

Brovkin, V. *Behind the Front Line of the Civil War.* Princeton, 1994.

Bronnikov, V.D. 'Sozdanie sovetskoi intelligentsii iz raboche-krestianskoi mlodezhi v gody grazhdanskoi voiny 1918–1920 gg. na materialakh Ukrainy.' In I.I. Mints, ed., *Oktiabrskaia revoliutsiia i molodezh.* Erevan, 1987.

Bruk, I., Kabuzan, V.M. 'Chislennost i rasselenie Ukrainskogo etnosa v XVIII – nachale XX v.' *Sovetskaia etnografiia,* no. 5 (1981) 23–4.

Budnitskii, O.V. *Rossiiskie evrei mezhdu krasnymi i belymi.* Moscow, 2005.

Bugai, N.F. *Chrezvychainye organy Sovetskoi vlasti: revkomy 1918–1921.* Moscow, 1990.

Buldakov, V.P., et al. *Borba za massy v trekh revoliutsiiakh v Rossii.* Moscow, 1981.

Butakov, Ia.A. *Beloe dvizhenie na iuge Rossii: kontseptsiia i praktika gosudarstvennogo stroitelstva.* Moscow, 2000.

Chop, V.M. *Makhnovsky rukh v Ukraine 1917–21rr.: problemy ideolohii, suspilnoho ta viiskovoho ustroiu.* Doctoral dissertation, Zaporizhzhia National Technical University, 2004.

Chyrkova, M. 'Vybory do Poltavskoi miskoi dumy 2 lypnia 1917 r.' *Poltavska petliuriana,* 2 (1996) 130–47.

Davydov, A.Iu. *Nelegalnoe snabzheniia naselenia i vlast 1917–1921 gg.* St Petersburg, 2002.

Dmitrienko, M.F., Lysenko, O.F. 'Natsionalna valiuta Ukrainy 1918–1919 rr.' *Ukrainsky istorychnyi zhurnal,* no. 6 (1994) 26–40.

Dillon, A. *The Rural Cooperative Movement and Problems of Modernizing in Tsarist and Post-Tsarist Southern Ukraine (New Russia), 1871–1920.* Doctoral dissertation, Harvard University, 2003.

Donchenko, S. *Liberalni parti Ukrainy 1900–1919.* Dniproderzhinsk, 2004.

Easter, G.M. *Reconstructing the State.* Cambridge, 2000.

Efremov, V., ed. *Rossia v mirovoi voine 1914–1918 goda.* Moscow, 1925.

Eklof, B. *Russian Peasant Schools.* Berkeley, 1990.

Emmons, T. *The Formation of Political Parties: The First National Elections in Russia.* Cambridge, 1983.

Figes, O. *Peasant Russia Civil War.* Oxford, 1989.

– *A People's Tragedy: The Russian Revolution of 1891–1924.* London, 1996.

Finkelshtien, Iu. *Za dela ruk svoikh.* New York, 1995.

Frenkin, M. *Zakhvat vlasti Bolshevikami v Rossii i rol tylovykh garnizonov armii: Podgotovka i provedenie oktiabrskogo miatezha 1917–1918 gg.* Jerusalem, 1982.

Fraiman, A.L. *Forpost sotsialisticheskoi revoliutsii.* Leningrad, 1969.

Gaponenko, L.S., Kabuzan, V.M. 'Materialy selskokhozaistvennykh perepisei 1916–1917 gg ...' *Istoriia SSSR,* no. 6 (1961) 97–115.

Gaponenko, A.S. *Rabochii klass Rossii v 1917 godu.* Moscow, 1970.

Gaudin, C. *Ruling Peasants: Village and State in Late Imperial Russia.* DeKalb, 2007.

Geifman, A. *Thou Shalt Kill: Revolutionary Terrorism in Russia 1894–1917.* Princeton, 1993.

Gill, G.J. *Peasants and Government in the Russian Revolution.* London, 1979.

Gimpelson, E.G. *Sovetskie upravlentsy 1917–1920 gg.* Moscow, 1998.

Gindin, A.M. 'Kak Bolsheviki ovladeli gosbankom.' *Istoriia SSSR*, no. 1 (1960) 224–37.

Gitelman, Z. *Jewish Nationality and Soviet Politics.* Princeton, 1972.

Golovin, N.N. *The Russian Army in World War I.* New Haven, 1931.

Golubov, A., Lokhmatova, A. 'Reformirovanie obshchestva i sudby liudei: popytki analiza psykhologicheskikh aspekotov preobrazovanii serediny XIX veka.' In H.V. Samoilenko, ed., *Istoriia ta kultura livoberezhzhia Ukrainy.* Kyiv, 1997, 77–8.

Gusev, K.V. ed., *Neproletarskie partii Rossii v trekh revoliutsiakh.* Moscow, 1989.

Guthier, S. *The Roots of Popular Ukrainian Nationalism: A Demographic, Social and Political Study of the Ukrainian Nationality to 1917.* Doctoral dissertation, University of Michigan, 1990.

– 'Ukrainian Cities during the Revolution and the Interwar Era.' In I.L. Rudnytsky, ed., *Rethinking Ukrainian History.* Edmonton, 1981, 156–80.

Hai-Nyzhnyk, P. *UNR ta ZUNR: Stanovlennia orhaniv vlady i natsionalne derzhavotvorennia (1917–1920 rr.).* Kyiv, 2010.

Hamretsky, Iu.M., et al. *Triumfalnoe shestvie sovetskoi vlasti na Ukraine.* Kyiv, 1987.

Hardeman, H. *Coming to Terms with the Soviet Regime.* DeKalb, 1994.

Hass, L. *Ambicje rachuby rzeczywistosc. Wolnomulartwo e Europie Srodkowo-Wschodniej 1905–1928.* Warsaw, 1984.

Hildermeier, M. *The Russian Socialist Revolutionary Party before the First World War.* New York, 2000.

Holquist, P. *Making War, Forging Revolution.* Harvard, 2002.

Holubovsky, O., Kulyk, V. *Ukrainskyi politychnyi rukh na naddniprianshchyni kintsia XIX pochatku XX stolittia.* Kyiv, 1996.

Hospodarenko, O. 'Zemske samovriaduvannia v Novobuzkii volosti Khersonskoho povitu 1917–1919 rr.' *Istoriia Ukrainy*, 16 (2001) 56–60.

– *Diialnist mistsevykh orhaniv vlady i samovriaduvannia na pivdni Ukrainy u 1917–1920 rr.: sotsialno-ekonomichnyi aspekt.* Doctoral dissertation, Mykolaiivskyi derzhavny humanistychnyi universytet, 2005.

Hrebennikova O. 'Komitety nezamozhnykh selian donetskoi hubernii v 1920–1925 rr.' *Pivdenna Ukraina XVIII–XIX stolittia*, 1 (1998) 184–9.

Hrynevych, V., et al. *Istoriia Ukrainskoho viiska 1917–1995.* Kyiv, 1996.

Hrytsak, Ia. *Narys istorii Ukrainy.* Kyiv, 1996.

Iablonovsky, V. *Vid vlady piatokh to dyktatury odnoho.* Kyiv, 2001.

Iarmysh, O., ed. *Istoriia mista Kharkova XX stolittia.* Kharkiv, 2004.

Iarymenko, O.I. *Administratyvna reforma hetmana Pavla Skoropadskoho.* Vinnytsia, 1998.

Ihnatienko, V. *Ukrainska presa 1816–1923 rr.* Kyiv, 1926.

Iroshnikov, M.P. *Sozdanie sovetskogo tsentralnogo gosudarstvennogo apparata.* Leningrad, 1967.

– *Predsedatel soveta narodnykh komissarov.* Leningrad, 1974.

Isakov, P. 'Spivvidnoshennia tsin ta realnykh dokhodiv hromadian v ukrainskomu seli na livoberezhyi Ukraini v 1919–1920 rokakh ...' *Siverianskyi litopys,* no. 4 (1998) 132–62.

Ivanov, Iu.A. *Uezdnaia Rossiia: Mestnye vlasti, tserkov i obshchestvo vo vtoroi polovine XIX – nachale XX v.* Ivanovo, 2003.

Kanishchev, V.V., Riazanov, D.S. 'Dekrety sovetskoi vlasti i gorodskie srednie sloi. Oktiabr 1917–1920 gg.' In A.L. Avrekh, ed., *Obschestvo i gosudarstvo v Rossii: Traditsii, sovremoennost, perspektivy.* Tambov, 2006, vol. 2: 159–69.

Kanishchev V.V. *Gorodskie srednie sloi v period formirovannia osnov sovetskogo obshchestva: Oktiabr 1917–1920 gg.: Po materialam tsentra Rossii.* Doctoral dissertation, Moscow University, 1998.

– '"Melkoburzhuaznaia kontrrevoliutsiia": soprotivlennia gorodskikh srednikh sloev stanovleniiu "diktatury proletariat" oktiabr 1917 – avgust 1918 g.' In S.V. Tiutiukin, ed., *1917 god v sudbakh Rossii i mira: Oktiabrskaia revoliutsiia.* Moscow, 1998, 174–87.

– '"Miatezhnyi obyvatel": Obobshchennyi portret riadovogo uchastnika antysovetskikh gorodskikh vostannii iunia 1918 g.' In P.V. Volubuev et al., *Revoliutsiia i chelovek.* Moscow, 1996, 170–5.

Kapustian, A.T. 'Ukrainskoe krestianstvo i vlast v pervye gody NEPA.' *Otechestvennaia istoriia,* no. 5 (2001) 165–73.

Karpenko, S.V. *Belye generaly i krasnaia smuta.* Moscow, 2009.

Kasianov, H. *Ukrainska intelihentsiia na rubezhi XIX–XX stolit.* Kyiv, 1993.

Kharchenko, T.O. Stanovlennia mistsevykh orhaniv vykonavchoi vlady ta samovriaduvannia v Ukrainskyi derzhavi kviten – hruden 1918 r. Doctoral dissertation, Poltavsky derzhavnyi pedahohichnyi universytet, 2000.

Kirianov, Iu.A., Shevyrin, V.M., eds. *Politicheskie partii i obshchestvo v Rossii 1914–1917 gg.* Moscow, 2000.

Kirianov, Iu.I. 'Pravye v 1915 – fevrale 1917 po perliustrirovannym departmentom politsii pismam.' *Minuvshee. Istoricheskii almanakh* 14 (1993) 145–225.

Kiselev, I.N., et al. 'Politicheskie partii v Rossii v 1905–1907 gg.: chislennost, sostav, razmeshchenie.' *Istoriia SSSR,* no. 4 (1990) 71–87.

Klepatsky, P. 'Holos kapitalu z Ukrainy pershoi polovyny XIX st.' *Ukraina* , (Dec. 1929) 71–81.

Koenker, D.P., et al. *Party State and Society in the Russian Civil War.* Bloomington, 1989.

Kohtiants, K. 'Tserkovno-parafiialni shkoly u Katerynoslavskii eparkhii v 1884–1916 rokakh.' *Kovcheh,* 2 (2000) 388–98.

Kolesnikov, B. *Professionalnoe dvizheniia i kontrrevoliutsiia.* Kharkiv, 1923.

– *Rabochee i professionalnoe dvizhenie.* Kharkiv, 1922.

– *Profsoiuzy posle oktiabria na Ukraine.* Kharkiv, 1923.

Kolesnyk V., Mohylny L. *Ukrainski liberalno-demokratychni partii v Rossiiskii imperii na pochatku XX st.* Kyiv, 2005.

Kondufor, Iu., ed. *Ukraina v 1917–1921 gg.: Nekotorye problemy istorii.* Kyiv, 1991.

Kovalchuk, M. *Nevidoma viina 1919 roku: Ukrainsko-bilohvardiiske zbroine protystovannia.* Kyiv, 2006.

Koretsky, V.M., et al. *Istoriia derzhavy i prava Ukrainskoi RSR 1917–1960.* Kyiv, 1961.

Korolivskii, S.M., et al. *Pobeda sovetskoi vlasti na Ukraine.* Moscow, 1967.

Korolivskii, S.M., ed. *Podgotovka velikoi oktiabrskoi sotsialisticheskoi revoliutsii na Ukraine.* Kyiv, 1955.

Kovanko, P. 'Biudget mista Kyiva.' *Zbirnyk sotsialno-ekonomichnoho viddilu,* no. 28 (1929) 36–40.

Krawchenko, B. *Social Change and National Consciousness in Twentieth-Century Ukraine.* London, 1985.

Kreizel, Iu. *Iz istorii profdvizheniia g. Kharkova v 1917 godu.* Kharkiv, 1923. *Professionalnoe dvizhenie i avstro-germanskaia okkupatsiia.* Kharkiv, 1924.

Krotofil, M. *Ukrainska armia Halicka 1918–1920.* Warsaw, 2002.

Krukhliak, B. 'Torhovelna burzhuaziia v Ukraini 60–ti roky XIX st. – 1914 r.' *Ukrainskyi istorychnyi zhurnal,* no. 6 (1994) 72–7.

Kryshyna, N. *Diialnist Nimetskoi viiskovoi administratsii v Ukraini u 1918 rotsi.* Doctoral dissertation, Kyiv National University, 2006.

Kryzhanovska, O.O. *Taemni orhanizatsii v hromadsko-politychnomu zhytti Ukrainy.* Kyiv, 1998.

Kulikov, S.V. *Biurokraticheskaia elita Rossiiskoi imperii nakanune padenniia starogo poriadka 1914–1917.* Riazan, 2004.

– 'Vremennoe pravitelstvo i vysshaia tsarskaia biurokratiia.' *Soviet and Post-Soviet Review,* nos. 1–2 (1997) 67–84.

Kulchytsky, Iu. *Shabli z pluhiv.* Lviv, 2000.

Kuras, I., ed. *Velykyi zhovten i hromadianska viina na Ukraini.* Kyiv, 1987.

Kurman, M.V. , Lebedinskii, I.V. *Naselenie bolshogo sotsialisticheskogo goroda.* Moscow, 1968.

Landis, E.C. *Bandits and Partisans: The Antonov Movement in the Civil War.* Pittsburgh, 2008.

Legiec, J. *Armia Ukrainskiej Respubliki Ludowej w wojnie ... 1920 r.* Torun, 2002.

Lebedeva, I. *Stvorennia uriadu Ukrainskoi Narodnoi Respubliky i formuvannia systemy vykonavchoi vlady cherven 1917 r. – kviten 1918 r.* Doctoral dissertation, Kyiv National Linguistic University, 2003.

Leonov, M.I. *Partiia sotsialistov-revoliutsionerov v 1905–1907 gg.* Moscow, 1997.

Lepeshkin, A.I. *Mestnye organy vlasti sovetskogo gosudarstva 1921–1936 gg.* Moscow, 1959.

Leshchenko, T., ed. *Kataloh dorevoliutsiinykh gazet shcho vydavalysia na Ukraini 1822–1916.* Kyiv, 1971.

Loza, Iu. *Ukraina. Istorychnyi atlas 10–11 klasy.* Kyiv, 2007.

Lozovy, V. *Ahrarna revoliustiia v naddniprianskii Ukraini: stavlennia selianstva do vlady v dobu tsentralnoi rady.* Kamianets-Podilskyi, 2008.

– *Vnutrishnia ta zovnishnia polityka Dyrektorii Ukrainskoi Narodnoi Respubliky Kamianetska doba.* Kyiv, 2005.

Lytvyn, V., et al. *Uriady Ukrainy u XX st.* Kyiv, 2001.

Mashkin O.M. 'Dvi ideii, dva svita: borotba mizh prybichnykamy Rosiiskoho samoderzhavstva ta national-demokratamy na terenakh Ukrainy v roky svitovoi viiny.' *Problemy istorii Ukrainy XIX–XX st.*, 9 (2005) 220–53.

Maistrenko, I. *Borotbism.* Ann Arbor, 1954.

Makarenko, M. 'Materialy Vseukrainskoho tovarystva politkatorzhan i zsylnoposelentsiv pro narodnytskyi rukh v Ukraini.' *Ukrainsky istorychnyi zhurnal*, nos. 10–11 (1992) 47–53.

Matkhanova, N.P. 'Formalnaia i neformalnaia ierarkhiia gubernskogo chinovnichestva v Rossii XIX veka' In V.A. Zverev, ed., *Sibir moi krai ...* Novosibirsk, 1999, 154–67.

Medrzecki, W. *Niemiecka interwencja militarna na Ukrainie w 1918 roku.* Warsaw, 2000.

Medvedev, V.G. *Politiko-iuridicheskaia sushchnost interventsii i gosudarstvenno-pravovaia organizatsiia belogo dvizneniia v gody grazhdanskoi voiny v Rossii.* Moscow, 2002.

Mikhailov, I. 'Getman i getmanshchina.' *Rodina* (Sept. 2000) 66–70.

Mikhutina, I.V. *Ukrainskii vopros v Rossii konets XIX – nachalo XX veka.* Moscow, 2003.

Miller, A. *'Ukrainskii vopros' v politike vlastei i russkom obshchestvennom mneni.* Moscow, 2000.

Mints, I.I. *Istoriia Velikogo Oktiabra.* 3 vols. Moscow, 1967–73.

Mints, I.I., ed. *Oktiabrskaia revoliutsiia i molodezh.* Erevan, 1987.

Mykhailiuk, O.B. *Selianstvo Ukrainy v pershi desiatylittia XX st.: Sotsiokulturni protsesy.* Dnipropetrovsk, 2007.

Mykhailychenko, D. 'Prodovolcha polityka radianskoi vlady na Ukraini i ii zdiisnennia u sichni-serpni 1919.' *Visnyk Kharkivskoho Universyteta. Istoriia, vypusk*, 32 (2000) 122–9.

Myronenko, O.M. *Svitoch ukrainskoi derzhavnosti.* Kyiv, 1995.

Naiman, O.Ia. *Ievreiski partii ta ob'iednannia Ukrainy 1917–1925.* Kyiv, 1998.

Narskii, I. *Zhizn v katastrofe: Budni naseleniia Urala v 1917–1922 gg.* Moscow, 2001.

Naumov, S. *Ukrainskyi politychnyi rukh na livoberezhzhi 90i rr. XIX st. – liutiy 1917 r.* Kharkiv, 2006.

Nesterov, O., Zemziulina N., Zakharchenko, P. *U pokhodi za voliu.* Kyiv, 2000.

Ohienko, V.I. *Diialnist Ukrainskykh national-kommunistiv 1918–1920 rr.* Doctoral dissertation, Kyiv National University, 2008.

Oliinyk, M.M. 'Diialnist partiinykh orhanizatsii po polipshenniu roboty derzhapparatu u vidbudovnyi period 1921–1925 rr.' *Ukrainskyi istorychnyi zhurnal,* no. 9 (1989) 64–71.

Osipova, T.V. *Rossiiskoe krestianstvo v revoliutsii i grazhdanskoi voine.* Moscow, 2001.

Ostapenko, S. *Ekonomichna heohrafiia Ukrainy.* Kyiv, 1920.

Ostrovskii, A. *Kto stoial za spinoi Stalina.* St Petersburg, 2002.

Pavliuchenkov, S.A. *Voennyi kommunizm v Rossii: Vlast i massy.* Moscow, 2007.

Petrov, V. 'Teoria "kulturnytstva" v Kulishevomu lystuvannia r. 1856–57.' *Zapysky istorychno-filolohichnoho viddilu,* 15 (1927) 146–65.

Pipes, R. *The Formation of the Soviet Union.* Rev. ed. Cambridge, 1964.

– *The Russian Revolution.* New York, 1991.

– *Russia under the Bolshevik Regime.* New York, 1995.

Plaskyi, T. 'Miske hromadske samovriaduvannia m. Oleksandrivska u 1917–1919 rr.' *Pivdenna Ukraina XVIII–XIX stolittia,* 1 (1998) 101–7.

Pomeranz, W. 'Justice from the Underground: The History of the Underground Advokatura.' *Russian Review,* no. 3 (July 1993) 321–30.

Predislovii, I.S., Stepanskii, I.S., eds., *Professionalnoe dvizhenie sluzashchikh Ukrainy 1905–1907.* Kharkiv, 1926.

Prysiazhniuk, Iu. *Ukrainske selianstvo XIX–XX st.: Evoliutsiia, mentalnist, tradytsionalizm.* Cherkasy, 2002.

Pyvovar, S. 'Truzheniki na polzu obruseniia kraia ... ' *Kyiivska starovyna,* no. 5 (1995) 58–71.

Radkey, O. *The Agrarian Foes of Bolshevism.* New York, 1958.

– *Russia Goes to the Polls: The Election to the All-Russian Constituent Assembly, 1917.* Ithaca, 1990.

Reent, O. 'Kryzovi tendentsii u silskomu hospodarstvi ... lypen 1914–1917r.' *Visnyk Akademii pratsi i sotsialnykh vidnosyn Federatsii profspilok Ukrainy,* no. 2 (2003) 86–101.

Revehuk, V. 'Lenin I borotba za khlib na Ukraini 1917–1921.' *Ukrainskyi istorychnyi zhurnal,* no. 4 (1986) 55–64.

Rigby, T.H. *Lenin's Government: Sovnarkom 1917–1922.* Cambridge, 1979.

Rodionov, P.A. et al., *Revoliutsiia 1905–07 godov v Rossii i ee vsemirno-istoricheskoe znachenie.* Moscow, 1976.

Rogger, H. *Russia in the Age of Modernisation and Revolution 1881–1917.* London, 1983.

Rosenberg, W. 'Social Mediation and State Control.' *Social History,* no. 2 (May 1994) 169–88.

Rowney, D.K. *Transition to Technocracy.* Ithaca, 1989.

Rudy, H. *Hazetna periodyka – dzherelo vyvchennia problem Ukrainskoi kultury 1917–1920 rr.* Kyiv, 2000.

Rubach, M.A., et al. *Radianske budivnytsvo na Ukraini v roky hromadianskoi viiny 1919–1920.* Kyiv, 1957.

Rybalka, I.K. *Rozhrom burzhuazno-natsionalistychnoi dyrektorii na Ukraini.* Kharkiv, 1962.

Ryndzionskii, P.G. *Krestiane i gorod v kapitalisticheskoi Rossii vtoroi poloviny XIX veka.* Moscow, 1983.

S.M. 'Gorodskaia duma i politicheskaia sytuatsiia na Ukraine.' *Kievskaiia gorodskiia izvestiia,* nos. 2–6 (1918) 28–44.

Samartsev, I.H. 'Chornosotentsi na Ukraini 1905–1917 rr.' *Ukrainskyi istorychnyi zhurnal,* no. 1 (1992) 90–7.

Sanborn, J.A. *Drafting the Nation: Military Conscription and the Formation of a Modern Polity in Tsarist and Soviet Russia 1905–1925.* Doctoral dissertation, University of Chicago, 1998.

Semenov-Tian-Shanskii, V. *Gorod i Derevnia v evropeiskoi Rossii.* St Petersburg, 1910.

Serebrianskii, Z. *Ot Kerenshchiny k proletarskoi diktature.* Moscow, 1928.

Serhiichuk, V. *Symon Petliura i Evreistvo.* Kyiv, 1999.

Shapoval, M. *Misto i selo.* Prague, 1926.

Shcherbakov, V. 'Zhovtnevyi period na Chernihivshchyni.' *Litopys revoliutsii,* nos. 5–6 (1927) 295–302.

Shelokhaev, V.V. *Kadety-glavnaia partiia liberalnoi burzhuazii v borbe s revoliutsiei 1905–1907 gg.* Moscow, 1983.

– *Partiia oktiabristov v period pervoi rossiiskoi revoliutsii.* Moscow, 1987.

Shelokhaev, V.V., ed. *Politicheskie partii Rossii konets XIX – pervaia tret XX veka. Entsiklopediia.* Moscow, 1996.

Shevchenko, V., ed. *Ukrainski politychni partii kintsia XIX – pochatku XX stolittia.* Kyiv, 1993.

Shevyrin, V.M. *Zemskii i gorodskoi soiuzy 1914–1917.* Moscow, 2000.

Ship, N.A. *Intelligentsiia na Ukraine XIX v.* Kyiv, 1991.

Sidak, V.S. *Natsionalni spetssluzhby v period Ukrainskoi revoliutsii 1917–1921 rr.* Kyiv, 1998.

Sidorov, A.L., ed. *Ekonomicheskoi polozhenie Rossii nakanune velikoi oktiabrskoi sotsialisticheskoi revoliutsii.* Moscow, 1957.

Sidorov, N.I. 'Mobilizatsiia reaktsii v 1906.' *Krasnyi arkhiv,* 32 (1929) 158–82.

Skaba, A., et al. *Ukrainska RSR v period hromadianskoi viiny 1917–1920.* 3 vols. Kyiv, 1968–70.

Skachkov, V.M., ed. *Periodychni vydannia URSR: Gazety 1917–1960.* Kharkiv, 1965.

Smirnov, N.N. et al., *Rossiia i pervaia mirovaia voina.* St Petersburg, 1999.

Smirnova, T.M. *'Byvshye liude' sovetskoi Rossii.* Moscow, 2003.

Smith, N. 'Political Freemasonry in Russia, 1906–1918: A Discussion of the Sources.' *Russian Review,* no. 2 (April 1985) 157–74.

Smolii, V., ed. *Tsentralna Rada i Ukrainskyi derzhavotvorchyi protses.* 2 vols. Kyiv, 1997.

Spirin, P.M. *Krusheniie pomeshchichykh i burzhuaznykh partii v Rossii.* Moscow, 1977.

Startsev, V.I. *Russkoe politicheskoe masonstvo nachala XX veka.* St Petersburg, 1996.

Stepanov, S.A. *Chernaia sotnia v Rossii 1905–1914 gg.* Moscow, 1992.

Stetsiuk, P. *Stanislav Dnistriansky iak konstytutsionalist.* Lviv, 1999.

Strilets, V. *Ukrainska Radykalno-Demokratychna Partiia: vytoky, ideolohiia orhanizatsiia diialnist kinets XIX stolittia – 1939 roku.* Kyiv, 2002.

Subtelny, O. *Ukraine: A History.* 3rd ed. Toronto, 2000.

Sudavtsov, N.D. *Zemskoe i gorodskoe samoupravlenie Rossii v gody pervoi mirovoi voine.* Moscow, 2001.

Sukhov, O.O. *Ekonomichna heohrafiia Ukrainy.* Odesa, 1923.

Tereshchenko, Iu.I. *Politychna borotba na vyborakh do miskykh dum Ukrainy v period pidhotovky zhovtnevoi revoliutsii.* Kyiv, 1974.

Tiutiukin, S.V., et al. *1917 god v sudbakh Rossii i mira. Oktiabrskaia revoliutsiia.* Moscow, 1998.

Trembitsky, V. 'Hroshi na Volyni 1917–1920.' *Litopys Volyni,* nos. 10–11 (1972) 58–64.

Tronko, P.T., ed. *Istoriia mist i sil Ukrainskoi RSR.* 26 vols. Kyiv, 1974–83.

Tsehelsky, L. *Vid legend do pravdy.* New York, 1960.

Tsvetkov, V.Zh. *Belye armii Iuga Rossii.* Moscow, 2000.

Tymofiev, V. 'Pro borotbu radianskoi vlady za revoliutsiynu perebudovu ustanov zviazku na Ukraini.' *Ukrainskyi istorychnyi zhurnal,* no. 4 (1978) 112–16.

Tymoshchuk, O.V. *Okhronnyi apparat Ukrainskoi Derzhavy kviten-hruden 1918 r.* Kharkiv, 2000.

Tynchenko, Ia. *Persha Ukrainsko-bolshevytska viina hruden 1917 – berezen 1918.* Kyiv and Lviv 1996.

Velychenko, S. 'Identities Loyalties and Service in Imperial Russia: Who Administered the Borderlands?' *Russian Review,* no. 2 (April 1995) 188–208.

– 'The Bureaucracy, Police and Army in Twentieth-Century Ukraine: A Comparative Quantitative Study.' *Harvard Ukrainian Studies*, nos. 3–4 (1999) 63–103.
– 'Local Officialdom and National Movements in Imperial Russia in Light of Administrative Shortcomings and Under-government.' In J. Morison, ed., *National Issues in Russian and East European History*. New York, 2000, 74–85.
Verstiuk, V. *Makhnovshchyna*. Kyiv, 1991,
Vikul, I. 'Liudnist mista Kieva.' *Zbirnyk sotsialno-ekonomichnoho viddilu*, no. 22 (1930) 224–8.
Vladimirova, V. *God sluzhby sotsialistov kapitalistam*. Moscow, 1927.
Volubuev, P.V., et al. *Revoliutsiia i chelovek*. Moscow, 1996.
– *1917 god v sudbakh Rossii i mira. Fevralskaia revoliutsiia*. Moscow, 1997.
Vyshnevsky, A., ed. *Naukov-dokumentalna zbirka do 90-richchia zaprovadzhennia derzhavnoi sluzhby v Ukraini*. Kyiv, 2008.
Vytanovych, I. *Istoriia Ukrainskoho kooperatyvnoho rukhu*. New York, 1964.
Wade, R. *Red Guards and Workers' Militias in the Russian Revolution*. Stanford, 1984.
Wartenweiler, D. *Civil Society and Academic Debate in Russia 1905–1914*. Oxford, 1999.
Yaney, G. *The Urge to Mobilize: Agrarian Reform in Russia 1861–1930*. Urbana, 1982.
Zaitsev, P. 'Zhmut spohadiv pro V. Vynnychenka.' *Ukrainska literaturna hazeta* (Aug.–Sept. 1959).
Zdorov, A. *Ukrainskyi zhovten. Bilshovytska revoliutsiia v Ukraini: sotsialno-politychnyi aspekt lystopad 1917 – liutyi 1988 rr.* Odesa, 2007.
Zhdanova, I.A. 'Problema federativnogo ustroistva gosudarstva v Fevralskoi revoliutsii 1917g.' *Voprosy istorii*, no. 7 (2007) 17–28.
Zhvanko, L. *Vnutrishnia polityka Ukrainskoi derzhavy v haluzi okhorona zdorovlia ta sotisalnoho zahystu naselennia*. Doctoral dissertation, Poltavskyi universytet spozhyvchoi kooperatsii Ukrainy, 2002.
Zyrianov, P.N. 'Sotsialnaia struktura mestnogo upravlenniia kapitalisticheskoi Rossii 1861–1914.' *Istoricheskie zapiski*, 107 (1972) 226–303.

Western Ukraine, Poland, Ireland, Czechoslovakia

Ajnenkiel, A., ed. *Rok 1918: Odrodzona Polska w Europie*. Warsaw, 1999.
Bakke, E. *Doomed to Failure? The Czechoslovak Nation Project and the Slovak Autonomist Reaction 1918–1938*. Oslo, 1998.
Bardach, J., ed. *Historiia panstwa i prawa Polski*. 4 vols. Warsaw, 1982.
Birmingham, G.A. [pseud. J.O. Hannay]. *Irishmen All*. London, 1913.

Borzyszkowski, J., Hauser, P. *Sejm Rzeczypospolitej o Pomorzu 1920 roku.* Gdansk, 1990.

Boyce, D.G., ed. *The Revolution in Ireland 1879–1923.* London, 1988.

Chajn, L. *Polskie wolnomularstwo 1920–1938.* 2nd ed. Warsaw, 1984.

Chimiak, L. *Gubernatorzy Rosyjscy w Krolestwie Polskim 1863–1915.* Wroclaw, 1999.

Chwalba, A. *Polacy w sluzbie moskali.* Cracow, 1999.

Collins, P., ed. *Nationalism and Unionism: Conflict in Ireland 1885–1921.* Belfast, 1994.

Culen, K. *Cesi a Slovaci v statnych sluzbach CSR.* Trencin, 1994.

Czepulis-Rastenis, R. *'Klasa umyslowa': Inteligencja Krolestwa Polskiego 1832–1862.* Warsaw, 1973.

Czepulis-Rastenis, R., ed. *Inteligencja Polska XIX i XX wieku.* Warsaw, 1987.

Day, W.A. *The Russian Government in Poland.* London, 1867.

Dudiak, O. 'Dynamika natsionalnoho skladu sluzhbovtsiv administratyvnykh organiv skhidnoi Halychyny u mizhvoiennyi period.' *Naukovi zoshyty istorychnoho fakultetu Lvivskoho natsionalnoho universytetu,* vol. 4 (2001) 363–72.

Gasowski, T. 'Struktura narodowosciowa ludnosci miejskiej w autonomicznej Galicji.' *Zeszyty naukowe Uniwersytetu Jagiellonskiego. Prace Historyczne,* 125 (1998) 91–105.

Glaser, O. *Czecho-Slovakia: A Critical History.* Caldwell, 1961.

Gorizontow, L. 'Aparat urzednicy Krolewstwa Polskiego w okresie rzadow Paszkiewicza.' *Przeglad historyczny,* nos. 1–2 (1994) 45–56.

Hantsch, H. *Die Nationalitätenfrage im alten Osterreich.* Vienna, 1953.

Hass, L. *Masoneria Polska XX wieku.* Warsaw, 1996.

Heflich, A. 'Walka o czytelnie Warsawskiego Towarzystwa Dobroczynosci.' *Niepodleglosc,* 6 (1932) 341–54.

Hoff, J. 'Podwoloczynska w XIX i pierwszej polowie XX wieku.' *Kresy poludniowowschodnie,* no. 1 2003 79–88.

Hon, M. '"Ievreiska vulytsia" Zakhidnoukrainskoi narodnoi respubliki.' *Khronika 2000,* vol. 21–2 (1998) 252–60.

Hopkinson, M. *The Irish War of Independence.* Dublin, 2002.

Hutchinson, J. *The Dynamics of Cultural Nationalism: The Gaelic Revival and the Creation of the Irish Nation State.* London, 1987.

Ihnatowicz, I. 'Urzednicy galicyjscy w dobie autonomii.' *Spoleczenstwo polskie XVIII i XIX wieku,* 6 (1974) 205–24.

Inglot, S., ed. *Zarys historii Polskiego ruchu spoldzielczego.* Warsaw, 1971.

Jaskiewicz, L. *Carat i sprawy Polskie na przelomie XIX i XX wieku.* Pultusk, 2001.

Kachor, A. 'Rolia dukhovenstva i tserkvy v ekonomichnomu vidrozhenni zakhidnoi Ukrainy.' In O. Baran, O. Gerus, eds., *Zbirnyk tysiacholittia khrystianstva v Ukraini 988–1988.* Winnipeg, 1991, 103–9.

Kania, L., *W cieniu Orlat Lwowskich. Polskie sady wojskowe, kontrwywiad i sluzby policyjne w bitwie o Lwow 1918-1919.* (Zielona Gora, 2008).

Kieniewicz, S., et al. *Z epoki Mickiewicza.* Wroclaw, 1956.

– *Powstanie stycznowie.* Warsaw, 1972.

Kolodny, A., et al. *Istoriia relihii v Ukraini: u 10–ty tomiv,* vol. 4, *Katolytsyzm.* Kyiv, 2001.

Kolodziejczyk, R., ed. *Spoleczenstwo polskie w dobie I wojny swiatowej i wojny polsko-bolszewickiej 1920 roku.* Kielce, 2001.

Kopczynski, K. *Mickiewicz i jego czytelnicy.* Warsaw, 1994.

Kozicki, S. *Historia ligi narodowej.* London, 1964.

Kozyra, W. *Urzad wojewodzki w Lublinie w latach 1919–1939.* Lublin, 1999.

Krochmal, A. 'Przemiany wewnetrze w kosciele Greckokatolickim w Galicji w drugiej polowie XIX wieku.' *Polska-Ukraina 1000 lat sasiedztwa,* 5 (2000) 69–74.

Kula, W., ed. *Spoleczenstwo krolewstwa polskiego.* Warsaw, 1965.

Laffan, M. *The Resurrection of Ireland.* Cambridge, 1999.

Landau, Z., Tomaszewski, J. *Gospodarka Polski miedzywojennej 1918–1939,* vol. 1, *W dobie inflacji 1918–1923.* Warsaw, 1967.

Latawiec, K. 'Ewakuacja cywilnej administracji ogolnej szczebla powiatowego z guberni lubelskiej 1915 roku.' *Wschodni rocznik humanistyczny,* 1 (2004) 157–70.

Lewandowski, J. *Krolestwo Polskie pod okupacja austriacka 1914–1918.* Warsaw, 1980.

Lewin, I. *A History of Polish Jewry during the Revival of Poland.* New York, 1990.

Libera, Z., ed. *'Konrad Wallenrod' Adama Mickiewicza.* Warsaw, 1966.

Loyka, J., ed. *Prasa Polsa w latach 1864–1918.* Warsaw, 1976.

– *Prasa Polsa w latach 1918–1939.* Warsaw, 1976.

Lukomski, G., et al. *Wojna Polsko–Ukrainska 1918–1919.* Warsaw, 1994.

Luzhnytsky, H., Padokh, Ia., eds. *U poshukakh istorychnoi pravdy.* New York, 1987.

Lytvyn, M. *Ukrainsko-polska viina 1918–1919 rr.* Lviv, 1998.

Macardle, D. *The Irish Republic.* New York, 1965.

Mahler, R. 'Jews in Public Service and the Liberal Professions in Poland, 1918–39.' *Jewish Social Studies,* no. 4 (Oct. 1944) 291–350.

Makarchuk, S. *Ukrainska respublika Halychan.* Lviv, 1997.

Mankowski, Z. ed., *Niepodleglosc Polski w 1918 roku.* Lublin, 1996.

Marczewski, J. *Narodowa Demokracja w poznanskiem 1906–1914.* Warsaw, 1967.

McBride, L.W. *The Greening of Dublin Castle.* Washington, 1991.

McColgen, J. *British Policy and the Irish Administration 1920–22.* London, 1983.

Medrzecki, W. *Wojewodztwo wolynskie 1921–1939.* Wroclaw, 1988.

Micinska, M. *Zdrada. Corka Nocy. Pojecie zdrady narodowej w swiadomosci Polakow w latach 1861–1914.* Warsaw, 1998.

Milinski, J. *Pulkownik Czeslaw Maczynski 1881–1935.* Warsaw, 2004.

Misilo, E. 'Prasa Zachodnio-ukrainskiej Republiki Ludowej.' *Kwartalnik Historii Prasy Polskiej*, no. 2 (1987) 53–76.

Mitchell, A. *Revolutionary Government in Ireland.* Dublin, 1993.

Molenda, J. *Chlopi Narod Niepodleglosc.* Warsaw, 1999.

Mykytiuk, D., ed. *Ukrainska halytska armiia.* 5 vols. Winnipeg, 1960–76.

Nikharadze, E. *The World of Imperial Provincial Bureaucracy, Russian Poland, 1870–1904.* Doctoral dissertation, Georgetown University, 1998.

Opocensky, J. *The Collapse of the Austro-Hungarian Monarchy and the Rise of the Czechoslovak State.* Prague, 1928.

Osadczy, W. 'Stosunki miedzyobrzadkowe a kwestia narodowa w Galicji wschodniej w XIX i poczatku XX wieku.' *Polska-Ukraina 1000 lat sasiedztwa*, 5 (2000) 69–102.

– 'Kler katolicki obu obrzadkow wobec Polsko-Ruskiej rywalizacji w Galicji wschodniej w XIX i XX wieku.' *Prace komisji srodkowoeuropejskiej*, 7 (2000) 86–90.

Pajak, J. *Konspiracyjne zycie polityczne w Staropolskim Okregu Przemyslowym 1882–1904.* Kielce, 1994.

Pajewski, J. *Odbudowa panstwa polskiego 1914–1918.* Warsaw, 1978.

Paseta, S. *Before the Revolution: Nationalism, Social Change and Ireland's Catholic Elite, 1879 –1922.* Cork, 1999.

Pavlyshyn, O. 'Orhanizatsiia tsyvilnoi vlady ZUNR u povitakh Halychyny.' *Ukraina Moderna*, 2–3 (1997–98) 132–93.

– 'Polske naselennia Skhidnoi Halychyny pid vladoiu Zakhidno-Ukrainskoi Narodnoi Respubliky.' *Visnyk Lvivskoho Universyteta*, 39–40 (2005) 203–52.

Peroutka, F. *Budovani statu.* 3rd ed. Prague, 1991.

Philpin, C.H.E., ed. *Nationalism and Popular Protest in Ireland.* Cambridge, 1987.

Pobog-Malinowski, W. *Jozef Pilsudski.* Warsaw, 1935.

Pohrebynska, I., Hon, M. *Evreii v Zakhidnoukrainskyi Narodnyi Respublitsi.* Kyiv, 1997.

Prusin, A. *War and Nationality Conflict in Eastern Galicia, 1914–1920: The Evolution of Modern Anti-Semitism.* Doctoral dissertation, University of Toronto, 2001.

Przenioslo, M. *Polska Komisja Likwidacyjna 1918–1919* (Kielce, 2010).

Sadowski, L. *Polska inteligencja prowincjonalna i jej ideowe dylematy na przelomie XIX i XX wieku* Warsaw, 1988.

Shankovsky, L. *Ukrainska halytska armiia.* 2nd ed. Lviv, 1999.

Shmeral, Ia.B. *Obrazovanie chekhoslovatskoi respubliki v 1918 godu.* Moscow, 1967.

Sobczak, M. *Stosunek narodowej demokracji do kwestii Zydowskiej w Polsce w latach 1918–1939* Wroclaw, 1998.

Sonevetska, O., et al. *Istorychno–memuarnyi zbirnyk Chortkivskoi okruhy.* New York, 1974.

Stempowski, S. 'Ukraina 1919–1920.' *Zeszyty historyczne,* 217 (1972) 64–88.

Suleja, W. *Tymczasowa Rada Stany.* Warsaw, 1998.

Szczepanski, J. *Spoleczenstwo Polski w walce z najazdem Bolszewickim 1920 roku.* Warsaw, 2000.

Szwarc, A., Wieczorkiewicz, P., eds. *Unifikacja za wszelka cene.* Warsaw, 2002.

Tyshchyk, B.I. *Halytska sotialistychna radianska respublika /1920 r.* Lviv, 1970.

– *Zakhidno Ukrainska Narodna Respublika 1918–1923.* Lviv, 2005.

Wiech, S. *Spoleczenstwo krolestwa polskiego w oczach carskiej policiji politycznej 1866–1896.* Kielce, 2002.

Wiskemann, E. *Czechs and Germans.* 2nd ed. London, 1967.

Wrobel, P. 'Barucha Mikcha Galicyjskie wspomnienia wojenne 1914–1920.' *Biuletyn zydowskiego instytutu historycznego w Polsce,* no. 2 (1991) 87–98.

Zarnowski, J. *Struktura spoleczna inteligencji w Polsce latach 1918–1939.* Warsaw, 1964.

Zeman, Z.A. *The Break-up of the Habsburg Empire 1914–1918.* London, 1961.

Index